SOAP BOX

S·O·A·P B·O·X

The Papermac Guide to Soap Opera

Hilary Kingsley

PAPERMAC

First published 1988 by
PAPERMAC
a division of Macmillan Publishers Limited
4 Little Essex Street London WC2R 3LF
and Basingstoke

Associated companies in Auckland, Delhi, Dublin, Gaborone,
Hamburg, Harare, Hong Kong, Johannesburg, Kuala Lumpur,
Lagos, Manzini, Melbourne, Mexico City, Nairobi, New York,
Singapore and Tokyo

British Library Cataloguing in Publication Data
Kingsley, Hilary
  Soap box.
  1. Television programmes. Soap operas
  I. Title
  791.45'75
  ISBN 0-333-46949-6

Typeset by Bookworm Typesetting Ltd Manchester
Printed in Hong Kong

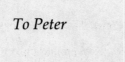

To Peter

CONTENTS

Acknowledgements

Many people assisted me with the preparation of this book. Frank Jeffery encouraged me, did the early historical research and supplied jokes. Geoff Tibballs beavered away on several subjects and made more jokes. Graeme Kay in Manchester added his expertise. Ian Brandes chipped in. Patient librarians at the *Daily Mirror* in Manchester and in London checked details and found photographs. Jennifer Kingsley typed until dawn. Anna, Daniel and Harriet, my children, brought me cups of tea and watched television tirelessly just in case it helped. My dear mother remembered 'Crossroads'. Thank you all very much.

INTRODUCTION

WHAT IS SOAP OPERA?

Ask a silly question and you get a lengthy answer. Everyone knows what soap opera is. We watch it all the time, don't we? Yes, but try defining it. 'Coronation Street' is plainly soap, but what about 'Howards Way'? Was 'Peyton Place' soap? Was 'Return to Eden'?

I believe that the essence of soap opera is this: it must be a continuing story with a family background aimed largely at women. It must deal not with ideas but with feelings and emotions. Above all it must be seamless, endless. Problems arise, problems are solved. Danger appears, danger is averted. Love arises, love dies. But always the central story must flow on like a great river. Individual story-lines are feeder streams, tributaries, creeks, backwaters, but the river goes on for ever.

Soap operas have no beginning and no end, like the universe perhaps. When a new soap begins the characters are shown already living their lives, dealing with their problems. When a soap ends the viewer must know that the story continues somewhere. It will just not be shown on television.

When 'The Colbys', a bad and batty American soap, ended, Aaron Spelling, tsar of the show, illustrated this in an almost mystical way. Fallon, the principal young love-interest, was kidnapped by aliens from space. She walked in a trance towards a shadowy spaceship where a hardly defined spaceman beckoned. The series was ending, but Fallon wasn't. She was going to a new life beyond the stars, perhaps to immortality. By inference, the viewer was being told that the rest of the Colby clan would continue to exist.

It is this continuance that really matters in soap opera. *Hamlet* isn't soap, because Hamlet's problems are introduced, complicated and then

1

ended by his death and the death of almost everyone else. End of story. In soap there is no end of story, ever.

Dennis Potter's 'The Singing Detective' wasn't soap. The story ran for many weeks. There were cliffhangers of the kind essential to soap opera. There were standard soap issues: love, betrayal, suffering. But the show wasn't soap because it dealt with ideas. (What is reality? Does anyone *really* care about anyone else? Is the child father to the man? How far does early environment shape our lives?)

In soap opera no eternal verities are questioned. Religion never plays a part in story-lines. Nor does politics – at least, not overtly. In soap conventional morality is never questioned. (It is often flouted, but the very flouting defines the morality.) In soap the goodies and the baddies are clearly defined, though characters may be shown to possess both good and evil impulses. JR may be the biggest bastard in creation, but he loves his momma and his son.

'The Singing Detective' could never be soap, because it used fantasy as a tool in telling its story. Soap cannot do that, because it must always seem realistic. Characters can fantasise in dreams – indeed, one whole season of 'Dallas' turned out to be a dream when it became convenient for Patrick Duffy to return as not-really-dead Bobby Ewing – but their lives must be lived in straightforward fashion. (This does not exclude impossibly glamorous lifestyles or wild melodrama. So long as the viewer or listener is told this is true, this is real, that is enough. Disbelief is never more willingly suspended than by the soap audience.)

At the centre of all soap operas there must exist the family. Sometimes, as in 'Crossroads', the family can be a social group, not a literal family. Everyone who worked at the motel belonged to this family. More often a real family is at the centre. The Fowlers are the main family group in 'EastEnders', though other families, the Wattses and the Beales, are important, too. The Carringtons of 'Dynasty' are a clan, a vast and powerful family, as are the Ewings of Dallas. In 'Coronation Street' the family is a close-knit community of neighbours, caring and feuding as real families do.

It is this feeling of closeness that matters most in soap. Outsiders are either a threat or a possibility of enlarging the unit. When Sammy Jo married Steven in 'Dynasty' she was both. She provided a new daughter-in-law for Blake and Krystle and a new grandson to carry on the dynasty. But she was wild and vicious, and her antics disrupted the whole clan.

New lovers in soap opera usually have a dual effect: they extend the horizons of the family we know, but they usually cause problems, too. Problems, of course, are soap's lifeblood. All drama is conflict; conflict causes problems. In soap the problems must be something like we have experienced ourselves, or problems we can imagine having. Everyone has been unhappily in love. Everyone has felt jealousy. Everyone has felt rage. Everyone has felt threatened. Everyone has rebelled against parents or similar authority-figures.

Soap deals in this simple currency. The drama may be more exciting than we have come across in life, but the basic emotions are the same. For instance, kidnapping of children is a recurrent soap theme. In 'Dallas' or 'Dynasty' it will certainly occur every other season. In the more down-to-earth British soaps less often, and usually it will be one parent who takes the child from the other (as Brian Tilsley stole Gail's son away). Few people will experience kidnapping in their own lives. But anyone who has children will have experienced fears for their safety. And the childless will certainly remember the anxiety their own parents showed when they came home three hours late.

Other big themes – infidelity, money problems, paternity uncertainty, childlessness, loneliness, betrayal, worry about loved ones who have gone off to some other part of the world – all delve deep into our unconscious and our conscious minds. *What soap does is to parade problems we either have or that we fear having*. Whether, like the classic drama is supposed to, they purge our minds of these fears, I've no idea. All I know is that we enjoy the process enormously.

HOW SOAP OPERA BEGAN

Soap grew out of American commercial radio, which was established by the early 1920s, after an argument about whether advertising over the air was seemly. The answer was yes, and broadcasting has never been the same again.

By 1927 the local stations were being hooked up to make national radio a possibility. By 1930 the pattern of radio and television broadcasting in the States was set, with the National Broadcasting Company and the Columbia Broadcasting System firmly established as rival giants, controlling stations across America.

Once all Americans – and especially American women – could hear the same programmes, advertisers began to look for shows that would sell their products by the megaton. The first answer they came up with was the daily drama, a continuing story about people the listener – particularly the woman listener – could identify with.

And since most of the early daily dramas were sponsored by the big soap firms (Procter & Gamble, Colgate-Palmolive were the big ones) the name 'soap opera' was coined. (No one knows by whom, though there have been claimants. The term has always been mildly derogatory and it has always infuriated the people who make soaps. To this day Granada refer to 'Coronation Street' as a Drama Serial.)

In 1929 two white actors put out a local radio show in Chicago called 'Amos and Andy', in which they played a pair of country-style blacks. The programme was essentially a situation comedy, but the stories continued day by day over several weeks. NBC began to put out 'Amos and Andy' nationally, and eventually the show claimed a regular audience of 40 million for its six-days-a-week fifteen-minute episodes. (Pepsodent toothpaste sponsored. Perhaps this one was a paste opera.)

'The Rise of the Goldbergs' followed, with Jewish characters substituting for Negroes. Again the aim was primarily comic, but advertisers quickly worked out that what hooked the audience was not so much the comedy as the fact that the story was continuous. To make you tune in tomorrow, the cliffhanger appeared. (*Will Mary tell Jim about her secret admirer? Will Dave tell Edna the truth about his long-lost son?* The device was pinched from the printed serial story, of course.) But neither 'Amos and Andy' nor 'The Rise of the Goldbergs' was a genuine soap opera. Probably the first true soap was 'Painted Dreams', a local radio show written by Irna Phillips. Irna was a bright girl who was a graduate of three universities. She became a teacher, then got work in 1929 with WGN, a local radio station in Chicago. She worked as an actress, often ad-libbing her part in hastily thrown together radio drama. She switched to writing and turned out 'Painted Dreams' for WGN as a daily serial drama aimed at women. No sponsor fancied it, and the show soon closed. But Irna Phillips had learned a lot, and by the time she was writing 'Today's Children' the soap formula was set: the family was the basis of everything, and the problems the family faced included love, money, betrayal, jealousy, misunderstanding and intrusions from the outside world.

Irna Phillips is important for many reasons. She invented amnesia as a recurring soap device. She conceived and wrote 'The Guiding Light', in 1937, a soap that stressed the importance of everyday morality. The show still runs on American television.

Irna Phillips sometimes wrote 2 million words a year and worked on six different soaps at once. Her main rivals were the Hummerts, Frank and his wife Anne, who started out as his secretary (a recurring soap theme – Krystle was Blake Carrington's secretary). Hummert was an advertising copywriter who moved from New York to Chicago and got caught up in the excitement of early radio in that city. Looking for a show that kept women at home glued to the radio – and his advertising messages – he came up with 'Stolen Husband' in 1931. 'Stolen Husband' flopped, but Frank and Anne kept going. They didn't write their programmes, they commissioned and produced; and eventually they came up with 'Betty and Bob', the first soap opera to go out to the entire American nation.

Irna Phillips gave soap its content. The Hummerts supplied its form. Most soaps on radio and television today follow the style of 'Betty and Bob', with different story-lines intertwined. The Hummerts also brought in melodrama, colourful events which the average real-life family never experiences. Betty was a shorthand typist who married her boss and thus provoked his millionaire father to cut him off without a cent. Bob then went to the bad, having affairs, drifting from job to job. The couple had a child, separated, divorced, remarried. Phillips and the Hummerts created soap as we know it, and we must be grateful to them.

The soap form burgeoned abundantly in the thirties and forties. It was reckoned that by 1940 every daytime quarter-hour in the States you could hear a soap on one station or another. In selling terms soap was rated the best advertising spot – apart from the very high priced evening comedy shows – on American radio. It went on like this until 1955 when television soaps began to grab the audience. Radio soaps struggled on for a time, but by the end of 1960 radio soap in the States was dead.

On television the form had arrived in a small way as early as 1947 when 'A Woman to Remember' drew pioneer audiences. But it was not until 1950 when Procter & Gamble put out 'The First Hundred Years' on CBS that tellysoap really got going. NBC countered with a family saga called 'Hawkins Falls', and the box turned into a soapbox. Daytime soaps, evening soaps developed all over.

The daytimers tended to be cheaper productions – radio with pictures, some critics called them. They went out live and often with inadequate rehearsal. The evening shows ('prime-time' in American terms) were better-rehearsed and more expensively mounted. They used filmed episodes to get them out of the studio, called on better-known actors, generally spent more money all round. Gradually taped shows began to take over from live transmissions. Standards rose in the sense that there were fewer fluffs and breakdowns, though some *aficionados* detected a lowering of emotional tension. By 1975 tape was the norm.

The next big change came with 'Dallas', which erupted on American screens in April 1978. 'Dallas' was a big-money production. Each episode was made on 35 mm film, like a Hollywood movie, and the quality rose dramatically. 'Dynasty' followed in January 1981, spending even more money and fighting 'Dallas' hard for top spot in the ratings.

The American soap scene now has three tiers: the daytime soaps, still mostly going out every weekday; the prime-time soaps, going out in the evening and often twice a week; and the supersoaps, 'Dallas' and 'Dynasty' style, going out once a week in prime time for a limited season each year.

In Britain soap arrived by accident. The BBC were not going to have any of that cheap American soap opera on their radio stations. Anything so popular must be bad. But in 1942 the Americans had to be convinced that ordinary Britons were standing up well to Hitler, so a soap opera was devised for the North American Service called 'Front Line Family', showing the Robinson family at war. Other areas in the Overseas Service began to take the show, and dial-twiddling Britons began to pick it up. Against the wishes of the BBC, the show began to gather a home audience. Eventually they had to give in and put the soap, retitled 'The Robinsons', out for home consumption. Listeners loved it; soap had crept in through a chink in the BBC's armour, and it has never gone away. 'The Robinsons' ran for nearly six years until it gave way to Mrs Dale and her Diary. Mrs Dale, so constantly worried about her doctor husband Jim, kept the soap flag flying alone for three years until a lusty band of countrymen joined the battle.

'The Archers' started with the worthy object of teaching farmers new agricultural techniques to help beat the postwar food shortage. Two writers who had been churning out a thick-ear crime series called 'Dick Barton' were called in to write the scripts. Edward J. Mason and Geoffrey Webb did such a good job on Dan and Doris Archer and their clan that in three months the hayseeds took the special agent's radio spots.

Since 'The Archers' began in 1950 the theme of spreading agricultural knowledge has continued. There is an agricultural story-editor, and townee fans are often subjected to lengthy chats on such themes as the proper way to dip sheep. Mrs Dale and the Archers were a two-horse team pulling soap opera along until 1969, when Mrs Dale closed her Diary for the last time.

'Waggoners Walk', a grittier series set in Hampstead, took her place and ambled along for eleven years before falling to the BBC's economy axe and sending the nation's soap fans into a frenzy of protest. The BBC took the view that they had 'The Archers' and, anyway, television soap had arrived. They could watch 'Crossroads' on Independent Television three times a week if they wanted to. ('Crossroads' began with five episodes a week, but was cut to four, then three.) The Archers ploughed their lone furrow – apart from a couple of weak and short-lived soap attempts by commercial radio stations – until the BBC unveiled their latest radio soap in October 1987.

Like 'Waggoners Walk', 'Citizens' was an attempt to draw in younger listeners, whose interest in radio tends to be limited to pop and rock music. The BBC claimed they would avoid Radio 4's instinctive middle-class bias, but the programme is based on the lives of young university graduates and has so far been a ratings' flop.

Television moved towards soap in the mid-1950s, when a weekly BBC serial called 'The Grove Family' told familiar family stories. Associated Television put out 'Emergency – Ward Ten', a biweekly and the first medical drama.

The first *real* soap opera, though, was 'Coronation Street', born in 1960. 'Coronation Street' set new standards in television drama, proving that a twice-weekly soap could occasionally achieve moments of drama as high as any of the posh playwrights could manage. The BBC came back with 'Compact', a fairly glossy soap set in the offices of a smart magazine. The BBC also tried two short-lived soap operas in the sixties: 'United!', which was about football and the men who play it, and 'The Newcomers', an attempt to show the problems of life in a new town.

And of course 'Crossroads' opened its motel doors in 1964. It had its ups and downs but never lost its mass audience until Central shut the old place down in April 1988. No soap opera has taken such a critical battering as 'Crossroads'. The newspapers lampooned, the comedians mocked (Jasper Carrott said that when the cast went on strike Central threatened them with rehearsal), but the fans stayed loyal to motel-keeper Meg and her descendants. In the end Central just became ashamed of it. They washed their hands of the poor old soap.

'Emmerdale Farm' took the genre into the Yorkshire Dales and established its own place as the sheepdip soap. 'Brookside' forced Britain to notice Channel 4 with gritty Liverpool stories, bad language and a left-wing subtext that upset a lot of people. 'Albion Market' traded for a short time, then the stalls were folded away.

But in 1985 'EastEnders' became the most important soap event since 'Coronation Street' first took us into the Rover's Return. The BBC had dithered a long time before coming back into television soap opera. 'EastEnders' was conceived as a sharp Southern counter to the Northern homeliness of 'Coronation Street'. The show worked at once, and soon became Britain's top-rated television show, with very strong story-lines and characters who became household names. (Even in posher households. Den and Ange are as big in Belgravia as in Barking Creek.)

Meanwhile the American supersoaps had moved into Britain. 'Dallas' first, then 'Dynasty', made the early eighties tingle as high-living oilmen and their molls battled it out in campy melodramas mounted and dressed in millionaire style. They were joined by 'Knots Landing', 'Falcon Crest' and 'The Colbys', highly scented soaps pressed in the same mould. American supersoap was and is enjoyed by the British, but in a special way. 'Coronation Street' and 'EastEnders' we take seriously.

Where will soap opera go in the future? My own belief is that the two styles – English down-to-earth storytelling and American glossy melodrama – will eventually merge. One day a strange hybrid will be born which will have the instant believability of 'EastEnders' and the bright exciting sheen of 'Dynasty'. I have a feeling the birth will be in America, but we shall see.

WHY SOAP OPERA IS IMPORTANT

For a start, soap fills a lot of television time, sometimes six or seven hours a week, and television is Britain's chief pastime these days. More than reading, more than watching sport, more than making love, more than knitting, more than fishing, more than going to the cinema or the theatre, more than all these things put together, we watch the telly.

Our children get more education from it than they get from school. Most of our information comes from the little screen, most of our entertainment, most of our political opinions, most of our notion about how the world is doing are all shot painlessly at us from little electronic guns behind a fluorescent screen. Just as the electrons make the screen glow with light and colour, the images produced set our minds and our hearts aglow. Whatever we say, we really *love* the telly.

And the figures show that what we love most of all in our beloved is her soap operas. The figures prove it. At Christmas in 1986, 30 million people watched 'EastEnders', easily the highest viewing figures of the holiday, despite the gift-wrapped tinsel shows (taped in July through tons of plastic snow gently falling) that were supposed to keep us awake after seasonal gluttony.

'EastEnders' and 'Coronation Street' are always in the top ten programmes, usually with 'EastEnders' slightly ahead. Scheduling often kept dear departed 'Crossroads' out of the charts, but even the less powerful soaps, 'Brookside' and 'Emmerdale Farm', 'Dallas' and 'Dynasty', pull in enormous audiences. You can put out Olivier defining Lear for all time, but he won't draw an audience a tenth the size that Hilda Ogden can command. I don't think that means Jean Alexander is a better actor than Olivier – though I'd be prepared to argue that one – but I do think for most of Britain drama *means* soap opera. I have to say this: I think this means soap *matters more* than Shakespeare. I think soap *matters more* than Dennis Potter. I think soap *matters more* than Fay Weldon. I think soap *matters more* than Jack Rosenthal. (I do not mean soap is *better*, just more important. The enormous shared experience watching soap represents is simply of tremendous social importance.)

I simply believe that an art form that can draw more than 40 million viewers a week is important. And I'd like to discuss how the most everyday drama in the world comes to achieve this high position. I would like first to present my credentials. I am a soap fiend, a soap addict, a soap nut, a soap *aficionado*. When I was young I denied this, of course, for it wasn't smart to worship both Mick Jagger and Stan Ogden. I became a secret soap-watcher, drawing the curtains in broad daylight lest sophisticated friends caught me watching Meg Richardson wrestling with half-remembered lines. Now I proclaim the simple faith: soap opera is good drama, soap opera is good for you, soap opera is good for us as a society.

A lot of academics have studied the phenomenon. Some of them agree with me, some don't. We'll take a swift canter through a few of their opinions, then I'll present mine.

Early American researchers into radio soap couldn't agree about anything. Two of them felt that we enjoy soap entirely for sado-masochistic reasons. We enjoy both the suffering of soap characters and the notion that we could be suffering in the same way. There must be a tiny nugget of truth here somewhere. Be honest: don't you actually enjoy it when JR is luring Sue Ellen back to the bottle? The power of the man is fascinating, the glitter of evil dazzles. And don't you at the same time put yourself in Sue Ellen's place and experience the fascination?

Other American academics decided that we like soap because it gives us the illusion that we can solve other people's problems. When Rita Fairclough was vacillating about remarrying, everyone in Coronation Street had an opinion and so did we. 'It's time she settled down again,' we said to each other; or 'That man won't do for Rita'. Rita couldn't hear us, of course, but we were in the superior position of knowing what was best for her.

Muriel G. Cantor from the American University and Suzanne Pingree of the University of Wisconsin collected a lot of ideas in a good book called simply *The Soap Opera*. Including: lonely people like soap because the characters provide them with friends and a family; for non-loners the soaps give an escape from real friends and family; day-dreaming and wishful thinking are given a focus by the delight soap characters take in their material possessions; soap can show that there's always someone worse off than you; soap becomes a habit and we enjoy it because it *is* a habit, like smoking; soap provides something to talk about to our friends; by showing problems similar to our own soap helps us solve those problems (if you believe that, you'll believe anything); soap is exciting because somehow the lives the characters live are on a more exciting level than our own (they fall in love more than we do, get mystery illnesses more than we do, they have more sex in their lives); soap teaches about practical matters – how to get a mortgage, how refuges for battered women work; soap can help us learn about ourselves.

Peter Buckman in his good book *All for Love* thought part of soap's power came from the fact that people love to gossip about the story-lines and the characters, for talking about them is like talking about, say, people you work with. Take 'the fact that the gossipers share with their subjects all sorts of common experiences and attitudes – unhappy love affairs, miserable love affairs, problems with sex and children and money – and you have a teeming pool to dip into,' wrote Buckman. 'It is also a pool whose waters are murky enough to be interesting, without being treacherous enough for danger.'

Tony Pearson, who runs a course in film and television studies at Glasgow University, says of soap characters: 'They become like friends, people you know because you watch them so often ... people adopt them as part of their own family, almost.' Pearson also believes that some soap operas – 'Coronation Street', for example – represent a kind of close-knit community that many of us no longer live in. 'Generally,' he says, 'the way we live has become a lot more complicated ... And in that context these programmes become enormously reassuring.'

Robert Grant, another academic from Glasgow, sees the soaps – he was thinking mainly of 'Dallas' and 'Dynasty' at the time – as modern morality plays 'ultimately differing little in their values from the traditional Christmas pantomime'. Blake Carrington's wealth and power, Grant feels, make him equivalent to a Shakespearian king. He sees Alexis's machinations as 'pasteboard wickedness', a sort of

9

symbolic evil. Her 'extravagant sexuality, like the Ugly Sisters in *King Lear*, adds a traditional, even puritanical, touch.'

The American sociologists George Gerner and Larry Gross thought that television and its soaps tended to move people, especially children, into standardised rôles and behaviour, though not intentionally. Two more American academics, Nancy Buerkel-Rothfuss and Sandra Mayes, checked people who watched soaps a lot and came to the conclusion that their view of society was coloured by what they watched. They assumed, for instance, that more women became doctors and lawyers than was actually the case, because of what they saw on the screen. In other words, soap can change the way we see the world.

My own view on the importance of soap is simple. I think it binds us together as a society. In the Middle Ages religion was the glue of society. Today television is the binding agent that helps us cohere. And the sticky quintessence of television (the superglue, if you like) is soap opera. To watch soap is an affirmation of social piety, a declaration that we share the beliefs, hopes, fears and prejudices of the rest of Western mankind.

People watch soap opera, talk and care about soap as a shared experience. Listen to them in offices, buses, clubs and pubs and you will find that whether Ange and Den will get back together is a more frequent topic than how Chelsea did on Saturday, whether Margaret Thatcher is a marvel or a monster, or even does God exist? We stick together for a lot of reasons, but one of them is our half-belief in these strange fictional worlds.

Popular newspapers spread the glue, and have done since they discovered that soap sells copies. The leaks about story-lines, the revelations about the actors' private lives, the gossip about how star X gets on with star Y – or, better still, doesn't – feed and comfort us when we are not actually watching the operas.

We watch, as I've said, because watching brings togetherness. But we get much more. Most important, a sense of the continuity of human life. Just as a soap opera can never really end, so we get this almost mystic sense of mankind moving on, whatever the troubles, the perils, the problems. We are reassured that the future is there, after all, Bomb or no Bomb. From soap comes hope. JR is the soapiate of the people.

It is true that if you ask the BBC or any of the ITV soap-boilers they will tell you they are merely making entertainment programmes, though entertainment programmes, they hope, of quality. It is true that the sage of Glasgow, Tony Pearson, warns against 'investing the soaps with more significance than they deserve', but I don't care. They are significant, they do matter, and if they disappeared tomorrow Britain would be a sadder place. And it would be an even less united Britain.

WHAT YOU CAN GET FROM THIS BOOK

What you *won't* get is the total uncritical fan worship you find in the official guides to individual soaps. This book tries to describe and profile the soap series, the characters and the actors truthfully. You get them soapwarts and all. You may disagree with my opinions, but you have the facts, too.

You won't get some university lecturer's recycled sociological study, either: slabs of comment from twenty housewives picked in the street one wet Wednesday and paid to say the first thing that comes into their head about television. Only sociologists need that and the jargon that goes with it. I've tried to use English.

SO WHAT IS THERE?

There is information to remind you about all the soap operas you ever saw (or missed because you were too young) on British television. What do I class as a soap? All the long-continuing series and all the smaller series which had soapy characteristics and were set to run and run (only viewers and producers lost interest). Some – such as 'Dr Kildare' – were never, strictly speaking, soap operas. But they led to soap operas ('Emergency – Ward Ten', for instance). I've ignored police series, although 'Z Cars' was possibly a candidate, and 'The Bill', which is poised to gain from the demise of 'Crossroads', certainly will be.

HOW TO USE THE BOOK

You can look up a soap you're keen on or are about to sample for the first time. Read about its history, creators, cast and crises. The soaps, the characters and actors in them are arranged alphabetically. You can also dip into my soap sections which give information on the oddities, traditions, continuing themes and side-effects (such as 'Fame', 'Censorship'). At the back there's a chronological table of when all the series were shown. The quotations used are mainly from interviews I've made. Some are from reported interviews with reliable writers. I hope you find it useful – and fun.

S·O·A·P B·O·X

'ACORN ANTIQUES'

'Acorn Antiques' became a running joke about amateurish under-rehearsed British soap opera in the BBC2 comedy series 'Victoria Wood – as Seen on TV'. Here the actors forgot their lines, the scenery shook and the camera went in and out of focus. Poor Noele Gordon must have been turning in her grave, because the audience immediately thought of 'Crossroads' watching the absurd events at an antique-shop run by queenly Miss Babs (Celia Imrie) with the help of fat Miss Bertie (Victoria Wood, who also wrote the script) and the baggy-stockinged, hump-backed, fawning charlady Mrs Overall (Julie Walters).

In the Christmas 1987 edition, the joke was taken further with a spoof behind-the-scenes report. Julie played the ludicrously grand and phonily humble actress behind the char, the star of the series: 'The nation have just taken me to their hearts,' she trilled. And Maggie Steed was hilarious as the paranoid producer terrorising the writers and refusing to reshoot scenes with fluffed lines and dropped props because 'Joe Public won't notice.'

ADULTERY

Adultery, in soap – betraying the one you love by loving another – is compulsory for every member of every married or unmarried couple, happy or unhappy, old or young.

It's obvious why. Adultery – or cheating – turns neutral characters into goodies or baddies temporarily. There's a chance for us to boo or cheer. Soap love comes and goes with sudden strength (characters don't vaguely fancy each other – it's obsession or nothing).

The morality is always clear. The morality of all soap is conservative, Christian and reactionary. Soap is a sneaky sort of Sunday school, revering God, the family and the *status quo*. It's all right for a character who isn't a baddie to have an affair so long as that person is seen to suffer guilt, and to Do The Right Thing in the end. Soap doesn't really discuss sex. Home-wrecking is the affront.

The other advantage of adultery is the way commentators in newspapers muscle in. My favourite soap hype was the love-affair between dreary Deirdre Barlow and Mike Baldwin, the Mr Flash of 'Coronation Street', in 1983. The question was: Should Deirdre leave her humourless but decent husband Ken for Mike? 'Don't do it!' one headline screamed after a readers' survey. Problem-page editors and agony aunts vied to put their views. Should Deirdre follow her heart? A London bishop writing in the *Sunday Mirror* warned the producers not to be too realistic. They weren't. There was only a kiss. But one writer asked: 'Did Mike and Deirdre do IT last night?' Columnist Lynda Lee Potter said an affair would rejuvenate Deirdre's marriage. Jean Rook wrote: 'Don't wander into the mire with Mike – stick in the mud with Ken.' The *Sun* asked a computer if Mike and Deirdre were compatible.

There were repercussions. The night Granada screened the kissing episode, a Chesterfield theatre sold just one ticket. There was panic in the North-East when Tyne Tees Television lost their pictures because of a transmitter breakdown. Even *The Times* ran a 'story-so-far' rundown for its readers. A Halifax housewife was reported to have given birth in the ambulance on the way to hospital – because she wanted to see Mike and Deirdre kissing. The *Daily Mail* consulted a psychiatrist. Poet Laureate Sir John Betjeman was moved to say: 'I think Ken's a nice man, he deserves better.' The *Daily Star* reported a baby boom because, it said, wives were staying away from family-planning clinics to watch 'Coronation Street'. The *Daily Telegraph* reported that Councillor Norman Smith – MP Cyril's brother – had tried to adjourn a Rochdale council meeting early 'so that we can all watch Ken and Deirdre'. His motion failed. The *Daily Star* set out to ask six-year-old Christabel Finch, who played Tracey Barlow, if 'your TV mummy should leave your TV daddy and go off with nice uncle Mike'. Christabel's mum refused to let them put the question. Granada's bouquet for the most enterprising press stunt of all went to the *Daily Mail*. Realising they had a captive audience of 56,000 for a Manchester United football match against Arsenal, they used the electronic scoreboard to flash a half-time message: 'Deirdre and Ken united again. Read tomorrow's *Daily Mail* for an action-replay of tonight's match and "Coronation Street"'s rematch.' The Stretford End roared its head off!

'ALBION MARKET'

'Albion Market', the twice-weekly £3 million soap launched in a blaze of publicity by Granada Television in August 1985 was a bit like most real street-markets – noisy, tatty and not much of a bargain when you thought about it. It was supposedly going to do for Independent Television weekend programme audience ratings what 'Coronation Street' had managed to achieve consistently midweek over twenty-seven years: grab 18 million regular viewers. 'Coronation Street' executive producer Bill Podmore was put in overall charge, and Denis Parkin – designer of the original Coronation Street – was invited to build the set.

On the big launch-day in Manchester, Granada managing director David Plowright invited the press to make a date twenty-five years hence in 2010 when, he predicted, 'Albion Market' would be celebrating its Silver Jubilee, and its stablemate 'Coronation Street' would be rejoicing in Golden Jubilee celebrations. Plowright also dismissed newcomer 'EastEnders' as 'no competition'. In fact, after a shaky start, the audience dwindled to a paltry 3.7 million – less than that enjoyed by 'Brookside' on minority-audience Channel 4. ITV acknowledged that strong competition from the BBC's newly launched 'Wogan' chat-show on Fridays and Top Ten Programmes leader 'Open All Hours' on Sundays had been too tough to beat. So 'Albion Market' was axed in August 1986 after exactly a hundred episodes.

Nevertheless, this story of down-to-earth Manchester market-folk made a brave attempt to exploit the kind of fast-moving complex story-lines used so successfully by 'Hill Street Blues'. Set in a £500,000 refurbished Salford warehouse, it dealt with the sociological and ethnic issues that involved forty regular stallholders, casual market-traders and their customers. David Hargreaves played tough market-boss Derek Owen.

18

Granada tried to inject an ethnic mix into the series by introducing Jewish, Vietnamese, West Indian and Pakistani characters amongst the stallholders. Like the token blacks and Asians of 'EastEnders', the Carpenters and Naima and Saaed, they were disappointingly two-dimensional most of the time. Here St Kitts-born Burt Caesar played fun-loving West Indian Phil who worked in the market café, suffered from his sharp-tongued woman boss and lived with his girlfriend and their baby. Actors Philip Tan and Pik-Sen Lim played Vietnamese refugees Lam Quoc Hoa and his cousin Ly Nhu Chan, a couple who could have been interesting had their story developed. Hoa was the stallholder, educated on the streets of Saigon. Chan, his older cousin, brought up in North Vietnam, had been foisted on to him by the family because she was more responsible. Brothers Raju and Jaz Sharma, Ugandans thrown out by Idi Amin, were ambitious market-traders, selling denim wear. Raju was well educated and serious, Jaz was the risk-taker with a weakness for English cream cakes and English girls. A sense of warmth and some humour (though not enough) came from the Jewish couple Morris and Miriam Ransome who ran the pottery-stall. Morris, played by former comedian Bernard Spear, was a worrier and a busybody. Miriam, played by Carol Kaye, a serious actress after twenty-one years' singing with the Kaye sisters, was the easygoing peacemaker.

Towards the end of its life Granada tried to revive it with new blood. Sixties pop singer Helen Shapiro came in as Viv the hairdresser, and former 'Till Death Us Do Part' 'Scouse git' Tony Booth was Ted Pilkington, landlord of the Waterman's Arms pub. But the market's life had already stalled.

THE CHARACTERS

Tony Fraser was the beefcake trader who sold ordinary cake in Albion Market. Played by heart-throb actor John Michie, he was a smooth-talking wide boy who lived in a touring caravan. Fraser was attracted to most pretty girls but pretended nineteen-year-old Lisa O'Shea, who helped her mum run the household-goods stall, was the only one. From Greenock, near Glasgow, he had hoped to become a pop star but he sold his gear and bought a van which enabled him to work the markets. All right so far, but *cake* . . .?

John Michie had a big female fan following during the programme's one-year run. A television newcomer, Michie – a former farm labourer and safari-holiday driver – quickly became the sex symbol of the series. To gain experience for the part, he worked for a while behind a real stall in a Manchester market.

Michie was born in Burma and has worked in many countries from Australia to Africa. He was an extra in the feature film *A Passage to India*. He came to Britain when he was thirteen, and his family settled down in Scotland. But by his eighteenth birthday he was wandering again. He worked his passage to Australia. Then he came back to Britain to study law, but dropped out to join the Edinburgh Traverse Theatre.

Lynne Harrison

Lynne Harrison was Albion Market's suffering woman. She sold hardware and, viewers soon learned, she had taken hard knocks in life. Lynne, aged thirty-six, played by Noreen Kershaw, had to support her daughter Lisa with a variety of jobs in the early years from cleaning to collecting pools coupons. Though one man after another let her down, she always remained a romantic at heart, even though she knew her ex-gaolbird husband Roy was a loser. A hard drinker and smoker in the Elsie Tanner vein, she had had to graft to get her own market-stall. Lynne enjoyed a close, almost sisterly relationship with her daughter Lisa, who helped her run the stall. Quick-tempered, but quick-witted, she was arguably the most believable character in 'Albion Market'. Trouble was, she wasn't sexy with it.

Noreen Kershaw left convent school in Bury, Lancashire, for a drama course at Manchester Polytechnic. That led to a fourteen-year stint in the theatre, mainly spells in Northern reps. She was a 'natural', therefore, for a number of rôles as Northerners in television series such as 'The Boys from the Blackstuff' and 'Coronation Street' – in which she appeared as the daughter of one of Annie Walker's 'lady victualler' friends. At one point she formed a women's theatre group, Bloomers, with two other actresses. 'We felt there just wasn't enough material being written either for, or by, women. So we put on a revue-style show aimed at women. It was a great success,' she said.

Roy Harrison

Roy Harrison was the Albion Market rogue. He sold household goods with a snarl. An ex-gaolbird, Roy's victims included himself. He was always a misery. Played by Jonathan Barlow, Harrison would have liked to be a professional soccer-player, but he wasn't good enough. He yearned for the good life with fast cars and holidays in Spain in posh hotels. He claimed to love his hard-working wife, Lynne, but two-timed her with another woman on the side – Kay Bannister. Unlike Lynne, Harrison believed in living from day to day. Booze and snooker were his priorities.

Jonathan Barlow also did a short stint in 'Coronation Street' as Geoff Singleton, Gail Tilsley's nice noble boyfriend during her 1987 marriage break-up from husband Brian. Jonathan, who comes from Telford,

Shropshire, trained at the Manchester Polytechnic Theatre School and played most Northern reps before making his television début in Granada's thriller serial 'The XYY Man'. His stage work includes an appearance as John Lennon in the stage musical based on Lennon's life, produced at Liverpool's Everyman Theatre. Jonathan, who married his wife Lynne five years ago, likes to relax by playing drums and singing with a Manchester band.

Lisa O'Shea, the pretty nineteen-year-old brunette who used to help her mum, Lynne Harrison, on the household-goods stall in Albion Market, was besotted with good-looking young market-trader Tony Fraser. Lisa, played by Sally Baxter, never knew her father and, as a result, never liked the men her mother brought home, mainly because they always left Mum in a mess. Lisa preferred the open-air life of market work to office jobs. Like her mother, she was a born fighter and survivor. There was a special bond between them – they were more like sisters. When her boyfriend Tony Fraser talked to other girls, Lisa tried hard to hide her feelings of jealousy. Their love-life was stormy and volatile.

Sally Baxter, the lively twenty-nine-year-old actress who played ten-years-younger character Lisa O'Shea in 'Albion Market', is from Cumbria, and broke into acting as a schoolgirl in local pantomimes. She worked as a BBC typist in London for a while before embarking on a three-year drama course at Bristol Old Vic Theatre School. Before television Sally was involved in the Bristol New Vic's Playwrights' Company and the Little Theatre Company in Bristol.

Derek Owen was the father-figure, the market-hall superintendent of Albion Market, a kind of feudal landlord. He had the power to throw traders out of the market-hall if they broke the rules. Owen, played by David Hargreaves, was a law unto himself. Hard, harassed, devious – but only to be fair – he was the man the traders loved to hate. When things went wrong he invariably blamed his young assistant Keith Naylor. Owen had worked his way up to a management rôle via several menial jobs like junior railway porter and town hall clerk. He took his 'O' levels at night-school. He cursed his teenage luck at having to pass up a career in the Navy because he got his girlfriend Barbara pregnant. Though he loved his three children, he was always thinking about leaving 'the wife' – but he never had the courage.

David Hargreaves played tough no-nonsense market-hall super-intendent Derek Owen in 'Albion Market' after another soap life. He played Suzie Birchall's father Bob in 'Coronation Street' in 1977. But viewers will probably remember him best for his rôle as the 'wet' probation-officer husband of the top female cop in the first series of 'Juliet Bravo'. Born in New Mills, Derbyshire, David Hargreaves trained as a teacher in Leeds before dropping out of college to join the Central School of Speech and Drama in London. After a two-year spell as a supporting actor with the Royal Shakespeare Company in Stratford-upon-Avon, he joined the National Theatre in the Olivier era. He appeared in Olivier's film version of *Othello*. The strong silent type, David got lots of television work in popular series like 'Z Cars' and 'Softly Softly'. He estimates that he has appeared in over 350 television productions or series episodes in twenty years. He is married to Chloe Ashcroft, actress niece of the great Peggy Ashcroft.

Duane Rigg was the chirpy little rogue in Albion Market who could twist his mum and dad around his little finger. Duane, played by Alistair Walker, used to help out on his parents' toy-stall but was always on the cadge. Sometimes he 'borrowed' goods from the stall to sell to his mates at school. His big joy in life was riding his motorbike. Duane was just beginning to get interested in girls but cringed at the thought of having to introduce them to his weird parents.

Alistair Walker was just sixteen when the series began in 1985. Born in Oldham, Lancashire, he went to the local Blue Coat School and joined the cast of 'Albion Market' after taking his 'O' levels. His sister, Wendy Jane Walker, played Susan, wife of Mike Baldwin, in 'Coronation Street'. As a child Alistair went to dancing classes and performed with amateur theatre groups and Oldham's Theatre Workshop. At nine he played Tiny Tim in Oldham Coliseum's production of *A Christmas Carol*. He was a panto kid in Liverpool Empire's *Babes in the Wood* at the age of twelve – a daunting business before an audience of 2000 people.

ALCOHOL

Alcohol lubricates soap opera. 'Coronation Street' and 'EastEnders' and the big American soaps would dry up and stop without it. The Rover's Return, the Queen Victoria and the Cattleman's Club are the settings for so much important action, useful places for characters to meet, a boon to the writers. Dot Cotton is looking for her nasty son Nick, so someone tells her he's in the Vic. Rita must come across Alan Bradley chatting up some other woman; she pops into the Rover's for a vodka and a confrontation. In 'Emmerdale Farm' the Woolpack is more than the home of that quaint married couple Amos and Mr Wilks. It is the natural battleground for Seth and Alan Turner, Jackie Merrick and his latest love-rival. Indeed, I sometimes think the BBC and the independent companies should get together and set up a Soap Cirrhosis Centre for the livers of these unfortunate characters who spend so much of their lives in licensed premises. In 'Crossroads' the motel had its own bar, a charmless place, and the drinks were often sloppily served. 'Brookside' manages mostly without a local, but that's only because Phil Redmond couldn't or wouldn't build one into the Liverpool close that became his set.

'Dallas', 'Dynasty', 'The Colbys', 'Falcon Crest', 'Knots Landing' always feature a great deal of eating and drinking. It's easy to see why. First, boring plot-points have to be made in complicated chunks of tête-à-tête dialogue. An elegant restaurant at least provides a glamorous backdrop. A pretty waitress pouring JR's Bourbon and branch water gives you something to look at while the turgid stuff about the cartel or what Washington thinks of the new oil leases is dispensed. Second, all this gracious living takes *time*, and soap opera has to progress at a leisurely pace. The story must unfold slowly, like those slow-motion films of a flower unfurling its petals.

Bars have a different function in American soap. They are frequently the place for fist-fights, a tradition inherited from Westerns. They are often used as shorthand for degradation. When Sue Ellen has been driven to drink once again by JR, we see her hanging on to her stool in some sleazy bar. When Ray Krebbs thought Donna loved another he, too, was seen in joints as low as a gnat's kneebone, filling his cowboy boots.

Drinking at home has its nuances. In home-boiled soaps it doesn't happen much, though old Lou Beale attacks the brandy-bottle occasionally in the Fowlers' parlour. The girls threw Bet Lynch a domestic hen party with an alarming mixture of drinks on the eve of her late-in-life wedding. Mike Baldwin is seen sipping a Scotch at home, but that is merely to emphasise that as one of the Street's few capitalists he can afford it. Good characters rarely drink at home. You don't often see Bobby Ewing take a snifter at Southfork. Or Miss Ellie. I can't ever remember Krystle Carrington clinking ice in a crystal tumbler, can you? Alexis, of course, can order Dom Perignon any time she chooses. Wickedness and extravagance go together. Sue Ellen is an exception. The pouting wife of JR is given to bouts of alcoholism, always brought on by JR's machinations. Her recurring pattern is to believe that JR really loves her after all, discover she's wrong and then immerse herself in vodka. JR often leaves the vodka conveniently to hand.

Another soap drunk is JR's brother Gary Ewing, who does his drinking in 'Knots Landing', though he occasionally pops home to see Miss Ellie at Southfork. Gary dries out from time to time. The actor Ted Shackelford does this most convincingly. He should do; he's had real-life experience of the process.

Adam Carrington hit the bottle briefly when he had to confess finally that he was an impostor, not a true Carrington. But he recovered fast when Blake and Krystle adopted him, which was nice, considering he'd tried to poison Jeff Colby. Nobody's perfect.

Drunks in British soaps are fairly unusual. Angie Watts tried to do herself in with booze and pills when she found out about Dirty Den's serious mistress, Jan. She still drank secretly – so the viewer knew she still had a dangerous weakness, her ex-husband had a weakness to exploit and her daughter something to worry about. Miss Diane had a fairly unconvincing addiction to the bottle for a short time in 'Crossroads'. She, too, tried to kill herself after breaking up with Vince. Like most 'Crossroads' plots the episode was handled so shallowly and was over so fast that it wasn't too important. The motel soap gave oldest inhabitant Jill Chance a drunken lover, Mickey Doyle, who was written out by being sent to a clinic. Presumably he's still there. Jack Rolfe in 'Howards Way' is a drunk rather than an alcoholic. The drink comes in handy when Jack makes a story-line work by doing something silly in an alcoholic haze. The drink gives him instant character. Without booze he'd just be an irascible old man. His geriatric girlfriend Kate Harvey has a matching occasional weakness – for gambling.

When the writing is bad enough, a Big Fault is a useful way of making a character stick in the viewer's mind.

WHAT'S YOURS?

In soap a character's taste in drinks is crucial to his place in the society of the series. In British soaps all 'real men' drink beer (yuppies have to drink real ale). Young characters drink mostly lager. Middle-class men drink whisky, women who've 'been around' drink vodka, and the drinking of wine is usually connected with romance. Here are some tastes I've spotted.

In 'Coronation Street' Ena Sharples, Minnie Caldwell and Martha Longhurst – the Holy Trinity in the snug – drank milk stout. Hilda Ogden drank light ale (bottled) most of the time when she treated herself. If asked, it's a port and lemon; but her favourite drink of all time is Planters Punch (she gained the taste while working on a cruise ship as a cleaner). Annie Walker had a Special Sherry (which was really Harvey's Bristol Cream); she liked cherry brandy or Tia Maria at Christmas. Mavis Riley and Emily Bishop take fruit juices. On special occasions it's sweet sherry (two for Mavis is one too many). Elsie Tanner liked gin; in the summer months she would have a lager with lime. Vera Duckworth and Ivy Tilsley drink bottled lager. Alec Gilroy drinks Irish whiskey. Mike Baldwin's is Scotch whisky, and champagne on special occasions. Rita Fairclough likes vodka and tonic. Audrey Roberts likes vodka or gin as long as it's a large one. Albert Tatlock stuck to rum. Alf Roberts, Brian Tilsley, Kevin Webster, Stan Ogden, Alan Bradley and Jack Duckworth are all beer men. Deirdre Barlow has lager or gin, Tracey Barlow has Coke, Ken Barlow half of Newton & Ridley's mild.

Of the 'EastEnders' stars Dot Cotton has pure orange juice or a nice cup of tea. Angie Watts takes gin, in large doses except when paying Pauline Fowler a visit; then it's light ale. When on the wagon, tonic water. Pauline Fowler likes light ale or a gin on special occasions. Ethel Skinner has Guinness. Lou Beale prefers milk stout and brandy or a Guinness. Pete Beale, Arthur Fowler, Barry Clarke, Rod, Charlie Cotton, Tom and Darren are all beer men (Churchill's). Wicksie, Ian Beale and Lofty have lager. Carmel Roberts drinks Guinness. Pat Wicks has gin. Den likes beer, Scotch, champagne or wine at Christmas. Michelle asks for soft drinks; when out on the razzle, she'll have a vodka or a gin. Sharon has soft drinks or, when out with the girls, a vodka. Mags has yuppy spring water or gin and tonic. Willmott-Brown enjoys beer and spirits. Dr Legg is a half-of-bitter man. Ali likes beer, or whisky – when playing cards. Sue has gin or soft drinks. Jan took Glenfiddich and Malvern water. Dr Singh was a half-of-bitter man. Colin prefers real ale.

In 'Emmerdale Farm' Alan Turner likes his whisky. Annie Sugden has a sherry on special occasions. Joe Sugden likes beer and whisky. When trying to get a young lady into bed, it's champagne. Jack Sugden sticks to beer. Jackie Merrick takes lager. Matt Skilbeck likes beer. Dolly Skilbeck occasionally has a lager, a gin or a drop of Annie's sherry. Henry Wilks likes whisky. Sandie Merrick has lager, cider or, when in the mood for love, wine. Phil Pearce drinks beer or, when warming up with Sandie, wine. Seth Armstrong is a beer man. The Reverend Donald Hinton takes a small whisky or soft drinks.

In 'Brookside' Bobby Grant likes whisky and beer. Sheila Grant likes fruit juice and (of course) holy wine. Doreen Corkhill likes gin or tea. The Collins family naturally were used to wine. Paul likes the odd gin, brandy or whisky. Annabelle likes a sherry after work. Billy Corkhill, Barry Grant, Ralph Hardwick, Harry Cross, Terry Sullivan are all beer-drinkers.

In 'Falcon Crest' the whole cast drink Falcon Crest wines. Except Richard Channing, who drinks only milk.

In 'Knots Landing' Gary Ewing has anything alcoholic he can lay his hands on and he drinks quickly. Abby Ewing drinks wine. There's not much drinking in this soap (Gary Ewing makes up for the rest of the cast).

In 'Dynasty' Alexis Rowan constantly sips champagne or cocktails but never gets squiffy. Blake Carrington likes a manly brandy, whisky or wine. Krystle Carrington takes wine or whisky or brandy, but rarely drains the glass. Steven Carrington drinks beer. Jeff Colby pours himself whiskies, wine, beer, champagne or cocktails. Fallon Colby likes wine, champagne or cocktails. Adam Carrington takes beer, wine and anything to get drunk on. Sammy-Jo wine. Dominique Deveraux likes champagne. Dex Dexter is a beer man but has wine with a meal.

In 'Dallas' Miss Ellie takes brandy or whisky before dinner as the clan gathers. She drinks wine with meals. Clayton has beer, whisky before dinner. JR has Bourbon and branch. Cliff Barnes takes Bourbon, whisky, wine or beer. Ray Krebbs is a beer man. Bobby likes beer and a pre-dinner whisky. Sue Ellen likes vodka, lots of it: when she's being good, she drinks Club soda. When not, vodka or even cheap sherry with the Dallas down-and-outs.

'ANGELS'

'Angels' kept medicated soap lathering in the late 1970s and early 1980s as the lives of six student nurses at St Angela's Hospital in London were followed intermittently in thirteen-week series on BBC1. Conceived as the hospital equivalent of 'Z Cars' (that is, with a documentary-like style), it won high audiences – averaging 12 million – despite being shown opposite 'Coronation Street'. Writers (mostly women) portrayed the young nurses' lives as hard and thankless, and there was a fast turnover of new actresses, each made to research the rôle by weeks of work on real wards. Fiona Fullerton was one who made an impact. In 1978, when Morris Barry took over as producer from Ron Craddock, his new intake included actress Shirley Cheriton (p.274). When Julia Smith (p.230) took over to produce the fifth series in 1979, not only were Judith Jacob and Kathryn Apanowicz (both future 'EastEnders' stars, pp.272, 271) put into uniform, but also the series was screened twice weekly on Tuesdays and Thursdays, almost making it the rehearsal soap for Julia's later triumph. Now filmed in unused wards of a Coventry hospital, the story-lines were perhaps the toughest yet for an early-evening (6.30) series. Joined by a token male nurse (Martin Barrass), the girls were now on the Pill, having affairs, hitting the bottle. One struggled to bring up a child and work. Inevitably there were protests. Julia Smith dismissed them. 'There are a lot of tensions in a young nurse's life; it's no wonder some turn to drink,' she said, adding: 'When you're just eighteen you've got a lot of growing-up to do.' Real nurses objected, claiming that the television versions were mostly idle, coarse and insensitive. Nurse Rose Butchins (Kathryn Apanowicz) was especially disliked. 'Angels' ended after nine series in the autumn of 1983, never having been granted the round-the-year status of a 'real' soap – perhaps because no group of characters was lovable enough or at least around long enough to become loved.

'THE APPLEYARDS'

The Appleyards were not true soap stars. More the forefathers of the Glums than trailblazers for the Fowlers or the Ewings, they were BBC Television's early idea of an 'ordinary, workaday family living in a little house'.

The twenty-minute episodes, written by Philip Burton, were shown sporadically as part of Children's Television at 5 p.m. on Thursdays, with a weekend repeat, from October 1952 to April 1957 in runs of six. The 'serial plays' as they were called were voted the most popular children's feature for two of those years, which may have put Muffin the Mule's nose out a bit.

Constance Fraser played homely Mrs Appleyard (after a spell in 'Mrs Dale's Diary' as Mrs Barr) and Frederick Piper played Mr Appleyard – later replaced by Douglas Muir. Their four children were Janet, a typist; John, an eighteen-year-old garage mechanic; Tom, 'a rascal'; and Margaret, his fourteen-year-old sister. In this pattern they were remarkably similar to the Grove Family living on grown-ups' television at the same time.

No sooner had the series started than a Derbyshire city councillor objected to the portrayal of young people betting on horse racing and teenagers shown smoking. (How would that councillor have survived 'Grange Hill', the BBC's 'blackboard jungle' series, one wonders.)

To young viewers, the Appleyards like the Famous Five were beyond criticism. To one newspaper commentator, though: 'The Appleyards seem to get no fun out of life. The series is more a documentary on the chores of family life.'

'THE ARCHERS'

'The Archers' is cowpat soap, daily whiffs of country life, fruity and frolicksome enough for townies to enjoy, harsh and humdrum enough never to incite them to camp on Lakey Hill or double-park outside the Bull in Ambridge. Whatever the slog, the problems and the pains, farming is fun every evening on BBC Radio 4 and has been, incredibly, since 1950.

Its Birmingham-based producers like to think it's a pure product, made (unlike the others) of real passion for the subject and true to the changing face of agriculture and rural society. Certainly, since the start 'The Archers' has hit all the right targets of entertaining serial-drama: the joys and heartbreaks of family life, romance, comedy and action-adventures. The chances are that the 'everyday story of countryfolk' (as the announcer always calls it) will be being told in another thirty-eight years when even the most oak-like television soap has withered or been axed down.

Its beginnings are often recounted. At a Birmingham council-chamber meeting, farmers were asked by Midlands broadcaster Godfrey Baseley what sort of programme they wanted. Henry Burtt of Lincolnshire rose and said: 'What we really want is a farming "Dick Barton".'

So Baseley and the writers of 'Dick Barton', the nightly radio serial about a special agent, Geoffrey Webb and Edward J. Mason, devised the adventures of Dan and Doris Archer, their sons Phil and Jack, daughter Christine, villager Walter Gabriel, businessman Jack Woolley and the Archer grandchildren, growing up fast. With a mysterious Baroness, Mike Daly, a secret agent, a crashing jet plane, hordes of vicious poachers, arsenists, kidnappers and rum 'uns, and a fair bit of romance and heavy breathing, it was hardly anyone's 'everyday story'. But there were lots of important cows – like Daffodil, the one whose labour was featured in the opening dialogue on Whit Monday 1950.

29

DAN (*to cowhand*): Well, Simon, what do you think?
SIMON: Ah well, 'er might and 'er might not.

By Easter the daily serial (budget £47 an episode) had moved into the 6.45 evening slot, killed off 'Dick Barton' and attracted 6 million listeners – a million more than 'Mrs Dale's Diary'. Ambridge, based on Worcestershire villages like Inkberrow, Ripple and Hanbury, near Borchester, based on Droitwich, became mapped in the national mind.

By 1953 listeners to the General Overseas Service could hear it, too. By 1955, Harry Oakes, who played Dan, was receiving £25 a week. The BBC argued that it was the formula not the actors which counted, and Noel Johnson, who'd played Dick Barton, had earned only £20. They also reckoned the audience had swelled to 20 million.

No wonder, then, that the death of Grace Archer, Phil's young lady wife, killed as she rushed into a burning stable to rescue a horse, completely wrecked the opening night of Independent Television. Grace made the next morning's front pages. ITV's opening ceremony was a minor event. It looked like a deliberate act of sabotage by the BBC. Isanne Churchman, the actress who played Grace, had been in dispute with the BBC and had been due to be dropped months before. More than a thousand listeners wrote protest letters. Wreaths, a shroud, six brass coffin-handles were sent. Later, news came that one listener was so shocked that she gave birth to a premature baby. It was the biggest (best?) rumpus the soap had until Tom Forrest was gaoled on a charge of murdering a poacher and 500 railway workers signed a petition to the 'judge' for leniency and money for a defence fund flooded in.

By the early 1960s the cosy class-snobbery-steeped world of Ambridge was being voted Best Radio Programme by *Daily Telegraph* readers for the fifth year running. Listeners adored Gwen Berryman, the Wolverhampton opera singer turned actress, who played the warm motherly Doris, who made Brookfield Farm the home of country goodness. (In reality she was unmarried and terrified of cows.) They thrilled to the burgeoning romance of John Tregorran (the only antique-dealer in the world never to fiddle a customer) and Carol, widow of the disliked absentee squire.

In 1967 the Director-General of the BBC, Sir Hugh Greene, granted permission for something of grave public concern. He allowed unmarried Jennifer Archer, the daughter of the Bull's alcoholic landlord, Jack, and his wife Peggy, to become pregnant by an Irish barman. The baby, conceived by Baseley over a cup of BBC coffee, caused worry and excitement throughout the land.

By 1969, Mrs Dale had been silenced and, with the death of Monte Crick, the second actor to play Dan, and a strong protest from the League Against Cruel Sports that 'The Archers' was condoning blood sports, the serial's future hung in the balance.

In 1970, Jock Gallagher was appointed editor and given three months to 'sort it out' or close it down. He sacked Godfrey Baseley. 'There was a kind of contempt for "The Archers" in professional circles,' he said. 'It wasn't really part of the Drama Department. A clique had been running the programme. The producer Tony Shryane had in twenty years never been allowed to attend the script meetings. There were vested interests with the Country Landowners' Association. There were great chunks of Ministry of Agriculture propaganda and the same two writers who'd become rather tired.'

He hired Malcolm Lynch, the editor of 'Coronation Street', new writers (eight at any one time) – some of them women, including novelist Susan Hill. He gently took the Archer family down a peg (they'd become gentry – far grander than they'd begun) and stopped caricaturing the peasant class. Some forelock-tugging stayed, because, said Gallagher, it existed for the real Jethro Larkins of the 1970s. Anthony Parkin joined the team as agricultural editor.

William Smethurst arrived as producer in 1978, introduced camp jokes, high farce and the Grundy family of hopelessly bad tenant farmers: oafish Eddie and Joe, his cantankerous old dad, whom listeners *knew* picked his nose and scratched his bum. Pat, Tony Archer's wife, became a Born Again Feminist; Sophie, David Archer's girlfriend, was a twittering Sloane Ranger.

Doris died in 1981 after Gwen Berryman's long battle against arthritis; and Jill Archer, the down-to-earth second wife of Phil – not pompous, not snobbish, whose lovely voice belongs to Patricia Greene – became the central Caring, Coping Woman.

The farming calendar was still a major concern. But so was Princess Margaret's visit to Grey Gables in 1984. Its owner, Jack Woolley, almost died of pride. Rich Brian Aldridge – such a go-ahead farmer – was revealed as a womanising rotter; Mike Tucker, the abrasive union man, went bankrupt and his family suffered movingly; and the Over Sixties' tea-money went missing, to everyone's alarm. Dan Archer died peacefully during lambing and Schula Archer finally stopped gadding about with upper-class twit Nigel Pargitter to marry her solicitor Mark Hebdon.

THE WRITERS

The writers were well paid (about £1400 for a week's scripts); the actors were well paid (about £750 plus repeat fees for the monthly four days of recordings); and the producers retained their secret weapon – the ability to slot in topical scenes, conversations about storms or stock-market changes, elections and disasters, despite recording episodes six weeks in advance.

By 1986, Smethurst had been headhunted by Central Television to administer artificial respiration to 'Crossroads'. (Actually that soap was just recovering from major transplants by Phillip Bowman.) Smethurst, with several 'Archers' writers and some 'Archers' actors, did major surgery, but the patient died of Controller's Whim.

Liz Rigby took over 'The Archers', brought in new writers (three of whom also write for 'EastEnders') and opened the windows to let realism in. Some camp humour stayed, so did the concern with swine fever and silage, naturally enough. But at the Bull prices were mentioned, Pat and Tony's children *spoke*, and Phil Archer had almost to sell Brookfield Farm to pay death duties. In the event he needed to sell only part of the land and when a housing development involving some old barns began, the Ambridge Ghost loomed up, alarming the locals for months.

More daring still, townsfolk moved in. Actress Carole Boyd's deliciously naff nouveau-riche voice as Lynda Snell became a comic success when she and her husband moved from Sunningdale into Ambridge Hall, formerly the home of the late, legendary Aunt Laura and Colonel Danby.

There was a late and much fussed-over baby for jolly Jennifer Aldridge who'd now completed her transformation from Ambridge's scarlet woman to its most insensitive matron and stranglable snob.

Mistakes still happened. Mrs Blossom died for the third time. One of the Vicar's children was stopped from catching the school bus when it was worked out that he was twenty-five years old.

The everyday story continued every day, and so did the listening. For all the wailing about changes, the audience increased by a third. This year almost one million people tuned in every day, a third of them under thirty-five. 'I think you can say we sorted it out,' said Gallagher.

And, as of going to print, Walter Gabriel, played by eighty-six-year-old Chris Gittins MBE, still said, 'Me old pals, me old beauties.'

BABIES

Baby anguish is big in soap. Babies rarely, if ever, arrive planned by two happy parents nine months after normal sex. Often the paternity of the baby is in doubt and of compelling interest; hence the huge interest in 'EastEnders' when Dirty Den was revealed as the father of schoolgirl Michelle's baby.

The pregnancy often results from a night of madness, or an act of violence, or is a mistake because the mother is too old, too delicate, too poor or too harassed. Pregnant soap women are always high-risk cases. In 'Crossroads' Glenda was a guinea-pig test-tube mum. They fall off horses and down stairs. (Both, if you're Krystle Carrington, the moist-eyed madonna of 'Dynasty'.) They miscarry, and doctors tell them they may never be pregnant again. They give birth in dangerous places without medical help. Imagine the birth trauma of Sheila Harvey's baby: delivered on the Crossroads' motel floor by Meg Richardson! The newborn's life frequently hangs in the balance during tense scenes in intensive care (see p.333).

In 'Dynasty', baby Christina was born to Krystle at home on satin sheets and had no umbilical cord. Krystle kept her knickers on, I swear. She survived only after several major operations involving about thirty specialists from around the world. A couple of seasons later the same child was found to need a heart transplant. When the agony of the donor child's mother could be fully explored, the writers had everyone's mascara running.

In 'EastEnders', little Martin Fowler (Lou's grandson and the unplanned child of frazzled fortyish Pauline) had a tummy bug and was rushed to hospital on his christening day. It was just as worrying. And when toddler Hassan, son of the 'EastEnders' café-owner and his wife, died a cot death gnarled old television critics cried.

'Dallas' loves baby problems. In the early days there was Sue Ellen's panic that her baby John Ross had the dreadful disease neurofibromatosis, inherited from his father Cliff Barnes. When Cliff was found out not to be the father, everyone was happy. Donna Krebbs had a 'late' baby (before Pauline in 'EastEnders' or Sheila in 'Brookside'). Donna's was diagnosed as a Downs Syndrome babe, so the problem was to terminate or not to terminate. In the event she miscarried after being gored at a rodeo. Happily that turned out to be a dream – as did all the events of the Bobby-less season of 'Dallas'. Donna became pregnant again, divorced husband Ray before the birth and quivered in court as he threatened a custody suit.

Ray dropped it. He was already entangled in the anguish of Jenna's baby – Bobby's love-child.

In 'The Colbys', Fallon's second baby had two possible daddies: Jeff or Miles. So, too, did Sarah Louise Tilsley in 'Coronation Street'. Luckily they have blood tests up there, too (even if they don't have neurofibromatosis).

In 1987 aborting babies was the thing – accompanied by much anguish and suffering. Susan Baldwin was thrown out by her husband in 'Coronation Street' after terminating her pregnancy. Debbie in 'Crossroads' was distraught but decided not to abort her frozen veg salesman's child. Michelle in 'EastEnders' fixed and went through with an abortion, then suffered because Lofty was heartbroken.

Soap babies don't poo or puke or have colic. They look divine. Women love soap and women love babies. A babyless soap won't lather.

BACK FROM THE DEAD

'Back from the dead' is a well-known route for soap characters. So many have taken it, it's obvious that no form of murder or heart-stopping injury need ever be fatal in soapland fantasy.

The most audacious was Bobby Ewing's rebirth in 'Dallas' after viewers watched Katherine Wentworth's car plough into his, watched him die in hospital, heard the life-support machines *ping* and then attended his funeral. Bobby had died at actor Patrick Duffy's request. But 'Dallas' turned out to need Bobby, and Patrick turned out to need 'Dallas' (see 'Life after Soap'). The show's writers decided to 'explain' his death in a dream – consigning the events of a whole series (the episodes without him) to Pam's Dream. Commentators in newspapers declared viewers would never forgive this 'cop-out'. But they did.

As Bill Bast, co-producer of 'The Colbys', said when Barbara Stanwyck left that show (declaring it a 'pile of garbage'), her character killed in a crash: 'Nobody ever dies conclusively in Hollywood soap operas unless they libel the show.'

Bringing back the dead is a good way to upset the living, and has often been done. Before Pam's Dream, when characters rose from their graves the explanation was usually misinformation. Fallon came back to 'Dynasty' because the news that she'd died in a plane crash was a mistake. (Actually the writers were stalling, hoping Pamela Sue Martin, the original actress in the rôle, would return.) When Fallon 'died' a second time, by going into space in an alien UFO, the explanation was that she'd had a temporary supernatural experience. We'd all guessed she was nuts.

Philip Colby came back to 'The Colbys' calling himself Hoyt Parker because reports that he'd been killed in the war were exaggerated. The human ashes found in 'Falcon Crest' weren't all that remained of Julia Cumson, it turned out. She escaped through a trap-door.

In 'Knots Landing' Ciji Dunne, a rock singer played by Lisa Hartman, was murdered. She did not come back from the dead, *but* Cathy Geary who looked very similar (because she was also played by Lisa Hartman) arrived. In the year Ciji had been dead, young viewers mourned. So a second coming was devised. Incredibly, viewers laughed, then carried on viewing.

British soaps have so far not performed miracles of resuscitation on their corpses. Though the early 'Crossroads' introduced a few characters viewers had never seen who were supposed to have died. It brought gasps from Meg when her second husband turned up as she was about to marry the third – but none from the audience. If Damon in the relatively realistic 'Brookside' were to swagger back, viewers might lynch executive producer Phil Redmond. Or they might weep for joy and watch on.

'BEN CASEY'

'Ben Casey' was the American medical drama which ran for 153 episodes at the same time as 'Dr Kildare' from 1961 to 1966. It was as big a success there and only slightly less popular here, shown on Independent Television in black and white. Dark-haired Vince Edwards was discovered by Bing Crosby (the show was made by Crosby's company) and put through a lightning course in handling scalpels and forceps to play brooding intense neuro-surgeon Ben Casey. He never had the boyish charm of Richard Chamberlain's Dr Kildare but he had sex appeal (well, he had hairy muscular arms). The series was seen as harder-edged, capturing the round-the-clock strains of dedicated doctors in a city hospital. It tackled some controversial subjects, darting into close-ups of operations. Sam Jaffe played Casey's mentor, Dr David Zorba, who guided and protected him in his battles with disease and the medical establishment. Like the Kildare series, 'Ben Casey' became soapier with age (although, unlike 'Dr Kildare', this series was not split into half-hourly shows). Stories ran on from week to week, and Casey was even allowed to fall in love with a beautiful patient who awoke from a thirteen-year coma. The series were rerun on some ITV stations this year to match the BBC's re-screening of 'Dr Kildare'.

BITCHES

The bitch is a perennial soap figure. She provides a focus of dislike for the viewer, a chance for wilful wickedness for the producers and an outlet for wild sexuality. Heroines can have sex, can even be involved (more often not *quite* involved) in extra-marital hanky-panky, but heroines have to *suffer*. Bitches do not. They enjoy it, the unprincipled hussies!

Heroines may sometimes be forced to deceit, to lie, to behave not quite the way Brown Owl would approve. But they hate it. Their lips quiver, their eyes show pain. Bitches dive right into bad behaviour, eyes glittering, cloven bosoms heaving. They *gloat* as they plot a rival's downfall. They *sneer* as the heroine is metaphorically tied to the railway lines. They *laugh exultantly* when one of their schemes succeeds. They *screw* any man they fancy, without thinking about it.

They have much more fun than heroines. It is probably true that most women like to fantasise about behaving like a bitch sometimes.

Joan Collins, the Wicked Bitch of the West as Alexis Rowan, always claims that her character is not a bitch, merely a strong-willed woman who fights for what she wants. The fact that sex is her main weapon just makes the fighting exciting.

Most soaps have bitches, but there are exceptions. 'Coronation Street' has always managed without. (Vera Duckworth is too stupid to be a bitch. She may be shrewish, but there's no real malice in her. Anyway, she's too homely.) 'Emmerdale Farm' is a non-bitch show, too. Perhaps there's no place for one among the sheep and the Northern rustics. Male villains stride the Dales, but bitches would probably be struck down at once by a lump of Annie Sugden's Yorkshire pudding.

Here is a gallery of bitches.

Betty Anderson in 'Peyton Place' was an early soap bitch. Dark and smouldering Barbara Parkins, a Canadian, made a fine foil to fey Mia

Farrow's Alison with her mane of golden hair (Alison Wonderland?). While Alison stood around looking little-girl-lost and squeaking out her lines in a Minnie Mouse voice, Betty set out to get her man, Rodney Harrington, by foul means or fouler. She tricked him into marriage by claiming he was the father of her unborn child, a very soap-bitch thing to do. Rod (Ryan O'Neal) really loved Alison (even after Mia's husband, Frank Sinatra, took the scissors to the golden mane), but Betty got him. Scuffing my winkle-pickers with anxiety at the drama of it all, I suffered with Alison. But I wanted to be Betty.

Claudia Blaisdale, played by Pamela Bellwood, was an interesting bitch, because bitchiness for her was a side-effect of insanity. Claudia was one of the nice girls of 'Dynasty' until husband Matthew disappeared. Claudia suspected Matthew of having an affair with Krystle and she kidnapped Fallon's baby, Blake's grandchild, ran to the top of a tall building and pitched the little mite off the top. Only it turned out to be a doll. Cynics suggested the doll out-acted most of the 'Dynasty' females. Claudia was unique among bitches because she suffered and looked miserable most of the time. Even when she was a mad, bad bitch, she was a sad, mad, bad bitch.

Constance Carlyle of 'Flamingo Road' is probably the most beautiful bitch in the soap firmament. Morgan Fairchild, who played her, has features so perfect that plastic surgeons use her as a pattern-book. Not surprising that no man can resist Constance. Not surprising that she was a spoiled rich bitch, a Southern belle who reverberated in the mind of every man who saw her, a blonde Scarlett O'Hara. There was a touch of the nymphomaniac about Constance and a list of broken marriages behind her. Ask most men which bitch they fancy, and the answer could well be Morgan Fairchild.

Sable Colby was a British bitch while 'The Colbys' was on the air. Stephanie Beacham made no attempt to hide her English accent playing the devious wife of Jason Colby (Charlton Heston). Stephanie had plenty of practice in bitchery as eponymous Connie in a bit of home-made soap about the rag trade 'oop North'. Stephanie enjoyed the money and the glamour of Hollywood for a time but wondered publicly where her face had gone under all that make-up. She made Sable more interesting than your average bitch by showing herself vulnerable to Heston's hectoring. When the hairpiece who was Moses fell for Sable's sister Francesca, Sable hit back by falling for awful Zach Powers, whose hair was his own but whose leer was fearsome. When her ancient sister-in-law Connie (Barbara Stanwyck) annoyed her by supporting Jeff, Sable tried to run her down. When Jason was about to run off with Francesca, Sable had him arrested for murder and wife-beating, even though she'd merely fallen downstairs. Not a bad bit of bitching, that. She was caught out but collapsed and had to remain in Jason's mansion, making unwedded bliss impossible for Jason and Francesca.

Abby Ewing – actress Donna Mills to you – is the bitch of 'Knots

Landing', the 'Dallas' spin-off. Abby had an affair with J.R. Ewing – he must be in *The Guinness Book of Records* by now, in the 'multiple mistress' section – and then went after his drunken brother Gary, who was married at the time. But he left his wife Valene and stood up with Abby till drink do them part. Abby could bitch for America if bitching were an Olympic sport. After Valene's twins were born, Abby secretly arranged to have them kidnapped and sold.

Anne Hammond was the smokily beautiful bitch in a long-lived soapy series called 'The Brothers', which was about double- and triple-dealing in business. Hilary Tindall made her sharp and waspish. Feminine Britain rejoiced as she shredded wimpish husband Brian with sharp words. Anne was never a conniving bitch, but she drank and took a lover and for a time was reckoned telly's wickedest woman.

Caress Morell was a visiting baddie, a doll who dallied in 'Dynasty' and did dastardly deeds. Britain's green-eyed Kate O'Mara played the girl, Alexis's younger and smarter sister. Caress started off in gaol, but she seemed to get time off for bad behaviour. Soon she was out and plotting against Alexis and Blake and anyone else she could get her long fingernails into. But her bitchiness was too similar to her screen sister's, and 'Dynasty' let her go. O'Mara came home to greater things – *King Lear* and 'Dr Who'. The pop press love O'Mara because she's another oldie-but-sexy. Kate says she owes it all to hormone therapy. We shall remember Caress because, in a genre where daft names breed fast, hers was the daftest.

Angelica Nero, played by Barbara Carrera, was one of the guest bitches who appeared in 'Dallas', for the Texan soap has no indigenous lady villains. To Britain, Angelica was hilarious. Her accent was incomprehensible – so was the plot which had her trying to ruin JR – and her acting over the top of over the top. There were suggestions of lesbianism, but who cared? The only interesting thing about Angelica was her clothes, which were uniquely hideous. I miss her.

Valerie Pollard, played by Heather Chasen, was a bitch who occasionally raised 'Crossroads' above the mundane. Valerie was the wife of J. Henry Pollard, a tycoon who became one of the motel's many owners. Valerie never actually did anything dreadful, but she said bitchy and amusing things while languidly operating a cigarette-holder. The style was Noël Coward but, alas, the 'Crossroads' scriptwriters weren't quite up to Cowardly writing. I used to think it a good night if the dialogue came in sentences.

Sammy Jo Fallmont is the number two bitch of 'Dynasty', a long way behind Alexis but pretty obnoxious just the same. White trash Sammy Jo, skinny and sexy, weaned Blake's gay son Steven off men, persuaded him to father a child, then used the boy to prise money out of the Carringtons while she carried on elsewhere. Steven backslid. We must all thank Sammy Jo (blonde Heather Locklear) for arranging the kidnapping of Krystle Carrington and the substitution of evil lookalike

Rita. This, the Spelling organisation proclaimed, would give Linda Evans, who plays Krystle, a Chance To Act. Linda took it with both feet, playing Rita without her soft expression, just using the other two.

Alexis Rowan from 'Dynasty' is the superbitch, the worst of an evil bunch. Joan Collins had an up-and-down career until she became Alexis, never quite in the front rank of sexy stars. She had made two terrible movies with one of her husbands, Ron Kass, as producer: *The Stud* and *The Bitch*. These films will probably enjoy a long life on those lists cinéastes produce of the Ten Worst Ever, along with *Attack of the Giant Tomatoes*. But they did show that Joan was very good at prancing around in designer clothes – sometimes in no clothes at all – being bitchy. Aaron Spelling, Duke of Dynasty, noticed this talent and remembered Joan when he was looking for a Thoroughly Bad Woman. And, once Alexis had walked into that Denver courtroom where her ex-husband Blake was on trial for his life, soap bitchery was never the same again. Alexis set the standard for others to attempt. She fired a rifle to frighten pregnant Krystle's horse and cause a miscarriage. (Just as well really, since the pregnancy was the result of husband-rape in a scene pinched directly from the Soames-Irene violation in 'The Forsyte Saga'.) She secretly financed a billion-dollar loan to Blake, then almost ruined him by calling it in. She gathered Cecil Colby's millions by marrying him through a hole in his deathbed oxygen-tent. She bedded more men than a National Health prostate ward. She drove the Jeeves of 'Dynasty', the butler Joseph, to suicide through blackmail. And because she was Over Fifty and Still Looked Sexy the British popular press loved her. Everything Collins or Alexis did was news. And the little Jewish girl from North London who started in showbiz when her agent father bought her a small repertory company moved into mythology. It helped that her private life seemed Alexis-like, a kaleidoscope of Hollywood homes, millions of dollars, husbands and lovers, public rows and private altercations. Joan-Alexis set a style. May she reign as Queen Bitch for ever.

Iris Scott in 'Crossroads' was a remarkably effective British bitch. She was nice Kath Brownlow's cockney niece, and Angela Webb made her such a mixed-up little creature that it was actually believable when Iris accused Kath's tedious husband Arthur of rape. (I remember it well, because not much in 'Crossroads' was believable.) Arthur was innocent, as Iris finally confessed. Had she accused him of boring her into submission, the jury would have convicted without leaving the room. Later she blackmailed Jill into giving her boyfriend a job and had a phantom pregnancy.

Kristin Shepherd, Sue Ellen's sister, was one of the early guest bitches in 'Dallas'. Played by Mary Crosby, Bing's daughter, Kristin tried first to seduce J.R Ewing – surely not difficult? – then shot him. She ended up floating dead in the Southfork pool, still causing trouble for JR, who was suspected of sending her to a chloriney grave. I forget who did actually do her in. Could have been a critic.

Katherine Wentworth was the bitch who kept trying to kill Bobby Ewing when he spurned her. When he lay first in Dallas Memorial refusing to croak, she crept in with a syringe of something lethal, only to be thwarted again. Finally, trying to kill Pam, she got Bobby. (And why not? He had Pam and Jenna. Even Bobby's not nice enough for three.) Except, of course, Katherine didn't kill Bobby. It was all a dream brought on by falling ratings and the politics of money, and Bobby was magically resurrected in a shower. Pre-dream Katherine was in a bin somewhere as a punishment for butchering Bobby, but she's out now, bitchy as ever. Morgan Brittany, who plays Katherine, is a beautiful brunette. Her madness when she was nicked after Bobbycide was wonderful to watch.

Angela Stavros of 'Falcon Crest' has to be included with the bitches, because there's no doubt she is one. She is also a heroine, holding her family together in the vineyard wars. Angela is played by Jane Wyman, as indestructible as her former husband Ronald Reagan. Wyman won an Oscar nearly half a century ago for *Johnny Belinda* and she will probably act for ever. Wyman is a graduate of the Joan Crawford School of Drama (motto: Let the customer *see* you're acting), so we're never in any doubt as to how Angela feels. Usually it's angry, though the anger is tight-lipped so as not to endanger the face-lifts. This woman tried to rob her nephew Chase Gioberti of his birthright. She spent weeks covering up an accidental death because she thought it was murder and one of her loved ones the murderer. Angela pushed her grandson Lance into marriage with a neighbouring vineyard just to get her hands on more acres of northern California grapes. She set moths free in Chase's vineyards, then reported the infestation to an agricultural inspector. The woman is rotten to the pips. Divorce kept Wyman from being the First Lady at the White House. But she's certainly the First Lady of the old soap bitches.

'BLACK FOREST CLINIC'

'Black Forest Clinic' ('Schwarzwaldklinik') may be *wunderbar* in its native West Germany, but it suffers from the same malaise as 'Châteauvallon'. Dubbed into the blandest English with atrocious lip-sync, it becomes more hilarious than harrowing. Teutonic melodrama could be powerful, uplifting. But with this stilted, stuttering translation into English Hitler would sound like Derek Nimmo. Still, the most successful German television series ever, attracting up to 25 million viewers an episode, 'Black Forest Clinic' arrived on Channel 4 in January 1988.

The head Hun was Professor Klaus Brinkmann (played by Klaus-jurgen Wussow), a distinguished surgeon who had taken over the directorship of the clinic in his home town. A widower, he couldn't get on with his son Dr Udo Brinkmann (Sascha Hehn), the token heart-throb who also worked at the clinic where he sent temperatures rising. Add a dose of passion three times a day and we had yet another 'Carry On Bedpan'. Except that the Germans play it deadpan.

When he was sixteen, Sascha Hehn starred in 'erotic films' to help support his impoverished pregnant mother. But Sascha, now thirty-three, refused to bare all in 'Black Forest Clinic'. 'Although the stories are about our love-lives, you see nothing on screen,' he said. 'We do not like to have exposed breasts and that sort of thing on television in Germany.' Quite so. Everything was orderly at the clinic. The place was spotless – none of the dangling entrails that make 'Casualty' such fun. Then there were the trees. Acres of them. Any lull in the action, and the camera panned across forests and lakes. I kept expecting to see Judith Chalmers emerge with details of a weekend break. If the going gets tough for young Udo, perhaps he should exercise a little Brinkmannship and set up as a tree surgeon. He'd have plenty of patients.

Germany's gem failed to attract viewers here, and in March 1988 the new controller of Channel 4, Michael Grade, axed the show, which he described as 'bloody awful'.

BLINDNESS

Blindness is a common affliction in soap, but it's always temporary. It allows the relatives of the afflicted to gasp 'Oh, my gaad!', for the victim to look helpless and pathetic, and for a dramatic surprise when bandages come off or sight is otherwise recovered.

Benny in 'Crossroads' added blindness to his other disabilities after a car smash. Vince Parker also went a bit blind after Meg accidentally knocked him off his bike (and went to gaol for it).

In 'Dynasty' Blake lost his sight after fighting with Dr Toscani, but it returned after Krystle cried enough. Julia in 'Falcon Crest' briefly added blindness to her other problems (she was a drunk, insane, prone to mass shootings, was on the run from a mental institution dressed as a nun and should have died in a cabin fire). Her eye problem was a side-effect suffered as a victim of an earthquake. Little Lucy Robinson in 'Neighbours' (Kylie Flinker) went blind after falling down a hole. She recovered her sight. Sadly the doctors never cured her other problem: her inability to blow her nose.

Augusta Lockridge in 'Santa Barbara' was the first soap-blindness victim to receive a letter from the White House. It should perhaps have gone to Bobby Ewing in 'Dallas', whose blindness after Katherine Wentworth shot him led to an 'experimental' operation to restore his sight. The emotion he stirred up was a sort of rehearsal for his next temporary affliction: death.

'BROOKSIDE'

'Brookside', Channel 4's 'Wild Child', exploded on to the television screen on 2 November 1982 – on the day that the new network began transmission. The resulting blast changed British soap opera for good.

The man with the cheek and nerve behind it was Phil Redmond, originator of the BBC's parent-scaring saga of school life 'Grange Hill'. He went for shocks again. Shunning 'Coronation Street' techniques, forgetting studios and plywood homes, he found and bought a set of newly built houses in Liverpool, installing in them all the newest television technology. He wanted realism. That ordinary people also live in Brookside Close (divided from the soap world by a barrier and security men) added to that realism. Only the post-box and, later, a hole in the road were fake.

But Redmond's fictional residents were too real for comfort. They were earthy, radical; they spoke unashamedly in thick Liverpool accents. The kids were obsessed with sex and other bodily functions and had respect for almost nothing. And they *swore*. They said everything you ever heard and more. And they used *that* word. There was uproar. Mary Whitehouse's clean-up lobby went into overdrive. They railed against a scene showing the attempted rape of a schoolgirl. Right-wing newspapers, notably the *Daily Express*, loathed the left-wing 'propaganda' and called for Jeremy Isaacs, Channels 4's boss, to resign. The media put the show under the microscope. The satirical magazine *Private Eye* lampooned it with a cartoon strip called 'Bogside'. Even the actors were shame-faced. One performer visited real residents of the Close, apologising for the show's controversial content.

Viewers turned off in droves. Shortly after launch, 'Brookside' faced its darkest hour, with just 250,000 viewers. A cot death for Channel 4's new baby seemed highly likely. So Redmond framed the *Daily Express* front page, stuck it on his office wall and changed direction. He stopped the swearing – sort of. 'People swear – they know they do,' he said later. 'But they have a deep-seated need to be offended by hearing swearing on television.' In came a few comic characters – Alan Partridge, a drunk (actor Dicken Ashworth), among them.

The approach to the media – formerly cautious and wary – changed. Story-lines were suddenly mysteriously leaked. A hype – using other soap operas – began. A 'Brookside' camera crew turned up outside Granada studios to film as part of a story-line. Some characters wanted to take back 'Coronation Street' souvenirs to their Liverpool home. Granada executives were not amused, and said so. As the hype grew, so the story-lines became more daring. Young widow Petra Taylor (Alexandra Pigg, later of *Letter to Brezhnev* fame) was written out. She suddenly disappeared, prompting a search by her family and friends. Soppier soap addicts loved this. Many wrote or telephoned with sightings. 'Brookside' milked the situation for all it was worth, until finally Redmond ordered the character's death – reported as a suicide in a Llandudno hotel.

The reaction to Petra's departure provided inspiration for 'Brookside' script teams when actor Cliff Howells, who played George Jackson, decided to go. The revolutionary idea that followed would put the character George in gaol, and give the show the opportunity to launch a real-life 'Free George Jackson' campaign. T-shirts and posters were printed with Howells's face on them; a 'Free George Jackson' record was released – with initial 'leaked' hints that the singers were Frankie Goes to Hollywood, then riding the crest of a pop wave. The snag was that Howells wanted nothing to do with the stunt. And there were more complications. The performers on the record were an obscure country-music band – unknown outside Merseyside and the North-West. The disc flopped. The T-shirts were withdrawn. Photographs for the posters – using a rear view of a chastened 'Brookside' PR man – were reshot.

Still, the campaign worked well enough. Viewers wrote letters of sympathy. One addict sent a cake for George with a file inside. Graffiti appeared in Liverpool. People even rang a special phone line to hear how he was coping in gaol. Ratings pushed up to more than 4 million.

'Brookside' was here. It was a Monday, Tuesday and Saturday (the omnibus) institution. Ratings rose. Soap could bubble over ideas, it showed, and those ideas could be downbeat or depressing. I once called it 'the soap to commit suicide to'. Every sort of despair seemed to be there. Unemployment was its constant backdrop. The frustrations of claiming money from the DHSS were fully explored. Characters debated who were the greater rogues – capitalist tax-avoiders or the jobless driven to go on the fiddle. They agonised over Youth Training Schemes – systems of slave labour more often than useful first steps, they said. Characters from Liverpool's shadowy underworld flitted in and out. Contraception, AIDS, loss of virginity, rape, homosexuality, drug addiction, prostitution – all were subjects discussed over breakfast.

And, yes, it did look and feel more realistic for being shot through a single hand-held camera on actual driveways, through the windows of proper homes with lavatories, dustbins, dropped clothes and Kellogg's Cornflakes packets on the tables. The writing style was low-key, but the action could be fast and furious. Only once did they resort to absurd melodrama, with a ludicrous siege complete with gunman and double death. It put ratings up to over 8 million.

There were plenty of other deaths. Gavin, Petra, Harry's wife Edna, Matt's wife Teresa, drug addict Nick, Laura and Damon. Viewers accepted it all.

The cast were and still are local heroes, mobbed and fêted in Liverpool wherever they go, deluged with requests to support local events and charities. To their credit, they readily accept as many offers as they can. Ricky Tomlinson and Sue Johnston worked so hard to help raise funds for miners' families during the 1985 strike that they were honoured by the National Union of Mineworkers.

It's commonly believed at Mersey Television that if the soap were shown on the main Independent Television network it would be near the top of the ratings, a serious challenge to 'Coronation Street' and even to 'EastEnders', the soap they claim to have inspired. I think they're right.

THE CREATOR

'Brookside' reached the screen because Phil Redmond *had* to succeed. He'd been badly let down by the BBC who had dropped a twice-weekly drama, 'County Hall', that he'd devised. He'd delivered story-lines for twenty-six episodes about which they'd been delighted: 'County Hall' had politics, romance, deaths, shocks, and characters based on real ones he'd seen researching the subject in the corridors and conference rooms of the Greater London Council (one was a then unknown politician called Ken Livingstone). Then the BBC drama bosses bottled out. The project was lost in the general malaise, the low morale and pre-'EastEnders' snobbery about soap.

For Redmond it was a blow. His series 'Grange Hill' had been hailed as a breakthrough, the series which brought children's television drama out of the ghetto. With its cameras at children's eye-level, it hadn't looked down on them. It had made shocked parents talk to their children about school life, sometimes for the first time, and, claims Redmond, discover that fact was far more worrying than fiction. The spin-off, 'Going Out', about teenagers was widely praised as a mould-breaker, too.

Redmond told me: 'I'd had the idea about "Brookside" since 1978. I realised I had to go independent. The BBC had shut the door, ITV had

"Coronation Street" and "Crossroads". I sought out Jeremy Isaacs [the chief executive of Channel 4]. He said: "Yes, we want a soap but we can't afford it." So I went to the Department of Trade and Industry and asked for a grant. I didn't qualify, because I wasn't a manufacturer, but they gave me £195,000 over three years as an assistance grant because I was setting up in Liverpool creating seventy jobs. They took £100,000 back in tax later, but that was another matter. I decided to keep all costs capital – not running. I decided to buy all the equipment and thirteen houses. Since then I've bought a further seven flats, another house and two Portakabins.

'I went back to Jeremy and said: "This is what it'll cost and this is also what it'll be about – these houses. It won't be anodyne, safe all the time, either." I told him I wanted it to be as realistic as possible: we'd use a real bank, a real shop. We wouldn't spend hours taking the labels off ketchup-bottles. I wanted to break hypocrisies – married couples would be seen in bed. And I wanted to be honest about swearing. Everyone swears in some form, even vicars. Jeremy agreed. I borrowed a million pounds, and Mersey Television was started. "Brookside" was born.'

Redmond's stories for 'Brookside' had to have one continuing quality. 'The audience isn't stupid and we don't treat them as if they were. I wanted to highlight the issues in society at that time. I wanted to attack the black economy, unemployment, the demise of manufacturing industries – what's wrong with trade unions, the position of women. Of course sociologists loved it. But they weren't important. What was and is important is giving people reassurance by debating issues. We deliberately take back the drama. I'd hate "Brookside" to become as frantic as "EastEnders" often is. If we didn't have bum episodes, we'd have to invent them.'

He added wryly: 'After our siege, we could have had an IRA cell in one of the houses or the Palestine Liberation Front at work or a jumbo jet crashing in the street. Or perhaps we could have made it all a dream. . . . I've tried to make sure we weren't seduced into escalating everything just to compete. We did rape last but we did it best in six episodes. We didn't rush to do AIDS – I think we were the first here – but we did it properly. It will run for over a year.' Well, it won't actually. Since Redmond made this claim Ian Bleasdale, the actor chosen to play the shop steward AIDS victim had to leave. Soap producers often mess up their best storylines by not checking actors' availabilities. Bleasdale was no sooner 'terminally ill', with Sheila Grant set to become his AIDS buddy, than he left for a prearranged role in Andy Capp. Exit AIDS issue.

Redmond enjoys suggesting the high level of 'everyday' crime in his community and Brookside has maintained its reputation as the most bent cul-de-sac in Britain.

As 'Brookside' approached its fifth birthday consistently at the top of Channel 4's viewing chart, many of its early supporters had begun to attack it for going soft on its socialism. Issues such as unemployment had been swapped for soppy yuppy love-stories. The working-class roots had been torn up and trampled on, critics said. Redmond replied: 'It never was a socialist soap – only a social soap. It reflected what was happening, how people felt in 1982. In 1987 it's a Tory society of conspicuous consumption with a sharp North-South divide. We must reflect that. You have to take change by the horns. I don't want "Brookside" to become a geriatric soap.'

Six years from the birth, Redmond is seen more as the tyrannical tight-fisted tycoon than as the boy-wonder of teenage drama. His actors and technicians work long and hard and, they claim, on minimum rates and miserly allowances. Unlike other television studios, 'Brookside' is 'dry': alcohol is banned. The soapsters' perks – fees of £2000 and more to attend the openings of shops – are allowed only if it suits the boss. Personnel are contracted to share fees with the company, Mersey Television, which regulates and vets the engagements. Redmond believes he has a right to his 'cut': he created the characters.

Several managers have left; there has been an exceptionally high turnover of actors – especially of actresses. This is partly because many were picked who'd had no previous acting experience. It's partly because some cannot stomach the dictatorial regime. On the other hand, many of the stars have been openly political – something most mealy-mouthed managements hate.

Redmond is now rich, living apart from his wife and children, so reclusive at times that staff nicknamed him 'Howard Hughes'. He's still the darling of Liverpool MPs, sociologists and media students. Liverpool's literary establishment are less welcoming. Writer Alan Bleasdale, for instance, has a low opinion of 'Brookside', claiming it belittles the city he loves. Redmond disregards criticism. By the end of the decade he is confident Mersey Television will have expanded. Feature films for television and the cinema are in his sights. By any standard, Redmond's achievement is impressive. His success was not unnoticed at the BBC. 'EastEnders' may have many Godfathers; one of them is him. Redmond has crossed soap boundaries. He has not been afraid to recast characters – both Gordon and Lucy Collins have had different faces in their time. He pioneered the idea of 'soap bubbles' taking a character into a separate but related mini-series. 'Damon and Debbie' was the first in November 1987, in three hourly episodes on Channel 4. It told how Damon Grant broke away from his family, ran off to York with his schoolgirl love, Debbie, pursued by her angry relatives. It summed up Damon's life and – to the sadness of his fans – detailed his death in a *Romeo and Juliet* style drama.

Tracy Corkhill's spell of growing up down South with her boyfriend Jamie was next.

Redmond has even suggested the end of 'Brookside' in that way – fittingly inspired and unusual. 'Perhaps we will watch a character leave and follow him or her. "Brookside" will continue with its daily life but not on screen any more,' he mused.

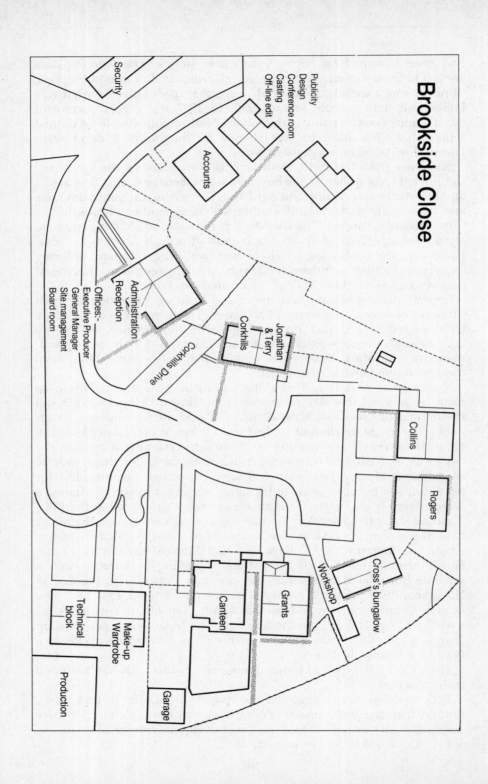

Brookside Close

Security

Publicity
Design
Conference room
Casting
Off-line edit

Accounts

Administration
Reception

Offices:-
Executive Producer
General Manager
Site management
Board room

Corkhills Drive

Jonathan
& Terry
Corkhills

Collins

Rogers

Cross's bungalow

Workshop

Grants

Canteen

Technical
block

Make-up
Wardrobe

Garage

Production

THE CHARACTERS

Annabelle Collins is the 'Brookside' do-gooder, middle-aged and middle-class, who suffers from bad smells under the nose. She used to be a snob, having come down in the world after Paul, her oil-company executive husband was made redundant and they were suddenly too broke for the stockbroker belt. A former French teacher, she found difficulty in relating to her working-class neighbours in the Close. She became depressed, sought solace in a ratepayers' group, teetered on the brink of an affair with the Council candidate – and slowly turned human. Her children traumatised her. Lucy changed political colours when she transferred from private to comprehensive schools. (She was arrested on a CND demo.) Then she left for a long holiday abroad. There was the married lover, too. But let's not mention that. Son Gordon says he's gay (Annabelle has only just forced herself to believe it).

She decided to become a magistrate and, by the wonders of soap, realised this ambition within weeks. She relished the idea of sterner sentences, but seldom got the opportunity to impose them. She tried catering, but the cook who wears washing-up gloves to chop onions (more bad smells) got in a stew. Then she suffered a trying time with her super-snob mother, who fell in the 'Brookside' hole in the road before being parked in an old folk's home run by uncaring crooks. She still dreams of a return to leafy luxury in the Wirral but she has mellowed. There's probably a heart of gold under her well-made clothes. Billy Corkhill will be able to borrow a cup of sugar any day soon. ·

Doreen Sloan, the elegant actress who suffers the slings and arrows as Annabelle in 'Brookside', lives on the Wirral (from whence Annabelle was forced to move in her slide down the social scale). There's a ghost in Doreen's house – perhaps of an ancestor of Annabelle. Doreen is a veteran of other soaps – ('Coronation Street' and 'Emmerdale Farm') and often brings mirth to the set by arguing volubly with her screen husband – actor Jim Wiggins – in a way uptight Annabelle would never manage. 'I'm a fan of Mrs Thatcher,' she says. 'I have the same beliefs and background as the Collinses and in a sense I'm glad to be able to stand up for my own group. Jim's just the opposite. He's very unlike Paul.'

In her spare time she rides horses, does the *Telegraph* crossword and enjoys snooker on television and brass band music. She also joins charity efforts with enthusiasm.

'I'd like Annabelle to dress with more flair,' she once said, 'but I suppose "Brookside" isn't "Dynasty".'

Paul Collins is the man 'Brookside' fans loved to boo. Now they probably like him. At least he's quiet (rare among this soap's males), and anyone who has to survive life with Annabelle, his lady wife, and (occasionally) her ga-ga ma deserves sympathy. He arrived with his family, the token middle-class residents. The others were working-class. He was a redundant executive of oil giant Petrochem, forced by his reduced income to leave his middle-class mansion in the Wirral stockbroker belt for a 'poky little' house in the Close. Pompous self-pitying Paul had his spell of depression (everyone in 'Brookside' has them) early. He was found wandering on a railway bridge, seemingly suicidal. He found a temporary job training young people and cheered up. Just as well. Soon his son Gordon, a strange withdrawn lad, confessed he was homosexual in a letter, stole money and ran away from home with a pal, a fellow school prefect. Daughter Lucy also returned home (in a different incarnation with a different actress playing the part) and immediately plunged into a torrid affair with a married man. Later she left the Close for a trip back to France with the young 'lout' Paul most detested, Barry Grant. Later he rescued a puppy from drowning, called it 'Lucky' – which it certainly wasn't. Gordon ran over it.

His setbacks – almost as numerous as Billy Corkhill's or Bobby Grant's – have made him less ridiculous. Decent and fair, he's hardly a baddie now, even if he does vote Tory. He has even accepted the 'embarrass-ment' of Gordon's gayness. But Paul's days in the Close could be numbered. He and his wife Annabelle could be heading for a cosy retirement home, well away from the hustle of Liverpool.

Jim Wiggins is a former deputy headmaster and one-time civil servant who is light-years removed from his pompous 'Brookside' *alter ego* Paul Collins. Paul is a fervent admirer of Thatcherism. Jim is a diehard socialist whose family have a formidable pedigree in the Labour move-ment. Jim enjoys Paul but shares with Doreen Sloan (Annabelle) the feeling that their scenes were less lively, less imaginative than the Grants' and the Corkhills'. 'Paul seems to be well liked by viewers now,' he said. And there are other differences. Paul is a conservative dresser. Jim often sports gangster-style fedoras, and cuts an elegant dash in matching overcoats. He chuckled. 'It is one way of disguising yourself from the fans.'

Billy Corkhill is the short-fused electrician who came to be

identified as the true image of the Liverpool Loser. Lured to live beyond his modest means by his daft demanding wife Doreen, he seems permanently poised for disaster, and has taken desperate measures to stay in Brookside Close.

Played with frequently frantic intensity by John McArdle, Billy has scabbed as a blackleg in an official dispute, laboured for a ruthless right-wing boss, travelled south to work, fiddled his 'leccy' meter (electricity to you) and then turned to crime. He faked a burglary in his own house for the insurance money. Later he drove a supermarket gang's getaway car – all to repay the family debts which, it's hinted, were growing at banana-republic rates. But for Billy – deep down a loving husband and father – it was all in vain. His wife Doreen, repelled by his risk-taking criminality, left him. His teenage children, policeman Rod and hairdresser Tracy, are growing more distant. His time at Brookside has been a nightmare. Tracy was seduced by a teacher, whom Billy punished with a beating. It landed him in court. Then she switched to modelling – until an unscrupulous photographer tried to persuade her to go topless. The family drifted deeper into debt when Doreen went on a credit-card spree and Tracy clocked up a huge 'Talkabout' telephone bill. It resulted in Doreen considering prostitution with her dentist boss and Billy resorting to crime. The constant domestic discord shattered the Corkhill family. Doreen, devoted wife and mother, is supposedly living with her mother. To 'punish' actress Kate Fitzgerald, who'd played her and had become discontented in 'Brookside', Doreen is referred to now as a heartless bitch. In May, Tracy went AWOL on a trip to London and the problems of Sheila Grant looked like being added to Billy's.

John McArdle is the thirty-eight-year-old actor whose soap life as Billy Corkhill is an almost permanent panic. Quiet John, who lives in nearby Lancashire, has become a major star, and rightly so. Billy's plight – his family's debts – touched people's hearts. Letters, food-parcels, small donations of cash arrive in the post weekly. Unlike Billy, who scabbed on his work colleagues, the actor was active in a long-running dispute in the steel industry during a five-year stay in Australia. He became an actor late, at twenty-six; and, while Billy stretches and interests him, film and television producers are knocking on his door.

Harry Cross, the grumpy pensioner of 'Brookside', lives up to his

surname. He is categorically Mr Misery of soap. Retired railwayman Harry owns two houses in Brookside – which must make him a baddie at base among the series' serious socialist followers. He bought one house, suffered a heart attack, then bought the bungalow next door. He has made himself comfortable in Brookside, though many residents wish he hadn't. From the moment he moved in, he became the scourge of the place. He watched the teenagers with eagle eyes. He regularly snooped on the tenants in his first house – hospital porter Pat Hancock, and nurses Sandie Maghie and Kate Moses – touring their house while they were out. He made life hell for his wife Edna with constant carping, yet he idealised her as 'my Edna' after her sudden death in 1985. Now old railway chum Ralph has filled the gap in Harry's life, and the Brookside 'odd couple' share Harry's neat detached bungalow. Prized gnomes smile in the garden. They're often 'Brookside''s only cheery souls.

Despite his repetitive whining, Harry has good points. Well, goodish. There's a certain loyalty. Genuinely fond of Edna, he was devastated when his only grandchild died shortly after birth (though, typically, he harangued his daughter-in-law, almost provoking premature labour). Harry saved Ralph from the clutches of an unscrupulous con-woman, Madge Richmond, the 'black' widow from the Wirral, who said she loved him. He sussed her out and sent her packing. Some of us wondered if he'd really done Ralph such a favour.

Bill Dean is the veteran comedian-actor in the owl-specs who made Harry into a cult figure. One Liverpool rock group have even christened themselves 'The Sons of Harry Cross' in tribute to the old so-and-so. Bill, once a local government officer, has television and film credits too numerous to mention. Happily for his friends and family, he's very different from Harry. Witty, enthusiastic and engaging, he has often left journalists at Liverpool's Press Club aching from laughing as he cracked gag after gag.

But the actor has suffered personally – because of Harry. During one shopping expedition in Liverpool with his wife, a 'fan' told him: 'Push off, you miserable old bugger, before I give you a good crack.' And Bill was virtually driven out of his home, near to the 'Brookside' set, by over-enthusiastic 'Brookside' addicts. Sagging under the strain of twenty-four-hour pestering, the elderly performer had to move from a house conveniently close to the Close to the quieter climes of Southport. Bill has also decided to restrict his appearances to wind down into 'semi-retirement' before putting his feet up completely. During the whole of 1988 he's unlikely to make more than twenty-five appearances.

Barry Grant is the eldest of the Grant offspring in 'Brookside', and the biggest disappointment to his hard-working parents, Bobby and Sheila. Despite their wishes to see him settle down, Barry has tried only one legitimate business, a tool hire company. It was wrecked by irate gangster Tommy McCardle, whose paid thugs also hospitalised Barry and his 'best mate', Terry Sullivan. More often than not, Barry has veered to the wrong side of the law. His innate dishonesty lures him to petty theft. He tried to con an insurance company, in the early days, by taking and driving his own car – a battered Jag – and later ditching it on Ainsdale Beach, near Southport. Barry once took violent revenge on a thug who tried to rape his sister Karen. But he's very much the ladies' man, though with varying success. He slept with widow Petra, who later committed suicide (unrelated). He seduced the boss's daughter, and persuaded her to open a tool hire business. He cuckolded his amateur league team's manager, and became the wife's toy boy. He tried and failed with glamorous Heather Haversham. To the horror of his mother and father, he became involved with a possessive heroin

addict, then left the Close for the Continent with luscious Lucy Collins –
leaving her posh parents grief-stricken. Barry's unfortunate obsession
also led him to bed a glamorous Golf-driving Yuppette, who happened
to be 'moll' to a vicious stuttering gangland chief called 'Sizzler'. He
loves his mum, but in this soap it's not enough. He's a wrong 'un.

Paul Usher is the young actor plucked from the dole queue to play the
pin-up of 'Brookside', Barry Grant. It brought him instant fame,
countless adoring fans, but personal disappointment, even despair. At
one point, when he feared he was losing his true pals because of soap
stardom, he bitterly declared: 'I hate Barry Grant; he has ruined my life.'
At the peak of his distress he became almost a recluse, afraid to go
shopping and forced to drive to the Pennines, where they could not
receive Channel 4 (so 'Brookside' was unknown) when he wanted a
peaceful pub drink.

Paul decided after the first year that he wanted to take breaks from the
soap, and his strongest wish was to be a rock musician. He sang at the
Soap Aid concert, which raised funds for Africa's famine victims. But
recording success has yet to come. Now an occasional visitor to
'Brookside' (rather like nasty Nick Cotton in 'EastEnders'), he still
receives about fifty letters a day from fans. But the days when drinkers
in pubs would challenge him to fights, confusing villainous Barry with
Paul, or schoolchildren stone his car seem to be behind him.

Bobby Grant of 'Brookside' is the first hero of a soap to care about

things other than his family and his firm. This one cares about politics,
the unglamorous factory-floor kind at that.

There's nothing glamorous about Bobby Grant. He's bearded, burly,
wears awful clothes and barks at his wife Sheila and his children. He has
been unemployed and depressed. His marriage all but broke up once and
is now on the rocks. His elder son's a crook, his elder daughter has disappeared; his younger son, who never found a job, was killed by thugs,
and his small daughter Claire, the quietest tot in soap, will bring him
heartache any day now. His life is no shining success, but his political
integrity in the early eighties – the dark dole-queue days – made him the
darling of the trendy left. 'Brookside' was 'Grantside'. Bobby was it.

A beer-guzzler, a good mate, a man's man, he is played with total
conviction by Ricky Tomlinson. At first a shop steward at the Fairbanks
engineering firm, Bobby later won an election to become a full-time
official. His far-left views led some workmates to brand him a Trotskyist,
but others called him a management stooge when he dissuaded young
militants from striking. At home his Roman Catholic wife called him a
sinner after he arranged a vasectomy without her knowledge. (He did it
after she'd had a difficult and unplanned late pregnancy.) When he
accused his wife of having an affair with a lecturer, then failed to
appreciate her suffering after a brutal rape, most female viewers called

him other things. Insensitive pig, was one.

A visit to Rome repaired the marriage and Bobby's faith, but when Sheila began an Open University degree course his male chauvinism welled up. From then on the decent man of Brookside became its main oaf, a change connected with the actor's many disagreements with Phil Redmond. Bobby behaved boorishly at Damon's funeral. He was callous when news came of Damon's girlfriend's pregnancy. He was found guilty of drunken driving just after the actor faced the same charge. Then, after a series of rows with Sheila, one of them violent, the couple were set for a messy divorce.

At Easter the unhappy actor could not tolerate Bobby The Beast. He walked out of Brookside Close leaving the writers to restructure three months' scripts. 'I have to go on living with the working classes,' he said.

Ricky Tomlinson is the forty-eight-year-old, stockily built 'hero' who plays 'Brookside' hero Bobby Grant. Ricky's real dramas mirror and even outdo Bobby's. Ricky was a building worker, gaoled for two years (spent mostly in solitary confinement) for offences in a bitter strike action. He became one of the Shrewsbury Two pickets whose plight became a *cause célèbre* of the Left. On an employers' blacklist, unable to return to building work, he turned to busking, working as a comic and banjo-player called Hobo Rick. A part in the Jim Allen classic film *United Kingdom* was his break into television. Phil Redmond chose him for the rôle of trade-union man Bobby, rightly guessing that there would be sympathy and commitment. Ricky holds that he *is* Bobby. They wear the same clothes, dream the same dreams. Ricky is a lot jollier with it. As he puts it: 'Bobby represents the worker who has come up the hard way, been on a million picket-lines, and had to face losing his job at the end of it. He sees himself twenty years ago in these kids and wants to stop them taking the same knocks.'

Success hasn't put Ricky off politics. He attends rallies of the Militant Tendency, supports the Labour Party and has thrown himself into the fight against unemployment, passing on his acting skills to jobless Liverpool kids. Sadly his long marriage, which survived gaol, broke under the strain of his soap fame. Now divorced, he lives in Wrexham, North Wales, and hopes to develop into a writer.

Damon Grant – one of the sunniest citizens of the Close. When the soap started he was already approaching school-leaving age, and with his pals Ducksie and Gizzmo provided much of the humour, though their language had to be toned down. Through Damon, writers were given the perfect opportunity to reflect the bitter reality of growing up in Liverpool. He got himself a place on a jobs scheme and worked his fingers to the bone for a year, hoping that the job would become permanent. It didn't. His resulting anguish provided the soap with some of its finest scenes. He left the Close to seek work in holiday resorts in the South-West. But he always came back, dispirited. Damon's final scenes in 'Brookside' paired him with a pretty teenage girl called Debbie, with whom he eloped to a new life in Yorkshire. This featured in a three-part drama called 'Damon and Debbie' shown in November 1987, also on Channel 4. But the 1987 love-saga ended – like Romeo and Juliet's – in tragedy. He was stabbed by a youth almost by accident. A gang was trying to burgle a houseboat Damon and Debbie were staying on.

Simon O'Brien was the acceptable face of youth unemployment. Clean, short-haired, Simon played the cheeky, cheery teenager dogged with bad luck. Having Damon for a name was only the start. As a Liverpool schoolboy, starting his 'A' levels, Simon went along to a 'Brookside' audition to keep a mate company. The casting director spotted him larking around, and the job of Damon Grant was his.

Five years later, he'd decided to give up a £30,000-a-year salary and the status of a saint in his home town, knowing that, while he might find bigger and better rôles, he might finish the 'A' levels and study botany at university, and he might also rejoin his classmates on the dole.

What made Simon say tarra to Damon? Damon bored him. He'd become more a wally than a scally. He announced: 'Damon's backward; he never goes to the pub, he hasn't got any friends, he's a pretty strange guy.' Damon's mind wasn't on sex, which, Simon argued with the writers, wasn't normal. When the Grants went on holiday Damon invited his girl round – for a *meal*. 'In reality you'd be straight round to the chemist,' said Simon. When the time came to sign a new contract, Simon decided Damon must die. He did – stabbed by a hooligan in York – in November 1987.

Normal, nice and witty was exactly how everyone found Simon during his five years in the Close. His student girlfriend from pre-soap days had survived the thronging teeny fans; his parents still talked to him, though he's prospered and bought his own home. Sue Johnston, his screen mother, and other colleagues praised his acting talent and predicted a great future.

Perhaps there can be 'life after soap' (p.347) if you always took it as a bit of a laugh – and a way to bunk off school. We'll see.

Karen Grant was Bobby and Sheila's big girl, Brookside's first precocious teenager. At first a sulky schoolgirl, whose sexy come-hither manner almost ended in rape, she blossomed into a serious-minded academic, last seen at university. She clashed with her mum over going on the Pill – to ease painful periods, not to sleep around. Then she gave her parents a hard time over the birth of baby Claire – because she thought sex between older people was 'disgusting'. After many false starts 'Kagsy', as her brothers called her, had her first experience of sex – a rather touching, tasteful scene – with intense fellow-student Guy.

Happiness, of course, was not to be. Karen became sick of Guy, and was devastated by the rape attack on her mother – though she proved a tower of strength to her. Finally, after long family discussions (and when the actress who played her, Shelagh O'Hara, wanted to quit), she transferred to a course at another university, and was last seen heading for London.

Shelagh O'Hara was possibly as mixed-up and unsettled as Karen Grant, the 'Brookside' character she played. It was hard to know, because Shelagh also played the mystery woman of the soap. This working-class Garbo, from the Liverpool inner-city region of Toxteth, was proud of her roots and keenly interested in local politics, serious cinema and theatre. She refused to be interviewed by newspaper people largely because she disapproved of the papers' proprietors, and a journalist who dared to mention her could count on a phone-called earful of reprimanding vernacular the next morning. In one rare interview, to *Gay Times*, Shelagh said she'd grown to like her character but was worried that 'Brookside' had gone 'blander'. She said: 'Personally I'd like it to be a bit more of a shock. It toes the line a bit.' When she joined a demonstration against cutbacks in the health service one Tory MP thought she set a bad example. It certainly didn't offend her producers. When she decided to leave, to explore film work, they were shocked. They hoped she might make return visits. But the mystery girl left at the end of 1986 and has not darkened a Brookside door again.

Sheila Grant is the matriarch of 'Brookside' and, boy, does she suffer for it. As a mother of four, she has four big worries. As sexist Bobby's wife, she has another set of problems. All her attempts to work and study are doomed to disaster or setbacks. The writers have made her pregnant, a rape victim, depressed, bereaved and distraught. Why she hasn't packed a bag and fled to somewhere relatively cosy – like Beirut – remains a puzzle.

Her first son, Barry, fights with his father and consorts with crooks. Damon, his brother, could never land a job and was brutally murdered by thugs at the end of 1987. Karen, her once wayward daughter, went on the Pill (a problem for Catholic Sheila), and her husband had himself sterilised. Only little Claire brings unclouded joys – but who is there to mind her when Sheila goes out? In March came news which temporarily lifted her spirits. Damon's girlfriend Debbie was pregnant with Damon's child. Because Debbie was diabetic, her father was urging her to have a termination. Sheila agonised but argued for the child. Then Debbie miscarried, and Sheila felt a small hope of happiness had been dashed. Her misery worsened as Bobby's behaviour became totally unreasonable. When she went dancing one night with Jimmy Corkhill's girlfriend

Kath, Bobby put her belongings on the street and locked her out, forcing her to spend the night at the Corkhill house. After Bobby left, Sheila's closeness to Billy Corkhill grew. Unimaginable though their pairing would have been a few months earlier (and despite the two actors' initial disbelief), it solved a problem. One house in the Close became empty and could be used for badly needed new characters.

Admired by neighbours for her devotion to the family, her plain-speaking and obvious good sense, Sheila ranks with Pauline Fowler, Rita Fairclough and Annie Sugden as the coping, caring core of their dramas. Of all of them, her life is the most tragic, but her manner the most quietly appealing.

Sue Johnston looks smaller, less harassed and a lot less frumpy than Sheila Grant, the 'Brookside' mother-martyr she plays. She smiles more and hasn't the thick Liverpool accent. But they have much in common. At forty-four, Sue was a respected stage and television actress before 'Brookside'. Her personal life hasn't been easy. Shortly after 'Brookside' began, she went through a difficult divorce. Now she brings up her only child, Joel, who's eight, on her own. Sometimes she has to double-check he knows Sheila is not the same as his mummy. When she filmed Sheila's rape ordeal, for instance, Sue wore the painted-on mud and stuck-on cuts and bruises home so she could prove to her small son the wounds he might see on television were 'pretend'. In the event, neither Joel nor any viewers saw much of the exhaustingly filmed woodland struggle with the taxi-man attacker. The Independent Broadcasting Authority decided they were too harrowing and ordered them cut. The story-line also revived painful memories for Sue of an ugly event in a dark alley fifteen years earlier. A man exposed himself and grabbed Sue by the neck. 'I had to fight like a tiger to get free. I never knew I had such strength,' she said.

Sue used to live on a new housing estate outside Warrington but autograph-hunters hounded her. 'I've crawled around on my living-room floor to convince them I'm not in the house,' she said. She moved to a more secluded spot in Cheshire but remains a keen supporter of Liverpool events, especially their theatre productions. Strongly committed to soap, she admits she sometimes disagrees with details of the plots. 'We complain every now and then. The writers listen, say thank you and suggest we just go away and get it done.' Ah well, they said thank you.

Heather Haversham was perhaps the most beautiful, certainly the most fantasised-over woman in 'Brookside'. Naturally, with so much charm and intelligence, the yuppy accountant had to be unlucky in love. Her first husband, sly solicitor Roger Huntington, seemed a weed but turned out a two-timer who slept with a woman client while he was dealing with her divorce. Her marriage promptly fell apart – to the consternation of the neighbours. Things got worse. A gay female boss made a faint pass. A relationship with a doctor fizzled out. A rampant Romeo almost tricked her into bed. She was saved by the bell – the doorbell which his wife was ringing! An intense affair with computer whizzkid Tom Curzon almost ended at the altar – but the romance collapsed and she found second husband Nick Black.

Every viewer watching must have been shouting 'Don't do it' as she set off to the register office. For divorcee Black (actor Alan Rothwell) came complete with three stroppy children and a lesbian ex-wife, and he was a secret heroin addict. After lying, stealing and promising to give up, he died from a drugs overdose and hypothermia. Heather drove off into the night, leaving 9 Brookside in the hands of an estate agent.

Amanda Burton became a thinking man's sex symbol from playing Heather Haversham. She did the profession of accountancy a power of good, and the Londonderry-born actress enjoyed it a lot. Amanda's pull was such that she was the first member of the cast to be approached with 'the soap bubble' theory; and plans, which later fell through, were well advanced to give her a glamorous mini-series of her own. By 1986, Amanda – fiercely protective of her character Heather – began to clash with the producers. She argued that a sophisticated fancy-free Heather would play the field, and wanted story-lines to match. She strongly disapproved of Heather's marriage to no-good Nick. But scriptwriters were adamant, and Amanda decided to go. She remains on friendly terms with the Liverpool-based soap and could well return. In the mean time she has taken a flat in London, a new boyfriend and parts in television series and a situation comedy.

WHO LIVES WHERE

Number 5's original occupants were Bobby and Sheila Grant with children Barry, Karen, Damon and later Claire. For most of the time.

Number 6: the bungalow's first resident was computer expert Alan Partridge, who married Samantha his sweetheart at the second attempt and then emigrated. Harry, Edna Cross, and later their friend Ralph moved in. Edna later died.

Number 7 was empty until bought in 1984 by Harry and Edna Cross. But they bought next door, too, after Harry suffered a heart attack. They rented the property to nurses Kate Moses, Sandra Maghie and Pat Hancock. But gunman John Clarke killed Kate in the siege. Terry Sullivan joined the duo, but was left on his own when Sandra moved out and Pat left to seek stardom. Terry moved to number 9. Frank and Chrissie Rogers and family moved in.

Number 8 was the come-down-in-the-world house for the Collins family: Paul, Annabelle, Lucy and Gordon. Annabelle's mother Mona stayed for a short time, before going into a home.

Number 9 belonged to Heather and Roger Huntington. They were divorced; Heather married heroin addict Nick Black, who died. Heather left the Close and returned home to Northern Ireland. Newlyweds Jonathan and Laura Gordon-Davies moved in. Laura died. Terry Sullivan moved in with widowed Jonathan.

Number 10 is another jinxed house. Gavin and Petra Taylor married and moved in. Within weeks, Gavin was dead from brain haemorrhage. A depressed Petra asked sister Michelle to move in. Petra disappeared and later committed suicide. Petra's elder sister, Marie Jackson, was left the house in the will, and moved in with husband George and their twin sons to share the house with Michelle. Fireman hero George was framed for a crime he did not commit, and received a gaol sentence. Marie and kids left Brookside. Terry Sullivan moved in with Michelle, but Michelle cheated on him and left. The house was sold to the Corkhills. The Corkhills – Billy, his wife Doreen and their two teenagers, Rod and Tracy – took over. But within two years the marriage had broken up, Billy had faked a burglary there and Doreen had left for good.

BROOKSIDE SPEAK

One thing they don't warn you about: Brookside Speak. It's a strange nasal sing-song language foreign to all who live south of the Mersey. You can muddle through, but here are a few translations which might help.

antwacky: old-fashioned. Karen used to refer to her mum's clothes as being 'dead antwacky'.
bevvied: drunk. From *bevvy* (beverage): beer, spirits, etc.
bizzies: the police
bladdered: extremely tired
blurt: a person who welshes on a deal
boxed off: fixed up, sorted out, finished
bubbled: reported on (grassed on, in another slang). Bobby Grant once asked Paul Collins if he'd bubbled on Pat and Terry for fiddling their dole money.
cabbaged: confused
case: (as in he's a case): a real character, sometimes a con-man
cop off: to arrange a date with a desirable member of the opposite sex
destroyed: extremely tired
divvy: idiot
doing my head in: unable to cope (as in *it's doing my head in*: it's getting on

my nerves)
down the banks: a rollocking
get me head down: going to sleep
in bulk: laughing a great deal
jacks: detectives
jangling: gossiping
kecks: men's trousers
leccy: electricity
made up: extremely pleased
minesweeper: one who trawls other's drinks or eats leftovers in restaurants
minted: rich, well off
minty: nutty, unbalanced
not worth a carrot: worthless
odds: loose change
off your cake: mad
queen: wife, girlfriend or mother
queer feller: a slippery character or a Jack-the-lad
scally: a young rogue
scran: food, nosh
the Soche: the Department of Health and Social Security
soft lad: an idiot
sound: great, marvellous
three sheets to the wind: mad
Tom Pepper: a liar
woolly backs: Northerners such as Mancunians or Wiganers, those who do not live in Liverpool

'THE BROTHERS'

'The Brothers' was the BBC's most important and successful soap in disguise. Officially about a road haulage firm and the sons of the late owner, its success from its first ten-part run in March 1972 to its end after seven series at Christmas 1976 owed nothing to lorries and very little to the men of the title. What made it compulsive for about 11 million viewers was the manipulating women characters, created by writer N. J. Crisp, projected by producer Gerald Glaister (later to devise 'Howards Way'), and acted with sustained strength and style by Jean Anderson as Mary Hammond, the meddling matriarch; Hilary Tindall as Anne Hammond, her languid daughter-in-law (the best bitch of the seventies); and Jennifer Wilson as Jennifer Kingsley, the dead man's secret mistress who, the family were shocked to find, inherited half the business. As the three sons, one gruff and hardworking, one wet and worrying, one a charming playboy, bickered in the background, the decent practical mistress struggled for acceptance, the proud mother struggled to oust her, and the beautifully dressed bitch schemed and shocked us (see 'Women Love Soap'). Pretty Gabrielle Drake, later to revive 'Crossroads' (p.150), arrived as the playboy's girlfriend, then wife, and was finally killed in a car crash. In the 1975 series Kate O'Mara entered vamping as the tough boss of an air freight business. Colin Baker followed as ruthless whizzkid Paul Merroney, rapidly earning the title 'Nastiest Man on Television'. Later still a French girlfriend was brought in for the new reformed playboy (Robin Chadwick) and the mistress married the eldest son (Patrick O'Connell, who'd replaced Glyn Owen after the first series). This couple then had problems both with her daughter (by his father) and in producing a child of their own (see 'Babies'). Amazingly the wet brother (Richard Easton) survived his wife's affairs and tantrums. Middle-class, snobbish, often arch, 'The Brothers' built on the success of 'The Forsyte Saga' to develop that very solid British brand of soap. It prepared the ground for 'Dallas' and the other American series and ensured a place for ever for feuding family drama on television.

'CASUALTY'

'Casualty' was the BBC's carbolic soap: a hospital drama which provoked such a rash of angry protest from politicians and doctors' and nurses' associations that viewers could feel fairly certain it touched on truth. Screened first in September 1986, set in the disillusioned mid-eighties in a night casualty ward in a Bristol-area National Health Service hospital, suffering from the Conservative government's financial cutbacks, it was aggressively different from the BBC's 'Angels' and closer to the American hospital-amid-chaos series 'St Elsewhere'. Written by Jeremy Brock and Paul Unwin, it was produced on a £2 million budget in fifteen-week series of self-contained hourly episodes by Geraint Morris, who'd made the police series with the woman inspector, 'Juliet Bravo'. 'Casualty', too, had rôle reversal: Julia Watson played Dr Baz Samuels, beautiful, tough but so overworked she needed amphetamines to combat the strain – she was having an affair with jokey but dedicated charge nurse Charlie Fairhead (Derek Thomson). There was a fierce but fatherly consultant, Dr Ewart Plimmer (Bernard Gallagher); Megan, a sympathetic sane Irish nurse (Brenda Flicker); Kuba, a Polish porter, alternately blabbering and brilliant; and King, a male nurse who boozed on duty. There was fast action as the road-crash, riot, pot-holing and fire victims, attempted suicides, injured drunken brawlers and heart-attack sufferers were dealt with in the cubicles. Unlike 'Angels', too, were the rude and rough language (bolshie customers were told to 'shut up'), the buckets of blood, gallons of tea brewed in the staffroom and the healthy helpings of passion.

Junior Health Minister Edwina Currie indignantly claimed the series was left-wing propaganda; nurses choked over King's boozing; doctors fumed over Baz's pill-popping. The Casualty Surgeons' Association dissociated itself from the series, and a Welsh Community Health Council objected to the fact that Baz was shown to have had two lovers –

a bad example in the age of AIDS, they thought. Modest ratings for a Saturday series (8 million) improved by the second series in September 1987. Dr Baz had moved on; Charlie nursed his unhappiness with whisky; and a steely woman administrator, Elizabeth Straker (Maureen O'Brian), set herself against Dr Plimmer and his team – only to fall under his spell and, by mid-series, between his sheets. When a pretty girl ambulance driver was stabbed by a drunk and died, viewers were gripped. Ratings topped 10 million and a decision to drop the planned series for autumn 1988 swiftly reversed.

Then, as if grimly to confirm 'Casualty' as our most topical soap, the episode shown on Saturday, 8 November 1987 centred on the hellish aftermath of an Irish terrorist bombing. On Sunday, 9 November in Enniskillen, during a Remembrance Day service, fact tragically mirrored soap fiction.

CENSORS

Censors of soap are the viewers, in the main. The television companies and the producers have fairly accurate ideas of how much sex, sin and suffering we want washing in on the soapwaves. Susan Tully, who is Michelle in 'EastEnders', told me her hardest-ever acting scenes were those when she was filmed in childbirth (Michelle was then an unmarried schoolgirl). The shots were never explicit or 'revealing', but despite everyone's labours the sequence was cut. The producer knew they were too 'strong' for soap.

Violence always brings protest: when Den smacked his daughter in 'EastEnders', Mrs Mary Whitehouse, Britain's pet Clean-Up Television campaigner, was affronted.

When the early episodes of 'Brookside' contained something like the level of swearing in the language of real Liverpudlians, viewers were gobsmacked with horror. Phil Redmond, the creator, became the censor for his own show. It was that – or risk its survival.

The power to demand cuts of stories, scenes and scripts belongs to the television companies. In America the Standards and Practices Department of the ABC network, anxious to protect sensitive viewers in the Midwestern Bible Belt, had many a victory over 'The Colbys'. A scene in which Fallon and Jeff undressed each other behind mottled glass in preparation for a shower together was reshot seventeen times then cut out for good on the grounds that it was too strong for soap. Another, in which Jeff affectionately kissed Fallon's foot after removing her shoe (both were fully dressed apart from the shoe), was deleted on the basis that it might inflame foot-fetishists everywhere. Ear-nibbling is another no-no.

Swearing is restricted in American soaps – by order of the Standards and Practices Department, too. In 'The Colbys' an allowance of six 'hells' or 'damns' a show was given. Nothing 'worse' was permitted. For

'Dynasty' the quota was lower still and falling. By this year it was one curse a show. 'And they counted,' said writer-producer Robert Pollock.

Jim Davis, who played Jock in 'Dallas', gave that soap's producers headaches. 'There were a lot of "hells" and "damns" in his natural speech pattern,' said producer Leonard Katzman. 'We have a strict count of four to five "cuss" words a show, and Jim could get us off count easily. The network [CBS] let us say "bastard" under certain circumstances. "Tramp" is OK, but "whore" is not.'

In Australia, television producers had to be aware of their sensitive and easily upset viewers in Melbourne. Their first television soap, 'Number Ninety Six', made in cosmopolitan Sydney, contained bedroom scenes thought so risqué that for transmission in the Melbourne area a thick black band was superimposed on the bottom half of the screen. When the Grundy Organisation sent episodes of 'Prisoner: Cell Block H' to America they were warned of American viewers' sensitivity. 'We had to cut scenes out and pick episodes carefully so as not to upset them,' Reg Watson, the writer-producer told me. By the time Reg produced 'Neighbours' for Grundy, the habit of self-censorship was strong. No one in Ramsay Street curses or smokes, and few drink more than the occasional (small) glass of beer. As for sex – it's all in the mind. Or, at least, off-camera.

'CHÂTEAUVALLON'

'Châteauvallon' landed in Britain in 1987 with the reputation of being the most dramatic thing to come out of France since William the Conqueror. But it travelled as well as a duff Beaujolais. Dubbed 'Dallas-sur-Loire' and, more appropriately, 'Châteauvalium', its dubbing was part of the problem. The passion of the French language was replaced by matter-of-fact English. It definitely lost something in the translation. Even so, the dubbed version still attracted twice as many viewers as the subtitled one shown in the same week on Channel 4.

Yet 'Châteauvallon' had been incredibly successful in its home land, where it was a veritable French revolution for the staid world of Gallic television. The most expensive series ever made there, it pulled in 35 per cent of French homes each week when the twenty-six-part series was shown on Antenne 2 in 1986. It was even sold to China.

French intellectuals had previously denounced the threat of 'cultural imperialism' posed by 'Dallas'. 'Châteauvallon' was their riposte. Jacques Dercourt, the show's executive producer, pronounced loftily: 'We couldn't be accused of succumbing to cultural imperialism with our series. In fact we tried to combat it with something distinctly French, a series in the literary tradition of Balzac and Dumas.'

'Châteauvallon' was a story of intense rivalry between two families: the rich and powerful Bergs (who were the Ewings with garlic) and Yugoslav immigrants the Kovalics, all set in a quiet Loire valley town. Being soap, it was quiet only on the surface. Beneath it was the usual diet of sex, political corruption, power struggles, and lots and lots of murders.

The head of the Berg family was Antonin (played by Jean Davy), who owned the local newspaper *La Dépêche (The Dispatch* to us). His daughter Florence (Chantal Nobel) was a Sue Ellen lookalike who put it about *un peu*. When Antonin died, Florence took over the paper.

At first, sex scenes were confined to the opening titles but they eventually infiltrated the rest of the show, causing Channel 4 to shift it to a late-night slot. Jacques Dercourt added: 'In France it is not a scandal to see a bare chest, but our naked scenes were something you would not see in US or British soaps.' The actress who sent male pulses racing was the striking Chantal Nobel, who in 1985 was involved in a mysterious car crash which shattered her career. She was, as the song says, 'a friend of Sacha Distel'. The heart-throb singer was driving Chantal's car at the time with her as a passenger. Distel was only dazed and bruised, but Chantal lay in a coma for months. She slowly recovered and managed to marry actor Jean-Louis Trintignant from her wheelchair. But she became a recluse and vowed never to return to 'Châteauvallon'.

'CITIZENS'

'Citizens' tried hard to be a radio version of 'EastEnders' after it was launched on Radio 4 in October 1987. It is aimed primarily at a young audience and is not afraid to tackle contemporary issues. One of the main characters is a single parent, another is unemployed. Through the overstretched Indian doctor come stories and conversations touching racism and the crisis in the National Health Service. Sex, money shortages and the problems of rubbing along are discussed with excellent dialogue and outstanding acting – but the effect is slightly dull.

Broadcast twice a week with an omnibus edition at the weekend, 'Citizens' is the story of four families from Norwich, Birmingham, Liverpool and Kilmarnock. Five young people from these families met at college in Leicester and have come to the capital to share 5 Limerick Road, a ramshackle house in South-West London. The five, all in their twenties, are: landlady Alex Parker (played by Kate Duchene) who is the mother of baby William; doctor Anita Sharma (Seeta Indrani); Liverpool twins Julia and Michael Brennan (Beverley Hills (!) and Russell Boulter); and merchant banker Hugh Hamilton (James MacPherson).

Brian Murphy (of 'George and Mildred' fame) plays twinkly tenant Ernest Bond, a betting man, living none too comfortably on the ground floor with Salome, possibly the first Siamese cat of soap. And a very classy miaow she has, too. The serial follows the famous five on their frequent long journeys home to their families. 'EastEnders' highlights inner-city decay. 'Citizens' features Inter-City delay.

By May 1988, though, there was talk of a re-launch because BBC radio's young and sparky soap was attracting only one third of the listeners who follow the more old-fogeyish 'Archers'. Michael Green, Controller of Radio 4, ordered more cliffhangers, more action and perhaps more attention to older characters. He also promised that if fizzier, soapier scripts didn't revive the ratings, 'Citizens' could be arrested next year.

71

CLOTHES

Clothes maketh the soap man and do wonders for the soap woman. Well, they do in America where tuxedos and ball-gowns, silly hats and sparkly jewels dress up the fantasy, and never mind the cost.

British soap-makers have scarcely cared how their 'ordinary' characters have looked. It suited the low budgets not to. So enter the typical British soap bloke as Man From Millet's and the average soap female as Oxfam Fatale. These days, the clothes are more clever, thanks to the wardrobe people's eye for bargains, but chain-store fashion and odd items from jumble sales and street-markets still account for most of what's worn. Actresses may yearn for designer garb, but it'll never be seen down Albert Square or Brookside Close.

When I visited the wardrobe department for 'Brookside' – lodged in one of the houses in the Close, in a room the size of the Grants' kitchen – I was taken to task. I'd joked that Doreen Corkhill had been handed £100 by her dentist boss to buy an outfit and turned up in a dress I estimated cost £8.99. The wardrobe lady told me, hurt, it had cost £11.99. What did I take them for – cheapskates?

For 'EastEnders', designers went to army surplus stores for some of Lofty's clothes and those worn by Tony Carpenter. They found a secondhand bomber jacket for Ali – very nice it is, too. Pauline's best blouse (interestingly the same as one of Annabelle's in 'Brookside') came from a chain store and cost £9.99. Shelves in their wardrobe department contain items for the old codgers labelled 'naff shirts', 'naff jumpers', plus space for Pete's hats and Sharon's fluffy tops.

'Neighbours' clothes are startlingly bright; no one is allowed to look drab. Everything is bought new and, if necessary, 'broken down'. The overalls used by Tony in the garage are strategically greased and creased. There's a fairly clean one for mornings, a grubby one for lunch, a dirty one for mid-afternoon and a disgusting one for the end of the day. Many of tiny Kylie Minogue's clothes are bought from children's departments, and the swimsuits and surfing-shorts are bought in large batches. There isn't a big call for bikinis in 'EastEnders' or 'Coronation Street', I suppose.

The soap with the least interest in its cast's clothes used to be 'Crossroads'. The poor actors had to wear their own. Jane Rossington, who was Jill, says: 'I used to provide all my screen clothes myself. They didn't pay me for it. It cost me a packet, and I used to end up drifting round sales for bargains.'

The Hunters, alias Ronald Allen and Sue Lloyd, griped at their miserly £6 a week allowance. It meant that Ronald had to pay for David Hunter's expensive suits out of his own pocket. When David was shot by his mad wife Rosemary they *had* to buy him not one suit but two. It caused a terrible row. The producer wanted blood to pour all over him. Janet pulled the trigger and nothing happened. Ronnie had already broken the blood bag and was turning red. They had to do the scene again, new suit, new blood. Sue had to borrow friends' clothes. She says: 'Six pounds didn't even pay for me to have my hair done, let alone buy "Dynasty"-style outfits.' It might just have bought a shoulder-pad.

Even Benny's hat belonged to actor Paul Henry. And Joy Andrews, who was Tish Hope, remembers when 'Crossroads' changed from black and white to colour. 'None of us had much idea what to wear. On our first day in colour, we all turned up in varying shades of beige. The motel uniforms were beige, too. We looked awful.'

At least from 1985 onwards, when Phillip Bowman took over as producer, the cast were able to choose their attire from up-market chain stores. So Gabrielle Drake, who played Nicola Freeman, could look glamorous even though the wardrobe budget was still a pittance in comparison to the American soaps. There were no £1500 gowns for Gabrielle.

Just before Central announced that 'Crossroads' was to end, their wardrobe department went out and bought a range of sexy outfits for Jane Rossington to wear on the show. Jane could have done with them earlier. She recalls: 'After the motel burned down, I had to start wearing a whole new wardrobe. One of my favourite colours was navy blue. But the new bar was decorated in dark blue, so if I wore a navy outfit I just vanished against the walls when being filmed. I had to search for much lighter colours.'

The weekly wardrobe budget for everything for around twenty characters in 'Coronation Street' is laughably low, well under £500, and was an unbelievable £15 a week as recently as fifteen years ago. Theirs is a 'make do and mend' policy, supplemented by astute buying by wardrobe supervisors who go about leading chain stores anonymously, finding items for Bet, Gloria, Rita and Co. Around £30 is the going rate for a new dress, and up to £75 for a good coat, often found in a sale. The system works because many members of the cast prefer to hang on to the same familiar costumes and stage props that they have worn for years and which have made them famous. Bryan Mosley absolutely refuses to be separated from Alf Roberts's original shabby brown suede trilby. Between recording days it is clinically sealed in a plastic bag in a storeroom called the Cave. Nearby is Albert Tatlock's threadbare suit which the late Jack Howarth stubbornly refused to let wardrobe press or dry-clean. It is an Aladdin's cave of memories, from Ena Sharples's old plant-pot hats to Hilda Ogden's pinnies (bought for two or three pounds from markets).

Amazingly, Jean Alexander's entire wardrobe of coats, hats and dresses, worn over twenty-three years of playing Hilda Ogden, fits easily on to just one half of a six-foot rail.

In 1960 when the series began, the costumes for twenty-seven regular cast members were accommodated easily on six six-foot clothes-rails. Now the room is packed to the ceiling with rails for over sixty characters. Nothing is thrown away except clothing that has been washed so often that it is on the point of disintegrating.

The flash dressers in the Street? Mike Baldwin has more suits than any other character, and Percy Sugden is a peacock with his gay waistcoats and cloth caps. Actor Bill Waddington who plays Percy is one of the few who is allowed to wear his own clothes, or at least headgear. He gives dozens of caps away to charity and has had his own supply manufactured privately.

Now that Bet is married, her barmaid's tat is redundant. At one time she could choose from a thousand pairs of earrings fashioned in the most outrageous shapes including dangling lavatory-bowls, most of them sent in by fans. But Bet has gone posh these days, in keeping with her image as the better-off landlady of the Rover's, and it is designer costume jewellery for her when the budget can stand it.

No such worries in American soaps. Nolan Miller, the designer credited with putting the flash into their most popular trash ('Love Boat', 'Charlie's Angels', 'T.J. Hooker', 'Hotel' and many more), has been spending about £20,000 on clothes on each episode of 'Dynasty' since the soap began. The spending ties in with the idea of the show: everyone's fantasy of what wealth and power mean. Anything Joan Collins wants as superbitch Alexis – from a copy of a Princess Diana Russian-style hat, coat and muffler, to hired diamonds and rare fur coats – she gets. Of the half-million pounds spent each series, Joan's gear costs about £100,000. And no outfit is ever worn twice; they are simply returned to the Spelling Productions wardrobe department – as big as an aircraft-hangar – to be used on other series with smaller budgets. 'It sounds expensive,' the tall Texan told me, 'but the cost is much less than it would be in the shops. I'll design maybe a dozen costumes per episode, costing an average of twelve hundred pounds each.' He adds that he couldn't buy off-the-peg clothes for Linda Evans even if he wanted. Linda has large shoulders, a large bust and no behind. 'We'd have to buy size-twelve tops and size-six trousers and skirts.' The actresses are also given the right of veto. 'It means my job is twenty per cent design and eighty per cent psychology,' said the man who dressed Joan Crawford, Liz Taylor and Barbara Stanwyck.

Miller's magic and the producers' munificence made actresses on rival shows jealous and angry. First the women in 'Dallas' protested; a 'Cinderella' delegation led by Victoria Principal complained that their show's dresses' budget was far too small by comparison. They weren't in the least interested to be reminded that 'Dallas' has to pay out for livestock and stetsons!

Bill Travilla, the man who made Marilyn Monroe's cream dress in 'The Seven Year Itch', was Lorimar's answer. He made Victoria, Linda Gray, Priscilla Presley and the other 'Dallas' dolls into shoulder-padded fashion-plates and he turned Barbara Carrera's Greek tycooness into a fantasy vamp in outlandish feathers, floppy hats, sweeping capes and flouncing sleeves. His average cost for a garment was £1500 – one of Victoria's outfits cost £5000 – but he stressed there was no waste. 'If I had a scene where cameras would be filming from the waist up, I didn't buy two-hundred pound shoes. They wore tennis shoes, and I put the money into a three-hundred pound hat,' he said.

In turn, the actresses on 'Knots Landing' heard what was being spent on their sisters in 'Dynasty' and 'Dallas' and stormed the producer's office. 'I screamed and howled,' Donna Mills said. 'We're still not up to their level but we don't have to wear anything twice. Face it, people tune in to see how we look and what we are wearing.'

My vote for the best soap clothes? Of the glossies, 'Howards Way' manages on a fraction of the budget of the American soaps. The plots may not be brilliant, but Jan Harvey's chic outfits make the 'Dynasty' models look like fancy dress. Of the humble homespun soaps, Sally Whittaker in 'Coronation Street' always looks young, fresh and fashionable.

'THE COLBYS'

The Colbys of California, cousins of the Carringtons, proved that as far as super-rich soap families are concerned there *is* such a thing as viewer fatigue.

Aaron Spelling, co-producer with Richard and Esther Shapiro of 'Dynasty', created 'The Colbys', the exploits of just but not jolly Jason Colby, tycoon; possessive but not passive Sable, his wife; and three grown children 'finding' themselves and fouling up in 1985. 'The Colbys' was 'Dynasty II', similar enough to the then hugely successful 'Dynasty' but different enough, they hoped, to have a style of its own. They reasoned that if 'Dynasty I' was making them pots (and it was, over £100 million a year in syndication fees) why not go for it and be greedy? What emerged was why not.

First came the stupendous hype. Then came the starry cast. Then came the stupid plots. The hype was that 'The Colbys' would be more exotic and more X-plicit. We were talking serious delirious sex and serious designer sportswear, here. This fabulous family would be more outgoing than those stay-at-homes in Denver. The established darlings of 'Dynasty' – Blake, Krystle, Alexis – would 'visit'. Jeff and Fallon (who would arise from the ashes of her plane crash) would move to California to stay.

Half of Hollywood was clamouring to take part. Burt Lancaster, Katherine Hepburn, Angie Dickinson, Gregory Peck, Faye Dunaway, all picked up the bait but then put it down. Angie, considered for Jeff Colby's mother, didn't like the character development, she said. Susannah York and Diana Rigg were tested for Sable but were turned down. In the end Charlton Heston signed for Jason, for £45,000 a week (two or three days' work). Barbara Stanwyck, then seventy-eight, signed for his sister, Constance (the veteran movie star had just made an impact in the television mini-series 'The Thorn Birds'). And English Stephanie

Beacham, who'd twisted so brilliantly in ITV's camp series 'Connie', won Sable, the superbitch rôle. The children were to be played by Maxwell Caulfield, Tracy Scoggins and Claire Yarlett. Who? Who? And who? Never mind.

On the soap that was to be 'Richer, Prettier and More Shocking' (according to the publicity blurb) than its rivals, salaries were higher – Heston's was £10,000 a week more than John Forsythe's for Blake (his counterpart in 'Dynasty') – the weekly wardrobe allowance was £15,000, nearly £4000 more than for 'Dynasty', and the budget for the whole show at £900,000 was £150,000 a week more than for 'Dynasty'.

So strong was the desire to make 'The Colbys' glossier and grander that, despite an outlay of £6 million in the first week of production, more than £1 million worth of furnishings and scenery were torn apart because Spelling and his executives thought them only run-of-the-mill rich.

The show was screened from November 1985 in America. By December, BBC boss Michael Grade had bought it for £40,000 an episode. It was screened in the 8 p.m. Wednesday 'Dallas' slot here from January and did passably well with around 8 million viewers. In America it was shown later, at 10 p.m. – the notion that it was an 'adult' show was taken seriously by the ABC network.

On the rival NBC network the comedy 'Cheers' was running. Audiences didn't switch. The first episode rated only fiftieth in the American lists, the second thirty-seventh and the third thirty-ninth. 'The Colbys' was being tagged a 'turkey' before it arrived here.

Rumours of salvation schemes began to flow. They were said to be ready to ship over Dominique Deveraux, Diahann Carroll's scheming hussy from 'Dynasty' (p.209), with – wait for it – rock idol Michael Jackson as her long-lost son.

From reviewers there was little enthusiasm for early plots revolving around Jason's fatal illness, Sable's fury that Constance gave half the Colby company stock to her nephew Jeff, and the two Colby daughters' boyfriends, one a blind folk-singer, the other a save-the-earth activist. Barbara Stanwyck's geriatric cowboy lover Hutch helped not at all.

Emma Samms, rushed in as the new Fallon – she was introduced to John James (Jeff) one minute and kissing him on camera the next – brought flak from critics. And more than one observer noted that the year was not Aaron Spelling's best. His 'Matt Houston' and 'Glitter' series were dropped in Britain. Other series were cancelled in America, and his long-buoyant 'The Love Boat' began to sink in the ratings.

By April 1986, Barbara Stanwyck had freed herself from her contract, declaring that 'The Colbys' was 'the biggest pile of garbage I ever did.'

The ABC network's Standards and Practices Department made sure the promised sexy shocks were never more than promises. A shower scene featuring Emma Samms and John James was removed by their order, and Jeff was not allowed to kiss Fallon's foot.

Episodes for the second season were prepared, and the producers, cast and writers hoped for an upswing like that enjoyed by 'Dynasty' (when Joan Collins arrived) to confound the cynics.

Stephanie Beacham's Sable seethed beautifully. Charlton Heston made Jason (no longer fatally ill, magically) a touching tyrant torn between his wife and his true love, Francesca (Katherine Ross), her sister. Maxwell Caulfield raped Fallon and regretted it, remarried and regretted that. Fallon quivered, and Jeff frowned.

Ricardo Montalban, as Zachary Powers the villainous shipping tycoon, yearned for Sable and schemed sinister schemes. The younger Colby girl, Bliss, in her ignorance, fell for an alcoholic runaway Russian ballet dancer ('more wodka, pliss'). And Monica, her elder sister (as a lawyer, she was the soap's token liberated woman), agonised over her returned long-lost illegitimate child which Sable wanted to buy.

The upswing didn't come. John James appeared on radio and television chat-shows to defend 'The Colbys'. Writers Robert and Eileen Pollock reaffirmed their belief that the show dealt with 'human values not the riches' and that it would be accepted and loved given time and a decent spot. The series was then sandwiched between two news programmes and had to pick up viewers 'cold'. If that wasn't bad enough, the rival network had 'The Cosby Show', America's favourite series, at that time.

The summer 1987 cliffhanger – a flight of fancy devised by Richard Shapiro – finally sealed the soap's fate. In what may have been seen as a way to rocket the show to the top, the genius behind the *Star Wars* film, John Dykstra, was hired to mastermind the special effects of an alien spaceship landing. The craft appeared in the desert, where the still-quivering Fallon had driven, pursuing her abducted mother-in-law. An alien – an extra in a body-stocking with bloodshot eyes – appeared in a haze of smoke and beckoned Fallon aboard. She clambered up in her high heels, stood bosom to bosom with her new friend as the craft's door rolled down and lightbulbs round the giant saucer-shell flashed for lift-off. The five-minute scene was said to have cost half a million pounds.

It struck some critics and many viewers that this – like the rebirth of Bobby in 'Dallas' – was a sign that They thought We would accept any old nonsense. Others suggested the idea was pinched from the send-up series 'Soap'. Others asked: 'What was in it for the Martians?'

Its writer, Robert Pollock, told me later that the idea had been that of co-producer Richard Shapiro. 'Apparently Richard had had a dream. He was tremendously excited. At the time the novel *Communion* was a smash hit. The supernatural was being discussed over dinner-parties everywhere. I couldn't discourage him. I was very worried about our writing ourselves into a corner. How would we get Fallon back? Richard said: "We'll worry about that next season." The scene was not received with enormous enthusiasm, as I expected. It will never be done again.'

The decision to drop 'The Colbys' was announced soon after the alien landing. Of 'The Colbys' stars only John James and Emma Samms survived to return to 'Dynasty'.

The UFO scene was repeated as flashbacks in 'Dynasty' this year, on the orders of an unrepentant Richard Shapiro.

THE CHARACTERS

Jason Colby, the patriarch of 'The Colbys', was not a happy man. For one thing Jason, played by Charlton Heston, was suspiciously similar to Blake Carrington in 'Dynasty', ruthless, proud, sentimental, misunderstood and *loaded*. (Was he cloned?) For another, family life in his palatial hilltop estate overlooking Bel Air was like something out of *The Brides of Dracula*.

His beautiful wife Sable suffered from acute advancing greed. His sister Constance was a geriatric nymphomaniac (dashing away for dirty weekends with Hutch, her elderly buck). His daughters were on their nineteenth nervous breakdowns. And his playboy son Miles looked like the Fonz and thought himself cool!

Jason was down to his last $2 billion as the series began. His nephew Jeff Colby held half the shares, and there were parts of America, Hong Kong and the South China Seas he didn't own. Bah! On top of that the doctors told him he had six months to live. Terminal paranoia, I dare say.

They were wrong about the six months. Doctors are so careless in soap, one just hopes they're insured. He had two years. Then the show was dropped.

In that time life rarely improved. Shiny pop-up Jeff turned out to be his son. Francesca, the wife's sister, loved him after all, but fainted at the wedding just because her dead husband showed up, too (see 'Weddings'). His own sister died mysteriously, and they held this really mawkish funeral. His son Miles looked awful in a suit. And Sable, who'd run off with his worst enemy, filthy foreigner Zachary Powers, threatened to come back. Worse than all that, every so often he had to dress up and pretend to play polo. Jason Colby would probably have swapped places with Arthur Fowler, but we'll never know now.

Charlton Heston, the big man who'd played Ben Hur and Moses, didn't consider the rôle of Jason Colby a come-down. 'I took a look at what was happening in the movie industry,' he said at the start. 'Last year they were making films for twenty-year-olds by twenty-five-year-olds. This year they're making films for fourteen-year-olds by fourteen-year-olds. I'm damned if I'll end up playing the father of a teenage computer genius. So for better or worse I'm back on the little tube.'

The sixty-four-year-old Illinois-born actor, a friend of President Reagan and a long-serving president of the Screen Actors' Guild, decided to become an actor after appearing in the school play at five. With over fifty starring rôles in films to his credit, and many more in theatre (one recent success was his portrayal of Thomas More in *A Man for All Seasons* in London), he has enjoyed work on television since 1948. 'When I started to do television', he recalled, 'theatrical actors of any reputation wouldn't do it because it didn't pay anything and film actors were contractually prohibited from doing TV. So I was competing in my own category – out of work!'

He won an Oscar for *Ben Hur* in 1959 and many equivalent awards in other countries since. But it was playing Moses in *The Ten Commandments* which has left its mark. The conscientious, highly disciplined actor was called 'Moses' by his co-stars in 'The Colbys'. Maxwell Caulfield was one 'sinner' to discover his laws could still be broken.

Miles Colby was the idiot of 'The Colbys'. He messed up. Always.

Played by English actor Maxwell Caulfield, he was supposed to be the rich kid, hunky, hip and heir to Colby Enterprises. While his twin sister Monica studied law, spoke Chinese and slaved over a hot blind folk-singer (in the interests of business) from nine to five, Miles drove his red sports-car like Mr Toad and toot-tooted at the world. And he looked about as comfortable as Mr Toad in tuxedo and tails.

When Fallon forgot her name (and we couldn't blame her) she called herself Randall Adams, and Miles married her. This upset the folks. Mother Sable did like to be warned of these things so she could scratch the girl's eyes out, then arrange a million-dollar 'do'.

Miles tended to comb his quiff and smirk. But he lost his cool when Jeff arrived, gleaming from 'Dynasty'. Jeff inherited half the company and said Fallon was his, too. So, being six foot two of tanned muscle (most of it between his ears), Miles raped her. And he *would* keep fighting with Jeff. It always ended with Jeff, the forgiving hero, nobly saving Miles as he dangled, holding Jeff's hand, from a cliff-edge.

Miles moaned to mummy Sable. But she couldn't stop him looking for a new bride with an even sillier name than Fallon: Channing. Not only was she scheming and poor, she was possibly the plainest girl in glossy soap. Fallon's baby wasn't his. Channing could, then couldn't, then didn't get pregnant. And between all this the police kept arresting him for murder.

He didn't do it. He probably lost the address. Colby Enterprises deserved him.

Maxwell Caulfield seemed to suffer from Miles Colby's bad luck when he played that rôle in 'The Colbys'. Miles kept displeasing his dad,

Jason. Maxwell kept displeasing Charlton Heston who played Jason. Robert Pollock, co-writer of 'The Colbys' with his wife Eileen, told me: 'Chuck Heston treated his rôle as a major project, and gave the young people all the support he could. Max wasn't as professional as he might have been. He was a little late once or twice, and this caused tensions. But Max seemed so unlucky; often it wasn't his fault. It was in his contract to make sure he looked good. We often have to remind the men – usually through the people in Wardrobe – that they're soon to appear stripped to the waist, so they must work off the flab. One afternoon Max checked he wasn't required for a few hours, looked to see which stage [part of the studio] was being used, then got into his togs to run on the studio roof. Unfortunately, the stage had been changed. Chuck was working when this terrible sound of thundering hoofs stopped everyone dead. Chuck yelled to security: "Get that madman down!" We knew it just had to be poor Max.'

Maxwell, who is twenty-eight, will no doubt put it in his memoirs. He may also include highlights from his pre-Hollywood days, when he accompanied the ladies on stage in Raymond's Revue Bar in Soho and other striptease clubs as a way of paying bills between acting jobs. After leaving London for New York in 1978, he began a successful spell of stage assignments, winning an award for his rôle in *Class Enemy*. He played the lead in *The Elephant Man* in a national theatre tour and won acclaim in such productions as George Orwell's *1984*, appearing with his wife Juliet Mills. His film début as the leading man in *Grease 2* led to a series of film parts, but the theatre seems to be his first choice.

Sable Colby is probably out there somewhere now, sucking in her

cheeks, narrowing her eyes and looking for old ladies to run down in her car. The silly bitch of 'The Colbys' is gone but not forgotten.

Sable, played by British Stephanie Beacham, was so similar to Alexis, played by British Joan Collins, you wonder if the writers really tried to make her original at all. Both women married their sugar daddies, had their children alarmingly young (Sable must have been in the Brownies at the time), then lost out to another woman. Sable wasn't promiscuous like Alexis. She couldn't have had the energy after stepping out of the shower to entice Jason ten times a day. Both loved their children in a power-mad kind of way. (Pity the sons – and daughters-in-law.) And both loved changing clothes and organising little soirées for two or three thousand guests.

Hating her sister-in-law Constance for giving nephew Jeff Colby company stock, she tried to finish the old trout by first loosening the footstraps on her saddle, then reversing the car fast to try to iron her flat. But the old trout bounced back. Later she hated her sister Francesca for stealing Jason when she had Roger, a perfectly good, starched, rich husband at home. And with his own hair, too.

Stephanie's Sable did stand out among the others in the gems-and-temper brigade. Her clothes and hair were never as ludicrous as her actions. And she never laughed at poor Jason. Not when he was being pompous. Not even when he was the oldest, portliest polo-player in soap.

Stephanie Beacham spoke with clenched teeth during most of the two years she played super-wealthy Sable in 'The Colbys'. Possibly this was because the forty-year-old Hertfordshire-born actress had to stifle the laughs at the preposterous plots. (Soap bitches are not allowed a sense of humour; it can spoil the make-up.) Possibly it goes with the slink.

Stephanie went to America and 'The Colbys' after co-producer Aaron Spelling saw her in ITV's 'Connie', in the rag trade. Before that she'd been splendid as Rose, in rags in the prisoner-of-war series 'Tenko'. Before that she'd been impressive in very little in the film *The Nightcomers* with Marlon Brando.

Picked for Sable – sandwiched between two 'legends', Charlton Heston and Barbara Stanwyck – after Diana Rigg and Susannah York had been considered, Stephanie spent her first months alone in Los Angeles feeling nervous and worried about her daughters (then aged ten and twelve, at school in England). And she found a marked difference between working in British television and American soap: 'Nobody rehearses in an American soap. They just learn their lines and go straight in. It's like a boxing-ring – outrageous.' Unsure how – or if – to breathe life into Sable, her problems were increased because Stephanie must lip-read. She is deaf in one ear with only partial hearing in the other.

She told listeners to BBC radio's 'Desert Island Discs': 'When I kept going to the right-hand side of Charlton Heston, they thought it was because I was rather more fond of my right profile than my left. But it was nothing to do with that at all; it was because old Mother here is deaf. It's not a real problem, because I know everybody's script and I listen very hard.'

The beautiful actress describes 'The Colbys' as 'The Old Cobblers – lovely escapist nonsense' and was sad and surprised when it was dropped. But she had found highly charged, wicked Sable a strain to play. 'When the series was scrapped I'm told I shed ten years from my face overnight.' Last year she appeared on the London stage in *The Rover* and made a mini-series in Paris: *Napoleon and Josephine*.

Sable may live on. She may make guest appearances in 'Dynasty', the parent soap, if allowed by the writers and Joan Collins, who plays the rival bitch and allegedly guards her territory like a Dobermann pinscher.

Alive or in that Great Soap Opera in the Sky, Sable did Stephanie favours beyond the £20,000 a week the part paid. 'Being in California made me a more confident positive person. When I made *The*

Nightcomers there I was twenty-two and a victim, terrified of all the terrible men in smart suits with "business advice". I'm not a victim now. I'm a predator.'

'COMPACT'

'Compact' was the BBC's highly scented soap about a women's magazine which ran from January 1962 to July 1965, Tuesdays and Thursdays after the legendary 'Tonight' show. It was the high-minded Corporation's first proper attempt at continuous storytelling since 'The Grove Family' ended in 1957. Dreamed up by Hazel Adair as she sat waiting to deliver an article to *Woman's Own*, written with Peter Ling, with whom she was to create 'Crossroads', the stories concerned 'the talented and temperamental people' who worked on this 'topical magazine for the busy woman'. There was very little busy work amidst the pot-plants and the artfully untidied desks, of course. But nine romances, including three marriages, took place in the first six months, and audiences of 9½ million followed the series loyally. Critics unanimously scoffed, called it 'empty-headed', 'worthless' and 'hollow'. BBC Television controller Stuart Hood tried to drop it in its first month (he didn't like it: the plots were unrealistic and the people too good-looking, he said). An archbishop tut-tutted at the story-line of a single girl, secretary Maggie, becoming pregnant and another depicting marital discord. Teenagers could copy this behaviour, he claimed. In fact viewers responded warmly, thousands writing in with advice and sympathy. The scripts had typically good BBC intentions, needless to say. Characters didn't smoke or swear; a chaste goodnight kiss was the sexiest moment (the foot of a bed was seen only once, when a character had flu). When the then popular dance, the Twist, was to be included in an episode, checks were made and, yes, a doctor somewhere had warned against sprains from the craze. A new, safe dance, the Method, was devised instead. When the 'Compact' glass doors first started swinging there was even a faint feminist quality. Neat bouffant-haired Joanne Minster (Jean Harvey) was the editor, coping with prejudice against women bosses and her inner conflict of career versus wifely duties. After six months she left the job, chose her husband only to find he didn't want to be chosen. This allowed Ronald Allen (p.166), playing Ian Harmon, son of Sir Charles, the magazine's industrialist proprietor, to step in as editor and become the soap's remote gentlemanly heart-throb. (All the other men were woolly bears.) Great was the relief when impish secretary Sally (Monica Evans), with whom he was smitten, rejected him and left. Later she returned (the actress said that after earning £50 a week on 'Compact' it was hard living on fifty bob unemployment pay). Ian and she married and both left, supposedly for America. Among an ever-changing cast (500 in the first two years), favourite characters included art editor Richard (Moray Watson), so good with the dry Martinis; warm-hearted gushing Gussie, the features editor (Gareth Davies). There was an agony aunt in a hat, a fat girl in the typing pool and a comic barrow-boy. But in the ratings 'Compact' lagged behind Independent Television's 'Emergency – Ward Ten', so producer Morris Barry was sent from 'Z Cars' to tidy and speed it up. There was more excitement: a boy falling asleep near a gas-fire caused protests; two youths being offered reefers caused shock. The critics said it was still terminally twee, claustrophobic and soppy. When the decision came to drop it – because journalists aren't as interesting as doctors – Hazel Adair said: 'People got us wrong. We did not set out to make a documentary about life on a woman's magazine. What we put over is the stuff the women's magazines are selling themselves.'

'CORONATION STREET'

**'Coronation Street' is the most remarkable success-story,
not only in the history of soap opera but
also in the history of television.**

THE HISTORY

It was born humbly, unheralded, with a cast of elderly unknowns, many
in the twilight of obscure careers in repertory, in black and white and in
the unfashionable, unglamorous North-West of England in December
1960. It was a hit. It's a hit today.

It's creator was a young unhappy actor-writer, paid £30 a week to
adapt scripts. Tony Warren (p.89) gave them the idea, wrote twelve
scripts, and British television soap opera became a fact of life.

Episode 1, transmitted live, went out on a Friday night, and the
programme went out on Wednesdays and Fridays until the spring of
1961. Then it switched to Mondays and Wednesdays – the 'dates' it has
kept for twenty-seven years.

A critic who viewed episode 1 looked forward to its end: 'The
programme is doomed . . . with its dreary signature tune and grim scene
of a row of terraced houses and smoking chimneys.' A death somewhat
exaggerated, it seems.

Regional audiences sent it soaring to the top of the local television
ratings. But some parts of Britain were unaware of its existence until the
following spring. Lew Grade, for instance, refused to let his Midlands-
based company Associated Television take the series at first. But along
with Tyne Tees Television, who had vetoed the first thirty programmes
or so, he had to back down as soon as he realised how deeply it had
bitten into the BBC's audience rations.

Johnny Briggs, later to play Mike Baldwin in the series, recalls visiting the Manchester studios and asking Violet Carson what she was doing. She was amazed he hadn't known. Carried away by the rapturous reception the programme had received up north, Vi and the rest of the cast had forgotten that not everyone had heard of 'Coronation Street', let alone seen it.

Because there were only two channels then, last night's television 'play' was next morning's topic of conversation on every bus and train. Viewers followed 'Coronation Street' in such enormous numbers that by the time Elsie Tanner got married to United States Army sergeant Steve Tanner in 1967 some 20 million viewers were glued to the edge of their seats – the sort of audience that only a royal wedding would normally command.

'Coronation Street' was bought by Australia in 1963 and shown five times a week. Sales deals were made in Holland, Gibraltar, Hong Kong, Singapore, Nigeria, Sierra Leone, Thailand, Greece, Sweden, Finland, Canada and even Hawaii. On the Polynesian island of Oahu where 'Hawaii Five-O' was made, the locals apparently preferred Elsie and Ena. Granada had high hopes of a sale in America, too, but the Yanks felt the Northern expressions and accents would baffle their viewers. But they were impressed; they came up with their own soap – 'Peyton Place'.

If things were 'warm' for Granada, they were red hot for the cast. Pat Phoenix and Philip Lowrie were mobbed when they made a personal appearance at a Leeds store and had to be rescued by mounted police. A fur-coat-clad Lynne Carol went 'incognito' to the Ideal Home Exhibition, but hundreds recognised her as Martha Longhurst and she was advised by police to leave for her own safety. Thousands thronged the sea-front at Blackpool when leading members of the cast, posing like film stars, switched on the resort's illuminations. Harold Wilson gave the cast a sherry party at 10 Downing Street, and James Callaghan dubbed Pat Phoenix 'the sexiest woman on TV'. When Pat, Doris Speed and Arthur Leslie toured Australia, a crowd of 20,000 fans was waiting to greet them in Adelaide. Two years later, when Violet Carson went there, 250,000 people rolled out the red carpet for her. Famous fans ranged from Sir Laurence Olivier to Sir John Betjeman, the Poet Laureate, who likened the series to Dickens's *Pickwick Papers* and declared: 'At 7.30 p.m. on Mondays and Wednesdays, I am in heaven.'

In 1964 came the bloody purge – a whim of new, young producer Tim Aspinall. He decided that Martha Longhurst should die in the snug bar of the Rover's Return. All through rehearsals on the date of the fateful recording, actor Peter Adamson, who played Len Fairclough, refused to say the line 'She's dead', firmly believing that someone at Granada would 'reprieve' Martha at the last moment. It didn't happen. She perished.

Other familiar faces who disappeared included Harry and Concepta

Hewitt, Leonard Swindley and Ida and Frank Barlow.

There is no doubt, though, that the series was at its zenith in that first decade, and the high spot for the cast was probably when they were invited to appear on the Royal Variety Show. As Tony Warren said: 'Yes, the stories were harder, grittier then because life was harder. "Coronation Street" didn't go soft – life did.'

In the seventies the original line-up began to disintegrate. Television companies are always soberly pointing out that actors' jobs are not pensionable, however popular individuals might be with the public. Granada meant it. Arthur Leslie (Jack Walker) died suddenly in 1970. Jennifer Moss, victim of a broken marriage and a miscarriage, disappeared to sort out her personal life. Violet Carson, then in her seventies, took a whole year out to rest. Actress Anne Reid asked to leave the series in 1971, and her character, Valerie Barlow, was electrocuted by a faulty hairdrier. Arthur Lowe (Mr Swindley) had already soldiered off to find greater fame in the BBC comedy classic 'Dad's Army'. Neville Buswell (Ray Langton) asked to be released from his contract. In 1973, Pat Phoenix and Alan Browning left the series to chance their luck with a forty-three-week theatre tour. Graham Haberfield (Jerry Booth) died suddenly in 1975. Peter Adamson (Len Fairclough) was suspended from the programme for three months to sort out his problem with alcoholism. And Ernie Bishop was killed off with a shotgun blast in a wages robbery after actor Stephen Hancock had staged a one-man pay dispute. Fleet Street speculated about the ability of 'Coronation Street' to survive at the top of the ratings with so many famous faces gone. The producers and the cast were quick to point out that the Street itself was the real star. A corny line, but they were right.

The eighties were littered with anniversaries from the 2000th episode and the twenty-first birthday, to a Silver Jubilee champagne celebration and a visit from the Queen.

But more famous faces were disappearing. The death of Violet Carson, Jack Howarth, Bernard Youens and Patricia Phoenix left William Roache (Ken Barlow) as the sole survivor from episode 1. New accusations were hurled: the show had lost its sparkle, the characters were living in a time-warp and bore no resemblance to present-day people living in the North of England, or anywhere else. The producers said there were still rows of back-to-back terraced houses with cobbled streets and corner pubs throughout the industrial North. Fan Russell Harty wrote: 'There was life before "Coronation Street" – but it didn't add up to much.'

The programme *was* finally toppled from its lofty perch by BBC's 'EastEnders' in 1985. The noisy, nosy cockneys beat the cosy Northerners. But its audiences remain loyal. Executive producer Bill Podmore says: 'We still set out to entertain and amuse, whereas "EastEnders" has a very different approach. But not everyone wants to sit down and watch the brutal realities of life after a day's work. This is why the Street remains popular.'

How long can the programme continue? Its future is in the hands of a new generation of characters from Gail and Brian Tilsley and Kevin and Sally Webster, to battle-axe Amy (Fanny Carby), Jack Duckworth's dreadful mother-in-law and battered wife Sandra Stubbs (Sally Watts), who replaced Hilda as the Rovers' cleaner.

'Coronation Street' is perhaps the most easily digestible of all Britain's soaps. Every moment of conflict is balanced by a scene of fun, every dashed hope matched by a spot of good news. If it can keep enough young viewers, it can keep its amazing success. Its Golden Jubilee? I'll drink a pint of Newton & Ridley to that.

THE CREATOR

Tony Warren wrote the first episode of 'Coronation Street' overnight. He then spent two days composing a memo about it to give to his Granada Television bosses who employed him at £30 as their writing starlet. The memo described 'a fascinating freemasonry, a volume of unwritten rules. These are the driving forces behind life in a working class street in the north of England. The purpose of Florizel Street is to examine a community of this kind and to entertain.'

They liked it. Tony was relieved. It meant he could stop adapting Biggles adventures (which he loathed) and start the next eleven episodes of his new creation. But, first, one change. He said: 'Agnes the tea lady said Florizel sounded like a disinfectant, so we changed it. It would have been Jubilee but there was already a series with that in the title, so Coronation was it.'

'Coronation Street', a twice-weekly soap began on 9 December 1960, steered a hugely successful, steady, safe course for twenty-eight years and is still going strong.

Tony Warren was twenty-three in 1960. He steered a wild, unsuccessful, almost disastrous course and is now back and going strong. Considering his achievement, he ought to be rich, fat and famous. He's none of those. But he is still pleased with 'Coronation Street'. 'They offered me a seven-year exclusive contract after the opening success,' he told me. 'I didn't want to be exclusive. Exclusive had brought me Biggles scripts and then this massive hit for thirty pounds a week. I wanted a life, and I certainly had one.' The life involved years of ructions with Granada, long trips to America and to Europe, and the squandering of vast sums on drink and hard drugs. 'They regarded me as exotic,' he laughs. 'Yes, if I'd had a percentage I'd have had loads more money. But I would be dead. It was a classic case of too much too soon. No twenty-three-year-old could handle all that. I certainly couldn't. Then it was all rather frightening. I'd invented a style which suddenly became everybody's style, public property. If you are full of vodka and drugs, as

I was for a long time, you tend to see life through a mucky window, you tend to be rather paranoid. I saw articles about "Coronation Street", read interviews with the cast, heard people talk about it on the bus. It was almost as though it was real life and inescapable.'

After three years Tony left 'Coronation Street'. He wrote an unsuccessful stage-play, *Strumpet's Daughter*, then turned to films. Brian Epstein, the Beatles' manager, asked him to write *Ferry Across the Mersey*. Tony wrote several versions, none of which he liked, then quit in a state of tension.

A period of self-doubt followed. At one stage he snubbed the soap's 500th-episode party, and told reporters he'd burned all his scripts, disowned the series and said it bore no relation to his original idea. Now he laughs at those accounts. 'I may have done that. I seem to remember kicking in a TV screen in Amsterdam because I didn't like seeing "Coronation Street" there. I did most of the things drunks do. I had this theory that the Street was an albatross. Today I think it's a glittering albatross, and it doesn't worry me.'

Tony wrote his autobiography, *I Was Ena Sharples' Father*, which upset Granada. He made friends with them again, wrote more scripts, had more fights. He went to Hollywood and hated it. 'I spent my time telling producers why I couldn't work for them, and they kept upping the money. It was crazy. But I had only to stand on Hollywood Boulevard for two minutes and I missed "Coronation Street".' After nearly dying three times from alcohol, he stopped boozing and hasn't had a drink for ten years. He made his peace with Granada and became the soap's consultant, a rôle he has to this day.

The middle-class boy from Eccles near Manchester who began as an actor but outgrew his talent by getting too tall looks back and laughs a lot now. 'I didn't come from a Coronation Street, but my grandma did. I used to go to her house and watch. My father was a fruit importer. I was the little boy who talked posh, and this made me the outsider. In 1960 the Northern Resurgence was happening in the theatre and in films. I wanted to bring it to television. I wanted to see something written from the heart, acted by genuine Northerners. "Coronation Street" isn't reality. It's adjusted reality; its strength is that it lets people belong to it. It's mine, and I belong to it. At thirty-one I was burned out as a writer. I spent twenty years just living. At fifty-one I suddenly find there's a great deal I want to write about.'

Tony Warren is still a flamboyant presence around the Granada studios. He launches a new big project in 1988.

THE CHARACTERS

Mike Baldwin, the crafty cockney of Coronation Street, is the most eligible middle-aged Casanova of Weatherfield. Much more eligible than Percy, Jack, Alec, Tom – and Albert Tatlock when he was alive. But is that saying much? Baldwin, played by Johnny Briggs, has a second-hand Jaguar and a cheap line in smalltalk that usually ensnares gullible females into corny candle-lit dinners for two with soft music and low lights.

Baldwin is a born hustler from Bermondsey. He discovered a natural bent for business, moved into the rag trade with a denim factory in the East End of London and a branch factory in Weatherfield: Baldwin's Casuals. Early in 1988, Mike turned mini JR and changed his business from clothes to curtains – to the alarm of his staff, whom he paid less to do more. The trade union movement isn't exactly strong in Weatherfield. When he was arrested for drunk driving he accused Vera of tipping off the police. He sacked her but cynically agreed to reinstate her when the stupid woman promised to blacken the character of Ida, the real informer, sacked months before and threatening a suit for unfair dismissal. Tough in business, he is a real sucker for the ladies. Suzie Birchall and Bet Lynch have sampled his whisky-and-sofa technique in his flash flat. If his chunky green leather sofa (he must have seen one like it in *Playboy*) could talk. . . . Mike's roving eye has wandered from Maggie Dunlop, with whom he had a love-child, to Ken Barlow's bored wife Deirdre, with whom he had a torrid affair in 1983 (see 'Adultery'). The Barlow-Baldwin triangle ended with Deirdre going back to her husband. But bad feeling festers between the two men.

Ken Barlow was horrified in 1986 when forty-four-year-old Baldwin began to court Ken's twenty-three-year-old daughter Susan. When they decided to marry, Ken threatened at first not to give her away, but he did his duty on the day and made an uneasy truce. Mike remained a male chauvinist, believed Susan's rôle in the marriage was to bear children and frustrated her efforts to work. When she did become pregnant he was delighted. When she took off to London and had an abortion (because she 'wasn't ready') he raged and threw her out, poured several whiskies, sacked Hilda and looked upset. By the time you read this, I expect several lucky ladies will have heard the whole story – over candle-lit dinners and nightcaps.

Johnny Briggs, born in Battersea, was a boy soprano who won a scholarship to the Italia Conti Stage School at the age of twelve. As a teenage actor, he appeared in feature films like *Quartet* and the Joan Collins movie *Cosh Boy* in which he played opposite the young starlet herself. His first professional engagement was as a boy soprano singing in *La Bohème* at the Cambridge Theatre on Boxing Night, 1947. At sixteen Johnny, the son of a BBC carpenter, got his first real television break in a Granada series called 'The Younger Generation'. Television parts followed in 'Z Cars', 'The Avengers', 'Softly, Softly', and 'Crossroads', before he became established as Detective Sergeant Russell in 'No Hiding Place'. He put lifts in his shoes to get the copper's rôle because he isn't very tall.

In 1972, Johnny, aged forty-two, married Christine, a schoolteacher fourteen years his junior. They have three children. He has a teenage son and daughter by his first wife. Johnny admits he has a lot of Mike's traits: self-confidence, a great instinct for self-preservation, and he attracts letters from women fans. He admits he *was* a womaniser before he got married but says he has now settled down to more mundane 'pursuits' like golf and squash, and raising money for the Variety Club of Great Britain. But in 1987, when he had a fling with a barmaid in a Manchester club, the ensuing press publicity led to a split between him and Christine. For several months she lived in Stourbridge and he lived in a Manchester hotel. They've now made it up.

Susan Baldwin, née Barlow, Ken Barlow's twenty-three-year-old twin daughter, played by Wendy Jane Walker, caused a stir in 'Coronation Street' in 1986 when she married forty-four-year-old middle-aged Romeo Mike Baldwin, the cocky cockney factory-owner.

Ken Barlow and Mike had come to blows earlier when ladies' man Mike began an affair with Ken's third wife, Deirdre. Ken tried hard to break up Mike's relationship with his daughter, even threatening not to turn up at the church to give her away. Susan walked a tightrope between her dad and her smooth-talking new husband. It seemed painful. Her lines were always whines. She had a strong independent streak. When she worked for the *Weatherfield Recorder*, the newspaper that Ken edits, they could never agree on how the news should be presented. Mike Baldwin has also had trouble stifling her ambitions to revamp and update the range of clothing that he manufactures. Their marriage ended in 1987 after a series of rows. She had become pregnant as was his wish, but she left for London and had the pregnancy terminated. When she told him he threw her out. She's now working in Newcastle and unlikely ever to return.

Wendy Jane Walker, the tiny twenty-three-year-old Manchester-born actress, actually made her début in the programme in 1969. She was cast as Ken Barlow's five-year-old twin daughter Susan – a juvenile rôle that she played on and off for seven years. But at twelve she left 'Coronation Street' to concentrate on her education. Drama school in Liverpool was followed by television rôles in 'Brass', 'The Practice' and 'The Adventures of Sherlock Holmes'. When Granada planned a major story-line for the new, grown-up twenty-one-year-old Susan in 1985, they turned to Wendy Jane again. Child actors rarely get the chance to play the same rôle in maturity, especially when there's a nine-year break between appearances. But by the autumn of 1987 the writers felt the couple were so mismatched that viewers were merely irritated by them. So they devised the soap's first abortion (not even 'EastEnders' had 'done' abortion then). Wendy Jane was furious. Rightly she claimed the instant abortion decision was not in keeping with Susan's character. As usual the actor's words fell on stony ground. Wendy Jane was dropped, and Johnny Briggs, who plays Mike, was eagerly awaiting his next screen romance.

Deirdre Barlow is one of the makeweight characters of 'Coronation Street', terminally passive. She has been the ordinary girlfriend, wife, mother, shop assistant since 1972. Now she's also a very ordinary local councillor. Not for nothing is she called Dreary (it's easier to spell, too). Played by Anne Kirkbride, she became famous for her large picture-frame specs and her low, flat-as-a-pancake voice. But she became a megastar in 1983 thanks to a plot-line which made her the *femme fatale* in a triangle of passions. The Deirdre-Ken-Mike-will-she-won't-she saga was the best adultery episode ever pulled off in British soap, so good that I've given it a section of its own. (See 'Adultery'.)

Deirdre first appeared in 1972 as Deirdre Hunt, Ray Langton's girlfriend. She married Ray, but he turned out to be a rat. After she found him cheating with a café girl and threw him out, Deirdre and her daughter Tracey were on their own. A new friendship blossomed with widower Ken Barlow, and they married in 1981. Deirdre soon discovered Ken was no raver but a set-in-his-ways male chauvinist. When her one-time lover Mike Baldwin sensed a chance to revive their relationship she was tempted. So began a hugely enjoyable British newspaper hype that rivalled 'Dallas''s Who Shot JR 'beat-up'. A spellbound nation watched Deirdre meet Mike furtively behind Ken's back. Mike asked her to leave Ken; Deirdre wavered. In sexual terms the affair on screen never went further than a kiss in a car. The eventual confrontation between Ken and Deirdre was delicious drama. Three years later when Ken's daughter Susan began an affair and then married Baldwin, the reverberations and reopening of wounds made 'Coronation Street' gripping again.

Meanwhile Deirdre proceeded as the not very inspiring mother of Tracey. Weeks went by without a mention of the girl. Indeed, she was not seen for nine months at one stage because of problems with the young actress. The scriptwriters clearly were not grooming Deirdre for a Mother of the Year Award. She has never discussed having a second child, perhaps wisely. In 1987, Ken toyed with the idea of opposing Alf as a local councillor. When he was warned he'd lose his job as a newspaper editor by doing so, Ken fixed it for Deirdre to stand and win as an Independent candidate. Her (mainly off-screen) council work, which has included trips away from home, is a source of strain in the marriage. But a repeat of the Big Affair with Mike or anyone else now seems unlikely. Worse luck.

Anne Kirkbride was born in Oldham, Lancashire, the daughter of a local newspaper cartoonist. She made her television début at the age of seventeen after acting in school productions. A few months later in 1972, she was cast as Deirdre Hunt, new girlfriend of Ray Langton in 'Coronation Street'. Granada were impressed enough to give her a long-term contract as Deirdre first married and divorced Ray, and then became the third Mrs Ken Barlow.

Anne's big moment came in 1983 when she was involved in the love-tangle story-line which had 17 million viewers on the edge of their seats for weeks. Would she leave her husband for Mike Baldwin or not? The saga was an acting triumph for Anne and fellow-actors William Roache and Johnny Briggs that brought special recognition for them at the Pye Television Awards. The judges congratulated them on their 'massive impact' on the nation's viewers. Five months later, however, Anne Kirkbride attracted headlines of a different kind. Detectives raided her Manchester flat and charged her with possessing cannabis resin. She was fined £250 after pleading guilty, but Anne told the court that the drugs belonged to someone else.

She has had regular boyfriends in the past but has no plans to marry. Among the cast she is something of a loner.

Frank Barlow, a genial local Post Office supervisor, made his début in 'Coronation Street' in episode 1 on 9 December 1960. Father of Kenneth and David Barlow, he was widowed early on in the series when his wife Ida was knocked down and killed by a bus.

In those days 'Coronation Street' wasn't afraid to be political and class-aware. Pipe-smoking Frank, played by Frank Pemberton, was staunchly working-class and proud of it. He voiced deep disapproval when his university-educated son Ken arrived home with middle-class ideas and a middle-class girlfriend. Sauce-bottle plonked firmly on the table, Frank tucked into his food noisily with a gusto that made Ken cringe. He liked a cup of tea with his meal 'because I like food swilled down properly'. Father and son never saw eye to eye again.

Frank Barlow retired to a detached house in Wilmslow, Cheshire, after a £5000 Premium Bond win. He died there in 1975 shortly after actor Frank Pemberton died.

Frank Pemberton was a victim of soap opera, as was Noele Gordon. Born in the shadow of Manchester United football-ground, he worked in rep in Yarmouth and Morecambe, then did some television extra work with artists including the great Tony Hancock. Granada signed him up in 1960 to play a middle-aged dad in 'Coronation Street'. After 400 episodes, Frank was axed in the great cast purge of 1964. Deeply shocked, he never recovered – professionally or privately. He was thrown on to the dole in 1965, and collapsed from a heart attack on his way to the labour exchange. In 1967 he tried bravely to resume his rôle as Frank Barlow when Granada invited him back for one episode. But he was so ill he could hardly walk. Frank Pemberton died in 1975, and his character was killed off the same year.

Ida Barlow, hen-pecked wife of Frank and mother of Ken and David in 'Coronation Street', was a former mill-girl who worked as a kitchen help in a local hotel. Ida, played by Noel Dyson, was devoted to her family, but worried about the growing rift between her working-class husband and intellectual son Ken who had returned from university with 'fancy middle-class ideas'. In 1961, Ida died when she was crushed under the wheels of a bus as she crossed the road.

Noel Dyson, who played Ken Barlow's mother Ida in episode 1 of 'Coronation Street', was educated at Roedean and trained at RADA. She married her actor husband Kenneth Edwards three weeks after they met in a Terence Rattigan play in the West End. Noel made it clear from the start that she didn't want to play Ida indefinitely. In 1961 she actually asked for a gory end when she heard that Ida was going to be killed off. Not a heart attack, please. Scriptwriter Harry Kershaw suggested an accident with a double-decker bus. 'Marvellous,' said Noel. And so Ida was gruesomely flattened, and Noel loved it.

Irma Barlow was the dead-common daughter of Stan and Hilda Ogden, who married Ken Barlow's brother David in 1966. A girl for whom bright bad taste in clothes was an art, and whose voice could bring on instant migraines, Irma was a try-out model for Bet Lynch. Where Bet's trouble was life, Irma's was her parents. Both were wonderfully witty with it.

Irma and David took over the corner shop in Coronation Street from Lionel Petty, then emigrated to Australia in 1968. When her husband and son were killed in a car crash, Irma flew home to Mum in Weatherfield. She left Coronation Street in 1972 for Llandudno in North Wales, then emigrated again and is now building a new life in Canada.

Sandra Gough was even more zany than the larger-than-life character she played in the Street. Funny how soap actresses seem to lead wild lives or very quiet ones. Rarely do they choose a middle path (see Wendy Richard, p.246; Pat Phoenix, Julie Goodyear, below). The daughter of a Lancashire market-stall greengrocer, Sandra did all manner of jobs before television, including modelling for the 'Daughter of Jane' strip cartoon in the *Daily Mirror*. Even so, she felt unable to cope with the fame that followed her huge 'Coronation Street' success. After opting out of acting to go to Australia, she returned to Manchester and resumed one of her previous jobs as an ordinary shop assistant. Then she went to Spain and married a Spanish nightclub-owner.

Ken Barlow, the schoolteacher turned local newspaper editor is the decent prig of 'Coronation Street'. Long labelled 'boring old Ken' by the critics, William Roache, the actor who has played him for twenty-seven years since episode 1 in 1960, believes passionately in Ken's qualities and powers of endurance. Roache insists that it is Ken's third wife Deirdre who is dreary: 'She is a crashing bore. All she is interested in is the corner shop and gossip. She had dragged Ken down to her level and never shown any interest in his work.' Brainbox Ken got a second-class honours degree in history and English at university. He never considered conquering the world; he's a stick-in-the-mud who prefers the 'small pond' life of Weatherfield. His late father Frank, a retired Post Office worker, objected to Ken's toffee-nosed attitude on his return from college. But personal criticism is like water off a duck's back to Ken – he's that stubborn.

He has tried all manner of jobs in his time, from personnel officer and teacher, to junior warehouse executive and, now, local newspaper editor. This summer he looked set to become its proprietor too. But Robert Maxwell needn't lose sleep.

Ken is currently on his third marriage. He's hardly a model father to his children, mentioning them about once every three years. In 1971 his first wife Valerie, niece of Albert Tatlock, was electrocuted by a faulty hairdrier-plug. His second wife Janet committed suicide with barbiturates after their divorce. He certainly has a powerful effect.

Ken has had several affairs, too – during and between marriages – but the tables were turned on him with a vengeance in 1983 when Deirdre had a smouldering affair with old flame Mike Baldwin. The whole nation watched as the television romance blossomed behind Ken's back. When he found out, the worm turned. Ken blew his top and told a tearful Deirdre to pack her bags and go. She lost her nerve and decided to stay with predictable Ken. It was a remarkable victory over the man that Ken called 'a little creep and a spiv'. Deirdre didn't listen to my advice to ditch them both, that's for sure.

On the credit side, when daughter Susan's marriage to Baldwin started to go wrong, Ken refused to interfere or give her house room. He didn't condone her abortion or lecture her. By then he was too busy badgering Deirdre, who had done as he bid: stood for the council and won. When she proceeded to work for local causes, he accused her of neglecting her daughter Tracey and not being a proper wife. It earned him the Male Chauvinist of 1987 Award.

William Roache, born in Ilkeston, Derbyshire, is a doctor's son who intended to take up medicine himself. Educated at Rydal School, North Wales, he gave up medicine for a regular commission in the Royal Welsh Fusiliers. His military service took him to Jamaica, British Guiana and Germany, before he finally embarked on a two-year posting to Arabia. Roache worked with Bedouin tribesmen and lived as an Arab, riding camels. The only English officer amongst 125 non-English-speaking Arabs, he was pressed to settle innumerable tribal disputes. But after five years with the colours he resigned his commission to try acting. A burst of letter-writing won him a small part in the Michael Redgrave film *Behind the Mask*. Then came rep in Clacton, Nottingham and Oldham, then parts in the ITV drama series 'Knight Errant' and 'Skyport'. Doris Speed also appeared in the latter.

Today, at fifty-four, Roache is the sole screen survivor of the original cast of 'Coronation Street'. 'If I had known it would run for twenty-eight years I would have run a mile. I didn't even want to sign up for thirteen weeks in 1960,' he said. After the first ten years in the part he admitted freely that he was now too scared to leave the series because he would miss the security, the money and the luxuries. Type-casting was something to be feared in the early seventies; not now. Today he is very protective towards the character and denies that Ken is boring. 'I regard myself as Ken's caretaker. He has got through several traumas – lost both his parents, his brother, nephew, and two wives. This has made him wise to life. He is a man of principle who fights for those things he believes in.' Bill Roache has a grown-up son and daughter from his dissolved first marriage to actress Anna Cropper. He now lives in a large detached house in the Cheshire stockbroker belt and has two children aged six and two by his second wife, former 'Emmerdale Farm' actress Sara McEwen. 'Boring' Ken has made Bill very comfortable indeed. Bill drives a Rolls-Royce and lives an idyllic country lifestyle which includes invitations to play golf in pro-am competitions. He's extremely astute, quietly investing the proceeds of soapy labour for all these years. Like the outspoken Ken, Bill has never hesitated to speak out if he thought his television rôle was not going as it should. During the Deirdre Barlow–Mike Baldwin romance story, Roache said: 'I am extremely unhappy with the plot the way it is going. I don't think Deirdre should be having this affair. It's ridiculous. I've told the writers that the couple will never be the same again in the viewers' eyes. They should be growing together not drifting apart.' They don't seem to have listened, and he doesn't seem to have been right. But Bill Roache is his own man.

Valerie Barlow, née Tatlock, first met Ken Barlow when she left her parents in Glasgow to live with her uncle, Albert Tatlock, at 1 Coronation Street in 1960. Valerie, played by Anne Reid, married Ken Barlow in 1962 and three years later she gave birth to twins: Susan and Peter. A hairdresser and housewife, and something of a pudding, Valerie felt inferior to her schoolteacher husband and his intellectual friends. She enrolled at night-school to try to 'improve' herself, but she still leaned heavily on Ken for support and advice. Valerie died in 1971 – she was electrocuted by a faulty hairdrier-plug. Millions of viewers who watched the sequence were profoundly shocked. This famous television death was one of the big media stories of the day, and viewing figures soared for the episode.

Anne Reid, the Newcastle-upon-Tyne born actress, won a bronze medal at RADA in 1955 when she was nineteen. She made her television début two years later in a Benny Hill comedy series, and moved on to 'The Tony Hancock Show' and 'No Hiding Place'. She was playing principal boy in panto when she was recruited for 'Coronation Street'. Viewers liked the character because she was pure working class and they could relate to her. Anne Reid married the late Peter Eckersley, one of Granada Television's most talented scriptwriters and drama producers. In 1971 she left 'Coronation Street' to broaden her career, and the whole nation was shocked when she was electrocuted on screen.

Suzie Birchall, the flighty blonde who became Elsie Tanner's

'adopted' daughter and lodger in Coronation Street in 1978, had a queue of men interested in her company. Her love-life was always stormy. She could never find Mr Right. Suzie, played by Cheryl Murray, charmed Mike Baldwin into giving her a job as a window-dresser in his denims shop. After a series of flirtations, she left Weatherfield to try the high life in London. She returned in 1983, fleeing from a broken marriage. Her husband Terry followed her north and beat her up. Suzie was last seen heading out of town again with a suitcase.

Cheryl Murray, the pretty actress who played Suzie Birchall, turned down what could have been an important career-building West End theatre début in *Separate Tables* in preference for 'Coronation Street'. Born in Liverpool, she appeared in 'Billy Liar' and 'Within These Walls' before joining 'Coronation Street'. Her original contract from Granada was for only two weeks, but she seized her opportunity and stayed for three years, making a lengthy return again in 1983. Patricia Phoenix, who played her adoptive screen mother, in fact took Cheryl under her wing and treated her like a daughter when she was in Manchester. Cheryl is married with a five-year-old daughter, Louise.

Emily Bishop, née Nugent, is the worrier of Coronation Street.

She was born with an anxious frown on her face, I'm sure. The strait-laced widow of Ernest Bishop, murdered in an armed wages robbery at Mike Baldwin's factory in Coronation Street in 1978, Emily is superbly portrayed by intelligent actress Eileen Derbyshire. She has been one of the pillars of the programme since 1961. Whenever other residents become too outrageous, Emily's is the voice of moderation and morality. She hasn't had a lucky life. In 1964 she made a courageous leap-year marriage proposal to pompous Leonard Swindley, her boss at

Gamma Garments. Then she lost her nerve and left Swindley waiting at the altar. Next came a visit to a marriage agency and a brief liaison with a tough Hungarian roadworker over candle-lit dinners. But he chickened out of marriage and hurriedly left. There was a mild flirtation with a Weatherfield vicar, but it cameth to nothing. Then came Ernest. Then went Ernest. More strife came anguished Emily's way in 1980 when her second husband, Arnold Swain, turned out to be a bigamist. Now she seems to have abandoned all hope of finding a partner. She busies herself in the wages office of Baldwin's factory, and kept a maternal eye on her young lodger Curly Watts until in one of the most daring storylines of this year Curly moved out to live with black Shirley Armitage. Emily's response was drastic. She changed her hairdo of a lifetime. Out went the elegant French pleat, in came a softer, shorter style. At about the same time Percy Sugden was thrown out of his flat. He persuaded Emily to take him in. He began looking at her strangely. The new hairdo had brought out the beast in him, some said.

Eileen Derbyshire, an accomplished actress born in Urmston, Manchester, joined the cast of 'Coronation Street' in 1961. Within months of taking on the rôle of Emily Nugent, now Bishop, she was desperate to point out that she is nothing like that dithery worrying matron. A qualified teacher of speech and drama, Eileen originally joined a local repertory company as assistant stage manager and then toured with the Century Theatre mobile theatre group for two years. Today Eileen is married to a local businessman and living in happy seclusion in the countryside near Manchester, with five dogs, two cats and two goldfish. Her son is a university graduate. She enjoys music, good conversation, the arts, and exploring old buildings. She is extremely fond of, and grateful to, Emily, who has provided her with a secure and well-paid job for the last twenty-six years. Eileen boasts about having been lucky enough to have had her cake *and* halfpenny.

Ernest Bishop is remembered by viewers for marrying Coronation Street's shy spinster Emily Nugent in 1971. He's remembered by actors for his death. Ernie, played by Stephen Hancock, followed his father into photography for a while, and divided his leisure-time between lay-preaching and playing piano for Rita Fairclough in her days as a nightclub singer. When Mike Baldwin opened his clothing factory in 1976, Ernest joined him as payroll clerk and right-hand man. Viewers were shocked when he died on the operating-table at Weatherfield Infirmary in 1979 after being blasted with a sawn-off shotgun by two wages-robbers. The real culprits were the soap's producers. They'd passed the death sentence on Ernie because Stephen Hancock asked for a rise. It was – and still is – a lesson to others. (See 'Killing Them Off'.)

Stephen Hancock combined a theatre grounding at the Central School of Speech and Drama with a music degree from Durham University. His musical skill enabled the 'Coronation Street' producers to use him as a popular pianist in the Rover's, and as accompanist for actress-singer Barbara Knox for sequences in which Rita Fairclough appeared as a cabaret singer. Hancock left the series in 1979 after a dispute with Granada over his contract. He believed he was worth more. They didn't.

Jerry Booth was the stuttering tongue-tied twenty-year-old
plumber who started work for local builder Len Fairclough in 'Coronation Street' in 1962. Played by Graham Haberfield, Jerry met and married Myra Dickinson. He was uncomfortable in female company, and his marriage ended in divorce. After subsequent romances with 'barmcake' girl Sheila Birtles and librarian Sally Frost, Jerry left Coronation Street in 1968. Seven years later, news came that he had died of pneumonia.

Graham Haberfield was born in Chesterfield. Graham was nothing like Jerry, but lively, exuberant and often involved in scrapes in his personal life. A former Bristol Old Vic player, he left 'Coronation Street' after six years to try his hand at something new. He starred as Delilah in Jack Rosenthal's hit television sitcom 'The Dustbinmen'. In 1975, Graham died of a heart attack.

Alan Bradley is the suave mature widower who has set up home
with Rita Fairclough in Coronation Street and wants to marry her. Bradley, played by Mark Eden, has a teenage daughter Jenny, at that tricky stage, a schoolgirl and a lovestruck woman in one. Her former fiancé, French Patrice, was a problem he'd rather not have had. Rita is a useful influence. Alan has twice tried to marry Rita, but she keeps turning him down. On one occasion, he set up a secret register-office wedding behind her back and seemed amazed when she flatly refused to go through with it. The smooth-talking Alan has tried to influence Rita's business life, too. He has installed a videotape-hire rack in the Kabin, much to the dismay of Mavis who works there. But Rita manages to retain control. This year he became an instantly qualified burglar alarm expert and began a business with Rita's money.

Mark Eden is the suave, square-jawed, London-born leading actor who has swapped a successful film and theatre career for a regular rôle in 'Coronation Street' as Alan Bradley. He's the live-in boyfriend of Rita Fairclough and the nearest the soap has to a man's man since Len Fairclough was killed off. Eden himself lives with Sue Nicholls, Audrey Roberts in the series. A former member of the Royal Shakespeare

Company, Mark Eden's films include *Night of the Iguana* and *Claudia's Story*. His television credits include the biblical blockbuster 'Jesus of Nazareth' and the Granada period thriller 'Cribb'. A graduate of Swansea rep, he was a fairground worker, beach photographer and milkman before he made it in the theatre. He was divorced in 1983 and has three children.

Minnie Caldwell was the mild-mannered Coronation Street pensioner (an early model for mousey Mavis) who was bossed and bullied by her friend Ena Sharples. 'Moaning Minnie' – she was always bleating on about something – was played by actress Margot Bryant. Minnie was one of the famous trio of old dears – Ena, Martha and Minnie – who met in the snug of the Rover's Return to natter and contradict each other over their milk stouts. When Ena was in particularly tartarish mood, Minnie took refuge in the company of Bobby her ginger tom cat. She much preferred cats to people. Viewers felt sorry for her. When her mother died in 1962 she took in a lodger: Scouse drifter Jed Stone, affectionately known by Minnie as 'Sonny Jim'. Jed called her 'Ma'. Minnie Caldwell loved a flutter on the horses, and once, thinking that it might improve her pension, she agreed to marry Albert Tatlock – until she found out she would actually be financially worse off. Minnie left Coronation Street in 1976 to live in Whalley Bridge, Derbyshire, where she still keeps house for an old schoolfriend, Handel Gartside.

Margot Bryant was born in Hull where her father was a doctor. She began her stage career as a chorus girl in panto and later danced in the West End Fred Astaire musical *Stop Flirting*. Totally unlike the cowed Minnie, bullied into submission by Ena Sharples, Margot could be caustic and outspoken. She wouldn't tolerate rude people or bad manners. A bit of a globe-trotter, too, in her Street heyday in the sixties, she loved to holiday in world capitals and big cities, and was especially fond of New York. Like Minnie, however, she did have a weakness for animals – cats especially. Margot Bryant made her début in episode 3 of 'Coronation Street' in 1960 and was last seen on screen in 1976 after appearing in 560 episodes. Ill health caused her departure from the series, and she died in January 1988.

Ivan Cheveski, a handsome Polish refugee, played by Austrian actor Ernst Walder, was married to Elsie Tanner's daughter Linda in the early episodes of 'Coronation Street' in the sixties. The marriage was a procession of rows and reconciliations. There was a touching scene when Elsie had to say goodbye to her six-month-old grandson Paul when Linda and Ivan emigrated to Canada in a last-ditch attempt to save their marriage. But Ivan returned to live in Birmingham when Linda began an affair. It fizzled out, and she came back to rejoin him. They still live in the Midlands.

Ernst Walder, the Austrian-born actor who portrayed Polish refugee Ivan Cheveski in the first episode of 'Coronation Street' in December 1960, was brought up in a mountain village. He landed in trouble with the Russian authorities during the last war for helping refugees to escape across the border. Gaoled by the Russians, he managed to escape by swimming across a river. In 1948 he joined a Continental theatre group on tour, and a few years later he moved to Britain to find work. After working as a butler and valet, he returned to acting and his Germanic looks and accent got him work in several war films after 'Coronation Street'.

Linda Cheveski, daughter of Coronation Street's sexpot Elsie
Tanner, had just married Polish refugee Ivan Cheveski when the series started in 1960. Linda, played by Anne Cunningham, gave birth to the Street's first screen baby, Paul, who weighed in at 7 lb 2 oz. Quick-tempered like her mother, Linda's incessant rows with Ivan led them to emigrate to Montreal as a last-ditch ploy to save their marriage. But Linda had an affair, and Ivan returned home. She later rejoined him in Birmingham where they still live. Linda made a brief return to Coronation Street in 1984.

Anne Cunningham played Elsie Tanner's peppery daughter Linda Cheveski in episode 1 of 'Coronation Street' in December 1960. Born in Leeds, Anne emigrated to South Africa with her parents, but returned to England to start a stage career, working at the Bristol Old Vic. Married to producer-director Darrol Blake, she has two teenage twin daughters. She is still good friends with screen husband Ernst Walder, who played Ivan in those early days. They ran an antique-stall together in the Portobello Road for a while – and didn't argue.

Gordon Clegg, illegitimate son of Rover's Return barmaid Betty
Turpin, fell for rebel teenager Lucille Hewitt when he first moved into Coronation Street in the 1960s. They eloped to Gretna Green, but had second thoughts about marriage. Gordon, played by leading London theatre impresario Bill Kenwright, left the Street in 1969 when his firm transferred him to London, but he has made several return visits to Weatherfield since then. The most dramatic was when the scriptwriters revealed that his real mother was Betty Turpin. Gordon was brought up by Betty's married sister Maggie Clegg, to avert the danger of a family scandal in the strait-laced forties. The Cleggs ran the corner shop.

Bill Kenwright, the Liverpool-born actor who played Gordon Clegg in 'Coronation Street' in the sixties and seventies, has gone on to become one of Britain's most successful theatre impresarios. He took the plunge in theatre management twelve years ago with Reginald Marsh, another 'Coronation Street' visiting actor. His company, David Gordon Productions, have staged West End revivals of *West Side Story*, *Alfie* with Denis Waterman, and *The Marriage-Go-Round* with former Street stars Patricia Phoenix and Alan Browning. Kenwright, who was a child actor at Liverpool Playhouse, and was educated at Liverpool Institute where George Harrison and Paul McCartney once studied, now rarely has fewer than twelve plays and musicals in production at any one time. But he says he's always available for guest spots.

Jack Duckworth, the gravel-voiced leering layabout of Coronation Street, inherited the mantle of work-shy Stan Ogden. Like Stan, he has been a reluctant part-time window-cleaner and Jack-of-all-trades – one-time taxi-driver and market-stallholder. First seen in the Street at Brian and Gail Tilsley's wedding in 1979, 'Idle Jack', actor William Tarmey, has now settled down. Once the oldest swinger in town, he has ditched his open-chested ruffled silk shirt and gold medallion for a respectable new career as a cellarman at the Rover's Return.

Husband of the loud-mouthed Vera, and father of tearaway Terry, Jack is an opportunist. One Christmas he lopped off the top of Percy Sugden's Christmas tree rather than buy one of his own. But most of his moneymaking schemes end in disaster. A self-styled ladies' man – Dulcie Froggatt on his window-cleaning round is a favourite conquest – Jack thinks he is terrific. But wife Vera is not impressed. Neither are barmaids Gloria Todd and Bet Lynch with whom he tried to flirt.

He can be touchingly pathetic, too. When he bodged a fuse and it led to the Rover's fire which nearly killed Bet he deserved to be garrotted. Instead he was so movingly miserable he *had* to be forgiven. His son treated him as a joke and, by the end of 1987, Vera's battle-axe mother Amy had moved into the Duckworth residence – a formidable further enemy. Luckily she moved out after shoplifting at Alf's shop and arguing with Vera.

William Tarmey was given a life-or-death choice by a hospital surgeon in 1986. It was open-heart surgery or curtains. By smoking fifty cigarettes a day for years, puffing Bill had damaged his health so severely that he needed a quadruple bypass operation to replace silted-up arteries. The operation was a success, and a trimline Tarmey, a stone and a half lighter at thirteen stones, returned to the series from hospital having given up smoking for good. Unlike rascally Jack, Bill is devoted to his wife Alma whom he met at a local youth club in his native Manchester when they were both fourteen. They married at twenty-one and have two children. A former building-trade worker, greengrocer and hardware shopkeeper, he started in show business as a cabaret singer with a showband. Like Elizabeth Dawn who plays Jack Duckworth's wife Vera, Bill Tarmey has risen to stardom from the ranks of television extras. He still does cabaret work, sings and has made an LP.

Terry Duckworth is the macho son of Jack and Vera Duckworth in 'Coronation Street' – the only bit of 'beefcake' in a programme dominated by strong female characters. Tearaway Terry, played by viewers' heart-throb Nigel Pivaro, was rejected by the Parachute Regiment in 1982 and returned home to become the main breadwinner in the Duckworth household. Much to Vera's delight, Terry's job in an abbatoir 'produced' lots of choice meats for the Duckworths' dinner-table. All Jack got was the cold shoulder, however, since Terry had no respect for his father's work-shy lifestyle. Terry was a sharp talker and a fast puller of 'birds', as he would call women. But it was a severe blow to his ego in 1985 when he made Andrea Clayton pregnant and she refused to marry him.

Wayward Terry made a dramatic exit from Coronation Street in 1987 when he ran off with Linda – wife of his best pal, Peter Jackson. He left his business partner Curly Watts in the lurch.

Nigel Pivaro, the beefy twenty-one-year-old Manchester-born actor, was stuck with a real-life 'bad boy' image from the moment the press discovered that he had once served time for burglary. A second brush with the law led to a driving ban, and fans were shocked in 1987 when, just eleven days before the ban was lifted, he was arrested again for driving without a licence. He was fined £275 and given a suspended six-week gaol sentence. Nigel is contrite about his police record and says that he is too hot-headed at times. After the burglary sentence, however, he did manage to keep out of trouble for seven years.

Initially, Pivaro emerged from the amateur theatre ranks to enter RADA. He joined 'Coronation Street' in 1983 – a macho, muscular addition to the elderly cast who enjoys weightlifting and fitness training in his spare time. Terry Duckworth rampaged through the story-lines like Rambo. Pivaro quit the Street in 1987 because he was 'bursting' to do a new stage-play called *No Further Cause for Concern* in which he played a convict. He even backed the production with his own money. It began a modest run in Cardiff prior to moving to the Edinburgh Festival. The television scriptwriters engineered a suitably dramatic exit from the series by making Terry Duckworth run off with his best pal's wife. Actress Kazia Pelka, who played Linda Jackson, hit it off immediately with Nigel – on and off the screen. When they left the series, they stayed together.

Vera Duckworth is the lanky loudmouth of Coronation Street who chews gum and calls everybody 'kid'. She's dead common, dead cunning and dead funny with it. She drinks and smokes and is a gift to impressionists. Played under a blonde bubble-cut wig by Elizabeth Dawn, looking like a tired chicken, speaking in a hoarse quack, she's half of a low-life duo with her Andy Capp-style husband Jack. Jack frequently feels the lash of Vera's tongue, while their streetwise son Terry – who could do almost no wrong in his mother's eyes – went scot-free.

Vera is comic relief in the clothing factory, too. She often battles with her hard-hearted boss Baldwin over pay or conditions and argues with her best friend Ivy Tilsley, who is shop steward there. Someone has to. Like Hilda, though, there is an underlying truth about Vera. She's aggressive and angry because she's the breadwinner. She has to wear the trousers because Jack's a slacker, a womaniser and dishonest. When Terry was found to have broken into the corner shop and stolen bottles of drink for a party, Vera was distraught with shame and disappointment. Men let her down. Naturally her tongue is quicker than her brain but, thick as she is, it doesn't stop her having more opinions than Percy Sugden, enough to offend everyone.

Her schemes can be brilliant. One was to install her mother in Terry's room (after he left in 1987) to thwart Jack's dream plan for a sex-starved young woman lodger.

It's sometimes a shame she can't be a bitch or a tartar, but 'Coronation Street' doesn't 'do' them now. (See 'Bitches'.) It's probably enough that Vera has a nine-carat heart and she survives.

Elizabeth Dawn, the Leeds-born actress, is naturally funny off-screen, too. A talented singer-comedienne, funny things happen to her all the time, like the night she did a carbaret engagement in full 'war paint', curly blonde wig, and long false eyelashes. She heard someone in the audience say: 'Doesn't he make a lovely woman?' It turned out later that she had been a late replacement for a drag artist, but her agent hadn't told her.

Liz Dawn is a friendly generous woman who works hard for charity. She is an ordinary Leeds lass who came through the ranks of television extras to become a larger-than-life Vera. Whilst running a home and bringing up five children, she did the cabaret circuit at night, playing working-men's clubs. It was Alan Parker, director of the feature films *Fame* and *Bugsy Malone*, who spotted her potential and recruited her for a series of television commercials. Her work impressed Larry Grayson, who invited her to appear in one of his television spectaculars. Then she landed parts in 'Z Cars', 'Kisses at Fifty' and 'Leeds United'. Granada used her as a waitress in their variety-club series 'Wheeltappers and Shunters Social Club', presented by northern comics Bernard Manning and Colin Crompton.

When the 'Coronation Street' casting directors were looking for a new family to move into number 9 in 1983, Liz was perfect for the rôle of Vera with the brassy Brillo-pad hairdo and the corncrake voice. The character was an instant hit with viewers. There was trouble for the actress, though, in 1984 when her marriage broke up and details of her life with husband Don Ibbetson were luridly printed in a newspaper. Granada suspended her from the series for two months. Eventually they forgave her and took her back. She has been a model leading player ever since. Happily, she has also managed to repair the rift with her husband. They are now settled into a new home – a large detached house – just a couple of miles from Granada's Manchester studios where 'Coronation Street' is made. Liz lives the life poor Vera would sell her soul for.

Len Fairclough was the main man of Coronation Street for twenty-three years. He had balls and BO. He brawled, he caroused, he sweated and suffered. Men related to him, sympathised with him. Women saw in him the danger and the sexiness there is in 'EastEnders' Dirty Den. When Len was killed off in December 1983 (because Peter Adamson, who played him, had been involved in a shameful court-case), Granada gave the soon-to-emerge rival, 'EastEnders', a serious advantage. 'Coronation Street' has not had a Real Man since.

Len, an ex-seaman from the rough end of Liverpool, arrived in 1960, a divorced man, a bricklayer and builder, with one son, Stanley. His fits of temper, public rows and his willingness to fight made him the soap's tough guy for almost a decade. But he wasn't just mouth and muscles. With Annie Walker, Elsie Tanner and, later, Hilda he was the cornerstone of the show. At first – and off and on for seventeen years – he was attracted to Elsie. She liked his lived-in face and no messing. They had a fling, but she turned down his marriage proposals, treating him eventually more as a brotherly pal. In 1975, now his own boss and a responsible citizen, he had a torrid affair with Bet Lynch, but two years later the writers decided he should commit himself. He fell for and married nightclub singer Rita Littlewood. By then the brawler had matured into a respected local businessman and councillor.

Peter Adamson was trouble to himself, his family and friends, and trouble to the makers of 'Coronation Street'. He was quite probably soap's most troublesome actor and also one of its best. Len Fairclough, the quick-tempered hot-blooded character he played for twenty-three years, was a pussycat by comparison. Adamson drank and argued. A court-case for indecency and the publication of a newspaper series of 'confessions' washed out his soap stardom. It was sad.

In the sixties the Liverpool-born actor fresh out of rep was already in the fray. There were public slanging matches, an arrest for drunken driving, and upsets which put his television job on the line more than once. But then people did not know that the actor was grappling with alcoholism and heavy drinking was beginning to affect his performances and wreck his private life. Bryan Mosley, his pal and fellow 'Coronation Street' actor, used to stay at the Adamson house in Bury some nights after long studio sessions. But the two rarely went straight home. 'Some of our journeys home were like draymen's delivery runs, stopping at every pub on the way,' Bryan said many years later. Sometimes he was with Adamson when the fighting started in Manchester pubs or restaurants. 'Then he'd have to go back next morning, apologise and pay for any damage. It had to be done so that his capers didn't become public knowledge. One night we'd both been out on the razzle. We ended up at Peter's and he handed me a full bottle of Curaçao which we polished off together. I remember waking up the next morning feeling like absolute death. Peter said: "Don't you tell me I drink too much. Look what you knocked back last night." I replied: "Yes, but I won't be able to touch another drop for weeks. Look at you. You're at it again already."'

Adamson knew his drinking was taking over. He made several attempts to kid his colleagues that he had given up, ordering only tomato juice in the pub. Then he dashed to the gents' to knock back a glass of brandy. All this while his wife Jean had suffered pain from arthritis. In February 1973 he stopped drinking. He was later quoted as saying: 'The last place I wanted to be was at home with the problems of my wife, the children and the tax man. I wasn't a nice bloke. When I stopped drinking, I saw things clearer. If Jean could accept and live with her problems, I knew I could accept going without a drink. We're a couple of cripples.' Eventually he turned to Alcoholics Anonymous, and has not drunk since. He became a personal crusader, admired for his openness. He addressed dozens of gatherings for fellow-sufferers. His career ran smoothly for ten years.

In 1983, however, his luck changed. He was charged with indecently assaulting two eight-year-old girls in a swimming-pool. He was cleared, but the publicity put him and his family under deep stress. He said later he would have committed suicide had the verdict at Burnley Crown Court gone against him. But as he walked free he was whisked away by reporters to whom he proceeded to 'tell all' about the colleagues who had supported him for so many years – arguably a more damaging deed than any before. His fee was alleged to have been £60,000. Fellow-stars – notably Pat Phoenix – said openly that they did not want Adamson back and accused him of 'ratting' on his mates. Later that year Granada decided not to renew his contract. They said it had nothing to do with the court-case, and the received wisdom was that his controversial statements to the newspapers, written without consultation or authorisation, had brought about his sacking. Shortly afterwards the fifty-three-year-old actor went missing. He turned up on the South Sea island of Bali and sent cheeky postcards to his Street pals. When he did return to Britain it was to the stage. He took the lead in *Dial M for Murder* playing a detective. There was more sadness when his wife Jean underwent a series of operations for her arthritis and died. After a spell living in a caravan in the south of England, Adamson left for Canada where he began a new and successful acting career. But it could never be the same. (See 'Fame'.)

Rita Fairclough is Coronation Street's wisest, wittiest woman. A lively redhead played by Barbara Knox, Rita broke into show business as a teenager touring the North and Midlands in panto and mediocre revues. Her life is so settled now, she's so respectable. But there has been a succession of affairs, rows and reconciliations with men which has made her cynical about the future. A former nightclub singer – Alec Gilroy was once her agent – she lived with a construction worker, Harry Bates, before she began a furtive affair with Len Fairclough. When Bates found out he beat her up. She eventually married Len in 1977. Now widowed – Len was killed in a car crash – she has set up home with smooth Alan Bradley. Suspicious of marriage, she has twice rejected Alan. The last time was when he tried to cajole her into marriage by arranging a secret register-office ceremony. She stormed off in disgust. Rita, who owns the Kabin newsagent's shop, has never been without admirers. Alf Roberts and Alec Gilroy were both sweet on her before they got married. Sensibly the writers didn't turn her into a replacement for Elsie (though the hair colour's the same). Rita's line in middle-aged sexiness is more subtle. And she has what Elsie never had: common sense. Now she's the motherly friend and guide to Alan's teenage daughter, Jenny, and the tolerant sceptical straight man to Mavis dithering daftly about Derek. When she doesn't appear in episodes, she's missed.

Barbara Knox is a very private person off-screen. After the break-up of her first marriage, she married wealthy Cheshire businessman John Knox and changed her name from Mullaney to Knox – very unusual for an actress to do in mid-career. She has not given a media interview since. An accomplished ballad-singer, Barbara's version of 'The Party's Over' in a Rover's Return concert led to the issue of an LP of 'standards' called 'On the Street Where I Live'. Barbara made her acting début with Oldham rep and went on to work in television series such as 'Emergency – Ward Ten' and 'A Family at War'. She is also a fine radio actress who has worked with Les Dawson, Ken Dodd, Mike Yarwood and Jimmy Tarbuck.

Fred Gee was the barrel-bellied bully of Coronation Street. Almost all the men in this soap in the mid-seventies and early eighties were overweight. Stan, Eddie, Alf, Len and Fred all sported extra chins, paunches and the unhealthy pallor of a heart attack looking for somewhere to happen. Fred, with his potato face, was randy, too, which somehow made it more threatening. The cellarman of the Rover's Return, his catholic taste in women ranged from Rita Fairclough to Vera Duckworth. His crude approaches invariably ended in the cold shoulder. Annie Walker used to make him bridle with her comments about his crudity; Bet Lynch had a wonderful knack of putting him down. But tireless Fred, portrayed by burly actor Fred Feast, did manage to cheap-talk buxom barmaid Eunice Nuttall into marriage in 1981. It turned out to be merely a business ploy to land the tenancy of the Crown and Kettle pub. When business slumped, the couple moved to the community centre as resident caretakers. Fred was sacked for insulting people. When the Gees were offered the Park View Hotel in Weatherfield, Eunice accepted but Fred stayed on in the Street, so the marriage broke up. He got his old job back as potman at the Rover's but was sacked by Billy Walker in 1984. Before he left he gave Billy a leaving present: a punch on the nose. He was repulsively real. I miss him.

Fred Feast is an ex-RAF paratroop instructor who jumped into show business feet first. On an impulse, he auditioned at the Windmill Theatre and was engaged as a stand-up comic, working with a little-known comedian called Bruce Forsyth. Scarborough-born Fred ran the gamut of showbusiness before he joined the Street, from summer season and pantomime to cabaret and feature films including Alan Ladd's *The Red Beret*. He joined 'Coronation Street' in 1975, made a folk-hero of the slobbish Fred Gee, but left the programme controversially in 1984 when he refused to sign a new contract. Furious Granada bosses claimed he threw the show into turmoil twice. Ten scripts had to be rewritten the first time when he took three months' sick leave to get over a bout of depression. There were major rewriting sessions again when Fred walked out in 1984. In a series of newspaper articles later, Fred claimed that the strain of constantly having to learn lines had led to 'nightmares and uncontrollable weeping'. He said he had left the series because he was determined not to end up as a 'Coronation Street cabbage'. He has not been spotted flowering elsewhere. Currently, his whereabouts are unknown.

Alec Gilroy is the slightly sleazy club-owner turned landlord of the Rover's Return in Coronation Street who is always on the make. Gilroy, played by Roy Barraclough, used to be Rita Fairclough's agent in her cabaret singing days – and now she wouldn't trust him an inch. Alec's next venture was the Graffiti Club, which began as a threat to the conventional Rover's Return but, with overpriced drinks, didn't stay in favour with the locals. When the club failed, Alec turned his attention to the Rover's itself, coveting the 'nice little earner' that Bet Lynch had set up for herself. When Bet got into money difficulties, Alec staked her to the tune of £12,000, knowing that she would always be in his debt. When he found out that Bet had skipped off abroad to think over her problems, Alec was on the next plane, panicking about his money. He realised that the only way to secure his missing cash, and keep the tenancy of the Rover's, was to marry Bet. There followed the most unlikely marriage in twenty-seven years of 'Coronation Street': brassy Bet hitched to oily Alec, with not a hint of romance or sex between them. Likely or not, the ceremony was amusing, Alec resembling a man facing an income tax tribunal, Bet in a pantomime wedding dress with what looked like beer-barrels up each sleeve, shooting dagger-like looks. Shots of the sour-faced groom in Bet's shocking-pink bedroom in later episodes were even funnier. The couple bicker over who's boss in the bar. She's human; he's mean. Bet, I fear, is set to suffer some more.

Roy Barraclough is a Northern character actor much in demand. He has worked with the famous from Richard Chamberlain to Les Dawson. Born and brought up in Preston, Roy spent the first twelve years of his working life as a draughtsman, keeping amateur dramatics for his spare time. Then came a job as entertainments manager at a holiday camp where he also played piano and told risqué jokes in the bar. He started acting at Huddersfield and then at Oldham rep.

Fellow 'Coronation Street' regulars Barbara Knox, Julie Goodyear and Anne Kirkbride are old mates: they all worked with Roy at Oldham rep in the sixties. Roy was best-known for his comedy work in the BBC television series 'The Les Dawson Show': he and Les formed a partnership as two grotesque old women shoving each other around as they guffawed. He appeared in 'Coronation Street' several times, in minor rôles, before becoming Alec. 'It was like coming home,' says Roy, an easygoing genial man, nothing like his obnoxious screen persona. A confirmed bachelor, Roy's pet hate is watching himself on television. 'I simply can't stand it. I have to get up and leave the room.'

Concepta Hewitt was the first barmaid at the Rover's Return when 'Coronation Street' began in 1960. Concepta, played by Doreen Keogh, was a pretty auburn-haired Irish coleen, first seen in episode 4. Then Concepta Riley, she met and fell in love with bus inspector Harry Hewitt, a widower with a wry sense of humour and a precocious daughter called Lucille. Concepta and Harry married in 1961 and moved into 7 Coronation Street. They later left to live in Ireland, leaving Lucille to complete her education in Weatherfield in the care of 'Uncle' Jack and 'Aunty' Annie Walker of the Rover's Return. When Harry died in an accident, Concepta married Sean Regan and went to live in Castle Blaney, Eire.

Doreen Keogh was involved in a well-publicised on- and off-screen romance. Concepta met and married bus inspector Harry Hewitt in the television series. Doreen, already married, fell for actor Ivan Beavis who played her screen husband. She got divorced, and they were married.

Born in Dublin, Doreen Keogh went to the Abbey Theatre School at fifteen and moved to London in 1950. She married four years later but, after joining 'Coronation Street', she fell in love with Ivan Beavis who was later cited in her husband's divorce petition. Doreen had beaten seven other actresses to land the part of Concepta. The Hewitts were popular with the general public, but their characters were written out in 1964. Doreen and Ivan immediately formed a touring company with other former 'Coronation Street' actors Lynne Carol (Martha Longhurst) and Frank Pemberton (Frank Barlow).

Harry Hewitt was a darkly smiling widower, a real catch for Irish barmaid Concepta Riley who worked in the Rover's Return in the early days of 'Coronation Street'. Portrayed by Ivan Beavis, Harry Hewitt married Concepta, and a year later she gave birth to a son, Christopher, who was kidnapped but returned safely to his parents on their first wedding anniversary. The Hewitts left to live in Ireland, leaving Harry's rebellious fourteen-year-old daughter Lucille in the care of Jack and Annie Walker at the Rover's Return. When the Hewitts returned to Weatherfield in 1967 to celebrate Elsie Tanner's wedding to American Steve Tanner, Harry was crushed to death when a jack collapsed under Len Fairclough's van, poor fellow.

Ivan Beavis, who played Coronation Street widower Harry Hewitt in episode 1, was born in Liverpool and had a spell at sea as a young man. He graduated to the professional stage through the ranks of amateur theatre. After a few television appearances, he was recruited by Granada to play a typical 'bloke next door' in their new soap at a salary of £40 a week. The Hewitts were popular with viewers, but Ivan and Doreen Keogh, who played his screen wife Concepta, returned from a holiday abroad to learn that they were being written out of the series. Together, they formed a touring theatre company. Ivan played minor rôles in television series like 'Emergency – Ward Ten' and 'Z Cars', but he thought the Harry Hewitt image was holding back his career. So he contacted Granada and asked them to kill Harry off. Granada agreed, and Harry died – crushed to death under Len Fairclough's van.

Lucille Hewitt, precocious daughter of widower Harry Hewitt, was Coronation Street's first and best rebel teenager. Played by Jennifer Moss, she shocked the locals when she had her hair died bright blonde and her arm tattooed. (This was 1962!)

111

When Harry married the Rover's barmaid Concepta Riley and left to start a new life in Ireland, Lucille opted to stay and complete her education in Weatherfield, living with favourite 'Uncle' Jack and 'Aunty' Annie Walker at the Rover's. She had a fling with Gordon Clegg, but Gordon's mum refused to let them get married. Annie and Jack Walker were horrified when Lucille eloped with someone else, followed pop star Brett Falcon to London, and joined a hippie commune. Last heard of, she had joined her stepmother in Ireland following her father's death.

Jennifer Moss was a fifteen-year-old Wigan schoolgirl when the programme started in 1960. In order to play the ten-year-old that the script required, diminutive Jenny (4 feet 11 inches) was asked by the producers to bind her body with bandages to conceal her breasts. When Lucille reached her fourteenth birthday, Jenny celebrated by wearing a bra. In 1968, Jenny Moss, aged twenty-three (still only 4 feet 11 inches), married Peter Hampson, a nineteen-year-old six-footer. A year later, she left the series to have a baby – a little girl, Naomi Ruth. The newspapers reported Jennifer's own problems: drink and debt and doubt. But that's over now.

Tom Hopwood, Sally Webster's uncle in 'Coronation Street', brought cabbages, cauliflowers and a little sunshine into Hilda Ogden's dreary life in 1987 for the first time since her Stan died. Tom, a greengrocer, played by Len Marten, was her gentle but ardent suitor. The two have been on coach outings, joined Percy Sugden's old-time dancing formation team and taken tea. Timid Tom proposed to Hilda after she inspected his new bungalow; but she turned him down, saying: 'It wouldn't be right.' We all agreed.

Len Marten is a veteran of the heyday of British radio and variety. He was a member of Charlie Chester's gang for five years when 'Stand Easy' was top of the listening charts. Born in Manchester, his Second World War army call-up led to appearances in 'Stars in Battledress' where he first met another Street veteran, Bill Waddington (Percy Sugden). Marten trod the boards at the London Palladium and also enjoyed a Royal Command Performance. He writes and produces, too. His film credits include *Monty Python's The Meaning of Life*.

Alan Howard was the dapper Geordie businessman who swept Elsie Tanner off her feet and married her in 'Coronation Street' in 1970. Viewers knew him as the star of 'The Newcomers'. He had an appealing presence and seemed sexy enough for Elsie. But, while he was glib-tongued and plausible, he soon ran into money problems. Howard was played by Alan Browning, whose off-screen romance with Patricia

Phoenix, who played Elsie, led to a wedding between them that was more glitzy and showbizzy even than their fictional one. Bizarrely, as the screen marriage broke up, Browning and Phoenix also drifted apart. The television characters were divorced in 1978. Alan Howard married Elaine Dennet and now lives in Newcastle. Browning the actor died alone of liver disease in 1979. He was an alcoholic.

Alan Browning soon found his life inextricably tied up with the plot when he joined 'Coronation Street' in 1969. As television characters Alan Howard and Elsie Tanner fell in love and married; so did actors Alan Browning and Patricia Phoenix. The press were invited to a larger-than-life Christmas wedding, complete with top hats and tails, mink furs, champagne and horse-drawn carriages. But Pat Phoenix's life with Browning was always stormy. He was in and out of work after they left 'Coronation Street' in 1973. They appeared in a forty-three-week countrywide tour of the stage-play *Gaslight*. Browning had a drink problem. At one time he drank a bottle of whisky a day. Pat managed to break his habit, but the damage had been done and he died from liver disease in 1979. The couple had already drifted apart, and she was too upset to visit him as he lay in hospital on his deathbed. There were rumours that she had recently had a facelift and could not yet risk a public appearance. Browning, who had made his television soap début as much-loved Ellis Cooper in the BBC's 'The Newcomers', is remembered by his friends in Fleet Street. Before he took up acting, he was a foreign news reporter with Reuters in the Middle East.

Ray Langton, first husband of Deirdre Barlow in 'Coronation Street', rapidly became 'Ray the Rat' for his outrageous behaviour. Langton, played by Neville Buswell, was a former juvenile delinquent and Borstal boy who was sacked for stealing from Len Fairclough. Langton served two years in prison for breaking and entering. Later, lenient Len made him a partner in his building firm. Langton met and married Deirdre Hunt but, when she caught him cheating with waitress Janice Stubbs, Deirdre threw him out. He left her and their daughter Tracey for a new life in Holland.

Neville Buswell, who played roguish Ray Langton in the 1970s, grew up in Buxton, Derbyshire, and studied at RADA. After a spell with Bristol Old Vic, he did the television rounds from 'Emergency – Ward Ten' to 'Love Story'. Dark-haired, with sly good looks, Neville was a particular pin-up for teenage girls. The nastier Ray grew, the more smitten were his fans. Viewers were shocked in 1978 when Neville left Britain mysteriously and later turned up as a croupier in Las Vegas. Equally mystified 'Coronation Street' producers were forced to write his character out when he asked to be released from his contract.

Ian Latimer was the fresh-faced blond Australian nephew of Ivy Tilsley who put the cat among the pigeons in Coronation Street in 1987 when he went to bed with Gail Tilsley. Shortly afterwards, she became pregnant with her second child. Gail's marriage was shaky, and when husband Brian found out about the affair he refused to believe that the child was his. Eventually they separated and divorced. Ian Latimer, played by Australian actor Michael Loney, offered to marry Gail, but she turned him down. He subsequently returned to Australia. He returned when the child was born, summoned by Gail's mother. But a blood test revealed the baby wasn't his.

Michael Loney was born in Perth, Western Australia. He took an English degree in Australia and then worked in television and theatre. He later won a scholarship to the Bristol Old Vic Theatre School in England. Now he is trying to establish an acting career in both countries. British producers see him as an Australian and have cast him in series like 'Tenko', while at home his ability to do an English accent has led to parts in which he played a true Britisher.

Florrie Lindley, who bought the corner shop from Elsie Lappin in the first episode of 'Coronation Street', crossed swords frequently with waspish Ena Sharples. After an unhappy affair with widower Frank Barlow, Florrie, portrayed by Betty Alberge, suffered a nervous breakdown. Her engineer husband Norman worked away. When he returned, they solved Florrie's mounting money problems by emigrating to Canada. They sold the corner shop to Lionel Petty and his daughter Sandra.

Betty Alberge portrayed Florrie Lindley who walked into a head-on verbal clash with Ena Sharples when she took over the ownership of the corner shop in 'Coronation Street' in 1960. Betty, who began acting at school, trained with the Manchester Repertory School of Acting and worked for ENSA during the war. She was an experienced radio actress who appeared in all the famous Northern comedy shows. Her early screen credits included *Love on the Dole*.

Martha Longhurst was the one with the funny black-rimmed glasses in the Holy Trinity of old biddies in the snug of the Rover's Return in 'Coronation Street' in the early sixties. Ena Sharples used to bully her, but she fought back more than Minnie Caldwell. Played by Lynne Carol, Martha was the nosy Street gossip. She was a cleaner at the Rover's where she found a rich vein of tittle-tattle. When the scriptwriters decided to kill her off in 1964 it caused a television sensation. Millions of viewers watched her die on screen as she slumped over a glass of her favourite milk stout after a heart attack in the snug. She was discovered by Ena Sharples. Wreaths, flowers and over a thousand letters of sympathy flooded into Granada Television's Manchester studios. Shortly afterwards, the producers acknowledged that the killing of Martha was their worst mistake.

Lynne Carol played waspish old Martha Longhurst in the first episode of 'Coronation Street'. Born in Monmouthshire, she was pitchforked into the theatre aged three by her actor parents. She came from six generations of actors. Lynne was married to the late Bert Palmer, a leading Lancashire character actor of the sixties and seventies, and they made their home in Blackpool where she still lives. After a highly successful three-year run as Martha, Lynne was deeply shocked to learn from her morning newspaper that a number of regular characters were to be axed from 'Coronation Street' by new producer Tim Aspinall. Martha was one of them. Bitter about Martha's fate, Lynne refused to let reporters into her home on 13 May 1964 when the death scene was screened. She viewed it in private with her husband Bert, who made a cine-film recording of the action on screen. To this day she still believes it was a crying shame to break up the gang of three: Ena, Minnie and Martha. Perhaps she's right. Since Hilda Ogden left, only Phyllis and Vera's mum Amy fulfil the old battle-axe rôles and they are thinly drawn pantomime figures.

Bet Lynch is Coronation Street's lippy loser. For eighteen years the scriptwriters have been pulling rugs from under her stiletto-heeled feet. The barmaid turned landlady of the Rover's Return slips and quips – usually with the best lines of the week. She's carbon-steel tough outside, so she gets up, uncracked. But the dents show. The helmet of bleached curls, the bosom, the bright tight clothes, joke jewels and hand-on-hip bravado are her trademarks. But to see big-mouth Bet as Weatherfield's tart with a heart is misguided. She's a failed tart. That's what's so sad, and that's why the way she dresses is important, not just funny. All that over-dressing spells one thing: desperation. Week after week Bet is there beaming, done up like a Christmas tree, trying to look like some man's special treat. Some man who didn't know her would run a mile in fright. Some man who did would like her for her gags not for her hoisted bosom and corny come-ons. Perhaps she knows she never had Elsie Tanner's sexiness and style. Perhaps when she married Alec Gilroy last year she admitted this to herself. Mr Right? How could he be more wrong? And who could be more honest with herself than Bet?

Actress Julie Goodyear, who plays Bet so superbly, always claimed there are hundreds of Bets to be seen at bus-stops all over Britain. 'It's all there. The figure, the legs. They look twenty-one from the back but when they turn round you think, oh luv!'

Elizabeth Theresa Lynch was probably born cheap and cheerful. Viewers know she had an illegitimate son, Martin, at sixteen who was adopted when Bet's mum threatened to throw her out. She had various jobs and digs before she took up Billy Walker's offer to be barmaid at the Rover's in 1970. His mother, Annie, was against it. Bet was far too common. In 1973 she was mugged. A year later, when she heard her son had been killed in a car crash serving with the Army in Northern Ireland, she tried to commit suicide. Living in the flat over Alf's shop, Bet had loads of fellas. Len Fairclough, Billy and Mike Baldwin dallied, then dumped her. Customers came back for more than the beer. But none of them loved her. In 1985 when the Walkers moved from the Rover's, Bet forgot romance and worked hard to become the landlady herself. Brewers Newton & Ridley took a chance, and it almost paid off. Jack Duckworth set the pub alight, Bet nearly died in the fire, but what's a little scare like that to a tough nut like her? Then in 1987 an enforced absence for Julie (her mother was dying) meant a drastic change for Bet. Bet had to disappear. We'd known the strain of repaying instalments on her bank loan was hard. We knew she'd borrowed £12,000 from know-all businessman and pest Alec Gilroy. He took over temporarily at the Rover's while the mystery of Bet's motives and whereabouts remained. Then Alec learned Bet was in Spain – squandering his precious twelve grand, he assumed. He flew out, found her up to her cleavage in eggs and chips working as a waitress in Torremolinos. And the fool hadn't even spent his cash. In a crucial scene filmed there, Alec stunned Bet and us with a loveless proposal of marriage. That way, he got the money and retained hold of the Rover's Return. Bet kept her status in the pub with a wedding ring. It sounded soulless and sad. In fact the odd couple's wedding scenes and the home-building – Bet failing as a gracious hostess, nurse and helpmate – were hilarious. Julie's talents as a comedienne came to the fore with Roy Barraclough's skill at playing the sour-faced fusspot Alec.

They worked so well as a couple that in March the writers took a chance. Bet, almost forty-eight, returned from a short holiday with the unlikely news that she was pregnant. Alec was terrified and tickled. Then Bet miscarried, and he was heartbroken. The scene where he and Bet wept at her lost last chance should have been absurd. It was touching.

By then Bet's clothes were changing. The polyester cocktail collection, the earrings which ranged from parakeets swinging on perches to miniature lavatory-bowls, were giving way to smart striped blouses, plain skirts and tasteful costume necklaces. It could soon be twin sets and pearls for poor Bet. And where's that nylon leopardskin coat, I'd like to know . . .?

Julie Goodyear is now the most important single player in 'Coronation Street'. As bosomy, big-mouthed Bet Lynch Gilroy, she's the

116

champion of all the good-time girls who had bad times more often. Bet's history is full of foolishness and lousy luck. Julie Goodyear could match Bet setback for setback, with a pile of controversies and broken dreams for reserves. Her life reads like a soap opera – a chapter of 'Peyton Place', maybe, not very well written and with many story-lines dangling unresolved.

My favourite Julie story relates to Julie the Lancashire teenager who dreamed of being a singer with a band. She burst into 'Blue Moon' at Bury Palais only to be hit in the mouth with a meat pie. 'I just picked it up off the stage and started eating it,' she said. 'I got my first big round of applause.' She decided to try acting. But first she had to settle for security. The child of an unsuccessful marriage, she'd lived mainly with her grandparents till she married Ray Sutcliff at seventeen and was instantly pregnant. To support baby Gary, she did office work, then sold washing machines by day and did nightclub work in the evenings. Four years later they were divorced.

Julie's parents then owned a pub. She worked there twice as a barmaid and hated it. So Julie took a modelling course. She had and still has exquisite hands and feet (whatever happens in between), and this led to a bit part as a factory girl in 'Coronation Street'. She said she hung around the studios every day asking for work. They gave in. There Julie met Pat Phoenix, who recognised a young talent in need of training. Pat took her to Oldham rep where for £12 a week she became ASM, the code for dogsbody. But this dogsbody was also a fighter. Four years later in 1970, Julie returned to 'Coronation Street' as Bet. Veteran scriptwriter Esther Rose once said: 'Bet Lynch wasn't much of a part – Julie made the most of it.' The 36B-cup bra, the jangling earrings and the brilliantly tatty tart's wear were Julie's – not the scripts. Julie relished the rôle and joked about her qualifications. Her famous breasts she called Newton and Ridley, after the Rover's brewers.

Fame brought her money enough to buy a big house in a leafy part of the North-West. (For the past four years she is reckoned to be the top earner in 'Coronation Street'.) Julie preferred to stay in the Lancashire mill-town of Heywood with her mother Alice – her most important fan and critic, she said. The actress took her longest break from 'Coronation Street' in 1987 to nurse her mother through the last stages of cancer. When she died, Julie said she felt she would never laugh again. The partnership she returned to start with co-star Roy Barraclough (Alec Gilroy), later her screen husband, happily changed that. The two share the same sense of comedy – as is clear on screen.

In Julie's life marriage was never as funny, though. After her divorce from Sutcliff, she was engaged to Northern club comic Jack Diamond in 1970. There was no wedding – only tears. Diamond said later it was a nightmare relationship. He was besotted with her, but she hated his camp stage act in which he used to wear gold lamé suits. She suggested he saw a psychiatrist. Shortly afterwards he took a drugs overdose.

Eighteen months later, in 1973, Julie married businessman Tony Rudman in a lavish church wedding to which thousands of 'Coronation Street' fans came, crowding the streets. Unknown to the public and her fellow-actors, the pair quickly went their separate ways; the honeymoon was secretly cancelled and the marriage annulled a year later. Julie kept up the pretence of being a bride for eight months. It caused her to have a breakdown.

When she met Andrew McAllister in Tunisia it was, in soap tradition, love at first sight. Julie proposed on St Valentine's Day. McAllister, at twenty-eight, was eight years younger than Julie; he gave up his job and moved into her Heywood home. Very soon they argued; she threw him out.

Wealthy American Richard Skrob, an executive with Lockheed, was the next man in her strange and turbulent life. They met on a London–Los Angeles flight, took trips to Paris and some other European cities, after which Julie told her Manchester colleagues they were married. It seems they weren't. Julie announced later that she was to marry 'Coronation Street' director Bill Gilmour. Again, no such luck. Three days before Christmas 1983, Julie claimed he had jilted her and walked out. There was a bitter war of words. Julie 'told all' to a newspaper for a large fee. She called him a drunk. He called her a liar. Well, it wasn't dull, anyway. Richard Skrob stayed in America but he stayed in the picture. In January 1985 they were married in Barbados, Julie later claimed. Almost exactly two years after that she divorced him, she also claimed.

If Julie's relationships have been at best difficult, at worst disastrous, the rest of her life has not lacked drama. In 1979 she underwent surgery for cervical cancer, of which she is now clear. After two months' leave from television, she returned to 'Coronation Street' and threw herself into a vigorous campaign to spread the word about early detection of the disease. She raised over £60,000 to open a screening laboratory in Manchester's Christies Hospital, but couldn't do what the doctor ordered: give up smoking. A couple of years later she found herself in the dock at Manchester Crown Court accused of fixing a lottery for her cancer fund. She went through five days of anguish until the jury acquitted her. Meanwhile her son Gary, who works at a garage, frightened his mother by racing Formula One cars. Her mother's poor health preyed on her mind. Then in 1986 a series of newspaper 'revelations' by taxi-driver Duncan Ford, who claimed to have lived with the actress, made Bet's problems pale by comparison. The allegations were that Julie was a lesbian, had had several passionate affairs and that her housekeeper, Janet Ross, was in fact her partner in a gay relationship. Tony Rudman, husband number two, former fiancé Andrew McAllister and former colleague Fred Feast were quoted as knowing that Julie preferred women. Richard Skrob flew in to pose for lovey-dovey photographs with Julie to counteract the claims, but the

In soap opera, the path of true love runs bumpy as can be. There's usually
a smooth bit at the weddings, though, when we can all enjoy a good cry.
Hankies came out for 'Neighbours'' first nuptials. Daphne (*Elaine Smith*) wed
Des (*Paul Keane*). Lots more were to follow.

Elsie Tanner (*Pat Phoenix*) said 'I do' with Steve Tanner
(*Paul Maxwell*) among others.

Alf Roberts (*Bryan Mosley*) took Audrey (*Sue Nicolls*) to be
his lawful, awful wife.

Much-married Ken Barlow (*William Roache*) caught
Deirdre (*Anne Kirkbride*) without her specs.

The happiest if not the prettiest pair were Eddie
(*Geoffrey Hughes*) and Marion (*Veronica Doran*).

Alec Gilroy (*Roy Barraclough*) smiled with Bet
(*Julie Goodyear*) and not since.

'Emmerdale Farm''s Kathy (*Malandra Burrows*) keeps
Jackie Merrick (*Ian Sharrock*) from his sheep.

Weddings, more than money, make the world go around in soap operas such
as 'Coronation Street'. They've had twenty-six to date.

'Crossroads'' Meg (*Noele Gordon*) married Hugh Mortimer (*John Bentley*) but happiness didn't last.

'Crossroads'' Jill (*Jane Rossington*) wore a hat. Adam Chance (*Tony Adams*) wore a smirk.

A bigger hat for Jill (*Jane Rossington*). A bigger headache with Stan (*Edward Clayton*).

Adam Carrington of 'Dynasty' (*Gordon Thompson*) stopped seething briefly to wed Dana (*Lean Hunley*).

'Neighbours'' Moral Majority Jim Robinson (*Alan Dale*) found saintly Dr Beverly (*Lisa Armytage*).

Weddings are for proud mums too, like Eileen Clarke of 'Neighbours' (*Myra de Groot*).

They love getting dressed up for the brides and grooms in 'Crossroads', 'Emmerdale Farm', 'Dynasty' and 'Dallas'. Confetti salesmen in 'EastEnders' and 'Brookside' are not doing a roaring trade, though.

Len Fairclough of 'Coronation Street' (*Peter Adamson*), loved and lost by Elsie, Bet and Rita.

'EastEnders'' Dennis Watts (*Leslie Grantham*). The only thing not crooked about him? His teeth.

Pete Beale of 'EastEnders' (*Peter Dean*) knows a woman's place is in the wrong.

David Hunter (*Ronald Allen*) kept a stiff upper lip through crises at Crossroads.

'Sons and Daughters' (fathers, too) survived traumas each week. (*Tom Richards and Stephen Comey*).

All Jason Colby (*Charlton Heston*) of 'The Colbys' wanted was power, money, sex, subservience . . .

Men's men are a must in soap opera. Hard working, hard drinking, hard to catch and hard to keep.

Bobby Ewing of 'Dallas' (*Patrick Duffy*), almost too good to live, died a while.

'Dallas''s JR Ewing (*Larry Hagman*) is a cheating, twisting swine and enjoys every minute.

Mike Baldwin of 'Coronation Street' (*Johnny Briggs*) steals wives, chats up barmaids and barks at machinists.

'Dynasty''s Blake Carrington (*John Forsythe*) has inner strength on the outside too.

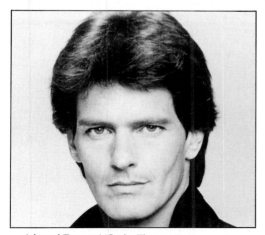

Adam of 'Dynasty' (*Gordon Thompson*) can use poison paint yet avoid the men in white coats.

How could Alexis in 'Dynasty' divorce devoted Dex Dexter (*Michael Nader*)? women everywhere asked.

Some beat their hairy chests. Some suffer in manly silence. Others swindle and swagger. Women love them all.

Alexis, 'Dynasty''s super bitch (*Joan Collins*), eats caviar
and men and prays Krystle Carrington will soon shrivel
and die.

Sable, 'The Colbys'' fur-, silk- and diamond-clad monster
(*Stephanie Beacham*), lost Jason and shacked up with Zac.

Constance in 'Flamingo Road' (*Morgan Fairchild*) wanted
to rule the southern States. She landed a wet Field.

'Dynasty''s Sammy Jo (*Heather Locklear*) tricked her
husband, helped kidnap Aunt Krystle and swindle
Blake. Then she reformed.

Bless the bitches of soap opera, the women who want their own way and
never feel guilty.

'Neighbours'' Nell Mangel (*Vivean Gray*), a snob, busybody and worse to lost husband Len.

Abby of 'Knots Landing' (*Donna Mills*) is a sex-hungry she-devil. Gary Ewing should sober up and escape.

Valerie Pollard, the rich bitch of 'Crossroads' (*Heather Chasen*). If only she'd stayed longer.

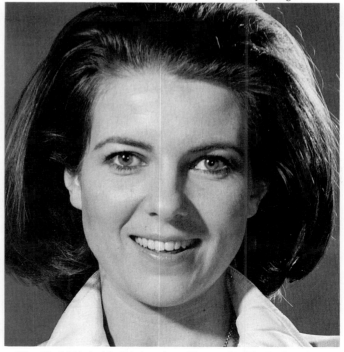

Kate O'Mara was businesslike in 'The Brothers', tough in 'Triangle' and Alexis's wicked sister in 'Dynasty'.

Hilary Tindall bitched for Britain as Anne Hammond in 'The Brothers' long before the shoulder pad. How well she cheated and lied.

Power mad, sex starved or simply rotten to the core, we've seen them all and booed and hissed.

Stubborn old Albert Tatlock (*Jack Howarth*) waddled around Coronation Street happily fuelled on rum.

The bowler hurt Alf Roberts (*Bryan Mosley*), a codger from childhood. His usual 'Coronation Street' hat's a trilby.

The Street's caretaker Percy Sugden (*Bill Waddington*) is a cantankerous old stick. Phyllis Pearce is stuck on him.

Harry Cross of 'Brookside' (*Bill Dean*) is smiling here. A temporary lapse. Don't tell the neighbours.

Soap's senior citizens – or codgers (if you must) – are a sturdy bunch. With many loyal older viewers, no producer dare overlook them. They remember, they advise and they keep families together.

When crabby Lou Beale (*Anna Wing*) in 'EastEnders' speaks her mind, grown men come away weeping.

'EastEnders'' Dot Cotton (*June Brown*) needs a smoke and a moan to calm bad nerves and hot flushes.

Ethel Skinner (*Gretchen Franklin*) is 'EastEnders'' game old girl. She likes silly hats and her pug Willie.

Annie Sugden of 'Emmerdale Farm' (*Sheila Mercier*) takes life seriously.

The publicans in 'Emmerdale Farm', Amos Brearly (*Ronald Magill*) and Henry Wilks (*Arthur Pentelow*), are among the rudest in Britain.

In American series, they're golden oldies, plucky, powerful and wise.
In British and Australian series they tend to be grumpier and frumpier and
they're martyrs to their aches and pains.

Oily JR (*Larry Hagman*) and boozy Sue Ellen (*Linda Gray*) of 'Dallas' are locked together in loathing.

In 'Dallas', Ray (*Steve Kanaly*) loves Donna. Jenna (*Priscilla Presley*) loves Bobby. But they make do with each other.

'Dynasty''s Blake (*John Forsythe*) loves Krystle (*Linda Evans*), and buys her jewels to prove it.

Among the upright Germans in 'Black Forest Clinic', Professor Brinkmann (*Klausjurgen Wussow*) loves Christa (*Gaby Dohm*).

Love's grand, innit? Only Michelle (*Sue Tully*) soon gave Lofty (*Tom Watt*) the 'EastEnders' elbow.

Meet the ex-trouble and strife. 'EastEnders'' shifty Den (*Leslie Grantham*) with alcoholic Angie (*Anita Dobson*).

Soap opera loves a lover. But happiness can never last. Bliss is boring to watch after a few episodes. A bit of harrowing is good for ratings.

Vacillating Victor Pendlebury (*Christopher Coll*) or dithering Derek Wilton (*Peter Baldwin*)? Luckily, Mavis Riley (*Thelma Barlow*), 'Coronation Street''s quivering spinster, eventually chose neither.

Jack Walker (*Arthur Leslie*) and his lady wife Annie (*Doris Speed*), together at the Rover's Return.

Muddy married love on 'Emmerdale Farm' for Jack (*Clive Hornby*) and Pat Sugden (*Helen Weir*).

Love with boring Ken (*William Roache*) or lust with flash Mike (*Johnny Briggs*)? Deirdre (*Anne Kirkbride*) had to decide while we all took sides.

Authoress Barbara (*Sue Lloyd*) booked in at Crossroads and married the boss David Hunter (*Ronald Allen*).

G'day, love! 'Neighbours'' Mike Young (*Guy Pearce*) saw Jane Harris (*Annie Jones*) at school.

'Crossroads'' fling for jittery Jill Chance (*Jane Rossington*) and macho Mickey Doyle (*Martin Smith*).

Life and love go on and on, new tangles, new heartbreaks, new bliss and old clichés. Some couples stay together out of spite.

Dedicated Doctor Kildare (*Richard Chamberlain*) practised in the sixties and became prescribed viewing.

Sister Washington of 'General Hospital' (*Carmen Monroe*) worked hard but wore a bedpan face.

Brisk Sister Carol Young (*Jill Browne*) of 'Emergency Ward Ten' made doctors better too.

Glyn Owen caught soap opera on 'Emergency Ward Ten'. 'The Brothers' and 'Howards' Way' followed.

Medicated soap has always been a favourite with its white coats, long words, sad cases and miracle cures. Scalpel! Forceps! Instant appeal!

They cured most things at the Black Forest Clinic except the out-of-sync-itis of everyone's lips.

Medicine was a struggle in run-down 'St Elsewhere', especially for perfectionist Dr Craig (*William Daniels*), top left.

Nurse Scott (*Marta Kertesz*) and Dr Elliott are all heart and progress in Australia's 'A Country Practice'.

Doctors are such gentlemen in soap. No wonder nurses, patients and we hypochondriacs at home keep taking the programmes.

Put on a brave face, chuck, say Bet (*Julie Goodyear*) and Rita (*Barbara Knox*).

What Vivienne Cooper (*Maggie Fitzgibbon*) didn't cope with in 'The Newcomers' was nobody's business.

Meg Richardson (*Noele Gordon*) went through calamities in 'Crossroads': fire, prison, kidnap, chef's cooking.

You name it, Jill Chance (*Jane Rossington*) suffered it with matching accessories at Crossroads.

Sad Sheila Grant of 'Brookside' (*Sue Johnstone*) was raped, bereaved, deserted but determined.

'EastEnders'' Pauline Fowler (*Wendy Richard*). Chirpy despite awful Arthur, grouchy Lou and problem kids.

How women suffer in soap! Men break their hearts and let them down.
Children cause anguish. Accidents happen and hopes are dashed.

No plain sailing at Howards Way for designer-dressed Jan Howard (*Jan Harvey*).

Miss Ellie of 'Dallas' (*Barbara Bel Geddes*) has needed handkerchiefs the size of Texas.

'Emmerdale Farm''s cows get more sympathy than single Sandie Merrick (*Jane Hutcheson*).

Pam Ewing (*Victoria Principal*) suffered so much at Southfork Ranch she dreamed Bobby had died.

Karen Fairgate Mackenzie of 'Knots Landing' (*Michele Lee*), a rock that sometimes crumbles.

Madge Mitchell née Ramsay (*Anne Charleson*) is Charlene's mother, so she's 'Neighbours'' martyr.

Soap women cope. They must. A new crisis is round the corner. The surgeon works miracles. The lost child returns. A good man turns up.

Flamin' Nora! Men? Elsie Tanner (*Pat Phoenix*) could tell Lucille Hewitt
(*Jennifer Moss*) a thing or two. Three husbands, umpteen fancy men and
where was she? Still in Coronation Street and skint.
Poor Pat died. But Elsie's somewhere in Portugal, solving the problem of men
with a fag and a gin. Lucille got dressed and made a few mistakes too.

stories were not repudiated. As Bet Lynch, Julie always had a large gay following. Her weekly mailbag (the largest of all the 'Coronation Street' cast) regularly contains enquiries from gay men about her clothes. Transvestites ask for guidance in modelling themselves on Bet. But, if a soap star is gay, he or she dare not Come Out it seems.

In time, perhaps, Julie will write her autobiography. The plot of the soap opera that has been her life will be resolved. I hope the ending will be happy – as soap endings always should be. One thing is certain: controversy will dog Julie Goodyear's life – as it does Bet Lynch Gilroy's.

Hilda Ogden was in 'Coronation Street' for twenty-three years from 1964 until Christmas 1987. It was a strange odyssey. On that long journey she changed from being the comic-relief sharp-tongued nosy char into the best-loved woman on television. For some reason, Britain took to her hair-rollers and headscarf, her flowered pinafore, her mincing walk usually clutching the edge of her mean little blue mac and all her small pretensions. Like the funny 'sophisticated' way she held her cigarette, the china ducks and the 'muriel' on her living-room wall. Perhaps the reason was simply that Jean Alexander, who played her, is a brilliant actress. Perhaps it is that Hilda, of all the women in soap, came to represent survival.

Like her friend and adversary, Bet Lynch, Hilda was a loser in life. Stan Ogden croaked on her. Her only son Trevor went up in the world and had no time for her. Mrs Lowther, whom she worked for and revered, died after a violent burglary. Hilda, also a victim of the burglary, received only a crack on the head and wondered why she had been spared. While work-shy Stan rested his glass back, Hilda unquestioningly worked to put the fish and chips on the table for 'tea' and pay the bills for the humblest house in Coronation Street, number 13. She skivvied for Mike Baldwin, 'bottomed' at the Rover's Return and 'did' for Dr and Mrs Lowther.

Her only truly treasured memory is of the time she and Stan won a 'second honeymoon' prize at a posh hotel. As she luxuriated in the furnishings of room 504 (the drawers didn't stick!) Stan got drunk on champagne and she trilled the forties song 'In Room 504'. Her only pleasures were shrill and tuneless singing, jumping to conclusions about her neighbours and telling fortunes: like Ethel in 'EastEnders' she read tea leaves. Luck? She had little. Respect? She had less. When Gail Tilsley needed a babysitter and Hilda was happy to help, Ivy Tilsley reacted as though Hilda was somehow unfit and unclean.

Bet Lynch fights life back with sharp wit, a jutting bosom, another bottle of peroxide; her carapace seems to grow thicker. Hilda has none of this equipment. Her eyes show pain. She weeps a little in private. She carries on. Nobody ever told Hilda life would be wonderful, but life must go on. Hilda had a nice cup of tea or bought herself a bottle of light ale at the Rover's, looked for a few blessings to count and went on, without making a fuss. That's why we loved her.

Jean Alexander surprised and saddened everyone who enjoys soap opera when she decided to stop playing Hilda Ogden in 'Coronation Street' in the autumn of 1987. She had created the 'little fighter' as she called Hilda, the prattling Mrs Mopp, from the part of a nagging wife married to a fat lout – the way the Ogdens were conceived in 1964. By 1987, then aged sixty-one, Jean said she wanted to put her feet up. She was tired of travelling daily from her Southport semi by taxi, train and taxi or bus to the Manchester studios. Granada had not offered their revered star the services of a driver. 'They'd *all* want one,' was apparently the reason. Jean wanted to leave in good health and spirits, fearing to follow other 'Coronation Street' actresses who were able to retire only to nursing homes or, worse, wait to die. She also wanted to try other rôles in television.

Liverpool-born Jean started her working life as a library assistant, but gave up her job to join a Macclesfield-based touring company. After rep in Oldham, Southport and York, she had a spell in London before joining 'Coronation Street'. Her trademark – Ena Sharples' was a hairnet – was her curlers and turban. When Jean brushed out her auburn hair at the end of a day's filming it gave her a degree of anonymity. She could shop in city centres unrecognised. For a woman once voted the fourth most popular female in Britain after the Queen, the Queen Mother and Princess Diana, she kept an extremely low profile, rarely gave interviews and never made public appearances except for charitable causes.

She is eternally grateful to Hilda. Before she joined 'Coronation Street', Jean claims she never had more than £15 in the bank in her life. She couldn't afford a television set until 1961. Over the years, she developed a taste for exotic holidays – particularly cruising. Unmarried, she lives an uncomplicated life in a comfortable semi in Southport. She never employed a char. Like Hilda she was a dab hand with a duster and a Hoover. Her joy was a rose-filled garden and classical music.

For the late Poet Laureate, Sir John Betjeman, playwright Willis Hall and television personalities Michael Parkinson and Russell Harty, watching Hilda was a joy. They formed the British League for Hilda Ogden. Betjeman declared his affection for Hilda and 'her ghastly husband Stan' and declared that, on Mondays and Wednesdays at 7.30 p.m., he was 'in heaven'. A rugby team in South Wales adopted her as their mascot, and members of their club had at all times to carry a Hilda Ogden curler – or be fined. She was also a pin-up of the Falklands fleet, and a request came from the South Atlantic for a photo of her in her curlers. She should, of course, have shed the headgear. Few women still bothered daily in the 1980s. When she landed in hospital after the Lowthers' burglary, I wondered if the head injury was really an in-growing curler. Over the years she had only four sets. 'I repaired them myself whenever the elastic perished,' she explains. 'And in twenty-three years I've only worn five pinnies.'

Jean rarely argued with the writers about Hilda. 'It wasn't my job,' she said. Her lines and her performance seemed always in tune. I once suggested that she deserved an Oscar, not for one particular scene or story-line, but for keeping Hilda bobbing back after every ducking. That year I was delighted that the Royal Television Society's Performance of the Year Award went to her. The scene which had impressed the judges so much came when Hilda was alone after Stan's death. She had not shed a tear throughout the funeral. In her living-room she unpacked the brown-paper parcel of Stan's belongings from the hospital. As she put his old spectacles on the table, she put her head down on her arms and sobbed.

On Christmas Day 1987, Hilda took off her pinny, took out her curlers, took down the ducks, and walked away from Coronation Street to live off-screen with Dr Lowther as his housekeeper. We miss her.

Stan Ogden was Coronation Street's large lump of lethargy, the uncrowned king of the non-working classes, an anti-hero to millions. For over twenty years, actor Bernard Youens worked hard to turn big 'Oggy' into the boozing, betting layabout the nation loved. 'He is my creation, and I am proud of him,' said Bernard. Members of the Stan Ogden Appreciation Society of Newton Abbot hailed him as 'the greatest living Englishman'.

Stan married Hilda Crabtree during the war. He worked as a lorry-driver from 1945 to 1964 – an amazing achievement considering his work-record from then on. He tried chauffeuring, but lasted only a day. Then there were brief spells as a coalman, a milkman and an ice-cream seller, before he bought a window-cleaning round. Stan's real work trouble was getting his back off the bed each morning.

Apart from drinking best bitter, he had only one vice – nipping round to see his fancy woman at 19 Inkerman Street. Hilda soon put a stop to that. She never dignified the relationship by speaking the woman's name. She always referred to ''er at number nineteen'. Despite this dalliance, Stan and Hilda enjoyed the Street's longest and most successful marriage. He was her cross, and she bore it well.

Superslob Stan's motto in life was to make the quickest quid with the least possible effort. Hilda criticised him long and loudly, but woe betide anyone else who raised their voice against him. She would defend him to the death. Although mostly stony-broke through their married life, the Ogdens always proudly paid their way – somehow. Usually thanks to Hilda's hard graft.

When Stan's health began to fail, Hilda skivvied twice as long, taking on extra cleaning work where she could. One of Hilda's most poignant scenes was opening letters to discover they were in debt and crying about it. Fat Eddie Yeats, the Ogdens' lodger, took on the window-cleaning round, but kept Stan on as a sleeping partner. Stan survived as best he could, by low-level trickery. When he stumbled over a paving stone, stubbing his big toe, he played on the injury and sued the local authority for compensation. There was an uproar from real local authorities all over Britain when dozens of 'copycat' claims were made by the general public.

Bernard Youens's death in 1984 compelled Granada to write out Stan from the series, and they decided to kill him off. Stan died in hospital, and Hilda bore the loss with great dignity, grieving in private. No one will forget the scene as she sat alone in her living-room with the brown-paper parcel from the hospital containing Stan's last few things. A great television double act had ended. Fat Stan was a kind of Hardy to Hilda's pipe-cleaner-thin Laurel. No wonder actress Jean Alexander said later that she would not be part of another partnership in 'Coronation Street'. There was only one man for her. His photograph remained permanently in her parlour.

Bernard Youens, who created a television legend as the mountainous moronic Stan Ogden in 'Coronation Street', was a darkly handsome leading actor in his theatre heyday in the forties and fifties.

When Independent Television first started in 1955, Bernard was hired as a velvet-voiced, cultured continuity announcer by Granada at their Manchester studios. Remember this when you recall the Neanderthal-like grunts of monstrous Stan, Hilda's heavyweight worse half. But because of this secure job – a boon to a married man with five children – Bernard almost didn't become Stan. He actually turned down a chance to audition for 'Coronation Street' in 1960 because it seemed like a gamble with a regular wage. Unlike Stan, Bernard had learned from his hard times. But, then, there were few comparisons. The man who played the archetypal gruff Northerner actually came from the South: tickety-boo Hove in Sussex. He finished his education in Newcastle-upon-Tyne, and it was there at the Players' Theatre that he was first employed, becoming an assistant stage manager. He met and married Edna, a ballet dancer, when he was just eighteen.

He worked in rep all over Britain before being called up in 1940 to serve in the Army's 1st Battalion, the Loyals' Regiment, in North Africa, Anzio and Egypt. After demob in 1946, there were acting jobs in a couple of Granada series, 'Shadow Squad' and 'Knight Errant', but the theatre was his first love. Sadly, it rarely paid all the bills. At one point he quit the theatre to take over a rambling old Manchester pub. There were punch-ups every Saturday night, and eventually the aggressive regulars drove him out. On his beam end, Bernard took a casual job as a bread salesman. When that ended, he laboured on a building site, starting work at 6.30 a.m. The Youenses bought another pub near

Preston, and that failed, too. So the staff announcing job at Granada came as a real lifesaver. Even so, a year later, when 'Coronation Street' had become a smash hit, Bernard was kicking himself with disgust for not accepting the earlier challenge. But in 1963 the casting directors were looking for a new family. Bernard grabbed this chance to audition, and he and Jean Alexander, who played Hilda, hit it off immediately. Not surprisingly, really; they were similarly cultured, sane people.

Stan's very first line, uttered in the bar of the Rover's Return, was: 'A pint of mild and twenty fags, missus.' Viewers loved the Ogdens from the start. Life for the Youenses perked up. Bernard cleared his debts, bought himself a smart car, and even joined a golf club. Life was sweet for Bernard and Edna until, in the late seventies, his health deteriorated. A forty-cigarettes-a-day man, he had several heart attacks, followed by two strokes that left his speech impaired. Bravely, he refused to give up acting and engaged a speech therapist to teach him how to speak properly again. Unfortunately Bernard had also been struggling for nearly twenty years with arthritis of the knees and neck. This led to his rather hunch-shouldered stiff-necked appearance on television towards the end of his life. It was a personal tragedy for a man who had been so slim and good-looking in his acting prime. His condition worsened, and his left leg had to be amputated when surgeons found gangrene. Bernard Youens died in hospital in April 1984, aged sixty-nine.

So many soap stars have cracked up under the continued pressure of being a household name, turning to booze, jeopardising their marriages or jobs by errors of judgement or taste, but Bernard Youens remained the complete professional – much missed by his fellow-actors, his lovable living cartoon, Stan Ogden, mourned by millions.

Phyllis Pearce, Coronation Street's bossy blue-rinsed matron who works at the café with Gail Tilsley, is played with gusto by veteran actress Jill Summers. Phyllis goes weak at the knees whenever the man of her dreams, 'action man' Percy Sugden, is around. She would like to get him to the altar. But Percy will have none of it, remembering, perhaps, that Phyllis once led Street dustbinman Chalkie Whiteley a dog's life. Chalkie provided a home for her grandson Craig when her daughter's marriage broke up. When Phyllis's home in Omdurman Street was demolished, she tried to move in with Chalkie. He panicked and fled to Australia, reuniting grandson Craig with his father. Phyllis's lone admirer is pensioner Sam Tindall, but he doesn't get a look in when Percy Sugden is around.

Jill Summers, the seventy-six-year-old Manchester-born actress who plays Phyllis Pearce, has just celebrated seventy years in show business. Her father was a circus tightrope-walker, and her mother Marie Santoi, a famous actress of her day, introduced all her five children to the stage at the first opportunity. Jill was six. During the Second World War, Jill entertained the troops with ENSA. In 1945 she returned to variety, playing every theatre in London, billed as 'the Lancashire Comedienne'. She joined 'Coronation Street' in 1982 and loves playing 'the old battle-axe'. Off-stage, Jill, Bill Waddington who plays Percy Sugden, and Tom Mennard who is Sam Tindall swap memories about their good old days in British music-hall.

Mavis Riley is the fluttery spinster of Coronation Street who has been described as the 'eternal virgin'. Probably the best-read, most intelligent woman in the soap, but her trouble was her upbringing in a strict Methodist household. Mavis had so sheltered an upbringing that it has made her totally indecisive in life. Played by Thelma Barlow, Mavis is the perfect foil for blunt outspoken Rita Fairclough who owns the Kabin, the newsagent's where Mavis lives and works. Rita gently teases and torments her.

Timid Mavis shares her flat above the shop with her budgerigar Harriet. She was shocked when Percy Sugden rudely suggested that Harriet should be mated with his cock bird, Randy. Mavis declined on the grounds that 'Harriet wouldn't like that sort of thing'. Although she would love to get married, she seems firmly on the shelf. In 1984, however, two men vied for her affections: old flame Victor Pendlebury, and mother-dominated Derek Wilton. Mavis said yes to Derek but chickened out on the big day by failing to turn up at the church. She was first relieved, then furious, when she found out that Derek had done likewise. He ended up marrying the boss's daughter and, to add insult to injury, he runs to Mavis to talk over his mounting marriage problems. She'd like to tell him to push off, but she lacks the courage.

Thelma Barlow, who plays mousey Mavis Riley the dithery spinster, is a bright positive person – the complete antithesis of her screen character. Born in Middlesborough, she grew up in Huddersfield and worked for several years as a secretary, acting in her spare time. Finally she took the plunge, quit her job and joined Joan Littlewood's Theatre Workshop in London. At the time, she says, she was 'as green as cabbage'. She graduated to West End productions and did long spells in rep in Bristol, Nottingham and Glasgow.

Thelma is a highly intelligent and articulate actress who has firm views on serious dramatists from Shakespeare to Chekhov. Her clever television portrayal of the dotty Mavis has been long admired and acclaimed by viewers and television critics.

Alf Roberts is one of the well-rounded characters of 'Coronation Street'. He's both solid Citizen Alf, the tubby corner shopkeeper who has always been a pillar of the community (and ever so slightly pompous with it), and he's the teddy bear, gruff on the outside, cotton-wool inside, who likes a woman to cuddle and mother him. He was born middle-aged and never changes. These days he is blissfully married to Audrey Potter when everyone feared she was taking him for a ride. But of course three-times-married Alf, played by Bryan Mosley, knew what he was doing – awkward Romeo though he is.

After his first wife Phyllis died in 1972, his marriage proposal to Maggie Clegg was rejected. Then pushy Donna Parker led him a dance, borrowed £500 and scarpered. In 1978 he married Renee Bradshaw, owner of the corner shop. When she died in a car crash two years later the business became his.

Alf fancied newly widowed Rita Fairclough and touchingly proposed. But she preferred friendship to marriage. Eventually, he was snapped up by scheming 'no better than she ought to be' Audrey Potter who liked his bank balance and saw him as her last chance of security. Sexy young-looking Audrey led him to the altar without a whimper.

Now he forgives her much – her shopping sprees, her flounces, even foisting Brian Tilsley on him as a stepson-in-law. After his heart attack in 1987 – realistically frightening but over with too soon and rarely mentioned since – theirs seems to be a marriage of true affection. What brought on the heart attack, it was suggested, was partly his portliness (too many fry-ups, pies and pints) and partly politics. Alf was an Independent local councillor, in an area where Independent means Tory. The obvious enemy of leftie Ken Barlow, he was shocked when in May 1987 Ken's wife Deirdre defeated him in the elections. She was a friend. This was betrayal. And, should his worries ever disappear, Percy Sugden or some other awkward customer could always browse around his shelves and wind him up to blustering-point.

Bryan Mosley, who plays solid stodgy shopkeeper Alf Roberts, has a constant battle with his waistline. He loves good food and good living. Just as well that Alf wouldn't be Alf without Bryan's Friar Tuck girth and double chins. Surprisingly, he was a stunt arranger and fight chor-eographer in his lithe young days twenty years ago. He's still a skilful fencer, who helped found the Society of British Fight Directors, and has arranged sword-fights for Tom Courtenay and worked with Terence Stamp on *Far from the Madding Crowd*. He presents his own stage-fencing awards at RADA. Bryan studied at the Northern Theatre School, and early credits included 'The Saint' and 'The Avengers', with parts in such highly praised films as *Charlie Bubbles*, *A Kind of Loving* and *Get Carter*. There were also several comedy rôles before he joined the regular cast of 'Coronation Street' in 1968.

Born in Leeds, he now lives with his wife Norma on the edge of the moors in Shipley, Yorkshire. They have six children. Quite unlike Alf, Bryan has always known how to enjoy life. He was a drinking pal of co-star Peter Adamson until Peter's heavy drinking alarmed him. And he was never afraid to thump on the producer's desk when he disliked the script – to little avail, he admits. When Norma had breast cancer a few years ago, Bryan seriously considered quitting the rôle. 'I'd often thought perhaps I should pack it in and go off to do Shakespeare on stage. But . . . well . . . here I am.'

One clash with the producers he *did* win was to drop a proposed row between Alf and Renee shortly after their honeymoon. He hated the way Peter Adamson's character was killed with shame, asked not to be involved in those scenes but was overruled. He says that scriptwriters do, however, respect the fierce loyalty and devotion actors have for their characters. 'For Alf I have stressed he should never be seen cheating or selling someone a duff product. It wouldn't wash,' he said. Bryan always wanted Alf to have a full-blooded romance. A little later, the writers paired him with common-as-muck Audrey.

Audrey Roberts is the scatty blonde hairdresser, mother of Gail Tilsley and wife of grocer Alf Roberts in 'Coronation Street'. She owns one of the least-lovely squawks in soap. But she can be fun – especially when she leads her tubby partner a dance with shopping sprees and barmy business ideas. One of the best was when Alf was forced to pay out damages on Audrey's behalf when she turned Hilda Ogden's hair orange on the eve of a local dance. Audrey, played by Sue Nicholls, hurtles round in Alf's treasured sports-car. She has crashed it once, but he will forgive her anything. They hardly seem well matched; she's as flighty as he is staid. But she's aware of her fading looks, and after numerous abortive liaisons with 'no-good' men she knows a good billet when she sees one. Before she charmed Alf to the altar, she had a good look at his business assets and declared him 'sound'. In her past, we're told, she was good-time Aud. Gail had no father and not much of a ma. When Gail split with her Brian over the pregnancy which her affair with Ian could have caused, Audrey was a brick. Mother-hen-like (or interfering-busybody-like – suit yourself), she contacted Ian in Australia and advanced the drama no end. Ian arrived to do the decent thing. Audrey sensibly told Gail to grab this good prospect while she could. Later, when the baby was born, Audrey did a nice line in coochie-coos, minding the infant and Nicky, her grandson, while Gail worked in the café. Early in 1988, Audrey surprised everyone, including herself no doubt, when she developed a long-lost son in Canada and disappeared to visit him, missing Gail's second wedding to Brian. (The reason had been the actress's sudden illness.) As a contrast to pursed-lipped Ivy, Gail's mother-in-law and the other grannie, Audrey's a must.

Sue Nicholls hides her rich County pedigree skilfully behind the flat Northern vowels that she projects on screen as Lancashire Audrey.

Daughter of Lord Harmar-Nicholls, the Tory peer, Sue was educated at boarding school and almost embarked on a languages career using her skills in French and German. After graduating from RADA, Sue had a long spell in rep. She made her television soap début as Marilyn Gates in 'Crossroads', but she's well remembered for her skill in comedies, particularly the Leonard Rossiter series 'The Fall and Rise of Reginald Perrin'. 'I think there's something about me that makes people laugh,' she once said.

Off-screen willowy Sue is as well spoken, beautifully dressed and suave as the man she lives with: Mark Eden, the 'Coronation Street' actor who plays Alan Bradley. At the time when her character was becoming a cooing grandma, Sue revealed her private sadness that she was unable to have children. She'd have liked nothing more than to be a housebound mum. 'I'm stupidly unambitious. I'd love never to work,' she said.

Renee Roberts, née Bradshaw, bought the corner shop in Coronation Street from Blanch Hunt in 1977. Annie Walker was livid when she applied for a licence to sell liquor. After a broken engagement, Renee, played by Madge Hindle, married Alf Roberts. In 1980, Alf and Renee contemplated selling the shop and went off to a country pub to celebrate. Renee drove home but stalled the car at traffic lights. Alf leaped out to take over the wheel, but the car was hit by a lorry and Renee died in hospital.

Madge Hindle is a fine comedy actress who has starred in 'Nearest and Dearest', 'The Two Ronnies', 'Porridge' and 'Open All Hours'. Blackburn-born Madge, a pal of Russell Harty, became mayoress of her home town in 1967 when her mother was elected mayor. She was originally trained as a teacher, but her close friend Alan Bennett invited her to appear in his television series 'On the Margin', and she has not stopped working.

Ena Sharples was the scowling old battle-axe, the feared matriarch of Coronation Street for eighteen years. Ena was magnificently portrayed by veteran actress Violet Carson between 1960 and 1978 when Vi retired, partly through ill health and partly because she had had enough of playing the old tartar.

Hairnet rammed tight over her head like a camouflage-net of a tin helmet, Ena charged into battle at the first sign of pomposity and authority. She could deflate old windbags like Leonard Swindley with a single word. She was bossy and brusque, but she was loyal to her friends and kindness itself to people in trouble. She had high principles. Ena, we were told, was put to work in a Lancashire cotton-mill at the age of eight, and later became a tram conductress during the First World War. She lived in Inkerman Street, but when her husband Alfred died she moved into the Glad Tidings Mission as caretaker.

With her old plant-pot hat jammed on her head like Grandma's in the Giles cartoons, she was one of the indomitable trio of old gossips who drank milk stout in the snug of the Rover's Return: Ena Sharples, Martha Longhurst and Minnie Caldwell. She bullied Martha and Minnie at times, but mostly vented her wrath on grumpy old Albert Tatlock. Quite right, too. They could also close ranks, especially against the impetuosity of the younger generation in the Street.

In the early sixties, Ena's stinging verbal battles with Elsie Tanner, on the pavement in full view of passers-by, left viewers gasping with delight. A God-fearing woman who was brought up by strict parents, Ena couldn't tolerate Elsie's sluttish ways. But, as time went on, the women developed a respect for each other which bordered on affection.

Ena nearly died in 1967 when a train crashed over the Coronation Street viaduct. She was buried alive, but the tough old bird emerged with only concussion and a broken arm. Violet Carson died in 1983, but Ena lives on in a holiday haven at St Anne-on-Sea, where she keeps house for wealthy Henry Foster. Perhaps the writers hadn't the heart to kill off the old lady who was loved by millions. Perhaps they simply forgot.

Violet Carson, OBE, who played the Coronation Street dragon Ena Sharples for eighteen years, was loved by millions – but in a different way from the other big stars of the series. Violet was a gracious lady of high principles, proud of her roots. Manchester born, bred, wed and widowed, she had several careers in broadcasting before she retired in 1978 through ill health.

Vi was born in a real Coronation Street type two-up-two-down terrace house in Miles Platting. Her father was a flour miller and her mother an amateur singer. She made her professional début at fifteen as relief pianist in a silent-movies cinema in Manchester. In 1926 she married her sweetheart, George Peplow, a road contractor. He died two years later at the age of thirty. She pressed on with her career, and in 1935 she started broadcasting for the BBC in Manchester, singing comic songs in Lancashire dialect, and even Italian arias. After the war, she became Auntie Vi in the BBC's popular radio series 'Children's Hour'. 'Coronation Street' creator Tony Warren (p.89) was a young actor in a children's play in which Vi was involved, and he remembered the no-nonsense actress whacking him on his bottom because he was making too much noise in rehearsals.

Next came her radio partnership with Wilfred Pickles and a six-year stint with 'Have a Go!', the meet-the-people quiz, a national institution in the fifties. Then, after twenty-five years in radio, she decided to 'have a go' in television at the age of sixty-one. Twenty-one other actresses had tried for the part of Ena Sharples. Violet thought it was a one-off play and wasn't bothered whether the part was hers or not. When the producer said that Ena might be difficult to play, she retorted: 'Don't be ridiculous. I have lived with this woman all my life. There is one in every street in the North of England.' The contract was for five weeks. Within a year one foreign correspondent said she was better-known than the Prime Minister. In 1965 she was proud to be awarded the OBE. At the investiture ceremony at the Palace, the Queen told her: 'I am a most ardent fan of yours.'

Violet Carson, an intelligent warm woman, didn't tolerate fools easily. A journalist who quizzed her about love and marriage was told curtly: 'I think sex is an absolute bloody bore. Why don't they leave it where it belongs – up in the bedroom?' In the same interview, her advice to young girls was: 'Listen to what your mother says, and don't expect too much out of life.'

Once, when Count Basie and his orchestra were blasting out jazz in the next studio, Violet simmered and then exploded in the middle of a scene. Finally, she yelled: 'Stop! I can't take any more.' The programme-recording ground to a halt, until the Count deferred to the 'Duchess' of Coronation Street.

During her eighteen-year spell with the series, Violet commuted to Manchester from her comfortable bungalow in Cleveleys, Blackpool, where she lived with her widowed younger sister, Nellie Kelly. Her indulgences were some jewellery, a mink coat, and she and Nellie immensely enjoyed sea-cruises. At the height of her fame, Vi and her sister took a cruise to Australia where she was mobbed by adoring fans.

In 1978, pernicious anaemia forced her to retire from the series. She was not well enough to join the programme's 1000th-episode celebrations, and was too ill to attend when the Queen and Prince Philip visited the soap's outside lot. In her retirement she enjoyed household chores and was philosophical about Ena. 'She had made me, but she has also destroyed me,' she once said, 'because nobody sees me – Violet Carson – or anything about me.'

The old lady, known to her close friends as 'the Duchess', died in 1983, aged eighty-five. Coronation Street, Blackpool and the nation mourned her death. Nellie said later: 'Vi never thought anything of the exaltation she received. She said she was just an ordinary actress. There was only one star – Coronation Street.'

Jed Stone was the good-hearted unsinkable 'whacker' who became Minnie Caldwell's lodger in Coronation Street in the sixties. Jed, who could sell snow to Eskimos, was played by Kenneth Cope. Minnie called him 'Sonny Jim' and he called her 'Ma'. He was into all things dodgy, from bent fruit-machines to stolen blankets, but he never, ever took advantage of Minnie. The law would like to talk to Jed, but nobody

knows his current whereabouts. If only they had a few nice crooks in it now. . . .

Kenneth Cope is no empty-headed Scouser like Jed Stone, his 'Coronation Street' character. He is a serious stage actor whose credits include a Shakespearian tour with the Old Vic Company. He is a successful television scriptwriter and runs a restaurant in the Cotswolds with his actress wife Renny Lister. They met while making 'Coronation Street'.

Percy Sugden is the interfering old know-all who is caretaker of the community centre. An ex-army veteran, pompous Percy, perfectly played by Bill Waddington, tries to run people's lives in a regimental manner that drives everybody mad. Power-crazy Percy holds forth bombastically on all manner of subjects, but is quick to take offence if people chastise him. He can't take criticism. Ena Sharples would have shot him down in two minutes.

A former chef in the Royal Army Catering Corps, his constant boast is: 'I've made gravy under gunfire.' Percy acts as a kind of unpaid policeman, hurling himself into the Street's Community Watch scheme with relish. Snooping is right up his street. Secretly he fancies Emily Bishop. When she took in Curly Watts as a lodger he was miffed. In May this year, though, he was sacked by the council as caretaker. He was sixty-five. Thrown out of his flat, he bludgeoned Emily into accepting him as a lodger.

Bill Waddington is the genial wisecracking veteran of old-time variety who makes humourless Percy Sugden bearable in 'Coronation Street'. Steeped in stories about the glory days of music-hall, Bill recalls working as a principal comedian in shows with Sophie Tucker, Lena Horne, Frankie Laine and Dorothy Lamour. He mourns the death of his wife Lilian, to whom he was happily married for over twenty years, but lives a very full life. He drives a BMW, owns racehorses and is a tireless worker for charity.

Bill's forty-year career in show business goes back to the time he joined the 'Blue Pencils', the first concert-party recruited from the armed forces at the start of the Second World War. From there he went into 'Stars in Battledress' billed as 'The Army's Number One Comedian'. He still treasures the memory of a Royal Command Performance in 1955. Bill's closest friends in 'Coronation Street' are former music-hall veterans Betty Driver, Tom Mennard, Len Marten and Jill Summers, who plays Phyllis of the foghorn voice. Yes, he really likes her.

Leonard Swindley was the pompous testy manager of Gamma Garments in Coronation Street – a superbly comic character not unlike

actor Arthur Lowe's other television creation, Captain Mainwaring of 'Dad's Army'. Swindley, like Mainwaring, was a puffed-up pillar of the community. A teetotaller, a lay preacher at the Glad Tidings Mission, he set his cap at crumpling spinster Emily Nugent in 1964. She sensibly jilted him at the altar. In 1969 he was summoned to Gamma Garments head office to work for the mysterious proprietor Mr Papagopolous. It was a black day for Coronation Street.

Arthur Lowe, unlike the corseted old windbag Leonard Swindley, was a shy retiring actor in his early television days. A kindly man, he nevertheless declined most press interviews for fear of being misunderstood. He was the first leading actor to leave 'Coronation Street' in the sixties. For him there was 'life after soap' (p.346): great success in other television series – notably 'Dad's Army', in which he played Captain Mainwaring.

Born in Hayfield, Derbyshire, he was in his mid-fifties when he became famous. He had a solid background in West End theatre hits including *The Pyjama Game* and *Call Me Madam.* He loved the sea. His favourite relaxation was sailing his own ocean-going yacht. By the time Arthur Lowe died in 1982 he was one of Britain's most popular actors. He had middle-class middle-aged pomposity licked.

Dennis Tanner, Elsie Tanner's roguish son, led his mother and sister a dance through the early years of 'Coronation Street'. His madcap pranks ranged from keeping a performing sealion in Elsie's bath, to some hair-raising brushes with the law. Dennis was played by Philip Lowrie, but when 'Coronation Street' was originally cast the part nearly went to Kenneth Farrington who eventually played Billy Walker. Work-shy Dennis tried countless schemes to make fast money, including a spell as rock singer Ricky Dennis. He once had a chimpanzee as a lodger, and struck up an affair with a stripper who used a snake in her act and asked Dennis to look after it for her. Elsie found it in a shoe-box. Dennis Tanner married Jenny Sutton in 1967. After a spell in Wormwood Scrubs for housebreaking, he is now trying to make his fortune somewhere in London.

Philip Lowrie was born in Ashton-under-Lyne, the son of a factory foreman. His mother worked hard to finance him through RADA, and he went straight into a West End play with Margaret Rutherford and Peggy Mount. His agent asked him to read for a new television series called 'Florizel Street' – later to become 'Coronation Street'.

Originally Dennis was conceived as a wastrel, constantly in trouble with the police, but the producers thought Philip Lowrie had a real penchant for comedy. But the actor was worried about being typecast in North Country rôles, so he left the programme after just one year.

Letters poured into Granada begging Philip not to leave. A year later he was back, but Lowrie didn't enjoy clowning around. He told friends: 'All I am doing is mucking around pulling funny faces.' He left for good in 1967. 'Otherwise', he observed, 'I shall still be playing Dennis when I am ninety-two.' He isn't. But he isn't doing much else on television, either. (See 'Life after Soap'.)

Elsie Tanner was what was great about 'Coronation Street'. She had three dimensions, few morals and no heart of gold. She was the red-haired sexpot of Coronation Street who shocked viewers with her button-straining cleavage and just-got-out-of-bed look when the series started in 1960. With a cigarette dangling from one side of her large loose mouth and a milk-bottle on the table, she was soap's most successful slut. Part of her huge popularity with viewers was that women could relate to the blousy good-time girl who had to cope on her own and lived on memories of past amours with wartime Yanks who were over-paid, over-sexed, over here, and over Elsie in the 1940s.

Elsie, portrayed by Patricia Phoenix, had a sharp tongue, and as the years went by she became a tart with a heart. Brought up in Gas Street, Weatherfield, Elsie Grimshaw got herself pregnant at sixteen, and the father, Arnold Tanner, married her. Three months later he joined the merchant navy, and that gave Elsie licence to enjoy the war in the big city of Manchester. Arnold returned just long enough to 'father' a second child, Elsie's son Dennis, and disappeared again until he turned up once more in 1961 to ask for a divorce. All this time, Elsie was struggling to bring up two children alone on low wages. She was always a soft touch for men keen on love but low on finances. Wasp-tongue Ena Sharples often chided her about her endless 'hospitality' to visiting American servicemen in the past. Hand on hip, fag dangling, and finger waggling furiously – in an argument, hot-tempered Elsie always gave as good as she got.

When old wartime sweetheart United States Army sergeant Steve Tanner walked back into her life in 1967, it looked as if Elsie's luck had changed. Unfortunately, soon after they got married, they both realised they were trying to live a dream. They drifted apart, and Steve was murdered a year later by another soldier.

Next, Elsie turned down two marriage proposals from Len Fairclough before falling for Alan Howard, a local businessman. But that marriage failed, too, when Alan turned out to be a heavy drinker. Elsie went to Torquay for a spell with new flame Ron Mather. But it was another old love, Bill Gregory, who finally brought some sunshine into her life when he swept her off to run a bar in Portugal's Algarve. She is still there today.

What endeared Elsie to millions was that 'the sexiest woman on television' was gullible: easily conned, susceptible to flattery, emotional, and quick to fall in love. She had twenty-three boyfriends, lovers or husbands in twenty-two years. It was Pat Phoenix herself who called 'enough'. Elsie had not only run out of eligible men by 1983; she had qualified for her pensioner's bus-pass. Pat thought it was time to move on. It was worth recalling one of Elsie's most famous lines. Peering into the mirror one morning after a particularly heavy night out, she retorted: 'Elsie, you're just about ready for the knacker's yard!' Pat Phoenix knew when Elsie's time was up.

Patricia Phoenix fought off all contenders to stay the Queen of British Soap for twenty-five years. The colourful and charismatic actress was described as 'the sexiest woman on television' by then Prime Minister James Callaghan. We followed her marriages, her miseries, her comings, her goings. She was never distant, she was never dull. Flame-haired, full-lipped and busty, she looked a poor man's Racquel Welch, probably too much to handle but a dream at the end of a hard day's work. Like Elsie Tanner, Pat packed an amazing amount of living into her sixty-two years before she died from lung cancer in 1986.

Before she was recruited for the soap in 1960, she knew what it was like to be hard up. Born in Port Humna, County Galway, she went to Manchester with her parents whilst still a tot. Her father was a newspaper reporter but, unknown to the family, he had married her mother bigamously. They were married for sixteen years before the truth came out and he was sent to gaol. Her mother married again whilst Pat was a teenager.

Pat made her acting début in a BBC radio play. It led to occasional broadcasts on 'Children's Hour'. At eighteen she left school to become a filing clerk with Manchester Corporation, acting with the Manchester Arts Group in her spare time. When she did go into rep full-time, she was advised to move south. Pat thought she would take London by storm. 'I did,' she recalled. 'I was a big hit at the London labour exchange.' Times were hard, and she looked back to a seven-year 'starvation' period in her career. Desperate for cash, she agreed to tour in a sex-crime play. She had her hair cut short, dyed it blonde, and changed her name. She also appeared in horror films such as *Blood of the Vampire* and *Jack the Ripper*. 'Well, I was always too big and busty to play an English rose,' she said sensibly.

For a while she wrote scripts for ventriloquist Terry Hall and comedian Harry Worth to earn a crust. Back in Manchester in 1960, virtually penniless, she broke down in tears when she met her mother. Then, Elsie Tanner rescued her from poverty and oblivion.

'I was very arrogant at the audition because I didn't think I had a chance of getting the part,' she recalled. 'When the producer asked me to take my coat off I told him, "You'll just have to bloody well guess, won't you?" ' But Elsie and Pat were smash hits with viewers. The crew of *Ark Royal* made Pat their pin-up, as did the first battalion of the King's

Own Yorkshire Light Infantry. She had an avalanche of letters from men which included an average of four proposals of marriage a week, plus numerous indecent propositions. She was the first British soap star. A year later, her first marriage to advertising executive Peter Marsh was dissolved, and Pat invested her money in a Georgian house with a kidney-shaped swimming-pool, in a smart Manchester suburb.

From now on it was spend, spend, spend. After those lean years, she was determined to pamper herself for the rest of her life. She believed fervently that money was meant to go round. Her wardrobe soon included mink, Persian and sable, 200 pairs of shoes, designer dresses and evening gowns from Paris. Pat could outdress Joan Collins any day. In 1967 she moved to a bigger house in Cheshire, once owned by Wilfred Pickles, with acres of land, a ballroom and a billiards room. Pat's parties were famous – it was open house to all.

Her business affairs and public appearances were now organised by former taxi-driver Bill Nadin, who eventually moved in with Pat. Later on, they bought a pub in Derbyshire. They eventually split up, and Pat moved out. At one point, even limelight-loving Pat, tired of fame. People expected her to be like Elsie. But she always preferred soda water to double gin and tonics.

In 1972, Pat married actor Alan Browning, who had joined the cast of 'Coronation Street' as businessman Alan Howard. It was a showbiz wedding with toppers and tails and Pat in mink, with horse-drawn carriages. But it was a showbiz love. Shaky. Browning had the same problem as the television character he played: he was an alcoholic. On impulse, the couple left the series together in 1973 to try their luck on a forty-three-week theatre tour with a revival of the melodrama *Gaslight*. But they had drifted apart by the time that Browning died of liver disease in 1978. Pat had returned to 'Coronation Street' two years earlier as the prodigal sex symbol. 'I didn't do it for the money,' she said. 'I was homesick for my friends in the programme.' No one disbelieved her.

It was not long before Pat resumed her old romance of twenty-five years previously with Anthony Booth, who was the 'Scouse git' in 'Till Death Us Do Part'. They had known each other as struggling actors long before. Pat made headline news again in 1983 when she suddenly quit the series once more. The fifty-nine-year-old actress had decided not to renew her £700-a-week contract, she said, because she was tired of being Coronation Street's lonely spinster. She told friends that she didn't want to play 'the old woman of the Street'. She was worried that the scriptwriters would run Elsie gradually down. 'At ninety, Elsie would still have stuck two blobs of rouge on her cheeks and gone down the pub and drunk milk stout. I couldn't allow that, it would have destroyed her original sexy image,' she said. So Pat worked as an agony aunt at breakfast-time on TV-am. She joked about being sixty and owning a pensioner's bus-pass. Later she took a rôle as a brassy seaside landlady in the ITV sitcom 'Constant Hot Water'. In a sense Elsie Tanner lived again. But the show was way beneath her. Before a better series emerged, unfortunately Pat made front-page headlines once more. In 1986 doctors diagnosed incurable lung cancer for this sixty-two-year-old woman who had smoked sixty cigarettes a day for most of her life. She fought it with style and humour, but the cancer had already sapped her enormous grit and strength. As her condition worsened, she agreed to marry Tony Booth in a dramatic hospital wedding. As she lay in bed, before the tearful ceremony, the frail star was given the last rites. Soon afterwards she told a friend: 'I'm Mrs Booth now, love . . . but not for long.' Surrounded by flowers and her favourite teddy bears, she drank a drop of champagne and ate a morsel of her wedding cake. Via one last photocall and press conference, Pat told her adoring fans: 'Thank you very much, loves . . . and ta-ra.'

Before she died on 17 September 1986, she had one more show-business flourish up her sleeve. She ordered a 'fun' funeral. A Dixieland jazz band played as her coffin was carried into a Manchester church for a requiem mass, and there was an old-fashioned knees-up for her friends and colleagues afterwards with the drinks on Pat. Fans packed the thousand-seater church, and lined the streets outside as if royalty was being laid to rest. All 'Coronation Street' rehearsals were cancelled, for the first time in twenty-six years. It was a send off for a star. A year later, it was revealed that Pat had died almost penniless, apart from the bricks-and-mortar value of her Cheshire country cottage which she left to Tony Booth. Few were surprised. Elsie wouldn't have done anything as boring as saving her money. And Pat was twice as much fun as Elsie.

Steve Tanner was the old flame from Elsie Tanner's past in 'Coronation Street'. A wartime American GI, he walked back into her life twenty years later. When he charmed her to the altar in 1967, 20 million viewers watched the wedding. United States Army Master Sergeant Tanner (the scriptwriters cleverly retained Elsie's surname) was portrayed by handsome Canadian-born actor Paul Maxwell. Steve swept Elsie off her feet at first, but she soon realised she had married a dream from her past. Their relationship soured, and the marriage was well on the rocks when Steve was involved in a brawl with a fellow-officer. He conveniently died from a fall down a flight of stairs. Elsie was free. Next!

Paul Maxwell was a Winnipeg-born Canadian with film-star looks. Originally trained at medical school, he switched to acting and settled down in America. He did a five-year stint in Hollywood, appearing in 'Bronco', 'Wells Fargo' and 'Highway Patrol'. But he wanted to work in Britain and Europe, so he came to London. He guested in action series including 'The Baron', 'The Saint' and 'Danger Man' before his one-year stint in the Northern soap. Actress Patricia Phoenix, who played Elsie, thought Paul would make an ideal permanent addition to the cast, but he wanted to go off to do other things, so the scriptwriters obligingly killed Steve Tanner off in a fatal fall down stairs.

Albert Tatlock was Coronation Street's chief codger, a cloth-capped Northern pensioner, portrayed by actor Jack Howarth. First seen in the first episode in December 1960, he was cantankerous and argumentative, but was also a do-gooder now and then.

Albert was an old soldier who loved to drone on about the First World War. He could bore at fifty paces about the Somme or Vimy Ridge. A former lance corporal who won the Military Medal, he once refused to ride in Ken Barlow's Volkswagen Beetle because it was a 'Jerry car'. One-time school 'lollipop man', he was the uncle of Ken Barlow's first wife Valerie. The couple lived with him at 1 Coronation Street. When Val died and Ken remarried, Deirdre and her daughter Tracey also lived under Uncle Albert's roof. (There was always something odd about that girl.)

A good neighbour to Ena Sharples, he nevertheless had many a fierce row with her, Minnie and Martha, the other old ducks in the snug of the Rover's Return in the sixties. His favourite tipple was rum, and when it came to free tots he was the artful cadger. Albert Tatlock died in 1984 whilst staying with his daughter Beattie in Cumberland Close, Weatherfield. He was eighty-nine.

Jack Howarth was the complete opposite of grumpy pensioner Albert Tatlock, his character in 'Coronation Street' for twenty-four years. A great practical joker and storyteller, he worked hard and played hard, raising thousands of pounds for SOS, his favourite spastics charity, and indulging himself on exotic cruises and holidays in Cannes accompanied by his devoted wife, former actress Betty Murgatroyd. They spent their weekends at their North Wales bungalow, and lived in four-star luxury in a Manchester hotel mid-week whilst at the studios. In forty years Jack Howarth played only two rôles: Mr Maggs in the long-running BBC radio serial 'Mrs Dale's Diary', and Albert Tatlock in 'Coronation Street'. A former touring player with Northern repertory, Howarth was born in Rochdale, Lancashire, and went to school with Gracie Fields. He began acting at the age of twelve. A founder member of the Northern soap, he clocked up 1700 appearances before he died in 1984. Jack, aged eighty-eight, had been playing Albert, aged eighty-nine. Ever the joker, he said he had great difficulty in playing an older man. His death severed the last link with the original gang of senior citizens.

Bert Tilsley, easy-going husband of wasp-tongued Ivy in 'Coronation Street', used to let his nagging wife do all the shouting – until it came to matters of principle. He put his foot down when she interfered too much in son Brian's married life. Bert, played by actor Peter Dudley, went through the torment of long-term unemployment long before Arthur in 'EastEnders'. When Peter Dudley suffered two heart attacks under the strain of an unfortunate court-case in 1982, he was so incapacitated that the scriptwriters had to devise a way of getting rid of Bert. After injuries sustained in an accident at Brian's garage, Bert suffered a mental breakdown. He was admitted to hospital near Southport where he died in 1984.

Peter Dudley, the Manchester-born actor who played Bert Tilsley in 'Coronation Street', began his working life in a cotton-mill. After breaking into acting in Northern reps, he got his big television chance in 1979 when the Tilsley family – Bert, Ivy and son Brian – bought 5 Coronation Street from Ray and Deirdre Langton. But after three good years Dudley's career began to go downhill rapidly in 1982 when he appeared in court charged with gross indecency with another man. A Crown Court jury failed to reach a verdict, and the judge ordered a retrial. But the strain of waiting, and the adverse publicity, was too much for Dudley. He was rushed to hospital with a heart attack after collapsing. The judge later ruled that he was too ill to face a second trial. Granada stood by the actor and gave him lines to say in camera positions where his physical disability would not be noticed. But he still couldn't cope. He had a second heart attack and had to be written out of the programme. Peter Dudley died in 1984 and, the same year, the character of Bert Tilsley was killed off by the scriptwriters.

Brian Tilsley is the macho-thicko of Coronation Street, the son of Ivy and the husband of Gail. He is touchy, tactless and swaggeringly vain with his bush of blond hair. He is also played (by Chris Quinten) like a man with his mind elsewhere. In his muscles, perhaps. I've suggested he is secretly Britain's first brain donor. It can't have been an accident that for several weeks in 1987 his name on the soap's closing credits was Brain Tilsley.

Headstrong Brian, once a motorbike fanatic, married Gail Potter in November 1979. Now they have two children, Nicky and baby Sarah Louise. Brian's marriage, outside the Catholic faith, upset his mother Ivy, who still has a strained relationship with Gail. It has always been a marriage of ups and downs, and their domestic situation reached crisis-point in 1987 when, with Brian busy at his garage, Gail began an affair with visiting Australian Ian Latimer. Brian tore off, set up with beautiful Liz, insisted the marriage must end. They were divorced but, when Gail met and became close to nice electrician Geoff Singleton, Brian snatched the boy Nicky and took him to the Lake District. Gail was distraught; the nation booed Brian.

On his sudden, crestfallen return, Gail agreed to take him back, and Geoff was shown the door. Brian works hard to make his garage a success, fired by Gail's ambition. But business isn't booming. I suspect people don't take their cars there, frightened Brian's hair could catch in the carburettor.

Christopher Quinten, the muscular ex-gymnast who plays Brian Tilsley, was born in Middlesborough, tried drama school at sixteen, but was persuaded to get a 'proper job' as an apprentice fitter at the local shipyard. Looking back, he says the only thing that kept him sane was his evening work with a local theatre company. At eighteen he tried his luck in London, answering an advertisement in the *Stage* for acrobatic dancers needed for cabaret work. Although he had never done any dancing, he was fit and knew a few acrobatic routines, so the theatre restaurant took him on. Three months later he broke into television with bit parts in series including 'Target' and 'The Pink Medicine Show'. He was recruited by 'Coronation Street' when the Tilsley family was being cast in 1976. Today, Quinten is a thirty-year-old bachelor who loves the nightclub and disco scene and is often seen escorting pretty young women – models, actresses and débutantes. Tabloid newspapers enjoy lurid stories of Chris's love-life, often based on the 'confessions' of these girls. He seems to enjoy press exposure and has taken his shirt off many times to show his well-developed torso for the cameras. He would have been wasted as a shipyard fitter. I think.

Gail Tilsley is the little coper of Coronation Street, the thirty-seven-year-old ambitious wife of garage owner Brian Tilsley. She copes with her bone-headed husband, her scatty mother, her huffy mother-in-law and her job running the café. Gail, played by Helen Worth, is the illegitimate daughter of flighty Audrey Roberts, now married to grocer Alf. Before that marriage, Gail had a stream of uncles, one of which tried to assault her. She bravely bit her lip under her rabbit-like teeth.

Because she never knew her father, Gail was determined to be a homemaker when she got married, and she dotes on her children, Nicky and baby Sarah Louise. She's fiercely independent and will stand no interference from Brian's mother, Ivy. The major crisis in Gail's life was in 1987 when she and Brian split up and were divorced. Brian had neglected her. Gail began an affair with visiting Australian Ian Latimer. Their affair coincided with Gail's second pregnancy, and Brian refused to believe that he was the father of Gail's daughter, Sarah Louise. A tug-of-love struggle over Nicky reached a traumatic climax for Gail when Brian abducted their son for a few days. But Nicky was returned home, Brian acknowledged that Sarah was his own daughter, and the couple began to court each other again. This time it was Brian who wanted to make it legal. Ivy, his mother, wanted a big white wedding, but Gail insisted on a small register-office ceremony. At least she had her own way on that.

Helen Worth, the small honey-haired actress who plays plucky Gail Tilsley, looks like an appealing hampster but is nobody's pet. A shy private person, she lives in London with respected Liverpool actor Michael Angelis and never plays the star.

Born in Leeds, she grew up in Morecambe. Her grandmother ran a theatrical boarding-house in Bradford where Vesta Tilley and other stars of the good old days of music-hall stayed. Helen's birthday treat when she was twelve was a part in *The Sound of Music*. Her parents had taken her to London for the day and discovered auditions were being held. It meant they needed to hire a chaperon for the nine-month theatrical run. After rep in the South of England, Helen picked up a television career which had begun at ten with a part in 'Z Cars'.

Ivy Tilsley is the tut-tutting, arm-folding little fighter who is the shop steward in Mike Baldwin's factory in Coronation Street. Ivy, played by Lynne Perrie, loves to champion the underdog; she may not look happy, but she enjoys waging war on boss Baldwin. As a mother she tries to smother her only son, Our Brian. As a mother-in-law Ivy could be poisonous. Her late husband Bert would have put her in her place. The trouble is Ivy has no one else to fuss over now except Brian and Gail and her two grandchildren, Nicky and Sarah Louise. A devout Catholic, she refused to acknowledge Brian and Gail's divorce, and it was a traumatic time for her until the two got together again. When Brian 'kidnapped' Nicky, Ivy sided with Gail. She may be prejudiced but she's not stupid. Why she puts up with Vera is a mystery. Ivy seems destined for permanent widowhood. When a well-meaning neighbour took her out for an evening or two, a jealous Brian quickly put an end to the relationship. But, at Christmas 1987, Don Brennan, a cheery taxi-driver she'd met on a disastrous 'girls' night with Vera, returned to pay court. In May she agreed to marry him.

Lynne Perrie is the perky pint-sized bottle blonde who plays Lancashire lass Ivy Tilsley. In fact Lynne hails from the other side of the Pennines: she was born in Rotherham, and now lives in Maltby, Yorkshire. The sister of television actor-comedian Duggie Brown, she has spent a lifetime in show business and appeared in television series including 'Queenie's Castle' and such feature films as *Kes* and John Schlesinger's *Yanks*. She is a dynamic cabaret singer, a little belter, who has worked in France, Germany, South Africa and America. She did concerts with Sacha Distel and twelve early concerts with the Beatles. In 1984 she celebrated thirty years in show business. She has a passion for horse racing and owns a colt, Maltby Lass, stabled at Market Drayton. In

1984 she underwent major surgery to correct a defective heart-valve after collapsing on stage. But plucky Lynne was soon back at work, feeling fully fit again.

Sam Tindall is one of the comic codgers of Coronation Street. The persistent suitor of bossy blue-rinsed matron Phyllis Pearce, it doesn't deter the thick-skinned fellow, portrayed by Tom Mennard, that she has eyes only for Percy Sugden. Conversely, Percy and Phyllis are united only in their dislike for Tindall. The result is a comic war of constant insults between this Street trio of jolly geriatrics. Who will accompany Phyllis on summer coach outings? Who will be her formation-team dance partner? Percy doesn't want to know, but Sam is mustard keen.

Tom Mennard is a veteran entertainer – a former Windmill theatre stand-up comic whose current BBC radio series 'Local Tales' has the dry-humoured flavour of Rob Wilton. Tom is a likeable prankster who keeps hampsters, tropical fish and all manner of caged birds (from zebra finches and canaries, to a wydah bird and a cockateel) in his Dorset home. He has a rare Llasa Apso miniature dog called Dougal who has appeared frequently in 'Coronation Street', has its own fan club and personal bank account. Together with Bill Waddington and Jill Summers, who play Percy Sugden and Phyllis Pearce, Tom was involved in music-hall and variety thirty years ago. Originally a bus-driver in Brighton, he wrote scripts for village-hall shows, and his big break came when the late Donald Peers recommended him to the BBC. They signed him up as a stand-up comic. He has appeared in 'Dad's Army' and 'Open All Hours'.

Gloria Todd is Coronation Street's blonde barmaid who clearly enjoyed Shirley Temple films at a formative age. With her long hanging curls, jammy pink lipstick, fluttering false eyelashes and frilly frocks, she brings out the smoothie in Jack Duckworth and Alec Gilroy when she's pulling pints in the Rover's Return. Gloria, played by Sue Jenkins, is probably the wrong side of thirty (I keep trying to work out her age by the rings on her neck), but she is clearly looking for the right man. Neither Drooling Jack nor Oily Alec is he. Nor was Alan Bradley, with whom she had a brief affair until Rita Fairclough did a 'her or me' on him and the poor man dropped Gloria fast. But despite her style Gloria is sensible, cheery and decent. A bit like every woman in the Street, in fact.

Sue Jenkins, the actress who plays Rover's Return barmaid Gloria Todd, first appeared on television as a schoolgirl in 'Z Cars'. Born in Liverpool and sent to drama school as a child, she appeared in the ITV drama series 'The Beiderbecke Affair' with James Bolam then a stage production of *Educating Rita*. She turned down a national tour in this rôle to appear in 'Coronation Street' in 1986. Sue is married to actor David Fleeshman, who made a cameo appearance in the Street as an estate agent trying to sell Elsie Tanner's house. In 1986 the writers sent her to Canada to find her long-lost mother. In fact she was skiving – having a Boxing Day baby, Emily Victoria.

Betty Turpin is the big cuddly barmaid of the Rover's Return in Coronation Street, another sensible Northern matron. She lives on a short fuse. A kindly soul, she's easily offended and she has a sharp tongue at times. Betty, played by jolly Betty Driver, has had a hard life. Approaching sixty-eight – she was born in 1920 – she goes to work only for companionship. She's the widow of police sergeant Cyril Turpin, who died in 1974. She felt ashamed when the locals found out that she had given birth to an illegitimate son, Gordon, who was brought up by her sister Maggie Clegg, not realising that these days nobody really cared. Bet Lynch and Alec Gilroy try to keep Betty sweet. She makes the best hotpot lunches for miles around.

Betty Driver is a cheery lady who has had a long and distinguished career in radio, theatre, records, films and television, with a seven-year spell as a singer with Henry Hall. A child star, Betty got a standing ovation at London's Prince of Wales Theatre when she was fourteen. Archie Pitt, first husband of Gracie Fields, was in the audience and he signed her up to 'double' for Gracie in a touring version of the hit show *Mr Tower of London*. A tomboy with a Lancashire accent, she travelled the world entertaining the troops in the Second World War, had her own show in Australia, appeared in the early Ealing comedies and numerous West End shows before she moved into television. Granada first used her in 'Love on the Dole', and they thought she would be perfect for the rôle of a matronly barmaid in 'Coronation Street'. Sadly, her singing days are over. She used to suffer from laryngitis, and a throat operation has permanently affected her vocal cords.

Annie Walker was the socially superior ever-so-refeened first landlady of the Rover's Return, who made her screen début in the first episode of 'Coronation Street' on 9 December 1960. Haughty Annie (she much preferred her Sunday name, Anne!) was played by Manchester-born actress Doris Speed, who came from very humble family origins and had no side to her at all.

Annie Walker liked to think of herself as Weatherfield's 'first lady', cultured, an intellectual. She cringed at coarse behaviour in the bar, and revelled in conversing with more eloquent customers like university-educated Ken Barlow whom she regarded as her equal. She spoke of herself as a Beaumont of Clitheroe, looking down on her clientele. What they didn't know was that her father was a humble mill-clerk and Annie was a loom operative in her youth. Luckily for her, her husband Jack tolerated most of the airs and graces in the interests of a quiet life. If pushed too far, a stern word from Jack could reduce her to quivering silence. Trained in the ranks of the Clitheroe Amateur Operatic Society in the 1930s, where she once played a 'memorable' Lady Godiva, Annie saw herself as a natural on stage. She determined to become a leading light in the Weatherfield Dramatic Society – whether the producers approved or not. She was Lady Bracknell in *The Importance of Being Ernest* and played the title rôle in *Lady Lawson Loses*.

When Ken Barlow had difficulty organising a float for the Jubilee pageant celebrations in Weatherfield in 1977, Annie offered to fix it with the brewery – on condition that she was allowed to play Good Queen Bess. Unfortunately for Annie, the lorry wouldn't start, and there was an undignified rush on foot to the park. When Bet Lynch's Britannia won a 'highly commended' award from the judges and Queen Bess was ignored, it was too much for Annie to bear. But her proudest moment came in 1973 when then widower Alf Roberts invited her to become mayoress to his Mayor of Weatherfield. She carried off the rôle with great dignity and charm, and was inspired to buy a secondhand Rover 2000 car. Indignant barman Fred Gee was her reluctant chauffeur.

On the credit side, Annie was a loving and sympathetic aunty to wayward Lucille Hewitt after her parents moved away. She patiently indulged the moral lapses of her no-good son Billy, who eventually wrested the tenancy of the Rover's Return from her in 1983. She still mourns the memory of her dearly loved husband Jack, treasuring his wartime love-letters which she keeps tied up with ribbon. Annie was written out of the series because of the ill health of actress Doris Speed. Annie now lives in comfortable retirement with her daughter Joan, who did well for herself – she married a teacher!

Doris Speed, the veteran actress who had played the toffee-nosed Rover's Return landlady Annie Walker right from the first episode of 'Coronation Street', was the subject of a television soap sensation in 1983 when the nation learned that she was eighty-four years old. The production team and members of the cast thought the sprightly Doris was only in her mid-seventies. In fact, unknown to her bosses at Granada, she had retired from one job as an office worker before taking up a new career in 'Coronation Street' in 1960 at the age of sixty. The shock of newspaper revelations about her age, complete with photostat copy of her birth certificate, coincided with a breakdown in health in 1983. After she had collapsed with a stomach illness, she had a long period of convalescence at home and never returned to the studios – except to attend the programme's Silver Jubilee anniversary champagne-party in 1985.

Doris Speed was practically born into the theatre. Mum and Dad – George and Ada Speed – were struggling music-hall artists, on tour when she was born. She joined the family stage-act at the age of three. Flaxen-haired Doris toddled on in her nightie, carrying a candle and singing a song about a golliwog. At five she played the velvet-suited child, the Prince of Rome, in a Victorian melodrama called *The Royal Divorce*. Doris eventually graduated to television via rep, musical comedy and radio. She was the tea-lady pushing a drinks-trolley in the early Granada series 'Skyport'. She had settled for life as a jobbing actress when the chance to audition for 'Coronation Street' came along. 'Until then I thought I was going to be another theatrical has-been.' Even then, she did not recognise the scale of the opportunity. She was doing a play in Bristol when the call came. She turned down the audition twice before her agent warned her that she would regret it all her life if she didn't turn up. What she didn't know was that 'Coronation Street' creator Tony Warren had written the rôle especially for her. He remembered her work from a BBC radio 'Children's Hour' play they once did, and he was impressed.

Granada chiefs, and viewers, loved Doris's interpretation of Annie Walker, which she had based on her aunt Bessie, who used to lead the family in Christmas charades – complete with withering look. Despite her instant stardom Doris, a lifelong socialist, remained cautious in her private life, choosing to carry on living with her elderly mother, Ada. The old trouper had a dreadful knack of putting her down from time to time just in case television fame ever went to her head. Once, she told Doris: 'I am eighty-seven-years-old, but thank God I never looked as old as you looked on TV tonight!' Doris refused to speak to her for four days after that.

When her mother finally died in her nineties, Doris lived on alone in Manchester, and it was that fact which gave Granada great concern after her breakdown in 1983. With no one to look after her, the company put her into a home for the elderly. Eventually, her health improved considerably, and she continues to enjoy retirement in a small community just north of Manchester at the age of eighty-eight.

Billy Walker, wayward randy son of Annie Walker of the Rover's Return, is the fly boy of Coronation Street. He has a quick eye for a fast profit. When Billy, played by Kenneth Farrington, makes his periodic visits to the Rover's it usually spells trouble, from late-night drinking sessions that put him in bad odour with the brewery to shady money-making deals. His 'flings' include Bet Lynch and Deirdre Barlow – before she married Ken. The last time he ran the Rover's, in 1985, he was under suspicion of selling his own booze instead of the brewery's. When Billy left the Rover's in 1985 – Annie Walker had already left the scene – it severed a fifty-year family association with the pub. Billy now lives in Jersey.

Kenneth Farrington is a Jack-of-all-acting-trades. After RADA, he appeared in dozens of television series and has tried his hand at most jobs in every acting medium. He has been player, producer, director and manager in his time. His visits to Coronation Street over twenty years have been fleeting. As soon as Billy got into hot water, Ken was off to play something else. Since his television mum, Annie Walker, has long retired from the series, his appearances in the Street are likely to be more scarce.

Jack Walker

was introduced as the affable easygoing landlord of the Rover's Return when 'Coronation Street' began in December 1960. A popular father figure in the Street, Jack, portrayed by actor Arthur Leslie, was a good listener to people's problems. 'Straight man' to his acerbic wife Annie, his mission in life was to ride her cutting, condescending comments and scotch her perpetual schemes to turn the Rover's into a hostelry for a better class of clientele. Once, she tried to introduce a Cocktail Hour amidst the meat pies and old ale. Sensible Jack talked her out of it. A model of self-control, on those rare occasions when he did blow his top even Annie was reduced to silence. The whole Street mourned him in 1970 when Jack died on a visit to see his daughter Joan in Derby. The scriptwriters, thrown into turmoil when the actor died suddenly, were forced to write out his character. There could be no question of recasting Jack Walker, pillar of the first decade of 'Coronation Street'.

Arthur Leslie, the bespectacled white-haired actor who couldn't sound his 'r's, was well loved by fans and fellow-stars as the cheery character he played for ten years: Jack Walker, first landlord of the Rover's Return in Coronation Street. Born into a show-business family – Leslie's actor parents were on tour in Newark, Nottinghamshire, when he was conceived – he spent most of his theatrical career in Lancashire, and until he was sixty he worked solely in live theatre.

When genial Arthur died suddenly on holiday in 1970 at the age of seventy, hundreds of viewers flocked to the funeral. Scriptwriters were left with a huge hole to fill. Jack was part of a great 'double act' developed by himself and accomplished actress Doris Speed who played his other half in the programme: haughty Annie Walker. Annie was to soldier on alone in the Rover's for another fourteen years, but Jack's photograph remained prominent on her living-room sideboard.

Curly Watts,

blinking behind unlovely specs, is the twenty-four-year-old 'egghead' dustbinman who was Eddie Yeats's mate when he first appeared in 'Coronation Street'. Continuing his association with wastrels, he then formed a dubious business partnership with Street yobo Terry Duckworth. They collected secondhand furniture and assorted junk, storing or reselling it from Len's old yard. Later they sold cleaning items door to door, posing as hard-up students. Called Curly because of his straight hopeless hair – he looks like an electrocuted cat – Watts is played by Kevin Kennedy. He lodged with Emily Bishop, who insists on calling him by his Sunday name: Norman. She wants him to get a white-collar job, but he fidgets at the thought of working in an office.

Curly has eight 'O' levels and two 'A' levels, but he turned down university in favour of hard cash. Tongue-tied with girls, he devotes his spare time to his telescope and astronomy. When Terry ran off with his pal's wife, Linda, in 1987, never to return, Curly decided to change his life. Emily was delighted when he resumed his studies – a business course at the polytechnic. So far, Mike Baldwin is not quaking from the fear of competition. At Easter this year Curly lost his virginity. So did Coronation Street, in a sense. The flat above Alf's shop became vacant when Sally and Kevin Webster moved into Hilda's house. Curly applied. Shirley Armitage (Lisa Lewis), a machinist at Baldwins, applied. They moved in together. He's white, she's black. The sexual revolution and racial prejudice were discovered at last in the same week. Alf mythered and blustered. Shirley's mum worried. But the Curly–Shirley hurly-burly was played for laughs. Curly quivered getting into bed the first night but Shirley was gentle with him.

Kevin Kennedy graduated from Manchester Polytechnic Theatre School, though he wanted to become a rock-music star. (Well, you don't *have* to look like Elvis, though. . . .) He played guitar with several groups around Manchester, and still hopes. He once lived in Spain, paying for board and lodgings with impromptu guitar recitals in local restaurants. Kevin's stage rôles include a part as Warren Mitchell's son in the Greenwich Theatre production of *Ducking Out*. Before he joined 'Coronation Street', he made his television début as a punk rocker in BBC's 'Hinge and Bracket'.

Kevin Webster is the young car mechanic in Brian Tilsley's garage. He always looks cheerful. This may be due to a constant tickle from the small hairy caterpillar under his nose. Kevin, played by Michael Le Vell, is the sole survivor of the Webster family who moved into the Street and bored viewers. Kevin's father and sister were moved south. In 1987, Kevin married pretty Sally Seddon despite competition from Terry Duckworth, who was bigger and brasher. (Maybe that's why he's smiling.) After sharing digs at Hilda Ogden's, the love-birds commandeered the flat over Alf Roberts's shop. When Brian and Gail's marriage went on the rocks, Sally tried to talk Kevin into buying the garage, but he had neither the nerve nor the experience. Cautious by nature, he is still learning about the traumas of married life.

Michael Le Vell, the twenty-three-year-old Lancashire actor who plays Kevin Webster, joined the cast of 'Coronation Street' in 1983. Michael began acting at school and went on to play the leading rôles in *Kes* and *Joby*. His real name is Michael Turner, but there is another actor with that name so he adopted his mother's maiden name, Levell, and split the syllables to make it look different. Michael is married to Jeanette Beverley, who played Sharon in the BBC sitcom 'Sharon and Elsie'. In May this year he decided to leave the soap, fearing he'd become typecast.

Sally Webster, née Seddon, is the fresh and pretty blonde wife of young garage mechanic Kevin. Sally, played by Sally Whittaker, is an utter charmer now but she started as a silly flirt sulking over landlady Mrs Ogden's house rules. But when she flutters her eyelashes at husband Kevin or grocer Alf Roberts, she can wheedle anything she likes out of them. It worked to get her a job with reluctant Alf, and the tenancy of the flat above his shop. A natural home-maker, she is ambitious for herself and Kevin and is always trying to push him further on.

Sally Whittaker, the pert blue-eyed blonde who plays Sally Webster, was born in Oldham, Lancashire. Aged twenty-three, she began her acting career with the Metal Mickey Road Show and then toured Canada and America with a London music-hall company. In 1985 she made her television début in 'Juliet Bravo' as a sixteen-year-old heroin addict. She played another teenager in Granada's twice-weekly serial 'The Practice', which led to a regular rôle in 'Coronation Street' in 1986.

Eddie Yeats is the burglar turned binman who should never have been allowed to finish his sentence in Coronation Street. He arrived in 1974 on parole from Walton gaol, a 'mucker' of Jed Stone with whom he'd once shared a cell. Looking like a badly made suet pudding, with a silly laugh and a daft gap-toothed grin, fat Eddie was the perfect mate for big Oggy – work-shy Stan Ogden – and a perfect 'burden' for Hilda when he became her lodger. He had, of course, a heart of gold.

Eddie, played by Geoffrey Hughes, had a dodgy start in the Street. Whilst helping Stan on his window-cleaning round, he earmarked a couple of houses for burglaries. After another six months in the nick, though, he declared his intentions to go straight. While others rejected him, Stan and Hilda took him into their home as a permanent lodger – the likeable son they would have preferred to their awful offspring Trevor. It was Eddie who affectionately dubbed Hilda 'Mrs O'. Eddie married his wife Marion after they met on a blind date. She had introduced herself over the airwaves as 'Stardust Lil' during his flirtation with CB radio. When Marion became pregnant, the Yeatses moved to Bury to set up home near Marion's mother, who suffered from ill health. They still live there. At the end of 1987 when Hilda lay in hospital following the mugging by burglars at the Lowther house, Eddie materialised at her bedside, still gap-toothed and giggling. Logically he should have been handcuffed then and there, made to move back into Hilda's number 13. But Geoffrey Hughes valued his freedom and made only a couple of appearances.

Geoffrey Hughes is the gawky gap-toothed sixteen-stone Liverpool actor who played Eddie Yeats and dovetailed in so perfectly with 'comedy duo' Stan and Hilda Ogden in 'Coronation Street' in 1974. Hughes has always remained serenely untroubled by his girth. He believes there will always be employment for fat actors, whereas the slim good-looking ones will wear and be short of work. After rep in Stoke on Trent and appearances in West End productions including *Maggie May* and Colin Welland's *Say Goodnight to Grandma*, he was a slobbish squaddy in two films, *The Virgin Soldiers* and *The Bofors Gun*. With his lived-in features, and Scouse accent, he was a gift to producers of 'Z Cars', 'The Likely Lads' and 'Curry and Chips'.

Geoff and his wife Susan live in a thatched house near Peterborough. He revels in country life and is often invited by local farmers to shoot game and rabbits. He left the Street because he wanted to explore new acting opportunities. But it was his love of the countryside which made him say no to a long-term contract offered after his brief 1987 return. He couldn't face the weeks in Manchester out of green wellies.

'Coronation Street' was a soap training-ground for many stars.

Diana Davies, now Mrs Bates in 'Emmerdale Farm', had a spell in 'Coronation Street' in 1972 as Norma Ford, a new assistant in Maggie Clegg's corner shop.

Arthur Pentelow, Mr Wilks of 'Emmerdale Farm', played George Greenwood, an old friend of Hilda Ogden's in 'Coronation Street' in 1971.

Peter Dean, Pete Beale in 'EastEnders', played haulage contractor Fangio Bateman in 'Coronation Street' in 1980.

Stan Stennett, Sid in 'Crossroads', played Norman Crabtree, Hilda Ogden's brother, in 'Coronation Street' in 1976.

'A COUNTRY PRACTICE'

'A Country Practice' is where Aussie doctors, vets, policemen and caring country folk discover and overcome all the most sensational social problems of the 1980s. As warm-hearted (and corny) as 'The Waltons', the formula has worked with great success for seven years, making it Australia's most watched television show in two hourly episodes a week and a favourite with afternoon audiences here.

James Davern created it as an antidote to the often violent police shows popular in the late seventies on Australian television, believing that viewers might tire of the sight of people who shot each other and go for those who helped each other. He wrote in every contentious medical problem around: euthanasia, abortion, VD in schools, teenage pregnancy, heroin addiction, brain death. Then he developed strong women characters: a female vet who didn't really need a man (but got several, of course), an independent-minded woman doctor and a town busybody. Then he added liberal rounds of romance.

'The glossy American soap operas had just started to arrive here,' he told me. 'I saw that the American dream – to be rich, powerful, drive big cars and wear fancy dresses – wasn't the same as the Australian dream. Ours is to get out of the rat race, own a bit of land and be your own man. I made my show for and about people with those ideals.'

His small company, JNP, sold the idea to Channel 7 (the station that was to start then stop 'Neighbours'), and viewers took slowly but firmly to the cheery souls of Wandin Valley (actually Windsor, on the outskirts of Sydney) while critics and judges of Australia's Logie Awards were quick to applaud.

The characters include Wandin Valley's GP, Dr Elliot (Shane Porteous), the Sydney surgeon, a recovered drinker who'd made a tragic mistake that cost a life; Vicky Dean (Penny Cook), the beautiful practical vet who married Dr Simon Bowen (Grant Dodwell), Dr Elliot's partner;

Maggie Sloan (Joan Sydney), the matron of Wandin Valley Bush Hospital – a woman who's as tough as goat's knees; plodding policeman Frank Gilroy (Brian Wenzel); Esme Watson (Joyce Jacobs), the busybody with the heart of gold; wacky Shirley Dean (Lorrae Desmond), Vicky's mum and the sister at the Wandin Valley Clinic; and madcap animal-loving farmer's wife Molly Jones (Anne Tenney), who developed leukaemia and died.

Amidst the laughter and tears, 'A Country Practice' celebrates the same traditions as 'The Waltons' and all the country soaps between. But the plots are often unpredictable. The wedding of Vicky the vet and Simon the doctor was a much heralded high spot but, as the guests assembled, the bride was operating on an injured horse in a farmer's field with the groom acting as anaesthetist. In later episodes an Aboriginal fruit-picker was seen in a drunken scrap and treated with coolness and prejudice at the hospital. And when Molly gave birth to her daughter feminists were interested to note her irritation with patronising male doctors. And, amazingly, in the important relationship between lovable Shirley and Frank the policeman he does the cooking – she won't. Women's Lib came to Wandin, and nobody noticed.

'CROSSROADS'

Since 1964, any comedian short of a quick laugh could always rely on mothers-in-law, seaside landladies – and 'Crossroads'. 'Did you hear about the actor who was sacked from "Crossroads"? He kept remembering his lines!' 'My wife's never been happy wherever we've lived. We've moved more than the sets on "Crossroads"!' 'My mother-in-law's really fat. Her thighs are as thick as Benny in "Crossroads"!' And so on. Radio Rentals even came up with a television commercial for a video machine that promised: 'It can take sixteen episodes of "Crossroads" (if you can!)'.

Like no other, this soap has been a target. It never failed to provide its many critics with ammunition. Some of the acting would have disgraced the humblest of village halls; many of the plots were so farcical they could have been written in a bad dream, and much of the dialogue was pathetic – like the hackneyed arresting line once used by a policeman to Benny: 'Come along now, lad. Let's be 'aving you.' Even the cast used to complain about some of the things they had to say. Max Wall, who'd been around a bit before he appeared in it, described the experience as 'Dreadful, just dreadful'.

Characters disappeared for ever without explanation. Others would go missing for months on end and would always be in the next room, on the other end of the phone; or, better still, just their back leg would be seen going out of the door. Non-speaking extras, terrified of making a sound (the producers would then have had to pay them more), would spend an entire scene shaking their head frantically like nodding dogs in the backs of Cortinas.

In defence of 'Crossroads', particularly in the early years, the budget was low and the workload punishing. The show was virtually done live. Actor Anthony Morton, who played chef Carlos Raphael for the first three years of 'Crossroads', recalls: 'It was all done on videotape, but

150

only very rarely was there a retake. They wanted it all done in one fell swoop. If you had to do a scene over again, you felt as if the Sword of Damocles was hanging over your head.' Even in the eighties, four programmes were recorded each week. Actress Clare Faulconbridge suggested that 'Crossroads' should have been shown with subtitles explaining that to produce two hours of television drama in a week from scratch was a near-miracle.

THE HISTORY

The first episode of 'Crossroads' was transmitted on 2 November 1964, but the idea had been floating around since 1958. That was when Associated Television's Reg Watson had casually told the station's boss, Sir Lew Grade, how impressed he had been by the live daily serials he had seen in America. Sir Lew said nothing – for six years. Then he asked Watson, an Australian, to produce a daily serial for ATV to be called 'The Midland Road', written by Hazel Adair and Peter Ling and centred on a widow named Meg Richardson and her two children who had turned their family home into a motel. Everyone at ATV liked the story but hated the title. So a Midlands newspaper ran a competition to think up a new name. 'Crossroads' was born. Watson, the producer of 'Lunch Box', didn't have to look far for an actress to play Meg. Noele Gordon, the hostess of 'Lunch Box', was the obvious choice.

'Crossroads' was scheduled to run for thirty episodes – six weeks – but it managed twenty-four years, to become a legend in its own tea-time. In some areas it was screened at 4.35 p.m., bringing complaints from worried parents about this adult serial being shown during what was traditionally children's hour. There was also unrest within ATV. Bill Ward, production chief at ATV, didn't like the fact that critics were already comparing it unfavourably with the company's other soap 'Emergency – Ward Ten'. He wanted to take 'Crossroads' off. Sir Lew wouldn't let him.

An important year for 'Crossroads' was 1967. For production reasons, the number of episodes was reduced to four a week. The big story-line that year was the explosion of an old wartime bomb which destroyed much of the motel. The 'bomb' was detonated by the producers, who were moving to new studios and wanted to feature new sets.

A year later, the London region decided not to transmit 'Crossroads'. Irate viewers sent a deluge of mail. Prime Minister's wife Mary Wilson was one of them. London succumbed, and 'Crossroads' was back on screen there – but six months behind the rest of the country. So characters who were alive and well in Watford were six feet under in Wolverhampton! London finally caught up in time for Meg's wedding in 1975 by means of a special hour-long episode. The wedding episode topped the television ratings. 'Crossroads' was at its peak. It was to go downhill from then on.

In 1979 the Independent Broadcasting Authority criticised the standard of 'Crossroads' and decreed that the number of episodes per week should be cut from four to three – a devastating blow, and one which seemed to panic ATV and its 1982 successor, Central.

The unthinkable happened in 1981: Meg was written out. Jack Barton, the producer of the time, had the motel burned down and Meg sailed off in QE2. The nation fumed and grieved. Charles Denton, Central's Director of Programmes, said the soap could not develop with Meg in place. He wanted to end 'Crossroads' completely but feared it would plunge newly formed Central into an awkward wrangle with the other independent companies. (See below, 'The Executioners'.)

A new-look motel, based on the Golden Valley Hotel near Cheltenham, failed to halt the slide in the viewing figures. Brash young producer Phillip Bowman was hired to cut out the dead wood and bring in new faces. He took charge in 1984, rebuilt the sets, switched the outside filming to Penns Hall Hotel in Sutton Coldfield and sacked the Hunters. The rot continued.

Eighteen months later, Bowman was replaced by former 'Archers' producer William Smethurst. He set out to put his stamp on the show, to move it up-market and, he said, make it 'unrecognisable in six months'. Out went Diane Hunter, Kath Brownlow, Nicola Freeman, Stan Hooper and others. Down went the ratings. A show that once boasted 16 million viewers was now down to 8 million. Before Smethurst's plan was complete in the summer of 1987, Central announced that the Crossroads Motel was to close for good nine months later – a move which, ironically, heralded an increase in the viewing figures. There was to be no reprieve. The 'joke' was over.

It would be wrong to say 'Crossroads' failed – it ran for twenty-four years. In that time it tackled many difficult subjects: alcoholism (regularly), test-tube pregnancies, bigamy, rape, abortion, mental handicap (remember Nina Weill, the Downs Syndrome child who ably played a part?), physical handicap (Sandy Richardson was soap's first paraplegic), adopted children and racism (Joe MacDonald was one of the first black characters to become a soap regular). So why did it finish? There is no doubt that the axing of Meg was the beginning of the end. Her exit alienated its loyal fans, who then had so much more to endure.

The 'Crossroads' epitaph has yet to be written. No doubt the sociologists and the media studies veterans will churn out millions of worthy words in their wonderful jargon. I can wait.

There are only a few certainties. It was taken off because Andy Allen, Central's Director of Programmes, felt like it. It wasn't attracting the sort of viewers the men who stick advertisements in its mid-show commercial break wanted to watch it. The faithful fans were mostly the unemployed, the retired or the lower-paid workers, who begin early in the mornings and are home and viewing by 6.35 p.m. The ABC1 spenders were still on their commuter trains or in their cars. You couldn't flog BMWs to 'Crossroads' fans.

People didn't *like* it as much, even if they continued to watch as a habit. They had felt comfortable with the show's familiar faces. Too many new ones too quickly was a mistake. And of the new ones who was there to *like*? Not Bomber. Not the ghastly Grice family; the long-suffering Mrs Grice was too weedy to care about. Mrs Tardebigge the comic cleaner was a pantomime figure. Charlie Mycroft was a buffoon. No one looked like the nicely mannered daughter the average older woman viewer yearned to see. And, for all the new plans, it remained – compared with 'EastEnders' and 'Brookside' – unstimulating. Compared with 'Coronation Street' it didn't make people laugh. And, with so many changes, it wasn't – as it had been before – relaxing in its basic soppiness. Cynics would say it wasn't bad enough to be good any more.

Certainly our comedians will have to find some fresh material. And that's no bad thing.

THE EXECUTIONERS

No soap has been reinvented as drastically and as painfully as 'Crossroads'. Behind the changes were tough men.

Charles Denton was the toughest. As Director of Programmes at Central, it was he who in 1981 decided to drop Noele Gordon from the cast. He was branded a 'murderer'. He received hate mail by the sackful and dog turds in the post. The senders would have been even more irate had they known that his one real regret was, he told me, that he didn't end the serial completely. He was never a fan of the soap.

He said: 'I had many conversations with Jack Barton, "Crossroads" producer. Central had not long taken over, but I had been doing the same job for five years at ATV. I knew how important "Crossroads" was. I knew Noele. Jack and I were in total agreement. Noele's large overwhelming presence bang in the middle of the series was such that it was fixed in a rigid formula. We despaired of ever changing things. Meg was a monster. I wanted to end the whole show, frankly. I thought it was past its peak. It's a British sin to let things go on too long. I very much regret I didn't bite the bullet then and kill it. But I didn't, Central was only just getting established. I thought it would cause a fuss they didn't need. But I knew Noele's character had to go. I didn't commit sacrilege lightly. Jack Barton couldn't take such a step. It was for me to do – and it had to be formal. I called Noele and her agent to a meeting and told her that all good things have to come to an end. She'd done magnificent work inside and outside the series for us but – she had to go. One person couldn't go on dominating a series. She didn't cry or make a scene – of course. She wasn't like that. She was simply speechless with disbelief. She accused me of murdering the best-loved woman in Britain.

'Later the general response amazed me. There was general furore. I had threatening letters, phone calls – and I can tell you that to receive dog turd in an envelope gives you a very strange feeling. The idea that people feel that strongly!

'I have no regrets about sacking Noele. I was sad, of course, that her leaving coincided with her illness. But I feel my decision was right. Her departure did do what was necessary, although it couldn't save the show ultimately. Maybe the slide had already begun.'

Jack Barton was proud of his 'Crossroads'. In the days he produced it, it was *the* soap – despite all the jokes. Mothers and grandmothers wrote to him begging him to consider the budding actors and actresses in their family for parts. 'Michael Crawford's mother wrote imploring me to give Michael a rôle. So did Gemma Craven's mother,' said Jack. 'To so many older women "Crossroads" was the most important, most glamorous show. They weren't impressed by the Royal Shakespeare Company or the National Theatre. To be in "Crossroads" meant you'd *made* it.'

Jack spent seventeen years working on the Birmingham soap, first as a director, then for twelve years as its devoted and fiercely protective producer. He wanted to leave in grand style after the show's twenty-first birthday. In fact he was despatched with no ceremony at all a year earlier, and to his shock and dismay had no say in the choice of his successor. Phillip Bowman, the man picked to follow him, was in Jack's eyes a misguided youth. William Smethurst, who succeeded Bowman, was even worse.

When the news came that 'Crossroads' was to end, he was dry-eyed. 'It wasn't "Crossroads" they took off. "Crossroads" had been killed off years before,' he told me. 'You cannot suddenly say I'm going to play to an entirely different audience, to ignore the existing loyal viewers who happened mostly to be housewives and elderly people. You can't slaughter the cast and take out all those familiar old friends.'

Jack was involved, however, in the removal of the most familiar old friend of 'Crossroads'. He agreed with Controller Charles Denton that Noele Gordon should be dropped. 'I agreed with Charles that she had to go because we could not have the show revolving around one person. She was a personal friend. I'd worked with her on two thousand to three thousand editions of "Lunch Box" and in the theatre before that. I felt she was frustrated anyway. Since her mother, who'd been her great support, had died, she'd seemed frustrated. She was hurt; of course she was. But I can categorically say that leaving the programme did not kill her. That's just the dramatic sort of thing actors like to say.'

Jack actually enjoyed Meg's leaving. He tried to ensure that the newspapers had no inkling of the story-line of her departure. While filming in *QE2* at Southampton he even wore a fake moustache to throw reporters off the scent. 'I was spotted by a group of journalists, and they asked me who I was. I said my name was Wolfenden and marched past. It was the stage manager's name; I'd plucked it out of the air.'

He positively hated what happened to the soap after he left. 'It was never a chore for me or the people I worked with. We loved it; that's why it hurt when people slagged us off. My aim was to make viewers happy, to help them while entertaining them. After all these years, I still derive satisfaction from the fact that there's a four-bedded unit in a Birmingham hospital for people suffering from kidney disease that "Crossroads" founded. We gave Downs Syndrome children a sense of pride when we showed a child and gave an idea what her life was like. Parents wrote to say they held their heads high after we did that. . . . My successors had a completely different outlook. They weren't interested in the family aspect, the caring aspect. It's all pretty pictures, smart speeches. Smethurst has changed it beyond all recognition. He destroyed all the illusions of the "Archers" listeners by bringing "Archers" actors and characters on to television. I can hardly believe what was done.

'"Crossroads" always had its critics. If it wasn't the media it was the IBA [Independent Broadcasting Authority]. The first time they cut us down from five episodes to four each week because they said they wanted something more cultural in that fifth slot. The cultural addition turned out to be "Opportunity Knocks"!'

Since 1984, Jack Barton has been writing and living in the country.

Phillip Bowman sacked Ronald Allen, who played the second most popular character in 'Crossroads', David Hunter. With him went Barbara Hunter (actress Sue Lloyd) and many others. Bowman, an Australian, then thirty-one, took cameras outside, introduced action and glamour. He was hated for it. The viewing figures rose; *The Times* gave him a good review. But after two years Bowman's affair with his young script-editor Kate Henderson (he was still married, although separated) caused uncomfortable publicity. She quit. He was moved to new projects. They are now married. He delivered the Hunters' death-blow in the elegant luxury of Brown's Hotel off Bond Street. What happened was bizarre, a nightmare for the executioner and the condemned.

'I had no inbuilt prejudices about "Crossroads",' said Bowman. 'I'd directed soaps in Australia. I was there because Ted Childs [Central's drama boss] knew me when he was at Euston Films and I was associate producer on "Minder". I just wanted to do a good job. I took a pack of tapes and scripts to France and decided I had to change the principal character, David Hunter. I flipped through *Spotlight* [the actors' directory] to find a leading lady. I had no favourites in mind. I saw so many people, then I found Gabrielle Drake.

'Once I'd got my queen in position, everything else fell into place. Being an Australian, I knew that once you're on the horse you gotta ride it. You know you'll come out of it covered in shit or glory. I invited Ronald Allen [motel boss David Hunter] and Sue Lloyd [Barbara Hunter, his wife] to tea at Brown's one afternoon. I told them I was going to change the series dramatically and they were not part of my plans. I gave them the prepared speech. Ronald – he's a lovely man. It killed me to do it. He cared incredibly about his work. He sat there that afternoon, white-faced, silent. Suddenly, this loud voice boomed: "My Gaad! It's you, Ronnie." Then: "Is it really true? You're fabulous. My Gaad!" It was a Canadian, a tourist – one of the Rothschilds, it later turned out. He was loaded with parcels and had been fussing about his driver. He was right there with us; he sat down and told us about watching "Crossroads" on cable there. It was just like a set-up. I was cringing, from the worst day of my life. Suddenly he said to Ronnie: "Who's the boy?" Ronnie said I was the producer, and he began congratulating me. I felt like an arsehole. Ronnie behaved like a perfect gentleman, politely talking for what seemed hours.

'Ronnie and Sue clearly didn't want to be left alone. When this outrageous man started pressing them to go out with him, have dinner and so on, they more or less went like children. I remember seeing their ashen faces through the back window of a taxi. . . . It was weird, awful.

'After Ronnie and Sue, sacking the others was easy. I did it without a moment's hesitation. Ronnie was terrific in his last weeks. He worked exactly as always. Sue, too. When they finally left, I gave them some antique vases. It was a very emotional time.'

Bowman also despatched Glenda, Kevin, Paul Ross, Mavis Hooper.

William Smethurst believes 'Crossroads' would be alive and well today had his revolution been allowed to run its course. What killed 'Crossroads' was impatience, he thinks. Had it survived, it would have been called 'King's Oak' and would have been quite different from the old motel saga born twenty-four years ago. So he has regrets. Perhaps he was arrogant. Perhaps he was naïve. But he has no regrets for the bloodshed – the characters he killed, the actors he sacked.

Smethurst put eight years with 'The Archers' behind him when he came in the autumn of 1986 to change corny working-class old 'Crossroads' into a witty middle-class young soap. He declared war with glee, slaughtered holy cows and male stars, too. He changed writers, sets, the music, the name. It should have worked, given time. But the corny working-class old viewers stayed and hated it. The trendy *Guardian*-reading new ones didn't show.

He went ahead with a relaunch of the new look in September 1987 just as his boss, Director of Programmes Andy Allen, announced the time was up. The execution would be total. 'Crossroads' was to die. The time it used in Central's studios – about 20 per cent – could be used better on something new (though no one knew what).

Smethurst, nicknamed 'Barmy Bill', stopped smiling and retired hurt but unrepentant. He said: 'When I was brought in the viewing figures were gently declining, the audience was older than for any of the other soaps and "Crossroads" still had the most awful reputation for shoddy quality. This wasn't really fair, because Phillip Bowman had made amazing changes to the way it looked. The lighting was superb, for example. But it was nowhere near enough. Perhaps I was naïve to think that if I improved the scripts, improved the acting I'd get a higher-quality product and escape the "Crossroads" image. The older viewers became very fretful, and I can't blame them really.

'We had a slump in the summer. We'd had the old characters dropping out at the rate of about one a week. I'm convinced it was the only way to do it. We had some terrific new writers and new characters. But then we did a survey of what newspapers "Crossroads" viewers read. It was depressing. More of them read the *Daily Star*, which was then going through its "Daily Bonk" phase, than the numbers who ever saw any of the quality papers. I realised there was no point in clever funny writing if no one would appreciate it. But we had to try to attract them. We went ahead with our new pub set, our new landlord and our new opening credits and title, "Crossroads King's Oak". We were working in the studios when we heard we'd been chopped.

'Over the next few months the ratings recovered, the audience profile changed, and I really do believe we had a literate amusing programme. If we'd stayed on, we would have been established somewhere between "Emmerdale Farm" and "Coronation Street". We had 11.5 million viewers, for heaven's sake. All right, we were never going to rival "EastEnders" or "Coronation Street", but I think we would have succeeded on our terms.

'I have no regrets about leaving "The Archers" and, no, I have no regrets about firing the actors. I hesitated only once – over sacking Sue Hanson, because she had been there so long. But unless I'd done something dramatic we could never have hoped to lose the old image. As for the others – well, every actor is a freelance artist, paid on a short-term basis. They aren't hired for life. When you end with one you replace him or her with another actor.'

Since October 1987, William Smethurst has been working on new drama projects for Central Television.

THE CHARACTERS

Jim Baines was an aggressive garage mechanic. His wife Muriel was a nervous agoraphobic. But together they were . . . awful. Brummie

Baines, played by John Forgeham, was one of the most unpleasant individuals ever to darken the doors of Crossroads Motel. He had an affair with the tart with a heart Sharon Metcalfe, who could never say no to a handsome man or Jim Baines, and he was even once suspected of attacking good old Vera Downend. The cad. He even won a jackpot on the pools but that only brought him misery, as well as the one he was still married to.

John Forgeham spent years trying to lose his Brummie drawl, but in the end it was that accent which won him the part of loudmouth Jim Baines. 'It was certainly ironic,' says John. 'I had been in over a hundred productions before "Crossroads", but that was the first time I'd ever needed my native Birmingham accent.' John is still a regular on television, invariably in villainous rôles.

Kevin Banks was married to Glenda Brownlow. A painter and

decorator by trade, young Kevin, played by David Moran, went into business partnership with Percy Dobson. When Dobson died leaving massive debts, Kevin took over the housework while Glenda went back to the motel to work full-time. His father Oliver bought the motel garage, and part of the deal was that Ollie had to have an affair with Sharon Metcalfe, the pushy bike of King's Oak. Eventually, in 1984, Kevin, like most painters and decorators, disappeared completely.

David Moran first appeared in 'Crossroads' as a postman back in 1976 before winning a longer part as painter and decorator Kevin Banks. David was born in Birmingham and first met screen wife Lynette McMorrough in repertory at Chichester. When actress Jo Anne Good joined the motel cast as female garage mechanic Carole Sands, romance blossomed between her and David and they set up home together.

Barbara Brady was one of the most caring characters of

'Crossroads'. A writer of romantic fiction, Barbara, played by Sue Lloyd, arrived in King's Oak as housekeeper to Meg's old friend, American psychiatrist Lloyd Munro. Six months later, she became engaged to David Hunter (which suggested that she needed a psychiatrist), and the loving couple were married in 1980. She comforted young Alison Cotterill, who had been made pregnant by David's dreadful son Chris, and then had to provide a shoulder for David himself to cry on when he discovered that Chris was not really his son after all. (Most fathers would have been relieved!) She helped David run the motel for a while before they left in 1985 to open a hotel in Bermuda.

Sue Lloyd found true love in 'Crossroads'. Her on-screen romance with Ronald Allen, who played her husband, David Hunter, spilled over into their private lives, and the couple now share homes in London and California. Since being written out of the serial in 1985, Sue admits she didn't watch a single episode. 'I just couldn't bear to,' she says. Like Ronald Allen, she found the £6 a week dress allowance on 'Crossroads' pitifully small. 'My character Barbara was supposed to be fairly glamorous, but it's not easy to look like Joan Collins on six pounds a week. It didn't even pay for my hairdo. I used to have to borrow all my friends' clothes!'

Born in Aldeburgh in Suffolk in 1942, Sue won a scholarship to the Royal Ballet School at the age of eleven. One of her first jobs was as a dancer with Lionel Blair. She went on to become one of Europe's leading models, adorning the covers of such glossy publications as *Vogue* and *Harper's*. Among her many films were *The Ipcress File* with Michael Caine, *Corruption* with Peter Cushing and *Revenge of the Pink Panther*. Television included 'The Two Ronnies', 'The Avengers' and 'The Baron' before she joined 'Crossroads' as Barbara Brady in 1975. One of the best actresses in 'Crossroads', Sue is also a talented artist.

Arthur Brownlow, played by Peter Hill, was born miserable. He was miserable to his wife Kath. He was miserable to his daughter Glenda. He was miserable to his son Ron. And he was miserable to his son-in-law Kevin. He was still miserable when he was accused of assaulting Iris Scott. And he was miserable when he was acquitted. He was even miserable when he thought he was going to die. When he discovered that his diagnosis had been mixed up with another patient's and that he wasn't going to die, he smiled – but he was miserable really. In 1982 when he was killed in a hit-and-run accident, nobody knew how Arthur felt. But we were all happy.

Peter Hill was the 'Crossroads' misery Arthur Brownlow, the man who was convinced he was going to suffer a slow painful death from an incurable illness. But he was wrong. He died very quickly under the wheels of a car. Fortunately Peter Hill is nothing like Arthur. Born in London and trained at RADA, he taught drama for many years before appearing in 'The Cedar Tree' and 'General Hospital'. Peter was in 'Crossroads' from 1976 to 1982.

Glenda Brownlow was the dumpy daughter of Kath and Arthur in 'Crossroads'. She first worked at the motel as a waitress in 1976 when she ran away from home. She was eventually reconciled with her family and in 1981 married Kevin Banks. Despite the fact that she looked permanently pregnant, Glenda had great difficulty in conceiving and had despaired of ever having children when, by the miracle of modern science, she had a test-tube baby, Katy-Louise, in 1983 at the same time as actress Lynette McMorrough had her baby in real life. Before viewers had the chance to discover if the babe had the same squeaky voice as her mother, Glenda and Co. were despatched.

Lynette McMorrough was delighted to find that her character Glenda Brownlow was pregnant in 'Crossroads' because so was Lynette, and her baby was able to play the part of her screen baby, Katy-Louise. Lynette had married television cameraman Simon Albu in 1982, but it had taken a blind date to get them together even though they had both been working on 'Crossroads' for five years. She was written out of 'Crossroads', along with screen husband David Moran, by producer Phillip Bowman in 1984.

Kath Brownlow was the plump motherly Crossroads Motel

housekeeper who took in all manner of waifs and strays. Actress Pamela Vezey must have despaired as Kath's natural kindness degenerated into madness. Among her less-inspired choices as lodgers were the wayward Iris Scott who had virtually seduced Kevin Banks shortly before his marriage to Kath's daughter Glenda, and who had also accused Kath's grumpy husband Arthur of indecent assault; Arthur's cousin Walter Soper, who turned up just after Arthur's death and proceeded to sponge off Kath; and travelling salesman John Latchford, a dodgy sort, who saw the spare room as a short cut to Kath's heart. Eventually, they all moved out of Kath's life and she remarried, this time snooty teacher Stephen Fellowes. Kath deserved to find happiness, because there could be few worse things in life than being married to Arthur.

Pamela Vezey has a distinctly musical background. Born in Bath, Pam is a trained singer like her mother and has therefore always been in great demand for musicals, including *The Pyjama Game, Oh What a Lovely War* and *The Threepenny Opera*. Among her television credits are 'Public Eye', 'Sounding Brass', 'Grange Hill' and of course 'Crossroads' in which she played the warm-hearted but soft-headed Kath Brownlow.

Adam Chance was the resident smoothie of 'Crossroads'. He had

breathless affairs with numerous women – often at the same time. Among those to fall for his charms were Deborah Crisp, Kate Loring (who was played by singer/impressionist Kate Robbins), Valerie Pollard, her daughter Miranda and Jill Harvey (née Richardson). Eventually after a 'will they/won't they/who cares whether they do or not' scenario with Jill the two married in 1983. They later separated, did a little dithering about reconciliation but remained good friends.

Adam arrived in 1978 to help sort out the motel's financial affairs. He was continually at loggerheads with David Hunter but with Jill's help he bought a half-share of the garage and went on to run the motel's leisure centre in his dinky tracksuit, and you'd *never* have guessed a cross word had been exchanged!

Tony Adams first joined 'Crossroads' ten years before he took on the rôle of Adam Chance. In 1968 he played an estate agent named Perkins who sold Meg's sister Kitty's house. In the mid-seventies he had a running part as Dr Neville Bywaters in 'General Hospital', which endeared him to millions of female fans. In fact Tony was an avid follower of 'Crossroads' while he was in 'General Hospital'.

Tony's feelings about Adam Chance leave little to the imagination. 'I couldn't stand him – he was a rat.' He also has strong views on the show in general. 'It was murder. It was not a show but an assault-course – terribly hard work. The show was popular for a great many reasons, but basically because of the time it went out. It was generally when people were waiting to cook their supper, and an awful lot of them saw it but didn't actually watch it.'

Tony resigned in September 1987 because he felt like doing 'other things'. Three days later he learned the series was to end. When Adam Chance appeared to be something of a wally nagging his leisure-centre staff, in episodes shown later that autumn, one wondered if revenge was being taken.

Vera Downend, played by Zeph Gladstone, ran the local hairdressing salon in 'Crossroads'. An attractive yet lonely woman (perhaps it had something to do with her initials), Vera lived on a houseboat where, appropriately, she went overboard for seaman Gus Harman. That fizzled out, as did Vera in 1977 when the inevitable skeleton – an illegitimate son, Clive Merrow – suddenly turned up.

Zeph Gladstone has little time for acting nowadays. Zeph (it's short for Zephyrine, which means 'gentle breeze') certainly had the wind put up her by the 'Crossroads' producers when they wrote out her character Vera Downend in 1977. But it gave her the chance to pursue other interests and, although she is still on an agent's books, nearly all her time is now devoted to running her antiques business in London.

Nicola Freeman was the attractive Strong Woman that 'Crossroads' needed after Meg went. In charge of the motel only from 1985 to 1987, she crammed a lot of drama into that short time. Played by Gabrielle Drake, this glamorous widow was dubbed 'the iceberg' for her coolness in business. But she soon began to melt. She searched for the mother she never knew and had an affair with married newspaper-boss Sam Benson. There was also the exposure of a past 'bunny-girl' affair with a Lord Wilminster over which her charming stepson Daniel tried to blackmail her. In fact Nicola's family were a right bunch. Her stepdaughter Joanna had to be rescued from a religious cult, and bonehead brother Mickey had a steamy affair with Jill Chance of all people. He was also a hopeless alcoholic. The last straw for Nicola was when her illegitimate daughter turned up. So she went on holiday and sent her resignation in the post, leaving Tommy Lancaster to take over the running of the place. She did pop back later in 1987 – originally to stay and tantalise Bomber, whose wife had conveniently departed this world. By the time she was to begin, however, the death-knell had been sounded on the soap. Gabrielle Drake got back in her fast car and drove off for good.

Gabrielle Drake played Nicola Freeman, the expensively dressed, sophisticated managing director of the Crossroads Motel from 1985 to 1987. Gabrielle, forty-one and married to artist Louis de Wet, made her name in the popular BBC drama series 'The Brothers'. In the early seventies she went topless in the film *There's a Girl in My Soup* and she bared all for the movie *Au Pair*. But she stayed covered up in 'Crossroads'. 'It was a family show,' says Gabrielle. 'I think two buttons undone was the furthest we were ever going to go.'

She was highly paid for her part and well liked by her fellow-actors, and William Smethurst tried and almost succeeded in luring her back in autumn 1987 after she had completed two successful runs in West End plays. Before she re-signed, though, the axe fell on the show. She appeared briefly in only two episodes.

Marilyn Gates was a bubbly Brummie waitress from the early days of 'Crossroads'. Having already toured as a beauty queen, Marilyn packed in her job at the motel in 1966 to become a singer with a pop group. But two years later she underwent a remarkable personality-transformation, first by marrying the local vicar, the Reverend Peter Hope, and then when the original Marilyn, actress Sue Nicholls, left the show and her part was taken over by actress Nadine Hanwell who looked and sounded nothing like her predecessor!

Sue Nicholls nearly played Jill Richardson in 'Crossroads'. The daughter of Lord Harmar-Nicholls, Sue was in rep when the audition came up for the part of Jill. 'I thought I'd stand a better chance if I ploughed my way through the script in a thick nasal Brummie accent,' recalls Sue. 'Very convincing I was – but not for the rôle of Jill. I ended up as waitress Marilyn Gates.' Marilyn's excursion to become a pop singer led to Sue appearing on 'Top of the Pops' when 'Where Will You Be?', a song written by Tony Hatch, who composed the original theme for 'Crossroads', entered the Top Twenty. Sue left 'Crossroads' in 1968, but the forty-four-year-old actress has been in constant demand ever since. She was Reggie Perrin's secretary Joan in 'The Fall and Rise of Reginald Perrin', and for the last few years she has played Audrey Roberts, wife of Alf and mother of Gail, in 'Coronation Street' (p.126).

Janice Gifford met her future 'Crossroads' husband, Brian Jarvis, while she was a secretary at the car-hire firm run by his father Dick. Janice, alias actress Carolyn Lyster, married Brian in 1965. But it was a stormy relationship which ended in divorce and Janice being written out of the show. See, women always come off worst in divorces.

Carolyn Lyster is married to actor William Gaunt. Following her departure from 'Crossroads' as Janice Gifford, wife of Brian Jarvis, Carolyn drifted away from acting to raise her two children. Now she is hoping to resume her career.

Benny Hawkins was the proud possessor of the most famous hat in soaps. Woolly in hat and woolly in mind, Benny, played with considerable compassion by Paul Henry, was the most original character in 'Crossroads'. He even had his own version of English. 'I do be,' he said, helpfully for impressionists. He meant 'I do' or 'I am' or 'I did'. I think. When he arrived at King's Oak as a farmworker in 1975, Benny couldn't read or write. He was slow, dim-witted and totally naïve. Unkempt and doe-eyed, like a Labrador that had fallen on hard times, he was the subject of ridicule by the less savoury members of the community. But that same child-like innocence won him legions of sympathetic fans and brought Benny some devoted friends at the motel. His closest friend was 'Miss Diane' as he called her. She taught him to read and write (after a fashion), and he responded by naming a donkey after her following her sudden death. It was a fitting tribute (if a cruel one by the producers). Benny was very fond of animals, and while he was at the farm he formed an extremely close liaison with a goat called Starry. Unfortunately, once he left the farm, he and the scriptwriters forgot all about Starry. Did Starry end up as the Chef's Surprise at the motel, I kept wondering. Benny had bad luck like others have spots. He was due to be married to a beautiful gypsy girl, Maureen Flynn, in 1977, but she was killed on the morning of their wedding day when she was knocked off her bicycle. When he was left some money, the nasty Josie, who was pregnant by another man, pretended that she wanted to marry Benny. When it all fell through, Benny was deeply hurt. He was then falsely accused of murdering Josie's sister, Lynda Welch, and spent some time on the run. There was even a 'Benny Is Innocent' campaign. Then, in 1981, he was temporarily blinded after being the victim of a hit-and-run accident. Finally he lost his beloved Miss Diane. But it was not all bad news for Benny, for despite his severe limitations he found that a total lack of intelligence was no bar to a steady job at the Crossroads Motel. Luckily the other characters never found out that the dopiest among them actually earned the most.

Paul Henry turned half-wit Benny Hawkins into a national institution. There were those who thought Benny should have been in a national institution, but the vast majority of viewers adored him and sent him woolly hats, his 'Crossroads' trademark, in abundance. All the hats sent to Paul were auctioned for charity, and he always wore the same one in the show that he wore on his début in 1975. The hat was Paul's idea and it helped make him an overnight success. With his natural bulk and one 'sleepy' eye, he needed only a pair of dungarees and the tea-cosy hat. He explains: 'I was working at Birmingham Rep over the road from the ATV studios with the man who dreamed up Benny as a character. He sold the idea to the "Crossroads" producers and recommended me for the part. I turned up at the audition with my weekend stubble, a woolly hat and a simple smile. And Benny was born. I finished rep on the Friday and started with "Crossroads" on the Monday.' Paul describes Benny as 'a child, someone who took each emotion to the limit. People loved him. I never had one nasty letter. Women wanted to mother him, while men liked to feel superior to him.' A renowned joker, forty-two-year-old Paul is absolutely nothing like Benny.

The Birmingham-born actor was heard on 'The Archers' before joining 'Crossroads', and even while at the motel he took six months off each year to do Shakespearian plays and panto. It was one such break that caused Benny's famous six-month disappearance to search for a spanner! Paul is married to Sheila and they have two children. Paul even recorded a song, 'Benny's Theme', which crept into the Top Forty in 1977 but earned him a ticking-off from ATV bosses as the lyrics revealed the outcome of Benny's doomed romance with Maureen. He also got into hot water with Central, ATV's successor, when he tried to sell woolly hats outside their studios. After all, they argued, he was their highest paid star.

Producer William Smethurst hated the character, however, because a half-wit had no place around the sort of swanky hotel he wanted Crossroads to become. Benny's scenes were cut back. Finally he made another disappearance after helping with preparations for Christmas – an episode shown in December 1987. This time he really was lost.

Sid Hooper arrived at the Crossroads Garage as a mechanic in 1982. Sid, played by Stan Stennett, was a kindly chap who had a bit of a problem with gambling but an even bigger problem with his weird wife Mavis who always looked as if she went prowling around graveyards in the dead of night. He and Mave once took in Benny as a lodger, but when Mave died Sid married the scheming Ivy Meacher and they left in 1987 to run a boarding-house in Sidmouth.

Stan Stennett wanted personally to kill off Noele Gordon from 'Crossroads'. A popular Welsh comic, Stan made his acting début in 1970 when he turned up at the motel as deranged GI Harry Silver and held the staff hostage at gunpoint. Stan says: 'When I heard that the producers wanted to write out Meg Richardson [Noele Gordon] I rang them up and suggested: "Why doesn't Harry Silver come back as a hit-man to kill her off?" But they signed me up as mechanic Sid Hooper instead. Perhaps it was just as well as I would have become one of the most hated men in Britain and I'd never have lived it down.' Stan was compère of 'The Black and White Minstrel Show' for a record seven years and now runs a chain of theatres.

Tish Hope ran an antique-shop as well as helping out at the Crossroads Motel. A close friend of Meg Richardson, Tish, played by Joy Andrews, worked her way up to becoming a director of the motel. Tish used to be an actress and, under her stage name of Venetia Dawn, was often recognised by guests. In 1970 she married Captain Ted Hope of the merchant navy. He later had the obligatory affair, but Ted and Tish patched things up and sailed off into the sunset in 1977 and were never heard of again.

Joy Andrews has switched from 'Crossroads' to crosswords. For sixty-seven-year-old Joy, who was Tish Hope in the serial for twelve years, likes nothing better than to solve crossword puzzles at her Chelsea home. Joy first joined the motel in 1965 in a couple of minor parts, but it was when she became Tish two years later that her career took off. Now a widow, Joy also lost her daughter Jane who died of leukaemia in 1975.

David Hunter was the most famously dull character in the history of soap operas. With the charisma of an ashtray and all the life of Sooty without Matthew Corbett's hand, David droned on at 'Crossroads' viewers for sixteen long years. Played by Ronald Allen, David joined the motel as a director in 1969. His voice and manner rarely rose above the funereal, and most of his lines consisted of just one word. Particular favourites were 'Hello', 'Meg', 'Jill' and 'Goodbye'. Occasionally, if he felt particularly dynamic, he would string two together, like 'Hello, Meg'. Of course he had his moments of high drama, although he seemed blissfully unaware of them at the time.

Globe-trotting journalist Kelly stole his heart (and, by the state of him, probably a few other vital organs as well), and in one of the show's most ludicrous plots he became a compulsive gambler for a week in 1977. David had family problems, too. His Uncle Timothy had already been responsible for Meg's son Sandy being confined to a wheelchair, and then his son Chris, who had a Saturday-morning job as an international terrorist, was involved in the death of Meg's husband Hugh. Needless to say, neither of these trivial incidents in any way affected Meg's close working relationship with David. He was also required to produce an instant ex-wife, Rosemary, who was a neurotic, a drunkard and a shoplifter. In a unique display of emotion, David actually hit her once. She later got her own back by shooting and wounding him. All this excitement was probably too much for David (though it was hard to be certain). He settled down to marry novelist Barbara Brady in 1980. To describe him as wooden would bring a libel suit from the Forestry Commission. Suffice it to say he was felled in 1985 when he and Barbara sailed off to Bermuda to run a hotel.

Ronald Allen may be sad that his long-running rôle as David Hunter came to an end three years ago, but at least it will save him some money. Ronnie explains: 'The clothes allowance on "Crossroads" was only six pounds a week. David Hunter was very conscious of how he dressed and wouldn't dream of wearing a suit costing less than three hundred pounds. So for years I had to dip into my own pocket and fork out money for David's expensive suits.'

Fifty-seven-year-old Ronald, whose matinée-idol looks have hardly changed in thirty years, is living proof that there *is* life after 'Crossroads'. He has built up an unlikely youth cult following appearing in new-wave comedy, notably Comic Strip films such as *The Supergrass* and *Eat the Rich*. Ronald said: 'On a recent visit to London, this punk came up to me and said, "Man, you were real cool in *The Supergrass*. Real cool," then he whispered, "I liked you in 'Crossroads', too."'

Although he admits that David Hunter was a pretty dreary character, Ronald was deeply committed to the soap for sixteen years. He has no doubt as to where the programme's demise began. 'The first nail in the show's coffin was writing out Noele Gordon. She had been its mainstay from the start. It was totally unnecessary to get rid of her. From then on, the show gradually went downhill as many of the popular characters were written out.' Before 'Crossroads', Ronnie had a spell with the Old Vic, encompassing *Henry V* with Richard Burton, a six-month stint in Hollywood where he made the film *Hell Boats* and, of course, a much longer stay as Ian Harman with another sixties soap, 'Compact'. Despite his heart-throb status, the actor lived for many years quietly in London with actor Brian Hankins. When Hankins died from cancer, friends were surprised when his friendship with Sue Lloyd, his screen wife, developed into a strong attachment. When the two characters were dropped, the couple left together for America. They now have homes in Beverly Hills and London. (See above, 'The Executioners'.)

Brian Jarvis was one of the 'Crossroads' originals. David Fennell played Brian in the very first episode and stayed in the show for ten years. Brian was Jill Richardson's cousin and the son of Dick and Kitty Jarvis. A morose architect, he married Janice Gifford in 1965 and they had a son, Richard. Their marriage was a tempestuous affair, mainly due to Brian's moods, his heavy drinking and his tendency to kill people. He was fortunate in the last instance, being acquitted of manslaughter after a fight with Janice's ex-lover John King had resulted in the latter's body being found in the motel pool. It was not altogether surprising, therefore, when Brian and Janice were divorced.

David Fennell left 'Crossroads' in 1974 after being in the show for its first ten years, but he hasn't a clue what's supposed to have happened to his character, Brian Jarvis. 'I think Brian's still probably around Crossroads somewhere,' says David. 'He was often referred to.' David has retired from acting now and runs a construction employment agency in the Midlands. He is married with four children. Born at Lucknow in India, David came to England at the age of four. He had a couple of interesting jobs before joining 'Crossroads': namely, assistant to a top London fashion photographer and ... bull-fighter. For some unknown reason, David had always wanted to be a bull-fighter and actually trained at the famous Alicante School. But after being badly gored David admitted ruefully: 'I just didn't have what it takes.'

Tommy Lancaster, known to all as 'Bomber', was a local steak-bar owner who arrived at 'Crossroads' late in 1986 and took over the motel shortly afterwards, changing its description to 'country hotel'. Played by Terence Rigby, 'Bomber' was a blunt cove, not dissimilar to Jack Woolley in 'The Archers'. (Since half the former scriptwriters of 'The Archers' were by then writing for 'Crossroads', it wasn't surprising.) He suffered the standard 'Crossroads' grief of a dying wife, Mary, and also an unruly daughter, Debbie, who seemed intent on running off with a dodgy frozen-veg salesman. At one point another daughter, Lisa, appeared. She, too, dallied with the frozen-veg man among others. By then Debbie was landed with a frozen bun in the oven.

Terence Rigby ran the Crossroads Motel for its last year in his rôle as Tommy 'Bomber' Lancaster. Born in Birmingham, bachelor Terence starred in numerous television and stage productions but is probably best-known for his rôle as taciturn dog-handler PC Snow in 'Softly, Softly'. An ardent tennis fan, he agreed to return to the Midlands and 'Crossroads' on one condition: that he could take time off to be a line judge at Wimbledon.

Diane Lawton was an all-purpose soap character, extremely valuable to the 'Crossroads' producers. Whenever a new character arrived in King's Oak with nowhere obvious to stay, they shared Diane's flat, which consequently became something of an annexe to the motel. This, of course, saved building any new sets. In what seemed like a reciprocal deal, Diane was frequently allowed to disappear for months on end and not only come back to a job at the motel but also be given a better one than she had before. By this unique method, she was able to rise from humble waitress to a middle-management position. Diane's closest ally in the early days was Jill, and sadly some of the latter's habits rubbed off on her. After giving birth to an illegitimate son, Nicky, by film star Frank Adam, Diane married dependable King's Oak postman Vince Parker. Having got her male, she lost him a year later when Vince, discovering that Frank Adam was sending Diane money to support Nicky, divorced her – presumably delivering the papers personally. Worse was to come for Di when, twelve months later in 1973, Frank Adam had Nicky kidnapped and taken to America. In the true spirit of 'Crossroads', she turned to drink and embarked on endless affairs. Her most spectacular coup came in 1979 when she agreed to a marriage of convenience to Chris Hunter, the part-time terrorist who had been involved in the death of Hugh Mortimer, husband of Meg, Diane's loyal employer and friend and the woman who kept giving her those jobs. They later obtained a quickie divorce without, so we are told, ever having consummated the marriage. But Diane was to bite the hand that fed her once too often. When the actress who played her, Susan Hanson, had a row with new producer William Smethurst, Diane suffered an instant brain haemorrhage and died. Callers phoned up in tears, but Diane's only consolation was to have a donkey named after her.

Susan Hanson was second only to Jane Rossington in the 'Crossroads' longevity stakes. Born in Preston in 1943, Sue joined the cast as Diane Lawton in 1966, originally for two weeks. She ended up staying for twenty-one years. Even before she booked in at the motel, Sue had made a name for herself in films, including *A Kind of Loving* with Alan Bates and *Catch Us if You Can* with the Dave Clark Five. Music was to play an important part in Sue's life, for in 1974 she married former Move lead singer Carl Wayne who appeared in 'Crossroads' for a while as Colin the milkman. Sue and Carl have a son, Jack, aged three. During her life sentence on 'Crossroads', Sue managed to tunnel out regularly to do television and theatre work. She once said: '"Crossroads" has given me a good lifestyle. But if I stayed in it all the time I couldn't progress as an actress. The reason I like playing Diane is that the scriptwriters never run out of things to do with her.'

After Sue had crossed swords with new producer William Smethurst, she asked to be paid as much as Gabrielle Drake, about £60,000 a year. The writers came up with a wizard wheeze which gave her a lot more time off than she had bargained for. So, in 1987, Diane suffered a brain haemorrhage and went up to that great reception area in the sky. Sue was miffed at the manner of her exit but found she had a royal fan in the Princess of Wales, who told her a few weeks before her departure: 'I'll be watching when you go.'

Mr Lovejoy never acquired a Christian name during his reign as the pompous chef at Crossroads. The late William Avenell made Mr Lovejoy an aloof perfectionist – when he could remember his lines. A scene featuring only Mr Lovejoy and Amy Turtle used to sound like a minute's silence. There was a shady side to Mr Lovejoy which was revealed in 1969 when he was the victim of attempted blackmail. This concerned some dubious business dealings when he lived in India before the war.

William Avenell once summed up his career thus: 'If you name stars, I've worked with 'em.' William, who is now dead, was born in South Africa in 1910. The son of a soldier, he made over 2000 appearances in plays, musicals and pantos in Birmingham alone. But to most people he was best remembered as Mr Lovejoy, the arrogant chef in 'Crossroads'.

Doris Luke, the sour-faced but soft-hearted spinster of 'Crossroads', first appeared in 1978 as housekeeper at Ed Lawton's farm. Doris was probably untouched by man – but not by goat. For Benny's pet Starry once ate Doris's best straw hat – an incident which did not, happily, prevent her from becoming good friends with Benny. If people's looks reflect their jobs, it was quite appropriate for Doris to become a vegetable cook at the motel. During that time, she caused a stir by going to the ballet with another lonely heart, chef Shughie McFee. Her sad existence deteriorated when an old flame, Tom Logan, turned up at the motel in 1982. But Doris was to be denied happiness. As she was to marry at last, he died. I'm afraid Doris then went a bit loopy. She wandered off with Glenda Banks's baby for a time. She was not a candidate for soap psychiatry and eventually drifted away from King's Oak for good in 1985.

Kathy Staff is best-known as battle-axe Nora Batty from the BBC comedy series 'Last of the Summer Wine', the woman whose wrinkled stockings put obscene thoughts under the woolly hat of Compo, the show's geriatric delinquent. But Kathy is just as fond of Doris Luke, whom she played in 'Crossroads' for seven years. The Manchester actress says: 'As many people knew me for Doris as they do for Nora. I loved being in "Crossroads" and I had a lot of sympathy for poor Doris.' Kathy actually first came to 'Crossroads' in 1971 as Miss Dingwall. Now aged sixty, Kathy is married to a maths teacher and they have two grown-up daughters. She once trained as a shorthand typist but says: 'Even when I was a little girl, I dreamed of being an actress.'

Shughie McFee was for three years the Invisible Man of 'Crossroads'. Having been a regular in the show for ages as the irascible Scottish chef, Shughie, played by actor Angus Lennie, became referred to but never seen. The reason for his disappearing act was simple: the producers had dismantled the kitchen set. Thus we could hear that Shughie had flambé'd a new waitress, danced the hokey-cokey in a giant cauldron of asparagus soup or made a full-scale model of the motel using only pineapple chunks and gherkins, but we never saw any of it.

Angus Lennie can be seen on most Sunday afternoons in the living-rooms of Great Britain. For the fifty-eight-year-old Scot who played chef Shughie McFee in 'Crossroads' made cameo appearances in endless films, among them *Tunes of Glory* with Alec Guiness and John Mills, *633 Squadron* and *The Great Escape*. 'I seemed to get a lot of forces rôles for the cinema,' says Angus, 'which was a far cry from how I started out in show business – as a tap dancer at the age of fourteen!'

Vince Parker was the genial postman and part-time barman at Crossroads. Played by Peter Brookes, he married Diane Lawton, baby and all, in 1971. He later divorced her, but this was a costly error as Diane stayed in the show until 1987 whereas Vince immediately disappeared off the face of the earth.

Peter Brookes opted out of acting completely after leaving 'Crossroads' and his rôle as postman Vince Parker. These days he teaches French at a school in Birmingham.

Carlos Raphael was Crossroads Motel's volatile Spanish chef from 1964 to 1967. He arrived by mistake. Motel-owner Meg Richardson had asked an agency to send an English chef, but a mix-up brought Carlos instead. Played by Anthony Morton, Carlos left Crossroads to return to Spain where he was killed in a fire, heroically trying to save some trapped children. The news of his death was relayed in a letter to his beloved wife Josephine (pronounced 'Hosayfeena') who still worked at the motel.

Anthony Morton was the temperamental Spanish chef Carlos Raphael, yet he was born and bred in Birmingham, didn't speak a word of Spanish and couldn't tell paella from pizza. Tony, now a burly fifty-three-year-old bachelor, had been cast as villains in programmes such as 'The Saint' and 'No Hiding Place' before he shot to fame as Carlos. Since he left the motel in 1967, he has rarely been idle, appearing as a gangster in the Mick Jagger film *Performance* and starring in plays all over the country.

Jill Richardson had the distinction of uttering the first words ever spoken on 'Crossroads' when in 1964 she spoke the beautifully written line: 'Crossroads Motel. May I help you?' Unfortunately, that was just about the only thing Jill got right over the next twenty-four years as she staggered from crisis to crisis. Played by Jane Rossington, Jill was Meg's daughter. She had one weakness: her brain. Jill was hopeless when it came to men, made Joan Collins look like Mother Theresa.

First on the hit-list was John Crane. He turned out to be a bigamist, and Jill had a miscarriage and contemplated suicide. Next came electrician Stan Harvey. They married in 1970 and unofficially adopted Stan's sister Sheila's baby. When Sheila married the baby's father, Roy Mollison, she took the baby back, causing Jill to get depressed again. She snapped out of it by having a fling with her stepbrother Anthony Mortimer and they had a son, Matthew.

Now, steady Stan decided this was a bit much even by 'Crossroads' standards. So he took his and Jill's daughter, Sarah-Jane, to Germany. Meanwhile, Anthony took Matthew to New York, leaving Jill with no men and no children. Naturally she had to deal with this. So she became a drug addict. She had a one-night stand with a television repair man (well, you do, don't you?), nearly ran off to the Middle East with an oilman and then . . . enter next mug, Adam Chance. After a long on/off romance with plenty of tears, they eventually tied the knot in 1983.

Jill showed she'd lost none of the old magic by having an affair with macho muscleman Mickey Doyle, who clearly kept his brains in his biceps. Well, it was the usual thing: she got pregnant by Mickey, split up from Adam, found out Mickey was a violent drunk and had a miscarriage. The natural common sense which Jill displayed throughout her life earned her a position of great power in the running of the motel – which says more about 'Crossroads' than words ever can!

Despite her mistakes, Jill remained a favourite with the viewers, who both warmed to her weakness and were inspired by her strength always to pick herself up and head for the next calamity. She always found time to have her blonde hair set, and her ability to colour-coordinate her clothes – even during a breakdown – was admirable.

Jane Rossington was the only member of the original cast of 'Crossroads' still with the show at the bitter end. As Meg Richardson's daughter Jill she survived many a drama but was also responsible for one of the show's least-heralded innovations: the eleven-month pregnancy. By a happy coincidence, at the same time that Jill was expecting in the show so was Jane in real life. But then Jane had a miscarriage. However, producer Jack Barton told Jane: 'We're getting such a good viewer response, we'd like to keep you pregnant in the show. Would you mind being padded up?' Jane duly obliged, then two months later she herself became pregnant again. So Jill's pregnancy had to carry on, and in all lasted eleven months. Jane recalls: 'Strangely, hardly anyone noticed!' To add a touch of uncharacteristic reality to 'Crossroads', Jane's daughter Sorrel played her screen baby Sarah-Jane. Sorrel was a bridesmaid when Jill later married Adam Chance. And the honeymoon following that wedding caused more problems for Jane and her co-star Tony Adams. Jane says: 'A honeymoon in Venice may sound very glamorous, but it's not when we were being filmed at the top of a very high belltower and both Tony and I are petrified of heights. Only a small guard-rail stopped us falling over the side. There was so little space, there was no room for the director. The only way he could give us directions was to climb to the top of another belltower. So he held a red handkerchief in one hand, a white one in the other, and the one he waved indicated which way we should turn. It was the first episode of "Crossroads" to be done by semaphore!' Born in Derby in 1944, the daughter of a bank manager, Jane played probationer nurse Kate Ford in 'Emergency – Ward Ten' before joining 'Crossroads'. Even her audition for the rôle of Jill was chaotic. 'My train was late, and I was in a right state when I arrived,' remembers Jane. 'To make matters worse, my shopping-bag burst and tins of baked beans rolled all over the floor. And my agent had told me to be natural! Yet I still got the part. With hindsight, they probably thought I was the ideal person to play poor Jill.' Jane married Tim Jones, a director on 'Crossroads' in the sixties. They were divorced, and she is now happily married to chartered surveyor David Dunger. They live in a Georgian mansion near Lichfield with their children Sorrel, aged thirteen, and Harry, seven. Jane was always cheerful about her stay at the motel. 'I'm glad my own life hasn't been so fraught as Jill's', she said. One reward was being able to spend £2000 on having bags removed from under her eyes. 'I looked like a panda and had to stay indoors for weeks until my eyes faded. But it was worth it.'

But 'Crossroads' stars, like the soap itself, attracted little praise. A rival on another soap saw the 'new' eyes and remarked: 'Who did it? – the Council?'

Meg Richardson was the matriarch of Crossroads. As owner of the motel, she helped it grow from a little acorn to a mighty King's Oak. Played by Noele Gordon, Meg was the dominant figure at the motel from the start in 1964 until, seventeen years, two marriages, a murder attempt, a spell in prison, a terrorist attack and a fire later, she quit. She was very much the linchpin of 'Crossroads', an isle of sanity in a sea of chaos. Meg was hugely popular. For example, when she was imprisoned for a month for dangerous driving after knocking postman Vince Parker off his bike, hordes of fans phoned Winson Green Prison to ask about visiting hours and whether flowers could be delivered.

Meg was the most powerful woman in British soaps, a tough shrewd businesswoman but also a coping, caring mother. She wasn't particularly warm, never sexy, had little humour, but she had what the women watching her admired the most: the ability to carry on. Whatever crises beset her family (and there were a few), Meg was always on hand to provide support. Without her strength, there is little doubt that her family and the motel would have fallen apart.

But in true soap tradition, although Meg was a success at business, her love-life was a shambles. Her first husband, Charles Richardson, a newspaper cartoonist, had died some years before the serial began. She was then twice engaged to local businessman Hugh Mortimer before he suddenly married one Jane Templeton. On the rebound, Meg met and married Malcolm Ryder who, as husbands in soap do, promptly tried to poison her before fleeing abroad. Jane Templeton having conveniently died, Hugh was free again and, eight years after their first meeting, he proposed to Meg for the third time. It looked like being third time unlucky until she discovered that Malcolm Ryder, who was thought to have been killed in a car crash in South America, was still alive. The shock caused poor old Meg to lose her memory. But Ryder made the elementary mistake of returning to England and was arrested for Meg's attempted murder. The divorce followed and finally, in 1975, Meg married Hugh in the show's grandest-ever spectacle. A special congregation of 300 fans was invited to Birmingham Cathedral, and the streets were crammed with wellwishers, bringing the city centre to a standstill.

ATV used a technique hitherto unheard of on 'Crossroads': outside filming. But, just when it seemed as if Meg and Hugh would live happily ever after, the scriptwriters intervened. Hugh was kidnapped by a gang of international terrorists and died of a heart attack. Heavily involved in the plot was her business partner David Hunter's errant son Chris who, amazingly, continued to pop into the motel over the next few years. No doubt Meg made sure Chris no longer got the best chalet.

When the motel burned down in 1981, Meg was thought to have been inside. But instead she'd sailed off to New York in *QE2* to start a new life. And who could blame her! Meg's final appearance was in 1983. She had a brief rendezvous in Venice with daughter Jill who was on honeymoon there.

Later there were references to her having gone to Australia, then that she had died.

Noele Gordon was the most popular woman in British soaps. It hardly mattered that she couldn't act. She played Meg Richardson, the leading character in 'Crossroads' from 1964 until 1981, a rôle that endeared her to millions. Noele, or 'Nolly' as she was known to her friends, was a star even before she took over the motel. Born on Christmas Day 1923 in East Ham, London, she was a child prodigy and made her stage début at the age of two and a half. Before the war she danced in musicals, and in 1938 had the distinction of being the first actress to be seen on colour television when she modelled for John Logie Baird's early experiments at Crystal Palace. From 1949 she starred in a thousand performances of the West End production of *Brigadoon* (as another Meg) before joining the newly formed ATV as an adviser on women's programmes.

Within a week she was hosting her own show, 'Tea with Noele Gordon', admitting: 'I'm far too much of a ham to stay away from the screen.' She went on to present 'Lunch Box', displaying the talents of an early Anneka Rice by riding an elephant, entering a cage of lions and going down a mine – about the only three story-lines the 'Crossroads' writers didn't dream up for Meg.

Her importance to 'Crossroads' was immeasurable, particularly in the early days when she held the show together while everything else (cast and scenery included) was falling apart. She was the series public spokesperson (it was in her contract), and she tirelessly defended it against the critical attacks and such jokes as that the cast could be punished with the threat of rehearsals.

After three thousand episodes, she was unceremoniously sacked, a move which created national outrage and 'Save Our Meg' campaigns. It was to no avail. Resilient as ever, Noele bounced back and resurrected her stage career in *Gypsy, Call Me Madam* and *No No Nanette*. She made a surprise return to 'Crossroads' in 1983 for a brief scene in Venice on her screen daughter Jill's honeymoon, and the show's new producer, Phillip Bowman, had planned to bring her back as a permanent 'occasional'. She didn't get the chance. After two operations, she died of cancer on 13 April 1984 in a Birmingham nursing home at the age of sixty-one.

Noele never married. The closest she came was during the war when she was due to marry a young army officer; but, in a twist reminiscent of 'Crossroads', she was jilted a week before their wedding day. She had a long affair with impresario Val Parnell and was great pals with camp entertainer Larry Grayson. She jokingly accepted a marriage proposal from him on 'This Is Your Life', a move which prompted hundreds of bouquets and flowers to be sent from viewers who thought the pair were serious. Above all, she was devoted to her late mother Jockey – and to the Crossroads Motel. As her co-star Tony Adams put it: 'Noele Gordon was "Crossroads" and always will be.'

After her death many of her friends spoke of Noele as having died as a direct result of Meg's end in 'Crossroads'. Ronald Allen, sacked four years later, said this in a magazine interview. Jane Rossington told journalists she believed that being fired killed Noele. Only the doctors knew for certain when cancer first afflicted Noele Gordon, but all who knew her agreed she never recovered from the blow. I was reminded of Frank Marcus's *The Killing of Sister George*. Sometimes truth can be stranger and sadder even than soap fiction. (See above, 'The Executioners'.)

Sandy Richardson was soap's first paraplegic. As Meg's son in 'Crossroads', he was on his way back from a wedding in 1972 in a car driven by David Hunter's Uncle Timothy. Not for the last time, a relative of David was to have a devastating effect on Meg's family (son Chris was later involved in the death of her husband Hugh). The car crashed, and Sandy was confined to a wheelchair. But Sandy wasn't an object of pity; he was brave, and had a dry wit which belied his monotonous voice. Despite his disability, he helped run the motel and was even made a director. For once the writers of 'Crossroads' treated a situation sensibly, and Sandy became an inspiration to those in a similar position. He even led to the formation of the Crossroads Care Scheme to help in the care of disabled people. When the actor who played Sandy, Roger Tonge, died in 1981, Sandy simply disappeared on holiday. A year later someone casually remarked that he was 'deceased'.

Roger Tonge, slight and sandy-haired, played Sandy Richardson in 'Crossroads' from the very first episode in 1964 until his death seventeen years later. Sadly, fiction and reality overlapped in Roger's case. As Sandy, he learned to play scenes from a wheelchair but later he needed one himself as he fell victim to an incurable cancer which was to take his life at the age of thirty-four. Birmingham-born Roger appeared in Post Office amateur dramatics before winning the part of Sandy. He got that only because of a cleaner's mistake. He was on his lunch-break from drama school and had popped in to ATV to see if there were any parts going. But a cleaning lady, thinking he had come for an audition, hurriedly sent him into a 'Crossroads' script conference (yes, they *did* have them). Roger created such an impression that they offered him the rôle.

Paul Ross was oily, slimy and creepy. But enough of his good points. Played by Sandor Elès, this odious toadie of a restaurant manager at Crossroads somehow managed to worm his way into the affections of numerous women. He had an affair with Miss Diane (who thus made an ass of herself before she died and became a donkey); he was living with Miranda Pollard at the time of her rape; and, to keep it in the family, he flirted with her mother, the awful Valerie. He entered into a marriage of convenience with a Polish dissident, Anna Radek, and from a different romance he had an illegitimate daughter, Lisa Walters (played by Francesca Gonshaw of "Allo 'Allo' and 'Howards Way' fame). The only decent thing he ever did while at the motel was to get seriously injured foiling a wages snatch. He was in a coma for weeks, but no one bit their nails to the quick. Finally, Ross made a slick exit and went to work in France.

Sandor Elès fled to England from his native Hungary in 1956 when the Russians invaded. He was nineteen at the time and has since appeared in well over a hundred television productions, including the part of the Crossroads oily restaurant manager Paul Ross from 1982 to 1986. Sandor says: 'When I first came to England, I had a very thick accent which meant that I only played villains. But as my English improved I graduated to Prince Charmings, handsome mid-European lovers and even the occasional aristocrat.' Now fifty-one, Sandor was written out of 'Crossroads' in the Phillip Bowman purge. (See above, 'The Executioners'.)

Amy Turtle symbolised everything that was unintentionally hilarious about 'Crossroads' in its heyday. Played by Ann George, who had the same memory for lines that Reagan had for Iranian arms deals, Brummie Amy was straight out of 'Acorn Antiques'. Every time the camera panned in on her, viewers knew they were in for a treat. There would either be silence, a garbled version of the script or, on a really good day, interruptions to everyone else's lines and a total wrecking of the scene. All this served to make Amy immensely popular with the public. The writers didn't let her down, either. One story-line had her accused of being a Russian spy, Amelia Turtlovski. She was also imprisoned, accused of shoplifting.

Amy first took the nation by storm in 1965 when she was working in Meg's sister Kitty Jarvis's shop. She moved to the motel as a charlady and general gossip and stayed for ten years until she was packed off to America to visit her nephew. There must have been an air traffic controller's strike, because she didn't come back until 1987.

Ann George introduced improvised acting to 'Crossroads' in her rôle as popular Brummie charlady Amy Turtle. Poor Ann used to have terrible trouble remembering her lines and had them scattered all over the set. One of her favourite hiding-places was the backs of beer-mats, which is why Amy always cleaned the cocktail bar so thoroughly. Some actors described working with her as a nightmare, but the public loved her. Born in Erdington, Birmingham, Ann's real name was Ann Snape. She made her stage début at the age of four and went on to be a singer with D'Oyley Carte in operas and musicals. Her main spell in 'Crossroads' was from 1965 to 1975, but out of the blue new producer William Smethurst invited her back to make a few guest appearances in 1987. One couldn't be certain he was making fun, but.... When she walked on the set for the first time in years, the cast and crew applauded, bringing tears to her eyes. Now in her eighties, Ann hadn't changed that much during her absence except perhaps for a few more lines around her face. But she'd forgotten most of them.

Anne-Marie Wade had a figure that drove men mad and a voice that drove everyone mad. This Scottish goody-goody arrived at Crossroads as a receptionist in 1985. Played by actress Dee Hepburn, Anne-Marie became engaged to Roy Lambert but at the last minute he called the wedding off, probably fearful of having to hear her say even simple words like 'I do'. She then succumbed to the nonexistent charms of motel assistant manager Charlie Mycroft. They had a lot in common.

Dee Hepburn made an instant impact on 'Crossroads'. On her first day behind the reception desk as Anne-Marie Wade, Dee promptly fainted. Twenty-five-year-old Dee hails from East Kilbride and sprang to fame in the hit film *Gregory's Girl* which won her an Actress of the Year Award in 1981. But she found that success hard to live up to and was out of work when she was asked to join 'Crossroads' in 1985. Ironically, at the same time as Anne-Marie was preparing for her screen wedding-that-never-was to Roy Lambert, Dee was calling off her proposed wedding to salesman Brian Ruane.

Benny Wilmott breezed out of the Crossroads Motel kitchen in 1967 to fetch some sugar – and hasn't been back since. Perhaps the scriptwriters just forgot him. Deke Arlen played Benny, the teenager who ran a local coffee bar as the 'Crossroads' producers tried to prove they were 'fab swinging cats'. Deke, now a big name in show-business management, recalls: 'My last scene was in the motel kitchen with Meg. She said: "Benny, go and get some sugar." I went out and was never seen again!' This absence of twenty years shatters the Crossroads Disappearing Benny record, breaking the previous best, held by Hawkins of that name, who once spent six months searching for a spanner. This must be a soap record.

Deke Arlen was an eighteen-year-old singer when he appeared in 'Crossroads' as Benny Wilmott, the Espresso Kid, from the second episode until 1967. He was sent to get some sugar but found a way to become a millionaire entrepreneur instead, handling such stars as Dennis Waterman and Elaine Page. His wife and business partner is Jill Betts whom he met at the motel when she played Josephine, wife of chef Carlos Raphael. On leaving the show, Deke first went into record production. Now he and Jill, who have two children, live in an Elizabethan farmhouse in Buckinghamshire and have two homes in the South of France. Not bad for someone whose 'Crossroads' career started in a coffee bar. So there *can* be 'life after soap' (p.347).

Many famous faces have been seen at Crossroads, among them Larry Grayson, Ken Dodd, Bob Monkhouse, Kate Robbins, Joe Loss, Arthur Marshall, Max Wall and Don Maclean. Others started at the motel before going on to (much) better things: Malcolm McDowell was a PR man, Crispin Ryder; Diane Keen made her television début in 1969 as waitress Sandra Gould; and Elaine Page appeared way back in episode 880 as Caroline Winthrop.

THE BITTER END

Bomber Lancaster decided to sell the motel-turned hotel. Adam, twiddling his moustache and narrowing his eyes, saw his chance finally to take control of the place with Jill, after raising money in London. He told Jill they might as well resume living together too. Jill's romance with frightfully jolly John Maddingham (Jeremy Nicholas) appeared to be over when his glamorous wife returned. Adam began to gloat. Jill twitched. Meanwhile Big Chef and Little Chef had decided to run a restaurant; ghastly slob Ray Grice had been kicked out by his long suffering wife and their daughter Beverly dithered choosing between Maddingham's son Jamie and her loyal Indian boyfriend Ranjit. Ranjit turned up with an expensive engagement ring so she decided she loved him, poor chap.

The moment of signing the new ownership papers arrived and Jill failed to turn up. Instead a newly-returned-from-heavenknowswhere Daniel Freeman (Philip Goodhew), former boss Nicola's sneering stepson, announced he'd won the takeover bid. Adam stopped gloating. Bomber and his daughters strode off into the sunset. Hearty laughter. Jill whizzed by with Maddingham in his sports car discussing opening a little hotel in the west. 'I always thought "Crossroads" was an awfully good name,' said Jill. Tinkling laughter.

Almost thirteen million people watched the final extra-long episode on Easter Monday, 1988. Some were sad. Many were asleep. In May Central TV auctioned many items from the 'Crossroads' sets including, mysteriously, a bath. No one in twenty-four years had ever so much as mentioned a bathroom in the place. Perhaps it was the secret Meg took to her grave.

'THE DALES'

See 'Mrs Dale's Diary'.

'DALLAS'

'Dallas' is the big daddy of lavish American soap. If it wasn't quite the return of 'Gunsmoke' and the Wild West, it proved that prairies and skyscrapers mix, that 'lerve' is lovely and that people in at least ninety-one countries will watch one wicked man till the cows come home. Without 'Dallas' and its success, the world would not have had the copies: 'Dynasty', 'The Colbys', 'Knots Landing' among the Americans, 'Howards Way' here, 'Châteauvallon' in France. And hundreds of millions of people would not have known about life with the Ewings.

The Ewings – for those who have been in a coma since 1978 – are a Texan family who live under the same roof in real fancy style. They eat breakfast together on a patio in gales. They marry and remarry in the drive. They stick together, take dinner together, go to the Oil Barons' Ball together and are deeply sentimental about each other. All this while they know that the eldest son spends most of his day plotting to disinherit his brother, wreck that brother's marriage, drive his own wife to drink and his rivals to ruin. The rest of the day he'll be with a mistress.

'Dallas' is about the continuing crimes of J. R. Ewing – soap's Idi Amin with a wink and a smirk – and the continuing virtue of Bobby and Pam. There are probably learned papers in university libraries everywhere explaining what 'Dallas' *means*. Perhaps it's the power of the biblical echoes – brothers JR and Bobby as Cain and Abel, Southfork Ranch as Sodom and Gomorrah. Perhaps sociologically we, the poor of the eighties, need to watch the rich screw up, so we can feel better for it. Perhaps the real reason we give 'Dallas' our time and attention is that it was original, it is often clever, and Larry Hagman as JR is always brilliant.

People who are strongly anti-American – loathe what they see as materialism and greed – can love to hate it. Wealth brings misery – isn't that a relief? People who believe in it all copy the dresses, envy the cars, think JR a hero. People who think it's tongue-in-cheek snigger and enjoy.

THE BEGINNING

'Dallas' started because David Jacobs, a New York writer of children's books and recently divorced, wanted to live near his twelve-year-old daughter. Jacobs wrote to his ex-wife, a literary agent (he has the letter framed on the wall of his Hollywood office), in July 1975 to say he was following them reluctantly to Los Angeles. 'At least can you find me some work?' he wrote. 'I don't want to make a career in screen or television writing just something that pays while I'm trying to write the adequate American novel. . . .'

He never wrote that novel. Two years later he wrote 'Dallas' for Lorimar Television. It was the first evening soap series to succeed in America since 'Peyton Place'. It didn't *just* succeed, either. 'Dallas' became the show that made us forgive that city for killing Kennedy. It became an obsession with the British, the Turks, the Lebanese, the Germans and the Israelis. When JR was shot it made an item in our nine o'clock news. A session of the Turkish Parliament was cut short so members could return home to view it. American hostages in Beirut watched their captors watch episodes. The Bonn Municipal Theatre produced a Ewing family ballet, and small shops in Wales did a roaring trade in JR dartboards.

David Jacobs, a witty balding man in a waistcoat, told me how it happened: 'The first television show I worked on was "The Family". I liked it, but I felt constrained. It was, in a way, like "The Waltons" [also a Lorimar production]. We had to keep "playing the past", running what happened before, to remind viewers. I'd been talking to Mike Filerman, a development executive with Lorimar, about my idea for something good. I had lofty ambitions. I'd loved *Scenes from a Marriage* with Liv Ullman, and my idea was an American equivalent; it came to be called "Knots Landing". The CBS network said "Knots Landing" was too middle-class and tame. How about something bigger and brasher? Would I think about Linda Evans, because they had her under contract? I didn't mind thinking about Linda Evans one bit. I thought of a semi-trashy character, Pam, a girl from the wrong side of the tracks, who marries Bobby, a boy from a rich family, and says: "Your family's gonna throw me off the ranch." Remember, I was an unreconstructed novelist! The next character was JR. He was so formidable. Jock Ewing, his father, was honourable but corrupt – or, rather, the corruption was the corruption of the society. Bobby was the apple of his eye, so that explained JR's resentment and warped outlook.'

In Jacobs's original scheme Bobby was to die early, leaving the stage clear for Pam and JR – good and evil – to fight it out. The original schemes in files marked 'Untitled Linda Evans Project' were never shown to Linda. Jacobs says this was because they realised the character of Pam was not classy enough for Linda; others say because Linda was too old. (She was just the right age for 'Dynasty'.)

Jacobs decided on the city, in the heart of rich redneck Texas, then he constructed his network of characters in a day. He hesitated before he wrote the pilot episode, but only briefly. It occurred to him: should he perhaps *go* to Dallas? He spoke to his friend Mike Filerman, who said get it written before CBS cool on the idea. 'Go to Dallas *after*.'

'So I wrote the first five episodes when I'd never been to Dallas,' Jacobs told me. 'When I went there for the filming six weeks later I found I didn't have to change a thing. Larry Hagman, who is from Texas, told me I didn't go far enough.'

Jacobs says he feels he's the parent of JR, Pam, Bobby, Sue Ellen and the rest, and added modestly: 'They're my children, but I sent them to camp early. If I'd been in charge of "Dallas", it would probably not have been the success it is. I have this tendency to bring things down to earth. "Dallas" is up there. When I went on the set I was shocked to see some people taking it seriously. I suppose someone has to. I don't think I could have.'

Jacobs has no pat theory to explain the international success of his baby. 'There is something about this decade. The world was just ready for this kind of portrayal of an American family, whose money and power is so vast it doesn't mean anything. I guess countries where there was a strong anti-American bias just threw in the towel.'

Jacobs was still working on 'The Family' when 'Dallas' was launched in America in the spring of 1978. He went on to produce 'Married' ('where my heart was'); then, when that flopped and 'Dallas' took off, to develop the idea that started it all: 'Knots Landing'. He and his pal Michael Filerman are still the executive producers of that series.

The real citizens of Dallas, Texas, America's eighth-largest town, dedicated to commerce, weren't at first too happy with what a Californian-made television series was doing in their name. They hated the image of Dallas businessmen as conniving adulterous oilmen who maybe worked in sleek high-rise offices but had cow manure on their boots. It may be true that Dallas has the highest divorce rate in America but, hell, they don't go to the city in stetsons! They pointed out to the producers that a strip of blue ocean could be seen from the window of JR's office on 1 Main Place (Dallas is landlocked); a palm tree was growing in the street (there are none in Dallas); and the Ewings had suffered a hurricane (Dallas has tornadoes). They also pointed out that in the soil of Dallas County there's not one drop of oil. So the writers invented Braddock County as the setting for the Ewings' Southfork Ranch. (This is in fact Duncan Acres, in Plano, Texas, used for the six weeks' location filming a year and an expensive but popular target for tourists the rest of the time.)

Larry Hagman, from the small town of Weatherford, twenty miles from Dallas, came under attack. (Heck, he shoulda put them pesky writers right!) He said: 'Some Texans say I don't know what I'm talking about. But I know the oil interests. I've worked for an oil tool factory and I've seen what those big shots do to one another. If we told the real story, they'd blow up CBS.'

By 1985 the most visited attraction in Dallas was no longer Dealy Plaza where JFK was assassinated, but the Southfork Ranch.

Larry/JR is now a local hero. Here, briefly, is the story they did tell.

THE STORY

The Ewings' doings began with a feud between Jock Ewing and Digger Barnes. Digger claimed his former friend had stolen his land and his girl. The 'girl' was Miss Ellie, who had tamed Jock, the oil wildcatter, because she had breeding and the Southfork Ranch.

As Jacobs's five pilot episodes began (each a self-contained story), viewers met their family: scheming JR and his vapid former beauty queen wife Sue Ellen; beaming Bobby and his voluptuous new wife Pam, Digger's daughter; and randy little Lucy, child of Gary, the wastrel son who lived out West (in Knots Landing, it turned out). With Digger was Cliff Barnes his resentful impulsive son and, later, Digger's wife Rebecca Wentworth, owner of Wentworth Tool and Die, and Pam and Cliff's evil half-sister Katherine.

There was also ranch-hand Ray Krebbs whose hat was glued on and who turned out, a few years later, to be Jock's illegitimate boy.

The serial form took over: a small story-thread was resolved each week, but the bigger stories took twenty-six or even thirty weeks to tangle, untangle and be resolved – ending, of course, in a cataclysmic cliffhanger. (This format was used by all the 'Dallas' imitators, too.)

Unlike 'Dynasty', 'Dallas' became a hit in its first year. We sat open-mouthed as Sue Ellen sank into her first vodka-vat and was soothed in the arms of Cliff Barnes. We watched enthralled as JR enjoyed six mistresses (in the first series), double-crossed his business colleagues and taunted Pam, then pregnant, till she fell off a barn platform, lost the child and was (of course) declared unable ever to conceive again. (Alexis did a similar thing to Krystle in 'Dynasty', and Krystle, like Pam, confounded the doctors later on.)

Then Sue Ellen produced a baby whose father could have been Cliff (but wasn't) and could have had neurofibromatosis, the fatal genetic disease that Digger had (but didn't). Terry Wogan, then a radio personality in Britain, found especial delight in that.

Jock stood trial for a twenty-eight-year-old murder; Digger confessed to it. Sue Ellen took up with lusty Dusty Farlow, a rodeo rider. Up-market Donna married Ray and his hat. And then in March 1980 a shot was heard round the world. Someone crept up on mean JR in his office and plugged him full of holes.

Was it Sue Ellen whom he'd been driving to a mental home? Was it Kristin, her sister, who'd been one of his mistresses? Was it the wife of a business partner he'd driven to suicide or another he'd led to bankruptcy? There were at least half a dozen good suspects whose guilt was rated by bookmakers, discussed in newspapers and miraculously kept warm for the following six months.

The most successful cliffhanger in television history, provoking '"Dallas" fever' in fifty-six countries (among an estimated 300 million viewers), was resolved in November 1980. That episode attracted 27.3 million viewers in Britain alone (3.3 million more than had watched him being shot).

The idea of shooting their magnificent bad guy had come almost by accident to the 'Dallas' bosses. The CBS network asked for an extra two episodes. Producers Leonard Katzman and Phil Capice threw out their original cliffhanger and wrote a scene in which JR was shot. Then they worked backwards, writing two complete scripts implicating a string of characters. 'We didn't really know ourselves who did it,' said Katzman. 'We said: "To hell with it! Let's shoot him and figure out who did it later."' And later Mary Crosby (Bing's daughter), who played Kristin, Sue Ellen's sister, turned out to be expendable. So Kristin did it. Mary's television career reached a peak. She survived another series, then JR drowned her in the Southfork swimming-pool. She hasn't really surfaced on television since. (See 'Life after Soap'.)

Later incidents included Pam and Bobby's search for a baby; in the end they adopted (bought) Christopher, an infant whose turnip-like features provoked a great many giggles. Divorced Sue Ellen had flings with Cliff (again), Dusty (again) – this time he was crippled and impotent – and Dusty's father Clayton Farlow (who later married Miss Ellie) before remarrying JR in 1983.

Pam divorced Bobby (though still in love with him) and was soon pursued by Mark Graison who later contracted a fatal illness which wasn't. Lucy married, divorced, was voted Miss Young Texas, was raped by a photographer then later romanced by Ray's cousin Mickey who was injured in that season's cliffhanger: the Southfork fire.

Sue Ellen took a lover who looked about fourteen years old; Bobby's old sweetheart Jenna, played by Priscilla Presley, arrived; and, in what tried to be a repeat of the Who Shot JR success, Bobby was plugged by black-hearted Katherine Wentworth. She later visited him in hospital to inject him with poison. He still refused to die. In 1985 she thought (and we thought) she'd got lucky when, still determined no other woman should have him, Katherine drove her car into Pam but killed noble Bobby as he pushed Pam out of the way. Patrick Duffy, who played Bobby, had decided to leave.

So determined was Duffy to make his exit final that he insisted on a death scene with full schmaltz. First he whispered to Pam about time wasted when 'we should have been married'. Then, with the family gathered around his hospital bed, he told them: 'Be a family.' As the world blubbed, he expired.

The year that followed was remarkable for the 'Dallas'-style manoeuvres off-camera. First, in Britain, there was the Great Dallas Robbery in which Brian Cowgill of Thames Television gazumped the BBC's price to the 'Dallas' distributors. He offered £54,500 an episode for the seven-year-old series instead of the £29,000 the BBC was paying. This naturally infuriated BBC Controller Michael Grade, though he hadn't been averse to pulling a similar stroke years before when he was at LWT and wanted the Saturday-night 'Match of the Day' rather badly. Grade pulled the remaining episodes of 'Dallas' off BBC screens, promising to run them in the autumn concurrently with the 'poached' new series. Ultimately, Thames overlords at the Independent Broadcasting Authority put pressure on Cowgill to withdraw. He did so, the BBC won the new 'Dallas' episodes at the old price, but Thames had to pay the difference between that and the price they'd agreed. For Brian Cowgill, who left Thames the week Bobby was seen to die, it was not at all like striking oil.

Meanwhile at Southfork there was Bobby's funeral in a field, JR's tears and Miss Ellie's stoical strength. Pam's world-wide search for the Remains of Mark Graison could cease when a very together-looking Graison (John Beck) turned up to rekindle their romance. Two long-lost Ewings turned up, too – though we wished they hadn't. Jack (Dack Rambo) was clearly there as a new Mr Nice (replacing Bobby) but managed only to be Mr Dull. Even a plot involving him and a lesbian Greek shipping tycoon was dull. Sue Ellen took to drink and joined down-and-outs on skid row.

Ray and Donna expected a Down's Syndrome baby. She miscarried but, in a rare moment of 'Dallas' – with-a-social-conscience, a boy with Down's Syndrome joined the cast as a child they wanted to adopt. (The only other messages 'Dallas' has felt inclined to deliver were those for breast-cancer checks when Miss Ellie had a mastectomy and, in the wake of the AIDS scare, when JR told young Casey Denault to 'be sure to stop by the drugstore' before sex.)

As we watched Pam prepare to marry Mark, Larry Hagman was doing a little wheeler-dealing of his own to bring Bobby (Patrick Duffy) back. The show had fallen to an all-time low in the ratings (placed sixth in the year in America). In the final episode, therefore, Pam found a familiar wet body in the shower. Bobby wasn't dead any longer.

With a Texan-sized helping of cheek, the 1987 series began with Pam concluding that all the previous year's events were a Dream. (See 'Back from the Dead'.) The couple remarried in the drive; Jenna gave birth to Bobby's baby boy; Donna and Ray divorced after she had a girl (and left the soap); Clayton's heart started missing its beats, to Miss Ellie's alarm, and Sue Ellen's new-found success as a lingerie empire tycoon (originally employing JR's mistress) grew and grew.

The season ended as JR was made bankrupt and Pam, having just learned she could, after all, become a mother, was mown down by an eighteen-wheeled truck. The reason was that Victoria Principal's time to 'do other things' had now come. Her badly burned body – or someone's – swaddled like the Invisible Man in bandages, was the focus of the early episodes of the 1987–8 series. When the wrappings came off, viewers had to believe a disfigured Pam ran away asking all to remember her as she was. JR had triumphed, Katherine lurked unseen and Bobby wept.

Ray and Jenna married, almost split up and moved to Europe (the way for Priscilla Presley to do her 'other things'). A barmier than ever Cliff Barnes teamed with impish April Stevens to tour the world looking for Pam Ewing. Miss Ellie and Clayton parted then reconciled and in the final episode there was a shoot-out between JR and Sue Ellen's gangster boyfriend Nicholas Pearce. 'About seventy per cent of the "Dallas" plots are dumb,' David Jacobs joked to me. 'No, maybe that's a bit low.'

By 1988 the show's ratings were low and no one wanted to watch the repeats. 'Dallas', the big daddy, had all but overreached itself. It had to be cut down by the JRs inside CBS, the network which paid the mounting bills. The costs they have to meet now exceed a million pounds an episode – more than four times the costs when it started. Even an extra, standing on a street-corner, has to be paid more than £60 a day; and to dress the sets, not make them, costs over £25,000 an episode. Double that to hire all the cars. The actors alone pick up half the budget. (See 'Pay'.)

With costs the moneymen's main concern, 'Dallas' episodes have to stretch. So the autumn's episodes may be self-contained, with no plots hanging on interwoven threads, no build-up to an end-of-series cliffhanger. Fewer leading players will appear at a time. With free-standing stories which can be repeated anywhere, anytime, 'Dallas' will stay in business. 'Who Shot JR?' may never make a main item in the national news. But, with care and economies, 'Who Shot "Dallas"?' won't be an item next year.

THE CHARACTERS

Cliff Barnes is soap's most famous pop-up brother-in-law, the likeable loser of 'Dallas'. We may think the man's mad, sad and simple but Ken Kercheval who has played him so splendidly for almost eleven years thinks Cliff's a hero. He said: 'I read the pilot scripts on an airplane and I sat there thinking and said to myself: There's not one redeemable character in this show except Cliff. Cliff is the only one with the sense of morality.'

Cliff Barnes is motivated by anger and resentment just as JR is. Cliff knows old Jock Ewing fiddled his pa Digger by buying Digger's share of their oil company when Digger was drunk. Jock would no doubt answer, 'When wasn't Digger drunk?' but that injustice and the hundred and one mean stunts JR has pulled on Cliff since provide the basic conflict of the saga.

Ken went on: 'Cliff Barnes is the only one that JR keeps having to worry about. No matter how he gets Cliff down, he can be assured that he'll turn round and Cliff will be there. Cliff unfortunately is looking for an outside fix on his life but it never works out. Being happy is an inside job. I come to him with compassion.'

Compassion is certainly in order. Consider Cliff's catastrophes. The lawyer and one-time aspiring politician found JR had sabotaged his campaign for a seat in the Senate. He was arrested in 1982 for the attempted murder of JR and in 1984 for the attempted murder of Bobby. He'd attempted nothing. He organised the trial in which Jock Ewing was charged with a twenty-eight-year-old murder and, darn it, his own father Digger confessed then promptly died.

His luck with women was even worse. First Sue Ellen loved and left. When she went back the second time to JR, at a stage when he'd lost his mother's trust, his job, her money and his money, Cliff tried to commit suicide with tranquillisers and booze. The surgeon who saved him at Dallas Memorial said to expect a 'personality change'. 'What personality?' we said, and nothing changed.

After Sue Ellen came Afton Cooper, the dumbest blonde and the soppiest singer in the history of soap – and she wouldn't go away. Mandy Winger found Cliff so distracted she took the worst job in Dallas: JR's mistress.

When Cliff tried to be clever – paying JR's secretary Sly to spy on Ewing Oil – JR had Sly spy back. Even Mark Graison committed suicide when he heard Cliff was about to ask for a loan.

As an oil man, Cliff made a good poet. Always having trouble with his geologicals, when he put on his hard hat and went down to the derricks we knew they'd rust on the spot. No wonder he drinks.

Only Jamie Ewing, the girl with the ever-open mouth, loved Cliff enough . . . to push a custard pie in his face at the Oil Barons' Ball. Cliff just wiped it off and smiled his demented smile.

My theory? It's his flat. Next time, look at those sloping walls. As Cliff sits down for another takeaway Chinese meal washed down with a gallon of booze, they're moving in. He sees it, too.

Ken Kercheval has had tough times in his life. But unlike Cliff Barnes, the walking disaster of 'Dallas' he plays, Ken has coped and cured himself. When he first played Cliff, the actor was an alcoholic. 'I went through a period of terrible heartache and sought refuge in alcohol,' he said. Eight years ago he joined a self-help group and hasn't had a drink since. He has helped fellow-members of Alcoholics Anonymous. 'I've woken up in the gutter a lot of times. I used to drink constantly, hard stuff, beer, anything, a tremendous amount of it.'

The Indiana-born actor, who is fifty-two, studied drama and singing at university, then went to New York, taking odd jobs between acting and musical rôles. A friend of Dustin Hoffman at the time, Ken recalls how he worked in sewers under the city, sold burial-plots at a Jewish cemetery and peddled encyclopaedias door-to-door. Unlike Dustin, Ken had a wife and three children to support.

From there he went to California and success with parts in such films as *Network* and *Pretty Poison*, and several guest starring rôles in television series. 'Dallas' was his main break and he has never lost faith in his character 'Calamity' Cliff. He said: 'Cliff is all but lobotomised, but it's how you interpret the character that makes the difference.' When Patrick Duffy wanted to leave because he said Bobby was 'boring' he had no sympathy. If Bobby was boring, it was Duffy who made him so, he said.

Ken collects antiques, including early glass, thirties paintings and Packard cars which he restores himself. And he's always being given advice for Cliff. 'People say he ought to win now and then. I don't know about that but I like him – he's a guy who never gives up.'

Bobby Ewing is the Mr Nice Guy of 'Dallas', the handsome younger son, so forthright, fair and faithful we know just why he gets right up bad ol' JR's nose.

In the beginning Bobby, played by Patrick Duffy, was nice but not good. In David Jacobs's scheme he was the rich Ewing playboy who happened to fall for the gorgeous Barnes girl, marry her and then find out the force of their families' feud. Bobby was also doomed to die after five episodes to let Pam and JR – good and evil – fight it out.

Then the producers discovered people love love. The Bobby–Pam romance balanced JR's dirty deeds, so Bobby became Prince Charming, Pam's knight in a shining-white ten-gallon hat. From two dimensions, he was down to one. Audiences didn't mind but, almost from the start, Patrick Duffy did. 'When I took the part my character had all the forcefulness and panache of a three-day-old piece of lettuce,' he lamented. 'Bobby had two lines: "It's all right, Mom, I'll take care of it," and "It's all right, Mom, I took care of it".' Patrick, with his clear bright skin, warmly wet eyes and the sort of body small swimming-trunks go well with, made those lines live.

Like Sue Ellen, Bobby was sinned against. Both JR and Cliff Barnes tried to end the marriage; his childhood sweetheart Jenna turned up with Charlie, the daughter who could have been his; daddy Jock died, so Bobby had to fight JR for a stake in the company. This led to divorce between Bobby and Pam, though their love never died. (Don't ask *why*, then, did they divorce; this is soap!)

But while Bobby fell into Jenna's (Priscilla Presley's) arms and Pam into Mark's (John Beck's) the CBS network acted as chaperons. Their Romeo and Juliet must remain chaste – sorry, Jenna and Mark! Enter evil Katherine as a diversion to try to kill Bobby out of jealous love. She shot him, blinded him, tried to finish him with a lethal injection, but JR stopped her in time. Enter also Jenna's nutty ex-husband, nasty Naldo, who kidnapped her before she could marry our boy. Bobby somehow managed to fit in a term as a State Senator, perhaps the most honest politician America has known.

Duffy still wanted to go. He said: 'They weren't letting Bobby grow or do anything. He was really stuck and everyone else was chewing the scenery.' So Duffy had him killed by Katherine, nobly saving Pam just before they decided to remarry. He was completely deceased, dead, buried and gone.

Until he came back. (See 'Back from the Dead'.) The born-again, gleaming, sincere, selfless Bobby still didn't grow or do anything, but a richer Duffy didn't mind.

Patrick Duffy is more complicated than awfully nice Bobby Ewing of 'Dallas'. He's 20 per cent more. That's what the thirty-nine-year-old Montana-born actor himself says, and his many friends agree.

Bobby is saintly and forgiving; Patrick is more so. When two youths robbed and murdered his parents in their bar in November 1986, the actor drew on the Buddhist faith he adopted when he married seventeen years ago. He did not condemn them but said: 'I feel sorry for the two guys; it must be a terrible thing to have to live with.'

Duffy's life is one of contradictions. He planned to be a professional athlete, but fell for school dramatics. He specialised in Shakespeare, but is happy with soap and commercials. Devoted to Carlyn, his ex-ballet dancer wife, and their two children, he talked of the other women he has known on a television chat-show. He's a clever businessman who has invested well and grown rich, yet he wears only jeans and drives an old jeep.

In his final year at university, working in two drama productions, singing with the Seattle Opera and going to classes, he caught a throat infection which rendered him speechless for three months. He then moved to New York for the theatre work, then to Hollywood for films and television. From small film parts and two years as the web-footed underwater hero of 'Man from Atlantis', 'Dallas' claimed him.

The boy with 'dirt-poor' beginnings came to play the immensely wealthy favoured son until 1985 when he declined to renew his contract. 'I never felt appreciated,' he said then. Ratings fell for the season without him (and, perhaps more to the point, without the show's much respected producer, Leonard Katzman, busy with another project). A public-opinion survey suggested the killing of Bobby Ewing was 'the biggest prime-time blunder in television history'. People didn't know about Katzman, but they knew they wanted Duffy back. It convinced the 'Dallas' producers. They sent Larry Hagman as the first messenger. The friends discussed Bobby's return in the Hagman hot tub.

Duffy claims he made more money in the year Bobby was six feet under than when he'd been alive. For the record, he's made television movies, a comedy-show pilot, played Bobby with a stethoscope and Bobby with a psychiatrist's couch. He made land-development deals and almost invested in a European film company until he found it was a front for the IRA.

His new 'Dallas' money was big. Not only was he paid a million to return to playing a millionaire, but his salary also doubled to £50,000 an episode. At Duffy's request, Katzman came back. Victoria filmed a final scene for the final episode as Pam finding Mark in her shower. When viewers saw it, Bobby was in that shower.

Patrick Duffy's television character may still be a little lettuce-like. But the actor sure ain't green.

Miss Ellie Ewing is the dowager duchess of 'Dallas', her little flat feet set firmly in Southfork soil. Ellie owns the ranch and never leaves unless she is forced. Even her bicycle is for exercise and goes nowhere.

Miss Ellie is the rock, respected, loved and leaned on. Played by anyone less skilled than Barbara Bel Geddes, she would be absurd. How could a woman tolerate the crimes of JR or welcome two bickering daughters-in-law into her house? Can't she do something about that dingy woodwork and dreadful wallpaper? And, with all those millions, why is she still wearing her old maternity-smocks?

But Barbara plays her as an enduring stateswoman. She rises above illness – her own mastectomy, husband Jock's heart attack and second husband Clayton's threatened one. She was brave when JR was shot, Bobby was blinded and Pam was burned. She was reasonable even when Jock produced a first wife in an asylum and an illegitimate son, Ray, who would lose in an IQ contest with his horse. If I were Miss Ellie, I'd never pick up the phone; it's always bad news.

Barbara has made the most of her screen miseries. Is that glycerine in her eyes, or can she act the verge of tears for almost an hour? When she smashed the crockery in her grief at Jock's death, we cheered. When Clayton's crazy sister Jessica bundled her in the boot of her car, planning to kill her and stop the wedding, we booed. When Barbara came back (after an absence) and her stand-in, Donna Reed, disappeared, we cheered louder still. But when Ellie had to fall half in love with creepy Wes Parmalee, a Jock Ewing impostor and con-man we all yelled: 'come *on.'* Miss Ellie towered above it all. Just one thing we need to know. Does hubby Clayton (Howard Keel) sing a medley from *Oklahoma!* in the Southfork bath?

Barbara Bel Geddes has her roots as firmly planted in the entertainment world as those of her character Miss Ellie are planted in Texan soil in 'Dallas'. Her father was stage designer Norman Bel Geddes, and Barbara, now sixty-eight, played on the New York stage while still in her teens. During the Second World War she toured with the USO then returned to Broadway to take the leading rôle in the inter-racial love-story by Elia Kazan, *Deep Are the Roots*, for which she won the Clarence Derwent Award for Outstanding Young Actress of the Year.

Then came Hollywood – a rôle opposite Henry Fonda in *The Long Night* and an Oscar nomination for *I Remember Mama*. She partnered Danny Kaye in *The Five Pennies* and James Stewart in Hitchcock's *Vertigo*. In her second Hitchcock film, *Lamb to the Slaughter*, she got to brain her husband with a frozen leg of lamb – a treatment many would recommend for her 'Dallas' son JR.

Soon after her rôle in 'Dallas' was established, Barbara underwent surgery for breast cancer and later re-enacted her experience as Miss Ellie, also suffering a mastectomy. In 1980 she won an Emmy for her 'Dallas' rôle, the only cast member so far to be so honoured. In 1983 her health was again affected when a stroke meant a year away from the part. The actress Donna Reed stepped into the part but, under protests from fans claiming that Donna had not captured the salty Texan toughness, the producers persuaded Barbara to come back. An angry Donna Reed sued Lorimar but died shortly afterwards of cancer.

Aside from acting, Barbara paints and writes children's books. Now widowed – her husband was Windsor Lewis – she has two daughters and lives in New York when not at Southfork.

J. R. Ewing is soap's satan in a stetson, the high priest of evil in high-heeled cowboy boots, corruption dressed as a cattleman, the devil posing as a driller. JR learned Hamlet's lesson – 'one may smile, and smile, and be a villain' – and the reason the man has become a folk-hero is that he's such a thoroughgoing bastard, a baddie who gets real job satisfaction. JR just loves being wicked, and we just love watching him. Early on he told us his motto, 'Once you give up integrity, the rest is a piece of cake,' and for eleven years he has shared that piece of spicy cake with hundreds of millions of devotees all round the world.

The dastardly deeds of JR are not so much the point. For the record he has, among other things, double-crossed almost every other oilman in Texas. He taunted pregnant Pam, who fell and miscarried. He killed Kristin after having her arrested for prostitution; tried to wreck his brother Bobby's marriage; drove his own wife to drink (three times) and to a sanatorium twice. He tried to kidnap their son, using his mother as stooge for the snatch; caused Cliff Barnes's attempted suicide; corrupted politicians; bribed policemen and paid a mad Rambo to bomb Saudi Arabia (all right, he changed his mind, but only when he looked like being caught). And then there are the women, dozens of them, he picked up, played with and dumped.

None of this is important compared with the way he's wicked. Even when he's not on screen, spinning a web, we worry about him. His unseen crimes are almost his worst.

David Jacobs is the creator of JR, the eldest Ewing brother. Larry Hagman, the actor, is the author of all his malevolent charm. Larry sends up the smarm and the folksiness, looks happy as he deceives. We know in JR's black heart there's a 'yee-hah!' bursting to be heard, but the gloating is restrained; it's we who celebrate his nasty success.

The reason JR is wicked is resentment: his beloved pappy, Jock, favoured Bobby – his brother. Bobby the playboy, Bobby the dreamer. As JR tried more and more to be like Jock, Jock seemed to love him less. JR's virtue is his love of his own son, John Ross, the child he couldn't bear to touch till he was certain it was his. Later JR's bedtime pep-talks to the baffled boy, usually on the lines of 'Some day all this will be yours', became a regular feature.

Larry Hagman has said: 'I based him on real life. I know so many Texans who are the epitome of this dude. People get wealthy and they get mean.' JR isn't evil to Larry's thinking. 'He thinks he's doing the right thing. He's no more ruthless than the TV executives who moved our series around from one night of the week to another.' I bet there was an evil chuckle to follow.

Larry Hagman is not a mean bastard like J. R. Ewing, his delicious 'Dallas' concoction. But he is the source of JR's glee.

A fifty-seven-year-old Texan, he should have been a lawyer like his pappy. He chose to be an entertainer like his mom. She's Mary Martin, the stage and screen star who often rides pillion on the back of his motor-scooter. Or joins in the parades down Malibu Beach, when her boy wears a gorilla costume or one of his 500 funny hats. He's the man who doesn't speak a word on Sundays, often moves around the Lorimar lot on a skateboard, bought a bubble-making machine for Linda Gray when her marriage broke up and, for relaxation, joins his wife of thirty-four years in a hot tub. Larry Hagman isn't boring.

As a boy, he wasn't a prize pupil. He went through sixteen schools then balked at university. After doing odd jobs badly, the teenager found work in musicals in New York until he accompanied his mother to London in 1951, she to star in *South Pacific* at Drury Lane, he to join the cast as an extra for £12 a week. He stayed in Europe, serving with the United States Air Force, and married Maj, a Swedish dress designer, in 1954.

Back in America in 1961 he took his first taste of soap opera, playing a lawyer in the daytime serial done live, 'The Edge of the Night'. He left after three years for Hollywood and great success for five years in the part of sweet stammering astronaut Major Tony Nelson in the television comedy series 'I Dream of Jeannie'. He left that for big-screen work – films such as *Failsafe, The Group, Harry and Tonto* and, in the year before 'Dallas', *The Eagle Has Landed*, playing 'the ugly American'.

But his television work meanwhile had stalled. Comedy roles after 'Jeannie' just hadn't worked. It was time for a change when JR came into his life. He says he rejected the rôle twice – the pay was 'insulting' – and agreed only when he learned that esteemed stage actress Barbara Bel Geddes had agreed to play his screen mother. In fact Robert Foxworth was first choice for the rôle. He wanted JR's nastiness softened, which the producers refused. So the net was spread wider. David Jacobs recalls the casting sessions. He told me: 'They said Larry Hagman was testing. I said "Get serious!" I thought of him as a comedian. But, when he came, he came in character, wearing the big hat, standing in the doorway like a giant. And he smirked.' There was no dispute after that. Hagman *was* JR.

Producer Phil Capice said: 'As "Dallas" was developing there seemed to be a special audience fascination with JR – this guy they hated and loved. We kept getting letters asking "When is JR going to get his?" It seemed like a good idea. We never really considered killing him but we talked about several ways in which near-death could occur and make sense.' At first the plan was for Sue Ellen to plan to commit suicide with pills – only JR accidentally swigged the water in which they were dissolved. Then the producers talked some more. The result was the 1980 shooting – the episode which started the summer of 'Dallas' fever, with bookies giving odds on the most likely culprit. When the new series started, the whodunnit episode became the most watched in the history of television, topped later in America by the last episode of 'MASH' and by a Christmas episode of 'EastEnders' in Britain.

It also allowed Hagman to do something about the 'insulting' pay. As the shooting episode was screened he flew to Britain, having asked the network to quadruple his money. In retaliation, they began to leak rumours that the actor Robert Culp might take his place. When the rest of the cast gathered to begin filming again in June, Larry Hagman was not among them. Three days later a deal was done. Larry Hagman trebled his pay, to £50,000 an episode and took a cut of the profits from merchandising items which showed his picture. He went back to concentrate on JR and messing up people's lives.

Hagman, a fervent anti-smoker since a chest X-ray in 1966 convinced him to give up cigarettes, has remained popular with co-stars. Linda Gray (Sue Ellen) and Ken Kercheval (Cliff Barnes) hate him in the scripts, love him for real.

Is JR bigger than Dallas I asked him? Has he become a myth on the level of, say, Sherlock Holmes? 'Absolutely not. JR reaches more people than Sherlock Holmes ever did because this is television. Whether he will be remembered as long remains to be seen. I still can't understand the success "Dallas" has had – I'm just pleasantly surprised. The letters I get from Israel, Brunei, all over the Middle East and Europe, you wouldn't believe. There must be something in the concept – the extended family, generations living together and clashing – that seems to have universal appeal.'

When it ends, he says, he'll donate to a library 'some forty old scripts annotated with bullshit from a bunch of TV creeps at the network' and enjoy a huge tax relief.

Has JR been good for LH? Stupid question. 'I tell you, I feel compassion for the rich, now that I'm one of them,' he said.

Lucy Ewing is the knee-high nympho of 'Dallas' and one of the most unhappy waitresses they ever had at the Hot Biscuit.

Little Lucy, who was young (seventeen) as well as short (even in the four-inch high heels she always wore), was the sexiest kid in school when 'Dallas' began. Played by Charlene Tilton, Lucy is the daughter of runaway Gary Ewing, Jock and Ellie's black-sheep son, and Valene Ewing, a woman who wore puff-sleeve dresses and flared skirts to annoy. At first she was seen sulking at the breakfast table, flicking her long blonde hair or trying to take Ray Krebbs's mind off his steers.

Her taste in men went down after that. She married and divorced wimpy Mitch Cooper, a student doctor. She fell for drippy Mickey Trotter, Ray's nephew, who ended up on a life-support machine at good old Dallas Memorial until Ray pulled the plug on the squirt and put us all out of our misery. She became Miss Young Texas (those judges had a sense of humour) and a mad photographer pounced on her. She became pregnant and had an abortion.

When a number of critics suggested Lucy's was not the most successful study of a young girl's emotional turmoil, the script seemed to punish her. Rich Lucy was sent to work in a sleazy diner, the Hot Biscuit, where her mother Valene had once slaved. The place made Ali's café in Albert Square look like the Savoy Grill. Lucy's lip curled. She looked like a hamburger in her brown nylon uniform, too. Luckily Mitch materialised, they remarried and moved. 'Dallas' was Lucy-less for almost three years. Then Lucy returned, older but no bigger.

Charlene Tilton probably didn't deserve to be tagged the no-neck poison dwarf of 'Dallas'. She has a neck, and lots of people are only as tall as she says she is: five feet. But hers just seem five small feet.

No one denies that the twenty-seven-year-old Californian blonde who plays rich Lucy Ewing has a pretty face and lot of spunk. A tough childhood – her father walked out on her mother before she was born – left her with no self-pity. 'Everyone's got a story you could bring out the violins for,' she said. At school she was president of the drama club, the lead in all the plays as well as wardrobe mistress and scenery designer. At the same time she worked forty hours a week as a cinema usherette. 'It was the only way I could get to see the film and be paid at the same time. But, if I hadn't made it as an actor, the only thing I would have been qualified to do was to sell tickets and popcorn in cinemas, because I failed every exam I took.'

Charlene's first professional acting job was in the Walt Disney movie *Freaky Friday*. The ten weeks she worked on that earned her, she recalls, more than her hard-pressed mother had earned working non-stop for the previous two years. After several more films and 'a bunch of TV' the girl with the sexy sulk won the rôle of Lucy and spent seven years making the sort of money that buys a Beverly Hills mansion and all the trappings.

In 1985 she was sacked. Shocked and hurt, she said later: 'I loved playing Lucy, but they were turning her into a nun and I wouldn't want that.' Charlene, who was then divorced from country singer Johnny Lee, with a small daughter, married Scottish singer Dominic Allen five days after the bad news. She took a holiday and later took acting classes, but few producers came to knock down her door. There seemed, for her, no acting life after soap.

Almost three years later she returned to appear in the final couple of episodes of the series, as a newly discontented doctor's wife and pint-sized sexpot, now in even shorter mini-skirts. 'Lucy's stronger, she has grown up and she's going to get her own back on JR,' she told me eagerly. 'Coming back has been wonderful – like I never left.' That's soap.

Pamela Ewing is the bosomy beauty to blame for nearly 300 hours

of 'Dallas'. If Bobby Ewing hadn't met her, married her and brought her home to momma in his shiny red Mercedes, that Barnes–Ewing rumpus might have stayed unwritten and unfought. But David Jacobs had this notion of poor not-so-pure Pam and rich Bobby each with a big brother who wanted them apart. What with Pam's daddy Digger being Bobby's daddy Jock's old partner and Jock ending up stinking rich while Digger was only stinking drunk, there was enough bad feeling to fill . . . well, eleven years of soap.

Pam should have been played by Linda Evans, but Victoria Principal struck Jacobs and the producers as the sort of beautiful woman that women watching would like (and men watching would like even more). They did. *Penthouse* readers voted her Sexiest Woman in the World in 1985.

In the early episodes it was clear Pam had put it about a bit. A first husband turned up. Ray Krebbs was revealed as her beau before Bobby, and JR treated her like trash. But then Pam became a virgin again. Even when she was pregnant – even when, after her divorce from Bobby, she finally slept with Mark Graison – she was prim, prissy and sweet. Anyway, there she was, with her silky dresses, cut-away swimsuits and perfect make-up day and night, an outcast in her in-laws' house, turning into a peacemaker. She was the ideal aunt to Lucy, the rebellious schoolgirl. She helped Sue Ellen with her baby, helped Miss Ellie in her grief over Jock's death, and prevented Cliff from destroying Ewing Oil the first few dozen times. It was something of a shock when she suddenly had a breakdown and tried to jump from the roof of a skyscraper. Bobby grabbed her, and she got well soon.

When Jock died, Pam influenced Bobby to get stuck in at Ewing Oil. This cramped JR's style and made him hate her all the more. Pam persevered, politely putting up with the Ewings and their open-air breakfasts in the wind, not to mention her newly returned battle-axe mother, Rebecca, and psychopathic half-sister Katherine (whose modest aim in life was to kill Bobby).

She even managed to be a model mother to adopted bun-faced baby Christopher; help run a department store; then, as Dallas's answer to Jane Fonda, run a gym and, from time to time, put in service as an instant oil-company executive for or against Ewing Oil.

Pam wasn't just Juliet to Bobby's Romeo, she was Mother Theresa, Nancy Reagan and Wonderwoman, too. The only jobs she escaped (as did Sue Ellen) were the cooking and the laundry. Miss Ellie made cookies in the kitchen; and Teresa, the only Southfork servant ever to warrant a name, must have done the rest.

When last seen Pam was plastered – wrapped head to toe in stiff bandages, only one false eyelash peeping through. She'd been burned to a crisp in a car crash, and rumours were it was the producer's mother inside, done up like a mummy-dummy, not Victoria Principal. Miraculously, though bound and helpless, Pam managed to find a pen and paper to tell Bobby and Christopher she loved them. Then she scarpered – to mini-series new. That was 1987. Her doll-face will, she said, never again darken Southfork's door. Perhaps JR's henchmen got her in the end. Perhaps it was all another dream.

Victoria Principal said, 'Bye, bye bimbo, good riddance,' when she shed Pam Ewing's pouting persona last year and left 'Dallas' after more than nine years. 'I won't use the phrase "sick of Pam"; she was a decade out of my life which changed it completely so I never need work again,' said the thirty-eight-year-old actress. 'But I had to get out of her; the poor girl was starting to turn me grey. Towards the end she became so goody-goody and prissy, I could have kicked her.'

Nevertheless Victoria regretted that Pam was robbed of a death scene. When her television husband Bobby died, she said, 'he got to say goodbye to everyone but his horse.' The 'Dallas' producers had hoped to lure Victoria back, but the actress who'd spent two years in the mid-seventies as an agent guiding others' careers knew firmly she wanted to leave. Unlike other former soap stars, it's unthinkable that she will sink into obscurity.

Victoria's life seems always to have been a publicist's dream. At sixteen she ran away from home – her father had been a United States Air Force sergeant, and 'home' was many places, including Ruislip in Britain – to live with flamboyant financier Bernie Cornfeld. The affair ended in scandal when she took him to court on charges of physical abuse. She then went to Hollywood to play Paul Newman's girlfriend in the film *The Life and Times of Judge Roy Bean*, while pleasing the gossip columnists with her off-camera friendships. Among many close to the starlet were Frank Sinatra, Warren Beatty and Elliot Gould.

Then came 'Dallas' and backstage romance and marriage with actor Christopher Skinner, hired for a bit part. The couple split up after twenty months. Andy Gibb of the Bee Gees pop group was next in line. While rehearsing a television show, he confessed to a producer that he watched 'Dallas' religiously to catch sight of Victoria. Coincidentally she was in the next studio, also rehearsing, and the message was passed. Victoria was helped to pop out from behind the curtains as Gibb was helped to mention his devotion to Pam before a studio audience. The actress gave the startled pop star a kiss which began a two-year affair. It ended, she claimed, when the rock-and-roll life of parties, drugs and travel wore her down.

Victoria married plastic surgeon Harry Glassman in 1985 with almost as much pre-nuptial publicity as Prince Charles. By that time she was the author of two successful books on beauty and health (a third one, on diet, has followed). The wedding, in Dallas during filming of the series, was a 'private affair' with only the world's press waiting at the door. Afterwards came a 'wedding contract' to formalise the couple's financial arrangements (Dr Glassman had tax and first-wife problems). 'I'm not your average ding-a-ling!' joked Victoria at the time, and no one was arguing.

Since 'Dallas' the slim beauty (who insists her husband's surgical skills have never been used on her) has filmed a mini-series, 'The Mistress', and co-directed a series in which she starred as a woman aged from nineteen to fifty-six.

But let's end with Victoria as the girl who never aged past twenty-three: Pamela Ewing. Leonard Katzman remembers the audition. She came into the room wearing skin-tight pants, a clinging sweater with a gold map of Texas dangling into a plunging neckline. Said Katzman: 'The casting committee had difficulty looking her in the eye, but she was in.'

Sue Ellen Ewing is a sexy sufferer, a long-term loser who arouses lust both in her on/off husband and in the male half of the 'Dallas' audience. In the person of actress Linda Gray, her luscious lips have more quiver than Robin Hood, her poppy eyes give her the look of a battered bush-baby, but a beddable battered bush-baby, as fate and JR make her life insupportable. But, like all the suffering women of soap, she does support it, frequently with the help of alcohol or comforting cowboys and always with that stupid optimism that makes her believe JR's promises that 'It'll be different, this time S'wellin!' As rocky soap marriages go, theirs is a good one. We always know both can't live with each other and can't live without each other.

At the start Sue Ellen was a nothing part, two or three lines in the first episode; she didn't even rate a name. JR called her 'darlin'' or 'honey'. Leonard Katzman, the producer, said: 'She was just the brunette on the couch.' Her creator, David Jacobs, told me: 'I had this idea that the most popular girl in the school never gets to be the happiest housewife on the block. I saw Sue Ellen as this kind of girl, a girl who tried. She became Miss Texas, married the rich Ewings' son, the best catch around, then did absolutely everything right and couldn't fathom why it wasn't working.'

Mary Frann (now in the 'Newhart' comedy series) was pinpointed for the part. Unknown Linda Gray got it. Jacobs went on: 'I fell in love with Linda – so I immediately made the rôle bigger. I wrote a scene for her screen test in which she puts on some sexy underwear to try to interest JR. She was so effective.'

So Sue Ellen's life began with a failing seven-year-old marriage and a failure to get pregnant. Pam, her new sister-in-law, beat her to it, so Sue Ellen tried and failed to adopt – or buy – a baby for £10,000. Then came the affair with Cliff Barnes, the baby born prematurely (of course), the kerfuffle over the inherited disease neurofibromatosis, a new start with JR, the booze, drying out, Lusty Dusty, divorce, a toy-boy lover 'Peeder' (Christopher Atkins), another pregnancy, miscarriage, more drink, more Dusty, more everything.

It was only when Sue Ellen bought a scanty undies business from the Donald Duck-like Mr Valentine to exploit JR's mistress, Mandy Winger, that Sue Ellen seemed anything more than a victim. But the big battles with JR – the freeze-ups and the sexy reconciliations – remain constant. Linda Gray told me: 'Poor old Sue Ellen, she's been through absolutely everything. She represents a great deal of inspiration to a lot of women. We all have a human condition – we all have something we're trying to overcome in our lives – trying to stop eating so much, drinking so much, talking so much. She has overcome quite a few of them. She's not completely through to the other side, but she is a survivor. To me she's by far the most interesting character in the series.'

And there are women like Sue Ellen, said Larry Hagman. 'Texan women are treated like second-class citizens but they have their own way of getting back. They marry five times and acquire big chunks of property in divorce settlements. Besides, you can't exactly blame JR for the way he treats Sue Ellen. She ain't no angel.'

Are there husbands like JR? I asked Linda. 'No question. There are men who fantasise about treating women as badly as JR treats Sue Ellen. It goes back to their childhood and it's passed on in families, in Texas for sure and in lots of other places around the world.'

Linda Gray says she has been a split personality for eleven years thanks to sexy Texan Sue Ellen, dumbo of 'Dallas'. 'Most people in a television series, especially a long one, play themselves because it's easier,' she said. 'They don't have to work. But when the cameras start rolling I not only get an accent, I walk differently, talk differently, I look different. I've done that for almost eleven years; it's creatively important to me.'

Creativity is now vitally important to the Californian actress who worked as a model, and switched to acting at the age of thirty-two. She appeared in 'Marcus Welby, MD', played a transexual in the film *All That Glitters* and appeared in several television films including *Murder in Peyton Place*. Then came 'Dallas'. In 1982 she was named Woman of the Year by the Hollywood Television and Radio Society and won the Italian equivalent of an Oscar for Sue Ellen.

Shortly afterwards Linda and Sue Ellen fell out. 'When she was going through yet another alcohol bit I became bored. I thought about leaving but instead I went to a "Women in Film" course at UCLA on Sundays.' It proved important. She told me: 'My grandmother said to me before she died: "Don't ever sit on the front porch of an old folks' home and say, 'Why didn't I do that?' or 'Why didn't I try this?'" Then I asked the "Dallas" people if I could direct some episodes. Larry [Hagman] and Patrick [Duffy] have done it for some time – about three or four episodes a series. They said no. I asked again, and they agreed, but I knew they would be watching like a hawk because *she* was directing. But, because I was prepared, I didn't make mistakes.' Linda has now directed four episodes, and producer Leonard Katzman declares himself mightily impressed.

Now, at forty-five, her twenty-one-year marriage to art director Ed Thrasher over and her son and daughter grown and away, Linda lives with her dog and some chickens on a ranch in Canyon City, an hour's trip from the studios. She savours her freedom, unlike Sue Ellen. 'I'll just keep plugging away, forging ahead,' said the actress. 'I'm really loving the process. I don't care if I'm criticised. To hell with everybody else. You get tired of taking orders. I want to take control of a project, do something with merit. I don't know how long my friend Sue Ellen will last but, rather than waiting for the next script to come to me, I need to focus my attention and my clout and do something positive with my celebrity.' Enough to frighten S'wellin back to the booze!

DISASTERS

Disasters disrupt soap life decidedly less than they might ours. Houses burn down, planes crash, earthquakes ruin, wars rage. But soap-folk go on – with hardly a hair out of place.

The high number of natural and unnatural calamities is not a sign that God hates soap. Usually they're a sign that the producers are fed up with the pay demands of the cast (so why not kill him, her or them for the cliffhanger and end the rows?) or they want to change the sets and setting fire to them on screen adds a dramatic incident to the plot.

'Crossroads' had two memorable fires. With the first they needed to explain a new look (they were moving studios) so the script had an unexploded bomb found in the grounds when a chalet was being built suddenly explode. After the disaster the script had the staff sent off to Tunisia (Tunisia, Birmingham, that is). With the second the motel burned down after a children's fireworks party. It was a way of getting rid of the putrid mauve-painted décor when parts of the scenery were ignited at an airfield. It was also a way to get rid of Meg when Central decided Noele Gordon must go. After the audience gasped, believing her to have been burned to a crisp, she emerged in the next episode and was soon sailing away on the QE2 to New York.

'Coronation Street' writers enjoy a good fire, and they're very partial to guns. The Rover's burned down in 1986 to allow the twenty-six-year-old set to be renewed. In an excellent episode, Jack Duckworth's botched rewiring in the cellar started the blaze. Heroic little Kevin saved Bet, and Julie Goodyear had a chance to do heavy acting from a hospital bed without her eye make-up. In 1975 kids smoking set the warehouse alight. Edna Gee was killed. A new building, soon to become Baldwin's Casuals, could be built.

'Dallas' producers decided to redecorate Southfork but didn't miss the chance of a spectacular blaze in 1984. With the new paints and papers supposedly stacked in the house, JR and Ray began a fight, a candle was knocked over and turmoil began.

'Dynasty' killed two birds with one stone when they decided to economise on the number of show sets. La Mirage, the hotel, had outlived its usefulness, as had the character of Claudia (Pamela Bellwood). Claudia, who was mad most of the time, had slept with every male in the cast, and most viewers would have cheerfully ordered men in white coats to carry her off. Instead the script had her lighting candles and going up in smoke along with the hotel.

'Falcon Crest' is the soap that never misses the chance for a disaster which also provides a corpse-littered cliffhanger for the series. Mad Julia's mass-shooting spree was also, like Moldavian massacre in 'Dynasty', a warning to the members of the cast suffering from self-esteem problems that they'd best stop asking for more money or they'd stay dead.

The other way of negotiating pay is the shoot-out. 'Coronation Street' props include a small arsenal of guns. Elsie Tanner was held at gunpoint by one of her lovers. Stan Ogden had to do something strenuous once: put his hands up for a gunman. And Ernie Bishop died the victim of armed raiders at the post office (presumably a big snatch including Albert Tatlock's pension money) when the actor Stephen Hancock, who played Bishop, asked for a rise.

But *the* soap shooting has to be the 1980 plugging of JR in 'Dallas', which was to have been a warning to the actor Larry Hagman that demands for big money don't work. There were even carefully leaked stories that another actor was being groomed for the part of JR after plastic surgery. Luckily the producers realised that no Larry Hagman meant no show. But the bullets did effect an economy of a kind. The least-valued character was eventually revealed as the person who fired the gun. Kristin (Mary Crosby) was found floating in the Southfork pool.

DIVORCE

Divorce is a deeply serious act in soap opera, although it may not always seem so. The way soap opera works its way into our affections, after all, is by presenting us with different versions of one story: a family at war. Any act which harms the group is a serious matter, and a soap character must be seen to suffer when divorce is contemplated. He or she could be miserable for a number of episodes, possibly even a number of months! If you remember how quickly characters can be forgiven their crimes and accepted back into the family home, it's clear that marriage-breaking is a crime akin to attempted murder, abduction, blackmail, almost anything bad. The only way a divorced character can make amends is to remarry that partner.

In American soaps divorce and remarriage is quite common. Blake and Krystle, the 'goodies' of 'Dynasty', managed not exactly to divorce. Their marriage was pronounced invalid because Krystle turned out to be legally married still to her former husband. But they *had* split; there was great unhappiness which a new marriage ceremony cured. Alexis is allowed to suffer divorce because she is a 'baddie', but even she regrets it. She bitterly regrets that she and Blake were divorced and she occasionally regrets that she and Dex were divorced. Good Jeff is deeply miserable when he and Fallon are divorced – they've done it twice. I wouldn't be surprised if they married a third time to end the pain. (Soap misery, like soap happiness, cannot afford to last lest the viewer become bored.)

'Dallas' also features divorce and remarriage. JR and Sue Ellen appear to be heading for their second divorce. The first was shown to have a hurtful effect on Sue Ellen and their son John Ross and cause the blessed Miss Ellie heartache.

Poor Ray Krebbs was made seriously unhappy by his divorce from Donna. Donna had already broken from the family by returning to live with her sophisticated Washington political set. She, too, was made wretched (the woman was about to give birth at the time), but Ray's suffering and subsequent heroism in not demanding custody of their baby daughter were presented as the greater.

The divorce of star-crossed lovers Bobby and Pam in 'Dallas' was one long pain. It was clear both still loved each other but they each had to clear a number of hurdles (other suitors, the meddling of wicked sisters and brothers) before the *status quo* could be re-established and they could be a family again. Well, until the next crisis.

Divorce is more rare in British soap. When Den announced he was suing for divorce from Angie in 'EastEnders' it was seen as a far more serious move than his prolonged adultery. While they have not yet remarried, it is a subject they discussed frequently. Angie, who suffered more from the split, wanted it badly.

In 'The Archers' divorce is even more serious a disaster than double foot and mouth. Dan's daughter Christine was unhappily married to Paul Johnson for years but they killed him off rather than let them disgrace the family name with a divorce. The official 'Archers'' guide can't bring itself to note that Jennifer divorced upper-class cad Roger Travers Macey. She did but she'll never be allowed to divorce her current caddish husband, womaniser Brian Aldridge. 'Archers' fans couldn't bear it. 'Howards Way' may copy the American glossies but not in matters of divorce. Jan Howard divorced Tom in the third series although his adultery began in esidode one of the first. Both were cut up about it. Tom sat gloomily with a whisky bottle at work. Their remarriage looks a good bet.

In 'Neighbours' Madge is divorced because her ex-husband was a family-splitter. He left to live with his secretary and later treated that woman badly. Madge is shown to be the devoted mother, looking after her children, brothers and, at one stage, her parents. She is someone who wants to remarry badly. People who disregard the interests of their families are always the baddies in Australian soaps.

In 'Coronation Street' Brian and Gail Tilsley were divorced after her adultery but remarried when both partners repented. Brian may be guilty of putting millions off their supper but he's a family man, so all is forgiven.

'DR KILDARE'

'Dr Kildare' wouldn't be mentioned in a soaps' encyclopaedia (it was mainly a series of hour-long self-contained dramas) except that it's impossible to think of any medical soap since which hasn't built on its tremendous appeal. Made by America's National Broadcasting Corporation, it ran both there and here on BBC1 from 1961 to 1966.

Before television there had been a successful radio series, and before that a series of Hollywood films starring Lew Ayres as Kildare and Lionel Barrymore as Dr Gillespie. But it was Richard Chamberlain as the idealistic young doctor and Raymond Massey as his stern superior which made it an instant hit. Ratings in Britain grew from an impressive 12 million start to over 15 million in 1962. For the first two years, Kildare was one of a trio of interns (Jud Taylor played Dr Gerson, Eddie Ryder played Dr Agurski). Later the drama shifted to the ever warm-eyed James Kildare's relationship with his patients at Blair Hospital and, to compete with 'Peyton Place', its producer Norman Felton changed it to a continuing serial. In America it was shown twice weekly in half-hour episodes. Strangely it began and ended at the same time as its more muscular rival 'Ben Casey', starring Vince Edwards. Richard Chamberlain went on to success on stage, in films and most spectacularly in television mini-series such as 'Shōgun' and 'The Thorn Birds'. The BBC repeated the series several times. Episodes were shown this year. 'Ben Casey' was re-run in afternoon slots on ITV to match.

'THE DOCTORS'

'The Doctors' was the first BBC twice-weekly serial made in colour, screened from November 1969 to June 1971, about a group of doctors, nurses and health visitors working in a group practice in the Islington area of North London. Devised by Colin Morris, responsible for 'The Newcomers', it was to be modern, authentic and serious. Fay Weldon and Elaine Morgan were among the writers. No love-affairs between the doctors, no antiseptic sentimentality as in 'Dr Kildare' or 'Emergency – Ward Ten', they announced. Instead predictably it bore the stamp of pre-'EastEnders' BBC worthiness. But the trio of fraught doctors was instantly liked by audiences of up to 8 million. John Barrie was believably grave as crusty pipe-smoking Dr John Somers; Richard Leach (who was really a doctor before becoming an actor) was much praised as the strained Dr Roger Hayman (with neurotic wife); and Justine Lord was soon tagged 'the sexiest woman on television', playing the crisp efficient Dr Liz McNeal, in love with a married sociology lecturer. Nigel Stock joined them in the second year as an old-style Welsh GP. Seasoned actors and actresses (they included Richard Greene and Jean Kent) kept appointments as patients. Then, in the manner successfully used later in 'The Practice' and 'St Elsewhere', three or four longer story-lines occasionally mentioning ladies' unmentionables, mostly touching on social problems, were wrapped up over two or three weeks.

Despite loyal audiences, the serial was never promoted with great enthusiasm by the BBC (still somewhat snooty about soap opera). After its 1971 summer break, it was not brought back.

Justine Lord was a rare thing, a soap heroine with a career, in 'The Doctors'. She played impatient but efficient Dr Liz McNeal, battling against the odds to do good for her London problem patients, while snatching only fleeting comfort from her selfish married lover. As the

205

kissing started the doorbell always rang.

The slim sophisticated blonde arrived fresh from 'Compact', in which she played a receptionist, and other sixties television series including 'The Trouble Shooters'. A great favourite with both male and female viewers, she laughed off her label of 'the sexiest woman on television'. Her hobby, she said, was paint-stripping not shirt-ripping.

DRUGS

Drugs are always a Bad Thing in soap, and drug addiction is frequently used as a terrible problem which endangers family life. Mostly there are miraculous recoveries, sometimes a death; and sometimes a black-hearted villain, a dealer, appears. Addiction to prescription drugs is a plot-line used more and more to illustrate the sufferings of women.

In 1987, AIDS seemed to oust drug addiction as the worst of today's evils. 'EastEnders' whipped up an AIDS scare for its gay couple Colin and Barry. 'Brookside' had a real case, a heterosexual shop steward of whom few had ever heard before and about whom fewer cared. 'Dynasty' and 'Dallas' slipped in little references to the disease: Blake lectured his gay son Steven on it, JR reminded a young protégé to call at the drugstore before a sex session with that good ol' oil-girl Marilee Stone.

But, unlike AIDS, drugs-dependance has unlimited mileage and the sufferers have only to look dishevelled occasionally. They don't have to wither and die. 'Crossroads' has given many characters temporary drugs problems. Diane, Jill and Hugh Mortimer suffered and recovered. The soap did it best with the heroin-addicted son of Harry Maguire, a character brought in as a temporary manager at the garage. The disappointment, worry and sadness caused by his son Peter's addiction and the criminal behaviour which accompanied it were revealed as the cause of Maguire's appalling grumpiness. Eventually Peter died from an overdose and his father left, cautionary tale complete.

In the medicated soaps 'Casualty', 'The Practice' and 'A Country Practice' all manner of drug addiction is illustrated. 'Casualty' had a girl addict tricking a young doctor into giving her a pain-relieving injection, then flouncing out triumphantly. 'St Elsewhere' often showed the violence which accompanies any involvement with narcotics.

'Dynasty' introduced the wicked Peter De Vilbis, a cocaine addict and dealer, and showed him wreck Fallon's happiness and kill himself in a plane crash. It also showed the star of Blake's football team taking drugs and letting down the group. The man was shown as a fool and a reprobate. He died later from an overdose.

'EastEnders' made its demon Nick Cotton a heroin addict to explain his immorality in part. When he appeared later he announced that he'd kicked the habit. Perhaps because black-clad Nick is almost a panto-mime villain, a continuing drug addiction would be too real and too worrying a problem for viewers to accept.

'Neighbours' put dotty Eileen through a prescription-drugs misery; it gave actress Myra De Groot a chance to show her skills. Eileen recovered after she sensibly sought help. 'Emmerdale Farm''s new producer Stuart Doughty also promised a prescription pills drama. Suffering Sandie or depressed Dolly? We must wait to see.

'Knots Landing' used a similar plot for Karen. She handled it well in contrast to the tougher character of Abby who collapsed when she learned that her daughter Olivia had become hooked on illegal drugs. And in 'Dallas' this year calamity Cliff Barnes became addicted to tranquillisers. As if he hadn't suffered enough, poor soul.

'DYNASTY'

'Dynasty' was the fantasy soap series the women of America, Britain and all over the world had been waiting for. It was designed to be about luxury, romance, money, entrapment, clothes, children, power and more money.

The American writer John Keeler traced soap opera back to the English eighteenth-century novel, especially Samuel Richardson's *Pamela*, which is about a servant girl who marries her master. Krystle was a secretary who married her boss. She was beautiful and good. Blake was charming and rich. Not so much has changed in two and a half centuries.

By 1981 some things had changed, though, thanks to 'Dallas'. The oil industry was considered immensely exciting. 'Dallas' – partly about feuding families, partly about land deals and wiping the floor with women – had put glossy soap back in fashion. Three years later Esther Shapiro, former vice-president of mini-series for ABC ('Roots', 'The Woman's Room', 'The Winds of War'), was hired by television mogul Aaron Spelling to 'do' an alternative with her writer-producer husband Richard. The pair, contemporaries and friends with Eileen and Robert Pollock, began to write 'the bible' for the soap that was to be loved or loathed, but never ignored, for most of the decade.

They wrote it in the Warner Studios, which used to be Mary Pickford's studios, in Mae West's old dressing-room. Esther had loved 'I Claudius', the BBC series based on Robert Graves's novels about villainy among a dynasty of Roman emperors. 'I thought: These Roman families aren't very different from what I see about me. Basically I want to write about winners, people with power to control others' lives. I could see a sea of cars from the window. I thought: Someone in oil is controlling this. They have huge mansions, they're the nearest we have to kings,' she explained.

There were objections, of course. 'As long as I've been in television people have told me audiences don't identify with the rich, they don't like unsympathetic people,' said Esther. 'I needed to prove them wrong. So I laid horrendous problems on these people, problems that didn't go away. A young man, Steven, in search of his sexual identity. A daughter who has everything but is suffering because her life is a shambles. Blake, really a nineteenth-century moralist who knows the world would be perfect if everyone did what he wanted. Krystle – the quintessential sex-object, the epitome of what a lot of women would like to be. And then we had Alexis, the classic "other" wife.'

It was important that Esther's emperors and empresses weren't young. John Forsythe (Blake) is seventy, Linda Evans (Krystle) is forty-five, Joan Collins (Alexis) is fifty-four. 'On TV I saw all those kids in jeans jumping over fences. The basic heroine was an eighteen-year-old girl. Being an older woman, I wanted to see more women, more elegance. The only time older women got rôles was to play a housewife getting liberated or having an affair with a twenty-one-year-old man. That doesn't necessarily turn people on. . . .'

At first the media weren't turned on to Esther's cast, either. 'Linda Evans and Joan Collins were better actresses than they were twenty years ago, they looked wonderful, but nobody wanted to put them on magazine covers.' Some things do change.

THE DYNAMICS

The woman who taught Alexis all her dirty tricks is Eileen Pollock. Eileen may have been married contentedly to the same man, Robert Pollock, for forty years, and may never have ground a stiletto heel in a rival's face. But before she became, with Robert, a highly respected writer (the couple won the first ever Emmy for a soap, 'The Doctors', in 1971) Eileen was an actress. She played bitches. She knows bitches.

The Pollocks were brought into 'Dynasty' after fourteen episodes had produced low ratings and lower morale. They diagnosed what was lacking: a villainous first wife for Blake they called Alexis. With Alexis there was a triangle. Blake Carrington at the top, Alexis and Krystle, the second wife, on the base. Then they had to make Alexis effective. They moved her into the studio she claimed was hers, next door to the mansion. Then they had to make her powerful. Re-enter rich Cecil Colby, business rival of Blake, as her suitor who would conveniently croak as the wedding ceremony ended.

They began writing, introducing their villainess, veiled in the final scene of the first series. She had entered as a surprise witness at the murder trial of Blake, to testify against him. But Alexis had to win battles with two powerful men before she was properly born.

Under the veil was an extra. Sophia Loren, the Italian film queen, was set to emerge for three episodes when the new series began. Aaron Spelling, the unimaginably rich and powerful mogul behind 'Dynasty' and many other expensive American entertainment series, had himself approached her believing her name would save the show.

Eileen and Robert despaired. She told me: 'I'd worked for Aaron about twenty-seven minutes and I went in and told him he was about to throw away millions if he wasted the character like that. He said: "OK – but explain it to someone in the next office." I said: "All right." I went next door to face Carlo Ponti, Sophia's producer-husband.'

Ponti is no pussycat. Eileen tried to explain, her face pained, that this woman his warm and lovely wife was thinking of playing was so evil, so black, so vile she would even cause another woman to lose her baby. 'I broke into my best Anna Magnani accent,' said Eileen. 'Ponti paused and then said: "Magnifico! Sophia would love to play her!"'

What killed it – mercifully for the Pollocks – was lire. Ponti wanted the same 'guest' fee, $150,000 an episode, for every episode. As a continuing character that would be ruinous. Aaron Spelling could always do his sums.

So the Pollocks started looking at clips from the film library.

At that time, British actress Joan Collins wasn't a name from the past so much as a no-name. She'd recently appeared in what the Pollocks considered a couple of porno movies. Eileen said: 'We came across a clip from something called "Fantasy Island". It was hysterically camp. Under a Cleopatra wig with grotesque turquoise eye make-up was Joan Collins. She had so much energy. Robert and I said at once: "Alexis"!'

The Pollocks wrote every outline of every episode for the next three years. At the start of the second series in America, the show began to move up the ratings. By October it was number eight. It had been forty-one.

'We'd stopped the waffle,' said Eileen. 'We invented emotional complications – business is not a passion, even if being successful in it is. We used all the staples of daytime soap opera: illness, pregnancy, love, hate, yearning. The Carringtons weren't just the rich folks on the hill, they were the unhappiest folk in television'.

By the end of the fourth season 'Dynasty' had beaten 'Dallas' in America. (This did not happen in Britain.) The Pollocks took off for Europe, a new project on their note pads.

After the Moldavian massacre, the cliffhanger to the 1985 season, they came back to pick over the corpses of the cast, to revive the show, create (then bury) 'The Colbys'.

This year they were supervising producers of 'Dynasty' as the Shapiros – the soap's other godparents – moved into new projects.

THE HISTORY

The carryings-on of the Carringtons of Denver, Colorado, aren't easy to summarise. Esther Shapiro, creator of 'Dynasty', once said of the plots: 'We don't do reality.' She should have added: 'We do shamelessness.' No old notion, no camped-up catastrophe was left unused. To returning long-lost children, spouses, sisters and brothers, to blindness, amnesia, problem pregnancy, pottiness and presumed deaths add fires, falls, every kind of accident, kidnap and breakdown. There was even a wedding-eve heart attack and an attempted murder by poisonous paint. Blake failed to spot an impostor in his bed for weeks (Krystle was abducted by her white-trash niece Sammy Jo's friend – played by Linda Evans, of course). A barmy Congressman dressed up as Alexis (Joan Collins) to commit a murder, and the disguise fooled her son so that she was almost convicted of the crime. Later Alexis disguised herself as a nun. That, too, fooled an army of Moldavian revolutionaries. Yes, honestly.

Outrageousness seemed to win audiences. Esther claimed: 'People wrote saying: "We love it when it's wild. The next thing you're going to do is tie them [the characters] to the railroad tracks".' They haven't done it yet. But when mad Claudia dropped Fallon's baby from a skyscraper roof and it turned out to be a doll I thought it could come next.

For British viewers, who caught up with 'Dynasty' a year later, the Carrington residence was a large part of the fascination. With opening aerial views of Mansion Fioli in San Mateo (the mansion used in the film *Heaven Can Wait*) and clinging shots of some of its forty-eight rooms, halls, the gym, solarium, ballroom and library (actually, tthese were five or six sets, cleverly rearranged in the studios), the place seemed fit for any emperor. Liberace would have liked it, too.

Watching the clothes was also fun. 'Dallas' women had shoulder-pads and plunging necklines. 'Dynasty' women had those and wings, flounces, trains, bustles – the sort of dresses Danny La Rue and every other drag artist would die for. 'Dynasty' and the arch-flouncing of Alexis, in particular, became a favourite for gay club entertainment. The show was presented on big screens in many of them, and even today a showing at one of the gay bath-houses of California makes any night party night.

The widespread success was due also to the skilful renewal of characters. To the relatively small Carrington clan of Blake, president of Denver-Carrington Oil Corporation, his second wife Krystle, spoilt daughter Fallon, cultured gay son Steven, the snobby butler, the sexy chauffeur and the preppy Jeff Colby who was to marry Fallon (when she could put the chauffeur down for a moment), came many more. Alexis, the old wife; Adam the son, kidnapped at birth; Amanda the daughter Alexis had kept hidden at a boarding school; Dominique Deveraux, singer and Blake's black half-sister who also had a daughter hidden in a boarding school; Blake's brother Ben, who also had a daughter hidden somewhere (I forget); and a succession of men for Alexis to eat. 'Dex' Dexter, her third husband, whom she divorced (of course) seems to endure. Played by Michael Nader, he remains the most caring and yet the most macho of the males.

In 1985 two Hollywood stars – Rock Hudson and Ali McGraw – were brought in, Rock as rich racehorse-owner Daniel Reece who fell for Krystle (see 'The Kiss') and Ali as Lady Ashley Mitchell who fell for Blake. Both were unlucky. Meanwhile nutty Claudia, who'd succeeded Sammy Jo as wife of gay-turned-straight Steven, set her sights at Adam, who'd been accepted back into the mansion despite trying to kill Jeff and despite raping Kirby (who married Jeff) and making her pregnant. Fallon ran off with a coke-snorting playboy only to appear to die with him in a plane crash.

But at the height of its popularity 'Dynasty' overdid it. Esther Shapiro's fantasy about royalty led in the direction of Moldavia, a mythical kingdom (near to Transylvania, no doubt). She invented for Amanda, Alexis's forgotten daughter (played by Catherine Oxenberg with a passably posh English accent), Michael of Moldavia, her wimpy playboy suitor, and devious King Galen, an old flame of Alexis, who offered herself as part of the package. Perhaps the Moldavian Popular Front had heard about Alexis and didn't fancy her as a future queen. Anyway, as the Carringtons togged up and trekked out *en masse*, the revolution began. The wedding (see 'Weddings'), held in what looked like a greenhouse, turned into an ear-splitting bloodbath with every character collapsing apparently riddled with bullet-holes. Only Jeff was moving – because he had to make the start of 'The Colbys', in which he starred. By the next season most of the others couldn't stay dead. But Luke, Steven's gay lover, died mawkishly in the first episode. As one by one the Carringtons awoke, crawled away and escaped the gunmen to arrive back in Denver shaken but not stirred, audiences worldwide hissed 'Swizz' and began to switch off.

The frantic plots continued: Alexis made Blake bankrupt and took over the mansion. Claudia survived the massacre but died in the fire at Fallon's hotel, La Mirage. More relatives turned up with English accents: English Christopher Cazenove as Blake's embittered brother Ben, English Kate O'Mara as Alexis's scheming sister Caress (the Shapiros thought Brits added Class). Blake and Krystle's baby Christina underwent a heart-swap. Adam married Dana. But – in a defiant gesture – the writers produced more revolutionaries. This time nutty Claudia's presumed-dead nuttier husband Matthew Blaisdale, once Krystle's lover, turned up at the ceremony with machine-gun and pals. The ratings fell further.

In the series seen in 1988, Alexis married the handsome man who saved her from drowning and turned out a swine. Adam and Dana had a child by a surrogate mother. Fallon and Jeff divorced again, and as Blake and Alexis ran rival political campaigns for the governorship of

Dynasty and The Colbys

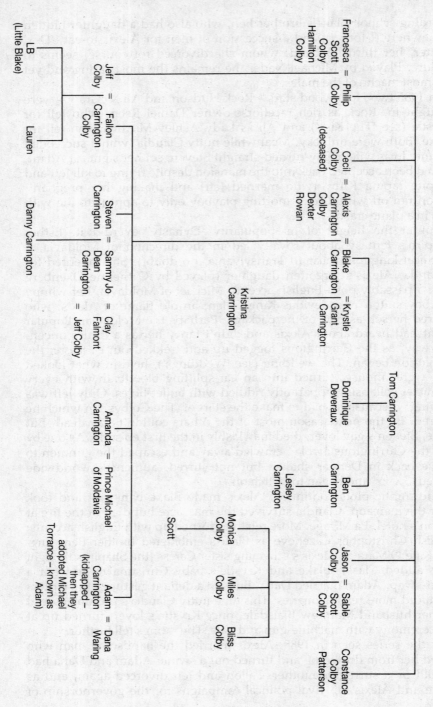

Colorado the younger characters fought in business. The Pollocks hoped their more topical and realistic story-lines would save their dynasty.

The ratings rallied slightly. A producer from 'Dallas', David Paulsen, was poached, given the job of beefing up male characters. But was it too late? The stars in the triangle – Joan Collins, Linda Evans and John Forsythe – each talked of leaving, and America's ABC network seemed slow to rebook. After the autumn 1987 stockmarket crash *Newsweek* declared: 'The Eighties Are Over, Down With Greed.' Sagas of the super-rich seemed sunk. As Alexis would say: 'We'll just see about that!'

THE CHARACTERS

Blake Carrington must be the oldest sex symbol in soap as the tough tycoon of 'Dynasty'. And the most self-satisfied. Conceived as a nineteenth-century man living in a twentieth-century world, a just dictator in a corrupt society, his early sins were neatly buried by the writers. But he did rape Krystle, his wife, in a fit of pique. From that she became pregnant, only to have Alexis cause her to miscarry. He did rail at son Steven for his homosexuality. He did cause the death of Steven's boyfriend Ted Dinard. As for his faithfulness – he did almost betray Krystle with new women as well as Alexis, his 'ex'. And he did (and still does) wear that dreadful double-breasted cardigan with the brass buttons.

Blake's real rôle was probably as the American woman's idea of a proper gent. He bought Krystle so many jewels the diamond mines must have been working overtime. He always noticed her clothes (and didn't laugh); called her 'darling' and phoned home. And he seemed to *like* dressing up in white tie and tails. At least once a series the lilac-haired heart-throb had to roll on the rug in the library and embrace Krystle by the light of the fire. (I don't know what happened next; I could never bear to watch.) At least once a year, too, he became a sort of senior citizen's Action Man, fighting a crazy psychiatrist on a mountain; surviving plane crashes, oil rig explosions, revolutions and sieges. And he had to talk sharply to Alexis whose wickedness he always under-rated.

John Forsythe, at seventy, is worshipped for his efforts as Blake, a character based on Marvin Davis, multi-millionaire oil wildcatter. But younger George Peppard was the first actor hired for the part, then sacked by Esther Shapiro. 'They reshot everything I did – it cost them two million dollars. They were very displeased. After that no one would touch me,' he said later. They did, though, a couple of years later. Peppard found his forte as a Viet veteran committing genocide weekly for children's amusement in 'The A-Team'. I've often suspected *they* were behind the revolutionaries who so nearly slaughtered the Carringtons in Moldavia.

John Forsythe won the part of clan chief Blake Carrington when 'Dynasty' creator Esther Shapiro saw him in a black leather garter-belt beating up naked girls for fun. He was playing a kinky sadistic judge in the film *And Justice for All*. Before that the seventy-year-old New Jersey former baseball-games announcer found his voice, rather than his body, made his fortune. He'd worked in radio soaps; then as a speech counsellor for shell-shocked pilots during the war; then, after several light-hearted television series, as the voice of never-seen Charlie in the series 'Charlie's Angels'.

John's wife of forty years, actress Julie Warren, confirms he is not ruthless or ostentatious like Blake. But he confesses Blake has realised many of his fantasies: owning a football team and an aeroplane, sleeping in silk sheets and having beautiful women wrestling in mud over him.

After a heart bypass operation nine years ago, John has followed a careful diet and exercise régime. He plays tennis well, sails, rides and owns sixteen racehorses. 'At my age,' he says 'I'm lucky to be still playing leading-man parts. What normally happens is you have a choice of becoming a character actor or running for president. I didn't want to run for president.' So far Blake has run for Governor of Colorado. President next series, perhaps.

Krystle Carrington is the moist-eyed madonna of soap opera, the beautiful, patient, good wife in 'Dynasty'. As Krystle Grant at Denver-Carrington Corporation, she married the boss, his mansion, four-posters, solarium, gym and private jet. But she found that his ex-wife, spoilt children, twisting business rivals and half a dozen calamities a week came with the job. So trying to live happily ever after is hard.

Played by striking actress Linda Evans, Krystle smiles radiantly through her tears; frequently whooshes up and down the grand staircase and changes outfits (from shoulder-padded hacking-jacket to shoulder-padded ball-gown, to shoulder-padded nightie – and back). Her revenge is that the ex-wife Alexis wears even more ridiculous outfits and has to change them more often. In the two wives' annual cat-fight, in water, mud and always in public, Krystle tends to win.

Her ex-husband Mark came back to wreck her new life. Her ex-lover Matthew came back to kill her and all the Carringtons. Her white-trash niece Sammy Jo had her kidnapped and leered over by George Hamilton, while her low-life lookalike (also played by Linda Evans, surprise, surprise) strutted the mansion.

Any day now her daughter, sweet little heart-swap patient Christina (Krystle went for unnatural childbirth – no umbilical cord, and her hair wasn't messed up), will turn and attack her. Krystle will look hurt, weep and smile her forgiveness.

Linda Evans should have been the star of 'Dallas' not 'Dynasty'. For ages the Texan soap was subtitled 'Untitled Linda Evans Project'. But the character earmarked for her – Pam Ewing – was too young, too low-class by the time scripts were completed. Linda was released from the contract and, three years later began work as Krystle Carrington, a rôle she described once as 'rich and dramatic' – with which no one could argue.

Linda, forty-five, tall, blonde and as wistful and sweet-mannered as her *alter ego* Krystle, now receives more fan mail than any other character in the seven-year-old soap. It confirms her view that the submissive wife of Blake Carrington is a character people admire. So Linda fights off attempts to change her. 'Linda's a tigress at protecting Krystle as she wants to play her,' writer-producer Eileen Pollock told me. 'I think Krystle is boring. You think Krystle is boring.' (I nodded.) 'Linda says she's not worried about being boring. She won't let Krystle get angry or lose her patience.' So there!

Linda, who grew up in Hollywood, married director John Derek who made her stop her career and pose for *Playboy*, then dumped her for Bo, a fourteen-years-younger model. She married real-estate tycoon Stan Herman, but they split a few years later. Businessman Richard Cohen has been hoping to become husband number three – he built her a £10 million mansion to help her make up her mind – but she remains undecided.

She is a close friend of John Forsythe, who plays her husband Blake; they met when they appeared together in the fifties and sixties series 'Bachelor Father'. She was seventeen. She toiled for years on the American series 'The Big Valley' before the 'Dynasty' rôle came up and, mid-series, Linda has also appeared in the Ingrid Bergman rôle in a remake of *Gaslight* and in 'The Last Frontier', a mini-series set in Australia. But the pleasure of playing Krystle continues: 'It's like your dear friend you talk to on the phone every day,' she said.

Fallon Colby was a spoilt little rich bitch who underwent total plastic and personality surgery in 'Dynasty' and 'The Colbys'. With a name that sounds like something you'd find in the garage (and at the start Fallon was often in the garage, tinkering with the chauffeur), and with the style of actress Pamela Sue Martin, Blake's girl was decadent and daring.

To live with her must have been tiresome. But to watch her, toying with men, twisting her besotted father round her finger, losing her memory or her baby son and breaking husband Jeff's heart, was the opposite. La Mirage, the hotel she decided to build, may not have been Claridges. But it sure looked more fun than the Crossroads Motel.

Then, when Pamela Sue wanted to leave to be a movie star, Emma

Samms came into the rôle. Where old Fallon had been raffish and elegant (no Nolan Miller clothes for her), the new Fallon was sweet, good and – fat. The flowery dress they found for her to marry Miles Colby in resembled the bedroom curtains, half-drawn.

Fallon lived in the Colby mansion in a permanent daze. She thought she was Randall Adams. Jeff and a psychiatrist put her right; while Sable, Miles's mother, tried to do her wrong. She had one of the longest pregnancies in soap, the baby's paternity – Miles or Jeff – being a matter of doubt. Then after the regulation emergency delivery, when Fallon seemed sane at last, she drove to the Mexican border in pursuit of Francesca (Jeff's mother, kidnapped by her back-from-the-dead husband Philip). Her car broke down and a bloke in a body stocking from a spaceship gave her a lift. Why an alien should have picked Fallon is open to speculation. My view is that aliens may be collecting soap characters for a zoo on Mars. They needed an exceptionally dumb brunette.

When Fallon and Jeff returned to 'Dynasty' for the series this year, Fallon's time was explained as another of her 'turns', an out-of-body experience. The aliens' spacecraft smelt of cinnamon, she said. 'Were they baking?' Jeff asked. The poor man's disbelief became grounds for another divorce.

Emma Samms had a rough ride when she first took over the rôle of Fallon in 'Dynasty' in the summer of 1985. Problems with the contracts for the soap rôle she was leaving, in the American 'General Hospital', meant that the young English actress had exhaustingly to overlap work there with that for the Carrington-clan soap. Then critics hated her 'Dynasty' performance. (One American reviewer said: 'She makes you want to crawl over jagged glass on your bare knees to plead with Pamela Sue Martin to return to the rôle she created.' In Britain she was referred to as 'fake Fallon' and 'fat Fallon'.)

Finally, while riding a horse for a 'Dynasty' scene, she was thrown, fell on her microphone battery-pack and injured her back. She couldn't work for a month. 'General Hospital' allowed her to record scenes sitting in bed, but Emma feared the Fallon rôle would be lost.

Her fears were misplaced. 'The Colbys' began in the autumn. No more pleading with Pamela Sue (over jagged glass or not) took place. In the scripts, Fallon's love of horses inexplicably disappeared. But, while Emma worked on, her publicity worked overtime. Her private life, it seemed, was steamier than a Turkish bath. Joan Collins-style myths (or possibly truths) began to grow, and the actress with the butter-wouldn't-melt face became famous for her allegedly torrid affairs, some 'marriage-wrecking', some just 'heart-breaking'. And there were rumours of rows with La Collins. Had Joan insisted that Emma's locks change shade to ensure Alexis stayed the only raven-haired temptress on the show? Pass. But the Fallon who went up in the spaceship was a brunette. The Fallon who came down was a redhead.

What is *not* merely rumour is that the girl from Harrow, daughter of a Jewish manufacturing company boss and a ballet dancer mother, studied at the Royal Ballet school until a year-long illness dashed her dancing hopes. Ballet-lovers will now probably never see Emma's bountiful bosom bounce around *Swan Lake*.

She went to Hollywood, had to serve behind the counter in a delicatessen before the rôle of Holly Sutton in 'General Hospital' saved her from the cream cheese and liverwurst for ever. Also indisputable is the tragic death of her brother Jamie from a bone marrow disease when Emma was ten. It inspired her to launch Starlight, a project to help incurably ill children. Shallow as her 'Dynasty' doll, Emma Samms certainly is not.

Jeff Colby is the gleaming goody-goody of 'Dynasty' who deserves

to marry saintly Krystle in another life and live happily ever after. Jeff, played by John James, was posted from Denver to 'The Colbys' in 1985 (he was the sort of chap people did things to) but was welcomed back with the Carringtons when the spin-off soap spun off the air.

Most of his early time in 'Dynasty' was spent opening and closing doors, looking puzzled. Alexis became his mother-in-law when Fallon was made to marry him (she really preferred Blake's football team) and Alexis was also his aunt when she was married to his Uncle Cecil (for a few moments before he died). He was bright enough never to call her 'Aunty'.

Adam Carrington, jealous of Jeff's position in ColbyCo., run by Alexis, tried to kill him by having his office walls decorated with poisonous paint. A nasty shade of blue, too. Fallon divorced Jeff, freeing him for other females (the game of musical beds in 'Dynasty' must make *The Guinness Book of Records* for Most Interchanged Partners). Kirby, the butler's daughter, was briefly Jeff's wife, but pregnant by Adam. Then Fallon agreed to remarry Jeff only to run off with her drug-crazed playboy lover Peter De Vilbis on the eve of the wedding and be 'killed' in a plane crash. (Pamela Sue Martin, who played Fallon, wanted to leave; see 'Life after Soap'.) Jeff buried Fallon but believed her alive a few scenes later, went to South America to search with Nicole, De Vilbis's widow, and married her while half-asleep. Luckily divorce is quick in soap.

When Fallon was reborn in 'The Colby's (Emma Samms now played the rôle), Jeff's luck didn't improve. She turned out to be married to Miles Colby. If this wasn't bad enough, he met his mother Francesca (Katharine Ross) for the first time to find she looked (and was) only a few years his senior. And his dead father Philip wasn't his father or dead. Jason Colby was his dad!

With Miles trying to drop him over cliffs and his Aunt Sable trying to have him disinherited, the puzzled look stayed. When Fallon disappeared and later said she'd gone up in a UFO he had just the look ready.

Last seen, he and Fallon had become joyful parents for a second time, so naturally they had to divorce. Musical beds continued, Lesley Carrington and Sammy Jo keeping Jeff Colby soap's most baffled boy. The only thing he stopped being baffled by was the fate of his poor mother, who was last seen being dragged across the desert by Philip. When 'The Colbys' ended, Jeff didn't mention his mother or his father again.

John James, who plays Jeff Colby in 'Dynasty' and 'The Colbys', might have done better if he'd played gay. John was tested for the rôle of Steven Carrington, Blake's homosexual son, cultured, moral and at least occasionally happy. When Al Corley won that rôle (Jack Coleman succeeded him) John landed the part of poor Jeff, manhandled by almost every woman in the cast.

Still, I doubt if it's through pity that John, aged thirty, has become the most popular and adored man in the soap. Joan Collins, who should know, called him 'the prettiest person on the set'. One appearance in a pair of tight jodhpurs three years ago still glows in the collective mind.

Jeff's character (I use the term loosely) had only six lines in the pilot, but the jobbing actor from New York was given a year-long holding contract to move to Los Angeles where 'Dynasty' is made.

Known as Jay-Jay, the tall brown-haired sports fan was already familiar to American viewers from a rôle in the daytime soap 'Search for Tomorrow', and between series of 'Dynasty' and 'The Colbys' he has appeared in 'Love Boat', 'Fantasy Island' and a couple of television movies. He had a chance to be the new 007 in the Bond films in 1986 but believes he was turned down because the Bond people knew 'The Colbys' was close to his heart. It certainly was. The actor made a personal crusade to twenty-three cities in a week in the autumn of 1986 to promote the threatened show. The network still dropped it a few months later.

With Emma Samms, John returned to the parent soap and his other crusade. '"Dynasty" is almost comic strip,' he says. 'I saw at the start that all the characters are after money and sex, so I figured I had to be different. I created this moralistic family-oriented man and stuck with it. He's less naïve now, but I think he's too diplomatic still, too eager to work everything out. I'd like to see him throw a tantrum.' Oh, yes – and in jodhpurs, please!

Dominique Deveraux should have been soap's first black bitch in 'Dynasty'. But decency kept creeping in, much to the chagrin of actress-singer Diahann Carroll who played her.

She arrived as a mystery figure in furs and funny hats – a famous singer, it turned out. 'Wasn't there a singing nun called Dominique?' asked Alexis, who loathed her at once. Later she revealed she'd come to Denver to prove she was Blake's illegitimate half-sister – news that temporarily amazed Blake and his (white) dying father. But after swiftly inheriting some of Carrington senior's cash she was able to annoy Alexis (formerly Carrington senior's pet) all the more. They enjoyed at least one wrestling session and several rows.

In time, her husband turned up. An up-till-now-hidden teenage daughter, by a lawyer she'd loved and lost, turned up. The lawyer turned up and was turned down, and the soap's action was punctuated by Dominique's passionately rendered ballads. She was a much better singer than Afton in 'Dallas', but with Dominique we weren't supposed to laugh. The white piano in the curiously titled La Mirage, Fallon's hotel (which Fallon had forgotten by then), came into service.

Dominique managed a medical miracle, too – she almost died, but revived after an operation (to stick her false eyelashes back on, I think). But her force as a villainess was not revived. She left with a young mining engineer for marriage and oblivion 'in New York' last year. They had to burn the piano and La Mirage first, though.

Diahann Carroll won the rôle of Dominique by being pushy. After thirty years of banging on Hollywood doors which stayed shut, she sang at an awards ceremony and gatecrashed a party afterwards held by soap supremo Aaron Spelling. He and co-producer Esther Shapiro agreed they needed a classy black woman for their three-year-old soap, someone on a level with Alexis to discomfort her like hell. Diahann, whose age, good looks and helter-skelter personal fortunes matched Joan Collins's, was ideal. Then aged forty-nine, Diahann had three failed marriages and spells of unemployment and frustration (she wanted to act, not sing) behind her. A long period of drug therapy using controlled doses of LSD ('I spent enough on LSD to buy the Savoy,' she said) helped her morale if not her finances. 'Producers cast black women as hookers or saints,' she said. 'We were never made believable villains because they were afraid of being accused of being racist.' Dominique should have changed it. Perhaps she helped. Diahann earned more than £20,000 a week in the rôle but left, upset that Dominique's bitching had never had enough bite. 'Wherever I went people said: "Get Alexis,"' she said. Perhaps Alexis got Dominique.

Dex Dexter is the wealthy honest mining engineer who is Alexis's chance of salvation in 'Dynasty'. She almost took the chance in 1984 when, after a little bother with a conviction for murdering Krystle's ex-husband, she married him, mostly for love and sex (though it meant a shrewd business merger, too). She soon divorced him after she caught him *in flagrante delicto* with Amanda, her daughter, who was going through a Lolita period at the time.

Dex, played by Michael Nader, was instantly so popular with viewers that the writers kept him in the picture, although with little to do except model his square jaw and act as a conscience for his villainous ex-wife. Repeatedly stating his love for her, saving her from baddies (he doubles as the James Bond of 'Dynasty' when wicked foreigners in distant lands have to be tricked), she repeatedly rejects him. Women around the world take this as proof that she's deranged.

Michael Nader plays Dex, the permanent middle male sexpot of 'Dynasty' (Blake is senior, Jeff is junior). Well suited for the part – he's tall, broad-shouldered, square-jawed, and his hair and teeth are his own – he is probably too good an actor to play doormat to the show's shrew (but don't tell him).

As a surfing-mad teenager in California, Michael was spotted for parts in a series of sixties beach movies. He moved to New York, to the Actors' Studio and took small off-Broadway rôles, supporting himself with work as a waiter and a model.

A three-year part in the American daytime soap 'As the World Turns' followed, a rôle in the mini-series 'Bare Essence' and, aged thirty-eight, an international impact in 'Dynasty'. He made an impact on Joan Collins, too. In one of their early love-scenes the powerfully built actor jokingly grabbed his slim co-star tightly and, in his words, 'planted a ferocious kiss on her'. Joan nursed a bruised lip with an ice-pack for the rest of the day.

Alexis Rowan, the villainess of 'Dynasty', is not a happy woman. She won't be happy until she is throwing the last lily on Krystle Carrington's coffin. Krystle is the 'ex-stenographer' (a phrase Alexis likes to roll and spit) who married Blake, without her permission.

Alexis's origins have never been made clear in 'Dynasty' (probably to allow a steady stream of long-lost relatives to appear when plot-lines ran thin). Played by British actress Joan Collins, there were references to her English birth and to the fact that she behaved so badly to Blake and their children (two were around, a further forgotten two turned up later) that he banished her from the house. He had caught her in bed with Roger Grimes, the estate manager.

When she strutted into the show at the start of its second series, she seemed like Lucretia Borgia, Evita Peron and the Wicked Witch of pantomime rolled into one. She perjured herself at Blake's trial to see him locked up. She moved into the artist's studio by the side of his house to murder some canvas and torment the new wife. She fired the gun that made Krystle's horse bolt and lost her the baby. She used her children as weapons, blackmailed, twisted, lied and grabbed. Later she lived on what looked like a lurex-swathed landing. She smoked, drank champagne and scoffed caviare by the tub. She petted pooches on the bed, but the pets she kept in it never lasted as long.

Husband Cecil's heart seized up during sex (he died as he said 'I do' the next day). Husband Dex was seduced by daughter Amanda. He was out like a shot. Husband Sean sinned first, but soon paid the price. And lovers between husbands were lucky to leave in one piece.

Certainly the Collins-style flounce, red-glossed pout, arched eyebrows and quick-change wigs became a target for fun in Britain. In America, the actress claimed, women admired Alexis's independence and were impressed by her style. She must have been right. In 1984 she was nominated for an Emmy as Outstanding Actress. The diabolical dame of 'Dynasty' had friends.

Joan Collins says she and Alexis, the wicked woman of 'Dynasty', have but two things in common. They both like clothes and they both like men. If that's true, I'm Mickey Mouse.

Joan Collins, born in 1933, daughter of a Jewish theatrical agent and early star of a string of forgettable British and Hollywood films, is now very famous. Very famous for playing Alexis and for being Alexis – or a non-malignant version of her. In America and the more than seventy countries where the glitzy soap is seen, the leading players share roughly equal adulation (Linda Evans, perhaps, just edging in front at home). In Britain the sayings, doings and screwings of Joan Collins have become a national obsession. Exaggerated, they may be. But you couldn't pay a writer to invent her.

Joan went briefly to RADA, but her skill (or lack of it) as an actress has hardly ever been the point. With her stunning looks, dark hair and clipped English vowels, she made an impact in, among many, *The Virgin Queen* with Bette Davis, *Seawife* with Richard Burton, and *Rally Round the Flag, Boys* with Paul Newman.

According to her autobiography, *Past Imperfect*, published in 1978, her first husband, Maxwell Reed, tried to sell her sexual services to an Arab sheikh; she scandalised Hollywood by living openly with Sidney Chaplin; she loved and lost Warren Beatty (with an abortion to follow); had a stream of tempestuous affairs, and a suspension by Fox for refusing to take orders.

When Elizabeth Taylor became ill just before filming on *Cleopatra* was to start, Joan was called in to take what would have been her first major rôle. Elizabeth Taylor recovered. Joan returned disillusioned to Britain, back to cheaply made horror films which paid the bills.

Her second marriage, to Anthony Newley, lasted seven years. They had a son and a daughter, now in their twenties, and Joan had a second daughter during her marriage to producer Ron Kass. With Kass, who died last year, Joan enjoyed a good deal of housewifely bliss in London until Kass moved them to California. There Joan signed on the dole and beat off the bailiffs until parts in soft-porn B-films, based on sister

Jackie's books *The Stud* and *The Bitch* made the housewife a siren again. The success, a few years later of a semi-nude spread of photographs in *Playboy* made Joan, then aged fifty-one, the most celebrated siren in Tinseltown.

As her third marriage failed 'Dynasty' was propelling her into global stardom and superwealth. The actress declared Alexis mostly fun, sometimes 'pure plod', but saw her as a character striking out for women's independence, treating ruthless men with the toughness they deserved. She resisted the image of a 'moustache-twirling baddie' the scriptwriters liked to promote – which seemed a shame. Alexis had also taught her to be a better businesswoman, she claimed, citing her sidelines in Joan Collins hats, glasses, perfume and jewellery.

But her next marriage, to a younger man, Swedish pop singer Peter Holm, showed Joan/Alexis at her worst (or should that be best?). The couple sold their wedding photographs to a newspaper for £200,000. The photographs of their divorce and bitter fight over money thirteen months later came free. He demanded (but was not granted) a massive slice of her new fortune. The tearful court-sessions, televised world-wide, made similar events in 'Dynasty' look tame. Asked what it had taught her, Joan said: 'What I need is a wife.'

In the autumn of 1987 the actress had to defend herself over two new scandals. The first was the mini-series 'Sins' she'd made in a break between 'Dynasty' series. Shown in Britain in a too-early slot, 'Sins' scenes of rape and violence in Nazi Germany angered many viewers. Joan declared herself on their side. The second was over her bust. Had it been boosted? Joan declared it had not.

By the beginning of 1988 she also declared herself indecisive about the future of Alexis. Is there fame for Joan without Alexis? Possibly there is as a party guest. Possibly there is as a producer of pulp mini-series starring Joan Collins as an Alexis clone. Possibly there is as the first sixty-year-old *Playboy* centre-spread. We'll see.

'EASTENDERS'

'EastEnders' made soap opera respectable by making it rough, raw and realistic. If the long steady life of 'Coronation Street' is remarkable, the so far short and sensational life of 'EastEnders' is staggering. It happened because creator and producer Julia Smith is talented and as tough as old boots; creator and script-editor Tony Holland is an intuitive genius; their then BBC bosses were loyal and had strong nerves; and a wasteland of sand and rubbish, Elstree studios, was empty.

At the start of 1984 a patch of land at the back of the BBC's newly acquired Elstree studios lay dormant and derelict. It had last been used six months earlier by the site's previous owners, Central, for their hit series 'Auf Wiedersehen, Pet'. At the same time, in the grey cubby-holes of the BBC's drama department, heads were knocking together. Pretending to ignore Granada's always top-rated 'Coronation Street' couldn't continue. They had to get back at the opposition with a twice-weekly serial and they had to get it right.

Just over a year later, that wasteland had been turned into the bustling Albert Square and the BBC's long-denied dream had become reality in the shape of 'EastEnders'. In another eight months it would be the most popular television show in Britain and eventually the Corporation's most successful ever programme.

THE BREAKTHROUGH

The origins of 'EastEnders' can be traced back to September 1971, to the first time that Julia Smith, director of 'Z Cars', met that show's new script-editor, Tony Holland. It was the beginning of a friendship and working relationship which was to flourish during five years of the biweekly serial 'Angels' and then 'District Nurse', both produced by Julia.

Then, in March 1983, the pair were summoned to London by the then head of series/serials at the BBC, David Reid. The Corporation had decided to stop messing around; they wanted a popular serial, two episodes a week, fifty-two weeks a year.

This was a big step. Back in the sixties, the BBC had tried to respond to 'Coronation Street' with the twice-weekly serials 'Compact', 'United!' and 'The Newcomers', but none of these was supported or successful enough. There was still that old snobbery within the Corporation that this was pulp drama for low-class ITV only. The word 'soap' was taboo. But with ITV and Channel 4 taking 60 per cent of the viewing audience and the Tory Party preparing to put the boot in and change the unprofitable BBC something had to be done.

Jonathan Powell had replaced David Reid. He passed on to Julia Smith and Tony Holland two ideas for the new wonder serial: life in a shopping arcade or in a mobile-home park. Both were non-starters.

At another meeting with Powell, the words 'East End' and 'Victorian Square' came up for the first time. In February 1984, Julia and Tony bashed out a rough format in twenty minutes in a Shepherds Bush wine bar, and Powell sold it to the then controller of BBC1, Alan Hart, in just half an hour. Nine weeks was usually the minimum.

'EastEnders' was born – but not with that title. For a long time, it was referred to as 'East 8'. Then it dawned on Julia that the word she'd used daily in conversation about the prospective series was also the ideal title.

Where could it be made? The real East End of London was too busy, so they settled on the back lot, as it is known, at the Elstree studios bought by the BBC for £7 million. This was converted into the Albert Square that we know and love with houses made of fibreglass and plywood and with real weeds in the gardens. To this day, the set is deliberately roughed up to make it look authentic.

Meanwhile Julia and Tony were in Lanzarote giving birth to Angie and Den, Sue and Ali and all, just as they had done in Crete for 'Angels'. They created twenty-five and returned with forty-seven pages of biographies. Tony used his own relatives for the Beales and Fowlers, while Julia based Dr Legg on her own GP. Some of the character names came from East End cemeteries.

As the wardrobe staff scoured Oxfam shops and jumble sales for characters' clothes, the great day was rapidly approaching. The casting was complete, and they were all set for lift-off on 19 February 1985.

THE HISTORY

The first episode of 'EastEnders', in which Reg Cox was found dead, was watched by over 17 million people. Three days later, the story that

Leslie Grantham was a convicted murderer broke, and the love–hate relationship between 'EastEnders' and Fleet Street began.

The national press were soon obsessed with the show. Anything (fact or fancy) remotely connected with 'EastEnders' made headlines. If Roly the poodle had been able to talk, he could have made a fortune -- except that Julia Smith would probably have had him seen to for his pains! This hysteria blew the programme's importance out of all proportion, but it did wonders for the ratings.

On 24 October, three weeks after Michelle told Den he was the father of her baby, 'EastEnders' topped the viewing figures for the first time, thereby ousting 'Coronation Street' (albeit with the addition of the Sunday omnibus programme).

The show continued to go from strength to strength in 1986. Viewing figures consistently topped the 20 million mark; Anita Dobson and Leslie Grantham won Pye's Outstanding Personality Awards; Den's mistress Jan turned up at the Queen Vic, Angie tried to commit suicide, Arthur was arrested and Michelle finally married Lofty.

Then, at Christmas, Angie and Sharon left Den and deeply depressed Arthur broke up the Fowler household. Those two episodes on Christmas Day attracted audiences of 29.5 million and 31.1 million respectively – the highest-ever recorded viewing figures. Bookmakers had been so confident that 'EastEnders' would top the Christmas ratings that they had refused to take bets.

The miracle continued throughout 1987. The cast and team won a Variety Club award given for the previous year, and 'EastEnders' cast its net further around the world. Already shown in New Zealand and Holland, it added Australia, Norway, Barcelona (where it was dubbed into Catalan) and parts of America to its list. On screen, Arthur went into hospital in January and came home in April, Jan walked out on Den and the Dagmar reopened. Gay Colin's Barry ended the affair. Ethel left the Square at the start of 1988, followed a few months later by Lofty and Angie.

So why has 'EastEnders' washed up so well? Is it because, as some said, it was the soap with the added ingredient: dirt? It's certainly dirty, and daring. More of that later. My theory is that 'EastEnders' is the first male soap. A man who watched 'Crossroads' and tried to talk to his workmates about it the next morning would be laughed at. A man who discusses 'Coronation Street' is thought a bit of a softie (and he's probably old). But a man who knows the score in Den's marriage, or how much Arthur owes the loan sharks, or if Dot has taken that creep Charlie back, is regular, non-suspect, discerning. He could be a pensioner or a fourth-former.

In other soaps men can feel sexual desire and jealousy, grief at a loved one's death and fear, frustration or despair at work. That's it. 'EastEnders' knows better. It has shown, with Arthur, how it feels to be unemployed, disgraced, to lose pride. Then what going barmy from anxiety is like. With Den it has shown what it's like to be trapped in a childless marriage with an alcoholic wife, unable to acknowledge a one and only child, born by mistake. With Lofty it has shown how being soft and sensitive can't make Michelle love him. With Colin it has shown that class and age differences can make a gay relationship collapse. With Pete it shows anguish over Wicksy not being his son. With Ali it shows a traditional macho man's fears about his fertility and his whole manhood. Male characters can sustain scenes together in 'EastEnders'. In 'Coronation Street', for example, all the real confrontations require women.

Women love 'EastEnders' because the men are more recognisably real. True, the female characters are mostly stronger (see 'Women Love Soap'), but this is the first soap to have a large male audience. They like the strong language and the strong emotions behind it.

Because of this maleness – this relative lack of soppiness – teenagers have taken to 'EastEnders' like to no soap before. To make a show educational is usually to give it the kiss of death. But 'EastEnders' educated young viewers about pregnancy, with Michelle; about sex, with Sharon; about getting along with parents, with Mark, Kelvin and very dramatically with Mary (whose narrowly religious mother 'stole' baby Annie). Teenagers and younger children loved it. Rival soaps were positively barren of young characters: 'Coronation Street' hadn't had a teenager, and certainly not a baby, for years; 'Brookside' had scored well with Damon and his pals, then ignored them.

'EastEnders' doesn't duck issues. It is frantically (sometimes perhaps too frantically) controversial. Already it has cot death, unemployment, mental illness, prostitution, schoolgirl pregnancy, suicide, AIDS, homosexuality and loneliness under its belt. It shows inner London as an unlovely place. It is never cute.

Most of the acting and writing are beyond reproach ('Crossroads' this ain't), and the show is so realistic that producer Julia Smith has to be constantly aware of her responsibilities. For example, when Sue Osman had a cancer scare, Julia had to make sure the story ended with a non-malignant tumour. 'Because I was sure that way we would send viewers rushing out to their nearest clinic for breast-screening. If we'd had malignant cancer, they'd have all stayed at home worrying themselves to death, thinking they'd got it, too.' Julia Smith was right. Women did flock for screenings, and the story-line won praise from Junior Health Minister Edwina Currie.

Susan Tully (Michelle) was used to introduce the NSPCC's better-parenting campaign, and Bill Treacher (Arthur) was involved in the Hands Across Britain day – further instances of how 'EastEnders' fiction has blended with reality.

Prisoners at Dartmoor staged a mini-riot when they couldn't see whether Michelle married Lofty; couples rushed to marriage guidance councils after watching Den and Angie's break-up; a vicar talked of forgiving Den in a parish-magazine article; Ken Livingstone once tried to make a political broadcast from the set of 'EastEnders'; and the programme is even on the school syllabus for thousands of inner-London children.

PUBLIC OUTCRY

'EastEnders' has attracted more than its fair share of complaints, a lot of them from Mary Whitehouse. She once said: 'It is at our peril that we allow this series. Its verbal aggression and its atmosphere of physical violence, its homosexuality, its blackmailing pimp and its prostitute, its lies and deceit and its bad language, cannot go unchallenged.' She also attacked the decision to repeat the show on a Sunday. Salisbury coroner John Elgar made adverse comments about Angie's suicide scene, saying it was 'regrettable' and could lead to copycat attempts. A girl died after apparently imitating the idea of Lofty's joke stag-night drink, and switchboards have been jammed on numerous occasions.

Producer Julia Smith defends the show vigorously. 'I think I'm just as moral as Mrs Whitehouse,' she says. 'And I care possibly more deeply. The difference is she generally believes in sweeping things under the carpet and pretending they don't exist. I believe in showing what does exist and preparing people for the world they live in. My prime aim is to entertain, my second is to inform. I do not preach. All I do is lead viewers to reach their own conclusions by having different characters representing different points of view. It would be nonsense to portray the East End without any semblance of violence. It is a very violent place. The people there are not very literate. They express themselves in raucous laughter and hugs, not careful discussion, and it can all turn into anger very quickly. It's a much more physical way of life. I've never been frightened of handling controversial subjects. You can tackle anything, however early in the evening, providing you do it in the right spirit.'

The BBC has stood by 'EastEnders' throughout, notably Alan Hart and his successor as controller of BBC1, Michael Grade. 'The concept has never been diluted by committee rule,' says Julia. 'I'm grateful for the BBC's bravery.'

LIVING WITH 'EASTENDERS'

I don't mean to sound cynical, but 'EastEnders' was lucky to reap endless press coverage from the skeletons in the cupboards of its stars, Leslie Grantham, Peter Dean and Sandy Ratcliff. Bad publicity is always better than no publicity. 'EastEnders' has been rocked by a number of other 'blows', too.

One actress was sacked even before the show went out. The part of Angie was to be played originally by Jean Fennell, but she was not happy with the way Julia Smith wanted her to play the part. Julia had to tell the bitterly disappointed Jean that she was miscast and paid her off. Within twenty-four hours, Anita Dobson took over the rôle in time for the first transmission. David Scarboro refused to speak racist lines as Mark Fowler and so his character had to leave home. But David returned to 'EastEnders' for visits before the young actor's tragic death. Black stars Shreela Ghosh, Sally Sagoe and Oscar James all accused the BBC of racism. Ross Davidson left saying he was 'fed up with being treated like a child'.

Even casting the show's two dogs caused headaches. Ethel was supposed to have had a pet Yorkshire terrier, but a suitable one couldn't be found so she had to settle for a pug instead. Den's dog was to have been an Alsatian called Prince. Again, no RADA Alsatians were available for audition, so the part went to Roly, an apricot standard poodle.

Mary Smith's baby was allowed by law to be on the studio floor for only twenty minutes at a time. She wouldn't stop crying, making filming hazardous. And Leslie Grantham threatened to quit in 1986 over a row about the Venice trip in which he claimed the BBC had tipped off photographers about his flight from Heathrow.

CAN IT LAST?

With strong characters and a strong style now established, the future of 'EastEnders' seems assured – providing they don't become too self-indulgent. Much depends on the success of Pat and Frank as replacement landlords at the Vic. They're older, less sexy than Den and Angie. Fireworks need to come from Den's new affairs and his spiky relationship with Michelle. Also, 'EastEnders' must make sure that the two-characters-only episodes, of which it is so proud, remain occasional and don't get too slow and boring. A little more humour wouldn't go amiss, either.

But these are minor points. There is no reason why 'EastEnders' should not maintain its grip on Britain's heart-strings until Michelle gets a bus pass, Den's in a Bath chair or Dot runs out of fags.

THE PRODUCERS

Julia Smith is known as 'the Godmother' for the way she rules the show with a rod of iron.

(1) She won't let any of the cast change their lines or suggest how characters should develop. 'Tony Holland and I have total images of the characters,' she says. 'They're our creations, not the actors'. Susan Tully almost cut me off for two weeks when she wasn't allowed to marry Lofty. She said I was cruel and called Tony a murderer.'

(2) None of the actors sees scripts more than a week in advance.

(3) Actors have to pay for taxis home unless they're working unusually late.

(4) Actors are forbidden to travel more than fifty miles outside London on any weekday.

(5) They must ask Julia's permission for every interview, public appearance, pantomime rôle, record, etc.

(6) The cast eat in the canteen and don't have limousines. 'They're working actors,' states Julia. 'It's important for them and the show that they remain human beings. That's the difference between the English and American approach.'

Nobody takes liberties with Julia. Shirley Cheriton, who played Debbie Wilkins, used to go to the ladies' after having her make-up put on and reapply it her own way. Julia found out and raged: 'Take that off. You're not a movie star.'

The actors don't do badly, though. For their six-day week, they are paid on average £30,000 a year (each episode costs £40,000 to make), but their earnings can be doubled by personal appearances and the other offshoots of super-soap stardom (see 'Fame').

Sixty-one-year-old Julia does have a softer side. She stood by Leslie Grantham, saying: 'Leslie rebuilt a life for himself, and I admired him for it.' She was able to reward him by giving him an unprecedented four days off when his wife had a baby. 'That meant a lot to me,' says Julia. She knits as she waits and watches rehearsals and recordings. And, according to Tony Holland, she comes up with more malapropisms than Ethel.

She was raised near Olympia in West London at the time of the Blitz, the only child of a musician father. She trained at RADA before joining the BBC and went on to direct 'The Newcomers', 'Dr Finlay's Casebook', 'Doctor Who' and 'Z Cars' and to produce 'Angels' and 'District Nurse'.

Long since divorced, Julia says she is 'terribly aware' of her responsibilities. 'Perhaps my marriage would have succeeded if I hadn't been so involved.' Now she lives with her elderly mother and Roly, Den's poodle in 'EastEnders'. 'He's a BBC dog but he boards with me. I take him on long walks and think of future story-lines. The ideas for the show come from the street, from buses, trains and pubs. I love to sit and eavesdrop. I am fascinated by what makes people tick. Charles Dickens was my teacher. He wrote serials for weekly magazines and had the gift of combining reality with fairy-stories. I don't think we are doing much that Dickens has not done before us.'

Tony Holland was Julia's co-creator of 'EastEnders'. The son of a soldier, Tony comes from an East End family. Forty-eight, mercurial and gay, Tony was once, in his own words, 'the most appalling actor in the world but an extremely pretty one'. For four years he was script-editor on 'Z Cars', where he met Julia, and they have worked together regularly since. Tony's temperament led to numerous rows between the two, and last year he walked out on the show, saying he just couldn't take any more. A few months later he re-surfaced and is now an occasional writer for the soap

THE CHARACTERS

Ian Beale Eighteen-year-old Ian Beale has forever had to live up to his dad Pete's great expectations. Ian, played by Adam Woodyatt, is a nice enough lad but he has suffered from living in his father's shadow and has been forced to grow up too quickly. His dad wants him to be a real man, so Ian took up boxing and bought a motorbike. But this desire to make his son macho backfired on pathetic Pete when he discovered Ian had acquired a knife to defend himself against would-be muggers. If left to lead his own life, Ian will probably do quite well. He is a talented cook. He used to be very shy with girls (when he first went out with tubby Sharon, he didn't know whether to kiss her or milk her), but he is gradually gaining in confidence. When he discovered Donna was his mother's child, he attacked his mother with a savage tirade. Later he had the brains to say sorry.

Adam Woodyatt might have become a butcher if the rôle of Ian Beale in 'EastEnders' had not come along. 'I had a Saturday job as a butcher,' says twenty-year-old Adam, 'and I learned an awful lot about the meat trade. All the regular customers knew me, and we used to have a laugh and a joke and I'd tell them what was best value.' Adam has lived most of his life in Chingford, Essex, although his parents recently bought a house halfway up a mountain in Wales. He made his stage début in 1980 as one of Fagin's gang in a West End revival of *Oliver!* Adam shares a couple of interests with his screen character Ian: he likes riding motorbikes and cooking – but not at the same time.

Kathy Beale is just about the nicest person in 'EastEnders'. Albert Square doesn't deserve her. She had a tough childhood in the sort of area where even the Alsatians went round in pairs. Kathy, referred to as 'Kaff' by her pea-brained husband Pete (not to be confused with Ali's 'caff' which is round the corner), ironically has had to battle hard to earn the respect of the Albert Square natives. Her father was an alcoholic, and her affair with Pete after his marriage to fat Pat failed branded Kathy as a scarlet woman. But in soap good wins through in the end, and Kathy, played by Gillian Taylforth, is a good friend, wife, mother, even (for a time) a good Samaritan. (The only thing she isn't that brilliant at is working her knitting machine. Each time she tries on screen, real machinists write in saying she does it all wrong.) Being married to Pete, she has had to fight through thick and thick. In the past, she went through the torture of being raped (she has a long-lost daughter, Donna) and having to win round her mother-in-law Lou, the only geriatric who could eat three Shredded Wheat. Kathy is totally faithful to Pete and went through agonies when Willmot Browne, her boss at the Dagmar pub, developed a passion for her. She's extremely practical, and she likes a laugh. She's sensitive with Ian, and having come up the hard way she doesn't want to do anything to tarnish her reputation. So she won't touch any stolen goods on Pete's market-stall like knocked-off nectarines or hot potatoes. Kathy's a good egg; unfortunately she's been poached by Pete – an idiot.

Gillian Taylforth enjoys a much-publicised off-screen romance with Nick Berry, one of her co-stars in 'EastEnders'. Gillian is thirty-three, eight years older than Nick (alias Wicksy), but she takes the age difference and Nick's legion of fans in her stride. 'When we go out, all the girls chase after Wicksy,' says Gillian. 'It's really strange to be standing in the supermarket when girls come over and kiss your boyfriend and turn round and glare at you. He gets very embarrassed about it, but I think it's funny and lovely for him.' They live in separate flats around Highbury, North London. 'I like a bit of space of my own to do the things I want,' she adds. 'That way we can go backwards and forwards between the two homes without either of us giving up our independence.'

Gillian's father is a master printer, and her mother is an early-morning cleaner at the *Daily Mirror*. She has a brother and three sisters, one of whom was already a member of the Anna Scher Theatre School when Gillian joined in 1973, while another is a policewoman. For ten years Gillian was in the unusual position of combining two careers: actress and personal secretary. 'I was lucky in finding office employers who would let me take my holidays or unpaid leave whenever I was called for a part. I worked for about nine years as a secretary in a firm of solicitors.' During this period, her talent for comedy emerged in such shows as 'Hi De Hi', 'On Safari', 'Shelley', 'Sink or Swim' and 'The Rag Trade'. She and sister Kim had previously appeared together in the BBC play 'Zigger Zagger', and when Kim was cast in the film *The Long Good Friday* but had to pull out she nominated Gillian for the part. And she got it. But Gillian nearly didn't get the rôle of Kathy Beale in 'EastEnders' because of fears that she looked too young. Producer Julia Smith recalls that Gillian was 'stunningly attractive with a husky voice that seemed incongruously at odds with her appearance'. After much soul-searching (more actresses were seen for the part of Kathy than for any other character), they finally offered Gillian the job. She is modest about her performance. 'I don't think I'm a very good actress. I won't ever be a star. I sort of sneaked into "EastEnders". I think they missed me at the gate and forgot to turn me away. One day they'll find me out! Kathy and I are quite similar in many ways, but I wish I was like her and spoke my mind. I just can't be bothered with rows.'

The normally bubbly Gillian had one anxious time in 'EastEnders'. 'My part was very low-key for a while. I was working behind the snackbar at the Queen Vic, and my only line of the week would be "Two pie and chips". I thought they were going to write me out; perhaps I was going to be crushed under three tons of King Edward potatoes falling off Pete's barrow!'

Kenny Beale, Lou's elder son, was head and shoulders above the rest of the Beale family, not only because he tried not to stoop to their petty squabbling but also because he was a good foot and a half taller than them.

Played by Michael Attwell, Kenny had emigrated to New Zealand on Lou's instructions over twenty years ago, but landed in Walford early this year without a trace of a down-under accent. Perhaps that had been misrouted to Gatwick. He was met with accusations, initially fuelled by Pat, that he was Wicksy's dad. But the threatened showdown with Pete (who'd been married to Pat at the time) ended amicably. Pat finally told them all she didn't know which was the father, which suited them both (and after a few bars of Wicksy's piano-playing you could see why).

Kenny's short stay brought out the best in Lou, the old tyrant. She was moved to see him, but not enough to get out of her chair.

Accompanying Kenny was his pretty daughter Elizabeth (Lucy Bayler), who stayed on to further her romance with cousin Ian. She brought a much needed touch of cheerfulness and glamour to Albert Square. She must have had Sharon and Michelle staring into their cracked mirrors.

Michael Attwell, the forty-five-year-old Leicestershire actor, had to give up his other job as Fleet Street cartoonist 'Zoke' to play Kenny Beale in 'EastEnders'. So strongly does executive producer Julia Smith dislike the popular press, she forbade him to give any interviews. Michael's editor at the *News of the World* insisted he write about life in Albert Square or leave. He left.

Michael's varied experience on stage and in film and television – he played a comic gangster in 'Turtles Progress' and was a memorable Bill Sikes in 'Oliver Twist' – happily keeps him constantly in work.

Lou Beale is the main ratbag of 'EastEnders', head of the Fowler–Beale dynasty and fount of all good old-fashioned wisdom. Well, old-fashioned anyway. Where Ethel is potty, Dot prissy, Lou is pompous and self-pitying. Played with gusto and a cockney accent no Professor Higgins could undo, by Anna Wing, Lou is the widow of market-stall trader Albert, buried nearby. She owns the house full of Fowlers and tries to rule the roost.

The comic Les Dawson might have had her as a mother-in-law in another life. She lashed her son-in-law Arthur for failing to find work, disapproved of her daughter's third pregnancy and declares, with a frown that could freeze sunshine, that most of the Albert Square goings-on are 'not right'. Worst of all, she favours her son Pete, who does little for her, above Pauline, his twin, who does everything. But during Michelle's pregnancy, Arthur's breakdown, Pete's trouble with the police and his ex-wife Pat she was concerned and caring. To her family she's She Who Must Be Obeyed. Even Pat waddles sheepishly over to Lou's parlour when summoned, and obeys her dictates like a lamb. Lou died in her sleep this summer as Anna Wing wanted to leave.

Lou's likes include bingo, buying bargains at jumble sales, brandy and speaking her mind to Ethel and Dot. Lou's dislikes include being ill – she has a heart condition and has morbid moments foreseeing her end – and being asked 'private' questions makes her noisily cross. When the June 1987 general election campaign was reflected in 'EastEnders' episodes, Lou's views were canvassed. 'Ask no questions, hear no lies,' she repeatedly squawked. I'm glad she's not my mum.

Anna Wing found fame at the age of seventy-one as that tough old bird Lou Beale in 'EastEnders'. 'When the producers asked me if I wanted to be in a soap opera and all it entails, I said: "All my life I've been an actress; now I want to be a household name." And dear old Lou has made me better-known than anything else I've done in fifty years of show business.' Although she now lives alone in a flat in the West End of London, Anna is a genuine East Ender. 'I knew the producers were looking for the real thing, so I turned up at the interview for the part with my birth certificate, my gran's picture and a family album. You see, I was born in Hackney, the daughter of a greengrocer, and although off-screen I talk with a proper English accent I still have an East End accent in my heart.' Now seventy-four, Anna (real name Eva Wing) was an artist's model before turning to the stage. When she was thirty she married actor Peter Davey, but they split up three years later. Their son is Mark Wing-Davey, who was in the television version of *The Hitch-Hiker's Guide to the Galaxy*. Anna later had a seven-year relationship with poet Philip O'Connor, and their son Jon is now a deputy headmaster.

It only takes ten minutes for Anna to change into her rôle as Lou. 'Except for the eyebrows, I have no make-up,' she says. 'So all the chins, wrinkles and cracks are my own!' Anna is worried that Lou might be going a bit soft. 'She started off full of prejudice, and the danger is that she might become too nice. As a grandmother myself, it's lovely when children tell me, "I wish you were my gran," but not for the character. She mustn't get too lovable. As something of a veteran actress, I realise that nobody's indispensable on "EastEnders". The day they tell me Lou is out, there'll be no tears from me. I shall say, "Thank you for such a lovely perk," and then start looking for another job. But as long as they want me I'll play Lou. And I hope some day Lou will have a fling with a man. She could have a jolly time going a bit wild.'

Pete Beale and his wife Kath are probably ideally suited to running a fruit and veg stall. For Kath's pretty fruity and Pete's a vegetable. On the surface, he's Mr Ordinary (and I mean ordinary), but behind his speech impediment ('woll up, wunner beans and wadishes') lies a man with a tormented past, a man who has had brushes with the law, a man who is not afraid to speak his mind, a man who is a wally. EastEnder Pete, played by Peter Dean, is usually the life and soul of the party, the sort of bloke who knows the words of 'Y Viva España'. The only good thing about his leading a sing-song at the Vic is that it drowns Wicksy's piano-playing and the landlord doesn't have to worry about throwing people out at closing-time. They've all left long before.

Pete has a secret sadness in the formidable shape of Poison Pat, his first wife. They were married when he was nineteen and, although they were soon divorced and he married Kath, Pat returned to taunt him by revealing that Wicksy wasn't his son. Pete hit her. Then, when Pat was later beaten up by the so-called Walford Attacker, Pete became the prime suspect. Having the brains of one of his turnips, Pete didn't exactly help his case by giving the Old Bill plenty of lip (he's got a north and south like the Blackwall Tunnel) and then physically resisting their invitation to come and help them with their inquiries. Unfortunately, he got off.

Pete does have his redeeming features. He's faithful and loving to Kath; he's a decent if not always sympathetic father to Ian; he thinks the world of his sister Pauline and his mum Lou. And he's not in every scene. Against that, he was horrible to Arthur when he was having his breakdown; he sometimes wears funny hats; and his melons are 3p dearer than in Safeways. At one point, the 'EastEnders' producers were all set to kill Pete off but they changed their mind. Pete's always been a dreamer – he was going to be a singer, a redcoat, run his own hotel. Oh dear, I dream of the day he's no longer in 'EastEnders'.

Peter Dean was 'discovered' doing Shakespeare in London's Petticoat Lane market while officially selling sheets. Like his 'EastEnders' character Pete Beale, Peter Dean has firsthand experience of running a market-stall. His family have had one in Islington's Chapel Street for years, but it was while working at 'the Lane' that Peter's acting career began to develop. He says: 'My grandmother Lily Randall was a music-hall artist and she used to teach me Shakespeare. So while I was flogging sheets I was reciting a speech from *Antony and Cleopatra*. Prunella Scales was passing, heard me and thought I had something. She suggested I try drama classes. I took her advice, and it all started from there. She was my Svengali.' Peter's second wife Jean, to whom he has been married for five years, also comes from a long line of market-traders. Peter Dean is a genuine East Ender. Born in Hoxton fifty-one years ago, he left school at fifteen and as a young man rubbed shoulders with the notorious villains the Kray twins. 'Ronnie and Reggie were nice enough fellas – we all sailed a bit close to the wind.' A bit too close in Peter's case. When he was nineteen he was sentenced to three months in a detention centre for possessing a knife, after a gang brawl outside a dance-hall in Holloway, North London, in which a young policeman died. A man was later hanged for the murder. Peter was less than pleased when the story came out two years ago. In his teens Peter became a printer but got bored with that and joined a holiday camp as a waiter. Still ambitious, he took a job on a ferry and performed in the shows on board to get his Equity card. He bought a shoe-shop and a stall in Petticoat Lane, and from 1976 his life fluctuated between work as a stallholder and various acting parts. 'No way was I going to settle for a market-stall and a council flat with a picture of a Chinese lady and three plastic ducks on the wall!' His first major acting rôle was in 1978 in the controversial series 'Law and Order' where he attracted considerable attention for his convincing portrayal of a crook named Jack Lynn. Two years later he popped up in 'Coronation Street' as Fangio, who had a penchant for pinching Deirdre's bottom. He has also appeared in 'Target', 'Shoestring', 'Minder', 'Give Us a Break' and 'Big Deal'. Peter's first marriage broke up after only three years (he has a daughter Leah, aged twenty, from it) and he wed Jean, who is thirty-four, in 1983. Yet he first met her twenty years ago when she was a schoolgirl babysitting for one of his mates. They haven't been able to have children of their own and have been turned down for adoption because of Peter's police record from over thirty years ago. 'We've tried to adopt a child,' says Peter sadly, 'but it's the law of the land and we have to accept that. But it's my wife I really feel sorry for.' Peter describes the man who has made him famous, Pete Beale, as the Bobby Ewing of Albert Square, the nice guy who tries to solve other people's problems. 'And after all those heavy parts it's nice to be able to smile for a change. Pete is a bit of a mummy's boy, the kind of bloke who makes a noise when he eats his celery. Finding out Wicksy wasn't his son after all must have been like having his guts ripped out. I wouldn't have slapped Pat – I'd have strangled her.'

Peter is under no illusions about his acting ability. 'I don't expect the National Theatre to come looking for me; I'm more likely to end up with National Car Parks!' For a townie who don't 'arf rabbit, Peter has a couple of unlikely traits. One is his conversion to Buddhism six years ago. He and Oscar James, who played Tony Carpenter in 'EastEnders', used to share a wooden prayer-stool in a dressing-room. The other is that his longstanding ambition is to retire to the country as a farmer and raise rare breeds of pigs and chickens. However, he returns to type by admitting: 'I love dog racing, too. That's my East End side.'

The Carpenter Family *See* The Ethnics.

Barry Clark was far more outgoing than his gay partner Colin Russell in 'EastEnders'. Whereas Colin liked to sit at home perfecting his design work, Barry was all for a night on the town. Barry, played by Gary Hailes, has a record-stall on the market. He was more carefree than Colin except where his father was concerned. For Barry had never told his dad that he was living with a man, dreaded telling him, but finally did off-screen at Christmas 1987. The only member of his family with homosexual tendencies (indeed, brother Graham is a local hood), the chubby little chap might eventually settle for a heterosexual relationship. Colin told him he'd be living a lie. But a working-class homo's life in the East End ain't easy.

Gary Hailes has found there are certain drawbacks to playing gay barrow-boy Barry Clark in 'EastEnders'. Gary, who is not gay, has twice been attacked and seems to get picked on in fights because of his television rôle. But Gary maintains: 'The part is a refreshing challenge for an actor.' Gary was born in the East End and now lives in Highgate, North London. The twenty-two-year-old actor made his professional début in 1978 in the BBC production of 'Pinocchio' and has followed that up with appearances in 'Grange Hill', 'Born and Bred' and 'Sorry!'

Charlie Cotton *See* The Baddies.

Dot Cotton, chain-smoking martyr to her nerves, survivor of the wickednesses of this un-Christian world, is the comic thread of 'EastEnders'. If the soap ended tomorrow, Dot would be woven into

popular culture like Hilda Ogden and Walter Gabriel, an original comic creation.

The success of Dot (she's now a 'must' for every aspiring impressionist) happened in the second year of 'EastEnders', owing largely to the shining skill of actress June Brown of the ratchet voice. Like a malnourished bird raised in city smog, she scratches around Albert Square pecking at people with her prejudiced ideas. And she worries.

She worries about appearances. When she was taken to court for shoplifting – a minor offence, put down to her change-of-life funny turns – she was deeply ashamed. Later when she was charged with breaking a window in Colin's car during a rumpus with the police, she was paralysed with shame. This offence earned her the sack from her job at the launderette (she did half the day there; Pauline did the rest). Later, when Mary proved a disaster in the job, she was reinstated.

She worries about her family – to use the term loosely. Charlie, her husband, makes guest appearances in her life. He's a pickpocket and parasite. But Dot is proud to show she has a Man and does her wifely duty – puts him up and gives him all her money. Then there's Nick, her criminal son, whose idea of loving his ma is to steal her chequebook and sneer at her in public. On New Year's Eve 1987, Dot announced she'd washed her hands of Charlie (who'd just done a bunk to one of his fancy women's homes). The women of Britain cheered.

A gossip, a small-scale gambler, prissily prejudiced against nonconformists, black people ('send 'em back where they belong') and homosexuals (until won over by gay Colin's nice manners), she's the woman you hate to love. But love her you do, because she has Standards and hot flushes; because she's an innocent; because she was kind to look after Mary's baby, right to disapprove of Mary's whoring and right to pray for her. She's a good friend to Ethel, who used to be a tenant in the same house, to whom she confessed her lasting shame about an abortion years before. And she was the sole mourner at neighbour Tom's funeral.

In her plastic rain-hat, smoking, listening to James Last tapes with the headphones of her Walkman upside down, putting on a posh voice to take telephone messages for Ali's Ozcab drivers, even spreading gloom and doom, she's ridiculous. And lovable.

June Brown is light-years away from her 'EastEnders' *alter ego*, the brilliantly batty Dot Cotton. The two have absolutely nothing in common whatsoever – except that June smokes forty cigarettes a day. Oh, and she talks nineteen to the dozen. Come to think of it, she leans towards the spiritual as well. And she is just a teeny weeny bit eccentric. But the similarities positively end there. June, aged fifty-five, is elegant, well spoken and infectiously happy. Born in Suffolk and educated privately, June's main link with the East End was her Jewish grandmother, 'a real East Ender who spoke just like old Ethel'. And June's family of actor husband Robert Arnold ('he found fame as PC Swain in "Dixon of Dock Green"') and five grown-up children are a far cry from Dot's delinquent duo, Charlie and Nick. Nevertheless, June is very fond of Dot. 'I love playing her – she's such a strong character. Dear old Dot, she's got strange moral views and odd religious ideas, but her heart's in the right place. She has that awful worried expression on her face all the time, so that when people meet me in real life they're amazed to find me always laughing.' Yet June has experienced more than her share of sadness. Before she was sixteen, five close relatives had died. 'I learned from a very early age what it meant to cope with the grief of death,' she says reflectively. Then June's first husband John, also an actor, committed suicide after they had been married for seven years. 'I was sitting in my sister's kitchen drinking tea when I suddenly felt "I must go home". The moment I got to the front door, I knew something was dreadfully wrong. I found my husband lying unconscious beside the gas-fire. He thought he was seriously ill and had talked about killing himself, but I thought people who talked about suicide were the ones who never did it. How wrong I was. Had I understood his problem earlier, I might have been able to save him.' June later remarried, to Robert Arnold, and had five children in six years and one daughter who died. That was Chloe, born prematurely, and the next child, also called Chloe, was born paralysed. June says: 'When she was fourteen months old, she couldn't even sit up, let alone crawl or walk. So I took her to a Christian healer and by the time she was two she was cured except for a slight limp. Now she has given me my first grandchild, Matthew.' But June has survived all these traumas and lives happily in Croydon with her husband, surrounded by cats, a dog and various other creatures brought home by her children Louise, Sophie (she used to be a monkey-keeper at a zoo), William, Chloe and Naomi, all of whom come and go as they please. Before 'EastEnders', June was a member of the Royal Shakespeare Company ('I'm basically a serious actress, you know'), and her long list of credits includes such classics as *Sunday, Bloody Sunday, Hedda Gabler* and Lady Macbeth. She got the part of Dot courtesy of Dirty Den himself, Leslie Grantham. 'We'd never met, but he saw me in an episode of "Minder" and told the producers that I'd be perfect as Dot Cotton.' Poor Dot hasn't too many designer labels in her wardrobe, therefore June, not being remotely like her in any way, must dress expensively. Correct? 'Well, I'm not used to spending money on clothes,' she confides. 'All my life I've scrimped, got things from jumble sales and Oxfam shops. And if anyone says anything I pretend I'm buying for Dot!' There. Nothing like Dot at all.

Arthur Fowler is the man without pride. He had it, but he lost it when he lost his job. It made him one of the saddest sights on television. Before he was made redundant Arthur worked in a factory. He loved his wife Pauline and kids Michelle and Mark. He was rock-solid and totally reliable, the sort of man you could always count on. He had no burning ambition – just to provide for his family. But without work and without the hope of work – as we saw him in the soap's first year – he went steadily downhill on a course towards self-destruction. Actor Bill Treacher captured Arthur's mounting despair in one of the most moving performances of the decade and one which proved once and for all that soaps are not second-class dramas. There was poor Arthur faced with the unthinkable prospect for a proud working-class man of not being able to pay for his own daughter's wedding. There seemed no way out. So he took the Square's Christmas Club money, £1500, and faked a robbery. A stupid thing to do, particularly as he was a rotten liar and soon found out by the police. He would have paid the money back. He never meant to hurt anyone. The listless blank days as a blob staring at his television set, the final frantic wrecking of his beloved family home, his time in the mental hospital and his subsequent trial were all chillingly realistic. Hundreds of viewers wrote in before his nervous breakdown, urging him to seek psychiatric help, and children even sent Monopoly money to help him out. Arthur didn't get much support from those around him when it really mattered, because – realistically – we don't hold with mental illness in Britain. Most thought it was high time he pulled himself together, and mother-in-law Lou was positively antagonistic. Pauline did her best but she had baby Martin to contend with, while Michelle was also preoccupied with her own problems. It was only when Arthur finally snapped that they began to rally round. What is particularly convincing about the treatment of Arthur in 'EastEnders' is what has happened to him since he has come home. He still has no steady job. There has been no miracle cure, no sudden personality-change. He has even borrowed money from loan sharks at crippling interest rates. He took a job with the Pakistani owners of the grocer's shop but continued to collect his Social Security money and, to Pauline's dismay, borrowed more to pay for a 'Goodbye, Kenny' party. Whereas 'Crossroads' would probably have turned him into an instant international playboy with a luxury yacht moored south of Wapping, 'EastEnders' has resisted the temptation to liven him up. Arthur remains a depressing figure and a man always likely to make the same mistakes again. The perpetual patsy, perhaps.

Bill Treacher found that playing Arthur Fowler in 'EastEnders' had a profound effect on himself and his family. Fifty-one-year-old Bill went through a great deal of anguish when Arthur had his mental breakdown. 'It got so depressing,' says Bill. 'I try not to take my work home with me, but when I was playing those harrowing scenes it was so bad that I once started crying while I was sitting at home in my armchair. I had to tell my wife that it wasn't me who was crying – it was Arthur. It's hard to escape from a character you are playing twelve hours a day, six days a week. Arthur went through hell, and I felt for him. My nine-year-old daughter Sophie is a big fan of the show, but she couldn't bear to watch when Arthur was at his lowest ebb. She hates to see her dad cry.' A psychiatrist advised Bill on how Arthur would behave during the traumatic scenes in the mental hospital and, in order to look suitably haggard, Bill went on a diet and lost two stone. 'I've never had a part that has been so physically demanding,' he adds. Bill's performance brought him critical acclaim and a flood of letters from unemployed people. 'They saw Arthur as the epitome of all their fears and problems and they looked to me for help. The letters were very moving. The writers poured out their hearts, their feelings of helplessness, their inability to cope.' Bill himself has had periods out of work. The longest was seven months, and he made ends meet by scrubbing floors; so he feels very strongly about the unemployment situation and has tried to help in any way he can. He was involved in the Hands Across Britain day and was made the first patron of Action, a charity aimed to help the long-term unemployed. He says: 'There are millions of Arthur Fowlers out there. Arthur is confused and frightened, strong at times but mostly weak. Sure he's a bit of a wally, but I like him. And he does have his qualities. However, being unemployed made his life a misery, and he felt he'd lost his self-respect.' Like so many of the cast, Bill is a true East Ender. 'We were a large family of six boys and two girls, and times were very lean round our way in the thirties. Me and my brother used to go down the market and scrounge boxes, broken nuts and anything else going. When I was six, I desperately wanted to belong to the Mickey Mouse Club at a Saturday-morning cinema but it cost threepence – well beyond our means.' During the Blitz, Bill's family lived in a block of flats in Hackney. He says: 'I can remember looking right across the docks one night after a bad air raid, and the whole skyline was ablaze.' Bill did National Service with the Royal Air Force then worked as a steward with the P & O Line to save enough money to go to drama school. During his two years at drama school, he tried hard to get rid of his cockney accent, 'which is ironic because I've played Londoners throughout my career'. He made his West End début in 1963, and four years later joined the Brian Rix Theatre of Laughter Company (slightly different from Arthur). At around the same time, he spent four years as Sidney the milkman in 'Mrs Dale's Diary'. But Bill's most important rôle was on the tour of *Let Sleeping Wives Lie*. For playing his wife was the lady who in 1972 became Bill's real wife, actress Kate Kessey. Bill was the first actor that the 'EastEnders' producers had thought of for the series – in fact Arthur had almost been invented with him in mind. The show's creators, Julia Smith and Tony Holland, had worked with Bill on 'Z Cars' and decided he had just what was needed for the difficult part of Arthur, namely 'warmth, directness and an ability to be convincingly ordinary without being dull'. Yet Bill agonised over whether to accept the part and sat the whole family down around the kitchen table and asked them: 'Do you want me to be in "EastEnders" or not?' Bill was afraid in case it would keep him away from home too often and too long. Home is a picturesque nineteenth-century cottage in Suffolk, and the family are wife Kate, son Jamie aged thirteen, and daughter Sophie aged nine. Bill Treacher is devoted to them. 'Unlike Arthur, I'm a very happy man. I don't think anyone in "EastEnders" is as happy and as settled as me.' So would he like some of this jollity to be injected into poor old Arthur? 'I'd certainly like to see him laugh, crack a few jokes and have a bit of fun. And I'd like him to put that bossy mother-in-law in her place!'

Mark Fowler is a sad case. As a teenager he was involved in dodgy dealings with Nick Cotton and eventually he left home. His mum, Pauline, desperately wants him back, maybe because she feels guilty that she and Arthur did not show Mark enough affection when he was at home. They tracked him down in Southend where Mark, played by David Scarboro, was living with an older woman. That relationship fizzled out, but Mark still preferred to drift around the country rather than come home permanently.

David Scarboro has twice discovered that 'EastEnders' fiction has overlapped uncomfortably with reality; for, like his screen character, unhappy wanderer Mark Fowler, David once walked out of his parents' home in Kent, vowing never to return, and also found the strain of being in 'EastEnders' took its toll when he had a nervous breakdown – like his screen father, Arthur. Twenty-year-old David started acting at the age of twelve and appeared in 'Grange Hill'. In some ways, he was fortunate to get the part of Mark, because Julia Smith, the producer of 'EastEnders', remarked after his interview: 'You couldn't see much of his face as most of it was obscured by a huge greased quiff that loomed dangerously down over his forehead and threatened to lop off the end of his nose!' Deeply depressed, he jumped to his death at Beachy Head in April 1988.

Michelle Fowler is only nineteen but she's about the wisest woman in 'EastEnders'. Her experiences have given her a maturity way beyond her years. Actress Susan Tully has made Michelle one of the toughest yet at the same time one of the most sympathetic characters in the soap. Michelle has paid dearly for one mistake – having one night of sex with Den. She became pregnant from it. Unlike some (her mum Pauline, for example), she doesn't constantly bemoan her fate. She knows she has been stupid but she gets on with her life. Against vociferous family opposition, she was determined to have the baby. Quite right, too. She was a model schoolgirl mum. She gave up riding her motorbike; carried on with schoolwork, even taking one exam in the maternity ward. If the writers were out to deliver a lesson to young viewers (which they certainly were, partly), it was to show that having a baby at sixteen need not be the end of the world. And Michelle has proved that she is a far better mother than either her own mum or her gran, Lou. Vicky always gets the best care and attention from Michelle.

Then there was Lofty. She was terrified of hurting him. He was crazy about her and Vicky, but Michelle knew that she didn't really love him – at least, it wasn't the sort of love she'd read about in *Cosmopolitan*. So she left him standing at the altar. Of course he'd be hurt in the short term, but over a longer period it would be for the best.

Then, silly girl, she relented and they married. That turned out to be a second mistake. Although she provided herself with a considerate husband and Vicky with a doting father, something was missing – and not just between Lofty's ears. As long as she lives near Den, he will cast a shadow over her relationship with men. She has been fair with him in spite of his occasional boorish behaviour. The painful thing is she loved him. She still loves him. He had far more to lose than she had if the truth – that he was Vicky's father – had come out. Yet she stayed silent on the subject. She's fiercely independent and tough. Just as in her parents' relationship it was Arthur who couldn't take the strain of the situation, so with Michelle and Lofty it's Lofty who can't cope. When she became pregnant for the second time at the end of 1987 and decided to have an abortion Lofty cracked. But these 'EastEnders' women are born survivors, built to last. Whenever Michelle is faced with a crisis, she simply puffs out her spotty cheeks and on she goes.

Susan Tully is the outstanding young actress in British soaps. Her portrayal of Michelle Fowler has never been less than excellent, and at times it has been quite exceptional. Hard to believe that when she filmed the emotional canalside scene telling Den that he was the father of her baby Susan was only eighteen. That scene, at the time the longest ever made in a soap opera, demonstrated Susan's remarkable affinity with the soap teenager. They do, it's true, have a fair amount in common. Michelle's 'cor blimey' accent is no performance. Both families are cockneys, and Susan's father, like her screen dad Arthur, was out of work for a while. Just like Pauline Fowler, Susan's mum had a baby late in life. And both Susan and Michelle are stubbornly independent; they're not going to be forced to do something they don't want to. For example, Susan states: 'I don't want kids. I don't think I'd be a good mum – I'm too selfish. And as I don't want kids I don't see the point in getting married.' So there. Susan points out: 'My emotional circumstances are not the same as Michelle's. She fell for Den because she had to go looking for affection. I don't need to. I get plenty from my parents. I don't really know anyone exactly like Michelle but I know lots of people with bits of her in them. What I like about her is her simplicity, her straightforwardness, the way she makes the best of a bad deal. She does things she believes are for the best. Even though she jilted Lofty, she believed in the long run that it would be for his benefit. For a girl her age, she's gone through a hell of a lot and come through it very successfully.' An indication of how true to life Michelle is for millions came with the stack of letters Susan received from pregnant girls. 'I was the first person these girls were telling, and their letters were pretty desperate. I had to refer them to people they could talk to, because I'm not in a position to give any girl advice about what to do if she finds herself pregnant.' With expert assistance, Susan did make a schools television programme, 'Too Young to Have a Baby'. She recalls the actual birth scenes in 'EastEnders' with some trepidation. 'I thought I'd just have to act a few labour pains and at the end there'd be a shot of me, with the baby in my arms, looking sweet and serene. Then when I saw the script I thought: Oh my God. I did a lot of research for the birth. I talked to my mum, went to a maternity hospital, watched childbirth films and listened to any woman who'd ever had a baby. I got so wound up about it that at the end of the scene I just burst out crying and sobbed on the bed for fifteen minutes. Yet I really enjoyed it. When we shot the next scene with the baby in my arms I was still crying, and Wendy Richard, who plays my mum, was, too. All I could manage was "Isn't she beautiful?" and Wendy could only nod her head!' Susan was born on 12 October 1967 in North London. She hosted a live television programme, 'Our Show', at the age of nine and followed this up by working on 'The Saturday Banana' with Bill Oddie. She then played Suzanne in 'Grange Hill' for four years. 'I always thought of "Grange Hill" as a paid hobby. I found it easy to shake off Suzanne when I got home, but it's much harder with Michelle. When I went for the interview for "EastEnders", I said I was pleased they were going to let Michelle have her baby because I'd never been allowed to grow up in "Grange Hill".' One thing Susan didn't have in common with Michelle was her refusal to name the father of her screen baby. 'I tried my hardest to find out who was going to be the dad. First I thought it was going to be Ali, then Tony. Then there were whispers about Andy or Den. I talked sweetly to the writers and assured the girls in the office that they could trust me. But as soon as I did finally find out I went straight home and told my mum.' A fervent Arsenal supporter who dotes on her younger sister Linda, now eight, Sue admits: 'If I sound sensible, it's only because I've been silly in the past. Without doubt, "EastEnders" is one of the best things that's ever happened to me, but I hope it hasn't changed me as a person. Anyway, I've made my friends and family take a pledge to tell me if I start getting big-headed.' Somehow I think Susan Tully's feet are planted too firmly in reality for that to happen.

Pauline Fowler would always lend you a cup of sugar or let you have her last jellied eel. There are times when she'd gladly let you borrow husband Arthur, mum Lou and daughter Michelle, too. Pauline's had a hard life and never tires of going on about it. Mum Lou is full of jolly East End bonhomie. When Pauline, played by Wendy Richard, announced that she was unexpectedly pregnant with Martin, Lou delivered the following motherly advice: 'Get rid of the kid or I get rid of you.' As if sharing a house with that old prune isn't enough, Pauline also has to put up with 'EastEnders' husband Arthur, the only man to look happier when he was having a nervous breakdown. Then there's Michelle, the unmarried mum who made matters worse by getting wed to Lofty – hardly a mother's ideal choice as a son-in-law. To add to her woes, Pauline's also got wayward son Mark – somewhere. All of these worries pale into insignificance beside having Pete Beale as a twin brother. Yes, Pete Beale, the man whose constant greeting of 'Awright, sis?' makes him sound like a sawn-off Michael Barrymore. Thank goodness Pauline hasn't taken the twin thing literally. Her cardies and pinnies may be dowdy but they don't look half so daft as Pete's hats. So Pauline's life is really grim. As long as Arthur hasn't got a steady job, all she will ever see at the end of the tunnel is another tunnel. Her only bright spot so far has been winning the Glamorous Granny competition at the Vic. She does her utmost to make ends meet, working at the launderette and doing cleaning jobs. But it's a never-ending slog with no visible reward. But she is strong. Whereas Arthur cracked up under the strain, Pauline battles on bravely. All she ever wanted was to keep the family together. In that respect, she has failed but she still stands by them and, even though she may not approve of everything they've done, she won't hear a word said against them. She was the first person to find out that Den was the father of Michelle's baby but she kept it to herself, taking the full burden of knowledge on her broad (unpadded) shoulders. In the circumstances, we should all feel desperately sorry for Pauline, but she loses house-points by continually griping on in that whingeing voice. Perhaps, after all, it's Arthur and Lou we should pity, particularly as they also have to stomach Pauline's cooking. Judging by the way that glutinous dollops of mashed potato have been seen struggling out of her saucepan in the past, she probably wouldn't even get a job at Ali's café. And that's saying something.

Wendy Richard was an exception to the rule when she was cast as long-suffering Pauline Fowler. The policy of the programme was not to use established stars, and Wendy was already a household name, fresh from over ten years as Miss Brahms in 'Are You Being Served?' However, 'EastEnders' producer Julia Smith had worked with Wendy on 'The Newcomers' and felt she would be ideal for Pauline. But would she accept playing such a drab woman after all her younger rôles? The answer was simple. 'I'm sick of glamour,' said Wendy, exhaling cigarette-smoke. 'I want to play my age. It's about time I did.' Born in Middlesborough, Wendy got her cockney accent from helping her mother run a guest-house in King's Cross for eight years. Her mother used to complain about Wendy's distinctive tones, but Wendy replied prophetically: 'You wait and see – one day I'll make a lot of money out of my voice.' How right she was. After recording 'Come Outside' with Mike Sarne in 1962 (she made a princely £15 from that), Wendy went on to play Joyce Harker in 'The Newcomers' and Doreen, a clippie, in 'On the Buses'. She also had a cameo rôle in the film *Gumshoe* with Albert Finney and appeared in 'Carry On' films, 'Dad's Army' and 'Not on Your Nellie'. Then came the busty Miss Brahms and, in 1984, 'EastEnders'.

Wendy, forty-four and a frogophile (she has collected 400 toy frogs), is proud of 'EastEnders'. 'It's bloody hard work and far from glamorous. The worse thing was having my hair cut short after having it long for nineteen years. I howled my eyes out, but everyone told me it made me look younger. And I was glad to be out of those high heels I used to wear as Miss Brahms. Mind you, the washing powder in the launderette plays havoc with my sinuses and gives me a runny nose half the time.' Last year BBC bosses had to tell Wendy to stop losing weight because it didn't look right for Pauline, though it won her a fat advertising contract for a diet food. 'She's certainly not glamorous,' admits Wendy. 'She's a bit dreary, her clothes are frumpy and her life is grim. That's why when I'm away from Pauline doing other shows I like to dress up a bit.' Wendy is very short-sighted. 'I can only see two foot in front of me. If they move a prop without telling me, I fall over it!' But she could see her television baby Martin. 'I nearly cried when they put this gorgeous baby into my arms for the first time. I even tried to avoid spending too much time with him, because it's so easy to become too attached. I suddenly realised what I'd missed by not having children of my own.' For, although Wendy has had a highly successful career as an actress, like so many leading ladies in soaps her private life has been less than happy. Her father committed suicide when Wendy was only eleven, and her first marriage, to Leonard Black, lasted a mere five months. When Wendy was twenty-eight, her mother died and Wendy attempted suicide. She then married advertising executive Will Thorpe, but that broke up eighteen months later in the most acrimonious manner. He was vindictive towards her in the press, and she responded by revealing how she had been a battered wife. 'One day on "Are You Being Served?" I came into work with three lumps on my head where he had hit me and clumps of hair pulled out. I had to have a make-up artist who was good at disguising black eyes.' Only her career pulled her through those dark days. She once said: 'Work has been my salvation so many times when my life has been hell.' These days, there is a new man in her life, Irishman Paul Glorney. If that relationship doesn't work out, perhaps she could look to her collection of frogs and find a handsome prince. . . .

Jan Hammond *See* The Yuppies.

George Holloway ('Lofty') was Albert Square's main misfit. Known to all as 'Lofty' (because of his height not his IQ), he shambled around like an Albert Square peg in a round hole blinking behind his granny glasses. Played by Tom Watt, Lofty looked as though he'd been caught in a time-warp. He was the sort of chap who wore Marks & Spencer string vests in June, rolled his trousers up to paddle on the beach, bought Roger Whittaker LPs – and whistled along to them. And judging by his weediness he definitely didn't eat spinach. Lofty hailed from an eminently respectable family, ex-Church of England and ex-Army. He was in his element in the Army until he was invalided out because he had dormant asthma. But he was never able to adjust to civilian life. He cared deeply about everything and everyone. His heart was in the right place, but his brain was not. Every sentence he uttered had 'eh?' at the end. Uncertainty? He invented it.

Apart from his Aunty Irene, who died in 1987, and Ethel, he had no real outlet for his compassion until he married Michelle. Millions expressed their disgust as poor, sweet, innocent Lofty was humiliated at the altar by that single parent. And they cried with joy when she changed her mind and allowed him to bestow all his love on her and her baby Vicky. Did Lofty deserve such public affection? Was he sympathetic or just pathetic? Did he marry Michelle simply to alleviate his own loneliness? Everybody said how lucky she was to have such a considerate husband, but what about him? He didn't do too badly, with a sensible attractive wife (just keep using the Clearasil, dear) and a lovely daughter. And was he that considerate? Because Lofty was old before his time, he expected Michelle to be the same. He forgot that she was still young. Lofty seemed incapable of mixing, relaxing and having fun, and begrudged Michelle an occasional good time. Did that apply in bed, too – particularly if he insisted on wearing that awful army jacket on manoeuvres between the sheets? The world's slowest barman, he moved at the speed of a caterpillar. He was the original pub grub. He let Den walk all over him, and when he finally made a meek bid for more pay Den sacked him.

The worm turned when he learned about Michelle's abortion. In a personality-change that was as sudden as it was unexpected, Lofty stormed out on her, snubbed the Fowlers and the Beales. Willmott-Brown employed him and gave him guitar lessons. It proved there were worse sounds than Wicksy's piano-playing.

His Rambo period proved temporary. Lofty was too wimpish to be truly lovable. He was an object of ridicule and a bit of an old woman. Like his asthma-spray, he got right up your nose. In March his paternal yearnings were partly satisfied when he coaxed Sue Osman through childbirth (from outside a closed bedroom door) and became one of the baby's godparents. In May he left Albert Square for ever to become a caretaker at a children's home. Would you trust Lofty with your blocked drains? Me neither.

Tom Watt was Lofty with brains. The part of George 'Lofty' Holloway was tailor-made for the thirty-two-year-old Londoner, the only major difference between the two being academic. For while Lofty had difficulty with joined-up writing, Tom had nine 'O' levels, two 'A' levels and a degree in drama to his name. What's more, his father is a retired headmaster, his mother was the first woman professor of economic history at Cambridge and his younger brother is a doctor. That apart, Tom was disarmingly like Lofty. 'EastEnders' producer Julia Smith remembers the first time she met him. 'The door opened and there he was – tall, pale and skinny. He looked vulnerably child-like and accident-prone, like Frank Spencer in spectacles. He was certainly different. . . .' Born in Wanstead on St Valentine's Day, Tom is shy, sensitive and deeply concerned about the problems of the world. He is a vegetarian, he doesn't drink much and he still scours Oxfam shops for secondhand suits. He drives a pristine 1953 Morris Minor, swims up to forty lengths a day and writes plays in his spare time. He even set up his own theatre company. Like his screen wife, Susan Tully, Tom is a keen Arsenal supporter and lives just around the corner from their ground in Finsbury Park. He and Susan are great mates and, although he strongly denied there was any romance, he admitted: 'There was a definite chemistry between us. She's a terrific girl.' He did have an unlikely love-affair with the extrovert Anita Dobson (Angie in 'EastEnders') which was somewhat akin to Lofty dating Madonna. Prior to 'EastEnders', Tom played such diverse rôles as Wally (!), a writer of poison-pen letters, in Granada's 'A Kind of Loving' and Duane, a punk, in Thames's 'Never the Twain'. Tom was quite attached to Lofty and even had two spare pairs of his distinctive National Health glasses in case of breakage. 'Lofty had a simplicity and an openness about him that kids especially could identify with,' said Tom. 'Growing up is a process of putting on defence mechanisms to deal with the outside world. Kids haven't acquired that tough shell, and neither had Lofty. He was a grown-up who hadn't grown up. At least falling in love with Michelle allowed him to stand up and be counted.' In one respect, Tom was actually envious of Lofty. 'I wish I could be as open and honest as him. Like most men, I have trouble revealing my feelings and emotions.' Although grateful to 'EastEnders', Tom was always anxious to further his career. He took time off from the show to appear in a Victorian melodrama 'to show I could do something other than "EastEnders".' He's certainly ridding himself of his Lofty image now. On leaving 'EastEnders' in March, Tom was due to appear in the thriller series 'Takeover' to play a secret agent and racing driver. Lofty would have been more at home in a Robin Reliant.

Naima Jeffery *See* The Ethnics.

Dr Harold Legg Actor Leonard Fenton has made Dr Legg, Albert Square's affable Jewish doctor, a respected member of the community, a man who is even prepared to listen to Dot's diagnoses. Although his young wife was killed when a German bomb fell on Albert Square during the war (he has never remarried), Dr Legg chose to stay in Walford and serve the people. He knows virtually everyone – indeed, he brought half of the Square's residents into the world. He's now in his sixties, looks older when he goes jogging and does sometimes seem dithery. Also, some of his remedies are a trifle old-fashioned. Anyway, Boots don't stock crushed newt any more.

Leonard Fenton is perfectly at home playing wise Jewish doctor Harold Legg. Leonard was born in the East End and used to live in Stepney. He remembers: 'My family's doctor in Bethnal Green was kind and caring. Dr Legg is in the same mould – an intelligent man who has chosen to remain working in the East End community in which he grew up.' Leonard qualified as a civil engineer before turning to acting in such programmes as 'Z Cars', 'Colditz', 'Secret Army', and as the Austrian Jew Erich Gottlieb in the long-running 'Shine On Harvey Moon'. Married to cellist Madeline Thorner, Leonard is also an accomplished artist and had ten paintings accepted for an exhibition at the National Theatre by actors who paint.

'Lofty' *See* George Holloway.

Rod Norman The least likely young goodie in 'EastEnders' is Rod Norman, played by Christopher McHallem. He arrived on the scene last year, seemingly just another punk prepared to push Mary a little further down the road to ruin. Yet he turned out to be a tower of strength with sincere feelings for both Mary and her daughter Annie. His sensible advice has prevented Mary from making a complete fool of herself on a number of occasions. This knight in ragged armour could turn out to be the best thing to happen to have happened to Mary since safety-pins.

Christopher McHallem has the enviable distinction of having three different birthdays. Christopher was born in Uruguay where his mother was a research chemist for a mining company. Owing to a bureaucratic mix-up, he has three birthdays – on birth registrations in Uruguay and in Britain and on his official birth certificate. Perhaps because of this, he is reluctant to reveal his true age, other than to say that he was born in the early sixties. Christopher came to Britain when he was two and in his time has had a variety of jobs, including toilet attendant, child minder, waiter (for twenty-five minutes) and cinema usher. He lives in Brixton, and 'EastEnders' marks his television début.

Andy O'Brien *See* The Yuppies.

Ali Osman is Albert Square's man not to rely on. He runs one of the least appetising establishments in television. I'd rather eat off the station floor in 'Hill Street Blues' or in the operating-theatre in 'Casualty' than go to Ali's café in Albert Square. Yet this spot that Ronay forgot seems to be a nice little earner for Ali, played by Turkish-Cypriot Nejdet Salih, and his domineering English wife Sue. Ali was born in Cyprus but came to London in the seventies and married Sue in 1982. Lazy but likeable, Ali will do anything for a peaceful life. If Sue wants a baby, Ali will go along with it. If Sue wants to scale the north face of the Eiger one lunch-time, Ali will happily supply the cheese rolls and a flask of tea. What he wouldn't be able to do is lay on a car to take her to the airport. For Ozcabs, the sideline that Sue and Ali run from the café, is pretty precarious. For a long time the Osmans were partnered in this enterprise by Ali's even less reliable brother Mehmet, but they finally bought him out. He gambled his share within days. In keeping with the 'EastEnders' interest in male emotions, the writers have regularly focused on Ali's bafflement about Sue and his feelings of inadequacy. When a fertility test resulted in his knowing he was not super-stud (a blow for a macho-minded Turk) he was a figure of pity. But things should start looking up for them, especially with their long-awaited baby, which was born in March 1988. That is, providing Ali doesn't gamble away the nappies or eat in his own café.

Nejdet Salih confesses to being 'more like Wimpo than Rambo'. At the interviews for the part of café-owner Ali Osman in 'EastEnders' he told producer Julia Smith that if she was looking for a Turkish-Cypriot Tom Selleck forget it. For Nejdet couldn't grow a moustache, and when he ripped open his shirt he revealed a distinctly hairless chest. But this follicular deprivation hasn't stopped him from being perceived as a sex symbol and sent nude photographs by admirers. Thirty-one-year-old Nejdet is, like Ali, a genuine Turkish-Cypriot and lives in the East End. He has a flat in Stoke Newington near Linda Davidson (Mary in the series) to whom he was once romantically attached. He was born in London but at the age of two he was sent to live with his grandparents in Cyprus because he suffered from asthma and needed a warm climate. He returned three years later but couldn't speak English until he went to school. He says: 'I still remember the shock of not being able to understand the teacher or talk to the other kids.' Young Nejdet gave early signs of a showbiz career when he used to do a folk-dance on the tables of his late father's London steakhouse. 'Everyone clapped like mad, and my dancing soon became a regular feature there.' His father came from a strict Muslim family, and Nejdet was to have had an arranged marriage. However, his father died when Nejdet was sixteen, leaving him as head of the house over two brothers and a baby sister. Nejdet went to drama school when he was twenty, but he hated it because they tried to make him talk with a plummy accent. Incidentally, he is still fluent in Turkish-Cypriot. He left drama school in 1982, played a Turkish bricklayer in 'Auf Wiedersehen, Pet' and won his first major rôle in 'EastEnders'. Of Ali he says: 'We are both happy-go-lucky, but that's where the similarity ends.'

Mehmet Osman *See* The Baddies.

Sue Osman is a born martyr. 'EastEnder' Sue is happy as long as she's got something to moan about. And with her irresponsible husband Ali, his crooked brother Mehmet and sometimes even Mehmet's shrew-like wife Guizin and her hoodlum kids to contend with Sue's got plenty of opportunity. But, thanks to the skill of actress Sandy Ratcliff, you can't help feeling sorry for her. Like so many women in 'EastEnders', Sue is very much the power behind the throne. She virtually runs the café singlehanded. She fights with their landlord, tells her customers (the other residents) the unvarnished truth about themselves and struggles to keep Ali from gambling away the profits. She loves him dearly, despite it.

Of course she has known tragedy. Her toddler son Hassan died a cot death early in the soap's first year – a story-line powerfully written and acted. (I've a lump in my throat just recalling it.) Later scenes – including one where she tried to give his clothes to pregnant Michelle – were equally moving. She thought she might have had breast cancer the following year (the scenes sent thousands of extra clients to clinics for breast screening). And she has been desperate to have another baby.

This year her wish came true. Whatever happens to Sue, though, you can bet she'll still be moaning.

Sandy Ratcliff hides a tragic secret every time she appears as Sue Osman in 'EastEnders'. For Sandy has been a heroin addict for eight years and has admitted to spending up to £400 a week, roughly half her wages, on drugs. The actress was actually gaoled for a year in 1983 for conspiring to supply cannabis. She served eight months of her sentence before being released from Holloway Prison in North London. In prison, she was locked up twenty-three hours a day. 'It was hell,' she says. Thirty-eight-year-old Sandy has always been something of a rebel. The daughter of an insurance salesman, she was expelled from school at twelve. She started taking purple hearts a year later and smoked cannabis by the time she was fourteen. Sandy drifted through jobs as a waitress, disc jockey, bass guitarist in a rock group and model while becoming a true sixties mod. 'I lived in Carnaby Street at the time,' says Sandy. 'I permed my hair, dyed it blue and had it sticking out at the side. My mother cried when she saw it.' Sandy had always worn outrageous clothes. She recalls making her own clothes when she was eleven. 'If people laughed when I went out, I knew I was doing the right thing!' When she was twenty, Sandy married photographer Peter Wright. They were later divorced. Her modelling career took her into commercials, and Lord Snowdon picked her out as his Face of the Seventies. In 1971 she beat 400 other hopefuls to get the lead rôle of Jan, a schizophrenic, in the widely acclaimed film *Family Life*. Her demanding father was played by Bill Dean, now equally mean as Harry Cross in 'Brookside'.

Sandy is unlikely to forget the part in a hurry, because she wasn't allowed to wash her hair for five weeks and had to bite her fingernails down to the quick. Television followed in the shape of 'Minder', 'Shelley', 'Target' and 'Shoestring' before 'EastEnders' came along. A staunch feminist, Sandy says: 'I was very pleased to see that "East-Enders" had a strong representation of women in the producer, several directors and writers.' And it was one of those women, producer Julia Smith, who stood by Sandy when news of her time in prison got out. Sandy offered to quit, but Julia knew about her past and persuaded her to stay. A truly talented actress, Sandy seems unhappily unable to kick drugs. 'They used to give me courage. I don't know if I'll ever be in the clear from them,' she says. These days Sandy lives with her son William, who is now fifteen. 'He is by far the most important consideration in my life.'

Carmel Roberts *See* The Ethnics.

Darren Roberts *See* The Baddies.

Colin Russell and his former boyfriend Barry Clark are, apart from Gordon Collins and his pal Chris in 'Brookside', the gay contingent of British soaps. Colin and Barry always had a high profile. Their relationship was dealt with in a sensitive realistic way. When they went to the pub, they were just a couple of mates out for a pint – without a shoulder-bag, a pink gin or a limp wrist in sight. The only sign of affection between the two was a quick kiss and cuddle. And that, sadly but inevitably, brought a storm of protests. Colin, played by actor

Michael Cashman, who is himself gay, came to Walford in August 1986 when he bought Tony Carpenter's flat. Before long, Barry moved in and, although the two tried to keep their relationship a secret from the rest of the Square, word soon got around. (Well, *words*: 'poofter', 'iron', 'Ginger' – they don't mince them down Albert Square.) At first the reaction was cool, even hostile. (Dot was shocked to discover in the launderette that they shared the same sheets. Eventually her Christianity got the better of her prejudice.) Gradually the less bigoted inhabitants came to realise that Colin and Barry were normal human beings. There was still abuse, but they were accepted into the community. A graphic artist by profession, Colin was considerably older than his partner. Probably for that reason, he was far more insecure. A shy sincere man, Colin is a natural worrier. He is obsessed with tidiness and can sometimes be a bit of a killjoy. For that reason, Barry found him hard work to live with. The 'EastEnders' treatment of this delicate subject has clearly benefited from the guidance and knowledge of the series co-creator Tony Holland, who is gay. It has already been disclosed that some American friends of Colin have died of AIDS. But Colin is in the clear and, not being at all promiscuous, he should be allowed to remain that way and not fall prey to a scriptwriter's idea for a dramatic story-line.

Michael Cashman is well placed to understand Colin Russell in 'EastEnders'. For, like Colin, thirty-seven-year-old Michael is gay. Michael lives in a splendid house in Bow, East London, not far from where he was born. In fact, he was born a few months premature after his mother had defended her husband in a Stepney street-fight. When he was twelve, Michael joined a stage school and was soon to make five West End appearances. The teenage Michael also did cabaret, and recalls one occasion when the entire audience walked out on him. 'It was only afterwards that I discovered a man had been drowning off the nearby cliffs. The audience clearly thought that was better entertainment than my rendition of "Mammy".' Michael overcame that setback to appear in numerous television shows, among them 'The Strauss Family', Jessie in 'The Jessie James Story', 'Enemy at the Door', 'Nobody's Perfect' and two series of 'The Sandbaggers' as brave agent Mike Wallace. His most publicised performance, though, was when he stripped on stage at a gay club to raise money for International AIDS Day.

Dr Jaggat Singh *See* The Ethnics.

Ethel Skinner was created in a Hackney pub where 'EastEnders' producer Julia Smith saw a vivacious old woman with bright ginger hair and a little dog. So enter Ethel, played by the actress with the Donald Duck voice, Gretchen Franklin, along with her wig, her malapropisms and her Little Willy. Ethel was a kindly old duck and a foil to fussy Dot, the other lone woman in the soap. Both had sad pasts. In one episode, featuring only the pair of them, Ethel relived her experience in the Blitz of discovering that all her family had died when a bomb hit their house. Free of all ties, she went on to have a 'good' war with plenty of passion in the blackout. She was the soap's gushing gossip and also something of a fortune-teller, studying everything: the cards, tea-leaves, palms, Russell Grant's sweaters, the lot. In fact, Ethel, Dot and Lou sitting together in the Queen Vic looked like the three witches. As for Little Willy, he may not have had the speed of a greyhound or the nobility of an Afghan but he could cock his leg with the best of 'em. Alas, time caught up with Ethel and she became more confused and less able to look after herself. So in January she took Dr Legg's advice and went to live in a 'sceptred housing' flat where hopefully she'll be 'quite continent'.

Gretchen Franklin kept quacking Ethel out of the old folks' home for a year. She hated the plot-line and told producer Julia Smith so. Julia relented, but insisted twelve months later. 'The day I read in the script that Ethel was being put away I went straight to the producer's office and resigned,' she told me. 'I disagreed with it entirely. I didn't want Ethel to be a sad old duck, being visited by the others. There was too much life in her for that.'

So sprightly Gretchen, aged seventy-six, left Albert Square and went on stage in Chichester. Earlier in her 'EastEnders' career she'd had a bone of contention with the producer. She discovered that, while she was travelling to the BBC's Elstree studios by bus, Ethel's dog Willy was arriving in a chauffeur-driven car. The situation was amended and, happily, the unsavoury incident did not sour relations between Gretchen and Little Willy, who shares a dressing-room with Roly, the poodle from the Vic. 'I loved him,' says Gretchen. 'The dogs were my best friends on the show.' Gretchen was born into a theatrical family seventy-six years ago and has done everything in show business except the circus. 'Mind you, I should have been in the circus – all my mother's people were in that line. My grandmother used to ride a horse round the ring, juggling.' In the 1940s Gretchen, who had married writer Caswell Garth, was the toast of the town with her glamorous looks. She reflects: 'If I'd become famous then when I was gorgeous, I'd have been a spoilt brat.' Her first television appearance was very nearly her last. 'I did this comedy revue and it was the silliest thing I'd ever done. I was just telling everyone so when a voice thundered from overhead: "Shut up, Gretchen, we've heard quite enough from you." It was the producer and he'd heard every word. I was sacked on the spot.' But she went on to work with most of the comedy greats before finding fame as Ethel.

Although she makes only occasional appearances in 'EastEnders' now, Gretchen still has a soft spot for old Ethel. 'I think she was popular because she was simple, kind, generous and brave. But the only thing she and I really had in common was our height.'

Mary Smith is the pathetic punk-styled pixie of 'EastEnders'. How this gawky Northern girl turned into the fallen woman of Albert Square is a sort of nightmare. A believable one. Played by Linda Davidson, Mary had an Irish Catholic upbringing in Stockport but after falling pregnant when she was eighteen she came to Walford to start a new life with her baby Annie. Illiterate, clumsy, disorganised, she could never earn enough money to make ends meet and drifted into stripping then prostitution to pick up extra cash. She had a crush on nurse Andy O'Brien, who tried to teach her to read and write and even persuaded her to remove her mask-like make-up. But he didn't want to be anything more than friends with her (and, anyway, he was run over soon afterwards). Mary used to leave little Annie alone all evening in their squalid bedsit while she went to the Vic to pick up clients. Eventually she was arrested and fined for soliciting. Mary genuinely loved Annie but neglected her appallingly. On one occasion when Mary was out, there was a fire in their room and Annie was rescued only just in time. While the flat was being redecorated, Annie went to stay with Mary's parents. What was supposed to be a short visit became a dramatic tug of love as Mary's mother refused to return the child saying that Mary was unfit to look after her. Finally, Mary got her back thanks to her father and, in no small way, her latest boyfriend, Rod, who belied his scruffy appearance by turning out to be just the sort of sensible man that Mary so desperately needed.

Mary with her Sputnik-styled hair and mask-like make-up was certainly not easy to like – she was far too belligerent and had a huge chip on her shoulder – but as a victim of society and of herself she provoked strong reactions from viewers. After a stable spell Mary's course turned to self-destruct again. She argued with her lorry driver father Chris, a dreary if decent bloke, threw out Rod and, unable to cope alone, took trips 'up west' and used her money on pills and drugs. In May she stomped out, grunting frustration after learning that her mother was heading south for good. I was glad she left. Perhaps she was too real, too depressingly unchanging for soap.

Linda Davidson admits there was a time when she could have ended up like her pitiful 'EastEnders' character Mary Smith. Canada-born Linda came to England and lived with her family in Lancashire until she left home at the age of sixteen and stayed in a bedsit in Toxteth, Liverpool. She recalls: 'There was fungus growing over the bed and it was so damp that the TV rental company removed the set because it kept blowing up. During that year on my own, I went completely mad. I was out at clubs every night, drinking at lunch-times and going out with boys, the lot.' But, like Mary, Linda travelled south to London to start afresh. Already a talented dancer (her mother was a soloist with the Ballet Rambert, and Linda herself had done cabaret work with the likes of Tom O'Connor and Freddie Starr), Linda went to drama school and appeared in 'Who Dares Wins', 'Bulman' and ultimately 'EastEnders'. Linda, who is the only principal artist on the show not to have any sort of East End background, goes to great pains to get the character of Mary right. When she first got the part, she went to London's King's Road to study all the punks, and when Mary became a prostitute she searched out real whores. 'I wanted to talk to genuine prostitutes, to learn how they felt and how people reacted to them. I saw girls of fifteen on the streets; it was so distressing I couldn't stop crying. I've even had kerb crawlers after me thinking I'm like Mary.' Linda deliberately makes herself depressed before recording 'EastEnders' by not talking to the rest of the cast or by reading a sad book. 'That makes me in the mood for Mary because I find her incredibly hard to play if I'm happy. Mary is one of the Square's saddest residents – a very challenging character.' Linda found Mary's strip scene particularly difficult. 'That was the hardest thing I've ever done as an actress,' she says. 'It was tough because I was having to be basic in public, sexually basic. I felt terribly vulnerable doing it and I was very upset afterwards.' She also had problems with her screen baby Annie. 'I'd never even handled a baby before "EastEnders". I was so nervous at first but now I'm more confident with her.' However, some fans were so incensed by Mary's neglect of Annie that they once threw stones at Linda. Twenty-four-year-old Linda, who used to go out with Nejdet Salih (Ali in 'EastEnders'), has one other fear: being recognised. 'It takes me an hour to change into Mary, and most people don't recognise me off-screen because I look so different. But it's horrible if I am spotted. Other people can handle the attention. I just go bright red and get shy and stupid.'

Angie Watts, landlady of the Queen Victoria, brought something new to soap: suffering with gaiety. Angie does more than survive the slings and arrows of disgraceful Dennis, her ex-husband. She thrives on them and laughs in his face. Her motto is 'On with the motley, the paint and the powder'. So when things go wrong it's a gallon of slap and the brightest, tightest tat ever produced by the East End rag trade. Angie laughs as her heart breaks.

It was clear from the start that behind the over-scented jammy smile, the shrill 'What can I getcha, darlin'?' from behind the bar of the Vic, Angie was a mental wreck. Cockney sparrow, and proud of it, she'd wed Dennis her childhood sweetheart at eighteen, and the marriage had gone downhill from then on. When the soap began Mr and Mrs Watts had had separate beds for thirteen years. Presumably Den had always 'played the field'; presumably Angie felt she had to match his affairs with her flings (in the soap's first year she dallied with Tony, then Andy); presumably she started drinking years back to make it all seem fun.

But what was blindingly clear about Angie, played by Anita Dobson, was her hopeless addiction to Den.

Her moods, ranging from exhausting cheeriness to malicious triumph (when she'd momentarily outwitted Den) to total collapse, mascara splashing on to her high-heeled feet, make her soap's most neurotic heroine. When she could no longer fool herself that Jan, Den's mistress, was a passing fancy, her attempted suicide in the kitchen upstairs in the Vic in February 1986, jamming handfuls of pills into her mouth and washing them down with gin, seemed entirely logical.

The suicide scene may or may not have been copied by impressionable people unhappy in their love-lives. Two Hackney doctors claimed they treated three times the number of overdose cases in the week following the episode. The coroner in Salisbury claimed a seventeen-year-old-girl had tragically re-enacted Angie's deed – only, unlike Angie, she wasn't found in time. (The girl's parents denied a connection.) But the power of the story-line and of Anita's performance was undeniable.

Even when, later, she dared to tell Den a whopping lie, that she was terminally ill, had only months to live (knowing he would guiltily give up Jan to be with her), the silly stunt kept the millions riveted. (The soap's record viewing figures of around 30 million watched the end of it: Den passing Angie the divorce papers after discovering the lie.) We care about her because she's such an obvious loser.

During Angie's year out of the Vic (1987) when she and Sharon lived in a flat above the Dagmar, where Angie worked, Sharon became Angie's mother. She pushed Angie to admit there was a problem about the drinking. Angie and the gin parted for a while. The embarrassing binges stopped. It was very dull. By the end of the year, her bossy little boss, Willmott-Brown and the Dagmar's yuppy customers were getting on her wick so much that she had to thump one of them and knock him out (don't worry, he was an estate agent).

Her return to drinking and then to the Vic, a strictly business arrangement (she said) following fat Pat's confessed 'urges' for Den, marked an upswing in the soap's liveliness early in 1988. But the booze almost killed her this time. She was taken to hospital with kidney failure, causing Den to gulp guiltily a few times and fidget by her bedside. As she slowly recovered, she forswore drink for ever, decided that she and Den should move away and proposed that they remarry. His charming reply was that he wouldn't marry her if she were the last cockney bint in the East End.

Angie returned to convalesce at the Vic but left to run a bar in Majorca with her best friend's husband Sonny in May 1988 after Anita Dobson decided that 'greater' things awaited her. The writers hope she will return.

Quite what 'life after soap' (p.347) holds for Anita, Angie, with her toothy smile, her polyester prettiness, her love of 'nice things', nights up West and plenty of male attention, will be watchable whatever she does. To men she represents a good time or, at worst, a lot of dirty laughs. To women she represents that spirit of not letting the buggers get you down. Cheers, Ange!

Anita Dobson hasn't moved far geographically since she became Angie in 'EastEnders'. Born in the Bancroft Road hospital off the Mile End Road in April 1949, she now lives in a maisonette in Wapping. But the girl who worked as an actress for thirteen years making hardly a ripple made a very big splash indeed with the cockney soap.

Until she started touring with small-time reps, she lived with her parents Alf and Anne in a council flat. Now she has bought them a posh flat close to her own. (Daughters don't move far from mothers in the East End, geographically or emotionally.)

She's an odd one, really, to become the most famous actress in Britain. She's 5 feet 3½ inches, she weighs 8½ stone when the worry of it all doesn't slim her down, her hair is naturally dark auburn and was straight before the crimpers got at her. In her teens she was influenced by Dusty Springfield, and the influence lingers in the eye make-up.

Anita left school at sixteen with four 'O' levels and the need to be an actress. She joined an amateur drama group, appeared at the Bethnal Green Institute. She had a few boyfriends, became engaged to Alan Bayley, a mod by night, a brewery messenger by day, called off the wedding a month before the day.

She was nineteen years old when she gave up her job as a clerk at the Prudential in Holborn and got herself a grant to study drama at the Webber Douglas Academy in South Kensington. One of her teachers was Julia Smith, later co-creator of 'EastEnders'. Julia was impressed. Anita did her first professional work at the Glasgow Citizens Theatre, then worked in almost every rep in the country. She played everything, including panto, managed a little dancing when it was called for, did bits and pieces on television. Then when Jean Fennell, the original choice for Angie Watts in 'EastEnders', was dropped Julia Smith thought of the skinny cockney kid she'd taught in South Kensington. The rest, as they say, is history.

The girl earned enormous fame – deservedly so. No one in the 1980s on television could smile through the tears, switch to anger and back to tears, as she could. She also earned a lot of loot, endorsing products and places. Despite a singing voice totally lacking in muscle (and quite un-Angie-like), her version of the soap's theme tune, 'Anyone Can Fall in Love', in the summer of 1986 reached the top of the charts. I'll be charitable about her next two records and say simply that they didn't.

She appeared in pantomime, almost daily in the newspapers, was made a 'Rear of the Year' as well as a favourite face. She talked about needing to do 'other things'. She decided to leave 'for a while' and left Albert Square in May.

Anita had an affair with Tom Watt, who plays Lofty the loser in 'EastEnders' and she's had other boyfriends from time to time ('I'm not a nun'), some of whom have kissed and told. But the woman with the longish nose – so far she's resisted rhinoplasty – the million-watt smile and the principal-boy legs seems to be married to her profession. Unlike Angie Watts, she doesn't let men get in the way of the really important things. Like work, fame, money.

Dennis Watts, landlord of the Queen Victoria, is part-rat, part-mouse and undoubtedly the most powerful male figure in British soap opera. The reason is the man who plays him: Leslie Grantham, convicted murderer. The actor, the BBC and many of his fans will angrily dispute this. But the truth is that, while the most violent of Den's deeds to date has been slapping his flirtatious daughter across the face or punching Wicksy out of jealousy over Mags, in the average viewer's eyes Den is a man with Leslie Grantham's highly dramatic past. He's aggressive, sometimes sour. There may be a problem with control. . . .

Often we viewers are guilty of laying a soap character's deeds on the innocent actor. Here, I'm convinced, the reverse has worked in the collective subconscious, to Den's benefit, if to Leslie's despair. Den was a strong character before Leslie Grantham's prison sentence was exposed in the papers. Based on a pub landlord friend of script-editor Tony Holland he is flash, dishonest, snappy with his staff yet capable also of generosity, insight and disarming frankness about himself. He needs love but can't cope with it. He's the divorced husband of Angie, the alcoholic shrew, devoted but inadequate father to adopted Sharon and natural (but secret) father (after one drunken session of sex) of Vicky, the baby born to Michelle at sixteen. Womaniser, occasional messenger for the local 'mob', there's scarcely a dodgy deal he hasn't tried, a lie he hasn't told. No wonder he was dubbed 'Dirty Den' and has, since the soap's start in February 1985, inspired waves of admiration and disapproval, lust and disgust.

The root of his problems, it's hinted, lay in Angie's sexual rejection of him early in their marriage. He became edgy and embittered with the strain of her drinking and of keeping up appearances in front of customers. From the start he was seen sneakily telephoning other women from the hall of the Vic or getting into his Rover, looking guiltily around before disappearing to keep a rendezvous. He enjoys the deceptions as much as the sex. Jan, his main 'other' woman, loved him but not his pub. Mags, her replacement, couldn't stand his old-fashioned possessiveness. Pat, who narrowed her piggy eyes at him last

Christmas and yearned, repelled him (which was lucky – with her bulk she might have flattened him). He lets Sharon, his daughter, down and gives time to Michelle, mother of his child, grudgingly (though he passes over the tenners generously). The brewery is always poised to catch him buying booze 'illegally' from the cash-and-carry. His rival landlord, 'Lieutenant' Willmott-Brown, would like to confine him to barracks. Pauline, Michelle's mother, would like to brain him, and Angie would like to kick him where it hurts most.

His failings, personal and in business, are so many that he seems more a victim than the villain of the piece. When the Angie–Den barneys had to stop (because Anita Dobson left), the producers hurriedly ordered the construction of Henry's Wine Bar, Albert Square's third watering hole (in competition with the Vic and the Dagmar). The local mob promptly bought it and installed Den, a bloke who wouldn't know his Alsace from his elbow, to run it. Still, as he would snarl, 'It's a tough old world'.

With the wine bar came a new woman for Den, lady-like Joanne (Pamela Salem) and a deep involvement with local villains. Den took the blame when Wilmott-Brown's pub, the Dagmar, burnt down after he failed to pay protection money. Den went to gaol for a spell, a sentence Leslie Grantham served by filming roles in other series.

Leslie Grantham, who plays 'dirty' Den Watts, the pub landlord in 'EastEnders', pays a price for his soap superstardom. Every time he is written about in newspapers or magazines, the life sentence – eleven years served in prison – for the murder of a taxi-driver while a soldier in Germany, in 1966, is mentioned. At the time, Leslie Grantham was seen as a cold-blooded monster. The phenomenal popularity of 'EastEnders' regularly recondemns him. The actor has never tried to minimise the seriousness of this crime. But over the years since Den, he and it became famous the nightmare hasn't diminished. I doubt if it ever will.

Leslie became an actor in prison. Growing up as a 'mod' in mohair suits in St Mary's Cray, near Orpington, he hadn't considered anything so airy-fairy. He left school at fifteen with no qualifications, few ambitions. After a few jobs he joined the Army, soon to be posted to Osnabrück in West Germany. Within a year he was starting a sentence in Wormwood Scrubs. When two prisoners leading the drama group were despatched for electric-shock treatment, Leslie stepped in. His new career and Dirty Den were on the way. Fellow-prisoner, architect T. Dan Smith, gaoled for his part in the Poulson corruption scandal, described him then as a natural – 'like he is in "EastEnders", highly volatile, always on edge'.

Leslie left gaol with £17 and a determination to carry on acting. He studied at the Webber Douglas Academy, where he met Julia Smith and actress Jane Laurie, who became his wife. He took theatre work, then small television parts, including a cockney army sergeant in 'Jewel in the

Crown', a convict in the play 'Knock Back', a villain in 'Bulman' and a policeman in the comedy film *Morons from Outer Space*.

When 'resting' he took odd jobs, bartending, selling suits, painting the VD clinic at St Thomas's Hospital. Julia Smith remembered him when casting 'EastEnders' and hired him for what was then planned as a relatively minor part. He accepted, then told her he'd better step down. There was this murder. . . . Her attitude, and the BBC's, was that he'd paid the penalty. It was over. How wrong they were!

In the autumn of 1986 he paid another penalty of soap success. His younger brother Philip died of AIDS. The secret could not be kept.

Despite his gaunt face and thinning hair, Leslie became the sexpot of soap. Anxious to make as much money from Den's possibly short life he accepts offers to appear at discos and clubs for fees of £1000–£3000 a night. Often he's mobbed by women who are encouraged to bare their boobs for Leslie to autograph. 'I feel embarrassed and try to cover them up,' said Leslie. 'I'm no heart-throb. But what can I do? People have paid to see me. I can't run away.'

Soon to be seen as a spy in a BBC thriller, filmed in Northern Ireland – a job squeezed into a fortnight's leave from the soap – Leslie remains modest about his talent. 'I'm not even a minor star,' he said. 'I belong to the NAN school – "no acting necessary". I've got two styles: I can look surly and miserable or miserable and surly. I don't find it difficult to keep my feet on the ground, because I know I'm the same awful bloke I've always been.'

Sharon Watts

Sharon Watts is the tug-of-love child in 'EastEnders' between mum Angie and dad Den. It's quite a tug. Den's podgy princess hasn't just got puppy fat; she's more like a full-blown St Bernard. When she sang in the rock band, she looked like Earth, Wind and Fire all rolled into one. If fat people are supposed to be happy, Sharon should be the jolliest soul this side of Bernard Manning. But she's not. Played by Letitia Dean, Sharon is eighteen and confused. It's hardly surprising. She was adopted by Angie, a woman who becomes unpleasant when she drinks too much, and Den, a man who doesn't need the drink. They bounce her around between them, like an over-inflated beach-ball, and toy with her affections. Sharon's a kind-hearted girl, and all she seems to want is a settled home life with genuine warmth from Den and Angie. She tried everything to get them back together. (Personally, I'd rather win the Ayatollah Khomeini on 'Blind Date' than live with those two, but it takes all sorts.) Sharon's best mate around Albert Square is Michelle. Michelle's no oil painting but she is bright. Next to Sharon she glows. A few years ago, Sharon discovered sex suddenly. Her virginity was a burden, it seemed. She wanted to go on the Pill at fifteen and used to flaunt her assets at all and sundry. She went out with Ian Beale for a while and with Wicksy for a bit. Wicksy arranged to take her away to the country for a weekend, and it was going to be the important First Time. But Sharon wouldn't go all the way – and I don't mean they only got as far as the Dartford Tunnel. The scenes on their return, in which Sharon explained she hadn't slept with Wicksy (because it hadn't felt right), were among the most preachy in the soap's history. Later Sharon's canine leanings came to the fore. For not only has she got her puppy-fat problem; she seemed to be trying to win favour with Roly, the family poodle. She even copied his top pom-pom and fluffy earmuff hairstyle. Then it was Duncan the curate to whom she became unofficially engaged. Anything in a dog collar. . . .

Letitia Dean got the part of Sharon Watts in 'EastEnders' because, in the words of producer Julia Smith, 'she had the dirtiest laugh in the world'. Not that she's had that much to laugh about in the soap. Sharon has had something of an emotional battering to date. 'I feel so sorry for her,' says Letitia. 'One minute she was getting attention from Den; the next minute he was off with some other woman. Then Angie, who'd been ignoring her, suddenly needed her and flooded her with affection. I know Sharon's a bit young and stupid, but it's no wonder she's confused. Fortunately I'm nothing like Sharon; for a start, my home life is far better than hers.'

Born in a cottage at Camfield Place, the Hertfordshire estate owned by Barbara Cartland, Letitia was named after a kindly old alcoholic who offered her own tattered christening-robe for the ceremony. Letitia used to be in a dancing act with her brother Steven, and on one holiday weekend in Blackpool they won no fewer than four talent shows. At the age of twelve she was in the West End production of *Annie* and in 1984 appeared as Dawn in 'Brookside'. Music plays an important part in her life. Her dad had the dubious distinction of designing all the clothes for the Bay City Rollers, and she used to be a singer with a rock group, the Young 'Uns. After two earlier records flopped Letitia fared slightly better when she swelled the ranks of 'EastEnders' recording artists by teaming up with Paul J. Medford (Kelvin in the series). Now twenty, Letitia lives with her mum, dad and brother in a West End mews house. On and off screen, she is great mates with Susan Tully, who plays Michelle, but is understandably a little wary of men after a former boyfriend had 'told all' to the press and photographs of a nude lookalike appeared in a girlie magazine. Letitia does have one other problem on 'EastEnders': her weight. She explains: 'I'm not actually allowed to lose weight. It's written into my contract that Sharon has to have puppy fat. If I lost weight, they would have to pad me out.'

Pat Wicks, soap's supersized slag, hit 'EastEnders' with the force of an SAS raid. Built like a Russian beauty queen, this bulldozer of a woman proceeded to crush everyone who came into contact with her.

Within a week of her arrival in June 1986 she had bluntly told her ex-husband Pete Beale that his beloved son Simon was not his son after all. Pete slapped her, but would have liked to do more permanent damage. Her son Simon hated her, too – so imagine their horror when poison Pat, played by Pam St Clement, was taken on as a barmaid at the Queen Vic. Lofty hid in the cellar for a week. Pat was trouble, big trouble. Nobody argued with her at chucking-out time. She made Nora Batty look like a shrinking violet, and even made Den look almost human. When she fell victim to the uninspiringly named Walford Attacker it was like *Murder on the Orient Express* – it was hard to find someone who didn't want to thump her. She encouraged Mary in the business of fleecing men for sex and treated Ethel like dirt. She has calmed down a bit since then. She and Angie were great mates until, in a shared drunken stupor, she confided that she fancied Den. She caused a rumpus when Kenny Beale returned, eventually confessing that she had slept with both brothers around the same time and simply could not tell which was Simon's father. She added with obvious glee that both were hopeless lovers. Pete tried to say that was wubbish, but he crumpled none the less.

Pete and Simon can just about stomach her now, and in Angie's absence she has become the power behind the bar at the Vic. Den couldn't open the fridge without her. Possibly because he couldn't get in the kitchen.

The truth is that, behind all her bluster and apparent immorality, Pat was a lonely woman, desperate for a man – if only to eat. That man could turn out to be an old flame, Frank (Mike Reid); looking rather like Alec Gilroy with a failed hair transplant, he came back into her life in March 1988 and proposed marriage.

Pam St Clement is as forthright in her opinions about her 'East-Enders' character, fat Pat Wicks, as Pat is about everyone else. 'I wouldn't give her house room,' says Pam. 'I think she's quite ghastly. She just opens her mouth and it all comes out. She doesn't think about anything she says. She likes to be the life and soul of the party, noisy and the centre of attention. I can't bear women like that. But, underneath it all, Pat's very sad and vulnerable. She's been hurt and she doesn't want it to happen to her again.' Forty-six-year-old divorcee Pam, is much smaller and less intimidating than Pat Wicks, and doesn't even smoke. At her request, the cigarettes that Pat draws on are herbal. But Pam St Clement is used to playing women who are larger than life. 'I always get landed with big forbidding women with rolling-pins,' she says. 'There's fifty beautiful girls for every part that's going, but there are very few who can play the likes of Rolling-Pin Pat and even fewer who can act.' Pam's father hailed from the East End, and Pam herself used to live in Stepney. Her many television rôles have included 'The Onedin Line', 'Enemy at the Door', 'Private Schultz' and Mrs Eckersley in 'Emmerdale Farm'. She was also in the film *Scrubbers*. Pam's brilliant creation of Pat is undoubtedly one of the high spots of 'EastEnders', and the actress herself is very keen on the part. 'I love playing Pat if only because I seldom get rôles where I can show my femininity. The great thing about being Pat is that I'm allowed to be brassy and quite attractive. I get the chance to shake the old cleavage about!'

Simon Wicks, known to all as 'Wicksy', soon became the Square's heart-throb, leading to actor Nick Berry being mobbed by legions of female admirers wherever he goes. Wicksy is the son of the mighty Pat Wicks but not from her marriage to Pete Beale. His sudden arrival in Albert Square caused great ructions in the Beale household. Pete, thinking he was his son, welcomed him with open arms, much to the consternation of wife Kathy and real son Ian. It soon emerged that Wicksy owed a lot of money, but Pete, always a soft touch, came to the rescue. In spite of, or maybe because of, having such an embarrassing mother, Wicksy is very popular. He used to work as barman at the Queen Vic until Den sacked him. Now he's got a similar job at the Dagmar. For someone who is young, good-looking and fancy-free, it's surprising that Wicksy has stayed in the area for so long, particularly in such poorly paid jobs. However, there'd be a huge teenage outcry if he was written out. He used to date Sharon Watts but moved on to Den's ex-mistress Mags. Den was not happy about that liaison and sacked Wicksy. Mags is too bright for simple Simon, who is basically just a pretty face. But he can behave alarmingly when roused. For, just as a rattlesnake rattles its tail threateningly when cornered and a skunk lets off a foul smell, Wicksy 'plays' the piano. It has much the same effect: people run for cover.

Nick Berry is the girls' favourite EastEnder. Twenty-five-year-old Nick has made barman Simon Wicks the show's pin-up, yet a horrific car crash four years ago could have scarred him for life. Nick, who was not wearing a seatbelt, was thrown through the car windscreen and fractured his skull. He had to have splinters of glass removed from his eyes, and his head swelled to twice its normal size. Fortunately, he made a complete recovery, and he and his girlfriend Gillian Taylforth (Kathy Beale in 'EastEnders') are besieged by fans whenever they venture out. However, they did find one haven of retreat, when they went on holiday to Florida. Only two people recognised them all the time they were there.

Nick joined a stage school when he was only eight and has since appeared in two West End productions of *Oliver!*, such television shows as 'The Gentle Touch', 'The Audition' and 'Box of Delights', and films like *Party Party* and *Forever Young*. However, his greatest success apart from 'EastEnders' came in October 1986, when his record 'Every Loser Wins' stayed at the top of the charts for three weeks. And Nick was modest enough to admit: 'My singing on it was awful.'

Debbie Wilkins *See* The Yuppies.

James Willmott-Brown *See* The Yuppies.

The Baddies

'EastEnders' has more meanies than all its cosier cousins in British soap put together. It's crawling with villains. The Firm are never far away, and many of the regular characters are on first-name terms with Shaw Taylor. Den dabbles and double-deals. In fact the only things that aren't hot at the Queen Vic are the meat pies.

Charlie Cotton If ever there was a case of 'like father like son', it's Nick's parasitic dad Charlie Cotton, played by Christopher Hancock. Like Nick, Charlie is a small-time villain who only comes to visit Dot when he can sponge off her. But, whereas Nick has animal cunning, Charlie is bereft of any intelligence whatsoever. There is absolutely no love lost between father and son – in fact Charlie's so repulsive that you could almost feel sorry for Nick. Neither Charlie nor Nick would hesitate to shop one another – if the price was right.

Christopher Hancock is the elder brother of Stephen Hancock, who was Ernie Bishop in 'Coronation Street'. Stephen was 'killed off' after making a crusade for better pay, and Christopher, better-known as loathsome lizard Charlie Cotton in 'EastEnders', is anxious not to follow in his brother's footsteps. 'What happened to Stephen has weighed heavily on my mind,' says Christopher. 'When I'm on "EastEnders" I'm very careful about what I say and do. Stephen learned that nobody's indispensable.' Christopher, aged fifty-nine, was recently divorced from his wife Ann after twenty-eight years of marriage, a split that he blames partly on Charlie Cotton. 'I was so desperate to get the part right that I didn't care enough about those who should have mattered most.' Christopher dons stick-on sideburns to become Charlie, of whom he says: 'He's a truly revolting character, a loser.'

Nick Cotton But far and away the most evil EastEnder is Nasty Nick Cotton, son of Dot. Actor John Altman has created a mini-monster in Nick, a sinister racist thug who hates everyone. His scowling, sneering face changes to a wicked grin only when he is hurting somebody, mentally or physically. Dressed in black, Nick is a character straight out of Victorian melodrama. All he needs is the waxed moustache. His standing in the Square sank to an all-time low when he

broke into Dr Legg's surgery and found medical notes revealing that Kathy Beale had once been raped and had a baby. Being the creep he is, he tried to blackmail Kathy about it. Not surprisingly, he has been on the receiving end of a couple of hidings from the locals. Because Nick is constantly on the run from somebody, he usually travels by night, but whenever he deigns to return to the Square he can be sure of a warm welcome from one person only: dotty Dot. For in spite of all that he's done, including stealing cheques from her and forging her signature and regularly pilfering from her purse, Dot dotes on her son. Dot still sees him as her baby boy, and probably reminisces about bygone days when little Nick used to demand rusks with menaces or mug classmates for their Crackerjack pencils.

John Altman would make his 'EastEnders' character Nasty Nick Cotton as sick as a stolen parrot. For, whereas Nick thinks kids are only any good to steal blackjacks from, thirty-five-year-old John is a devoted family man, madly in love with his two-year-old daughter Rosanna. 'It's brilliant being a dad,' enthuses John. 'It's brought out the softy in me. To be honest, I'd be happy to stay at home full-time and look after Rosanna.' Nor would racist Nick be at all pleased with John's choice of wife: Asian model and actress Brigitte Poodhun. John also takes Nick to task for the way he treats Dot. 'I'd never dream of speaking to my mother the way Nick talks to poor old Dot.' John adds: 'I use the anger in me to play Nick. He's like a rat in a corner. He grew up in a tower-block with urine in the lift and graffiti on the front door. He became a rebel and a bully and left school with no qualifications. In a way, I feel sorry for him: he's a victim of Britain in the eighties. He looked for work, couldn't find it and turned to drugs and blackmail.' Yet, although he plays such an abhorrent creep, John gets inundated with letters from girls wanting to know when Nick is coming back. 'People like a villain,' says John. 'It's a strange quirk of human behaviour.' John was born in Reading, the son of a City banker. He graduated in photography and spent a year as an odd-job man for an Arab oil sheikh before becoming a professional actor. He has been in demand ever since, and his film rôles have included *An American Werewolf in London, Quadrophenia* and *The Return of the Jedi*. And John has one more confession which would shame Nick: he used to be afraid of the dark.

Mehmet Osman is the most charismatic of the 'EastEnders' baddies. He's the handsome Turkish-Cypriot brother of café-owner Ali. Actor Haluk Bilginer has built up a considerable following as Mehmet, who has been dubbed 'the Terrible Turk'. Probably because he's married to the rodent-like Guizin, Mehmet is a real womaniser. When Mary Smith was going through her roughest phase, Mehmet charmed her into submission, purely to win a £10 bet he'd had with Ali that he could get Mary into bed. A not too devoted father of two, Mehmet tries it on with all the women, which means there are a lot of men after his blood. Ali's wife Sue hates him, too, and was not that upset when rough justice, in the shape of Pete and Den, caught up with Mehmet after he'd swindled Pete's wife Kathy. He even once made a pass at the Queen Vic barmaid Donna – only, I suspect, because he thought her surname was Kebab.

Haluk Bilginer reckons even the postman blushes when he delivers mail to his North London home. For Haluk's rôle as Terrible Turk Mehmet Osman in 'EastEnders' has brought him an avalanche of fan mail – most of it leaving little to the imagination. 'I get all kinds of suggestions,' admits Haluk, who lives with girlfriend Maddie. 'I think it's because women regard me as a challenge – my Mehmet image will live on for a while.' Those fans caused Haluk to be fined for speeding on one occasion. 'I was driving in London when a car pulled up beside me and all these women inside recognised me and started yelling at me. I decided the only thing to do was escape, so I put my foot down and the next thing I knew the police pulled me up for doing seventy-nine miles per hour in a fifty miles per hour area. In court I was fined seventy-five pounds.' Haluk defends Mehmet, the Romeo Rat. 'He's not an evil person; it's just that he's a total gambler with life and gets himself in situations where he is judged as a nasty piece of work.' Haluk, Turkish-Cypriot, first read for the part of Mehmet's brother Ali in 'EastEnders'. But his performance at the audition was so physical that at one point the producers thought he was going to hit Sandy Ratcliff, who plays Ali's wife Sue. They decided he was too hot for Ali but created the character of Mehmet for him instead. Now thirty-four, Haluk came to England thirteen years ago. When he was in Turkey, he worked at the State Theatre, and in this country he has appeared in *The Glory Boys* with Rod Steiger. One of Haluk's great loves is singing. 'I've done a few Turkish concerts in London, singing classical songs. And during my national service days in the Turkish army, I was actually the battalion singer!'

Darren Roberts

is a fairly recent arrival in Albert Square. Played by Gary McDonald, Darren is the brother of do-gooder social worker Carmel and is a sort of dusky Arthur Daley. He's always wheeling and dealing, trying to keep one step ahead of the law and Carmel. He has a son, Junior, and a daughter, Aisha, but that doesn't cramp his style, for Darren is a flashy dresser with an eye for the ladies. He is what is known to some as 'streetwise'. To others (including me) he's also a berk.

Gary McDonald joined 'EastEnders' in July last year as the roguish Darren Roberts. Yet Gary found himself on the right side of the law in the film *Burning an Illusion* where he played a policeman. Gary's other credits include 'London's Burning' in which he was 'Ethnic' Lewis, 'Now – Something Else' and the National Theatre production of *Macbeth*. Gary won't forget 'London's Burning' in a hurry. While filming Jack Rosenthal's television play, Gary bravely put out a real fire and then, during a riot scene, his character was hit on the head with a slab of concrete and killed.

The Ethnics

'EastEnders' tried to make itself 'EthnicEnders', the soap which reflects the cosmopolitan mix of races and nationalities in poor parts of London. It wasn't too successful. By early 1988 it was as though the Ku Klux Klan had held rallies in the Albert Square Gardens. There was hardly a non-white face to be seen.

The Osmans are dealt with elsewhere, but for over two years the principal black family in the show were the Carpenters, a motley crew comprising parents Tony and Hannah, who lived apart until they unaccountably decided to give their marriage one last try, and kids Kelvin and Cassie.

The Carpenter Family Tony was by far the most popular with his neighbours and viewers. Played by Oscar James, Tony was a too gentle giant. He let his odious offspring run rings around him and allowed Hannah to behave like Hitler in drag. Tony was born in Trinidad and clearly felt the cold in Britain as he continually wore a sheepskin-lined flying-jacket – even in the middle of June. (Perhaps he simply couldn't take the jacket off; maybe Hannah had nailed it to his skin.) Tony was the Albert Square handyman, and it's a testimony to his work that most of the place looks as if it's about to fall down. A burst pipe? Tony would be round immediately with a reel of Sellotape. Or he'd staple you up a nice set of shelves or even install an entire central heating system using only sticky-backed plastic and detergent bottles. It was therefore a great relief to the home-owners of Walford when Tony decided he'd had enough and returned to the Caribbean in May 1987.

Hard-hearted Hannah, played by Sally Sagoe, liked nothing better than a good row. When she was young, she was a black beauty. Now she's just an old nag. Where once she could turn water to wine, now she turns wine to vinegar. Her marriage to Tony was on the rocks when the series began and, although Tony and Kelvin lived in the Square, Hannah and Cassie had a place elsewhere. It was near enough for Cassie to be a regular visitor, though, when she was being beaten up by Hannah's fella. Eventually, Hannah left her man and she and Cassie moved in with Tony and Kelvin to make one big unhappy family. She knew Tony was a lousy judge of women (he'd even had a brief fling with Angie) and she made his life hell. An arrogant snob, she was always on at Tony to better himself. In the end he did. He left her. It was amazing that Tony never took an axe to her. Perhaps he did – one he'd repaired, and the handle dropped off just as he tried to use it.

Cassie, played by Delanie Forbes, was in danger of graduating from a little brat into a big one. She had been caught smoking pot, so was despatched to boarding school. Her elder brother Kelvin, played by Paul J. Medford, was too cocky by half. First he thought he was God's gift to music, as he and his mates formed an ill-fated rock group, and then he fancied himself as a great womaniser. He tried to prove his manhood by moving in with social worker Carmel Roberts, who was some years older than him. In time she saw through his dreadlocks and ditched him. It couldn't have happened to a nicer bloke. Eventually, in October 1987, he left to go to university where he is probably rewriting history.

Oscar James feels that the BBC missed an opportunity to improve race relations in this country by the way in which the Carpenter family were portrayed in 'EastEnders'. Oscar played West Indian Tony Carpenter until the character was written out in May 1987 and says: 'The Carpenters were always arguing and at each other's throat. Having a black family in a top TV show should have been a wonderful method of educating the nation to treat each other as individuals, not according to their colour. That is the way to world peace. "EastEnders" has done a lot of good. It's just that the BBC could do so much better – and recognise that the ethnic minority in "EastEnders" deserve better.' Oscar also used to get letters from West Indian fathers complaining that he was too soft with son Kelvin. 'They're very strict,' says Oscar, 'and wouldn't have tolerated such behaviour. Oscar is forty and a big chap (six feet tall and weighing fifteen stone), a Buddhist and a pacifist. Born in Trinidad, he ran off to sea at the age of fourteen and travelled the world before ending up in London. A bachelor father of two daughters, the flamboyant Oscar is a keen singer as well as being a familiar face on television. His long list of television credits includes 'Emmerdale Farm', 'Love Thy Neighbour', 'The Fosters' and 'Angels', and he is one of the few actors prepared to admit he was in London Weekend Television's horrendous 'comedy' series 'Bottle Boys'.

Sally Sagoe got her showbiz break on a six-month cruise to the South Pacific. 'It was a bit of a cheek for me to audition in the first place,' confesses Sally, 'because they wanted an experienced cabaret singer and all I'd done at that stage was play an angel in *Jesus Christ Superstar*. But I got the job. Thirty-four-year-old Sally left the soap in 1987. London-born Sally, who has a Nigerian father, also has a blossoming singing career. She used to front the Sally Sagoe Band with five men until their gear went up in flames and Sally was £6000 out of pocket. Her singing has certainly made an impact – an Arab sheikh was once so impressed by her that he flew her out to Dubai for a special performance.

Paul J. Medford was one of the most popular young actors in 'EastEnders', playing Kelvin Carpenter for nearly three years. Twenty-one-year-old Paul was born in West London, although his parents come from Barbados. Apart from acting, Paul's great passion is music and, in company with virtually every other member of the cast except the dogs Roly and Willy, he released a record, 'Something Outa Nothing', with co-star Letitia Dean. It didn't change the world or his lifestyle, but it was pleasant.

Naima Jeffery
Actress Shreela Ghosh showed Naima to be an intelligent independent woman, under no illusions about the difficulties encountered by an Asian girl running an inner-city shop. Most of the locals were friendly towards Naima (although the shop was once daubed with racist slogans), but she was always distant. It was usually a case of service with a snarl. Naima was Bengali and a Muslim. She entered into a marriage of convenience with Saeed, who was played by Andrew Johnson, so that they could run the store together, but the marriage didn't work, and when it was revealed that Saeed had been visiting prostitutes Naima walked out. Saeed returned to India. Naima battled on, aided and abetted by Debbie Wilkins and Rezavi, a decidedly shifty cousin of Naima who came to keep an eye on her but eventually took over the shop. For, in November 1987, Naima and a more distant cousin Farrukh went back to Bangladesh with the intention of getting married. She might even smile for it.

Shreela Ghosh described the Saeed prostitution story-line as being a slur on Asians, and both Oscar James and Sally Sagoe have expressed their disappointment at the way in which the Carpenter family were depicted. 'I think the BBC played us down,' said Oscar. 'They could have done a lot more.'

Shreela Ghosh caused confusion when she went to court for a licence for a wine bar she was planning to open with fellow-EastEnder Paul J. Medford. For in the same week Shreela's EastEnders character, Naima Jeffery, had been granted an off-licence for her shop. 'What do you need another licence for?' asked one of the panel. 'You've already got one!' Fortunately, Shreela succeeded in her quest and the wine bar, called Cobblers, in Bethnal Green, is a thriving concern. Shreela, aged twenty-six, was born in India and educated in England. She married film director Jonathan Curling after a whirlwind romance and left 'East-Enders' for a few months to have a baby daughter who is now three. A noted Indian classical dancer, Shreela has appeared in 'The Chinese Detective' and 'The Jewel in the Crown' and was in 'EastEnders' for almost three years before she left in November 1987 saying: 'I didn't want to become typecast.' She certainly wasn't typecast when she appeared in Sue Townsend's play *The Great Celestial Cow* at London's Royal Court Theatre a few years ago. Shreela played nine different parts including the back end of a pantomime cow!

Carmel Roberts
Carmel, played by Judith Jacob, was certainly much too good for Kelvin. Anyway, she's got enough to worry about keeping an eye on her dodgy brother Darren. Carmel worked tirelessly to get Mary and her daughter Annie reunited in spite of considerable abuse from Mary. Carmel is a good caring citizen and, to date, the only West Indian in 'EastEnders' to be portrayed totally sympathetically. The others have all been either weak, crooked or just downright nasty.

Judith Jacob joined 'EastEnders' in the summer of 1987. Judith, aged twenty-six, whose parents hail from Grenada, trained with the Anna Scher School and appeared in three series of 'Angels' as well as episodes of 'The Gentle Touch' and 'Maggie and Her'. She has a daughter Aisha, aged three, who has made her television début as Carmel's niece.

Dr Jaggat Singh
A new doctor arrived in the area in 1987, the Sikh Dr Jaggat Singh, played by Amerjit Deu, but moved on by Christmas to a job 'up North'. (No sighting in Coronation Street, yet.) His appearance maintained the Asian balance in 'EastEnders' after shop-owner Naima Jeffery left.

Amerjit Deu, the turban-wearing Dr Jaggat Singh in 'EastEnders', is a real Sikh from India, but he admits: 'I can't even tie a turban. So some friends of mine made me one in white and then starched it so all I had to do was pop it on my head after gelling my hair.' Amerjit was born in India twenty-seven years ago. He came to Britain in 1967 and went to school in Leeds. He worked in provincial theatre; his only television work before 'EastEnders' was in an episode of 'Never the Twain'.

The Yuppies

Amidst the cockles and mussels and cor blimeys of the Walford natives, a new breed has steadily burrowed its way in: the yuppies. Armed to the teeth with Filofaxes, the upwardly mobile brigade have made great inroads. Already the Dagmar has been revamped by one of their leaders to cater for their particular requirements and Henry's Winebar looks like the window of Habitat. How much longer before Ali's café becomes a Japanese restaurant and the launderette turns into a dry-cleaning branch of Laura Ashley?

Magda Czajkowski ('Mags') Jan was succeeded in Den's bed
by the half-Polish, half-Yorkshire Magda Czajkowski, thankfully known
as Mags. Played by Kathryn Apanowicz, Mags turned up at the Vic in
May 1987 to arrange the catering for the party to celebrate Debbie
Wilkins's engagement to Detective Sergeant Rich. She soon caught
Den's roving eye and moved in. However, she soon made it clear that
she was too independent to be tied to Den, so when Wicksy came along
with a better offer she went off with him. Wicksy got the sack – and got
Mags in the sack, too. Smug-mug Mags is clever and hard-working, I
grant you, much too good for all the men in Albert Square. I still hate
her.

Kathryn Apanowicz is well known as Mags Czajkowski, but is in fact a
show-business veteran at the age of twenty-seven. She made her
television début when she was nine as presenter of 'Junior Showtime', a
job that lasted for four years. She moved on to Yorkshire Television's
'Calendar Kids' and the film *Bugsy Malone*. She has also worked with
such fine comedians as Victoria Wood and Lenny Henry, but her most
famous rôle was as the not-so-angelic nurse Rose Butchins in 'Angels'
for three years. Like Mags, Kathryn is half-Polish (her father comes from
Poland) but brought up in Yorkshire. 'My voice has probably got a hint
of Yorkshire,' says Kathryn, 'which is why I'm glad Mags doesn't need a
cockney accent. I've got no connections with the East End at all.'

Jan Hammond Two of Den's ex-mistresses were decidedly
professional. The first, and most significant, was PR lady Jan Hammond, played by Jane How. Jan had been Den's bit on the side for nigh
on seven years, and for a year in 'EastEnders' she was on the other end
of clandestine phone calls to and from mine host. Out of the blue, she
turned up at the Queen Vic during a drag show in January 1986. The
effect was devastating. Angie tried to kill herself. Jan was a compassionate lady, but when it came to tugging heart-strings she was no match for
Angie. At first, it seemed as if she would simply replace Angie totally in
Den's affections (such as they were) but when she met up with her
ex-lover Dario on a Venice trip it dawned on her that there were more
desirable men in the world than Dennis Watts. Even so, when Angie
and Sharon moved out of the Vic, Jan left her posh flat and moved in.
But, just as she had wanted to be more than just Den's part-time lover,
she now realised that she wanted more than Den could offer. Not
surprisingly, Miss Silk Knickers, as Angie called her, was not over-keen
on living in a tatty room over a tatty pub; nor was she best-thrilled at
being expected to smile at the riff-raff that passed as clientele. So, in
February 1987, Jan moved out. Basically, she was too superior to Den –
but so is Roly.

Jane How has little sympathy for her 'EastEnders' character, Den's classy mistress Jan Hammond. 'A woman who goes in to break up a marriage is despicable,' says Jane. 'Anyway, I wouldn't last five minutes, let alone seven years. I just could not put up with an affair like that with a married man. I'd be far too demanding.' Jane, thirty-six, has been married for eleven years to actor Mark Burns, who appeared opposite Joan Collins in *The Stud*. They have a six-year-old son, Jack, and live in London. Jane was raised in Scotland, educated at a Paris finishing school and became a débutante (very Jan Hammond!). Jane's television rôles include 'The Foundation', 'Dr Who', 'General Hospital', 'The Spoils of War' and 'Don't Wait Up'. Ironically, she attended drama school with the girl who was to become her love-rival in 'EastEnders': Anita Dobson.

Debbie Wilkins and Andy O'Brien

The first of the new set to arrive in Albert Square were Debbie Wilkins and her live-in lover Andy O'Brien. Debbie, played by Shirley Cheriton, gave up her steady job in a bank to start her own business. This led to endless rows with Andy, who was still slaving away as a nurse at the local hospital. The pair were looked upon as 'outsiders' in Albert Square, mainly because Debs had a tendency to be a bossy madam. But her business dreams were shattered when Andy was run over and killed while trying to push a child clear from the path of a lorry. She worked at Naima's shop for a while before her 'get rich quick' plan finally paid off – in reverse. After being romantically pursued by Detective Sergeant Quick, she decided to marry Detective Sergeant Rich. She left the Square in May 1987.

The ill-fated Andy O'Brien, played by Ross Davidson, was better-liked than Debs. The strapping Glaswegian nurse unintentionally won the heart of Mary Smith whom he tried to teach to read and write and was a popular figure in the area. His death was fittingly heroic – but a blow to his fans.

Shirley Cheriton found that policemen played an important part in her life while she was Debbie Wilkins in 'EastEnders'. Off-screen, she left her policeman husband (they have a son, Mark) to live with her 'EastEnders' lover Ross Davidson. On-screen, her character married Detective Sergeant Rich. That part was played by actor Gary Whelan. When Shirley was Katy in 'Angels', which was also produced by 'EastEnders' supremo Julia Smith, her character married a policeman, played by the same Gary Whelan. Londoner Shirley, who left 'East-Enders' in 1987, started her show business career as a dancer on sea-cruises. She has featured in over forty television shows but still worried about 'EastEnders'. She was so anxious during the first three months of filming that she shed seven pounds.

Ross Davidson was hugely popular as Andy O'Brien in 'EastEnders' but he crossed swords with producer Julia Smith and quit the show in

1986, saying he was 'fed up with being treated like a child'. Ross, aged thirty-eight, was born in Airdrie, Scotland. He taught physical education and played water polo for the national team. He came down to England to further his career. 'It was ironic', says Ross, 'that when I came south I decided I didn't just want to play Scotsmen and for most rôles I dropped my Scottish accent. Yet I needed it for Andy.' After leaving 'EastEnders', Ross began a new career as co-presenter of the BBC lunch-time series 'Daytime Live'.

James Willmott-Brown The most prominent yuppies are Colin Russell and the owner of the Dagmar, James Willmott-Brown. Ex-Army and ex-married, Willmott-Brown, played by William Boyde, arrived on the scene in March 1986 as Den's brewery boss. Totally honest, he was the complete opposite of Den and was quick to stamp on any of his fishy deals. Nevertheless, the two men had a sort of respect for one another. Suddenly, hyphen-Brown decided he wanted to open his own pub and bought the Dagmar, a real dump frequented by drug addicts and prostitutes. This meant he would be in direct competition with Den, not only because of the nearness of the Dagmar, but also because the Queen Vic attracted drug addicts and prostitutes, too. The rival pub could ruin Den's trade. But with a resolve as stiff as his upper lip Willmott-Brown completely transformed the place into a plastic fun pub, serving overpriced coloured swill as cocktails. Trade flourished, and to rub salt into the wound Angie was a driving force behind its success. But Willmott-Brown is a little man with a short fuse. He does not suffer fools gladly – which is why Pete Beale rarely goes in the Dagmar. Anyway, it wouldn't do. Willmott-Brown likes to drool over barmaid Kathy, Pete's wife, much to her horror. Eventually his army precision got on people's nerves, and even Angie returned to the Vic. He had it coming, I reckon. Who wants to be caught drinking with estate agents and double-glazing reps? I'd sooner buy the *War Cry*.

William Boyde has come to the conclusion that acting isn't as glamorous as it's made out to be. Before playing James Willmott-Brown in 'EastEnders', thirty-four-year-old William seems to have made a career out of being in productions where nobody could recognise him. 'In the film *Treasures of the Snow* I had to abseil down a mountain; I spent eleven episodes of "The Spoils of War" just driving a jeep; and in "The Secret Army" I was thrown into the Peterborough Canal. Even in "The Jewel in the Crown" I was an intelligence officer who didn't merit a name. But I was really excited when I read the script, because it said my scene took place in Burma. It was filmed just outside Manchester where I was surrounded by lots of jungle-type pot-plants!' William acquired his upper-crust accent from Cheltenham College. He went on to train at Bristol Old Vic. He still has links with the West Country, for the Boyde family home is a tranquil Devon farmhouse.

'EMERGENCY –
WARD TEN'

'Emergency – Ward Ten' was British television's first medicated soap and a huge success for ten years. Independent Television's first twice-weekly serial, it was started and stopped almost by accident. In 1957, Tessa Diamond, then a lowly £15-a-week continuity-writer for Associated Television, casually suggested to her boss that 'something about doctors and nurses' might fill an empty 7.30 slot. The plugs were pulled in 1967 when old age and weakness in the ratings area were diagnosed – an action subsequently rediagnosed by ATV chief Lew Grade as one of his worst mistakes.

Diamond, a doctor's daughter, thought of a hospital called the Oxbridge and a six-week serial entitled 'Calling Nurse Roberts'. The racier 'Emergency – Ward Ten' title was preferred to hers, but the emergencies coped with every Friday and Tuesday for half an hour were never as important as the romantic entanglements of the handsome doctors and pert young nurses. Within its first year over 10 million viewers were taking the treatment. Oxbridge's patients were remarkably healthy and lucky.

The number of deaths a year was set at five (later cut down to two), and no worrying or incurable illnesses (such as cancer) were allowed. The writers occasionally did tug heart-strings. When the wife and baby of Dr Anderson died in a flood, for instance, tearful viewers protested in droves.

The series won praise in a British Medical Association report for allaying people's fears about hospitals. In 1962, Enoch Powell, then Minister of Health, congratulated the soap on its 500th edition, commenting on the useful job it did in reminding people of the need for immunisation and for taking precautions at home. There were critics, too, in the medical world. A Manchester St John Ambulance Brigade commissioner forbade his cadets to watch it, because, he claimed, it portrayed nurses as 'feather-headed flibbertigibbets'. This didn't worry too many viewers, though. They seemed happy with the winsome girls and dashing doctors.

The latter included Charles Tingwell (surgeon Alan Dawson) and the twenty-one-year-old John Alderton (Dr Richard Moore), who left after one year supposedly to marry Carol Davies, one of the nurses. In fact he married Jill Browne, who played another nurse, Sister Carole Young. Others still being asked by strangers for medical advice are: John Carlisle (Dr Lester Large); Ray Barrett (Dr Don Nolan); Desmond Carrington (Dr Chris Anderson); and Richard Thorp (Dr Rennie), later to star in 'Emmerdale Farm' (p.305), who was once invited to watch a real operation but had to leave halfway through, shortly before fainting. Many famous actors played small parts: Albert Finney, Ian Hendry and Joanna Lumley were passing patients.

The soap was halted in 1962 during a five-month actors' strike. Actress Jill Browne was quoted afterwards as glad to return to the wards, to earn £130 a week instead of the former modest £75. In 1964 her character was dropped and a move began to counter slipping ratings with more serious story-lines.

Jamaican actress Joan Hooley was cast as Dr Louise Mahler, and a romance arranged between her character and Dr Giles Farmer (John White). A planned kiss in a bedroom was suddenly cut from an episode after ATV executives thought the black–white love-story too hot for them to handle. The kiss (p.341) was finally planted two months later, reduced to a peck and happening in the hospital garden. More money was injected in 1966, and the soap was changed to an hour-long once-weekly story.

Spectacular scenes were recorded – a plane crash was one. Topical social problems were discussed. One plot had a prisoner brought to the hospital from gaol to use a kidney machine. Even cases of cancer were treated – although the patients recovered.

Sadly, the ratings didn't. The hour slot was changed to forty-five minutes. But only 6 million viewers seemed inclined to keep taking the Oxbridge medicine. After nearly 1000 episodes, when 5 producers, 25 directors, 16 writers and 1200 actors had worked to keep 'Emergency – Ward Ten' open, ATV decided to close it in April 1967. Five years later, Sir Lew Grade (not a man to admit readily to error) said: 'One of the two biggest mistakes I have made in my life was taking off "Emergency – Ward Ten". The other was taking off "Sunday Night at the London Palladium".'

Whether more money, tougher stories, more sex or anything would have served as a life-support for the soap, I doubt. Its absence during the actors' strike was a bad blow. Perhaps something had always been missing: characters viewers could wholeheartedly rely on to pull through any and every emergency. And where were the strong women among the 'feather-headed flibbertigibbets'?

'EMMERDALE FARM'

'Emmerdale Farm' has sex, violence, drunks, adulterers, long-lost children, crashes and crises like any other soap. It also has sheep, burly men stamping their boots on Ma's kitchen mat asking each other very slowly if there's ' 'owt oop'. There are two added ingredients for slow-lathering deep action: culture and country beauty.

The culture was discovered by the Ilkley Literature Festival in 1979. The organisers invited producers and writers of 'Emmerdale Farm' to take part, and they still swell with pride at the memory of it. The undeniable beauty comes from the Yorkshire Dales on which it's set.

Most important, it has an audience so loyal they'd watch it if it were shown at 3 o'clock in the morning. It has been shown at lunch-time, tea-time, supper-time and bed-times. Of all the major British soaps it is the most moved. But that doesn't matter, because it's the most moving, its creator, story-editors and writers believe. The characters are the most genuine, clear-thinking and decent soap-folk you can find.

THE HISTORY

It was begun by Yorkshire Television in October 1972 as television's reply to radio's 'The Archers'. It was never to have been a copy of 'The Archers', but a tale of country family life which contrasted strongly with the other Independent Television Northern soap, 'Coronation Street'.

They showed it at 1.30 p.m. to distract housewives from the washing-up. And distract them it did. It was soon moved to tea-time to catch a larger audience.

Kevin Laffan, a townie but a passionate country-lover, devised a strong if downbeat start. There was a family funeral. No grief for the departed but a widow's resignation at the death of a wastrel husband.

278

It wasn't worth taking your curlers out if you lived at number 13 Coronation
Street. That's what Hilda Ogden decided. Her Stan didn't notice, anyway.
Hilda, played by award-winner Jean Alexander, got on with cleaning the
Rovers and spreading the gossip.

Milk stout with the Holy Trinity in the Rovers Return snug. Minnie Caldwell, Ena Sharples and Martha Longhurst (*Lynne Carol, Violet Carson and Margot Bryant*).

Sadly, Elsie Tanner (*Pat Phoenix*) is one rover who can't return. She left for the love of Bill Gregory and his bar in '84.

Bet Lynch (*Julie Goodyear*) played games with Alf (*Bryan Mosley*).

Deirdre Barlow (*Anne Kirkbride*) and Ken (*William Roache*) have just remembered they haven't seen Tracy in months.

'Coronation Street', the cosy saga of north-country folk.

Ivy Tilsley (*Lynne Perrie*) always has advice for Our Brian.

Remarriage for Brian Tilsley (*Chris Quinten*) and Gail (*Helen Worth*). Now't so queer as folk!

Alec Gilroy (*Roy Barraclough*) is devious, penny-pinching and pompous.

Rita Fairclough (*Barbara Knox*) is sanity itself in the Kabin.

If anyone deserves the voice of Vera Duckworth (*Liz Dawn*) in his ear, it's husband Jack (*William Tarmey*).

Going strong since 1960 and likely to outlive us all.

Southend smiles from the Fowlers: jobless Arthur (*Bill Treacher*); runaway Mark (*David Scarborough*); coping Pauline (*Wendy Richard*) and single mum Michelle (*Sue Tully*).

Albert Square smiles from Sue (*Sandy Ratcliff*), away from her café, Andy (*Ross Davidson*) before his road death and Lofty (*Tom Watt*), away from the Vic.

'EastEnders', the Cockney upstart, arrived in 1985.

Drink could be the death of Angie Watts (*Anita Dobson*), Den's ex-missus.

Sharon Watts (*Letitia Dean*) grew up in the Vic as Den's Princess.

Fat Pat Wicks (*Pam St Clement*), barmaid, bouncer and Frank's intended.

Colin Russell (*Michael Cashman*) is glad to be gay when the insults stop.

It cursed and shocked its way to the top.

Girls go for Shane Ramsay (*Peter O'Brien*) and Scott Robinson (*Jason Donovan*).

Madge (*Anne Charleson*) and kids Charlene (*Kylie Minogue*) and Henry (*Craig McLachlan*).

Rotter of Ramsay Street, Paul Robinson (*Stefan Dennis*) with Gail (*Fiona Corke*) by the pool.

From Down Under came 'Neighbours'. They hooked young viewers each day.

Des Clarke (*Paul Keane*) and Daphne (*Elaine Smith*) have tragedy in store.

Charlene (*Kylie Minogue*) and Scott (*Jason Donovan*) show that young love succeeds.

Jim Robinson (*Alan Dale*) is the wise man of the street.

Helen Daniels (*Anne Haddy*), the grandma with brains and style.

Life among the residents of Ramsay Street wasn't always sunny, though.

'Dallas' was the first American super-rich soap to lather in Britain. We fell for JR Ewing's wicked laugh and loved the limos, the lip-gloss and family breakfasts by the pool in the wind. LEFT TO RIGHT: Cliff Barnes (*Ken Kercheval*); Clayton Farlow (*Howard Keel*); JR (*Larry Hagman*); Sue Ellen (*Linda Gray*); Bobby (*Patrick Duffy*); Ray (*Steve Kanaly*); Miss Ellie (*Barbara Bel Geddes*) and Jenna (*Priscilla Presley*).

OPPOSITE: 'Dynasty' came next, flashing its mansions, jewels and shoulder-padded gowns. Again a family was at war with itself and the world. Power and money were all the Denver folk asked. SEATED: Fallon (*Emma Samms*); Alexis (*Joan Collins*); Blake (*John Forsyth*); Krystle (*Linda Evans*). STANDING: Jeff (*John James*); Sammy Jo (*Heather Locklear*); Steven (*Jack Coleman*); Dana (*Lean Hunley*); Adam (*Gordon Thompson*). ON STAIRS: Dex (*Michael Nader*); Lesley (*Terri Garber*); Sean (*James Healey*).

Farming is serious stuff for Jackie (*Ian Sharrock*), Matt (*Frederick Pyne*), Jack (*Clive Hornby*) and Pat (*Helen Weir*).

Baby Sam Skilbeck was christened. Mother Dolly (*Jean Rogers*), Joe (*Frazer Hines*) and Ma (*Sheila Mercier*) look proud.

'Emmerdale Farm' is the country soap where the scenery is a star.

Alan Turner (*Richard Thorp*) has a rare hug from Mrs Bates (*Diana Davies*).

Beckindale's vicar Donald Hinton (*Hugh Manning*) has time for his flock.

Nay, Nay, Nay, Mr Wilkes, says Amos (*Ronald Magill*) to his partner (*Arthur Pentelow*).

Naughty Nick Bates (*Cy Chadwick*) hugs his pretty sister Kathy (*Malandra Burrows*).

That doesn't mean they don't have murders, divorces, fires and feuds too.

More smiles than usual from the Grants, Jimmy Corkhill, Gordon Collins and Chrissie
Rogers and her kids.

The Corkhill clan: Doreen (*Kate Fitzgerald*), Rod (*Jason Hope*), Tracy (*Justine Kerrigan*) and
Billy (*John McArdle*).

Brookside Close in Liverpool is where soap went serious.

Much missed Heather Haversham (*Amanda Burton*) gave accountants a good name.

Poor Damon Grant (*Simon O'Brien*), Brookie's best scally. He died in a soap bubble.

Paul Collins (*Jim Wiggins*) and queenly Annabel (*Doreen Sloane*) came down in the world.

The houses are real and so are the issues.

Miss Diane (*Sue Hanson*) waited in the restaurant but
Mr Right never came.

Jill Harvey (*Jane Rossington*) with Stan (*Edward Clayton*)
was not a model mother later.

David Hunter (*Ronald Allen*) pretends Amy Turtle
(*Ann George*) isn't really there.

The old motel days! Benny (*Paul Henry*) and Sandy
(*Roger Tonge*) in his wheelchair.

'Crossroads' was the soap we made jokes about. But millions watched it for
twenty-four years.

Nicola Freeman (*Gabrielle Drake*), Queen of the chalets for a while.

Brummie Bomber Lancaster (*Terence Rigby*) barked and blustered. He didn't have Meg's touch.

Don't be fooled. Friendly they weren't. Adam (*Tony Adams*); Jill (*Jane Rossington*); Barbara (*Sue Lloyd*); David (*Ronald Allen*).

When it ended, we missed Benny and Jill, Bomber and Debbie. Well, some of us did.

The Grove Family started a trend. Mother (*Ruth Dunning*), Dad (*Edward Evans*) and cheeky young Lenny (*Christopher Beeney*).

Between heady romances, 'Compact' staff Gussie (*Francis Bennett*), Edmund (*Robert Flemyng*) and Ian (*Ronald Allen*) published their magazines.

'Peyton Place' was America's answer to the success of 'Coronation Street'. Young passion supplied by Alison (*Mia Farrow*) and rich Rodney (*Ryan O'Neal*).

British soap arrived in 1941 . . .

There was a shock in the will. The farm had been left to Jack, the son who'd turned his back on it. There were rivalries, money worries, disappointments, a serial within a series each three weeks with a different strong story.

More death and difficulty followed. Jack's sister Peggy died in childbirth. Her twins were then killed in a railway accident. Jack's younger brother, Joe, married and divorced. The audience loved it.

Not even the disappearance of Jack (the actor who played him, Andrew Burt, wanted to return to the theatre) cooled it. When late-evening repeats were shown in the home area, they won more viewers than 'Match of the Day'. By April 1977 it was screened in the early evenings. By the following year it was networked on Tuesday and Friday, featured regularly in the ITV Top Twenty lists and drew over 12 million fans. For about six months in 1985 it shared its 7 p.m. time-slot with 'EastEnders' on BBC1. By August of that year it claimed victory: 'EastEnders' was moved to a 7.30 slot.

Kevin Laffan said the success was due to the country locations, which appealed to city-bound viewers, and – especially after frequently frantic 'EastEnders' – to the low-key scripts. But he was soon arguing bitterly with the producers when 'Emmerdale Farm's' action seemed to be rivalling the cockney counterpart.

The year's first big event was the shooting of Mrs Bates's dog Bundle for sheep-worrying. The dog's agent had to reassure shocked viewers that the death was merely a performance. In November, Jack Sugden, married with a pregnant wife, had a steamy affair with Karen Moore, and viewers saw them kissing and cuddling in a hotel room. In 1985, Pat Sugden was producing contraceptive pills from her daughter Sandie's drawer. Later Dolly was discussing the best time of the month to try for a baby. Jackie Merrick was gorily injured on the road as he stopped to tinker with his motorbike, and lay in intensive care falling for an Asian nurse. But the love had turned sour and, to ensure that Jackie had a Really Bad Time, Beckindale's bearded baddie Harry Mowlam returned and ran down Tess his dog.

It had been quite a year for the 'gentle' soap. Just as they waited for Mary Whitehouse to slam 'Emmerdale Farm' as a den of vice (she did that in 1987), a member of the royal family managed to chip in and put the show in the headlines. Princess Michael attended the 1000th-episode celebrations in October as guest of honour. She proved unlike Princess Diana, who is always immaculately well briefed about soap (either one watches 'Crossroads', 'EastEnders' and 'Dynasty' in the palace or one's aides fill one in). This princess failed to recognise any of the cast, later confessed she'd never heard of 'Emmerdale Farm', much less watched it, and left early. The snub won sympathy for the soap-stars and few new fans for the royal family.

The year 1986 began violently with Mowlam's murder in a ditch, and Matt was accused of it. The vicar was held hostage by a gunman. Dolly miscarried but, unfortunately for those hoping that Matt, soap's most boring man, would go down for a life-stretch, he was soon released.

To add to Dolly's bad luck, her long-lost love-child Graham stalked the woods like a bogyman, then revealed he was a deserter from the Army. Dolly had a new haircut, and Matt got over it all.

Pat Sugden's screen child, Robert, played by Richard Smith – well, the initials are the same – made his début in April, some months after the actress's real bulge had become a Thomas. Within months Pat (Helen Weir) was despatched in a hit-and-run road accident, so the producers never had to argue about baby names again.

More violence came when badger-baiters kicked Seth unconscious. More sex came when new arrival Phil Pearce dumped his wife and child for Sandie and put up with backache every time he kissed her (she's 4 feet 10 inches; he's 6 feet 2 inches).

In 1987 the soap was chosen as the first Euro-soap, beamed abroad by Super Channel satellite. Soon it was dropped. No advertising could be sold for the show.

Back home things were better. Accident-prone Jackie fell down a mineshaft; new baddie Eric Pollard arrived to steal from the auctioneers and brandish a poker at Sandie; Joe Sugden fell for Ruth, the vet who looked so stunning and straightforward but turned out to have a hidden fiancé and a rich funny father; and – most important – Beckindale villagers fought off a plan to dump nuclear waste on their doorsteps.

The story-line – hailed as a major advance in the politicisation of soap – was based on the struggles of campaigners in Fulbeck, Lincolnshire. As Gordon Naismith, a real fighter from Fulbeck, said: 'Soap-opera characters shouldn't live in a world where there are no four million unemployed, there is no AIDS epidemic and the space shuttle did not blow up.'

Jackie and his new girlfriend Kathy Bates were arrested after a demonstration, Jack Sugden went to gaol for pulling down a fence at the dump, but the plan was scrapped.

By 1988, 'Emmerdale Farm' was on the move again to a 6.30 slot on Tuesdays and Wednesdays. Stuart Doughty, it's new producer (from 'Brookside') arrived and promised to increase the number of dramatic cliffhangers, keep it up-to-date and to introduce plots about an extra-marital affair and drug-dependence. But, with a pretty wedding for Jackie and Kathy, a crisis in the close-down of NY Estates and the continued brooding of selected Sugdens, 'Emmerdale Farm' forges on with 10–12 million followers, relevant, robust and, of course, cultured.

THE LOCATION

Beckindale, the fictional village setting for 'Emmerdale Farm', has been located in two different places in its time: Arncliffe and Esholt, West Yorkshire.

Originally Arncliffe, deep in James Herriott's Dales country, was chosen for location filming when the series began in 1972. The locals soon found they were unable to cope with television fame – there is only one shop there and one pub, which doesn't have a Sunday licence.

Yorkshire Television moved on to Esholt because it is also more accessible. They promised local residents that they would not reveal where Amos and Co. live, to try to keep nosy tourists away.

But when the office of tourism in Bradford featured the Commercial Inn, Esholt (which doubles as the Woolpack), on the front cover of its official brochure the secret was out. Coach operators were quick to exploit the situation. Esholt's lazy days of soaplessness were over. Now, at the height of summer, you can count as many as twenty-five coaches parked in the village at one time – far too many for a little community which measures just 100 yards from end to end, with eighty-two houses.

Local opinion is sharply divided. Some local shopkeepers have made a killing, selling Emmerdale rock, souvenir T-shirts, mugs and beer-mats. At weekends there is often a queue waiting to sample a pint in the Commercial. But when tourists get inside they are usually disappointed. Interior scenes for the series are shot in the studios, and the fictional bar looks completely different. At this busy time of the year, the locals have been known to boycott the pub for up to six months.

Others, like Farmer Joe Whitham, are not impressed by rubberneck-ers. Mr Whitham has posted a sign outside his farm that says: 'This is NOT Emmerdale Farm.' It has had the opposite effect from that intended. People are more convinced than ever that it is and invade the yard with renewed enthusiasm. Mr Whitham recalls nightmare days like the harvest-time when three of his tractors were marooned in the middle of buses and cars that had paralysed the village street.

Visitors to Esholt have, however, managed to locate Jenny the farm's donkey that featured in the Seth Armstrong story-lines, the vicarage used by the Reverend Donald Hinton, and the church where the Skilbecks were married. When Bradford Corporation advertised seven houses for sale, they were swamped with offers from all over the country.

The real Emmerdale Farm is miles away from Esholt. Filming takes place on Lindley Farm, a 200-acre farm in Washburn Valley near Harrogate, owned by Arthur Peel. Sheep and cattle – usually about 140 Friesians – feed on the lush grasses, and many an unsuspecting lamb or calf has been born in the glare of television cameras. Arthur Peel recalls the day in 1972 when photographers first tramped through his yard looking for a site for a thirteen-episode serial. He told them he didn't mind a few cameras and cables around but they'd have to work around him – not vice versa. Sixteen years later he has stopped minding the cables, but the noise in the yard – which can mean 150 sightseeing trippers are straining at the gates – he'll never enjoy.

THE CREATOR

Kevin Laffan bitterly rejects 'Emmerdale Farm', the soap opera he created and nurtured for twelve years. He hates its producers for including scenes of violence and explicit sex, and for compromising on the principles he set down for it. ' "Emmerdale" climbed in the twelve years I was writing for it with very little publicity and no hype. I was proud to have ignored the press,' he said. In August 1985, Laffan, farm labourer turned actor and playwright, angrily accused Yorkshire Television of injecting the essentially (to him) ordinary non-hysterical story with increasing amounts of 'sex, sin and sensationalism'. 'My original idea was that this was a group of people trying to live together to avoid quarrelling. The fact that this sometimes breaks down is part of it. To me you're a failure if you have to resort to violence, to kick someone in the balls. What do you do afterwards? Kick him again. "Emmerdale Farm" was from the start about the cruelty of man to nature. The opening had references to pollution of the river by manufacturers, fish dying off – generally issues of conservation. The hero Jack left because he disagreed with battery hens. It was never to be a shouting match. Of course as the writer I had to give the characters something to do, but I wanted to show them at work or at home, not to have everything shouted out. And the violence, as in Greek drama, was always to happen off-stage. You don't need conflict and violence of course. You can have good dialogue about having a cup of tea or not having a cup of tea – just as you can have bad dialogue about the end of the world.'

Laffan, now sixty-five, argued repeatedly with script-editors (who were often, he claims, kids straight out of university, trained for nothing). He hated that Annie Sugden, his earth mother, his hard-working holder-together of the family, was seen as in any way a sentimental figure. 'I based her on a lot of Yorkshire landladies I knew, and there was nothing soppy about them,' he said. But in August 1985 he had more than a row. He was so unhappy with the soap he suddenly stopped writing for it. What caused the unhappiness? Family head Jack seen in bed with his young mistress. A vicious brawl between Jack and Tom Merrick. Sandie's sexual encounter with Alan Turner's objectionable son Terence. The blood and gore seen when Jackie was hit on the road. For starters.

'The writer in television is shit,' Laffan told me in 1988. 'I won't allow my scripts to be altered whether they are stage-plays or soap opera – and I never look down on soap opera; I see it as a one-year play – after which I write another year's play. But producers and script-editors are the enemies of good long-running drama. Unless the writers have power, the poetry can't work.'

Kevin Laffan remains a consultant for 'Emmerdale Farm'.

THE WRITERS

Annie Sugden will never take a toy boy. There'll never be an outbreak of international terrorism, AIDS or race riots in 'Emmerdale Farm', says Andrew Holden, the soap's story-editor. 'We're not trying to shock or scandalise or be particularly relevant. "Emmerdale Farm" is about people who feel deeply for each other and want to get on with each other. People often criticise it on the grounds that it's uneventful and slow. But this just shows they haven't watched it enough. It's the most cultured and literary of all the soap operas, and the characters are unusually reflective. Someone once suggested a six-episode blockbuster about Annie thinking she had breast cancer and not having it. I decided it was dishonest and undignified, so it didn't happen. We try to show rural life as it is today; the class structure has changed, the squires have gone, impersonal new managements are organising the work of estates, and some of them – like our NY Estates – are not always successful. Many of the old customs have gone; we are not interested in being quaint.'

Andrew Holden, who is thirty-two, works with two script-editors and a team of between eight and twelve writers. Unlike other soap operas, 'Emmerdale Farm' gives writers blocks of four or six scripts to write, encouraging them to be inventive, to follow their instinct. 'Soap opera is an enormous compromise for quality, time for rehearsals, writing and shooting. The constraints are severe and frustrating. To produce fifty hours of drama a year on a relatively small budget is quite different from trying to make a couple of perfect plays. But I think "Emmerdale Farm" has removed the stigma from soap opera.'

WEATHER

If the weather were on the payroll of 'Emmerdale Farm', it would get the sack. Weather doesn't understand soap opera and the advance recording that is always necessary. It wrecks the continuity of scenes time and again. Because of the high costs of location filming, farmyard scenes for up to six episodes tend to be recorded over a couple of days. Similarly village scenes. This means, with our changeable winters, that Jack could leave the farm in brilliant sunshine and arrive at the Woolpack in thick fog or a hailstorm. Snow machines have been booked in cloudless October for scenes to be screened in January, only to arrive in the middle of a blizzard. Viewers have seen Matt with his sheep in one field thickly carpeted with snow and later in the same episode walking on dry grass. And former producer Richard Handford recalls the time he almost had to buy a field of corn in which a scene was scheduled to be recorded ten days later. Exceptional good weather had brought harvesting forward. The field's owner wanted to start, but a landscape of stubble would have been useless. On the day the field-buying deal was to be signed – rain began. It lasted two weeks, saved the budget and Handford's bacon.

THE CHARACTERS

Seth Armstrong, the hawk-nosed poacher-turned-gamekeeper with the droopy handlebar moustache and hangdog expression, has become established as one of the best-loved characters in soap during his twelve-year stint in 'Emmerdale Farm'. Viewers relate to the rogue played with Yorkshire relish by veteran comedian turned actor Stan Richards. He is an opportunist whose hobbies are cadging free pints from unsuspecting tourists and visitors; and baiting either Amos Brearly, mine host of the Woolpack inn, or Alan Turner, Seth's pompous boss. Seth's reaction to officialdom veers between the kind of deliberately provocative comments that enrage and inflate the corpulent Turner to bursting-point, and turning on a gormless grin that army officers once used to refer to as 'dumb insolence'. Either way, Seth rarely loses the initiative. Excitable Amos is another easy target for Seth, who likes an audience for his mickey-taking and deliberately waits until the saloon bar is full before he starts his banter.

Seth often gives the impression of not being too bright, but he has the same cold and calculated approach to life possessed by most country-men who live by striving to outwit nature. Joe Grundy and Walter Gabriel of 'The Archers' combine the same rustic charms with country cunning. Shrewd, devious and work-shy, Seth totes his shotgun around the estate, always looking for easy ways to make a quick quid. One of the best-known poachers in Beckindale in his time, his knowledge of wildlife made him a natural first choice when NY Estates were searching for a gamekeeper. Seth rather likes his 'rascal' image, but *we* know he has a heart of . . . well, silver, and had on occasions dropped off the odd brace of pheasant to needy families. Poking out from underneath the woolly hat that is as famous as Benny's in 'Crossroads' is a nose for gossip that is quick to sniff 'owt' that is happening in the village. Whatever is going on, Seth (like Hilda Ogden in 'Coronation Street') knows first and stirs first.

Seth's worst moment came in 1986 when he was beaten and kicked unconscious by a gang of poachers and badger-baiters in a big 'Emmerdale Farm' cliffhanger. They left him for dead, and viewers watched anxiously for weeks as he slowly recovered from severe head injuries and badly damaged ribs.

Seth is married to long-suffering Meg. She has tossed scores of spoilt dinners into the dustbin over the years as a legacy of Seth's late-night

Emmerdale Farm

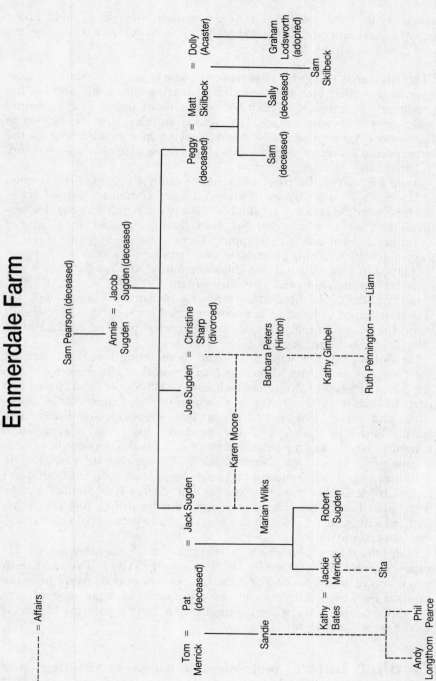

------- = Affairs

Sam Pearson (deceased)

Annie = Jacob
Sugden Sugden (deceased)

Peggy = Matt
(deceased) Skilbeck

= Dolly
(Acaster)

Graham
Lodsworth
(adopted)

Sam
Skilbeck

Sam
(deceased)

Sally
(deceased)

Joe Sugden = Christine
Sharp
(divorced)

Barbara Peters
(Hinton)

Kathy Gimbel

Ruth Pennington ----- Liam

----- Karen Moore

Jack Sugden =

Marian Wilks

Robert
Sugden

Jackie
Merrick

Sita

Tom = Pat
Merrick (deceased)

Sandie

Kathy = Bates

Andy
Longthorn

Phil
Pearce

binges at the Woolpack. Even on a rare night when Seth went home early to make amends, he bought Meg a bottle of port as a peace offering and drank it all himself.

Stan Richards leaves his false teeth at home to play the country rogue. It isn't a gimmick. Stan just doesn't like wearing false teeth, and has the producer's permission to play the rôle without them. Stan's gummy looks are now his trademark. His famous toothless grin has helped to keep him a star turn on the Northern working-men's club circuit for the latter part of his thirty-year show-business career. He also has a fan club in Tanzania.

Aged fifty-seven, Barnsley-born Stan is really a musician (he studied at London's Trinity College of Music), turned comedian, turned actor. Even Seth would concede he still plays the piano with expertise. He was given lessons as a ten-year-old, and five years later the Barnsley Grammar School boy was skipping homework playing the piano in pubs, sneakily downing pints of beer and smoking the odd fag. Later on he played in a dance-band. He still loves music, and his Barnsley home contains a grand piano and an electric organ.

One of Stan's jobs after school was as a Ministry of Labour clerk. He was transferred to London but soon scurried back north – he couldn't stand the place. To him, Barnsley is the greatest place on earth, and he intends to stay there for good. Sorry, Tanzania.

He took a great risk with 'a wife and three young mouths to feed' in the 1960s when he turned professional comedian. The three turned to six, but after years of struggling he became a bill-topper, and landed bits parts in such television series as 'Coronation Street' and 'All Creatures Great and Small'. Engaged to appear in five episodes of 'Emmerdale Farm', both the public and the producer liked his interpretation instantly. He became a permanent fixture – a break Stan compares with winning the pools. 'I love "Emmerdale" – it's our own little family.' He still does club dates, amusing audiences with lines such as: 'Nah don't forget. If Mr Turner comes in 'ere tonight, charge him double!' Unlike Seth, Stan hates beer. He likes Scotch. But he drinks real ale on set without a murmur. 'Look at it this way. If you're getting paid to drink it, you can't complain!'

Stan tells tales against himself in a gravy-thick Barnsley accent. He recalls the night a local took him to task, asking: 'Why is it you talk posh when you're on the telly?' For once, Stan was stumped. Away from the cameras he is no countryman and he could never be a gamekeeper. 'I'm too soft. I couldn't hurt a fly. I couldn't kill a thing to save my life, and I would never carry a gun.'

Caroline Bates – better-known to millions as Mrs Bates – had millions of 'Emmerdale Farm' watchers on the edge of their seat in 1985

when she teetered on the brink of what would have been the unlikeliest television romance of the year. Would she fall for her bumptious boss, fat man Alan Turner, the JR of Beckindale? After all, she was vulnerable, a woman alone, struggling to bring up two kids. To everyone's relief – many women viewers wrote anxious letters to actress Diana Davies, who portrays Mrs Bates – she didn't succumb. Diana reckons that romance is very unlikely. 'I think she finds Turner appealing in a little-boy-lost kind of way. He brings out the mother in her. But I don't see things going any further. If they did, it would spoil their secretary–boss working relationship.' It's Emmerdale's best light comedy. Every now and again Mrs Bates says 'enough', rather like a nanny, and Turner backs off. She keeps him in order, and he would be lost without her.

Back in the little house she shared until recently with her two children, Caroline Bates nurses her private grief: the breakdown of her marriage to schoolteacher Malcolm. After a two-year separation she secretly hoped that they might reunite. But in 1987 he turned up to demand a divorce and announced that his new girlfriend was pregnant.

Caroline takes comfort in helping her two nice children, student Nick and Kathy, who married Jackie Merrick in February 1988. Their modest lifestyle contrasts with the growing wealth and influence of the Sugden family.

When actress Diana Davies joined the series in 1983, Mrs Bates was a minor character. Her popularity grew, so scriptwriters gave her more and better lines. They also had to reveal her hitherto missing Christian name: Caroline.

Diana Davies, the fifty-one-year-old actress who plays Caroline Bates, is no Joan Collins on screen in her plain grey clothes and sensible pullovers. But she has the nicest smile in soap.

Diana joined the cast of the series in a minor rôle in 1983, but viewers warmed to her, she stayed and grew in importance. Manchester-born Diana, the daughter of a big-band musician, started her television career as an extra for Granada Television for eleven years before she worked her way up to speaking parts. It was a superb cameo performance as Doris, Freda Ashton's friend, in Granada's long saga 'A Family at War' which caught the eye of the casting directors. As a result, her rôle in that series was extended to twenty episodes. Diana appeared in 'The Liver Birds', 'Juliet Bravo' and 'Shoestring'. When she landed a part as Norma Ford, a corner-shop girl in 'Coronation Street' in 1972 it was like a dream come true. She stayed for eighteen months. Norma seduced Ken Barlow, but left the Street in a huff when he married his second wife, Janet Reid. Diana's stint in the Street coincided with the mini-skirt era. With her elegant long legs, she was given the nickname 'Di the Thigh'.

Poignantly, Caroline Bates's broken marriage is a mirror of her own sadness. Her husband Peter left her in 1978, and she was emotionally shattered. 'I will never remarry,' says Diana. 'I've not even had a date since then. That's been my choice. For a long time I was too raw even to think about it.' She was forty-two when it happened, with a fifteen-year-old son Stephen. 'It's not the best time – you think you are over the hill. Now I'm content with my own company.' She describes herself as 'retired hurt'. 'I think I've lost the recipe for romance,' she said.

Diana lives in a quiet Manchester suburb with her son. She feels that being in 'Emmerdale Farm' has the edge on 'Coronation Street' for her. 'It's a smaller cast, and if people are going to the theatre or out for a meal they always ask if I want to join them. That's nice for me, because when I'm alone all I do is put my feet up and watch telly.'

One of the greatest thrills of her career was co-starring with Glenda Jackson in the West End production of *Rose*. They tried to take it to the United States, but American Equity wouldn't allow it. 'So, instead of Broadway, here I am in Beckindale, turning all the pensioners on as Mrs Bates.'

Amos Brearly,

landlord of the Woolpack inn in 'Emmerdale Farm', sports the most famous whiskers in soap: big bushy mutton-chop sideburns of great character and distinction. Underneath them, Amos, played by Ronald Magill, is a blustering old windbag who is easily riled and quickly takes offence. He puffs up like a pigeon when his feathers are ruffled. Seth Armstrong, his chief tormentor, can get him going in a minute.

Basically, Amos is a bit of a snob who harbours romantic ideas. In 1982 he had visions of becoming Member of Parliament for Halifax. He is also a writer with literary pretensions. A correspondent for the local rag, the *Hotten Courier*, he churns out flowery prose. Local gossip is his speciality.

For all his faults, he is dearly loved by viewers and admired for his staunch Yorkshire loyalty. Some Southerners wonder if the larger-than-life Amos is a joke on the part of the production team.

What fascinates millions is the bizarre relationship between Amos and Henry Wilks, his partner and lodger at the Woolpack. Why does he call him 'Mr Wilks' instead of 'Henry'? Yorkshire Television are content to frustrate viewers with this.

Amos and Henry bicker and bustle about in the back kitchen of the pub like an old married couple. I've joked that they're soap's senior gays – only to be sternly rebuked by fans who recall Henry's fondness for Annie. Theirs is a strange 'double act' matured over thirteen years. Someone counted that in the first thousand episodes of the series Henry said 'For 'eavens sake, Amos!' to which Amos replied, 'Nay, nay, Mr Wilks!' 450 times.

Amos has been landlord of the Woolpack for over twenty years, is immensely proud of the pub and feels that his is a noble calling.

Particular about his clientele, and fastidious in his habits, Amos feels that the laid-back Henry often puts a damper on his grand plans and is too generous to boot. Woe betide him if he catches Henry giving away a free pint. One sure way to wind Amos up is to suggest that Ernie Shuttleworth's pub, the Maltshovel, is more go-ahead.

Sartorially, Amos is a shambles. He wears some of the worst cardigans and knitted shirts in soap: only Ray Grice in 'Crossroads' has worse taste. Amos seems to have no female friend or family around to advise him. A confirmed bachelor, Amos has only broached the subject of marriage once, when he asked Annie Sugden to marry him. For some years the Woolpack regulars had been telling him that the pub lacked a woman's touch. Amos grudgingly accepted the point and decided that the only likely candidate within miles of Beckindale was Annie, who had recently lost her husband. Amos confidently considered himself an excellent catch. What more could a woman want? But Annie turned him down. He had no stomach for marriage after that.

Ronald Magill, the balding bewhiskered actor who plays Amos Brearly in 'Emmerdale Farm', is so easily recognised in public that he reckons every journey takes twice as long as it should because so many people stop to talk to him. One woman who stopped him in a London street asked him to make up a sentence – 'just for me' – when he appeared on television that night. He didn't have the heart to tell her that the programme had already been recorded before. A man in Marks & Spencer grabbed his arm and said: 'It is you, isn't it?' Before Ronnie could confirm it, the man dashed off, saying: 'I know I'm right, because I'm a bugger for faces!' Magill has tried disguises. Hats and dark glasses are no use. It's the sideboard whiskers that are the giveaway. He grew them for an Edwardian costume drama and when he auditioned for 'Emmerdale Farm' the producer told him to keep them sprouting.

Ronald Magill was born in Hull. His parents were schoolteachers, and his father was so keen on literary standards that he refused to let Ronald read comics. It was whilst he was in the Royal Corps of Signals that he got involved in troop shows and joined 'Stars in Battledress'. That whiff of the theatre spurred him on towards the professional stage in Civvy Street. For nine years he was an actor-director at Nottingham rep. Extremely well read, he has appeared in plays by Goldoni, translated from the Italian by himself. He appeared in the Charlton Heston film epic *Julius Caesar* and has an unfulfilled ambition to play King Lear at Stratford.

Ronald Magill is a quietly spoken, thoughtful man, totally unlike the bombastic blathering character he plays; and he and Arthur Pentelow, who plays Mr Wilks, are firm friends. They tackle the daily crossword together at rehearsals and both enjoy a pipe between lines. They were once jointly nominated for the title of 'Pipe Smoker of the Year'.

Ronald takes his bar duties seriously. It's real ale in the Woolpack, and the Licensed Victuallers' Association advised him about staying sober behind the pumps. Off duty, pubs are places to avoid. Says Ronald: 'Every time I go in one they always want me to go behind the bar and start pulling pints.'

Unlike Arthur Pentelow who plays his television partner, Magill is a bachelor who lives alone in South London – a total break from his television life in Leeds. And unlike Amos he's a snappy dresser. 'I'm a peacock when it comes to clothes.'

The Reverend Donald Hinton, vicar of Beckindale, is the wise kindly man of 'Emmerdale Farm' whose door is ever open to anyone in need of comfort or counsel. He is an old-fashioned clergyman with deeply held beliefs who, nevertheless, doesn't try to force his ideas on his parishioners. Respected as a good listener, Donald Hinton, played by Hugh Manning (6 feet 2 inches, and weighing 20 stone), is equally at home in the pub or a tied cottage – he has the common touch. His dignity and quiet humour have earned him the respect of everyone in Beckindale.

A widower, Donald Hinton has an uneasy relationship with his son Clive and his headstrong daughter Barbara, who once had a fling with Joe Sugden when her marriage collapsed. Hinton lives alone in the vicarage now, surrounded by his beloved books and his butterfly collection. Since the death of old Sam Pearson, he has become a closer friend of Annie Sugden.

Hinton was shattered when Barbara tried to use the vicarage as a sanctuary when her marriage foundered. It was a great personal blow since he firmly believes in the sanctity of marriage and doesn't countenance divorce. He had previously refused to marry Pat and Jack Sugden in church because Pat was a divorcee. When the broken-marriage problem landed on his own doorstep he was perplexed. The news that Barbara and Joe Sugden were lovers swept through Beckindale and also embarrassed Annie Sugden, who is a church warden. It was a great relief to both Annie and Donald when Barbara declined Joe's offer of marriage and left for a new life in London.

No one would call Hinton a cardboard character. But Hugh is tickled by the fact that a life-size cardboard cut-out of him, with collection-box, placed outside the Esholt vicarage (it doubles as Hinton's home) has raised thousands for Ethiopian famine relief. The cut-out stops tourists knocking to ask the real vicar, the Reverend Arthur Wilson, if Hinton is at home and is a convenient spot for rubberneckers to pose for pictures.

Hugh Manning, who plays the Reverend Donald Hinton, is one of the veterans of the series. At sixty-seven he is just one year younger than his contemporary Sheila Mercier who plays Annie Sugden.

Since a major hip operation, Hugh has tended to feature less in the series. Nevertheless, he has one of the best-known faces on television. For many years he was the Jeeves-type old retainer in white gloves, with silver salver, in the Robinson's barley-water commercials. One of his early television rôles was as Kathleen Harrison's adviser in 'Mrs Thursday'.

He is one of the linchpins of the actors' union, Equity, once its president, now a trustee. Although he was never a militant, this screen vicar did preach the 'gospel' of the closed shop to his fellow-actors, including his flock in 'Emmerdale Farm'. Hugh was concerned that there are too many actors chasing too little work.

Away from show business he has been a keen tennis- and bridge-player, and also loves to garden at his London home. A dedicated traveller, India is his great favourite. He toured with a Shakespearian theatre group for six months and longs to go back.

Jackie Merrick, the large clumsy son of the late Pat Sugden in 'Emmerdale Farm', married Kathy Bates (Malandra Burrows) in February 1988 after an amazing 'macho man' act. He won her away from a smoothie rival by smashing up his own beloved banger of a van as a demonstration of his affection. Kathy had ended her relationship with Jackie, played by Ian Sharrock, because she thought it had become stale and passive. Jackie, driven crazy with jealousy, mooched moodily around Beckindale for months until he could control his frustration no longer.

Jackie's fiery temperament stems from his unhappy childhood. His mother Pat was originally married to hard-drinking wastrel Tom Merrick. The marriage finally foundered when Tom took off for Aberdeen to take a job on an oil-rig. Pat was left to bring up Jackie and Sandie as best she could in a caravan rented from NY Estates. When Jackie was sacked by Alan Turner, boss of NY Estates, he burned down the caravan in frustration. He was later found guilty of arson and sentenced to do community service. After a spell under vicar Donald Hinton's roof, Jackie took a job at Emmerdale Farm. The only man he couldn't stand was Jack Sugden. Jack turned out to be his real father. When Jackie found out he went on a 'drown-it-all' drinking spree.

Jackie was always accident prone. Dashing back to Demdyke with his girlfriend, he was knocked off his motorbike by Alan Turner's land-rover. Ironically, the five months in hospital with a badly fractured leg gave him time to think. He came home a more responsible person, touched by the way the family rallied round him. In 1987, in another accident, he fell twenty feet down a disused mineshaft and was saved by a mountain rescue team. No sooner well than he was demonstrating with others against a plan to dump nuclear waste. He was carted off in a police car.

The heart-throb of 'Emmerdale Farm', he has had plenty of girls. After the accident, Alison, his latest flame, was forgotten for Asian nurse Sita Sharma who helped Jackie through his convalescence. In typically impetuous fashion, he announced his engagement to Sita, but her protective father refused to recognise their relationship and the romance collapsed. Jackie then turned his sights on Caroline Bates's fast-maturing teenage daughter Kathy. Theirs is a stormy up-and-down relationship, and even marriage seems unlikely to change that.

Ian Sharrock, the hunky twenty-eight-year-old actor who plays volatile Jackie Merrick, was once dubbed Yorkshire's answer to James Dean and voted 'the sexiest man in soap' (possibly by the ladies of the Ambridge Over-Sixties). His petulant traits, rugged looks, and hot screen romances have brought him shoals of proposals from admiring female viewers. In fact he is happily married to Pam McDonald, a former Yorkshire Television publicity assistant who used to answer Ian's fan mail at the studios. Four thousand fans besieged Leeds Cathedral when they married in 1985. They now have a two-year-old daughter, Natalie Clare. 'Like Jackie,' says Ian, 'I think I have matured since I joined the programme in 1980. When you've got family responsibilities it changes your outlook.'

Ian was acting at twelve. Still at drama school, he appeared with Jodi Foster and David Niven in the Walt Disney film *Candleshoe*. Ian played the title rôle in the television musical 'Smike', and appeared in the series 'Games'. After eight years with 'Emmerdale Farm', he is typecast but has no regrets. But he is baffled by Jackie's appeal. 'To my mind he is not particularly smart, handsome or appealing. His relationships with women have been a disaster. I get embarrassed by all the attention,' he said. One thing Ian shares with the screen character is a love of motorbikes. If he hadn't been an actor, he would like to have been a motorcycle trials rider.

Kathy Merrick is the pretty fresh-faced blonde who married Jackie Merrick in 'Emmerdale Farm' in 1988 – but led her new husband a merry dance first. Kathy, played by Malandra Burrows, was a nineteen-year-old heart-breaker who had a long list of admirers. Joe Sugden was smitten when he returned to Beckindale from France in 1986. Kathy preferred the company of his nephew, hunky Jackie – though he wasn't interested at first. When love happened, they went to bed in the Emmerdale farmhouse while Annie was away in hospital – a steamy scene for this soap.

The daughter of Caroline Bates, Kathy took a job at Emmerdale to learn about farming. She found it too much like hard work. A later spell in the NY Estates battery-chicken unit scared her out of her wits. Kathy drove Jackie out of his mind when she temporarily ended their relationship to start a fling with smooth-talking educated Tony

Marchant, an NY Estates management trainee. She was out of her social depth. As she dithered over ending that relationship Jackie made her mind up for her with a flamboyant demonstration of passion. He smashed up his own van with an iron bar outside the Woolpack. Kathy got the message – he was her man.

Pleasant with an infectious giggle, Kathy can easily win round Henry Wilks and cantankerous Amos when she helps behind the bar. But with Jackie's unpredictable temperament her marriage will be full of ups and downs.

Malandra Burrows, the blue-eyed blonde who plays Kathy Merrick, in 'Emmerdale Farm', is a bubbly twenty-one-year-old 'Scouser' who previously starred as Pat Hancock's girlfriend Lisa in 'Brookside'. Malandra, who claims she was bitten by the acting bug when she was four, went through dancing classes and theatre school as a youngster. She did fringe theatre rôles in productions such as *Frankenstein and Dracula* before she was recruited by 'Brookside'. She sings, too, and has belted out rock numbers at charity events.

She joined the cast of 'Emmerdale Farm' in 1985 and blossomed. 'The prettiest girl in soap,' one reporter decreed. Marriage proposals, many from younger viewers, flood into Yorkshire Television's offices, despite the fact that she is often thigh-high in manure on screen. Malandra would like Kathy to be more glamorous and initially hoped for steamy scenes in the hay-loft. She was seen in bed with Jackie before their marriage, but you missed it if you blinked.

A city girl, she tackles her rural rôle bravely, learning to drive a tractor and a motorbike and look fearless among cows. But she quakes among cattle and went weak at the knees when she was asked to milk a cow in the early episodes. There was worse to come. . . . When Kathy took a job in the poultry unit at NY Estates to escape the dole queue, Malandra had to play scenes inside a battery-hen house. 'It was horrific. I went in for a few seconds and just heaved. I had to come out,' she recalls. 'Then I had to force myself to go back in and do a week's filming in there. Those poor hens – twenty thousand of them packed in, six to a cage. The RSPCA assured us that this was one of the better units. But I still have nightmares about the place and it has put me off eggs completely.'

Malandra, who lives in Liverpool with her father, is single but has a steady boyfriend.

Sandie Merrick is the moody dark-haired daughter of the late Pat Sugden, and the nearest thing 'Emmerdale Farm' has to a sensual woman. She has no interest in farming and – alone among the residents of Beckindale – admits that country life can be boring. She's tough but tiny – just 4 feet 10 inches. (Who knows, perhaps she was a rôle model for little Lucy, the 'Poisoned Dwarf' in 'Dallas'.) The toughness, it's suggested, grew from emotional hardship: her parents' broken marriage, her illegitimate child, the shock news that Jackie Merrick is only her half-brother, and her mother's tragic death in a car accident.

Viewers have watched Sandie mature into a confident capable young woman. Mind you, played by Jane Hutcheson of the sad spaniel eyes, she has always looked too old to be Pat's daughter. Perhaps they start younger in the country. Like her brother Jackie, she was a rebellious teenager, never encouraged as a youngster. When she was under stress in 'A'-levels year, no one wanted to know.

Sandie's search for love ended in disaster, of course. In her (hardly believable) first fling with lanky bespectacled Andy Longthorn, a sixth-former at Hotten Comprehensive School, Sandie not only lost her virginity; she got pregnant on a one-night stand. She was just eighteen. The almost comic seduction scene between 'the short and the tall' happened after Sandie and farmer's son Andy consumed too many sherries at a social held by the vicar. When Andy refused to own up to his responsibilities, the impetuous Jackie blacked his eye and broke his glasses. Later he offered to marry Sandie, but she rejected him. In order to avoid wagging tongues in Beckindale, Sandie went off to live with her no-good father Tom, who was working on an oil-rig off Aberdeen. When the baby was born, she had it adopted on the advice of Dolly Skilbeck who had also had a child adopted in her youth. Will this long-lost child crop up in future story-lines? The script editor says no, but. . . .

Sandie later fell for the charms of Alan Turner's tearaway son Terence (Stephen Marchant). Terence, just down from Oxford, wasn't her type. And it wasn't quite the love in the hay-loft it promised to be. He didn't seduce her, and it didn't last.

Settled with a decent job as an auctioneer at Hotten market, Sandie was reconciled with her mother before the car accident, but was soon in hot water again. She broke up the marriage of local builder Phil Pearce (Peter Alexander), another 'giant'. Emmerdale's little 'scarlet woman' was called a tart by Philip's wife. Sandie boldly moved in with Phil, faced stern grannie Annie and the Woolpack guardians of morality. Will it last, though? A blight on their relationship is that Phil has gone into business with wicked Eric Pollard, a local antiques dealer. Pollard used to be Sandie's boss until she found out he was stealing from auctions and cooking the books. One night he broke into her home and threatened her with a poker. She put her coat on and drove him home. (Well, in soap opera as in life, you have to get on with people. You'll be bumping into them again and again – and again.) In March she found that she was pregnant but miscarried after the vet visited. Even in the Dales a soap woman was born to suffer.

Jane Hutcheson may be a secret Diddywoman, which would account for her size (tiny). The Stockport actress who plays sexy Sandie Merrick made her acting début on a show with comic Ken Dodd, disco dancing with his 'Diddymen'.

Jane, aged thirty-one, has been acting since she was five, played a pantomime principal girl at fourteen and has a cupboard full of drama competition trophies. An early asset to soap, she crossed the Pennines from Lancashire, and a small part in 'Coronation Street', to a major rôle in the Yorkshire Television saga. Between acting rôles she took a drama degree at Birmingham University and worked with a theatre group in France.

Jane lives in Leeds, is single, has a steady relationship with a London-based freelance television director, but no plans to marry. She has had hundreds of proposals from viewers over the years. Some 'fan' letters are less than admiring, though. When Sandie fell for Phil Pearce, who was already married, viewers informed Jane she was a tart and a home-wrecker. 'It proved what I thought,' said Jane. 'As far as Sandie is concerned, they were the best scripts I had received for five or six years. They breathed new life into the character. I'm glad they are bringing out the softer side of Sandie, but I don't want her and Phil to get too cosy. They mustn't get into the old married-couple syndrome.'

Jane has had to play some tricky scenes with her six-foot screen lover, played by Peter Alexander. Peter has to bend his knees to create the 'two-shots' the director often needs. What should be serious romance is often giggle-making and uncomfortable.

Like Sandie, Jane is no great country-lover, although she enjoys horse-riding on days off. City shops, clubs and restaurants are more her style. There's a problem with fresh air, she explains: it makes your hair frizzy. The 'Dynasty' people would understand. At Emmerdale it's not so easy.

Dolly Skilbeck is the bubbly blonde ex-barmaid from the Woolpack who is married to clodhopping farmer Matt in 'Emmerdale Farm'. The question every viewer wants to ask is 'Why?' They forget that Dolly, like all good soap heroines, has a Past. In Dolly's there's the love-child by a flash businessman who refused to marry her. The child was adopted. Dolly is nice, placid and grateful to Matt. He puts up with the fact that she cannot say 'was'. She always says 'were'.

Played since 1980 by Jean Rogers in too-tight jeans, Dolly were from Darlington (sorry, *was* – it's catching) and came to Beckindale on a brewery training scheme. Cantankerous Amos coolly called her Miss Arcaster for months but warmed. He was thrilled to be asked to give her away at her wedding to sheep-loving Matt. They soon had a son, Sam.

A natural homemaker who *never* argues with Annie Sugden, Matt's mother-in-law from his first marriage, despite living cheek by jowl, she wouldn't last long in 'EastEnders'. Practical and sensible, she helps part-time at the village playgroup and was soon on the warpath when, after a playschool nature ramble and picnic, Sam and his friends became sick. They were victims of a corner-cutting crop-spraying exercise by NY Estates that went wrong. Alan Turner got the rough edge of her tongue.

In 1985 actress Jean Rogers pleaded with the scriptwriters to let Dolly have another baby, as a build-up to the 1000th episode of 'Emmerdale Farm'. She was allowed to get pregnant, but had to have a miscarriage when actress Helen Weir produced a child in real life and the writers were forced to give Pat Sugden the pregnancy story-line. (There was room for only one howling child on set.)

Dolly's past caught up with her in 1986 when her illegitimate son Graham came back to torment her. He turned out to be a wrong 'un on the run from the Army.

Basically the Skilbecks have had a hard life. Things began to look up in 1987 after they befriended Metcalfe, an old recluse. He shot himself and left his cottage and effects to kindly Matt. Will this mean a second rich family to rival the Sugdens, a spin-off soap as 'Knots Landing' was to 'Dallas'? Unlikely. Crossgill, the cottage they inherited, suffered a fire in May. Dolly was allowed to become emotional. She *shouted* and *broke* a plate! She also seemed to be heading for a fling with the new forestry man, Stephen full-of-himself Fuller (Gregory Floy). But, now they have come into money, will Dolly buy herself a pair of better-fitting jeans?

Jean Rogers, the glamorous blonde divorcee who plays Dolly Skilbeck, is dying to breathe new life into a character who seems doomed to lead a humdrum existence down on the farm with her boring husband Matt. If Jean had her way, she would turn Dolly from a frump into a man-eater.

When Worthing-born Jean took over the rôle from actress Katherine Barker in 1980, she inherited a wardrobe of old clothes that seemed set to last Dolly for ever. They presumably included the famous pair of skimpy faded jeans that make Dolly look like the oldest teenager in town. In an attempt to cheer up the character, Jean bought a black evening dress – 'the sort of little number that every blonde in Yorkshire has in her wardrobe', she claimed. She hasn't been allowed to wear it. The producers felt it would glamorise Dolly too much.

Jean herself is not prepared to give in to the ravages of middle age quite so easily. She was still posing for leggy cheesecake pictures in the hay as recently as 1986, aged forty-five. If Yorkshire Television ever relax their rules to allow 'Emmerdale Farm' stars to appear in pantomime, she could still play a smashing principal boy. Her great love is disco-dancing. No wonder she gets frustrated with dull Dolly at times.

Trained at the Guildhall School of Drama, she moved to the National Theatre before working in rep in Coventry and Chichester. For three years she presented the BBC programme 'Watch', and worked on 'Listen with Mother' for seven years. No stranger to soap, her television credits include 'Crossroads', 'Emergency – Ward Ten' and 'General Hospital'.

Jean split from her school-caretaker husband in 1983, then moved to Leeds to live with her father and two teenage children. In 1986 her affair with forty-three-year-old television unit manager Philip Hartley, who had left his wife and two children, made newspaper headlines. Jean has no plans to remarry.

She is godmother to the blonde-haired scene-stealer Benjamin Whitehead who plays four-year-old Sam Skilbeck, one of the best child actors in soap. Ben walks on to the set and chatters naturally.

Matt Skilbeck, the mild-mannered sheep-farmer who shares the donkey work with Jack Sugden on the Sugden spread in 'Emmerdale Farm', has been called 'the most boring man in soap' (I was putting it mildly). Even actor Frederick Pyne, who plays him, agrees Matt has been 'too nice and goody-goody' over the years. Slow-moving and slow-talking, Matt tends to speak at dictation speed. A plodder, stubborn when his temper is aroused, Matt knows real tragedy. He was married to Annie Sugden's daughter Peggy. She died from a brain haemorrhage shortly after their twins, Sally and Sam, were born. A year later the children were killed in an accident on a level crossing. Both times Matt was totally grief-stricken. With his second wife, former Woolpack barmaid Dolly Arcaster, came happiness and a second Sam.

Placid Matt is decent, honest and straight; true to 'Emmerdale Farm' creator Kevin Laffan's ideal, he tries to see the other person's point of view. But there's a limit. In 1986 viewers saw Matt repeatedly trying to pacify his obnoxious neighbour Harry Mowlam (Godfrey James). Mowlam had openly flirted with Dolly. Then, when the sneering Mowlam turned sheepstealer, Matt pitched into him in a blind rage. He soon found himself fighting for his life. Mowlam died, and Matt was charged with manslaughter. He was released when the real culprit (who'd arrived on the scene later) was found. The case soon forgotten (well, in soap, murder is quickly forgotten), Matt returned to his hobby: breeding Masham sheep.

His finances improved the following year when Metcalfe, a recluse he'd briefly befriended, shot himself, leaving Matt his house and its contents. Whether he and Dolly will move from the converted barn next to Emmerdale Farm that they live in is not clear. Stick-in-the-mud Matt won't want to be far from his sheep. If Dolly has a serious affair with Stephen Fuller, Matt could just decide to join them.

Frederick Pyne, the easy-going fifty-year-old bachelor who plays Matt Skilbeck, was for many years the only member of the cast who knew one end of a sheep from the other. Although Frederick was born in London, he spent much of his youth on the borders of Cambridgeshire and Hertfordshire. His verdict on farming? 'It was such a tough and mucky job I swore I would never go back to it.'

As a young man, he wanted to teach, but when he won a place at RADA acting became his natural choice. Before he joined the cast of 'Emmerdale Farm', he had spells at the National Theatre and four years at the Old Vic, working with Sir Laurence Olivier, Frank Finlay and Maggie Smith.

He is fond of the phlegmatic Matt, whom he has portrayed since the series started in 1972. But Freddie himself is by no means as placid. 'My constant fear is forgetting my lines. I am very irritable when I'm learning them – bad tempered even. I must be left alone.' He has not forgiven the writer who said 'Matt could bore for Britain in the Olympics' (me), but agrees that Matt *is* boring at times and should go out and get drunk occasionally or have an affair.

He is one of the kindest men in show business, vigorously supports many charities and worthwhile causes. He has been involved with CND and Greenpeace, he personally raised over £25,000 for hospital charities and the disabled, and is trustee of a home for elderly entertainers and chairman of the Committee for Disabled Performers. 'I'm so lucky to be fit and well!'

He loves the theatre, and opera in particular. His most cherished theatre notice starts: 'Freddie Pyne, as Bottom, strode the stage well. . . .'

Annie Sugden, known around 'Emmerdale Farm' as 'Ma', is the agricultural matriarch of soap. She was born to iron and to endure crises. Whatever happens, she can be relied on to make a pot of tea. Stony-faced and stern, Ma smiles only at coronations and takes her pinafore off only slightly more often.

Played by veteran actress Sheila Mercier, the phlegmatic Annie, head of the Emmerdale household, has learned about life the hard way. Her late husband, Jacob, used to booze the farm profits away in the Woolpack. Then elder son Jack left the farm after a furious row with his father. So it was Annie who kept the business going on a hand-to-mouth basis. Later Annie had to cope not only with financial crises, but also with the sudden death of her daughter Peggy from a brain haemorrhage, the death of her twin grandchildren and a constant war of words between sons Jack and Joe.

After Jacob died in 1972, Annie ruled the family with a rod of iron. But when the rebellious Jack returned to claim his inheritance and make a success of the farm, and old friend Henry Wilks joined the board of their new limited company, Annie began to mellow. She still 'speaks her mind' to her family, but she's wisdom itself.

Annie's confidant for many years was her father, Sam Pearson, who featured prominently in the story-line until the death of actor Toke Townley in 1984. Her relationship with Henry Wilks has never advanced beyond the platonic, and scriptwriters have avoided melodramatic story-lines for her. An idea to inflict suspected breast cancer on her was thrown out. 'We don't want to make her a martyr,' said the story-editor. But a few niggles with her daughter-in-law Dolly over housekeeping mightn't go amiss.

She did, however, make a small chapter of soap history. She underwent surgery for an arthritic knee on and off screen. Until then ailing actors and actresses simply disappeared for operations, and no one mentioned their absence.

Sheila Mercier, the sixty-nine-year-old East Yorkshire actress who plays Annie Sugden, is one of a handful of actors who have survived right from the first episode of the series.

The sister of former Whitehall farce impresario Brian Rix, her whole family was in love with the theatre. Her mother had a fine singing voice and used to appear in church charity shows. 'Brian and I used to hide under the piano and listen to them rehearsing,' recalls Sheila. Her father used to make the scenery for amateur productions as a hobby. Family get-togethers inevitably involved everyone doing a party piece. Sheila, who had elocution lessons as a child, was keen on poetry-reading. During the Second World War she became a WAAF with RAF Fighter Command and entertained the troops in her off-duty moments.

It was whilst she was at drama school that she was spotted by Sir Donald Wolfit and invited to join his touring company. She recalls spending more than a few nights in seedy digs. After making numerous appearances in touring comedies with brother Brian, Sheila was happy to swap irregular hours for the more stable life of television work. Sheila, fiercely loyal to the soap, says Annie Sugden is 'kind, wise and placid under stress. I am not so even-tempered. Once the story centred around the farm, and the key scenes involved Annie and her father. Since Toke Townley's death and the exit of Grandad, Annie has taken a back seat. The accent is more on the younger cast.' She had great faith in the series right from the moment Kevin Laffan showed her the first script. 'Magic! There was no way it could fail.'

Sheila has suffered painful arthritis in her knees for a number of years, which is why she is largely seen indoors and sitting down on set. But she has always tackled difficult film location scenes gamely, like the time she had to make friends with a flock of geese so that they would behave on camera later on.

London based, married to former actor Peter Mercier, Sheila once tried her hand at running a pub in Tunbridge Wells. It didn't last. 'I can't add up. We used to have to ask the customers to do it and we lost out.' Until recently she was a regular smoker. Oh, to see prim Annie puffing on a fag!

Jack Sugden is the kingpin of Emmerdale Farm, only you wouldn't know it. He's not puffed up with his own importance, isn't our

299

Jack. He doesn't waste words. Sometimes he barely uses them, which makes his 'other career' from farming – writing successful novels – all the more remarkable. Sometimes arrogant and abrasive, he is part poet, part grafter, a hater of the cruelty of man, a lover of nature.

His on/off relationship with Beckindale has been as colourful as his love-life. The elder son of Annie, he returned home at the start of the series for his father's funeral. He'd left for London after rows about intensive farming. To his surprise and the rest of the family's dismay he inherited the farm (so there hasn't yet been a sequel to his literary masterpiece *Field of Tares*). After another absence (in Rome) he returned to take charge on the farm. This led to a stormy relationship with his brother Joe, later followed by a stormy relationship with his stepson Jackie (later revealed as his own son), to be followed by occasional verbal punch-ups with brother-in-law Matt and Annie and actual punch-ups with Tom Merrick. Having stormy relationships is what Jack does, as well as work hard and think slow.

He's not slow in bed, though, and has no trouble winning women in his flat cap and anorak. His steamy affair with auctioneer Karen Moore whilst his wife Pat was pregnant put the hot into Hotten. Most viewers enjoyed it, but the hate mail that poured in for Clive Hornby (who plays him) and Annie Hulley (Karen) suggested that some town folk couldn't accept Jack's excuse: his need for solace to escape mounting criticism of a rash purchase of cattle to upgrade his pedigree Friesian herd. Not so much 'my wife doesn't understand me' as 'my wife doesn't understand my cows', perhaps.

His mentor Kevin Laffan hated the Hotten hotel scenes and stopped writing for the soap after several rows. But he wholeheartedly approved when Jack later waged a campaign against dumping nuclear waste in Beckindale. After a six-month protest he served a week in gaol for contempt of court. He won (the site was moved elsewhere) but victory left him dour as before.

He did manage, though, to fit in a fling with an old flame, Henry Wilks's daughter Marian. They slept together while her Italian husband lay critically ill in intensive care (of course) after being shot by the 'Emmerdale Farm' villain of the time, antiques dealer Eric Pollard.

For a time Jack's life centred on bringing up Robert, the child Pat had shortly before her death in a road accident, and building up the business for the family, but a decision by new producer Stuart Doughty sent Jack on his world travels again in 1988. For the time being his commitment to his farm and Beckindale is off.

Clive Hornby, the forty-two-year-old Liverpudlian who plays Jack Sugden, is married to actress Helen Weir who played Jack's late screen wife Pat. Both divorcees, they met and fell in love shortly after he joined the series in 1980. They married on-screen in 1982, off-screen in 1984.

Clive originally trained as an accountant, then worked as a drummer in the Dennisons pop group which played alongside the Beatles in the 1960s. Clive graduated to acting via Liverpool Playhouse and the London Academy of Music and Dramatic Art. After repertory theatre, he appeared on television in 'Minder' and the feature film *Yanks*. Clive succeeded Andrew Burt in 'Emmerdale Farm', and his introduction to country life was quick and startling. Within hours of starting work on location he had to deliver a calf in front of the television cameras. 'A farmer showed me what to do; it was a wonderful moment.'

'Emmerdale Farm' changed Clive's life. He was going through a rough patch in his career, wondering if he was ever going to get anywhere. 'I was thirty-five, without a wife or a home, when I met Helen. She has brought changes in my life I would never have dreamed of. We are blissfully happy.'

Joe Sugden, the fresh-faced farm lad who matured to become the rising star of NY Estates, vies with his brother Jack for 'the most eligible bloke' title in 'Emmerdale Farm'. Joe, portrayed by Fraser Hines, is the younger son of Annie and a pragmatist – unlike Jack, who is an emotional idealist. Annie likes Joe's cheerful and willing disposition, but she does worry about him.

A callow youth of eighteen when the series started in 1972, Joe was a thorn in the side of the 'Mr Nasty' of NY Estates, Alan Turner. Joe is a shrewd if unorthodox businessman, and Turner resented his success. Now, however, with the demise of NY's Beckindale operation, the two men have formed an uneasy business relationship setting up a country club.

Joe's relationship with Jack is an uneasy one. Joe was devastated when his rebellious elder brother returned like the prodigal son to take over Emmerdale Farm, left to him by their father in his will. It shattered Joe's dream of taking over the farm. (It's now a limited company with five equal partners.)

Like Jack, Joe's problems with women concern him just as much as fowl pest or liver fluke. His marriage to Milk Marketing Board inspector Christine Sharp was doomed before it started. Christine, who drove a trendy sports-car, couldn't cope with the humdrum life down on the farm. She was the daughter of Robert Sharp, a wealthy businessman who ran a dairy farm as a hobby. (This made him a Bad Lot in this soap, which believes everyone should take the country seriously.) Sharp was against the marriage from the start, and when Joe refused his injection of cash into the ailing Emmerdale business things went from bad to worse. After the honeymoon, Joe had little time for social occasions. It wasn't long before he and Christine split up and sold Hawthorn Cottage.

As divorce proceedings started, he began another ill-fated affair with farmer's daughter Kathy Gimbel (Polly Hemmingway). When Kathy's father disowned her, it soured their affair. Their relationship ended with the tragic news that Kathy's father had killed himself with his own shotgun.

Joe has also 'tangled' with Barbara Peters, daughter of the Reverend Donald Hinton and Karen Moore (actress Annie Hulley), the woman who almost wrecked Pat and Jack's marriage. Joe was smitten again by new vet Ruth Pennington (portrayed by Julia Chambers) who came to Beckindale in 1987. He should have realised that he was out of his depth with upper-class Ruth. A dinner-party at her rich father's country home was a disaster. Joe was crestfallen to learn that she was engaged to a wealthy international art dealer.

Joe's farming career has been much less fraught and improved by a period working off-screen, supposedly in France – the cover story when Fraser Hines's marriage to Gemma Craven began to break up in 1983 and Fraser asked to leave the series at short notice. He returned in 1986, made the occasional cross-Channel phone call in Edward Heath French and knuckled down to the job of upsetting Alan Turner, his underling at NY Estates, before NY's changing fortunes nudged the two men into an unlikely business relationship.

Fraser Hines, the sensitive forty-two-year-old actor from Horsforth, Leeds, who plays Joe Sugden, has been fighting to emerge from the shadow of his broken marriage to actress Gemma Craven. It ended in a blaze of publicity in 1984 and briefly blitzed his acting career. After their relationship had been put under the microscope by the press Fraser left 'Emmerdale Farm' in 1983 to spend more time with his vivacious wife. When the marriage crashed a year later and Gemma left him, he was too upset to continue acting so filled his time with horse racing, his hobby. He bought a half-share in the racehorse Ingham, stabled at Middleham near Catterick, and followed the fortunes of the Turf.

In show business since he was eight, Hines was at stage school at ten with Richard O'Sullivan, Dennis Waterman and Susan George. By the time he was thirteen he had been in half a dozen feature films. He appeared as the truculent Scot Jamie, assistant to Dr Who in the BBC television series. He still gets fan letters for Jamie from all over the world.

He appeared in the first episode of 'Emmerdale Farm', in 1972, and has a great fondness for the series and for his Yorkshire roots. The chance to rejoin the cast of 'Emmerdale Farm' in 1985 was a real pick-me-up. Stories that he was being paid a £1500-a-week salary seemed unlikely to be true. He needed 'Emmerdale Farm', and it needed him. 'I thought there might be some resentment from the cast, but they were great. When I walked into rehearsals it was just like old times,' he recalls. A champion of his soap, he hates 'EastEnders'. 'I'd rather go to the dentist than watch it,' he told me.

Pat Sugden, the late wife of forceful farmer Jack in 'Emmerdale Farm', seemed born to suffer. For ten years she had one of the most complicated love-lives in soap before she was killed off in 1986 after a typically 'Yorkshire' barney between Helen Weir, who played her, and the producers.

In March 1986, after the birth of a son, Helen wanted him as her screen baby (the pregnancy had been written into the plot to suit her). But she also wanted him called by his real name, Thomas. The writers had called the Emmerdale tot Robert. They might have changed it – but not to Thomas, because it would have been mad to call the child after Pat's hated ex-husband Tom Merrick, the soap's main monster. When Helen insisted and refused to sign her contract, Yorkshire Television decreed that Pat must die – and had her bumped off by a hit-and-run driver. 'We had no alternative,' said story-editor Andrew Holden, adding with masterly understatement: 'It made good drama, but Helen didn't like it.'

Originally the teenage sweetheart of young Jack, she married loutish Tom (played first by Edward Peel, then by Jack Carr) on the rebound when Jack hurriedly left Beckindale. (The actor who first played Jack, Andrew Burt, hurriedly wanted to return to the theatre.) Tom disappeared, went to gaol, drank and rarely worked. Pat was the soap's Woman Alone, struggling to bring up Jackie and Sandie in a caravan. She finally divorced the brute, and love blossomed again with the newly returned Jack. Son Jackie became hostile. Then Pat sprang her Big Secret to Jack: he was the lad's real father. Jack hadn't known she was pregnant when he left. Fortunately, neither had Tom. Jack gambled and told Jackie the truth, sending him completely off the rails. He ran away from home on a boozing spree. Pat was furious with Jack, then distraught when she learned that the whole of Beckindale knew her sixteen-year-old secret. Jack and Tom had a good brawl over it outside the Woolpack.

Like any good soap sufferer Pat was soon putting her pride behind her and marrying Jack. Considering Annie, Emmerdale's She Who Must Be Obeyed, had blessed the partnership, what else could she do? There was happiness, pregnancy, happiness, then more suffering when Jack rekindled an old romance with Karen, the raven-haired auctioneer of Hotten. Pat knew but said nowt until one night when she followed the lovers to Karen's flat and confronted them. 'Come home with me or never see me again,' she said. He came.

Pat settled back at Emmerdale, tended Grandad Pearson's vegetable patch and heroically never uttered a cross word to her mother-in-law or her sister-in-law, Dolly. Then she followed the trend for late babies set by Sheila Grant of 'Brookside' and Pauline of 'EastEnders', giving birth at forty-three. Lovely for Helen, who'd really managed it. But a teeny bit troublesome for poor Pat. . . .

Helen Weir had the best rôle in 'Emmerdale Farm' until she lost it after a row about her baby's first name. It ended her soap career. Before the birth in December 1986, Helen and her husband on- and off-screen, Clive Hornby, were adamant that they would take the baby everywhere – on location, into the studios. Yorkshire Television were happy with the idea and, because the couple, Pat and Jack Sugden, were so important and popular in the country soap, wrote the baby into the story. Everything was sweet until they named the baby Thomas and Helen insisted the screen baby also be called Thomas because it would be confusing for the child to be called one thing by day and another by night. But Helen had forgotten her first screen husband: Tom (the Rotter) Merrick. Thomas was the one name the scriptwriters couldn't accept. Pat wouldn't do such a thing. Helen, from Ilkley, Yorkshire, stood firm, refused to sign her contract and was dramatically dropped. (See 'Killing Them Off'.) The producers broke the news to the couple over a restaurant meal that Jack would soon be a widower and Robert motherless. It left Helen short of a good income and Thomas without his chance of early stardom. Baby Richard Smith landed his part. Had both parents and their babe worked, it would have made soap history. 'But it could have been a nightmare,' said a cynical member of the hit squad.

Helen, trained at RADA, had repertory and West End successes behind her before she was brought into 'Emmerdale Farm' as Jack Sugden's long-lost love, and for most of her screen life she sported the best-cut hair in soap opera (she wore her thick auburn locks in a tapered 'page-boy' – perhaps a shade too sophisticated for the cow-shed).

When Clive joined the cast in 1980 the couple, both divorcees, began to hit it off in private, too. They married on-screen in 1982, off-screen in 1984, moving into a six-bedroom Georgian farmhouse in North Yorkshire with Helen's ten-year-old son from her previous marriage. The couple share a common love of country life from rummaging through antique-shops to walking their two Border Collie dogs Barker and Dobson.

Alan Turner is the nearest this genial soap has to a swine. Not very competent, a bully and a snob, the Bunteresque manager of NY Estates was also the butt of comic scenes because of his clumsiness and cluelessness as to the feelings of his staff – particularly his saintly secretary Mrs Bates. (Will he ever melt her sensible heart? No. But he'll keep trying.)

Conceived as the Outsider when he arrived from the South in the spring of 1982, his many conflicts with the Sugden family over farming and village matters have been bitter. Hostilities peaked when he badly injured Jackie (Jack Sugden's son) in a night-time road accident. A thorn in his side is gamekeeper Seth Armstrong, who frequently tells Turner where to stick his grand ideas. Turner rages at Seth and the other estate workers for slacking but enjoys nothing so much as slipping off for the golf-course or the racetrack. He's good at boozy business-lunches, too, though a conviction for drunk driving in May has cramped his style.

Thanks to the twinkly appeal of actor Richard Thorp, Turner has mellowed and is seen by viewers as funny but sad, a well-rounded character in all senses. He suffered the selfish behaviour of his would-be whizzkid son, Terence, two years ago but is otherwise lonely. Perhaps under the bluster he knows his social, romantic and career prospects aren't exactly rosy.

Richard Thorp is the biggest man in soap and getting bigger. Stout when he joined 'Emmerdale Farm' in 1982 as bumptious Alan Turner, Richard gained three stones in as many years in the rôle. It exasperated the wardrobe mistress and prompted the scriptwriters, worried for the health of their star, to construct a diet plot-line for him. It failed dismally.

Completely different from the screen loner, Thorp is an easygoing witty family-man. He lives in some splendour in Sussex with his third wife and five children. Born in 1933, the once slim, handsome actor was a natural as well-bred heroes in such films as *The Dam Busters* and *The Barratts of Wimpole Street*. He became a heart-throb on television as Dr Rennie in the sixties soap 'Emergency – Ward Ten' and was in 'A Family at War', 'To the Manor Born' and 'The Cedar Tree'. He played the lead in the West End stage production of *Murder at the Vicarage*.

Playing the sometimes nasty NY Estates boss made him famous but brought trouble. People berated him rudely in the street, and the tyres of his Range Rover were slashed by someone who left a note expressing hatred for Turner.

Henry Wilks, the retired businessman who is a partner and lodger at the Woolpack inn in 'Emmerdale Farm', is the wise elder statesman of Beckindale. A retired Bradford wool merchant who settled in the village after his wife died, his is the calming voice of reason, heard not only in the comic 'Amos and Henry' verbal jousts in the pub, but also on the board of Emmerdale Farm itself where family squabbles break out from time to time.

Wilks, beautifully underplayed by Arthur Pentelow, took lodgings in the pub when his village home was destroyed by fire. He hadn't meant to stay, but he has been there ever since. He is blunt, but honest – a businessman who often lets his heart rule his head. He and Amos squabble amicably all the time just like an old married couple, but they are good for each other and share the companionship of two elderly men without a woman in their lives. Henry is genuinely fond of Annie Sugden. He has been a financial adviser ever since her no-good husband died and left her almost penniless.

When a family row broke out at Emmerdale and Jack threatened to quit, the future of the farm was secured by Henry Wilks. He bought the freehold and organised the family into a limited company. Together they have brought the farm up to date, and Henry has won his way into the hearts of the Sugdens.

Apart from Annie, the only other female that Henry cares about is his daughter Marian. As a teenager she fell in love with Jack Sugden and almost married him before fleeing to Italy to start a new life. There she married successful businessman Paolo. But when Marian and Paolo arrived in Beckindale to show Wilks his new grandson, Niccolo, Marian revealed her marriage was on the rocks. Henry came very close to leaving the Woolpack to set up home with his daughter and grandson. But when a tragic shooting accident crippled Paolo and left him disabled Marian decided she would stay his wife for ever (which can be very short in soap). So, despite his obvious wealth, Henry remains firmly installed at the Woolpack, suffering Amos's irritating fads and moods. He is the perfect foil for the temperamental landlord.

Arthur Pentelow, the laconic, pipe-smoking actor who plays Henry Wilks, originally planned to become a policeman in his native Rochdale, but the war intervened. He found himself in the Navy instead. With plenty of time to reflect, he decided to follow his first love – acting – after the war. Having first trod the boards in school plays at Rochdale Grammar, Pentelow went to study at the new Bradford Civic Playhouse Theatre School. In between parts, he sold sliced bread to earn a crust.

After rep at Bristol Old Vic, Nottingham and Birmingham, he appeared in an Orson Welles West End production of *Othello*. Arthur appeared in the Albert Finney feature film *Charlie Bubbles* and in *Privilege* with Jean Shrimpton. His television rôles include appearances in 'Z Cars', 'Emergency – Ward Ten', 'United!' and 'Coronation Street', in which he played George Greenwood, Emily's driving instructor and an old friend of Hilda Ogden.

He and his wife like pottering around antique-shops at weekends, and Arthur likes birdwatching and walking his dog. Like Ronald Magill, who plays his screen partner Amos Brearly, Arthur has learned to live with being stopped in the street by demanding fans. But he treasures the memory of one old man who tugged his sleeve in a Leeds street and said quietly: 'I'd like thee to know tha's given me an hour or two of real pleasure.'

He told me: 'I'm not a pub person at all and Ronnie (Amos) and I often laugh about the dingy living quarters we're supposed to share. We fantasise about a lovely lounge upstairs and luxurious bedrooms. We do have separate bedrooms, by the way, despite what people say.'

'FALCON CREST'

'Falcon Crest' is where they turn wine not into water but into soap, every week. And it's wine with body. There have been enough bodies in this tempestuous tale of North Californian vineyards to drive a workaholic pathologist like Quincy to an early grave. Those that haven't died have had numerous narrow escapes as buildings suddenly explode or catch fire, cars and planes crash and wronged parties run amok with machine-guns. Throw in the odd drowning and even the occasional death from natural causes and you've got a fair picture of life in the fictitious Tuscany Valley.

Apart from the insurance investigators, the most important person in the valley is Angela Channing around whom most of the action and a lot of the attempted murders revolve. Played by Ronnie Reagan's ex-wife Jane Wyman, Angela looks like an up-market Ma Sugden of 'Emmerdale Farm' but without the ironing-board. She is the tough all-conquering boss of Falcon Crest Wines who schemed to swindle her magnificently named nephew Chase Gioberti (it always sounds like a children's party game) out of his birthright.

Chase had inherited fifty acres of vineyards from his late father Jason, but Angela wanted that land and was prepared to go to any lengths to get it. Good guy Chase was played by Robert Foxworth until the character drowned last year. But Angela battles on to keep Falcon Crest and thwart her many enemies.

Made by Lorimar (the 'Dallas' and 'Knots Landing' producers) and filmed in California's Napa Valley, 'Falcon Crest' was first shown in America in December 1981. It has continually tried to outgun 'Dallas' and 'Dynasty' and, after a sticky start, has gone from strength to strength. It has never had the opportunity to emulate its American success in this country, usually being scheduled by ITV companies between lunch-time cookery programmes and such delights as 'One Hundred Things to Do with Raffia'.

Other major characters in 'Falcon Crest' are Chase's writer-wife Maggie Gioberti, played by Susan Sullivan; ruthless newspaper proprietor Richard Channing (David Selby), who discovered that he is the son of the woman he hates, Angela Channing, and is fighting to gain control of Falcon Crest; Angela's evil playboy-grandson Lance Cumson (Lorenzo Lamas), who was once convicted of trying to murder his dear old granny; and Lance's ex-wife, the equally shady Melissa (Ana-Alicia).

Among major stars to have guested in 'Falcon Crest' are Lana Turner, Kim Novak, Ursula Andress, Gina Lollobrigida, Morgan Fairchild and our own Simon MacCorkindale. In a spell of desperation when all the American soaps' ratings seemed to be in a tailspin, the producers even hired *Playboy* centrefold star Shannon Tweed. Supervising producer Bob McCullough recalled: 'We'd tested everyone when this six-foot girl with no bra and her blouse unbuttoned walked into the audition. She walked over to the table and threw down a stack of photos. "Excuse the nudes, but that's all I have," she said. They hired her that day. We had to give her acting lessons. She was getting fifteen thousand dollars a week.' She stayed for eighteen months.

The malevolence of the 'Falcon Crest' plots seems to have spread to some of the cast. Reports of open warfare frequently leak out. Robert Foxworth had a chance to direct episodes, which prompted Jane Wyman to ask to direct. Her request wasn't granted, but when he directs she gets a director's salary. Foxworth was angered to discover Jane Wyman's trailer was six inches longer than his. He demanded (and got) a bigger one. After Jane Wyman and Lana Turner's relationship became so hostile that their scenes together were filmed separately and a split-screen technique had to be used, 'Falcon Crest' was widely regarded as the most dangerous soap to work on. Happily there has not yet been a need to call in the coroner.

Ana-Alicia plays the twice-married rich bitch Melissa Cumson, a candidate for the Nastiest Woman In Soap award. Most 'Falcon Crest' fans foam at the mouth mentioning her. As well as bedding every male in the wine industry, she promises to sell her wine harvests to such people as Angela, only to refuse on a whim.

Ana has achieved her success in spite of having the sort of minor physical imperfection which would send most American actresses screaming for their analyst, their chequebook and their plastic surgeon. 'I have a bump on the left side of my nose from an accident when I was a child. When I first went for an acting job, the producer told me to fix it. I told him if he'd wanted a girl with a perfect nose he could have hired one. Since then me, my nose and the bump have worked steadily.' Now thirty-one, Ana-Alicia was born in Mexico City. She studied law before switching to drama and has appeared in programmes such as 'Quincy', 'Hotel' and 'Battlestar Galactica'. Like many other women, she was linked with her then 'Falcon Crest' husband Lorenzo Lamas.

Robert Foxworth was fed up with doing the standard scene as Chase Gioberti in 'Falcon Crest'. 'I complained to the producers that I did the same thing with Jane Wyman in every single episode. Jane said: "Chase, you don't belong here. I'm going to run you out of this valley and have Falcon Crest all to myself." And I yelled back: "Angela, you know that's not true. I care as much about Falcon Crest as you do and I'll always be here to fight you." I could do that scene without a script.' He's not there to fight her now – Robert left 'Falcon Crest' at the end of the sixth season, his character Chase being killed off. Born in Houston, Texas, Robert lives in Los Angeles with his wife, 'Bewitched' star Elizabeth Montgomery. He didn't always see eye to eye with his co-stars on 'Falcon Crest' – he and Jane Wyman spoke on set only if it was in the script.

Lorenzo Lamas more than lives up to the sexy playboy image of his 'Falcon Crest' character Lance Cumson. He has had a weakness for fast cars, fast women, drink and drugs. Born in Los Angeles, the son of the late romantic actor Fernando Lamas and actress Arlene Dahl, wild boy Lorenzo has constantly diced with death. In 1977 he cracked his skull in a motorbike crash. He was partially paralysed and couldn't speak for three days. In 1985 a 110-miles-per-hour racing-car smash left him with a broken collarbone, a dislocated shoulder and a warning from the 'Falcon Crest' producers to give up motor racing. He simply refused. 'I'm not stopping. I love racing too much.' Thirty-year-old Lorenzo, whose daredevil antics make Evel Knievel look like Lofty from 'EastEnders', later did a circus stunt with no fewer than eleven vicious tigers.

He's a bit of a tiger with the ladies, too. His first marriage, to model Victoria Hilbert, who was twelve years older than him, lasted under a year, and it wasn't long before the relationship between Lorenzo and his second wife, publicist Michele Smith, ran into trouble. 'We were heavily into cocaine,' he told American journalist Sharon Rosenthal. 'We hit rock bottom. I was going through five hundred dollars a week. I was high most of the time.' After divorcing Michele, he fell for his screen wife of the time, Robin Greer, who, it seems, has helped him kick drink and drugs. Robin revealed: 'We couldn't help becoming intimate – we spent months in bed together in front of the cameras. We didn't have wardrobe changes, we had sheet changes.'

David Selby, who plays nasty double-dealing businessman Richard Channing, got more than he bargained for when filming a love-scene with co-star Susan Sullivan. She went into the bathroom to 'get into something more comfortable' and emerged wearing a silk robe. As the passion reached fever pitch, she dropped the robe to reveal a body-stocking crammed with bottles, cans and tubes of toothpaste. David and the rest of the crew fell about laughing.

Born in Morgan Town, West Virginia, David was bitten by the acting bug at an early age and has appeared in many Broadway productions as well as films like *Rich and Famous* with Candice Bergen and Jacqueline Bisset. He was also a regular in 'Flamingo Road'. David lives in Los Angeles with his wife Claudeis and their three children.

Susan Sullivan is the Suffering Woman of 'Falcon Crest'. As Maggie Gioberti she has been on the receiving end of all the Channing barbs. She had a breakdown, amnesia, was widowed and then had the misfortune to fall for obnoxious Richard Channing, foolishly imagining she could change him. For her pains she was blown up twice in his house.

Susan once worked as a bunny girl in the Manhattan Playboy Club. She says: 'I had been a waitress before and I felt I would rather show my legs and make sixty dollars a night instead of twenty.' And she recited Shakespeare while serving the drinks. Born in New York forty-two years ago, Susan is attractive, intelligent and unmarried. When she was twenty-three she used to go out with Cary Grant. 'It was no big romance,' she admits, 'but you can imagine what it was like to have Cary Grant call you up!' Susan has no doubts as to why viewers like 'Falcon Crest': 'People want to see wealthy families, beautiful clothes and lovely women. But they also want to see that they're really miserable at heart in spite of all their wealth and power.' Susan is refreshingly honest. When filming the episode where she learned of her husband Chase's death, she shed real tears. Sympathy for the poor suffering widow? 'It was pre-menstrual tension,' she said later.

Jane Wyman didn't make it to the White House but she made sure she was the first lady on 'Falcon Crest'. Jane, famous for being Ronald Reagan's first wife, had a number of run-ins with her 'Falcon Crest' co-stars, particularly if they threatened to upstage her. She and Lana Turner were old adversaries dating back to 1939 when the then seventeen-year-old Lana nearly wrecked Jane's romance with Ronnie. When Lana was introduced to 'Falcon Crest' in 1982 as Jacqueline Perrault in a bid to boost sagging ratings, the two were soon at loggerheads. It got to the stage where Jane's character, the matriarchal Angela Channing, would not appear in the same scene as Lana. Finally, Jane issued an ultimatum to the producers: 'Either you have me back on this show for the next series or Lana Turner. Not both.' Lana was duly killed off.

Jane Wyman was born Sarah Jane Fulks seventy-four years ago in St Joseph, Missouri, where her father was the Chief of Detectives. It was Warner Brothers who changed her name, and she went on to appear in films such as *The Lost Weekend*, *The Yearling* and *Johnny Belinda*, for which she won an Oscar for Best Actress in her rôle as a deaf mute. In 1937 she married and divorced New Orleans dress manufacturer Myron Futterman. A year later she met actor Ronald Reagan while they were filming

Brother Rat. They were married in January 1940 in Hollywood and had a daughter Maureen and adopted a son Michael. Jane and Ronnie were divorced in 1949, and she blamed the failure of the marriage on his insistence that she share his interest in politics. Three years later, she married orchestra-leader Freddie Karger. They were divorced in 1954, remarried in 1961 and redivorced in 1965!

Jane is philosophical about what might have been. 'I've no regrets about missing out on the White House. It's definitely not my scene. But I was delighted when Ronnie was elected and quite ecstatic when he won again. We've always remained friends, and I have so many wonderful memories of our life together.'

Jane is in her element in 'Falcon Crest' and won a Golden Globe for Angela Channing in 1984. 'I just wish I'd had the chance to play meatier parts years ago,' she says. 'I love being bad.' Lana Turner will second that.

FAME

Fame from soap is hard to bear, many actors moan. It's tough having people pester you in the street or point on trains. What newspapers do – invading actors' privacy, printing details of their love-lives – is too, too terribly cruel. Any soap star invited on to a television chat-show will do that little speech. As yet I've never heard one complain about a good review, a flattering profile or mention the considerable sums some newspapers pay for the chance to publish selections from their memoirs.

Soap fame is different from film fame. Leslie Grantham and Kylie Minogue come into our living-rooms with unfailing regularity. They seem to belong to us. It's not so with Dustin Hoffman or Elizabeth Taylor. We'd rush to see them, too, if they came to open the new local Woolworth's. But we wouldn't expect them to be matey.

Peter Adamson, who was Len Fairclough for twenty-three years said in a BBC radio interview with Mavis Nicolson that he had seen both sides of fame: love and hate. Three years earlier he had stood trial accused of gross indecency with two eight-year-old girls. He was acquitted. 'I saw the adoration that is given to people like myself in "Coronation Street". And I saw what they imagined to be the filthiest act in this world. I saw the same crowd turn against me. That was just outside the court. The worst thing was the press. We had fourteen reporters at the front of the house, fourteen at the back. I was a big name. My wife and my two kids were not part of that. Am I bitter? No. I could well understand it. If I'd been out there, I'd have joined them. You see, at sixteen I wanted to be famous. I wanted to shine in something. I was the last in a family of six and I was possibly the least important. The strange thing is that I became famous not for what Peter Adamson did, but for what the character did. That made me slightly bitter. That made me rethink the whole thing – about what acting is supposed to be about – because Len is much bigger than I will ever be.'

Susan Tully, Michelle in 'EastEnders', has seen the strain of fame in other members of the cast. She told me: 'It's terrible. I've been lucky. I haven't had that much stick. But I've seen people in tears; I've seen people considering leaving it ["EastEnders"]; I've seen people go into very deep depressions about invasions of privacy. I know you have to sacrifice a hell of a lot if you're going into such a high-profile programme. But what cracks people up is the effect it has on your family. You get journalists knocking on your friends' and families' doors at six in the morning. I can deal with it. They can't. A lot of the time it's a lie. It's a build-up of lies; we're all being dealt so much shit, it's unfair. But the good things outnumber the drawbacks. When people come up and say they like what I do I get a kick out of it. If anyone says they don't, I don't believe them. And the financial benefits are great: I've a flat and a car, I travel, I meet interesting people. I love it.'

A young actor who admits he couldn't cope with the pressures of sudden soap fame is Darius Perkins who played Scott Robinson in 'Neighbours' but was replaced by Jason Donovan.

Darius was quoted in Australia's TV Week as saying: 'The whole thing of losing your identity, people actually believing you are Scott and girls constantly coming up to you in the street. . . . You feel isolated in a way, a bit untouchable, a bit alone. The whole thing freaked me out completely. I blew it. I was too young and inexperienced to handle it.' Darius went on to admit he was smoking dope but said, 'I don't think I was ever uncooperative. I might have been late a couple of times. I should've known better.'

He was out of acting work for eighteen months after his 'Neighbours'' contract was not renewed. 'When I went for an interview you could see what they were thinking: "Is he stoned?" Unless you've done it and had to cope with the pressures you can't understand.'

FANS

Fans of soap are a mystery to the companies who make them. It seems they are women, men, aristocratic, middle-class, lower-class, old, young, black, white, brainy and thick. People tell lies about the television shows they watch, and the cultural condescension to soap opera (despite its phenomenal success) continues unabashed.

As I stood with spectators in the Melbourne cul-de-sac watching a scene for 'Neighbours' being filmed, I talked to a few 'fans'. Had they always liked the show? I asked. 'Oh, not really. I prefer documentaries and news.' People say the same all over. Yet documentaries and news programmes never make top ratings. Odd, that.

'Crossroads' died because its fans were too old. Advertisers couldn't sell them Diet Coke or shampoo. The advertisers who want slots during 'Knots Landing' in America want to sell deodorant, tampons, cross-your-heart bras and dog food. So we can safely assume research shows the fans are female.

'Neighbours' is watched by middle-class women and millions of children. One child is particularly important in its success-story here. Sixteen-year-old Alison Grade mentioned to her father Michael that she watched 'Neighbours' with pals at lunch-time on the school's computer-room telly. The then controller of BBC programmes made a note to help kids who couldn't get into their computer rooms. He switched the morning repeats to 5.30 p.m.

My favourite fan story is this. It's true, I swear it.

A gravely ill grandmother of a staunchly Catholic family was sent home from hospital to die. Granny passed her last precious weeks surrounded by devoted children and grandchildren, doing all they could to demonstrate their love.

One evening, close to the end, moving in and out of consciousness, they heard her murmur: 'You know, I keep wondering....' The

314

sentence drained away. The children tried to rouse her, anxious to put her troubled mind at rest over perhaps one important family event.

The next day she stammered: 'Ee, it does bother me. . . .'

'What? What?' they coaxed.

'I can't help thinking', she said, adding more faintly, 'what's going to happen in "Emmerdale Farm".'

Then she died.

'FLAMINGO ROAD'

'Flamingo Road' showed that you can't make a successful soap out of any old bunch of sexy scandals. Based on the novel set in the American deep south by Robert Wilder, it ran for two seasons only in America, from January 1981 to July 1982, and was bought by the BBC for screening in 1982 and then eighteen months later in 1983 because it was colourful, melodramatic and seemed at first like 'Dallas' with politics, a brothel and mango groves. British viewers, like American audiences, soon tired of going down its pink-feathered paths and found none of the characters likeable or strong enough to tolerate.

Also their names – Lute-Mae, Eudora, Lane and Field – made us giggle. Morgan Fairchild as Constance Weldon was a spectacular bitch, it must be said. Spoiled by her rich adoptive parents, her marriage to the politically ambitious Field Carlyle (who, naturally, loved another) began the action. While Constance proceeded to rip the clothes off every man in the steamy little town (only Skipper, her young brother, escaped), Field dithered and dallied with Lane, a poor carnival queen with a heart of gold. Even though played by budding heart-throb Mark Harmon, Field was so wet he should have been called 'Swamp'. He seemed especially puny in scenes with Howard Duff as wheeler-dealer Sherif Titus Semple. The first series ended with Constance tumbling over a staircase. By the second series David Selby had joined as the energetically evil Michael Tyrone, to have an affair with Lute-Mae, the brothel-owner, so discovering Constance was really her child. Then he bedded Constance, shattering her with the truth, sending the now deranged Lute-Mae into a sanatorium, threatening Lane and her new husband and practising voodoo against Titus. In the last episode he faked his own murder, hid in a monastery and had Titus blamed. Field had contemplated suicide at one point, but was so boring I can't remember if he did it or not. David Selby and Morgan Fairchild lived to see better traumas in 'Falcon Crest'; John Beck, who played Lane's lover, went on to 'Dallas' and Mark Harmon to 'St Elsewhere'.

Morgan Fairchild is the actress (real name Patsy McClenny) who seems to have cornered the market in young blonde man-eaters in television series including 'Flamingo Road', 'Falcon Crest' and 'Paper Dolls' and in the long-running American daytime soap 'Search for Tomorrow'. She turned down the rôle of Jenna Wade (subsequently filled by Priscilla Presley) in 'Dallas', although she appeared briefly early on in that soap as a would-be breaker of Pam and Bobby's marriage. In 'Flamingo Road' she was the spoilt Constance who seemed to rip the shirt off every male in sight. She appeared in 'Falcon Crest', and in 'Paper Dolls' she was Racy, the head of a Manhattan modelling agency.

Born in 1950 in Dallas, married briefly at seventeen when already an actress, a rôle in the film *Summer of '62* marked the start of her career. A jolly jokey girl, skilled at karate but much smaller than she appears on screen, she is frank about the plastic surgery and other beauty tricks she used to acquire the stunning looks of a soap tease. She and her 'Flamingo Road' co-stars, she said, played it for laughs and, no, she never thought it was art. Of her image as man-mad: 'Whenever I walk into a room, every woman grabs her husband. Actually I'm still quite shy.'

'THE FORSYTE SAGA'

'The Forsyte Saga' has been amply analysed and praised elsewhere. This small section is merely to place the BBC's adaptation of John Galsworthy's family chronicles where it belongs – as the last British soap opera made in black and white. In terms of characterisation and acting, it was perhaps the finest. Producer Donald Wilson and four writers spent a year preparing scripts for the twenty-six-part series, made for a paltry £500,000, and screened for the first time on BBC2 (then very much the minority channel) from January to July 1967. An instant critical success, it was rapidly repeated on BBC1 and drew audiences of 18.5 million. American audiences who saw it in the autumn and spring of 1969–70 were similarly entranced. Set in the changing society of the late-Victorian era to the interwar years, it had classic soap ingredients. Packed with cliffhangers and shocks, it was the story of solicitor Soames Forsyte, his beautiful wife Irene, her affair, his claim on his property (by raping her), her lover's death, her divorce, marriage to 'young' Jolyon and later the fraught relationship between their son Jon and Soames's daughter Fleur. Among many brilliant performances, Eric Porter's desiccated Soames stays in the mind. So, too, do the grace of Nyree Dawn Porter as Irene and the brittle gaiety of Susan Hampshire's Fleur. Like the Ewings and the Carringtons, the Forsytes were materially and socially solid and secure. Emotionally they were fragile. That's why watching them was fun.

GAYS

Gay men in soap have come in to Come Out, be a problem to themselves or become problems for other people. While many gay viewers have criticised creations such as Gordon Collins in 'Brookside' and the 'EastEnders' couple Colin and Barry as unconvincing, few will begrudge the writers praise for effort. At least in the late eighties camp comedian Larry Grayson would not be invited to repeat his two appearances in 'Crossroads'. First, at Christmas 1972 he was a flouncing 'difficult' customer. Later he was the pursed-lipped chauffeur at Meg's wedding.

It certainly seemed brave and original of the American writers of 'Dynasty' to portray gay Steven Carrington at first as a thoughtful cultured man, eager to make peace with his homophobic father Blake. His later 'conversion' to heterosexuality and then his dithering over his preferences made him ludicrous. It seemed the writers had lost their nerve. Steven's gayness had caused the Carringtons grief. Blake was charged with murdering Steven's early lover, Ted Dinard. Later his friend Luke Fuller was drawn as another troublemaker. In the wedding massacre in Moldavia, Luke was the only character to be killed and to stay dead.

The Australian soap 'Number 96', which ran from 1972–77, had a gay man, Don Finlayson, the most honest, wise character in the cast. 'We were daring, I suppose,' said producer Peter Benardos. 'But we didn't have him teapotting around the studio. He was a very butch homosexual.'

'Brookside' was the British soap to 'do' homosexuality first, with Gordon, son of the come-down-in-the-world Collinses. Discovering he was gay was a further blow to the parents, another hope dashed. Gordon agonised over wearing a gay badge, fretted when his *Gay Times* was delivered to a neighbour by mistake.

Jonathan Sanders, television critic of *Gay Times* commented: 'His gayness was almost irrelevant.' Jim Wiggins, who plays the father Paul

Collins, said: 'The opportunity was completely wasted. I do think it's totally unrealistic that parents wouldn't talk to each other about something as important as that.'

Of the 'EastEnders' gay couple, graphic designer Colin and young barrow-boy Barry, Sanders comments: 'After the AIDS publicity campaign early in 1987 they tried to integrate Colin and Barry into the story more. In terms of heterosexual audiences it was well done. The character of Dot was used to ridicule the attitudes of the "moral majority". And they tried to move him on from his goody-goody start. But for me they are quite uncaring – hardly able to touch, let alone kiss or do anything remotely sexual. You never get any sense of warmth or intimacy. You certainly do with the other "EastEnders" couples.'

For 'EastEnders' scriptwriter Tony Holland, gay himself, an important character was the drag artist played by David Dale who twice performed at the Vic and shocked the regulars. 'I'd seen David in a documentary in which he said it was his life's ambition to appear in "Coronation Street". So I thought we'd get in first,' said Holland. 'I loved his parting speech about gays not being sexually neutral – that "you mustn't assume because I'm half in make-up, wearing a wig one minute, dressed as a man the next, I'm not a whole person myself". And I liked the way the other men were disturbed by him; some found themselves almost sexually involved. Then he tarted up Sharon, the publican's daughter, with make-up like his – just to twist genders all over the place.'

Whatever viewers or David Dale himself thought of the drag queen, there was more than titillation in the story-line. In the tacky 'Santa Barbara' story of transvestite Dominic/Sophia there wasn't.

By the beginning of 1988 the 'EastEnders' couple Colin and Barry had split after a series of bitter rows. Barry was unable to face a future of ridicule from his working-class father. His attempts to form relationships with girls – one was dithery Donna – continue with difficulty. Colin continues as one of the sages of Albert Square.

In 'Brookside', Gordon and Chris became heroes in 1988 when they sprang Gordon's slightly senile grandmother from an old folks' home where the matron mistreated the inmates.

Lesbians have yet to figure properly in soaps. 'St Elsewhere' had a visiting gay woman doctor who lasted only one episode. 'EastEnders' gave Dr Legg a woman friend in a yellow mac who declared herself gay and then disappeared. In 'Dallas', Barbara Carrera played a murderous Greek shipping tycoon who was having a lesbian affair with her secretary when not seducing JR. With her flamboyant clothes and flying-saucer hat, she was a ridiculous figure. Australia's 'Prisoner: Cell Block H', made in the 1970s, included two characters written as lesbians, their homosexuality being part of their social unacceptability. Carol Burns was Franky Doyle, a biker and a misfit, a tough tormentor and ultimately someone to pity. The second, Joan 'The Freak' Ferguson (Maggie Kirkpatrick) was simply a brute. Lesbians need 'Brookside' or 'EastEnders' to write them as people.

Actors who are gay are often cast completely against type in soap almost as a joke. I can't name all the names because 'coming out' is still liable to limit an actor's future prospects. It's still a brave thing to do. But I can say that in almost every soap there's a gay man playing macho. One of the married men in 'Coronation Street', one of the sturdy chaps striding across the dales in 'Emmerdale Farm', two of the crooks in 'Brookside', for instance. The gay friends of actor Tony Adams used to smile at his role of randy womaniser Adam Chance in 'Crossroads' and Ronald Allen, cast as butch David Hunter, surprised his friends when his relationship with his co-star Sue Lloyd developed.

Far more interesting, though, is the important contribution gay men have made in the development of soap opera. The best 'strong women' characters seem to have been written by them. Three of the most successful soaps seen in Britain were the cherished creations of homosexual men.

'GEMS'

'Gems' is not quite a jewel amongst daytime soaps, but it is certainly a passable imitation. Created by the not so aptly named Tessa Diamond, 'Gems' has nothing to do with emeralds and sapphires but everything to do with the rag trade. Set in the Covent Garden workshop of a young fashion design company, whose label is Gems, this afternoon serial from Thames Television began in January 1985 and has now achieved three series and over a hundred episodes.

The clothes for Gems have been designed by students from the Royal College of Art and are expertly made up. Viewers get the chance to see real collections early, and the cast are able to keep some of the outfits.

Tessa Diamond also created 'Emergency – Ward Ten', while the associate producer on the first series of 'Gems' was Michele Buck who presided over the last rites of 'Crossroads'.

The main characters are the Stone brothers, Stephen and Alan, initially played by Steven Mann and Cornelius Garrett. They ran Gems until Stephen went off to teach at art college. He also had a new actor playing him for the 1988 series: Stuart Fox, who, typically for soaps, bears little resemblance to his predecessor. Other principals include David Savile as Charles Banks, who took over the running of Gems with Alan, and Anjela Belli as design director Christina Scott; and among guest stars was Tracey Childs, the refugee from 'Howards Way'.

Australian audiences enjoy its moderate pace and decent acting. But here 'Gems' just doesn't shine.

'GENERAL HOSPITAL'

'General Hospital' opened five years after 'Emergency – Ward Ten' closed, and, much as Associated Television denied it, it was the same prescription: pretty nurses, handsome doctors and peculiar patients. From September 1972 until March 1975 the course of romance and disease in a Midlands hospital was taken in half-hour doses twice weekly after lunch. Despite the small-scale set (a critic said the action was so cramped it should have been called 'Cottage Hospital') the average 3-million-strong audience felt it did them good. ATV promptly built a bigger, permanent set at Elstree and changed the treatment to thirteen hourly supper-time doses. By now the first batch of actresses playing nurses had left (they included Judy Buxton and Lynda Bellingham), but David Garth as consultant Dr Armstrong, Lewis Jones as prickly Dr Parker-Brown, James Kerry as Dr Baxter, and Tony Adams (p. 161) as Dr Bywaters were firm favourites. For a short time there was a black doctor, and Carmen Munroe was immensely popular as West Indian Sister Washington.

By January 1979 the series was tired, the scripts lifeless and the characters less than addictive. Medical soap had lost its appeal – due partly perhaps to the BBC's documentary series 'Your Life in Their Hands', which showed that there was more gore than glamour in medicine and surgery. In the mid-1980s, 'St Elsewhere', 'The Practice' and 'Casualty' began to revive the appeal of illness drama.

GRANNIES

Soap opera often seems to be the granny society – thick with grand old ladies.

By tradition British soap grannies are crabby. Grandma Grove, played by Nancy Roberts, set the tone in 'The Grove Family': a toothless pest in a shawl who became very popular. 'The Archers' has disapproving Granny Perkins.

'The Newcomers' featured a similar grand-matriarch. 'EastEnders' kept to the style with Lou Beale, a battle-axe who cuts her whole family down to size. Lou's softer side appears as she reminisces about the old days, when the East End seemed to be one giant friendly society. Grannies can be male, too. Albert Tatlock filled the rôle for years in 'Coronation Street'. Most of the time he was a daft and rambling old fool, but sometimes he was used as a wise and cooling influence on headstrong Ken Barlow. (Fascinating to think that Ken is a grandparent himself now.) 'Crossroads' provided a silly-old-bag style of grandmother when Beverley Grice's terrible fault-finding mother appeared.

In 'Dallas' Miss Ellie, mother of Bobby and JR, granny of Lucy, John Ross and Christopher, shows that transatlantic grannies are made of different stuff. Miss Ellie is wise and fair, always ready with quick sympathy for a cut knee or a lost oil empire. Most of us would be happy with a Miss Ellie granny, but they don't seem to exist outside the little square box. Even JR respects Miss Ellie, though he did come over all Oedipal when she married Clayton. Meanwhile, up in the Dales, Annie Sugden shows a different style of grandmotherhood, bossing her children and grandchildren (some of whom seem curiously close in age) with no-nonsense Yorkshire common sense. When Jack's wife Pat was killed in a car crash, Granny Annie brought up their son Robert herself while Jack brooded heavily over the sheep-dip.

In the 'Colbys', Barbara Stanwyck's Connie was white-haired and wise, though not strictly a granny. When her nieces and nephews were in trouble, Sable, their mother, could be guaranteed to make things worse. Connie neutralised her. Alexis in 'Dynasty' must be the world's worst grandmother. She doesn't look the part, for a start. (Grandmother, what big boobs you've got, and it's the wolf who's in danger.) Her idea of being a granny is to arrive with a train of servants bearing expensively wrapped gifts for the grandchild. Before the shiny paper is unpeeled Alexis is snarling at Blake or Krystle. She couldn't change a nappy if she went on a course. 'Neighbours' scored a first with Helen Daniels (Anne Haddy). Not only is she a non-nagging mother-in-law, she is saintly, fair and chic.

'THE GROVE FAMILY'

'The Grove Family' was BBC Television's first soap family for grown-ups. The series, the 'EastEnders' of the 1950s, was born unplanned by a happy accident and was a huge success until it was killed off hastily – its producer's mistake – just over three years later.

Writer Michael Pertwee recalls how he said to his Light Entertainment Department boss, Ronnie Waldman, one day: 'Why don't you have a family?' and was amazed to be told: 'Good idea. Write it.' So he did, with his father Roland, his partner in writing plays. He expected the job to be for thirteen episodes. The first twenty-minute Friday-night story was transmitted live in black and white at 7.50 on 2 April 1954. With short breaks they were writing almost until its end in June 1957.

They called the family the Groves, after BBC's Lime Grove studios, although the exterior shots of their home were of a sturdy double-fronted house in Hendon, North London. The Pertwees aimed to show the small ordinary things which happened to the typical British family who might be watching – a lower-middle-class couple who'd worked hard to build a home for themselves and their family after the war and were just beginning to feel comfortably off after the years of thrift. At one point a wage of £16 a week was mentioned. Mum and Dad – he a jolly, sometimes harassed jobbing builder, she a warm and forthright housewife (Edward Evans and Ruth Dunning) – had just paid off the twenty-year mortgage on the house (repayments £13 8s/£13.40 a month) raised when he began his own business. Their children were Lenny, bright but fib-telling, played by Christopher Beeney, then twelve; scatty Daphne, two years older, played by Margaret Downs; Pat a twenty-year-old assistant librarian, played by Sheila Sweet, who soon became the country's dream girl-next-door. Finally there was Jack, 'one of the lads', doing National Service in the Army. A nosy know-it-all neighbour, Rusty a mongrel puppy, and Nancy Roberts as a crotchety toothless grandmother in a shawl (catchphrase: 'I'm starved for want of nourishment') who stole many a show, completed the permanent cast in the self-contained, often very topical stories the Pertwees devised and scripted at £125 a time.

Instantly liked, it was watched after its first year by almost 9 million people, a quarter of the population. It was second in popularity to the soft-hearted 'Ask Pickles' show, and viewers of all ages wrote angry letters to the BBC about atrociously ungrateful Gran, asked for estimates for building work from Bob Grove, advised Gladys about slimming, Jack about his girls and Pat about her admirers. They held their breath when Ruth Dunning was rushed to hospital with appendicitis. After four weeks, the BBC extended its run and gave the actors a pay rise. The press admired it, and the Queen Mother, who visited the studios, declared herself a fan, calling the family 'so English, so real'. Their only detractors were the Independent Television companies, which had opened in 1955 and tried without success to find a show to match it. Loyal viewers enjoyed, among other stories, Lenny's switch to long trousers, Dad's attempt to give up smoking and the discovery of Gran's true age. She wasn't entitled to a hundredth-birthday party: she was only ninety. (Nancy Roberts was only sixty-one.) Sheila Sweet left; she liked the money to buy taffeta gowns, she said, but she was fed up with Pat. Carole Mowlam took her place. Only a story about two escapees from a lunatic asylum forcing entry into the Grove home, one wielding a meat-axe, upset the fans at home.

Then came the blow. The Pertwees asked to take a break, telling producer John Warrington they were tired. New writers were hired, the slot changed to an earlier one: six o'clock on Wednesdays. Soon the first soap's premature death was decided – to everyone's surprise.

Michael Pertwee recently looked back on events: 'My father and I were just written out after three years. But we felt they were our characters, we'd created them, let them develop according to the way viewers reacted. Gran, for instance, became much more important than we'd first imagined. We asked to oversee the scripts of other writers, but the BBC wouldn't agree. It all got a bit awkward, sour. In a matter of weeks after we'd stopped they decided to end it. I felt sorry; it could have gone on. It was a waste. The people at the BBC then didn't have the foresight, the commercial sense, to see what the people making "Coronation Street" and "Crossroads" saw – that these series can go through quiet spells, but they can survive and last and be important.'

He and Roland declined to write another television series. Edward Evans and Ruth Dunning never achieved such stardom again. Only Christopher Beeney continued, becoming fondly known as the accident-prone under-butler in ITV's 'Upstairs Downstairs' and the gormless nephew in the funeral-parlour comedy 'In Loving Memory'. All that remains of 'The Grove Family' is a short film. No copies of the series exist.

HAIR

Hair in soap opera can be its crowning glory or another story. Cuts and styles are so noticeable in the characters we see week in, week out.

No one could forget Mia Farrow's long blonde tresses in 'Peyton Place' – especially after she switched to a moth-eaten crew-cut. No one could fail to spot and remark on Ivy Tilsley's brown hair which turned golden blonde over night – except all the other characters in 'Coronation Street'. Even Bert, her husband, failed to mention it. (It wasn't in the script, and the potty producer didn't add a quick comment.) Many actresses have new drastic cuts, and their husbands don't even grunt the usual 'How much did that set you back?' let alone pass judgement. Dolly in 'Emmerdale Farm' had one such; so did Sally in 'Coronation Street'.

In 'Coronation Street' and the American soaps, the high proportion of red-headed women never fails to surprise. Is it rust, a side-effect of the scripts, or a conspiracy among television studio hairdressers to make the world ginger?

In 'Dynasty' almost every woman wears a hairpiece. Joan Collins seems to wear several at once (she won't have them called wigs), and her styles switch from short to long with breathtaking speed. Vera and Bet in 'Coronation Street' wear acrylic blonde bubbles, but the dames of 'Dallas' insist their locks are their own. Priscilla Presley's concession to real acting was positively saintly. When Jenna, her character, was gaoled for murdering nasty Naldo, she allowed dark roots to be seen. Three inches of them. Were we glad when she was released, and back on the bottle!

Linda Gray's hair is another 'Dallas' wonder. The stylist must have it in for her. This year Sue Ellen's hair has appeared spouting above one ear or frizzed with fright or scragged back. Donna Mills of 'Knots Landing' wins the Battle of the Bleach hair bravery award, with Linda

327

Evans of 'Dynasty' and her platinum straw coming second.

'Crossroads' has enjoyed a few hair jokes in its time. Remember Rosemary Hunter chopping off her own hair when going nuts? The best giggle (intended) was Mrs Tardebigge's carrot-coloured beehive, burned one day when she cooked her Ron's fish fingers – a great relief to actress Elsie Kelly who bore the weight of it so well. As Barbara Hunter, Sue Lloyd wore a bird's-nest cut and won Telly's Worst Barnet award several years running.

Soap men have always taken to toupees, with varying success. Larry Hagman's hairpieces in 'Dallas' were especially worrying when he repeatedly bubble-bathed with Mandy Winger. Was the glue steam-proof and waterproof, we all puzzled. Alas, it seemed it was. Lloyd Bockner, so briefly Cecil (or 'Seesil' as they called him in 'Dynasty'), kept his brown rug in place between the sheets with Alexis and inside his oxygen-tent. Poor chap, he could never relax. No wonder his heart gave out.

Proving soap opera is good for your scalp is Kevin Dobson. As Mack in 'Knots Landing' his pate is perfectly covered with curls. As Crocker in the earlier-made 'Kojak' (often repeated on the same days as 'Knots Landing' is shown here) our Kev's a baldie. British soap men mostly steer clear of false hair. But Martin Smith as Mickey Doyle, the muscleman of 'Crossroads', wore a convincing wispy fringe. Mike Reid as fat Frank, a heavy in 'EastEnders', sports a threatening flat weave. While Leslie Grantham as Den recedes with resignation.

Amos in 'Emmerdale Farm' wins the Worst Whiskers award, and Ken Masters of 'Howards Way' cops Stupidest Sideboards prize. Were they ever fashionable, I wonder.

Soap's senior hair-salon success? Blue-rinsed Blake in 'Dynasty'.

HEART DISEASE

You've gotta have heart in soap operas. Heart disease, that is, for angina and the coronary are perfect for soap plots. Give a character a heart condition and you've got built-in drama. He may live, he may die, he may collapse at any shock the writers care to engineer.

Stubborn old Lou Beale in 'EastEnders' sits in her chair, irritates her family and blackmails them with the threat of a sudden and dramatic attack. In 'Dallas', Clayton Farlow has a weak heart despite that big tough frame, which means that Miss Ellie always has something to worry about. (So did we, when Clayton cavorted with a girl young enough to be his grand-daughter.) We feared Clayton was in for a really heart-stopping climax, but the old ticker performed well, even if Clayton didn't. Podgy grocer Alf Roberts in 'Coronation Street' had the most convincing heart attack I've ever seen, just after Deirdre Barlow toppled him from the local council. Alf could be used in government health-warning ads: 'overweight, raised on fatty foods and given to apoplectic outbursts'. The collapse was well done, the recovery a little too rapid. Martha Longhurst, as I recall, died of a heart attack by falling into her beer in an early episode, right there in the Rover's. The complaints taught Granada a lesson. People don't enjoy well-liked characters dying without warning. They like a little build-up, for a really satisfying demise. 'Crossroads' managed the most melodramatic coronary when Hugh Mortimer, one of Meg's husbands, produced it while being held by kidnappers. Double points there, I think.

'HOWARDS WAY'

'Howards Way' is the awfully British one about boats, boardrooms, expensive frocks and fraught affairs. From its start in September 1985, around 12 million devotees pretended to laugh at the torrid entanglements of Tarrant, a fictional south-coast gin-and-Jag town, while secretly taking it seriously. By its third season in 1987 it was an established BBC hit, the on- and off-screen pairings of the cast reported in the tabloids and followed almost as avidly as the nightlife of Joan Collins (on whom it can probably be blamed). 'Howards Way' was created in answer to glamorous American sagas about the rich, such as 'Dynasty' and 'Dallas', by that seasoned soap and suspense purveyor Gerald Glaister, who produced the similar saga 'The Brothers' a decade before. With writer Allan Prior and a £2 million budget he brought us another family in crisis: square-jawed and successful aircraft-designer Tom Howard (Maurice Colbourne) made suddenly redundant; a decorous homebody wife Jan (Jan Harvey) about to blossom; a statuesque sailing-mad daughter Lynne (Tracey Childs) and student-son Leo (Edward Highmore) about to drop out. There was also a brick of a mother-in-law Kate (Dulcie Gray) who gambled. Into their lives came beautiful Avril Rolfe (Susan Gilmore) and her gruff Scotch-swigging father Jack (Glyn Owen, formerly of 'The Brothers' and 'Emergency – Ward Ten'), owner of the failing Mermaid Boat Yard. There was also a collection of boats, insured for £40 million, notably *Flying Fish* and *Barracuda*, the choppy waters of the Solent and several grandly furnished drawing-rooms to admire. Soon Tom had sunk his money into the Mermaid and fallen for Avril; Jan had become a boutique manageress and the mistress of her boss Ken Masters, a ghastly go-getter with jewellery (Stephen Yardley); listless Leo had discovered his girlfriend, awkward Abby, was pregnant by someone else; and Lynne, who'd earlier declared, 'Daddy, I don't think I could ever love

330

any man as much as I love the *Flying Fish*,' had tumbled into an affair with millionaire tycoon Charles Freer (Tony Anholt). The thirteen-part series ended as she discovered Freer making love on his yacht to a stranger in black lacy underwear – his wife! Lynne ran tearfully along the jetty and fell into the harbour.

In the year she spent apparently underwater, awaiting rescue, tourist trips at £60 a head around Bursledon, Hampshire, the real Tarrant, were in great demand, much to the annoyance of the local council. (A steep rise in property prices in the area helped to calm them.) The second series began in September 1986 after a repeat showing of the cliffhanger – a sign that the BBC at last accepted the fun of soap. With the exception of a ship's figurehead used in the opening titles (too many critics had joked that it looked like a man with an impressive bust), it was the recipe as before. Lynne completed a lone Atlantic voyage, arriving in New York looking so neat and well groomed that pigtailed Claude Du Pont (Malcolm Jamieson), her mother's French dress-designer partner, fell instantly in love with her. Tom's boat was sabotaged. Jack drank the Mermaid's profits. Kate lost her home on a horse, and Abby had her baby then gave it over to its American father. Jan and Ken pretended to sunbathe in Cannes in 90° (clearly it was somewhere near Southampton in 45°), and after a lavish wedding for Lynne and her small pigtailed Frenchman he was run over by a speedboat while water-skiing and killed. By now the fans also knew that off camera Tracey Childs and Tony Anholt were a couple as were Jan Harvey and Stephen Yardley.

By the third season Tracey Childs had quit, claiming fame was too stressful. But it started well, beating ITV's opposition, Joan Collins in 'Sins', by more than 2 million in the ratings. Tom and Avril split. Jan and Ken split. Leo acquired a beautiful rich wife promised to another. Nigel Davenport came in as the stately-home-owning swinish tycoon father of Freer. Gerald Urquart, Abby's father, Freer's accountant, produced a dying gay lover; and Jan invested in the Mermaid Yard, snapping her manicured fingers and sending Jack back on the booze. With healthy audiences, a 1988 series was assured, the whole thirteen episodes budgeted at under £3 million – approximately the price of one episode of 'Dallas'. 'It's quite a bargain,' said Gerald Glaister.

Jan Harvey is the neat Cornish-born actress who became Britain's favourite housewife turned tycoon turned sexpot as Jan in the boats-and-beds soap 'Howards Way'. The fact that the former school-teacher had been twice divorced and, by the second series, had allowed her on-screen affair with wide boy Ken Masters (Stephen Yardley) to spill over into her private life added piquantly to her allure and swelled her fan club's membership.

At first the wife deserted for a younger woman, Jan Howard dried her tears and began running a fashion boutique. By the third series she had survived several affairs and business and family disasters. Flanked by her genteel brick of a-mother (a sort of plucky Mrs Dale played with a point-to-point accent by veteran stage-actress Dulcie Gray), she passes all the Soap Strong Women tests of toughness, frankness, fairness and guilt. And her clothes sense scores honours.

Jan Harvey reckons the soap is a success because half the cast are women, all gainfully employed. 'They aren't just putting the food on the table when their man comes home at the end of the day.' She adds: 'I'm not like her. I forget the phone calls, drive off and leave my handbag on the pavement.' Her first outing on a fast-moving trimaran for the show proved she was no natural sailor – a failing she shared with most of her co-stars, whose weediness on the waves gives the locals who loan the boats many a laugh.

A seasoned television actress before 'Howards Way', the forty-year-old actress hopes to return to the classics one day. 'Hopefully Mrs Howard will only be a little capsule in my career,' she said.

INTENSIVE CARE

Intensive care, medical treatment with knobs on, is what almost always follows soap accidents. More of our sympathy can go out to the victim when he or she lies still in a hospital room, attached by wires to banks of sinister surgical boxes, eerily plinking and pumping. There's no call in soap for ordinary medical care in wards with bedpans, sour-faced nurses and cups of terrible tea from auxiliaries.

American soap opera has always been keen on intensive care, giving almost every character a turn amidst the machines. 'Dallas' is set almost as often in Dallas Memorial as it is at Southfork. British soaps use this main line to melodrama more and more. Here are a few intensively enjoyed intensive-care episodes.

In 'Emmerdale Farm', accident-prone Jackie Merrick was laid up in intensive care after stopping by the roadside for a pee and being run down by a slightly tipsy Alan Turner. In 'Coronation Street', Bert Tilsley (actor Peter Dudley) played his last scenes horizontally in 1984. He'd been the victim of a garage explosion, a mental breakdown and then a stroke. In 'Crossroads', Diane also left the series via intensive care. Her fate was a cerebral haemorrhage. After the first shots of her strapped up to the machines the drama then shifted to the other characters who had to decide when to turn them off.

'Brookside' added to this plot-line in 1987. Its heroine, Laura, became the second woman in soap to electrocute herself (the first was Valerie Barlow in 'Coronation Street' in 1971). Beautiful new bride Laura touched a wrongly wired light-switch and qualified for intensive care. Over several weeks of the plinking and blinking, her handsome husband Jonathan had to decide when to order the plugs to be pulled. Finally he gave the word, but heroically he did not tell Laura's heartbroken father the truth about her accident. This was that it was he who'd caused the death by tampering with the light-switch.

'EastEnders' put Angie in intensive care when her gin consumption caused kidney failure early in 1988. Unlike American soap queens, Angie had to look like a patient, too. She had to have her eye make-up surgically removed for two episodes.

All the principals in 'Dallas' have been wired up at some time, but you can't see the scars. Jock had a heart bypass; Miss Ellie had a mastectomy; JR had everything following the shooting by Kristin; Bobby had to recover from both a shooting and an operation to cure his blindness; and Pam had the works following her car accident and burnings. Only little Mickey Trotter, Ray's nephew and Lucy's boyfriend, had the plugs pulled. He landed in Dallas Memorial after trying heroically to save Sue Ellen from driving when drunk. The car they were in was hit by another, and Mickey was paralysed. Mickey decided he no longer wanted to live, and Ray switched off his life-support, landing himself in gaol for his pains.

'Dynasty' uses intensive care less often, but wrings more from every plink. Dominique underwent throat surgery without an eyelash disturbed; Fallon's prematurely born and sickly baby Lauren looked helpless amid the machines; and Krystle's baby Christina not only endured treatment after birth involving the best medical brains of the world but also underwent a heart transplant, causing the mother of another child to grieve dramatically over her decision to stop the machines keeping her daughter alive.

But 'Knots Landing' wins my prize for the most affecting hospital death, that of road-crash victim Sid Fairgate. He was seen covered in a green operating-theatre sheet on a trolley as the camera panned away, leaving him pathetically alone.

INTERNATIONAL SOAP

Soap goes around the world. From Rochdale to Rio, viewers get themselves in a lather about soaps.

America is the home of the soap opera, and its programmes are sold world-wide. It has been estimated that 50 million Americans (that's one in five of the population) watch a soap at least once a week. The major American soaps ('Dallas', 'Dynasty' and the like) are dealt with elsewhere in this book, but others worthy of mention are the most popular daily soap, 'The Young and the Restless', which has clocked up over 4000 episodes since its creation in 1973 and which is known as 'Febbre d'Amore' in Italy; 'Rituals', which flopped in America but is proving far more successful in Italy, Spain and most of Latin America; 'Loving', sold to France and Italy; and 'Ryan's Hope', which can be seen in Ireland.

Brazilian serials are called *telenovelas* and the television company Globo has cornered the market in them. Every night Globo transmits three and a half hours of back-to-back *telenovelas*, and their programmes have been shown in eighty countries. The *telenovelas* are used like commercials to sell products and are sponsored by various companies. Honda sponsored one called 'The Steel Horse', so a Honda motorbike was heavily featured in nearly every episode. Merchandising has long since taken control of the narrative in Brazilian soaps. It has now got to the stage where it commands the plots, too. A couple of *telenovelas* have been screened here on Channel 4: 'Dancin' Days', set in a disco, and 'Slave-Girl Isaura' about a white slave on a Brazilian plantation in the nineteenth century.

Other leading lights are Australia, France, Germany and Japan, where soaps are termed 'home dramas' and where the most famous is 'Oshin' about a girl in slavery at the turn of the century.

Apart from 'Châteauvallon', the most popular 'soapy' series in France is 'Maguy' (pronounced 'Maggie'), a comedy about a middle-aged matron. It is based on the American sitcom 'Maude', which itself was a spin-off from 'All in the Family', which in turn was a transatlantic version of our own 'Till Death Us Do Part'. By my reckoning, this makes Maguy a cousin twice removed of Alf Garnett!

'Maude' was shown in the States from 1972 to 1978 and starred Bea Arthur (tall deep-voiced Dorothy in 'The Golden Girls') as the posh outspoken cousin of awful Archie Bunker's wife. Maude was living with her fourth husband. 'Maguy', set among the Paris middle-classes, stars former stage-actress Rosie Varte with Jean Marc Thibeault as her stupid husband. This witty series was originally shown weekly, but public demand has led to it being screened daily for the past four years. One out of four French viewers watches 'Maguy' on Antenne 2, giving it better ratings there than the likes of 'Dallas' or 'Dynasty'.

KIDNAPPING

Kidnapping is so common in soap opera, you could swear the writers hate kids. Obviously they know the intense fear and agony parents have of losing a child. Adults are abducted, too, in soap, but it's rarely as scary.

In British soaps the kidnapping tends to be the more everyday tug-of-love kind. In 'EastEnders', Mary's baby Annie was taken by her mother and not returned for months. In 'Coronation Street', Brian Tilsley dashed off with son Nicky to wife Gail's distress. Neither event had the emotional charge of the irrational snatching of the Hewitts' son Christopher from his pram in 'Coronation Street' in 1962 – not surprisingly, an episode with one of the show's highest-ever ratings. In 'Crossroads', Diane's son Nicky was kidnapped by his pop-star father, taken to America and never seen again. Similarly Jill's children in that soap lived always with their father abroad. It certainly made things simpler for the producers. Babies on sets are difficult, noisy and expensive (minimum fees are £100 an episode), and recording scenes involving them is often a painfully slow process. (They will keep looking at their real mothers and covering the props with chocolate, and they're bad at learning their lines.) In 'Coronation Street', Tracey managed to 'kidnap' herself. She disappeared somewhere in the Barlows' little house for almost a year, then reappeared with a new face.

In the American soaps the richer children are snatched, but rarely for ransom. In 'Falcon Crest', Richard Channing's son Michael, nabbed by gangsters for money, was an exception. Crazy Claudia stole Fallon's first baby and pretended to drop him from a skyscraper roof. In fact she dropped a doll. Power-mad JR snatched his own son John Ross from Sue Ellen when divorcing her and was behind the removal of Christopher, his brother Bobby's adopted son, by the child's real aunt. In 'Knots Landing', Abby's husband 'stole' her children, Olivia and Ben, then

Abby was kidnapped herself by Mark St Claire. Later, to even the score perhaps, she arranged the theft of Valene's twins.

In 'Dallas', Miss Ellie was taken to a motel by Clayton's mad sister in the boot of a car; while, in 'Dynasty', Alexis was grabbed by soldiers after the Moldavian massacre, but escaped disguised as a nun. Poor Krystle, also taken, was left to wail.

Both 'Dallas' and 'Dynasty' ended series this year with kidnapping dramas, for vengeance rather than ransoms. JR whisked John Ross to a boarding school 'somewhere' to spite Sue Ellen who had just thwarted his attempts to take over Weststar Oil. A desperate Sue Ellen enlisted her mafia man lover Nicholas Pearce to help reclaim the boy.

In 'Dynasty' the kidnap of Adam's newborn son by a surrogate mother was a water drama, building on the success of the previous series' cliffhanger, 'drowning' Alexis. This time the villain was the hero of the 'drowning' – Alexis's new husband, Sean, secretly out to avenge the death of his father, the Carrington's former butler Joseph Anders. The babysnatch led to a fight by a river's edge and the infant, tossed into a canoe, was swept away by the current. Perhaps because the months of suspense would have been too harrowing for viewers, we saw Adam save the babe and former enemy Steven tenderly dry him. Pity he was so obviously a doll, though.

But my favourite soap kidnapping – inventive, funny and sad – was the 1979 snatch of Coronation Street's Bet Lynch during Weatherfield Rag Week. She was held to ransom for £20. The Rover's regulars raised only £4.56 to set her free!

KILLING THEM OFF

Killing them off is usually the producer's revenge in soap opera. When an actor asks for more pay or more say the reply can be a violent death for his character.

Actor Stephen Hancock asked to renegotiate his contract when he played Ernie Bishop in 'Coronation Street'. The producers believed he was leading a small revolt among the cast, many of whom felt an unfair two-tier pay-structure existed. Hancock was a musician, too – he played the piano accompaniment when Rita Fairclough sang. He considered that made him special. The producers decided he was specially pushy. In a short time Bishop was facing a sawn-off shotgun in a post office raid. He fell dead – and the rumblings over the cast's pay stopped dead, too.

Susan Hanson, Miss Diane in 'Crossroads', asked for the same pay as the former leading lady Gabrielle Drake. Producer William Smethurst had a better idea. Miss Diane developed a headache. That turned into a brain haemorrhage and farewell! To seal the producer's revenge, the show's dimwit Benny named a donkey after her.

Jane Cunliffe who played Laura in 'Brookside' incurred the producer's punishment after she asked to leave. Her character had only just arrived but Jane was unhappy in Liverpool and less than smitten with Steven Pinner, who played her husband. To humiliate her, she was killed off after several months of vegetable life in intensive care.

It's not always a row over money. Helen Weir's character, Pat Sugden, in 'Emmerdale Farm' died swiftly when she refused to have her baby son, also a character, called a different name from his own.

The adding of shame to a character's formerly good reputation is a sort of double killing when a soap star and his bosses fall out. In 'Coronation Street', Len Fairclough was killed in a car crash and his character besmirched when it was revealed that he had a mistress. This was a second blow to his widow, the much-admired Rita. The reason for Fairclough's death was known to be the sacking of actor Peter Adamson, who played him. His soap crime was to have sold his views to a newspaper, something which was forbidden in his contract. The real cause of his television death was the 'swimming-pool' court-case, in which he was accused, then acquitted, of indecently assaulting two children.

Actors 'die' sometimes of their own free will – a sort of character suicide. In 'Knots Landing', Sid Fairgate expired on a hospital operating-table, a moving scene. Don Murray, who played him, wanted to leave. Daphne in 'Neighbours' also died in hospital after a car crash. She wanted to leave and suggested to the writers that her death leaving her soap husband to bring up their baby would be a strong plot. They agreed.

Linda Evans gave the writers a headache at the end of the last 'Dynasty' series. She was uncertain about her future in the rôle. (The rival CBS network had offered her a mini-series deal.) They coped by giving Krystle a headache – a strange, persistent one which could be turned into something fatal. If she does die, though, you can bet she'll do it smiling.

Occasionally a character has to die because it's time for a death in the script. Andy in 'EastEnders' was killed because he was happy. In soap, happiness can't last, because happiness is boring to watch.

Sometimes when an actor dies the character is not continued. It may be decided viewers would hate him to be played by another actor. Jim Davis, Jock in 'Dallas', died in 1981 of heart disease. The character was kept alive at the end of a telephone for several episodes, then lost in a jungle, presumed dead. His portrait – medallion and hat glistening – hangs in J.R. Ewing's office still. A respectful tribute, yes. But it didn't mean Jock's possible return from the dead had been ruled out for a later date when Jim Davis had been forgotten. One impostor – Wes Parmalee – has already wormed his way into Miss Ellie's life. Perish the thought, but Jock's death could still be revealed as a dream.

THE KISS

The Kiss in soap has to be soothing, suggestive and satisfying. Because, as far as sex goes, it's all there is. Soap sex is something that happens to make families happen, keep families going or break them up. True to the old-fashioned morality soap operas push, sex is rarely just pleasurable. If young characters think about it too much, it's an illness to be cured straight away.

'Emmerdale Farm' is the least sexually inhibited of British soaps. Jack Sugden was seen between the sheets with a range of women and he was still their Good Guy. But Jackie Merrick and Kathy Bates were exponents of the classic Young Soap Lovers' Kiss. Theirs was by a lock with a waterfall, to swelling music, one long kiss followed by puppy-like smiles, rubbed noses and another long kiss as the cameras fade. Aah!

In 'Crossroads', Jill and Adam Chance's wedding-day kiss was another classic: hesitation, lowered eyes rising to a devoted trance, then the kiss as the frame is frozen.

In 'Knots Landing', Gary Ewing and his ex-wife Val enjoyed an extra-long smacker on their one-night reunion. We were meant to remember it. Val became pregnant and had twins.

Oldsters get to kiss passionately, too, because producers know many regular fans are pensioners. Among those kisses teenagers squirmed at were Miss Ellie and Clayton's in 'Dallas', and, in 'The Colbys', seventy-nine-year-old Barbara Stanwyck as Connie kissing her ancient cowboy Hutch. He was urging her to come away with him in his caravan 'while we're still young enough for everything'. *Everything*?

Among the protested-about kisses were the twin puckerings in 'Coronation Street' of Elsie Tanner with Alan Howard and Deirdre with her then husband Ray 'the rat' Langton. Both couples were clamped at the mouth as Rita Fairclough sang. Disgusting, they called it! Another shocker was Sue Ellen kissing her toy-boy lover Peter in 'Dallas'.

Had Alexis in 'Dynasty' merely kissed Cecil Colby the night before their wedding, he might still be here to count his millions. But, guarding her lip-gloss, the couple swirled in the satin sheets. The anxiety he suffered in keeping his toupee in place caused a heart attack. She couldn't even kiss him at their wedding. He was in an oxygen-tent, a mask on his mouth.

Soap's most notorious kiss – tagged the 'kiss of death' – came when Rock Hudson kissed Linda Evans in the hay in 'Dynasty'. Hudson knew he had AIDS when he began his cameo appearances as the millionaire adventurer Daniel Reece. He did not inform his co-stars. It's not clear how much danger of contracting the disease Hudson put Linda Evans under. Hudson's long experience as a screen lover paid off. He knew how to plant his mouth on her cheek near her mouth (indistinguishable from the real thing on camera). But his death, less than six months after the filming, in October 1985, led the American studios to cut down the kissing. Donna Mills, who plays Abby in 'Knots Landing', the nymphomaniac of American soap commented: 'AIDS has spread so much I don't want to kiss anyone new on the show.'

'KNOTS LANDING'

'Knots Landing' is the nearest the Americans can bear to get to a soap about ordinary people. By 'ordinary' they mean no one in it has a private jet. Yet.

The five neighbouring families who live on a plateau in the hills of the southern Californian coastline in a cul-de-sac may be the poor relations of the super-loaded Ewings and Carringtons – some of the women have their original noses! – but their houses are large luxury versions of the 'Neighbours' homes, and the Grants' house in 'Brookside' could fit into one of the 'Knots Landing' kitchens. Still, if the creator, David Jacobs, and his Lorimar bosses want to bang on about Gary and Val, Karen and Mack, Abby, Laura, Lilimae and all being 'middle class', let them. We know that if they had less money and leisure, cut the psychobabble, went to football and watched 'Coronation Street' they'd be lots happier. But, then, happiness can be fatal in soap, as we know.

Happiness nearly sank the 'Knots Landing' nits. But, first, the beginning.

The ground was cleared in America in 1979 by the success of 'Dallas'. That show had proved, for the first time since 'Peyton Place' ended ten years before, that people would follow serials in the evenings. There, 'Dallas', 'Dynasty' and the other glossy soaps are considered 'adult' entertainment, suitable only for screening after 9 p.m., usually at 10 p.m. (In more mature Britain, they are always shown in the semi-serious 8 p.m. slot.)

'Knots Landing' was dubbed 'Son of "Dallas"' but was, if anything, 'Dad of "Dallas"' because Jacobs had outlined his saga, based loosely on the Swedish *Scenes from a Marriage*, before something bigger and brasher – 'Dallas' – was ordered. When 'Dallas II' seemed like a bright idea to the CBS network, the 'Knots Landing' presentation came out of the bottom drawer. Jacobs went to work.

343

The starting-point was Gary Ewing, alcoholic no-good son of the millionaire Ewings, who remarried his waitress teenage bride Valene after Miss Ellie's intervention and moved south to where Bobby Ewing had constructed a bunch of houses on twenty acres of family-owned land. Gary and Val left their troublesome daughter Lucy at Southfork, though she and her uncles dropped in from time to time.

The neighbours were Karen and Sid, who owned the local garage where Gary worked, Richard and Laura, a crazy lawyer and his battered wife who had to pick up men at a military base for revenge, and a young recording executive and his wife who moved away. Later Abby Cunningham, Sid's divorced sister, a scheming blonde man-eater, arrived to tantalise and terrify all the men. Like 'Dynasty', 'Knots Landing' improved with a large dash of female nastiness.

Gloom descended with the death of sober solid Sid in hospital after a road crash. (The actor who played him, Don Murray, had wanted to leave.) Wonderful Julie Harris was brought in as bible-bashing Lilimae, Val's mother; and, as Gary submitted to Abby's sexy ploys, Val became a bestselling novelist, discovered Gary's betrayal and left him.

At this point American audiences began to yawn, the network was about to cancel the show and the BBC, which had run it since 1980 in its main Saturday-night slot, lost interest completely. Audiences for 'Dallas' had fallen, and ratings for 'Dallas-on-Sea' slumped, too. David Jacobs told me: '"Knots Landing" is about modern marriage and trying to live in a community, but there was nothing to laugh at, it was too straight. We'd lost our most sympathetic male character, and our women viewers weren't getting what they wanted: misery.' The solutions made 'Knots Landing' the most improved of the American soaps. In its sixth year it beat both 'Dallas' and 'Dynasty', to become that nation's favourite night-time soap.

The solutions were simple. In came a new Mr Nice, Mack Mackenzie (Kevin Dobson), for Karen (Michele Lee); in came a sexpot, Ciji (Lisa Hartman); in came a new Mr Nasty, corrupt politician Greg Sumner (William Devane); and in came two celebrities, Ava Gardner as a mischievous widow, wreathed in sinister cigarette-smoke, and film heart-throb Michael York as a devious publisher.

After Karen's near-terminal happiness with Mack, she suffered every disaster in the soap book. The triangular traumas of Gary, Val and Abby multiplied. There were murders, trials, drug problems, custody battles, kidnappings galore. And they doubled their spending on the dresses after Donna Mills requested it. 'I screamed and howled,' she said. (See 'Clothes'.)

Michele Lee said the reason the show works is that 'Knots Landing' still has 'ordinary' believable people living in it. 'We are adults dealing with situations anyone can believe,' she said. 'My character went through the heartache of losing a husband. She didn't swan around in slinky négligées, eat caviare and gaze droopy-eyed into young men's eyes.' H'm.

So far the new improved action of this biological soap hasn't washed with the BBC. They did bring it back from 1987, but they run it at lunch-time, and British viewers are years behind. Only if 'Dallas' or 'Dynasty' is dropped in America will these poor middle-class folk be famous in Britain again.

Michele Lee did something important for soap opera when she badgered the 'Knots Landing' producers to feature female friends.

Michele plays earth mother Karen Fairgate Mackenzie, whose list of misfortunes is nearly as long as her neighbour Valene Ewing's. (In not necessarily this order, Karen has been widowed, has overcome drug dependency, been seriously wounded, given only months to live, been kidnapped, trapped in a blazing house and made to panic as Diana, her daughter, ran off with the dastardly Chip.)

All of this Michele has enjoyed. But what sent her back and forth to the producers' office was her belief that the show's vast numbers of women viewers needed to see women depending on other women. She insisted on at least one scene between Karen and Valene each episode. 'You have the Cagneys and Laceys [the television women cop buddies] of the world, but in the soap opera genre you have no other girlfriend relationship like Karen and Valene's,' she said.

'Knots Landing' is perhaps the only soap opera where the actors are encouraged to tell the producers and writers what they think their characters should do. There are even episodes which are largely improvised – the actors providing their own dialogue as they think fits the situation. One such improvised episode was the one, yet to be seen in Britain, portraying events after Laura (Constance McCashin) dies of a brain tumour. One result is that Karen and Mack get to adopt Laura's new baby.

Michele, is a former Broadway star, a singer, and the 1982 winner of an Emmy for her 'Knots Landing' rôle, takes all this in her stride. 'So long as I know where Karen is going, I tend to like it,' she said.

Donna Mills plays a special kind of soap bitch in 'Knots Landing'. This one likes sex as sex, not sex as power. She also wears more eye make-up than Boy George. 'I love Abby,' said the slim forty-four-year old Chicago actress. 'I love her naughtiness, her open sexuality and her intelligence. If people get in her way, she just brushes them aside. But she's manipulative in a way that's charming.' Abby first pursued Richard, then Gary, moved on to Greg, back to Gary, seduced JR when he dropped in and managed meanwhile to run a cable television super-station, arrange the kidnap of Val's twins and try to break up the marriage of Greg and Laura.

Donna was originally a dancer, hit New York at eighteen, quickly getting into commercials and soaps, including a three-year rôle which may have been a sort of training (by deprivation) for Abby. In 'Love Is a Many Splendored Thing', she played a nun. Then she did a short series with Larry Hagman, 'The Good Life', followed by twenty-one television movies in eight years. 'No girl on TV has ever been raped, strangled, assaulted, kidnapped, beaten or killed more than I,' she said. 'You can see why I wanted Abby so badly.'

Ted Shackelford plays the sexiest wimp in soap opera, but his character Gary Ewing in 'Knots Landing' would go back to the booze if he knew.

Tall blond Ted, who was educated in Denver, won his soap spurs in the daytime serial 'Another World' before moving to Hollywood on Christmas Day 1975, where television rôles came thick and fast. David Ackroyd (a co-star on 'Another World') originated the rôle of Gary Ewing, the thin-skinned washout of the Ewing family in 'Dallas', but Ted took over, becoming the main man of 'Knots Landing' from 1979.

Gary was a weak son, a failed husband, father and friend, an adulterer, an indifferent garage mechanic, but a spectacular drunk. He could fight and rage like Sue Ellen, Angie Watts and the regulars of the Rover's Return rolled into one. Then they sent him to Alcoholics Anonymous, he sobered up, became a dedicated environmentalist and managed to be charged with murder and mess up his life in other ways. He drank again and was dried out, again.

Like Gary, Ted is a recovered alcoholic – he makes educational films on the subject – and he's also a campaigner for wildlife and the ecological state of the world. In episodes yet to be shown here, Gary becomes tougher. 'He becomes the Ewing he never wanted to become: power-mad, compulsive, ruthless,' he said.

One thing they couldn't change was his height: six feet three inches. When his diminutive television daughter Lucy visits Knots Landing, she has to stand on a box or look him straight in the navel.

Joan Van Ark deserves sympathy for her soap sufferer, Knots Landing's good wife, Valene Ewing.

Our Val was married at fifteen; had a daughter of restricted growth; was turfed out to California by JR; and lost her alcoholic husband to a minx who wears make-up by the kilo. Her nagging mother moved in; her long-lost psychotic television-evangelist brother turned up. She had a breakdown and thought her name was something even worse than Valene – Verna. And, if that wasn't enough, she spent about twenty episodes fretting about the reported death of her newborn twins which her ex-husband's wife had fixed to be sold. Valene wears the sort of folksye cotton frocks the Stepford Wives wore after their operations. In other words she needs help.

Happily, award-winning Yale Drama School graduate Joan Van Ark doesn't. She has been married to the same man for over twenty years, has never lost her teenage daughter, and never thought her name was Verna. But she believes Valene is 'real' and her situations are those 'the audience can relate to'. She added: 'Money isn't the central theme – that distinguishes our show.'

LIFE AFTER SOAP

Life after soap? There isn't any. Well, not life with fame and money. The actors and actresses who walk out of soap parts expect new offers to pour in. Mostly they don't. What almost always awaits the household name who decides to move on is a long rest, a theatre tour and perhaps a guest spot in someone else's television series.

It was always so. Whoever heard of anything from Maggie Fitzgibbon (p.383) after she walked boldly away from 'The Newcomers'? Or from Justine Lord (p.205) when she decided 'The Doctors' was cramping her style? Lewis Jones had to go on the dole after six years of stardom in 'General Hospital'. Robin Chadwick, the pin-up of 'The Brothers', was reduced to labouring on a building site. Patrick O'Connell, who played his brother in that, also dropped out and was never top of a television bill again.

We soap fans, it seems, are an unforgiving lot. When a favourite actor or actress quits, we feel snubbed. The soap is still good enough for us. Why has this bighead rejected it? Was it simply greed for more money? Producers know this and realise that the novelty value of ex-soapers wears off fast. At the height of 'EastEnders' mania, former cast members Ross Davidson and Shirley Cheriton (p.274), a glamorous enough couple, reasonably expected their tour with the play *Monkey Years* would bring in the crowds. It flopped.

There were no glittering new opportunities for once-adored Pat Phoenix after she let Elsie Tanner emigrate. Fellow former 'Coronation Street' favourite Peter Adamson had to go to Canada to find regular work – a search which has so far been unsuccessful for Fred Feast, the former Rover's barman. After life as fat Eddie for ten years, Geoffrey Hughes is almost unknown to television, even if the theatre always has room for fatsos.

Total obscurity awaited Ronald Allen and Sue Lloyd after 'Crossroads' despite their wide experience in television and films before it. Possible parts in American series came to nothing. In Australia, Francis Bell was 'rested' from television despite being the best thing in the early 'Neighbours'. Carol Burns, so impressive in 'Prisoner: Cell Block H', failed to impress television producers after that.

In American soaps, it's the same story. Al Corley and Pamela Sue Martin didn't make it in the movies after quitting 'Dynasty'. Patrick Duffy may, as he claimed, or may not have made more money in the year he was dead in 'Dallas'. He certainly achieved nothing to convince film or television audiences that he was anything more exciting than a reborn Bobby Ewing under different names. No one signed him for a major series. Charlene Tilton struggled 'taking acting classes' in the years she was out of favour as Lucy Ewing, and I'm glad Susan Howard, Donna in 'Dallas' for so long, has a strong religious faith. She was dropped. She'll probably need it.

Even a bright and pretty actress such as Amanda Burton, who left 'Brookside' relatively early, has appeared only in small cameo rôles in more than two years. Will Jean Alexander be forgiven for dumping Hilda Ogden? Perhaps – but I doubt whether the 'serious work' in plays she fancies will be easy to find. Hilda may live in the memory; Jean will be forgotten.

One exception to this, one system-beater, may be Victoria Principal, loved as Pam in 'Dallas'. By the time we watched them bring her to hospital after her car smash, burned to a crisp and never likely to be the same again, she had produced and co-starred in a mini-series and was confident of greater deals to come. We'll see.

LONG-LOST RELATIVES

Long-lost relatives turn up so often in soap opera, I can only conclude that carelessness over losing family members is catching. I suppose we can't blame Alexis and Blake in 'Dynasty', for example, for losing two of their four children (Adam and Amanda) then forgetting to mention them for twenty-odd years. Blame it on the scriptwriters, who reckon a dramatic entry of a newcomer likely to arouse strong emotions, disrupt pecking orders and property claims every now and then is no bad thing.

'EastEnders' hasn't been above this most unlikely device: planting young Donna in Albert Square and after months of hinting, revealing that she's the child Kathy Beale gave birth to after a rape. This soap has also unearthed Pete's long-lost first wife (Pat) and his long-lost (or long-emigrated) brother Kenny. Their arrival successfully produced fights, guilt and raised hackles.

In 'Emmerdale Farm', Dolly's illegitimate son Graham Lodsworth yomped over the dales and seemed sinister for weeks before revealing his identity. And, if the writers are ever stuck for a story-line about Sandie Merrick, the child she had adopted will be there on her doorstep with a suitcase.

'Crossroads' probably had more long-lost relatives in its time than any others. Doris Luke's spooky sister and niece, Edna and Gloria Tilling, moved into Long Brough Cottage. Stan Harvey's supposedly dead brother Len reappeared, as did Meg's second husband Malcolm Ryder (also thought to have died abroad). He tried to stop her marriage to Hugh Mortimer, then to poison her. Naturally. Miss Diane's cocky cockney brother Terry and uncle turned up. So did Paul Ross's instant daughter – by coincidence, of course. In 'Coronation Street', Audrey Roberts developed an unexpected long-lost son in Canada. It served to liven her up.

Krystle in 'Dynasty' had rotten luck with returning long-lost relatives.

349

Enter first her trashy niece Sammy Jo; then her first husband, Mark Jennings. Blake had his share of shocks. A long-lost brother from Australia and Dominique Deveraux who declared herself his sister. All right, so she was black. But did she have to sing those awful songs, too?

And, in 'Dallas', JR greeted his cousins (not so much long-lost as never heard of before) Jamie and Jack Ewing as warmly as he would a pair of lepers. Yet all they did was to demand a share in the Ewing fortune and divide the family. So Jamie married Cliff Barnes, the enemy, and Jack involved JR with two murderous lesbian Greek shipping tycoons. That's all.

LOSS OF MEMORY

Loss of memory happens so often to people in soap opera, it's a wonder JR hasn't had a mind-block and turned up surfing in 'Neighbours' or Lofty didn't blurt out his feelings for Alexis. Amnesia must be high on the list of soap plots (when writers are stuck) – so useful to tag on to the end of a disaster or explosion, providing such relief when the victim's brain clicks back.

Good characters suffer memory-losses so that baddies can trick them and we caring viewers can worry. When characters can't remember their name and what has happened in their life, the writers can have people remind them – and us.

Blake Carrington, hero of 'Dynasty', lost his memory partially, after an oil-rig blew up. Saved by brother Ben, kidnapped by awful Alexis, the poor bloke thought he was still married to her (a delusion she encouraged, wearing fifties frocks and even more make-up), while Krystle, his real wife, wept.

In 'Falcon Crest', heroine Maggie lost her memory after underground villains blew up the house of Richard Channing with whom she was starting an affair. In the shock and emotional turmoil, she forgot who, why and where.

Fallon lost her memory at the start of 'The Colbys'. Actually she never had it. Emma Samms had just arrived to replace Pamela Sue Martin in the rôle, so viewers had to be reminded who this 'intruder' was. Fallon was supposed to have crashed in De Vilbis's plane and in her confusion given herself the name Randall Adams. When Jeff, her husband, arrived to say 'My Gaad! It's Fallon, my wife, mother of Little Blake,' and then Blake arrived to say 'My Gaad! It's Fallon, my daughter, sister of Steven,' we were all put in the picture.

'Crossroads' is the only British soap which has resorted to this corny trick. Paul Ross forgot his own identity (I was going to write 'character'

351

but that would be stretching it) after armed robbers stealing the motel staff's wages beat him over the head.

I hope scriptwriters can remember to forget memory-loss in future. It's almost always forgettably boring.

'MARCUS WELBY, MD'

'Marcus Welby, MD', proved that women loved old doctors, too (even when they looked a bit like tortoises). Seen in America from 1969 to early 1976, the series ran as an afternoon show in some ITV regions in Britain steadily through the seventies. Robert Young was sixty-two at the start, having come out of a seven-year retirement after starring in the fifties American series 'Father Knows Best'. He played the careful, kindly, thorough Santa Barbara GP who became smilingly entangled in the lives of his patients whose illnesses were rewardingly dramatic: tumours, strokes, blindness, an overweight jockey, a diver with the bends. Strangely, for an American doctor, he never mentioned dollars. Bucks were always bypassed as he clashed with his young assistant, Dr Steven Kiley (James Brolin), who was often proved the more old-fashioned. A great success for ABC television at the time (Young won an Emmy and the esteem of several medical groups), its success was possibly due to Welby's fatherly approach and simply psychiatry, together with the reasonable certainty for female fans that no woman would ever steal him. Welby was wedded to his work.

MEDICAL MIRACLES

Medical miracles occur in soap opera, and we're meant to rejoice not scoff. The cures are always complete; no one gets only a bit better. Sometimes the aim is to show the doctors as wonderful clever people, or the nurses or relatives of the patient as inspirations. With soap love, anything and everything is possible, and all emotions including grateful relief must be shown.

Often a character's miracle cure is nothing more than the correction of a mistake. It's hoped that, with tragedy averted, viewers will be so relieved, they won't shout 'Swizz!' But it *was* a swizz when Arthur Brownlow, Mr Misery of 'Crossroads', was found *not* to be dying. We knew he always looked that way. The computer had boobed. Bah! Such was the audience annoyance when the error was discovered that the character was killed off in a road accident shortly afterwards.

Jason Colby in 'The Colbys' was given similar news: 'tests' proved that he had only six months to live. Luckily few of us believed it, otherwise we may have chucked bricks at our screens when the pompous patriarch announced the muddle. It was a mistake, too, when Sue Ellen in 'Dallas' thought baby John Ross had neurofibromatosis, a fatal genetic disorder. He turned out to have different genes.

Karen in 'Knots Landing' was given only one year to live, but brilliant doctors taking risks made her completely well.

Many medical miracles concern newborn babies, which score well on the Richter scale of 'Aahs'. Almost every soap baby is born in the wrong place, too early and with 'complications' only very special surgeons can put right. In 'Dynasty', Krystle's baby, Fallon's baby, the baby a surrogate mother had for Dana were all born with a great deal of bother. Even Dolly's baby in 'Emmerdale Farm' began to arrive on the farm. Krystle's baby, Christina, went one further and had a heart transplant. She must be one of the few transplant patients who never needs a pill or a check-up.

Also in American soaps psychiatrists perform miracles. 'Paralysed' Fallon was made to walk again by Dr Toscani's shock treatment (he had her jump up to stop her child running near the pool).

People have speedy recoveries in British soaps, too. Alf Roberts's heart attack was forgotten in weeks, for instance. Full marks to 'EastEnders', though, for making Angie's kidney damage serious enough to last, and to 'Brookside' for making Annabelle's mother's senility incurable.

But the greatest miracles have been the recoveries American soap stars have made from violent injury. Alexis, shot squarely in the head by a sniper at a political rally, emerged from hospital one day later with a two-inch plaster by one eyebrow. Half the cast, gunned down in Moldavia, scuttled off with barely a scratch. Krystle, held hostage, bound, starved, frightened for weeks by wicked Sammy Jo's friends, came out smiling. The healing power of soap, you see.

'MIRACLES TAKE LONGER'

'Miracles Take Longer' had the devastatingly unglamorous location of a Community Advice office as a backdrop. Thames's daytime soap, not surprisingly, lasted only four months from January to May 1984. Patsy Byrne played organiser Betty Hackforth, backed by Polly Hemingway, Richard Warner, Rosemary Williams and Lynette Davies cast as her team.

MOTHERHOOD

Motherhood in soap is never about washing four tons of baby clothes a day, shovelling in the mashed banana dessert, helping with the French verbs and running in the egg and spoon on sports day. Not much trauma there. It's about kidnapped twins, contested paternity, custody-fights and how to tell Janet she can't sleep with John because he's her brother.

It's always a problem. The women are either absurdly young, like Val Ewing in 'Knots Landing' who had Lucy at fifteen and Francesca in 'The Colbys' who must have had Jeff, her son, when she was aged about eight; or they're knocking on. Women who looked as though they produced nippers a year or so before collecting their bus passes include Annette Andre as Sarah, David Hunter's mistress in 'Crossroads'; Val Ewing, who had those kidnapped twins; Sheila Grant in 'Brookside'; Pauline Fowler in 'EastEnders'; and Maggie Gioberti in 'Falcon Crest'.

In 1987 non-motherhood was a trend. Soap *did* abortion. Susan Baldwin in 'Coronation Street' had a termination which terminated her marriage. As did EastEnder Michelle. Soap decided abortion was a Bad Thing.

'Crossroads' did test-tube babies for Glenda and Kevin. 'Dynasty' did surrogacy in 1988 when the cause of Dana Carrington's lip-twitch turned out to be infertility. The surrogate mother did not miss out on the stock wobbles: fainting fits; early contractions; tears and tantrums from a returning no-good husband paid to upset the deal and make everyone's lips twitch.

Motherhood must have been invented for soap opera.

357

'MRS DALE'S DIARY'/ 'THE DALES'

If anyone was the mother of soap opera, it was genteel doctor's wife Mary Dale whose family life was the subject of BBC radio's much-loved afternoon serial. Next to the Queen she was the most popular woman in Britain for most of the 1950s, and her changing views of middle-class life during the serial's twenty-one-year run from January 1948 to April 1969 provide treasures for BBC historians and sociologists alike. In the history of soap opera Mrs Dale is a classic Woman Who Copes. BBC policy insisted that she was a model of Christian goodness, so trusting she sometimes seemed a total twit. But, like Meg in 'Crossroads' and the soap heroines to follow, her job was to survive and to cope with any and all family upsets. Harrowing tragedy and death (apart from the demise of a dog) weren't allowed to happen, though, until the early 1960s (when listeners were assumed to have 'got over' the worst of the postwar sadnesses). The serial started after 'The Robinson Family' ended a successful six-year term. Lord Ted Willis and Jonquil Anthony were among its team of fine writers. (Playwright Tom Stoppard applied and was accepted. Novelists Olivia Manning and Doris Lessing were, incredibly, turned down.) The first episode set Mrs Dale, played by Ellis Powell, at a writing-bureau in her drawing-room at Virginia Lodge, Parkwood Hill, a leafy suburb of London. Soon 4 million Light Programme listeners, 90 per cent of them women, were gripped by fifteen minutes' worth of dramatised events concerning Jim, her GP husband, children Gwen and Bob, mother Mrs Freeman (called gravely 'Mother-in-law' by Jim), Mrs Maggs the char, Sally the glamorous sister, grandchildren, neighbours and all. When Gwen, the daughter, married in 1951 and there was a worry over her wedding dress being ready in time, anxious listeners offered to lend her their own. (And this was on radio, remember.) Mary's often-repeated introduction, 'I'm worried about Jim', became an affectionate national joke. The purpose of 'Mrs

Dale's Diary', as the BBC saw it, was to reflect middle-class family life. The lower classes – the char, Monument the gardener, the not-quite-posh-enough neighbours – were brought in (as in Shakespeare) for comic purposes.

Then, in 1962, Mrs Dale went modern. The title was changed to 'The Dales'; the scriptwriters managed to get some freedom to be more realistic; the theme music, played on a harp, was changed; and Dr Dale's practice was moved to Exton, an industrial town where patients contracted more fashionable illnesses. Mrs Maggs (Grace Allardyce) was transplanted, too, after listeners' protests. In 1963 producer Glyn Dearman sacked Ellis Powell (she was known to be an alcoholic), and Jessie Matthews, the 1930s film and musical-comedy star, took over the rôle and triumphed in what Laurence Olivier later called 'the greatest piece of miscasting'. With Charles Simon as Dr Dale (he had succeeded James Dale and Doug Burbidge before him) and Dorothy Lane splendid as Mrs Freeman, Jessie worked on for the princely fee of £80 a week until Robin Scott, controller of Radios 1 and 2, called 'time'. Among horrified listeners was Liberal MP Peter Bessell, who tried to introduce a parliamentary bill to reprieve 'The Dales'. He failed. After 5431 episodes Jim told Mary, 'I'm going to retire,' and all around the land listeners dropped knitting or slopped tea into saucers. An era ended, but the work of Mary Dale in showing women as the force for stability (in life and soap) went on.

'NEIGHBOURS'

THE HISTORY

'Neighbours' is the Australian soap which proves that lather lasts longer if there's never any dirt. Everything in sun-blessed Ramsay Street is as clean and straight as its schoolkids' teeth. 'Neighbours' has neat houses, quickly tidied problems, strong young bodies, strong old biddies, token grown men and a hint of sex. Watch it and you can believe gritty 'Grange Hill' and earthy 'EastEnders' never sullied our screens: unemployment, alcoholism, racial tension and homosexuality do not exist. Here the sermons are simple: do the decent thing; don't take any flak; come straight out with it and stop that whingeing. With its 'No offence, mate', 'Fancy a bit of tucker?', 'No worries' bluster, it's faintly foreign and faintly funny, but it never disturbs and it never depresses.

Too right 'Neighbours' is the cheapest brand of soap we can buy (it costs the BBC just £5000 a show), but for over 14 million teenagers and their mums five nights a week it's also the best. And, without doubt, the little show the Aussies twice almost dumped is the most spectacular success in the history of soap opera in Britain. Pure or puerile entertainment, it's a smasheroo.

'Neighbours' tells of the mini-misunderstandings, rapid romances and hastily mended heartbreaks of the Robinsons, the Clarkes and the Ramsays, their lodgers and long-lost relatives, as they nip in and out of each other's homes in a leafy cul-de-sac in suburban Melbourne. Think of 'The Waltons' in swimsuits with all mod cons and you're close.

But, first, there was the man who thought it up, the man who nearly closed it down, and the men and women who battled to keep the doorbells of Ramsay Street ringing.

'Neighbours' is a creation of Reg Watson, the soapies' supremo of Oz. A softly spoken Queensland bachelor, he based Ramsay Street on the

Brisbane street he grew up in. And he'd had plenty of practice with plots and characters. He worked first as an announcer, then came to Britain in the fifties to work for the BBC as an actor, then to help Val Parnell and Lew Grade with their spectaculars and game-shows. At Associated Television he created, wrote, edited, produced and directed 'Crossroads' with unflagging dedication until a sudden yearning for sunshine and bright colours sent him back home in 1973. He found Australian television needed him badly. There was little or no home-made drama; almost every show was bought from abroad. Reg masterminded game-shows and drama for the Grundy Organisation with wild success. 'The Young Doctors', 'Sons and Daughters', 'Prisoner: Cell Block H' and many others not seen in Britain were created and shaped by him. He made it look easy. 'Neighbours', he says, was darned hard. 'It was the most difficult of all because of its simplicity,' he told me. 'I probably wrote the first episodes twenty times.'

The idea of three diverse families who are friends is simple, as is the idea of using all the small things which face adults and children in ordinary life. Making it entertaining was the complicated part. He was going to call it 'One Way Street', then 'No Through Road', but 'Neighbours' seemed better, more ordinary, in the end.

'I started with the Robinsons – a widower and four children. The mother-in-law lives with them,' said Reg. 'Everyone would immediately think she'll be interfering – but, no, I went the other way and made her back him to the hilt. I hoped to bring out warmth in those attitudes. I wanted humour and a likeable roughness with the Ramsays. And I wrote teenagers as adults, talking to each other and to adults, and adults listening to them and being guided by them. Communication between the generations was very important.'

Reg Watson insists he's not preaching. 'Quite often subjects we would consider handling are best left to be done as a documentary. I learned this years ago on "Crossroads". I considered doing a drugs story using Meg's daughter. But the honest thing would have been for her to die – not miraculously to recover – and I didn't want viewers upset and switching off. It doesn't mean I want happy endings every time, but there are no wild developments. A barking dog would be as likely to start a feud as anything.'

Gwenda Marsh, then a script-editor at Grundy, now stories-boss of Australia's glossy soap 'The Flying Doctors', remembers the birth of 'Neighbours' differently. 'Really "Neighbours" was the "What the hell do we do now?" show,' she said. 'Grundys had had a big expensive flop – a bad spy thriller called "Possession". Reg and I had grand ideas about a straight soap with laughs. We made two different pilots, wrote five pilot scripts. It didn't end up the comedy we aimed for.'

'Neighbours' opened on Channel 7 in Australia in the spring of 1985, a much more middle-aged, less glamorous show than it is today. Not surprisingly, it flopped. The all-important Sydney and Melbourne viewers switched off. Channel 7 had spent £4 million on its production, and after six months and 171 episodes – in their terms, a 'fair do' – they dropped it. Grundy were later to say the reason was that Channel 7 already had two soaps – 'A Country Practice' and 'Sons and Daughters' – and that 'Neighbours' was screened at the wrong time. The truth was that it was not much good.

Actor Peter O'Brien, who played Shane Ramsay, heard of the decision in the pub. He recalled: 'Two executive types in suits were standing at the bar and, not realising other actors and I were in earshot, one said to the other: "They don't know it yet, but we're here to axe their show."' Peter rang the disbelieving producer the next morning and, as they spoke, the other telephone rang. It was Reg Grundy, head of the Grundy Organisation, with the bad news.

Enter the second hero, Ian Holmes, a Grundy executive with enough of the pioneering spirit to think that, if one customer goes cool, another might be warmed up. It hadn't been done before, but so what? Holmes approached Channel 7's rival, Channel 10, who agreed on condition 'Neighbours' had a facelift and its problems – the heavyish social issues occasionally included in the plots – were removed. Only five of the original cast stayed: the way was cleared for new young characters who 'looked good with their gear off' by the swimming-pool. In came teenagers, cheeky Charlene (Kylie Minogue), a new shining Scott (Jason Donovan), to be followed by earnest Mike (Guy Pearce) and the gawky plain Jane who was to turn into a suave beauty (Annie Jones). And into the Ramsay home came Madge the mouth, a caring windbag who'd provide a good few of the laughs.

Furious Channel 7 executives pulled their remaining episodes off the air, refused to sell the 'Neighbours' sets – the story is they burned them – so Channel 10 made new ones, brightening and extending the wall-to-wall kitchens British housewives so love. In a seven o'clock slot, with great big smiles, 'Neighbours' was back in business. But not for long. By May 1986 the axe was poised to fall again. Sydney viewers were simply not interested in a Melbourne-based show.

This time the publicity people took up the cudgels. They dragged the cast from Melbourne to Sydney – 600 miles – every weekend, had them tramping the streets and shopping-malls of Sydney, presenting competition prizes, taking part in silly stunts, signing autographs, doing anything to persuade people that Ramsay Street could be their street, too. After four weeks, the cast were tired and the company nearly half a million pounds poorer – but the viewing figures had started to increase.

By the autumn, 'Neighbours' was watched by 5 million of Australia's 16 million people, BBC's daytime programmes were due to begin and Barry Brown, an Australian working in the Corporation's Purchased Programme Department, had been home, had watched it and was hooked. 'Neighbours' was 'tested' on samples of British audiences, and the responses were positive. He told me: 'I thought it would appeal to women because it's a classless society. Living standards in Australia are high, and it's good to see ordinary working people, like Max the plumber or Des Clarke the young banker, living well without money problems.' He was right.

Add to this the fact that the BBC can buy a week's worth of 'Neighbours', five twenty-three-minute shows (each to be repeated) for £27,000, while 'EastEnders' costs more than £40,000 for one half-hour episode, and you can see why they took the gamble.

Thanks to the efforts of Ian Holmes, viewers in France, Italy, South America, New Zealand, Sweden and parts of South-East Asia are also enjoying the classless non-political frolics of Ramsay Street.

British viewers, of course, didn't pause to wonder why there wasn't an Aboriginal face in Ramsay Street. They loved the old (Channel 7) 'Neighbours' and, when they'd survived the bumpy transition – the episodes Channel 7 confiscated – and the shock of Scott's new face, they loved the new 'Neighbours' more. Screened at 10 a.m. and 1.30 p.m., middle-class housewives decided it was the soap for them. Babies cooed to the Tony Hatch theme-song about love and harmony, often comically at odds with the bickering and fist-waving in the plots, and when children were home on school holidays the 6 million a day viewing figures soared.

'Neighbours'-watching in gangs at school began, children sneaking into the computer rooms and using the television sets. In boarding schools, groups gathered ritually in common rooms, not simply the daughters of those middle-class mums, but the sons, too. Teachers at Eton, Marlborough, Sherbourne and public schools all over Britain lamented that 'Neighbours' did not figure on the GCSE syllabus.

Then Alison Grade, a sixteen-year-old London schoolgirl, mentioned to her dad that sometimes she and her pals couldn't get into their computer room for their lunch-time 'Neighbours' session. Her father, Michael Grade, then in his last months as director of programmes at BBC Television, decided to move the repeated episode from 10 a.m. to 5.30 p.m. so that children could watch with mother or at least without wearing out the school's set.

It took the first three weeks of January 1988 to put 'Neighbours' into five places in the British Top Ten, attracting 14 million viewers a day. By the beginning of February, 'Neighbours' was more successful than 'Coronation Street', the soap that inspired it. Only 'EastEnders' beat it, and Arthur, Dot, Den and Co. were looking worried.

The man who thought 'Neighbours' would never last, and tried to put it out of its misery (well, lots of people make mistakes) was Channel 7 executive Ron Casey. 'Obviously my timing was a little out,' he said later.

The first year of 'Neighbours' stories was punctuated by the non-marriages of Des Clarke. The first time he was jilted, Daphne the sensible stripper moved in as a lodger to help pay the mortgage, much to the disgust of his neighbour, gasbag plumber Max Ramsay, after whose grandfather the street was named.

A car accident then dashed the diving career of the soap's sexiest man, Shane Ramsay, and Danny his brother ended up in hospital after a drink-and-drugs spree. Pretty Terri, Max's new assistant, began dating Paul Robinson, eldest of the quieter Robinson family, a student who'd dropped out to be an airline steward. They married, but Terri turned out a wrong 'un in a ridiculous plot about an evil ex-boyfriend who blackmailed her till she killed him, then tried to kill Paul but was driven away. Later she committed suicide in prison.

Max's marriage to Maria broke up – she ran off to Hong Kong with the insurance man, and Max disappeared, too, to Brisbane (the 'Neighbours' black hole) after Francis Bell, the actor who played him, fell out with the show's new Channel 10 bosses. Tom, an Identikit brother, arrived literally to speak his lines.

Bustling Madge, Max's sister, arrived and as the second year began her troublesome truant-playing daughter Charlene turned up, bringing news that her brother Henry was in gaol and setting her sights on Scott Robinson.

Meanwhile Daphne had developed a grandfather eager to leave her the Ramsay Street Coffee Shop – a place in which almost every member of the cast except nasty gossip Mrs Mangel would eventually take a job. She also decided to marry Des, but the bridal car driven by Shane, now a chauffeur, was unfortunately hijacked by a bank robber dressed as a gorilla.

Daphne switched affections temporarily to Shane, who was jealous of the Coffee Shop; while Paul, in his new J.R. Ewing guise, tried to buy her out. Reliable Des helped her, and she decided to marry him despite his sticking-out ears and mad mother Eileen.

Meanwhile came the death in a car crash of Tom's evening-class teacher girlfriend, whose husband, a Vietnam veteran, permanently paralysed, had been swiftly disposed of.

Gentleman Jim Robinson had an affair with Zoe, his son's secretary. It led to an ectopic pregnancy and Zoe's exit. Romance, too, came for grandmother Helen Daniels – but the art dealer was a con-man and she was almost ruined.

Madge's arguing parents appeared; she took a job in the Waterhole pub (which makes the Queen Vic look trendy), and in their grey school uniform Scott and Charlene discussed sex and the marriage of the year.

THE LOCATION

The Ramsays, Robinsons and Clarkes are paying three real mortgages in Pin Oak Court, Vermont, a short drive from the Nunawading studios outside Melbourne where 'Neighbours' is made. A deal with the residents of three of the thirteen-year-old three- and four-bedroom detached houses (valued at about £100,000) was struck three years ago, when the producers expected the soap to last a few years – if they were lucky.

The £200 a week Channel 10 pays buys the use of the neat driveways, gardens and the swimming-pool in the Ramsay house, while the owners lurk indoors behind net curtains agreeing never to hang washing on a line, allow children to play or park cars in the front on the two days a week outside recording takes place.

Since the show became a hit, the residents have developed a sort of siege mentality, living a life of desperately protected anonymity and silence. The television station posts security guards in the cul-de-sac at night to stop fans and tanked-up tourists knocking on those familiar front doors asking for Scott's or Charlene's autograph at midnight.

THE PRODUCER

Marie Trevor is the godmother of the 'Neighbours' cast, writers and directors, though she's more fairy-like than iron-willed. Since she took the producer's hot seat in July 1987 the comedy quotient has risen. 'I want it to be a lot of fun,' she said.

In appearance the sixty-five-year-old grandmother is not unlike Julia Smith, 'Mrs EastEnders', but while both began as performers Marie was a soap heroine and knew the rigours of continuous drama from the sharp end, too. 'I was Joan Field the lead in the radio soap "When a Girl Married – dedicated to all those who are in love",' she told me, laughing affectionately at the memory. 'Joan married a boy from the wrong side of the tracks, went through all the crises, had a baby – the pregnancy lasted eighteen months, I seem to recall. It was lovely!'

She came to Britain in the fifties to work for York repertory and BBC radio but after four years longed for the sunshine and came back to Australia, back to being Joan Field, then to another radio soap, 'Blue Hills'.

She went to Melbourne with her actor-writer husband Alan Trevor in the early days of television where her husband wrote crime and police shows and roped her in to help with the casting. When he died, Marie took over, directing and later producing. Work on the gentle series 'A Country Practice' was followed by over two years on Grundy's hard-hitting 'Prisoner: Cell Block H' before a reprieve – a posting to 'Neighbours'. 'It was so scary. I was afraid to change anything,' she said. 'But I'm so lucky with the cast.' As her four-year-old grandson skipped around her desk, she enthused about the musical talents of singer Kylie, guitarist Craig, saxophonist Guy and Paul, a demon drummer. 'They all come in here. I give them little notes. You can always improve.'

CHARACTERS

Daphne Clarke was the stripper with the hedgehog haircut who kept her clothes on in 'Neighbours'. A more prim and proper girl you couldn't hope to meet. She moved in as a lodger with jilted bridegroom Des Clarke, and it took the dope months to realise she was the girl of his dreams. When she was late to the church – a small matter of a burglar in a gorilla suit hitching a lift – he went into a sulk.

Meanwhile Daff had gone to work in an office, but left after telling a sexist boss he should jump in a lake. Then her grandad handed her a business – the coffee shop – which she ran like a pro.

A romance with Shane came to nothing – she was too bright by half. And when Des looked set to win her back his daft mother Eileen almost drove her away. Finally they married; but Elaine Smith, who played Daff, had decided to leave. The writers gave her a long-lost father with a convenient illness; she left to be his nurse, seeing Des at weekends. Then she returned to get pregnant, have one of soap's typical traumatic childbirths, then die in a car crash.

Elaine Smith made her hair stand on end, and the 'Neighbours' producers couldn't fail to take notice. By looking strange, she says, she won the part of the Aussie soap's stripper, the first favourite with the fans. 'I used to have straight, long, lady-like hair,' the pretty actress from Perth told me. 'I wanted a change and went to the other extreme: a short, spiky cut which amazed everyone. The casting director of "Neighbours" was looking for some outrageous image for Daphne, this stripper – he didn't quite know what, but my haircut was it!'

Elaine, who'd worked on stage and in small television rôles, including 'about five minutes' in 'Sons and Daughters', made friends and found fame and romance (with co-star Peter O'Brien) during two and a half years in the soap. But then she decided to quit. She even suggested her 'death' to the writers. 'I realised I was comfortable in "Neighbours" but bored,' she told me. 'It wasn't a challenge, and there wasn't the variety. At first it was fantastic. But you have to live "Neighbours" twenty-four hours a day. If you try to buy a loaf of bread, people ask you about it. When I went to Britain last year to see the members of my family in Scotland (she'd left, aged eleven, with her parents) it turned into a publicity tour. Everyone wanted to know about "Neighbours".'

When she went back to Perth there was the chance of a short stint on the stage. She loved the luxury of long rehearsals, found it satisfying and creative, and determined that Daphne must die. 'The "Neighbours" producers asked me to come back, but I said no,' she said. 'I've accepted the idea of unemployment – if that happens. I want to choose my own scripts if I can. I liked Daphne's confidence and stubborn streak, but she did her share of moaning, and that got me down. I'm glad she was

366

allowed to die in a car crash. It freed poor Des to start off again. I'll miss Daphne – and the money – and, most of all, the show's hairdresser who did my all-important hairstyle every morning.'

Eileen Clarke means well as the batty old bird of 'Neighbours', but if she were my mother I'd apply to be an orphan. Her son Des, the luckless long streak of bank manager, doesn't deserve her visits from Perth, which are usually impromptu, to disapprove of his actions and make him eat up his greens. But she has done good deeds. She discovered Andrea was lying – Bradley was not Des's boy. She was kind to lone Mike and decent to Daff. And when she was broke she risked ridicule to try work in an office. Like every other member of the cast, she has worked in the coffee shop. A social climber and crawler, British viewers think she's a laugh. Australia has seen her suffer and soften. First, she became dangerously dependent on pills. Then the husband she divorced years before came back and reproposed. Predictably he didn't match up to her standards. So the pest of Perth stayed.

Myra De Groot was the skilled actress who kept nutty Eileen Clarke this side of strangled. The meddling mother of Des was written as a one-week character, but Myra made her so comical the producer asked her to stay.

East Ender Myra – she left England in 1958 bound for America, then New Zealand then Oz – was sixty and had worked in all areas of show business from magician's assistant to writer, producer and performer. She agreed to stay if Eileen could come and go, allowing her time for the theatre, her first love. 'So I'm not going to escape the old bitch,' she joked when we met, a few months before her death. 'Eileen's mad as a meat-axe, saying one thing one moment, the complete opposite the next. She's old-school – a victim of her generation, a working-class snob who'll never change. She just has to criticise, with an instinct to go for the jugular.'

Myra was very pleased when the writers brought Eileen's husband back. 'It was strong stuff, a good change,' she said. The actress adds that she wouldn't like her ex-husbands to reappear – any of the three husbands she divorced: 'I'm no good at marriage – far too big a mouth.'

Broken ribs and a blood disease put Myra on the sick-list. 'It won't stop Eileen,' she vowed. But cancer killed her in April 1988.

Des Clarke is the Mr Misfortune of 'Neighbours', the man who does the seemingly impossible: makes us feel sorry for a bank manager.

Not only has this big bloke jug ears and a face like a half-deflated rugby ball, he also has a demented mother who thinks he's still seven years old, and the other women in his life trick him, jilt him and die on him. He ought to put himself in a safe-deposit box at the bank where he works and throw away the key.

Paul Keane plays Des with an understandable air of defeat. Des's dilemmas started the soap. Unlucky in love before, now his bride had jilted him on the eve of their wedding so Daphne, the straight-talking stripper, moved in to help pay the mortgage. When he tried to marry her, she was late to the church. The chump took it personally, then almost fell prey to awful Andrea and beastly Bradley, the buck-toothed boy she claimed was his (aged ten, he had a 'romance' with Lucy Robinson, causing widespread nausea). Luckily Des's mum Eileen popped over from Perth, sorted her out, and a Mr Moneybags carried her off. Daphne's problems at the coffee shop called Des back into her life, and after getting 'plastered' as a practical joke – an arm was set in a splint – the couple were spliced in style.

Happiness can't last in soap, so no sooner was the honeymoon over than Daphne was off, then she was pregnant and then, as Australian viewers saw early in 1988, she was gone. Hapless Des was left holding the baby, looking hopeless.

Paul Keane is still keen on Des Clarke, the likeable nerd of 'Neighbours'. 'Des may be set in his ways, but he's a good bloke – a good friend,' said the charitable chap. But, then, as his co-stars all say, the shy thirty-year-old from Sydney is an excellent actor, a man who likes a challenge.

On stage he played an old man in Chekhov and Romeo in Shakespeare, then television rôles began to roll in. 'Neighbours' was not his first soap. He played in 'Sons and Daughters' whose stories he thought 'unbelievable and sensationalist'. He prefers the Ramsay Street epic, and wouldn't have minded a part in the cop show, 'The Bill'. 'Television audiences are not in general as stupid as some people seem to think,' he said. 'A show must have credibility. Take "The Bill". The audience cares for the characters in that because they appeared as real people. To me "The Bill" is superb.'

Paul, a bachelor, says he's hopeless with money – unlike desperate Des, the manager of a bank. But he isn't worried about playing Des as a single father. He thinks he'll hold the baby the right way up. 'My sister has a baby, Patrick. I've practised on him.'

Helen Daniels is the gracious granny and model mother-in-law of 'Neighbours'. But as an artist she stinks. Series creator Reg Watson wrote her as a counter-attack on the myth of the interfering in-law and female fuddy-duddy.

As the woman whose heart went out to Jim Robinson when her daughter, his wife, died in childbirth, Helen is a brilliant housekeeper, perfect cook, patient listener and woman of the world. She helps run a property company, always looks chic and paints in her spare time.

Anne Haddy, who plays her, wants it known the paintings are done by someone 'in scenery'. 'They're awful, aren't they?' she confided. 'The most upsetting fan letter I've received was from a little boy who wanted me to paint his dead cat. I had to explain I wasn't a real artist.'

Widow Helen nearly fell for art dealer Douglas Blake, who turned out to be a swindler. The experience didn't sour her – perhaps because Blake was played by James Condon, Anne's husband.

Anne Haddy might never have become soap's warmest wisest grandmother Helen Daniels if Rolf Harris had had his way. Anne, from South Australia, came to London in the 1950s, dotty about films and the theatre, to take speech and drama classes. Her Aussie friend cartoonist Rolf wanted to send her photograph to his agent. 'But I got scared,' said Anne. 'I thought: I'll get married instead. So I did. What a fool! What a fool!'

Anne, now happily married for the second time to actor James Condon, and a besotted grandmother, isn't really complaining. 'I shouldn't say that about the father of my two children, I know,' she said. 'If I hadn't married and returned to Australia, I'd never have met my present husband or ended up in "Neighbours".'

Back home Anne made a name for herself in a long line of stage hits and became well known to soap fans as Rosie Andrews in 'Sons and Daughters' and as a dying mother in 'Prisoner: Cell Block H'. At the time she was appearing in 'Prisoner', she *was* practically dying of heart disease. It led to bypass surgery. Later she suffered major surgery for stomach cancer and, to round off her bad luck, treatment for a broken hip.

But the elegant fifty-eight-year-old actress does not find it strange that she should now work five long days each week. 'I thought no one would want to employ me after my heart attack, but I was pleasantly surprised,' she told me. 'My doctor – no one – has told me to take things easy, so I don't. I simply eat sensibly – there's a good deal of me pushing food about my plate at meal-times at the Robinson house – but generally I enjoy things. All people with wonky bodies feel they have to prove something, I suppose. And it's not hard proving Helen's real. She sometimes annoys me when she's always right. But she's a doer – and it's nice to show a grandmother can wear high heels and nail varnish, too.'

Jane Harris was 'plain Jane, super brain' to her classmates at school.

With Daphne and Helen's help before the school dance, the greased hair was washed, the swot's specs came off and . . . and . . . to the surprise of absolutely no one the ugly duckling was a swan.

Blonde actress Annika Jones, who plays shy Jane, was always rather obviously pretty; that was the snag. But her character, like that of her boyfriend Mike, is important to the 'Neighbours' writers' concern for lonely isolated teenagers (of which there are many, especially among immigrants to Oz).

None of the 'Neighbours' children manages to live a settled life with two parents. Jane, whose parents are in Hong Kong, and Mike, whose father beat him and whose mother was so hard pressed he's now on his own, are that much worse off. Jane lives with her grandmother, unpleasant Mrs Mangel. Mike moves around; his friends are his 'guardians'.

Australian viewers have watched Jane blossom into a swish model, the beauty of Ramsay Street, with the most stylish, expensive clothes. It's enough in 'Neighbours' to be good-looking and nice. In 'EastEnders' or 'Dynasty' it's unknown.

Annika Jones plays frump turned beauty Jane Harris, a quiet shy girl. But staying quiet and shy doesn't help a struggling actress, she found.

Annika (her parents are Hungarian) was a teenage model in Adelaide then won a rôle in the film *Run Chrissie Run*, then 'The Henderson Kids' and five months in 'Sons and Daughters' on television.

'I was out of work for four months and got sick of it,' Annie told me, 'so I started ringing up Grundy's every few days to tell them I was still alive. Eventually the rôle of Jane came up.'

Now twenty-one, Annie says she has learned a lot from her 'Neighbours' co-stars – especially from Vivean Gray, 'a fantastic actress'. In some ways she wishes Jane was still plain, gawky, four-eyed and unsure. 'I don't think there are enough good rôles for women. They should be given gutsier, dirtier rôles, not just be the pretty faces all the time,' she said.

Nellie Mangel is the resident Sourpuss of 'Neighbours', who looks as if she has a bad smell permanently under her nose.

Played by Vivean Gray in bright red lipstick, Mrs Mangel has a husband, Len, who has never been seen but to whom she frequently calls – irritably. As the humourless old cat disapproves of 'the young people of today' and isn't that fond of the rest, it's entirely possible she is punishing the man for a crime such as smiling and has locked him in the loo (or would have, if Ramsay Street houses ever had anything as realistic as a loo). At one point she thought he was dead, and buried his clothes in the garden, and when he turned up she pretended to have lost her memory.

Her grand-daughter Jane Harris she rules with a rod of iron. Jane's boyfriend Mike she was quick to denounce. Only Eileen, a fellow-snob, is ever welcomed for a visit. Like her red velvet chair, Mrs Mangel is tightly buttoned.

Vivean Gray understands her. She said: 'The Mrs Mangels of the world are people who are disappointed in themselves. Perhaps they are lonely, too. At any rate, they can't adapt to a changing society. Such people need counselling.' Or pushing over the nearest cliff.

Vivean Gray, Mrs Mangel in 'Neighbours', comes from Cleethorpes and worked as a nurse, a secretary and a matron in a boys' public school. Then with £13 in her pocket she went to Australia and stayed. That was over thirty years ago. Once she'd settled in Sydney with a job in the book trade, softly spoken Vivean began to act with amateur groups. When she moved to Melbourne she decided to call herself a professional and found theatre work and television spots before the rôle of Mrs Jessup, the Nosy Parker of 'The Sullivans' came along and made her a star for six years. 'Mrs Jessup and Mrs Mangel are sisters under the skin,' said the never-married actress. They were both gossips with too many opinions. But Jessup had saving graces, she would help people – Mangel is mean and bitchy.'

When 'The Sullivans' ended, Vivean had four years with only short parts – a genteel poisoner in 'Prisoner: Cell Block H' and an English matron in 'Anzacs' were two. Then came the chance in 'Neighbours'. 'I was keen – especially as Myra De Groot, who played my sister in "The Sullivans", was to be my best friend in this. Mangel was only supposed to be around for three weeks, but I think people like watching her. I think they say: "Isn't she dreadful – thank goodness she doesn't live near me".'

Charlene Mitchell is soap's teen queen, the truculent tomboy of 'Neighbours' and an inspiration to girls with mother problems everywhere. Charlene – she prefers 'Lennie' (and wouldn't anyone?) – is the smallest and cutest of the raucous Ramsay family, daughter of Madge the Mouth and an unseen father somewhere in Brisbane. Played by Kylie Minogue, she arrived toothy and tousled one day in the soap's second year, having run to her mum when her father moved in with his secretary, Susan. Mum said: 'Charlene, just what do you think you're playing at?' loudly and repeats it at least once a week. They're a marvellous double act.

By the time she arrived Lennie seemed to have left her life as Lolita. We were told she'd had an abortion, been a drinker and had gone on the Pill. Her on-screen crimes were bunking off school, lying to Madge and canoodling with Scott Robinson, the boy of her dreams. To her neighbours, especially the stuffy ones, Lennie enjoys speaking her mind, and at school she's the first to fight. St Trinian's would have suited her well. In her dungarees and baggy sweatshirts she became the darling of the show.

Earlier this year she appeared holding a baby, to give Madge a nasty turn. The tot was Susan's (Charlene's father had thrown them out), and

Lennie's soft heart was revealed. Kylie knew it was there. 'Charlene is really sensitive but doesn't show it. She'd rather die than be caught crying,' she said.

Australian viewers have seen Lennie and Scott's wedding, watched the young pair struggle on next to no money and solemnly discuss parenthood, and seen Lennie work part-time as a mechanic in the garage. 'I think people like her because she'll always come out on top,' added Kylie, 'and when you think about it her relationships with her mother and Scott are the most normal in the show.'

Kylie Minogue's teenage tantrums in 'Neighbours' made her a star at seventeen and a member of soap and rock royalty at nineteen. Unlike Joan Collins and Co., Kylie never had to fleece a tycoon or suffer the slings. All she had to do was be rude to her mum. 'That was on-screen only,' said the pint-sized actress who still wears child-size clothes. 'I'd never dream of talking to my own mother like that.'

Kylie insists her parents aren't pushy showbiz parents. 'They'd be just as supportive if I were a secretary,' she told me, and she still lives with them in Melbourne, near where the successful soft soap is made.

In 1986, Kylie recorded a version of the Little Eva song 'Locomotion' which topped Australia's charts for eight weeks, and followed it with the disco number 'I Should Be So Lucky' which soared to the top of the charts in Britain. It put Kylie's face on more magazine covers than she could count and left her blinking in two spotlights, slightly daunted by the fuss.

At the beginning it was shy Kylie's younger sister Danielle, now highly paid hostess of the children's show 'Young Talent Time' (made by the 'Neighbours' company, Grundy), who seemed more certain of fame. At eleven Kylie accompanied Danielle to an audition, but won the part herself, appearing in 'Skyways' and 'The Sullivans'. She put her career on hold then until 1984 when, with a tutor in her dressing-room, she played the tough tyke in 'The Henderson Kids'.

No sooner had she finished her school exams, than up came the rôle of Charlene, a teenager forced by her mother to study for her exams. The workload became so great that Kylie now barely has time to open a book or do the dressmaking she enjoys. She feels she must accept almost every offer to make a public appearance: 'I could be a nobody tomorrow.' Inevitably there has been speculation that her health may be suffering. 'It would be nice to lead a normal life, have friends and not be nagged about losing too much weight,' she said. 'It's hard to put on pounds when you're constantly active. I'm six and a half stones – I'm happy with that – I'd like to be taller [she's 5 feet 1 inch], but it's no hassle.'

Her out-of-hours friendship with Jason Donovan – her partner, Scott, in the show – has added to her fame. 'One day I'd like to have a normal sensitive caring husband. Isn't that what every woman wants?'

Madge Ramsay is the man-less mother hen of 'Neighbours', protecting her brood, scratching her living, tending her nest. She's the spirit of old Australia. Out in the bush a hundred years ago she'd have been the sunniest Sheila in the best-kept shack. Played by glamorous Anne Charleston, Madge is loud but likeable, meddlesome but cuddlesome, she has an opinion on everyone, ridiculous often but usually right.

Wisely, the writers brought in Madge Mitchell (she changed her surname in the second year) as Max and Tom Ramsay's elder sister who'd left her womanising husband in Brisbane. Blustering plumber Max (Francis Bell) had left the show, and bullet-headed Tom (Gary Files) was a poor imitation. She soon became the Ramsay of Ramsay Street, named after her grandfather, as the woman alone, unqualified in all but nagging, looked down on by her neighbours. In time she took over the house, and her burdens arrived. First Charlene, her awful, adolescent, undersized daughter, who sulked and lied and played truant from school. Then her comic-book parents, grumpy pa and puffed-up ma, on the brink of divorce. Later came Henry, the son out of gaol, who'd wear her out with his schemes and his uncouth charm. She clouts the kids round the head, but it doesn't improve them.

Madge never saw the funny side as she battled for work and something to boast about. Paul Robinson sacked her as a secretary and almost sacked her as the barmaid of the Waterhole where she dispensed drinks with disapproval and, later, treated temporary help Henry with the same courtesy Den showed his staff in the Vic.

Later, too, came the sort of romantic interlude favoured by the 'Coronation Street' scriptwriters for Mavis. Madge's man from the past, fussy fuddy-duddy Harold, appeared, proposed and then postponed the wedding when the value of his shares crashed. We knew Madge was too good for him. If only she'd played clever with nice Jim Robinson. . . . But playing straight is all she knows.

Anne Charleston says she understands why Madge, the character she plays in 'Neighbours', is the most popular monster mother on the screen. 'Firstly she's aggressive because she grew up with a dominating father and two great big bullying brothers,' the Melbourne actress told me. 'Then came this womanising husband, and would you like to have a dreadful daughter like Charlene? Madge is very physical – all that belting her children and nephew – I blame that on the brothers, too. But I think they all realise she's also compassionate. She's never dull. I don't want her to change.'

Anne has also been a single parent since her children were small. Now her teenage daughter is at school and a nineteen-year-old son 'is going to be a great big rock star'. Like sensible Madge, Anne made him work to pay for his singing lessons. She jokes: 'My smothering techniques are different from Madge's, though. I used to worry if my children had missed out because their upbringing was a bit unorthodox. Sometimes with an actress mother you live like gypsies. But they seem very happy.'

Anne describes herself as stagestruck from birth. 'I became an actress at eighteen after studying with a wonderful old actress called Lorna Forbes from the age of twelve.' Early live television work ('It would give me a nervous breakdown now') was followed by a long rôle in 'Bellbird', guest rôles in many Australian series including 'The Sullivans' and 'Prisoner: Cell Block H', as well as a long list of stage productions.

Anne enjoys 'Neighbours', despite the slog of long days and the irritation of children singing the theme song at her as she tries to rush around the supermarket. 'I think being recognised goes with the territory. Some people bellyache, but I often find it gratifying,' she said. She strongly approves of the emphasis on women as hard workers, never letting life get them down. I'd like to see more social issues brought into it, though I doubt it will happen. We had an Aboriginal boy in the cast for a while – the character worked in a bank – but there wasn't one reference to the fact he was black.'

Shane Ramsay made a sexy splash as the daring diver at the start of 'Neighbours'. There he was, blond streaks glistening, designer muscles rippling, 6 feet 2 inches of dedication. But a car accident dashed his career, and away from the pool his appeal seemed to pall. As a gentle gardener and a shambling chauffeur, he hardly made waves. Who wants a hunk with an identity crisis?

Daphne, the sensible stripper, fell for him but cooled when he seemed to want her to give up her job in the coffee shop. (Women in 'Neighbours' do so like to pay their own way.) When she went back to Des, Shane (played by Peter O'Brien) was down in the dumps. He dived further down when he drove his Uncle Tom's girl, crashed, she died and Shane was falsely accused of being drunk at the time. He was cleared in a ridiculous plot involving Ramsay Street's burglar of the month.

At least they let him win a motorbike in a darts match. He zoomed off to see his banished parents Max and Maria in Brisbane (both had long left the cast), met a girl in a caravan and decided to see the world. Or at least that bit of it beyond the Ramsay Street coffee shop.

Peter O'Brien, Shane in 'Neighbours', proves it's an ill wind that blows nobody any good. His ill wind was a cyclone which had him evacuated from an oil-rig where he worked. When safely in Perth he found his parents had been trying to contact the former teacher, swimming-pool digger, model and odd-job man to tell him he'd finally been offered the work he wanted: acting.

That was six years ago. The former farmboy from South Australia said: 'I guess I always knew I didn't want to be a teacher for the rest of my life. I'd done a drama course at university, so I thought I'd give acting a go. I do plan to travel, though, and perhaps settle in England.'

Audiences soon gave him a go in episodes of 'Special Squad' and 'Prisoner: Cell Block H', and three years ago Shane the diver turned gardener in 'Neighbours'. Last year he decided to leave to take up the rôle of Sam the pilot in the glossier filmed series 'The Flying Doctors'. Elaine Smith, his one-time girlfriend in 'Neighbours' and long-term partner in private life, left the soap soon afterwards. 'I said I'd stay in "Neighbours" for two years and that's what I did. I had enough of my shirts being ripped off my back,' he said.

Henry Ramsay is the new pin-up of 'Neighbours', replacement for both Shane, who got on his bike, and Clive who took up his stethoscope. Played by Craig McLachlan, Madge's ex-gaolbird son arrived in 1988 and showed immediately he was more than a pretty face and bulging biceps. Henry's a clown, a lovable one. His schemes are tiresome, but his liveliness is charming. The writers should have fixed him parole and brought him in sooner.

What took him to gaol isn't mentioned – nothing serious, it's hinted. Back with mum Madge and sister Charlene, he had to overcome the problems of an 'ex-crim', find a job and girl. For a time, troublemaker Sue was his date, but the romance didn't last. He had a passion for Jane but feels he's not good enough for her. Later he worked at the garage and at the pub. He even taught his mother to drive. And got out of the car joking!

Craig McLachlan won his rôle as Henry Ramsay partly because he looks like Kylie Minogue – with muscles. Kylie plays Charlene, Henry's sister. Like her, Craig, aged twenty-five, has curly blond hair, blue eyes, a short nose and perfect teeth. It makes you sick!

But Craig, a natural comedian, is more interested in the humour of his part than in his sex-symbol rating. 'Henry's a bit of an ox and a terrible womaniser,' he told me. 'About the only female he hasn't offered himself to is Bouncer the Labrador. He gets within a bull's roar of something romantic happening, then realises he's not a fit person and it's the cold shower treatment.'

Craig, a New South Wales country boy, always wanted to act but did many jobs first. He was a plumber's mate and labourer for a time. But he said he always had a nagging feeling 'that unblocking toilets' wasn't his ideal career. He left school early and landed a small rôle in 'The Young Doctors' and made several commercials – then scurried back home, unsure of what he wanted.

A couple of years later Craig moved back to Sydney, began playing guitar in a band called The Y-Fronts, married and began seriously searching for acting work. A small rôle in 'Sons and Daughters' led him to 'Neighbours'. Craig recalled: 'Someone in the studio said: "It's uncanny – with your looks you could be Kylie's real brother." His friend said cattily: "Or her sister, duckie." It's certainly true we get on like we're family. And I love Anne Charleston who plays Madge, my mother. But she doesn't act all that bashing me around the head. It's real. Mind you, I'm usually pinching her behind at the time.'

Jim Robinson

Jim Robinson is the Mr Nice of 'Neighbours', the sort of man anyone would want as a neighbour, father and friend. You could add that the Rock of Ramsay Street is often about as interesting as a bagload of ballast, but there's something weirder than that. How does this paragon pay the bills? Jim is an engineer who never does any engineering; the company boss who never talks to his staff or mentions a client. If this was 'EastEnders', he'd be revealed as a secret drugs dealer or a pedlar of porn. But in a land still fond of the beer-swilling okker, the widowed father of four, played by Alan Dale, is an ideal: reasonable, accessible, quiet and calm. He has never argued with his mother-in-law, who helps him bring up the kids in their immaculate home, and he was even polite when meddlesome Madge and hopeless Henry came to stay.

Only three children lived with him after the show's first year, his elder daughter Julie having gone to live with her widowed ex-boss. Then it was his turn for romance, to the disgust of his nine-year-old daughter Lucy, with Zoe, the young secretary who worked for Paul, his businessman son. Jim made her pregnant after one of those miracles of soap. The couple were never alone; even Lucy stayed in the room with them when they went off for a weekend, and he's far too large and correct to lunge at her in the back of the family Ford Falcon. Unlike Dirty Den in 'EastEnders', Jim discussed the secret pregnancy with all his children and every other character in the soap. Then he proposed; Zoe refused, then miscarried and left.

This year Jim's job has been to be tolerant and supportive as Scott swots for exams and prepares to marry Lennie. He had a small flutter – with a woman he met on a plane – but it ended in tears. No prizes for spotting a third-time-lucky coming up in the plots.

Australian viewers have seen him court, win and wed, against the odds, the new stern-faced GP, Dr Beverley Marshall. Perhaps she can diagnose why he never seems to work.

Alan Dale is nothing like the staid statesman Jim Robinson he plays in 'Neighbours'. He hopes. New Zealander Alan is divorced and, like Jim, a single parent. He has looked after teenage sons Matthew and Simon for six years. But, unlike Jim, he is always seen to work – long weekday hours making 'Neighbours', as a radio disc jockey on Sundays and dashing off to make personal appearances or help charity appeals whenever he can. Then there is sport – windsurfing, golf, cricket, you name it – and tinkering with old sports-cars, a craze all his life.

Alan says his frantic lifestyle is partly the result of knowing tough times. As a law student at university, selling cars part-time and working a milk-round he'd bought, he heard a clapped-out disc jockey on his car radio announce he was fed up and leaving. Alan shaved, went to the station, got that job and the part of a radio station manager in a television series.

In 1978 he left for Australia, with a few dollars in his pocket and a lot of nerve. He auditioned but was rejected for a part in Grundy's 'The Restless Years'. But it was when he cheekily went back to tell them their show was rubbish and, anyway, why hadn't they hired him that he won the rôle of no-nonsense Dr Forrest in 'The Young Doctors'. It lasted three years.

A flat period followed with Alan working most of the night on radio, seeing the sons he'd taken custody of only sleepily after school. When another actor dropped out of 'Neighbours' just before recordings began and the rôle of Jim was offered to Alan, it saved his sinking spirits.

Now the rugged forty-one-year-old lives in relaxed style with Tracy Pearson, a former Miss Australia, and doesn't have to sell himself. As the highest-paid star in the show – he earns around £1000 a week (see 'Pay') – he often speaks up for his younger co-stars, whose stamina he admires. 'We know we've been exploited,' he told me. 'We're paid a pittance compared with the Americans. We know the show's a huge hit in Britain, but it doesn't make us any richer.'

He's proud of 'Neighbours' and furious to learn that some 'East-Enders' actors, notably Linda Davidson, have criticised it as a cheaply made sausage-machine show. '"Neighbours" deals with many of the social problems we have in Australia – abandoned kids, drugs, sex – and it appeals to poorer people here. It's not heavy but it is relevant.' Anyway, Alan's a former 'Coronation Street' fan but doesn't like the sound of 'EastEnders', which he hasn't yet seen. 'I have letters from England saying I behaved like Dirty Den, making Zoe pregnant, or that with my short hair I look like gay Colin. I don't like the sound of either of those gents.'

Paul Robinson is the nearest 'Neighbours' has to a Mr Nasty. He'd like to become a junior JR but mostly he's just po-faced, power-mad and pompous. He blames it on a woman. Marry a girl plumber and what do you get but a spanner in the works of the cosy Robinson family?

Paul, Jim's elder son, was a serious student until he dropped out of college to become an airline steward and see the world. Still jet-lagged no doubt; he married Max Ramsay's boiler-suited blonde mate when he touched down. An evil ex-boyfriend soon turned up, and Terri was firing a gun at both men. Now she's dead after suicide.

An embittered Paul went to work in an insurance company and was soon running the international property business owned by granny Helen plus Lassiter's hotel. At twenty-four he was one of the biggest businessmen in soap – but what he did with his money was a mystery. Those grey suits and button-down shirts can't have cost that much, and he still lived at home.

Scott his blond brother probably wished he hadn't. For Paul was always bossing him or being beastly to women like Zoe, the droopy secretary he hired who had a fling with his father. When she left, a girl with a baby asked for her job; Paul showed her the door, and looked as if he'd like to kick the kid, too. Madge at the Waterhole took a drunk's car keys to save him from danger. Paul nearly sacked her. And when he married again his nice wife Gail found she couldn't conceive. We half-expected Paul to drown her in the pool.

Stefan Dennis says he picks up tips from mean-minded Paul Robinson, the whizzkid he plays in 'Neighbours'. 'I've learned to like property,' said thirty-year-old Stefan, proud owner of a 1920s house in the hills outside Melbourne, 'and I'm very realistic about things. I don't suppose "Neighbours", or at least my part in it, will last for ever and I know that the bigger you are in TV the more the people in films keep you at arm's length. So you can't sit waiting for the phone to ring. You must make it ring.'

Stefan was born in Victoria, but his naval-captain father is English so he retains a British passport, and he trained first as a chef on the Gold Coast. 'My father said I could be a ship's cook if acting didn't work out,' he explained.

Acting did work out. First theatre, then a break into television with 'The Flying Doctors' mini-series. Then came a part in 'Neighbours'. To keep it he gambled on the future of the series, despite its rocky start, to decline a rôle in 'The Flying Doctors' soap. 'Paul Robinson had an important function,' said Stefan. 'He had to bring in viewers aged between twenty and thirty; research had shown there weren't any, they were all younger or older. I liked the challenge.' The actor, who's married to television show hostess Roz Roy, doesn't agree that Paul is a JR baddie. 'Deep down he has a conscience,' he said.

Scott Robinson is the star schoolboy of 'Neighbours', polite,

perceptive, neat and nice. Probably he folds his clothes, too. In other words, he's like no teenager you ever met. But with actor Jason Donovan's bashful blond looks his millions of fans are prepared to overlook a detail like that.

Scott, younger son of Jim, was a different dish to start with. Played by dark-haired Darius Perkins, he wasn't such a goodie, either. First he was in trouble with the police over a suspected mugging, along with the boy next door, Danny Ramsay. They ran away to work on a farm. Then the friends battled for the favours of Wendy Gibson, and then Scott mysteriously disappeared as soap children do. In reality Channel 10 had taken over the show and wanted a golden boy. Enter a new-look Scott, played by Jason.

These days Scott's rôle is to argue with his hard-nut brother Paul, partner cheeky Charlene and be a normal young chap. He swotted hard for his exams, and in episodes seen in Australia married Charlene, and was almost divorced when he kissed neighbour Jane. Now he plans to be a journalist. In soap even a journalist can be normal, I suppose.

Jason Donovan almost didn't join the cultivated Robinson family of 'Neighbours' as schoolboy Scott. He was going to be a rough and ready Ramsay, a cousin to Charlene. The young actor auditioned for the part of Danny Ramsay in 1984, then decided he'd go back to school and swot for his Higher School Certificate. He passed well (with a score of 285 out of 410) and plans to pick up his interest in art and design one day.

His father, seasoned Australian television star Terence Donovan (best known as the detective in 'Copshop'), tried to dissuade his boy from the acting business – an insecure job with built-in heartbreaks, he said. But as Jason was finishing his exams the rôle of Scott, taken originally by another actor, was offered, and he couldn't resist.

Scott's one-parent family (his television mother was supposed to have died giving birth to Lucy his sister) is not unlike his own. Jason and his father were alone after his mother, television personality Sue McIntosh, left them when Jason was five and there was a bitter divorce. Sadly, he says, he saw his mother occasionally on birthdays and at weekends, but when Terence remarried five years ago (Jason was best man) the contact ended. 'I guess the break-up made me pretty independent,' he said. 'I've always done my own washing and I can cook up quite an omelette. Dad and I lived by ourselves, and I spent hours and hours with Dad on film and TV locations. I suppose it got under my skin.'

Jason first acted when he was eleven, in 'I Can Jump Puddles' and 'Skyways' – as the brother of his on- and off-screen girlfriend Kylie Minogue (Charlene).

Now twenty, Jason has finally moved into his own little house and enjoys singing and water sports when there's a gap in his seventy-hour 'Neighbours' week. The long hours have meant he had to abandon his plan to take part in surfing competitions. And the fame has meant he's pointed out and pummelled or asked for his autograph everywhere he goes. Even swimming, in goggles, at a public pool, fans ambush him waving soggy paper and pens.

NEW FACES

New faces are a funny phenomenon of soap – funny because we're all jolted when a character is suddenly played by a different actor or actress but no one in his or her fictional family notices. Are they stupid or something? Probably, but still. . . .

Long-running soaps are bound to wash away parts of their population: at any time someone in a cast wants to quit to play Hamlet, be the new Meryl Streep or have a quadruple heart bypass. In British soaps the characters tend to be written out or simply not mentioned again – although 'Emmerdale Farm' has had two Dollys, two Tom Merricks, two Jack Sugdens and two Marion Wilkses, 'Brookside' has had two gay Gordons and two troublesome Lucys.

In American and Australian soaps the services of unseen plastic surgeons are frequently used. Steven Carrington looked the image of Al Corley before his face was burned in an oil-rig fire. Then he turned up as a remarkably unscarred Jack Coleman. Shame, that.

British schoolgirls are finally forgiving the 'Neighbours' producers for changing schoolboy Scott Robinson from dark-haired Darius Perkins to blond Jason Donovan. (Many tell me they really want both.) Fans of 'Sons and Daughters', though, can never forgive Rowena Wallace – the woman they loved to hate as Pat the Rat – for having cosmetic surgery after a long trip away. When the (not very noticeable) wrinkles and double chin went, the face of actress Belinda Giblin emerged.

The Ewings of Dallas proved they all need spectacles when they failed to spot that their beloved momma, Miss Ellie, had suddenly acquired a waistline. Her pretty hair turned into a stiff meringue and her ever-tearful eyes suddenly dried up. They didn't even say 'Welcome home' when Barbara Bel Geddes, the original model, reappeared and the impostor, Donna Reed, was presumably returned to wardrobe.

Fallon Colby of 'Dynasty' underwent perhaps the most drastic rebirth

– not only a new face, a newly ballooned bust, a new body and a new voice. Fallon also changed character. Lanky languid Pamela Sue Martin, who had made a wonderfully classy cow of her before deciding to become a movie queen (see 'Life after Soap'), was metamorphosed into cute Emma Samms. The new Fallon didn't deflower football teams between chukkas of polo or tennis sets, or take a canter across Colorado each morning. She stared sweetly or she quivered. The inspiration had quite gone.

'THE NEWCOMERS'

'The Newcomers' was the BBC series, running from October 1965 to November 1967, about London families settling in a rural community, which replaced the more frivolous 'Compact' and complemented 'United!', which started in the same month and competed (unsuccessfully) with Granada's 'Coronation Street'. Devised by Colin Morris and in black and white, made in Birmingham, it was middle-class, worthy and often rather dull except when actress Maggie Fitzgibbon took centre stage as the independent-minded strong Vivienne Cooper. Set in a fictional East Anglian overspill town, Angleton (really Haverhill, Suffolk), it featured the newly moved Cooper family. Vivienne's husband Ellis (Alan Browning) was the shop superintendent of Eden Brothers, a computer components' firm. They had children Phillip, seventeen and brash, Maria (played by Judy Geeson before she became a film star), sixteen and dreamy, and cheeky Lance, thirteen; and there was also a glum Gran, who seemed riveted to the settee. Audiences of about 6 million were loyal if not ecstatic. Industrialists complained that the Eden Brothers chairman was a crook, its managing director an ass and the image of British industry was sullied. Mary Whitehouse's clean-up organisation gave it an 'honorary mention' in the annual awards for morally sound shows. (The kiss of death now?) Between a fair quota of births, deaths and marriages, children's health problems were favourites in the script. One child had tetanus, another lost a kidney, one almost lost an eye. The closing titles were forever rolling as parents bravely bit lips, eyes wet. Social issues were responsibly handled: tax tangles, business ethics, the upheavals when a ring road is proposed, and witchcraft. Heather Chasen, later to become noxious Valerie Pollard in 'Crossroads', played a posh witch. Many well-known actors came and went including Wendy Richard (p.246) who played Joyce Harker, a twenty-year-old cockney. Alan Browning quit in

382

December 1967 (because he was bored), so Vivienne became a widow. When the writers first scheduled a marriage to a new character Charles Turner but then switched the story to a whirlwind romance and wedding (unseen) in New Zealand, Maggie Fitzgibbon left, disagreeing with their decision. Only Raymond Hunt, who played Lance, the short-trousered schoolboy turned local-paper journalist, went all through. By the end the newcomers were thought oldcomers. They made way for 'The Doctors'.

Maggie Fitzgibbon spoke like a nicely brought-up English lady in the BBC sixties soap 'The Newcomers' until she had to raise her voice. Then her Australian origins became obvious; she sounded like Madge in 'Neighbours'. But viewers loved her. She became so popular as wife and mother Vivienne Cooper that one critic called it 'The Vivienne Cooper Show'.

Born in 1930, formerly a singer who starred in several West End musicals, she was unlike the character, being divorced with no children. But like the strong principled housewife she quit when the scriptwriters decided the character should have a whirlwind romance and marriage in New Zealand, instead of the earlier plan to marry her off with a colourful ceremony to Charles Turner. The strong stand shocked viewers, and provoked rival Pat Phoenix, star of 'Coronation Street' to say bluntly: 'If they asked me, as Elsie Tanner, to go and cut somebody's throat in Stoke Poges . . . well, it might not be according to my usual character but I'd do it just the same. An actress is paid to do a job, like anyone else.' (Some years later Phoenix left 'Coronation Street' because she was fed up with Elsie doing little more than sitting in the pub asking for gin and tonics.)

'The Newcomers' never recovered from Vivienne's disappearance. In its last episode, seven months later, there was a joking reference to her 'getting what she wanted'. She'd apparently married Turner.

PAY

Pay for soap stars is a subject which causes feuds and resentments that make the fights of Angie and Den seem tame.

Most soap actors are not paid film-star rates or even the rates of actors in leading rôles in other television drama. This may seem odd since soaps are the most successful shows on television, earning the commercial companies high advertising revenue. But the cultural condescension to soap is so strong that the attitude persists that acting the same part in a long-running serial is less artistically demanding even if the physical strain of six-days-a-week work can be immense. There is also a notion that the fees should be lower because soap work is secure work in an unstable industry. It can be long-lasting, but the end can come suddenly and bitterly.

Actors who have appeared in Hollywood films, on stage and in television soap say the artistic input is the same. Michael York, the Oxford-educated film star and regular appearer in 'Knots Landing' (he plays Charles Scott) said: 'I don't see it as a hierarchical thing. Soap is another discipline, and it's a very tough one. I enjoy it.'

Having said that, soap actors don't do badly. Chris Quinten, for example, who lives in a tiny terraced house as Brian Tilsley, has bought eight properties from his earnings and earlier this year declared himself 'Coronation Street''s first millionaire. But 'Brookside' stars are paid the Equity minimum and have to fight for out-of-pocket expenses. It still rankles with 'EastEnders' stars that they are paid £500 a week less than the other star regulars of 'Coronation Street' when they tend to work a longer week. While the cockneys earn around £1100 a week, their Northern rivals earn around £1600. The gulf is even greater between other BBC drama and ITV drama. If 'Howards Way' were an ITV production, instead of a BBC show, for instance, stars such as Nigel Davenport would double their pay. 'It's about time the BBC started paying actors what they're worth,' he said, announcing he would lead a campaign within the actors' union, Equity.

In American soaps, which earn their producers hundreds of millions in syndication fees, it is not unusual for a star to be paid around £50,000 for each of the twenty-five to thirty weeks a year they make episodes. These high pay-rates are threatening the future of the prime-time soaps, whose overall costs, met by the television networks, have spiralled to around £1 million an episode. In the first year of 'Dallas', in 1978, £50,000 paid the entire cast; now it's less than the amount paid to one of the top players.

Michael Filerman, an executive producer at Lorimar which makes 'Dallas', 'Knots Landing' and 'Falcon Crest', told me: 'Unless actors stop being greedy, they are going to push the costs up so high the networks will just refuse to take the soap. In America the networks are now run by businessmen who have no thought for the intrinsic values of their TV series. It's a hard world.'

PETS

Pets in soap are a threatened species. Actors and producers so hate their unpredictable performances that they're becoming rarer than babies.

Minnie Caldwell's cat Bobby in 'Coronation Street' used to be a star of the show. Is that him on the roof in the opening titles or the moggie from the fish shop? Nobody knows. Hilda's cat Rommel was hardly ever about. In fact there were three feline stars in that rôle. The first was run over; the second had bad breath, worse wind, and Hilda (Jean Alexander) had him swiftly removed; the third was so shy he spent most episodes hiding. Mavis's budgie Harriet is often mentioned but rarely tweets. Percy's bird Randy has been ignored for years.

In 'Crossroads' only Benny was allowed pets – perhaps to show there were dumber creatures around. He had a goat called Starry tethered then abandoned years ago. He then bought a donkey and called it Miss Diane in honour of his dead friend, the motel waitress. There was no resemblance I could see. He also had a large hairy dog, Moses, who upstaged the whole cast on many occasions with a woof and a shake.

'EastEnders' had two hounds: Ethel's pug Willy, her child substitute, victim of a kidnap plot, now with her in a home, and Roly the apricot poodle at the Vic. (Highly unsuitable, I always thought. Thug-like Den should have had an Alsatian. Anyway, such is the tendency of 'EastEnders' stars grandly to announce their impending departures 'to do other things' that by the time you read this he may have left to open a poodle parlour in Chelsea as well as to concentrate on his stage career.)

There are no pets in 'Dallas' apart from Ray's horse and several million head of cattle. In 'Dynasty' Alexis has a small hairy parcel of a dog called Rio. But I think she has recently divorced him.

'Emmerdale Farm' has had its quota of dogs. Mrs Bates's hound Bundle was shot for sheep-annoying in an early story-line. Matt has his collie to help with the flock, and his small son Sam has rabbits in a hutch. 'Brookside' is the totally petless soap; no goldfish, pussycat or tortoise has ever had a walk-on rôle. The reason must be fear. If they brought in a pet, one of the Corkhills would nick it.

'PEYTON PLACE'

'Peyton Place', the first major American soap and the first to travel to Britain, has a lot to answer for. It made complicated love-affairs with breathless sex its main ingredient, and made corny cliffhangers the rule for every episode and convinced British viewers that through the leafy backwaters of America strutted a race of glamorous but guilt-ridden women with cupboards full of skeletons and with children fathered by the wrong men and/or not turning out as they should.

It was screened in America from September 1964 to June 1969. Here it ran from 1965 until late 1970 (different ITV regions screened it differently, Granada held back and Thames tried to drop it, were forced by viewers' protests to restart and were one of the regions to begin repeats from 1971).

The seed from which this huge international success grew was in fact 'Coronation Street'. American gambler turned television producer Paul Monash heard of the grip 'Coronation Street' had on British audiences, considered buying that series but decided Americans would not understand Lancashire life or the accents. As a compromise he bought the rights to Grace Metalious's salacious bestselling novel which other producers rejected on the grounds that it was too sin-soaked and shocking for family audiences and, anyway, a film version starring Lana Turner had already been made.

It was a gamble that paid off. The 514 episodes made fortunes for its producers, writers and stars (there were sixty regulars) and launched young newcomers Mia Farrow and Ryan O'Neal into glittering film careers. British ITV companies bought a first batch of 104 episodes for £30,000, their first cheap American package, and could never have regretted it. Shot in the Twentieth Century-Fox studios, ABC netted $62 million from it; it spawned a daytime sequel 'Return to Peyton Place' and two more films.

Audiences of around 8 million here (60 million there) were instantly smitten by the deodorised reworked Metalious tale. Helpfully the main seductions and murders had happened before her stories begin but the series was still tagged television's first 'sex opera' and 'that situation orgy'. (Today it seems tame. Beautiful Allison stayed a virgin for 200 episodes.) Set in a squeaky-clean New England town, population 9875, the town's handsome Dr Rossi was the link between two interweaving sagas. One was Betty Anderson's pregnancy, miscarriage and loveless marriage to rich Rodney Harrington, who really loved virginal Allison (Mia Farrow). The other was bookshop-owner Constance Mackenzie's love for Rossi, who alone knew that Elliot Carson, the father of Constance's illegitimate daughter Allison, was serving eighteen years in gaol. Because of Mia Farrow's well-publicised affair and marriage to Frank Sinatra, Allison was written out two years later. First she fell into a coma, then she mysteriously disappeared. Leigh Taylor-Young was soon hired to play a similar wistful pure young character. Betty (Barbara Parkins) next married Steven Cord who had defended Rodney (Ryan O'Neal) in a murder, then two years later she remarried Rodney. Top-of-the-bill actress Dorothy Malone, who played Connie, was replaced for one year by Lola Albright after she almost died during an operation for blood clots in the lungs. When she returned Connie married Elliot, who'd become the town newspaperman and guru. But the couple were written out in 1968. A year later, with falling ratings, the soap ended with several loose ends including the fate of Dr Rossi, arrested for murder, Rita Harrington, who was pregnant, and Rodney, bound to a wheelchair. In the 1977 movie *Murder in Peyton Place*, Rodney and Allison died together in a car smash. In the 1985 movie *Peyton Place: The Next Generation* (shown here in September 1987), Allison had been in a twenty-one-year catatonic trance but had a lookalike long-haired daughter Megan, who fell for Dana, Betty's son, officially by Rodney but actually (phew, no incest) by Steven.

Mia Farrow was nineteen with waist-length blonde hair when she first grabbed the devotion of British and American viewers as whimsical pure Allison, illegitimate daughter of Constance Mackenzie in 'Peyton Place'. Off-screen she seemed the rebel child of Hollywood (her father is director John Farrow, her mother film star Maureen O'Sullivan). In December 1965, during her affair with Frank Sinatra, her famous hair was suddenly chopped off, leaving the writers to explain Allison's new Joan of Arc crewcut. Predictably it started a trend. Sinatra later told friends he cut it. Apparently on bad terms with some of her co-stars, she didn't endear herself to the producers by skipping recordings to cruise aboard the yacht *Summer Breeze* with Sinatra. She left the soap in April 1966 after several such tensions.

Soon she was the internationally acclaimed star of such hit films as *Rosemary's Baby*, *The Great Gatsby* and *Hannah and Her Sisters*. By the late

1980s the one-time rebellious waif, still fragile-looking and beautiful, was better-known for her marriages to Sinatra and André Previn, her long-term personal and professional relationship with Woody Allen, and as a model mother to nine children.

Dorothy Malone became a familiar face here and in America from 1964 to 1968 as Mia Farrow's television mother, bookshop-owner Constance Mackenzie in 'Peyton Place'. Millions of women admired her long (false) eyelashes and bouffant blonde hairstyle falling seductively over one eye, sympathising with her emotional woman-alone problems.

Born in Chicago in 1925, Malone was a fine experienced actress who, after pretty-girl parts in a string of RKO and Warner pictures, won an Oscar as Best Supporting Actress in the 1956 film *Written on the Wind* in which she played a man-chasing Texan millionairess. After several lean years, she won the rôle of Connie and later said of 'Peyton Place': 'People say the series is overdone but after all that has happened to me in my life, it reflects a great deal of reality.' One real cliffhanger in her life was her September 1965 heart–lung operation in which she nearly died. Her part in 'Peyton Place' was filled by Lola Albright for a year.

She married three times, had two daughters by Jacques Bergerac, whom she took to court for increased child support. He accused her of extravagances including buying a £60 pair of false eyelashes, and the judge rejected her claim. After being written out of the series (after Mia Farrow left to marry Frank Sinatra), she sued ABC and Twentieth Century-Fox for £666,666 for breach of contract but was believed to have settled for considerably less.

Ed (Edwin) Nelson is the New Orleans actor who played Dr Michael Rossi, the kingpin holder of secrets of 'Peyton Place' from 1964 to 1969. Honest, moral, he was also fatally attractive to women yet remained unmarried throughout the immensely popular series. When last seen in the soap he was standing trial for the murder of his latest conquest's husband. By contrast, Nelson was a happily married father of six, who drove a hundred miles each evening to be home in time to help with the children's homework. He was named Father of the Year in 1968. After 'Peyton Place' he combined television and film work with the job of President of the University of California Institute. He played Rossi again in the 1985 movie, *Peyton Place: The Next Generation*.

Ryan O'Neal was a struggling small-part television actor aged twenty-two, a Californian of Irish parents, when he landed the rôle of Rodney Harrington in 'Peyton Place'. As the hot-headed son of the town's rich man, irritable Martin Peyton (George Macready), he became famous as the all-American boy. Earnestly in love with pure Allison Mackenzie (Mia Farrow), he was trapped into a loveless marriage with bad girl Betty Anderson (Barbara Parkins). Later his fate included being ousted from the mansion and forced to live in a dingy flat while on trial for murder and being paralysed and wheelchair-bound.

Off set the actor dated most of the beautiful women in the cast, including Barbara Lana Wood (sister of Natalie), who played Sandy, and in March 1967 married Leigh Taylor-Young who'd just joined the cast to replace the departed Mia Farrow. After the series closed, Hollywood seemed at his feet. He became one of the top male stars of the seventies with films such as *Love Story, What's Up Doc?* and *Paper Moon* (in which he starred with Tatum, his daughter by an early marriage, who won an Oscar for her performance in it).

In the eighties he starred principally in gossip columns as Farrah Fawcett's lover and the father-in-law of tennis's John McEnroe.

Barbara Parkins was soap's first bad girl to become a rich bitch in 'Peyton Place' in which she had a leading rôle, Betty Anderson, for 425 episodes from 1964 until just before its close in 1969. Portrayed at first as a promiscuous teenager who got pregnant but miscarried, her first wickedness was to trap rich Rodney Harrington (Ryan O'Neal) into marriage by telling him she was to have his child. But unlike later soap bitches (p.38) Betty was shown as muddled, someone who'd do anything for love. She later married the town lawyer, then remarried Rodney.

When the soap was cancelled, the petite dark-haired Canadian-born actress, still only twenty-four, was to star in a spin-off, *The Girl from Peyton Place*, but instead went on to rôles in films including *Valley of the Dolls* and *The Kremlin Letter*. She then seemed to turn her back on Hollywood, moving to live in London for eleven years, lived alone, practised yoga and took only the occasional rôle. One was the Duchess of Windsor in the television movie *To Catch a King*. In 1985 she played an older but not wiser Betty heading for another disastrous marriage in *Peyton Place: The Next Generation*.

POLITICS

Politics used to be kept out of soap because politics smacked of the real world and only selected aspects of the real world can bubble to the surface in soap. Politics came in only as a general attitude among soap folk that 'it's politics that causes all the trouble'.

The centre of all successful soaps is the family (either actual families or groups of people joined in a common pursuit). The family must be shown always just overcoming threats to its stability, but there must be no hint of a real threat to the public *status quo*.

So the Moldavian massacre in 'Dynasty' was shown as an act of mass wickedness; there was no questioning of the fitness of King Galen (who turned out to be totally corrupt), and his son Prince Michael was evidently a playboy. The revolution was simply a bad thing because it upset the order as well as the Carrington family's wedding party.

In British soaps, the Falklands, Northern Ireland, the crises in the Middle East, the stock exchange crash never happen. It makes conversation in pubs and round dinner-tables unnatural. But by making its centre the family, where all members can be equal, soap dissolves the tensions of the world outside. Real differences in power, class and wealth are never in focus for long. Even at the Crossroads Motel, a workplace, conflicts between management and workers seldom arise. There was a strike in 1985, but it was not over pay but over a stolen pendant.

The situation changed slightly last year. 'Coronation Street' let politics in when local elections in Weatherfield were called. Ken Barlow, who had been a pacificist socialist in the early days but had seemed to forget his beliefs and become a wet liberal like everyone else in the cast, was suddenly fired with left-wing fervour again. He tried to stand against Alf Roberts, an 'Independent' (which usually means a Conservative). The story-line had Ken's boss at the local newspaper forbidding him to

392

stand and Ken's wife Deirdre, who had never made a squeak about an issue greater than what to cook for tea, standing in his place. When she won the seat it was the human conflicts (defeated Alf had been her boss) which were dramatised. In over a year she has not mentioned a political issue.

'EastEnders' acknowledged the general election by including a couple of episodes in which characters discussed having political allegiances but not their beliefs, and Lou Beale was seen comically avoiding the party political canvassers, leaning from an upper window squawking: 'Ask no questions, hear no lies.'

The American soaps had always allowed politicians to feature fleetingly, usually as symbols of power and often as men who could be corrupted. JR has bribed many, and both he and his good brother Bobby stood as candidates. Bobby was even selected and sat in the Senate but left politics to devote more time to something more important than affairs of state: his family.

This year, inspired by the theatre of political campaigning, 'Dynasty' put both Blake Carrington and Alexis in the running for the governorship of Colorado (God help Colorado!). Blake's motive is a pure desire to serve and bring justice for all. It has allowed touching scenes of the white-haired statesman, flanked by his lovely loyal wife and handsome children on platforms and in the streets. One-time villainess Sammy Jo has become a useful campaign worker, as has gleaming Jeff Colby, Blake's right-hand man. President Reagan couldn't wish for more.

Meanwhile wicked Alexis, motivated only by jealousy and the wish to do Blake down, spread smear stories about Blake's trips to a brothel and put herself forward as a rival. It allowed her to be shot in the head as she took the microphone at a rally. It was an injury from which she recovered speedily. But her image consultant forced her to wear pastel-coloured clothes ('My Gaad, I *hate* past-ells!') and to liken herself to Margaret Thatcher. Perhaps soap's new interest in politics is Reagan's and Maggie's fault.

'THE PRACTICE'

'The Practice' was the 1985 medical soap which never made perfect but which in its early days was certainly passable. Designed by Granada (producers of 'Coronation Street') to start in January just before the opposition's much-heralded 'EastEnders' and sabotage it, there were production rows and problems from the start. The first six episodes were made then scrapped after executives deemed them substandard. Then the ITV network refused them a second evening in the week, so the soap was seen on Fridays and Sundays. Nevertheless the picture of bustling life in a National Health Service clinic in a fictional inner suburb, Castlehulme, was realistic and varied. The mix of mature male GP Dr Lawrence Golding (John Fraser), unmarried dedicated woman GP Dr Judith Vincent (Brigit Forsyth) and their trendy, newly qualified partner Dr David Armitage (Tim Brierley) was balanced. Outside the consulting-rooms and into patients' homes went a sensible senior receptionist, a buxom district nurse and a kindly, harassed health visitor. Two real doctors devised the health problems, and the aim was to show the professionals warts and all. One early story-line concerned bus-driver Kevin Eccles, whose wife was insisting he have a vasectomy. Alarmed and convinced that this meant the end of his sex life, he repeatedly bolted from the surgery and set up home in his own garden shed. Critics diagnosed chronic over-acting all round and some misplaced comedy. Early high ratings of 16 million fell rapidly. The Sunday edition did badly. Perhaps this was due, as one critic pointed out, to the fact that even soap opera fans deserve a day of rest from others' labours, stomach aches and difficulties with the Cap. The producers had scrapped episodes dealing with cancer and cot death for fear of causing distress. A story in which a pregnant woman learns her baby has spina bifida and chooses to have an abortion caused viewers to protest. So by the second series in January 1986 there were no claims to reflect a realistic picture of illness and its treatment.

This time round, the soap was screened for one hour, later on Fridays. Out went searing stories. In came more domestic upsets for the doctors. Dr Golding's wife wanted to separate. Dr Vincent fell foolishly for the young new partner (Rob Edwards replaced Tim Brierley). A Downs Syndrome actor featured in a 'happy' story, and there was lots of fairly heavy-handed comedy. But despite ratings of 8 million and the interest in seeing so many former 'Coronation Street' actors and actresses re-employed as patients 'The Practice' was stopped. Plans for a third series were scrapped. Perhaps Granada were unlucky. Their second new soap, 'Albion Market', also closed that year. Perhaps they would have been more successful had they plumped for one of the other ideas they'd considered two years before: a series about soldiers' wives, a British 'Dynasty' based on a rich Cheshire family; or a soap about gamblers, called 'Casino'.

PRIMA DONNAS

Handling the soap stars can be difficult. Colbys' writer-producers Bill Bast and Paul Husar had to use tact and patience with Charlton Heston, their revered leading man and the only actor allowed to know future story-lines. Beautiful Stephanie Beacham's character, Sable, his young wicked wife, caused him to fume: 'This man Jason would not put up with this woman. She does terrible things to him. He would throttle her!'

Said Bast: 'Every time he wanted to get rid of her, we'd have a scene in which she stepped out of the bath, showed him her body and would hand him a towel forcing him to wrap it round her. After that he would be quiet for several weeks. He would understand why Jason was still interested.'

Actors had to handle each other, too. When Heston walked on to the set everybody fell into line – except, sometimes, Maxwell Caulfield, his screen son, who chose to drive ninety miles each morning from his home to the studios and was occasionally late. Heston made his strong disapproval plain, though he did not confront him. Barbara Stanwyck, however, angered by the tension and bad feeling, openly criticised Caulfield.

Later, when the twenty-six-year-old Caulfield argued and physically fought with a technician during filming, Heston wrote to him accusing him of unprofessional behaviour, sending copies to the rest of the cast. Diplomatic relations weren't sweetened when Heston subsequently passed a back room to spot Caulfield imitating him to the applause of the crew.

'PRISONER: CELL BLOCK H'

'Prisoner: Cell Block H' is the soap about a women's prison which first shocked Australian viewers, then sentenced them to follow it for seven years. There's rarely a 'G'day' at the fictional Wentworth Detention Centre for leering lesbian Franky Doyle and her fellow female 'crims' – murderers, armed robbers, poisoners and con-women. Mostly they're reduced to tears as the nice and the nasty warders make them follow the rules.

The almost laughably grim drama, now washing up as a cult on the soapwaves here, shown late at night on ITV, was created by Reg Watson, who devised and wrote the cleaner-than-clean 'Neighbours'. It was made at the same studios in Nunawading on the outskirts of Melbourne and, after its launch series in 1979 (it ran two hours a week), it was produced by Marie Trevor, now the godmother of the lightweight Ramsay Street saga.

'Prisoner' (as it was called there – the title was changed to distinguish it from our 'Prisoner', the Patrick McGoohan series) was meant to be heavyweight and harrowing. Butch biker Franky, inside for armed robbery, played by bright Brisbane actress Carol Burns, deliberately downbeat in dungarees, with fake nicotine stains on teeth and hands, was, curiously, an instant hit in Australia and here. When the series was sold to America (censored to protect their delicate sensibilities) Los Angeles lesbians picketed the studio protesting at the portrayal. Later they adopted Franky as a champion. When she died they held a wake.

Wentworth's other social misfits were also popular. They included beastly Bea Smith (played by Val Lehman), gaoled for murder and feared by all; man-hungry Marilyn Mason (Margaret Lawrence), convicted prostitute and the prison nympho who managed to have sex with the prison electrician in a recreation-room cubby-hole and on the roof; vicious Vera Bennett, the sadistic warden (Fiona Spence). They were matched by tragic dumb blonde Lyn Warner (played by former weather-girl Kerry Armstrong), accused of burying a child alive and urged to have sex with Franky; friendly 'Mum' (Mary Ward), the garden-loving long-stay prisoner, a mother-confessor for all; and chubby loser Doreen Anderson (Collette Mann), inside for forgery.

A favourite goodie was beautiful schoolteacher Karen Travers (played by Peita Toppano, glorious as the villainess of 'Return to Eden'), convicted for killing her husband. Karen managed to attract the show's other token man (though there were more later), when the handsome (of course) prison doctor, played by Barry Quin, resumed his earlier passion for her. Aussie audiences were thrilled when Peita and Barry's romance became real and they married. They've since split.

Critics at first called Wentworth 'a hell house of appalling animalistic behaviour' where 'morality is a mockery'. Actresses complained of emotional exhaustion and the strains of playing scenes of riots, cell fights, strip-searches, threats and forced attention – always with the lips curled. The television company, Grundy, made sure individual performers had breaks between such scenes, fearing a spate of nervous breakdowns. But Australian actresses – especially mature character actresses – fell over themselves to appear in 'Prisoner', so rare was it in an Aussie television production that rôles did not require them to 'get their gear off' and parade in a swimsuit.

Inevitably some prison officials attacked the soap for misrepresentation. Reg Watson said: 'I don't think we ever tried to make it totally realistic, although we certainly researched the stories thoroughly and two guards from a prison in the Melbourne area assisted us with plot-lines. The real thing would have been women sitting around drugged and depressed for most of the time. That would be deadly dull to watch. We made it like a girls' boarding school gone wrong; the practical jokes led to violence and more violence.'

Phil East, producer for early episodes, admits that the sets now look flimsy and the production techniques old-fashioned. But the cheap-looking fibreglass doors matched those in Australia's newer-style gaols at that time, he says.

Carol Burns left after the first run: her character, Franky Doyle, escaped from Wentworth with Doreen Anderson but, after only a brief taste of freedom, was shot dead by a police officer – which quite turned Doreen's head for a while. With the passing of sad tormented Franky, who was given to spiteful outbursts in her vain attempt to assert her authority – she once stole Lizzie Birdsworth's false teeth (not even Nick Cotton has thought of that one yet!) – Queen Bea was left to reign supreme until fresh challengers emerged in the contrasting shapes of lean sour Noleen and Big Monica, who came in shaking double chins and rippling her muscles.

Reg Watson says unhappy Franky was based on a real case – toned down – and he's rather proud of her. Carol Burns said: 'I liked her. She was a lost soul in a society where the bikie and the lesbian are misfits. She couldn't read. She couldn't communicate. She never had anyone to love her.' But the group who remember the soap best are probably Australia's teachers. Children followed life in Wentworth and used the crims' cruel taunts of the screws as conversation pieces with teachers. Pity the poor schoolmarm to inherit prisoner Vera's nickname: 'Vinegar tits'.

PSYCHIATRY

Psychiatry in soap is a wonderful science. It almost always works and it's almost always instant. It removes mental stains and strains and leaves characters clean and fresh. It was developed from the wonderful films made in the 1940s in which psychiatry sorted out problems quicker than the shrink could blink. They turn up on the telly all the time: *Lady in the Dark*, *The Seventh Veil*, *Spellbound* – all had a psychiatrist who sounded like Herbert Lom (and often was) probing into someone's subconscious and coming up with the answer the audience had spotted three reels back. No matter how nasty the neurosis, how subterranean the psychosis, a few yards of celluloid was all that was needed for a complete cure every time.

Soap psychiatry is still at the same level. Analysis may take years to help anyone in the fancy fauteuils of Fifth Avenue Freudians or the shabby sofas of our socialised shrinks, but that's real life. Soap doesn't have time for that sort of thing. A couple of episodes on the couch fix everything.

British soap is suspicious of psychiatry. (You must be barmy to go to a psychiatrist is the standard view of our soapmakers.) But 'EastEnders' boldly went into new territory when Arthur Fowler had a nervous breakdown. He had been shocked into deep depression by continued joblessness and arrest by the police when he stole the Christmas Club cash to finance Michelle's cancelled wedding. Arthur took to sitting around staring at children's television shows or staring at the walls of his allotment hut. Pauline couldn't understand, then couldn't cope, and Dr Legg got Arthur into a psychiatric ward. He was off-screen but on the pills for a few weeks and when he returned he told us he enjoyed his chats with the nice psychiatrist and cheered up almost at once.

Anne-Marie, Crossroads Motel's bit of bannock (Scottish crumpet to you) caused a lot of trouble when she stole a pendant. Suspicion fell on

400

Lorraine, their token black girl, but finally the bannock confessed. Swiftly a psychiatrist discovered she'd had an unhappy childhood, and Anne-Marie was soon back, chirpy as ever, well over her bout of pendant-pinching.

It was in 'Crossroads', too, that David Hunter's first wife, Rosemary, went barmy and tried to shoot him in the head. Luckily she missed, or there would have been a charge of woodslaughter at the very least. The psychiatrists moved in, but Rosemary never returned.

I think those are the only recorded psychiatric cases in British soap history. Across the Atlantic shrinks get in everywhere, and the rich girls of the prime-time soaps spend as much time with them as with their hairdressers. Sue Ellen, of course, recovers from alcoholism on average once a series, with the aid of skilled Dallas psychiatrists. In 'Dynasty', Fallon Mark I and Fallon Mark II both needed shrinking. Pamela Sue Martin's Fallon (the pretty one) went to the celebrated Dr Toscani (Britain thought of him as Dr Toscanini) and had an affair with him. Krystle took her sufferings to the same sofa, and the shrink fell for her, too. But Krystle's a good girl and she said no. Physician Toscani went batty, was unable to heal himself, and tried to kill Blake on a mountain. Krystle went searching for him on a fine horse and brought him home safe in a King Lear of a storm. Emma Samms (the Fallon with the fall-out bosom) lost her memory in a plane crash and became Randall, just as she was about to remarry Jeff Colby. So she married Miles Colby instead. Expert psychiatry restored her memory, and she exchanged Miles for Jeff, making the treatment well worth the money. In 'Knots Landing' twittery Lilimae Clements – wonderful Julie Harris, the finest actress ever to swim in soapsuds – is clearly saner than most of the other Knotters, but she, too, has been in the hands of the mind doctors. Of course, she did drive a car at Chip, and the police *would* call it attempted murder. Most people thought Chip deserved it. If Lillimae had been a better driver, he would probably have got it. Lillimae had to stay in a sanatorium for thirty-four days. Her successful defence plea was 'temporary insanity'. Temporary indeed.

In 'Falcon Crest' more women go to shrinks than don't, which proves that wine affects more than the liver. Julia, Melissa and Emma have all had therapy. Angela, the one who needs it, somehow escaped. Like JR, her madness is too important to the show to be tampered with by those who minister to a mind diseased.

PUBS

Pubs in soap ought to turn the nation teetotal. The landlords are rude, the bar staff are moody, the beer looks flat, the spirits cloudy, the décor is dreary and one shudders to think about the lavs. Hilda may have done her best cleaning them at the Rover's Return, likewise Ethel at the Vic, but both old girls are long gone. More important, there's so rarely a fresh face at the bar. The locals aren't locals. They're fixtures.

The best things about British soap pubs are the names of the ales. In 'EastEnders' the Vic has Churchill Strong and Luxford & Copley bitter which landlord Den handles with convincing aplomb. In 'Emmerdale Farm' the Woolpack has Efram Monks real ales, but landlord Amos can't avoid too much froth. In 'Coronation Street' the Rover's has Newton & Ridley's brew but, from the way Brian Tilsley always leaves his pint undrunk, it must be cold tea. In 'Crossroads' nothing ever came out of the fonts in the motel bar. But the new pub, the Stag, which emerged overnight as the series coasted home, looked realistic enough. The prospect of meeting superslob Ray Grice at the bar or having daft Jill Chance set in a tizzy with the change would put most customers off. The 'EastEnders' yuppie pub, the green-painted potted-palm-fringed Dagmar, serves lager (of course), and the customers run the risk of being serenaded by Willmott-Brown or, worse, Lofty on the guitar.

In American soaps pubs aren't needed as meeting-places. All the characters live together anyway. But the Cattleman's Club in 'Dallas' seems to have glamorous short-skirted waitresses, and there's always a cowboy bar where Ray or Bobby can go for a good fight.

Winner of the worst drinking-dive in soap, though, is the Waterhole in 'Neighbours'. Even with marvellous Madge at the bar, it's a cheerless dump. And customers should check their change. For three weeks this year the till was fixed at $3.30, and most of the customers only drink mineral water.

RAPE

Rape is committed with added criminal intent in soap opera. The crime is always included for sexy sensationalism, often with a whodunnit plot, and the victim always recovers with unnatural speed.

There were exceptions. 'Brookside' had a taxi-driver rape Sheila Grant in a plot in which several male characters were suddenly possible sex attackers. At least, though, Sheila was seen to be depressed, disorientated and fearful for months afterwards. Her relationship with her husband was damaged, too. The attacker's motive was never explored.

'Crossroads' had worldly Miranda Pollard raped and battered. We saw the bruises, and the man, a salesman staying at the motel, was not 'excused'. It was a bold story-line for an early-evening soap, but Miranda was sent away to mope off-screen.

'EastEnders' made their Walford attacker stop short of rape – perhaps because they dragged the plot out for months, hinting that Pete Beale was the man. When the modified monster appeared it was only for a moment. The rape of Kath Beale before the soap started is regularly referred to; Donna is the child born of it.

In 'Coronation Street', Gail Tilsley appeared to have been raped – or at least assaulted – by one of her then unmarried mother Audrey's fancy men at the end of an episode. By the start of the next the incident had been forgotten – apparently by Gail, too.

The classic forgotten rape was committed in 'Dynasty' by Blake Carrington on his wife Krystle. It was after this that she became pregnant and briefly happy. In the next series Alexis had been introduced as the wicked witch, and Blake developed a halo. The rape was curiously deleted from the official guidebook which publicised the show, although every other tiny plot-twist was included.

In a jealous rage Miles Colby raped Fallon in 'The Colbys' and was seen to be sorry afterwards. It didn't damage Fallon's sanity noticeably, perhaps because she was nuts from day one.

In American soap, rape is a fairly minor offence.

REAL ROMANCE

Real romance is often a sweet side-effect of soap opera. Inter-cast canoodling can copy the scripts. There are two reasons. First, actors and actresses in these round-the-year serials spend so much of their lives in television studios rehearsing, recording, being made up, dressed, directed and talked to about their work that there's little chance to form new friendships or keep old ones in the outside world. Often newspapers make too much of what's merely chumminess. Often they (and so we) miss the carryings-on because of strong inter-group protectiveness. But it certainly happens.

The second reason is that actors and actresses often take on the personalities of their characters or vice versa. The two *do* merge, though few actors would admit it – it's a sort of loyalty to what's partly their creation. So it's entirely understandable when a pair, playing husband and wife, or close friends, marry or become close in private, too.

The cases are too numerous to list, but our 'knowing' that Pat Phoenix and one of her 'Coronation Street' husbands, Alan Browning, really did argue about the top of the toothpaste or who should make the tea – they were really married – was a bonus. Other on- and off-screen relationships include John Alderton, married to fellow 'Emergency – Ward Ten' star Jill Browne. Clive Hornby married his 'Emmerdale Farm' wife, actress Helen Weir. Helen in 'Neighbours' was really married to James Condon who played a con-man, toying with her affections. Peita Toppano, Karen in 'Prisoner', married Barry Quin who loved her through the bars as the prison doctor. In 'Crossroads', David Hunter loved his television wife Sue Lloyd – they were even sacked together. In 'EastEnders', Debs (Shirley Cheriton) loved Andy (Ross Davidson) and left her husband for him. In 'Dynasty', John James was rumoured to be dating the television wife who divorced him twice, Emma Samms. Ted Shackelford had a screen romance in 'Knots Landing' with Terri Austin for eighteen months; then, after twenty-five episodes, the couple announced they'd 'clicked' in their private lives, too. Ted left his second wife for Terri. Kylie Minogue and Jason Donovan, who play teenage sweethearts Charlene and Scott in 'Neighbours', denied rumours of an off-screen romance until photographs of them on holiday together in Bali settled the matter. They weren't just acting.

Perhaps the most public fun from soap's private affairs came from 'Howards Way' – or 'Howards Have It Away' as one headline-writer put it. Tracey Childs teamed up off camera with Tony Anholt, her screen lover. Stephen Yardley left his wife to be with Jan Harvey, the object of his desire in the soap. No reports yet that Kate (Dulcie Gray) has ditched Michael Denison, her husband, to move into a secret senior citizens' love-nest with her television beau Jack Rolfe (Glyn Owen). But nothing would surprise me. I lie. *That* would.

'THE ROBINSONS'

'The Robinsons' was Britain's earliest soap, and like Spam and dried egg first appeared during the Second World War. Unlike Spam and dried egg, soap was an export, not an import.

Alan Melville, a comedy writer with a theatrical and radio background (he had broadcast for 'Children's Hour' in 1927) was given the job in 1942 of devising a radio soap opera to be broadcast to the United States and Canada on the BBC's North American Service. (Melville is said to have come up with the idea while sheltering under a table from a German bombing raid.) First called 'Front Line Family', it showed the Robinson family bravely coping with rationing, Hitler's bombs, their RAF aircrew son going missing, their daughter Kay falling in and out of love.

The Americans loved it. So did the Canadians. Other Overseas Services took it up and dial-twiddling Britons, patriotically avoiding Lord Haw-Haw, began to catch the show. Eventually the soap, retitled 'The Robinsons', was put out for home consumption on the Light Programme. The BBC were ashamed of it, for the sons of Reith had always set their faces firmly against this bastard form of drama from the United States.

Surprise, surprise. Britain took to soap like a rubber duck in a warm bath. The show ran altogether for nearly six years, finally bowing out to make room for Mrs Dale and her Diary. Poor worried Mrs Dale would never have happened without 'The Robinsons', and maybe we would have been a soapless island to this day. So 'Front Line Family' was more important in its way than even Spam or dried egg.

Val Gielgud was the BBC's director of drama when 'The Robinsons' crept on to the British air. Gielgud had put together the BBC Repertory Company, a group of actors who constituted a kind of National Theatre of the Air, and he wasn't going to have his high standards attacked by soap opera, something he thought cheap and nasty, if he could help it.

One of his ideas was that if an actor became a household name in a soap opera he would end up demanding more money, until he was being paid as much as the most distinguished of rep thespians. Serial actors were not in that sort of league, Gielgud thought. If they were good actors, they would not take a job in soap operas, would they? For Val had a very low opinion of soap. It was 'deliberately constructed to hit the very centre of the domestic hearth by playing variations on the theme of all kinds of domestic trivia'. Patrician Val was sure they shouldn't love soap. (The BBC in those days was very good indeed at knowing what was good for us and what wasn't.) He thought by these cheating methods soap would 'achieve a quite unreasonable influence'. So Val Gielgud got rid of 'The Robinsons'. He did allow Mrs Dale to fill the vacuum, probably because he was persuaded that nice middle-class doctor's wife Mrs Dale wasn't really a soap person. Indeed a BBC document said specifically that Mrs Dale 'is not a soap opera of the kind which abounds in American radio'. Well, no, but it wasn't a bad likeness.

Dulcie Gray was one of Britain's first ever soap stars, and she's still shining as grandmother Kate, aged seventy, in 'Howards Way'.

Dulcie met Val Gielgud at a party, and he helped her to find acting work in radio. By 1941 she was picked to play the daughter-in-law in 'Front Line Family', which became 'The Robinsons'. She told me: 'I remember it so well. We were a very ordinary family – a Scottish mother and a cockney father who was in the ARP. The stories were about all the problems people had during the war – and, remember, we were recording in London during the Blitz. We had food shortages, clothing coupons, worries about what was happening in the fighting. It was classed as propaganda, and we knew the aim was to get the Americans into the war. I was very committed. My mother had been killed by the Japanese, my brother was a prisoner of war. Michael [Dulcie's husband Michael Denison, the actor] was serving in Northern Ireland. Practically everybody we knew was affected by the war in some way. Almost immediately we got a tremendous number of letters from people in America and all over the Empire. They seemed really moved by the stories. I can't claim we were solely responsible for bringing in the Americans and winning the war, but I feel our little soap opera helped.'

'ROOMS'

'Rooms' was the afternoon serial from Thames Television which ran intermittently for three years between 1974 and 1977. The setting was 35 Mafeking Terrace, London W14, a house converted into bedsits with plenty of coming and going. Dorothy, the landlady, and Clive, who lived in the basement, were the only characters linking the house's floating population. Sylvia Kay was Dorothy with Bryan Marshall as Clive.

'ST ELSEWHERE'

'St Elsewhere', the American-made hospital drama is possibly not true medical soap in that miracles are rarely, if ever, performed on the operating-table; the patients aren't brave; the doctors and nurses are so deeply flawed you almost *know* them; and there are lots of jokes. It's included because I like it and probably, with its heightened emotions and emphasis on duty, it owes more to 'Dr Kildare' than to 'MASH'. Made by MTM and the team responsible for the police series 'Hill Street Blues', and directed at a similar fast pace, story-lines run over three to four episodes and the scenes at the fictional run-down Boston hospital, St Eligius, are intercut with scenes at the homes of the main doctors. Typically, these are young, brash, troubled or confused (Morrison, Fiscus, Erlich and others), contrasted with old, wise, troubled and confused (Westpall, Craig, Auschlander). Screened in America from 1982 and in Britain, on Channel 4 from 1983 to small but admiring audiences, continuing stories have included the love-life of Fiscus (at one point he was having sex on a slab in the morgue with a beautiful pathologist); the broken marriage of Dr Peter White, who turned rapist; Dr Auschlander's own cancer; the discovery by the womanising plastic surgeon that he has AIDS; and nurse Helen Rosenthal's struggle to make sense of her not always rewarding job. The violent uncaring world outside is always stressed. Among many excellent performers, William Daniels as the prissy, fanatically precise heart specialist Mark Craig deserves the highest awards going.

'SANTA BARBARA'

'Santa Barbara' is the soap to turn to when, dejected, you think there can be nothing worse than 'Crossroads' or 'Black Forest Clinic' or 'Gems'. 'Santa Barbara' is always worse. The first American daytime series to be shown in this country, it's soap scum. It is hard to know which is more rubbishy – the scripts, the sets or the acting.

The interior scenes sound as if they have been recorded in an echo chamber, while the supposed exteriors are the most blatant fakes imaginable. You can see the joins in the beach. Although it costs $30 million, 'Santa Barbara' looks cheap.

The acting defies description. A mass murderer was written in to get rid of some bad actresses, and an earthquake removed a few more. I think it's the corpses who are left, because there are some appallingly lifeless performances – most notably from Paul Burke as the powerful C. C. Capwell. He has now been replaced by Charles Bateman (in true soap tradition, the new face has not been noticed by any of the family). Burke's exit from the rôle follows those of Peter Mark Richman and Lloyd Bochner (Cecil Colby in 'Dynasty'). Bateman is the fourth CC. Perhaps they're trying for ten.

CC's a real no-no – in good company. Set in Santa Barbara in southern California, this epic follows the lives and loves of four families: the aristocratic Lockridges, the influential Capwells, the middle-class Perkinses and the poor Andrades. It boils down to a battle between the Lockridges and the Capwells, both of whom want to run the prosperous ocean-front town and will go to any lengths to achieve their ambition.

Among the locals are T. MacDonald Lockridge's weird widow Minx, played by eighty-seven-year-old Australian Dame Judith Anderson; her lazy eldest son Lionel (Nick Coster); his sex-mad wife Augusta (Louise Sorel), who, when temporarily blinded, was probably the first soap character to get a letter of sympathy from the White House; and Joe

411

Perkins (Dane Witherspoon), who was wrongly imprisoned for killing one of the Capwell sons and has since been struggling to prove his innocence.

'Santa Barbara' is nothing if not daring. It has featured male prostitution, and boasts soap's first transvestite in Dominic who was formerly known as Sophia Capwell. On a clear day, you can still see 'his' bra.

The series began in the States in 1984 and started over here in 1987, ITV's answer to 'Neighbours' on BBC. It attracts audiences of around a million in its morning slot.

Peter Mark Richman, who played CC for six months, summed it up: 'I enjoyed "Santa Barbara" because it is like improvised theatre. There is very little rehearsing, you learn your lines, then go on set and almost wing it.' I'd never have guessed.

SHOPS

Shops in soap are never likely to win their owners Queen's Awards for Industry. They're places in which to trade gossip or commit small crimes, but rarely make healthy profits. Usually the owners sell up or go broke.

In Coronation Street's corner shop run by Alf Roberts there are toffees in glass jars the actor knows are twenty-eight years old. In the early sixties a kid could buy a quarter-pound for threepence (2p), now that amount costs 50p. All the food is real, though the tins and packets (removed and stored every week) have whiskers on them. Viewers often write in asking for the coupons from the back of cornflakes packets. But they can be generous, too. When there was an actual sugar shortage in the seventies and the plot had Alf's stocks sold out, viewers sent him supplies.

In 'Crossroads', Roy Lambert's shop never had enough stock; it was no surprise when he sold up. In 'Dallas', Jenna had a fashion boutique. No customer was ever seen to make a purchase.

Another reason for soap shops' poor profits is the pilfering that's not in the plot. In Alf's corner shop the nicking for nibbles by members of the cast became so bad that the small edible items had to be sprayed with off-putting mothball-type material. In 'EastEnders' producer Julia Smith had to post notices: 'Pinching Fruit from Pete's Stall Is Strictly Forbidden.'

413

SMOKING

Smoking in soap is a dying art. In a few years from now no soap pub will have ashtrays, no hard-pressed housewife will be allowed to reach for her fags; Dot Cotton and Bet Lynch will be chewing nicotine gum and telling their neighbours of the harmful effects their former habit had on their health. None of the Aussie Neighbours smoke now. Or drink or swear. Strewth!

Fair enough, I suppose. Soap operas are morality tales, and tobacco has become a wicked temptation good folk must shun. But realism is suffering as producers fall in with anti-cigarette campaigners. If you watch a forties or fifties film in which almost every character is wreathed in smoke (even the sensible family doctor), you'll see how dramatically successful the lobby has been. In American soaps only unreliable or devious characters may light up. 'Dynasty''s Alexis smokes using a long holder, as befits her thirties movie-queen style. But not often. Joan Collins smokes much more. The Health Education Council in Britain has its eye on the smokers in 'EastEnders', 'Brookside' and 'Coronation Street'. Most of them are lower-class and female, and their habits are justified in terms of stress. No professionals smoke. The Council is worried about the effect on children who watch 'EastEnders' smokers: Dot, Pauline, Nick, Wicksy and policemen Rich and Quick were seen in the trial period to puff at a rate fourteen times greater than in the American dramas. The Council was alarmed that smoking was treated on a par with walking, reading or eating: normal, everyday activities. More anti-smoking propaganda was called for. Story-lines about characters giving up, perhaps? Or Ken Barlow campaigning to make the Rover's a Clean Air Zone? Hilda Ogden – wherever she is – is almost certainly puffing away, ciggie held backwards, cupped in her hand. And why not, eh, chuck?

'SOAP'

'Soap' was a send-up of American daytime soap operas screened in a late-night slot here by ITV from September 1978 to January 1982 and repeated by Channel 4 from 1983 to 1986. (In America it ran from 1977 to 1981 despite sustained orchestrated protests from religious groups, notably the Catholic Church, objecting to comic treatments of homosexuality, exorcism, nymphomania, impotence among many themes.) Created, written and produced by Susan Harris, it portrayed two families, the rich Tates and the less well off Campbells. Benson, the Tates' witty black butler, became so popular that he was given his own series. Jessica Tate (Katherine Helmond) and Mary Campbell were sisters who had four sons between them from previous marriages. One was a gangster, one gay (planning a sex-change), one a ventriloquist who thought his dummy was real, and Peter, a bed-hopping tennis coach killed early on in the shower. Jessica was arrested for the murder. Then in the second season her husband Chester confessed to the killing. Later crazy plots involved one daughter's marriage to a priest; the gay son's switch to heterosexuality; Jessica's romance with a South American revolutionary; and Burt, Mary's husband, being kidnapped by aliens, followed by Mary's affair with Burt's clone.

Each episode ended with a narrator asking a series of life-or-death questions with comic solemnity. Many soap fans hated 'Soap' on principle. Others disliked its often noisy hysteria, but Katherine Helmond was a sought-after frequent guest to British television chat-shows and 'Soap' earned a cult following here. Because of this a new series of repeats on ITV is planned to start soon.

SOAPTALK

Soaptalk is the language scriptwriters pretend does not exist, but those who produce dialogue for the American, the Australian and most of the British soaps (with the possible exception of 'Brookside' and 'East-Enders') secretly flip through a special phrasebook at the beginning of every episode. How else would the following lines appear so often?

In the shop, pub or restaurant

'Well, if it isn't [*full name, to help viewer*]! What brings you to these parts?'

'You haven't touched a thing.'
'I'm sorry – I'm just not very hungry.'
'But you *must* eat. . . .'

'Look, you can say it's none of my business, but. . . .'

'I hate to do this, but something important just came up. I must leave.'

'If that's true (*gasp!*), they can't get married.'

In the hospital

'Just tell me, Doctor, is he/she going to be all right?'
'I can't say. We're running some tests.'

'I know the treatment/drug/operation is new and untested, but it's all we have and without it he/she will die. . . .'

'He/she has just got to pull through. . . .'

'Look, Doctor, I don't care how much it costs. . . .'

'How quickly can [*name of world-renowned specialist who lives thousands of miles away*] get here?'

In the office or boardroom

'I built this business up from scratch. . . .'

'What's that supposed to mean?'

'Two can play at that game. . . .'

'I can explain everything.'

'This could destroy all I've worked for.'

In the bedroom

'Don't you understand . . . I love you . . . everything is going to be all right.'

'But what about your wife/girlfriend/husband/boyfriend . . .?'

'It happens, to everyone. . . .'

'You're still thinking about him/her, aren't you?'

(*When the phone rings*) 'No, don't answer that. . . .'

'SONS AND DAUGHTERS'

'Sons and Daughters' is the so-bad-it's-good feuding-families soap, Australia's answer to the over-the-top melodramas washing in from America in the early eighties. In some ways it was more daring. 'Dallas' didn't have incest; this did.

Made between 1981 and 1987, and still popular in afternoon slots in Britain and many other countries, it also solved a long-standing dilemma for Australian producers. This was the rivalry between the residents of Sydney and Melbourne. 'Sons and Daughters' bridged the gap, setting its richer, middle-class Hamilton family in Sydney and the poor Palmers in Melbourne and actually producing episodes in both cities. The link in the plot was that twins born to unwed David Palmer and Patricia Dunne were separated when the couple split. They met twenty years later and – you guessed it – fell in love. Meanwhile Patricia (Rowena Wallace) married into a wealthy Sydney family and her daughter Angela took her new husband's name. When Angela, played by dark-haired Ally Fowler (later to play Zoe in 'Neighbours') later met broody John Palmer (Peter Phelps) the scene was set for UST (unresolved sexual tension) plus a great deal of fighting from mum, who became 'Pat the Rat', and solid truck-driver dad.

When this pair remet, there was a torrid affair, kept secret from their respective partners, hen-pecked landowner Gordon (Brian Blain) and warm-hearted frump Beryl (Leila Hayes).

Audiences were able to hiss happily at Wayne Hamilton (Ian Rawlings) and coo over a number of babies, including the one born to Dave's other son Kevin (Stephen Comey). Kevin began as one of the cheap check-shirt brigade (as opposed to the suited Hamiltons), but after going temporarily deaf from a bomb blast he became a Sydney businessman and a stockbroker in London.

Throughout the saga, one of the few constants in a sea of changing faces – over 2000 actors shared the trials and tribulations – was Aunt Fiona, the worldly guest-house owner who raised baby John for his father, knew all the secrets and was the shoulder for every main character to cry on – a spirited performance by Pat Macdonald. Anne Haddy (later Helen in 'Neighbours') was almost as popular in her rôle as the Hamiltons' lovable housekeeper Rosie.

The undoubted hit of 'Sons and Daughters', though, was the bitchery of Pat the Rat Hamilton, played by two actresses. Coventry-born silver-haired Rowena Wallace established her as the iron-fisted roost-ruler, ranting and raving one minute, breaking down the next, but always the woman viewers loved to hate. (Not just in Australia. Rowena scooped Best Bitch awards in British viewers' polls, too.) After three years she left, exhausted. But the rôle survived. Pat left for Rio de Janeiro, escaping arrest for murder to undergo plastic surgery, in the script. Blonde Belinda Giblin, an actress known for Australia's earlier sexy soap 'The Box', came in six months later as the reconstructed Pat 'in disguise' under the name of Alison Carr.

Viewers there and here happily 'saw through' the disguise but accepted the impostor underneath.

THE STAIRCASE

The staircase is a major asset to a soap opera. If only the Crossroads Motel had had one, Jill might be tumbling down it now.

'Dynasty' has had the most mileage from its two-flight, thirty-two-step, wrought-iron-bannister job, the pride of the Carrington mansion. Alexis has flounced down it. Krystle has glided majestically or fallen catastrophically down it; she went into labour, prematurely (of course), after cascading down it, first slipping on marbles left on the midway landing by Little Blake. Dana descended it for her wedding to Adam, glowing among the flowers woven through the ironwork. The drama of any average scene is always doubled by a trek up or down those steps.

(Actually the stairs go nowhere. On the permanent 'Dynasty' set at the Warner Hollywood Studios, the last step leads to a mass of lights and a sheer drop. The downstairs hall is revamped and used as the upstairs hall, so that actors seen going down from the top do a graded crouching act to the amusement of all.)

Dallas's Southfork mansion has a less impressive staircase, but second rate or not it's frequently used to heighten fights. Characters are always coming down to use the phone at the bottom. Clayton took a twisted turn when his heart condition needed to be shown.

And 'Flamingo Road', which featured the Weldon mansion stairs, didn't hold back. Bitch Constance was pushed backwards from the top. A few episodes in a wheelchair and she was as right as rain.

British soaps haven't held back with stair dilemmas, either. Ethel in 'EastEnders' fell over an avocado and in 'Coronation Street' Alf Roberts fell over Bet's shoes when she was his tenant in the flat.

Most of the houses in 'Neighbours' are one-level, so dramatic falls are likely to be few. They do have a swimming-pool with drowning potential, though, so we mustn't grumble.

420

'STARR AND COMPANY'

'Starr and Company', about two families and a firm making buoys, was the BBC Drama Department's first twice-weekly serial ('The Grove Family' had been a Light Entertainment production). It might have been the last but for the energy and organisational flair of young Gerald Glaister, a BBC play-director from Chesterfield who was dragged reluctantly into producing it.

It began live transmissions on Mondays and Thursdays at 7.30 p.m. in March 1958, introducing viewers to the town of Sullbridge, fifty miles south of London; to Joseph Starr, a stern retired naval engineer, recently moved there to start the firm; his supportive wife Edith; their son Robin, who also worked for the firm; and Julia, their dashing daughter, a London public relations officer. Working with them was loyal Jim Turner from Lancashire and his far more humble family. Conflict between the families and with the locals, and dramas with the customers, soon became highly popular.

But Glaister had determined to work on this for only four months. 'No one had the faintest idea how to do live drama twice a week,' said Glaister. 'We fumbled through, and I have to say "Starr and Company" wasn't bad. It could have gone on for longer, but I wanted to do other things. After I left I cheekily sent a paper to Michael Barry, the Head of Drama, setting out what I felt was needed for twice-weekly series in full detail. To my amazement he sent a reply signed by himself and the Controller of Programmes. It said: "Agreed." ' Four years later, Alan Bromley, producer of 'Compact', withdrew Glaister's document from the vaults. Soap Method was laid down. Glaister went on to produce 'Dr Finlay's Casebook', 'The Expert', 'The Brothers', the hugely successful 'Colditz', 'Secret Army' and most recently 'Howards Way' among many series. 'I'm not a Family Soaps Expert any more than I was a War Expert when I made "Colditz",' he said. 'I'll do anything I think has a good entertaining story.'

'THE SULLIVANS'

The Sullivans have been fighting the Second World War in a small Australian town since 1976, and those patterned sleeveless pullovers and forties frocks are still going strong. In the soap tradition, the caring family of Dave, Grace and their four kids, Norm the rock-like best friend, voluptuous Maggie at the pub, the humble German family who run the shop, Mrs Jessup the busybody, and a good few more go on suffering but surviving. They deserve to. 'The Sullivans' was the first Australian series to travel the world – about 600 hours of it were made up to 1982 – and it's probably the finest yet. No wonder it's regularly repeated in daytime slots here (on ITV) and in more than thirty other countries.

The Bellamys of Belgravia, the family in our 'Upstairs Downstairs', were partly to blame. That series unleashed nostalgic cravings all over Oz when it was shown there in the early seventies. Granada sent over their 'A Family at War' saga, and the cravings got worse. So when the Crawford company sent one sheet of paper outlining a thirteen-week series to Australia's Channel 9 the television station executives didn't hesitate to accept.

Crawfords bought and restored an Edwardian house in Canterbury, near Melbourne, and Alan Hardy led a team of idealistic young writers to invent scenes of the global conflict: in Yugoslavia, Holland, Greece, the deserts and the jungles – all filmed in the scrublands, hills and quarries of Victoria. 'I think we were all in awe of the war,' Alan told me. 'We were able to add so many fascinating political and historical things. We raided army surplus stores and old clothes shops – and I don't think we made many mistakes.'

The first thirteen hours, which were to have ended as the two older Sullivan boys, John and Tom, went off to war, were soon extended. Viewers saw John, a medical student and pacifist, clash with his father, a First World War veteran and a foreman at a small engineering works. John had also fallen for lovely Anna Kaufman, who suffered prejudice from the town bigots, along with the rest of her family.

The adored star of the show was Grace Sullivan, played by Lorraine Bayly (now a radio personality in Australia). As the quiet, highly principled Catholic mother supportive of her husband she radiated warmth and stability, as have all strong soap women before and since.

Some of the best-written stories concerned events after the war. Kitty Sullivan (only thirteen at the start) married a photographer, went with him to Hiroshima and was so horrified by the aftermath of the atomic explosion that she committed suicide. Terry, her freckle-faced all-Australian brother, could not adjust to peace and turned to petty crime. His young wife Caroline, gainfully employed before the war, struggled to get work on the land, but was sacked to make way for a newly returned soldier – the law of the day.

Slow and sentimental at times, 'The Sullivans' bravely faced the issues of war while examining the morality of the forties. It provided romance, stock surprises, conflict, and characters viewers cared for deeply. When a V-bomb killed Grace Sullivan, mass mourning followed.

The show ended in 1982. Young audiences decided their parents' war was over.

'TAFF ACRE'

'Taff Acre' was 'Emmerdale Farm' with pit ponies. The first English-language serial to come from Wales, it was shown two afternoons a week for twenty-six episodes between September and December 1981.

Made by Harlech Television at a cost of £500,000, Taff Acre was the name of a fictional South Wales village, about twelve miles from Cardiff.

The central characters were the Johnson family. Actor Richard Davies (Mr Price in 'Please Sir!') was unemployed Max with Rhoda Lewis as his breadwinner wife Beth. They had two sons: Wayne, made redundant at seventeen (Stuart Davis) and PE teacher Gareth (Dewi Morris). The glamorous Beth Morris was Gareth's pushy wife Cilla. The Johnsons also had a daughter, nurse Sian, played by Sue Jones Davies.

'Taff Acre' was quickly laid to rest in the valleys.

'TAKE THE HIGH ROAD'

'Take the High Road' is Scotland's answer to 'Coronation Street', and it proves conclusively there's more than caber-tossing and listening to Andy Stewart records going on up there. It is shown in the evenings in Scotland, and it regularly attracts larger audiences than any soap except 'EastEnders'. Other areas screen it in the afternoons and, although viewing figures are up to the 6 million mark, the show's makers, Scottish Television, have yet to convince the English companies that it warrants an evening slot.

'Take the High Road' started in 1980 and has notched up well over 500 episodes. It is set in the fictional village of Glendarroch, which is really Luss on Lock Lomondside where the series is filmed. The village is owned by Glendarroch Estate which, until 1987, had been run for generations by the Cunningham family. In the biggest shock-horror story to hit 'Take the High Road', Elizabeth Cunningham, the lady laird, was killed in a car crash and her daughter, single parent Fiona, also left. The new laird and lady laird at the Big House are Sir John and Lady Margaret Ross-Gifford. They are English and therefore unpopular with the estate workers.

Glendarroch isn't a million miles from Dallas now. 'Take the High Road' has included rape, attempted murder, schoolgirl pregnancy, passion, car crashes and, of course, money problems. The most hated character is rival estate-owner Davie Sneddon who, the publicists would have us believe, is a worthy rival to Dirty Den and JR. Irish actor Derek Lord, who plays Sneddon, puts it into perspective: 'I wouldn't mind being compared to Dirty Den. But he gets a thousand letters a day – I get ten a year!'

Popular characters are local gossip Mrs Mack (played by Gwyneth Guthrie), solid and dependable shepherd Dougal Lachlan (Alec Monteath), village shop-owners Isabel and Brian Blair (Eileen McCallum and

425

Kenneth Watson), farmer Inverdarroch (John Stahl) and heart-throb Jimmy Blair (Jimmy Chisholm). Edith Macarthur played Elizabeth Cunningham (she was 'killed off' at her own request – she wanted to return to the theatre). Jan Waters took her place as super-bitch Lady Margaret Ross-Gifford, and Michael Browning (brewery boss George Newton in 'Coronation Street') is Sir John.

'Take the High Road' has learned a lot from previous Scottish soaps 'High Living' and 'Garnock Way'. Its success is such that it has been sold to Sri Lanka, Turkey, Zimbabwe and Saudi Arabia, all episodes shown in Saudi being carefully dewhiskied to ensure there is no evidence of alcohol consumption!

TOURIST SOAP

You tried to book a room at the Crossroads Motel. You tried to camp by Emmerdale Farm. You wanted to walk around Albert Square and nose in the windows and peep round the back. You wrote, you rang, you were told 'get lost'. But now Britain is catching up with Hollywood – slowly. You can stroll along Coronation Street's cobbles, visit a museum that houses Ena Sharples's hairnet, Albert Tatlock's cloth cap and Hilda Ogden's curlers. Perhaps you can even stroke the cat that curls up on the rooftop with the opening credits. You can drink a pint of ale – call it Newton & Ridley's – at the Rover's Return. Not *the* Rover's, but a replica a stone's throw away from the 'real' one, housed on a vast 'location tours' site on the banks of the River Irwell where Manchester joins Salford. The site opened this year, and 750,000 fans were expected to take the three-hour jaunt. At Elstree studios where 'EastEnders' is produced there were plans to allow the public to come and worship. But the security problems were too great: uninvited visitors, even some BBC staff, regularly remove items as souvenirs, not to mention the fruit from Pete Beale's barrow. And details of future story-lines could, it was claimed, be guessed from some props. So, sadly, the scheme was never developed. A great shame, some said. The BBC could have doubled its licence-money income with the popularity of the show.

'TRIANGLE'

'Triangle' was the BBC's 1981 all-at-sea soap about life and love on a passenger and freight ferry travelling between three points: Felixstowe, Gothenburg and Amsterdam. It should have been a success, coming after a public announcement by Graeme McDonald, head of series and serials, that the BBC was now seriously searching for an all-year-round soap opera – an ideal snootily rejected in the past. But because 'Triangle' was recorded expensively on location, on board a North Sea ferry, it never sailed all year round or full steam ahead. It sank with only 6 million viewers aboard after its first trip, January to April 1981. Refloated from April to July for two successive years, it did no better. The fault was not with the stars, however. Kate O'Mara, a favourite since 'The Brothers', was the ship's siren and purser Katherine Laker, who had bravely to pretend to sunbathe topless under grey skies in the first episode. Since the soap was screened at 6.55 p.m. on Mondays and Wednesdays, this caused protests, but unfortunately failed to bump up viewing figures. Michael Craig, fifties and sixties film star, played the distinguished-looking captain, but was given no scope to be heroic or lovable. Larry Lamb was ship's engineer Matt, eager for romance but denied it by the script. There were stowaways, thefts from passengers, men overboard, even an attempted rape, but the busier each episode the less addictive it seemed. Perhaps life aboard a ferry is neither cosy nor glamorous enough for a soap opera. And perhaps the squabbling crew were never a family.

'UNITED!'

'United!', the would-be gritty soap following the fortunes of a fictional football club, kicked off on Mondays and Wednesdays from October 1965, in the same week as 'The Newcomers'. Made at the BBC's Gosta Green, Birmingham studios, the series was set somewhere in the Midlands. Like 'The Newcomers', set in East Anglia, it was intended to contrast with the airy-fairy London-based 'Compact', dropped two months earlier. Devised by Anthony Cornish, written by Brian Hayles, the action revolved around the efforts of blunt, bearded club manager Gerry Barford (David Lodge) to lift Brentwich FC from the bottom of the Second Division of the Football League. He had to cope with a tycoon chairman with a snooty wife, an ingratiating club secretary, his own anxious wife and desperately keen footballing son, a prickly team captain (Bryan Marshall) and a womanising goalie (Stephen Yardley, later to leer at ladies in 'Howards Way'). Mitzi Rogers played Barford's pretty secretary; and Arthur Pentelow, later of Emmerdale Farm (p.306), played the supporters' club chairman. Although the actors were all said to be keen amateur players, and game sequences were filmed on the Stoke City pitch, there were loud complaints early on of too little play, too many women and too much tittle-tattle. Jimmy Hill, then Coventry City's boss, was hired to vet the scripts, yet footballer Danny Blanchflower lambasted it as wholly unrealistic. Wolverhampton Wanderers FC struggling at the time, complained that the plots were unfairly close to their real progress, and the BBC had to reassure them it was coincidence. By February 1966 seven of the cast were dropped and new writers Max Marquis and Dick Sharples brought in to make 'United!' 'sweatier' and less cosy. The team's woman physiotherapist was despatched, but with its usual decorum the BBC insisted that bathing-trunks were still worn in the after-match shower scenes. By March 1966, Barford was sacked (after the actor asked to leave) and later that year Ronald Allen (p.166), the pin-up from 'Compact', came in as Brentwich's new manager. This doubtless won more women supporters but prompted cynics to wonder if 'United!' would become 'Compact' in boots with Gussie as the next goalkeeper. After eighteen months, when it showed no signs of rising in the ratings league – audiences had stayed around 6 million – the production was put on the transfer list. It ended in March 1967. A brave attempt to make the muddy masculine world of sport a subject for soap had failed. In soap you need women playing centre forward or you can never win.

'WAGGONERS WALK'

'Waggoners Walk' usurped 'The Dales' as the BBC Radio 2 serial in April 1969, a soap for and about younger people, set in a town as opposed to the Radio 4 country soap 'The Archers'. Positively hated at first (grieving fans of 'The Dales' couldn't switch off fast enough), it featured three young women, Tracey, Lynn and Barbara, sharing a Hampstead flat. One had an illegitimate child and married a homosexual (who later 'reformed'), another's marriage broke up and the third lived in sin. In the flat below lived a married couple; and an elderly cockney pair, Stan and Alice Hickey, filled the basement. Determined to avoid the cosy, middle-class image of 'The Dales', 'Waggoners Walk' went for social problems – abortion, child custody, hypothermia, even murder – squabbles, confrontations of every kind, rather as 'EastEnders' was to do sixteen years later on television. Listeners protested, but five years later 4 million of them followed it (more than followed 'The Archers'). In 1974 listeners were asked to write their own plots in a competition (one suggested the whole cast board a bus which is then driven over the edge of a cliff), and critics regularly praised it for its liveliness and lack of condescension. But after eleven years the axe fell. 'Waggoners Walk' went as part of a BBC money-saving plan in June 1980.

WEDDINGS

Weddings in soap are even more wonderful than in life. They provide the perfect excuse to gather all the cast (or most of it), to dress up and get emotional. And any soap-writer worth his salt knows to add shocks, surprises, a little disappointment but the maximum chance for us, the guests at home, to enjoy a good cry.

Naturally there are far too many soap nuptials to mention. And, predictably, the Americans do weddings bigger. Not better, though. No one could envy Sue Ellen having to remarry JR in the Southfork drive in a force 9 gale. And they do them differently. The wedding in a Moldavian greenhouse for Amanda and Prince Michael in 'Dynasty' was the only mass-killings marriage I can recall soap celebrating.

There have been non-weddings, too. The 'EastEnders' event when Michelle turned back at the church door, didn't walk up the aisle and wasted all those sausage rolls her dad had stolen £1500 to pay for was perhaps the best, providing a flood of sympathy for non-bridegroom Lofty. 'Neighbours' had a non-wedding, too – a ridiculous affair with a burglar in a gorilla suit hijacking the bride's car. In both cases the non-married couple did the deed later, to great relief. In 'Coronation Street', Rita Fairclough's non-marriage to Alan Bradley (he tricked her into attending at the register office, but she angrily refused to comply) was an original version.

'Howards Way' produced an impressive do with a splendid gown for Lynne Howard (Tracey Childs) and her diminutive pigtailed Frenchie 'Clod' (Malcolm Jamieson). It looked as though someone would jump up from the pews to 'give just cause' why the couple shouldn't be joined, but, no, we couldn't have everything.

'The Young Doctors', the very moral Australian soap in which doctors and nurses had to marry before they could play doctors and nurses, did halt a wedding in this way. Dr John Forrest – played by Alan Dale (p.376), Jim in 'Neighbours' – intervened in the wedding of Liz and Ben. (Liz was played by Rebecca Gilling, future heroine of 'Return to Eden'.)

'The Colbys' managed to include a back-from-the-dead event to halt the wedding of Jason Colby and his sister-in-law Francesca. The bride spotted her 'dead' husband on the way down the aisle and fainted.

In 'Dynasty', Alexis married Cecil Colby seconds before he became a corpse. The chap was in an oxygen-tent following the heart attack she caused the night before in bed. When Alexis married Sean Rowan this year, the earth moved. Literally. An earthquake sent tremors rumbling through the Los Angeles studio, delaying filming for two hours.

'A Country Practice' went for a wedding with added animal appeal. Their vet Vicky married Simon her doctor, but only after guests had to wait for the bride to finish operating on an injured horse in a field while the bridegroom administered the anaesthetic.

The funniest do was the wedding of convenience between Bet and Alec in 'Coronation Street'. He looked dyspeptic, disgruntled and terrified; and Bet, in a dress with sleeves bulging so much I wondered if she had a barrel of beer in each, looked as though someone was pushing a pencil up her rear.

American daytime soaps are shameless with weddings. Lisa in 'As the World Turns' married Farley Granger in white with full veil and trimmings. It was her seventh marriage. But the Worst Wedding Dress prize must go to Cathy in 'Knots Landing', who married Josh in a short-skirted strapless number resembling a tart's underwear.

The Kathy in 'Emmerdale Farm' had her wedding dress ruined by a collapsed ceiling this January. In stepped the bridegroom's gran, miserable matriarch 'Ma' Annie Sugden. When she reached into the bottom drawer of her sideboard, I feared she was going to alter an old pinafore for the girl. Instead she produced her ancient wedding dress and slaved all night to take in the seams. In the morning, slumped over her Singer, Ma was the heroine.

WOMEN LOVE SOAP

It's strikingly clear that all the successful soap operas have strong women characters: women who cope with all crises; women who manipulate others – the famous soap bitches (p.38); women who demonstrably care about others, especially other family members; women who can be relied on to Do What's Right. Most of the men, by comparison, are out being powerful or selfish or dangerous or decent.

Having created these supermums, superbarmaids and supermotelmanageresses, the sensible soap-writer then obeys the next rule: never let the male characters stop thinking about the women characters. The women must be centrally involved at all times, even when this is highly unrealistic. In 'Dynasty', for instance, Blake's wife Krystle knows as much as I do about, say, oil leases in the South China Seas or big business generally. Yet she's somehow involved in every crisis at the firm, Denver-Carrington. When Blake faces ruin she sells the jewels he gave her, the symbol of their love (we have capitalist soap here). When deals come good, he gives her another set of jumbo-sized diamonds. She smiles through her tears. Life goes on.

So men in successful soap must always be aware of the women's feelings. They must desire them, fear them, hate them, do anything but ignore them.

Soap women emerge not as more liberated, luckier or happier than Miss or Mrs Average watching them. Mostly they suffer more – look at Sheila Grant in 'Brookside' or Bet in 'Coronation Street' or any of the poor cows of 'EastEnders'. But they are more important in the lives of their men and children. Can you wonder that this seems attractive to the soap fan rushing in from work, trying to watch, say, 'Emmerdale Farm' or 'Neighbours', cooking the family meal before taking her coat off or being jeered at for trying to listen to 'The Archers' on the radio when the teenagers are demanding 'The Network Chart Show' and Father wants 'Sports Desk'?

WRITERS

Writers of soap come in every shape, class and kind. You don't have to be a poet or a creative genius. Some of the best words to British sagas have been dreamed up by housewives, playwrights, actors, journalists, an army captain, a farmer, a solicitor's clerk – with not a single BA in Eng. Lit. between them.

Once they find they can write the simple speeches, the platitudes, the rows and the smalltalk of soap, their agents sometimes urge them to move on to 'better things'. For some there are no better things. A good soap half-hour's worth which makes all the compromises with cast and budget and recording times, which fits with all that has gone before and all that is to follow, but which adds indelibly to the lives and depths of the characters, is a true literary achievement. Charlie Humphries, for example, occasional contributor to 'EastEnders', created thirty minutes with that soap's Dot and Ethel (no other characters were seen) in which nothing happened apart from Ethel's dozing off and Dot's thinking, fleetingly, that her friend might be dead. It was, however, a perfect little play – two sad old women reflecting on their lives.

For their efforts, scriptwriters are usually well paid. An average fee for a half-hour script is about £2000 with more added if there's an omnibus or foreign sales. On 'Crossroads' in its latter stages, writers produced only the dialogue, all the scenes were mapped out for them.

On 'EastEnders' four scriptwriters meet the producer and script-editor together. At the end each writer is designated one script (sometimes they toss a coin) and has to deliver by the following day his or her synopsis of the developments for approval. After two to three weeks the first draft is produced; rewrites are hurried, and the writers attend recordings making small changes if they turn out to be necessary.

On 'Emmerdale Farm' writers are encouraged to be inventive. Only the outline of a story is decided in advance, and writers tend to work on sequences of four, sometimes six, scripts at a time. They're given 'elbow room'. James Robson, sometime labourer, factory worker, now one of the most versatile soap-writers we have, says: 'You have to be a chameleon – you are not asked to fill an empty stage with life and drama. It's quite a responsibility. The knack is to keep the tenor of the life of the soap, to fit in with previous episodes.'

Attending a 'Coronation Street' script conference, said one survivor, is like being shut in a room with a dozen secondhand-car dealers all trying to flog their own vehicles to the producer. James Robson agrees. '"Coronation Street" conferences were dreadful. People would shout and scream. Gay men would flounce around. Others would shrink from the bitching, walk out of the room and have to be brought back from the lift.' At these conferences two story-line writers take notes to summarise what should happen in episodes. They're nicknamed 'the Beano Kids' because they must reduce complicated events to cartoon brevity. One writer, for instance, spent twenty minutes eloquently describing the appalling mental turmoil and clash of desires and duty Deirdre faced during her affair with Mike Baldwin. After he finished, the group remained pensively and approvingly silent until a Beano Kid said flatly: 'So Deirdre's fairly upset, then . . .?'

The best soap writing, thinks Robson, comes when writers can draw on their personal backgrounds and experiences. He finds writing for 'Emmerdale Farm' and, before that, 'The Archers' the more satisfactory because it relates to his early life in similar villages. If the patois of country people ever eludes him, he can take a walk near his North Yorkshire home and speak to farmers 'every bit as outspoken and bloody-minded as Jack Sugden'. A writer's childhood is crucial, he thinks. 'Crossroads' never rang true quite simply because 'Whoever heard of a writer with fond memories of being brought up in a motel?'

Peter Batt, one-time 'EastEnders' writer, agrees that backgrounds are important. A sports columnist with a barrow-boy's accent and wit, his own life reads like a (bad) soap opera. Out of work and broke, his wife spotted a newspaper feature on the preparation of the first cockney soap. Batt sent off copies of two scripts for (never-made) gangster films he'd written and told producer Julia Smith that he had the jargon and knew the insides of most of London's snooker halls, dog tracks and pubs. He was summoned to the famous Shepherds Bush wine bar, told there wasn't much chance, then sent off to write an episode. He wrote a couple, then six more including one excellent and moving episode in which Michelle gave birth to Den's baby, and then slipped out of favour. Meanwhile he began to write a commissioned series for Penelope Keith and returned to success in Fleet Street. 'Julia Smith and Tony Holland are renowned for giving chances to unknown writers, and I shall always be grateful. I enjoyed the script conferences. They weren't for the timid, though,' he said. And he rarely watches 'EastEnders'. 'I wanted more humour in it. I liked it earthy. There were too many middle-class, middle-aged women writing for it at one time. But, then, working-class kids have to live and struggle a bit. Too soon they *are* middle-aged – and middle-class.'

'THE YOUNG DOCTORS'

'The Young Doctors' began on Australian television in 1976 with Craig saying to Marilyn, 'I'll never forget you, Nurse, you know that,' and Marilyn whispering back: 'And I'll never forget you, Doctor Rothwell.' Then the couple, embracing in the operating-theatre of the Albert Memorial Hospital, parted, sighing.

White-coated slap and tickle among good-looking young people was the prescribed treatment for this Grundy soap, which ran five nights a week until 1981 (almost 1400 episodes) and is still gratefully followed in afternoon repeats on ITV here.

Created by Reg Watson of 'Crossroads' and 'Neighbours' fame, it worked by injecting romance, comedy and melodrama in equal doses. Few of the complaints proved fatal, very little tomato ketchup blood was lost, and no plot-complication failed to respond to transfusions of concentrated soap corn. The medical staff suffered chronically from weddings, frequently from separations but never from divorce, which writer-producer Alan Coleman felt might damage viewers' health. He also banned sex scenes; the kiss was *it*.

The medics also suffered acutely from shootings, bombings and invasion by loonies. They proved resistant, though, to constant catcalls from critics. By the show's 1000th edition the producers were even boasting that, unlike almost every other Australian television series, they'd never won an award.

Main characters included the hospital superintendent Dr Denham whose wife was having an affair with another doctor, senior surgeon Dr Shaw. There was a clutch of young residents swinging their stethoscopes and waggling their syringes. Among these were the ambitious one, the over-confident one destined to make a tragic mistake, the playboy and the naïve female doctor (Peita Toppano, in training for 'Prisoner: Cell Block H' and 'Return to Eden') who found herself in emotional situations she couldn't control. 'Neighbours' star Alan Dale (p.376) came in as chauvinistic Dr Forrest.

The mostly female audiences experienced hot flushes watching the men and warm sympathy watching the coquettish young nurses, even bosomy Nurse Jojo Adams played by Delvene Delaney. When pop star Mark Holden joined to play young medic Greg Mason and Spanish-born Tony Alvarez joined as Dr Tony Garcia the producers seemed to have performed heart surgery on all the fans, even if no one in her right mind would have trusted either to unpeel an Elastoplast.

These days the fun of watching is partly the unintentional humour – the frequency with which the hospital staff ended up as patients in their own wards, for example, and the scream of the clothes. Yes, men really wore flared trousers, kipper ties and bushy sideboards, and even young girls wore their hair up like Emily Bishop in 'Coronation Street'.

By the way, Craig did forget Marilyn.

CHRONOLOGY

The following table traces the history of radio and television soap opera in Britain. Dates for imported series refer to their transmission in Britain. The origins of soap opera are explored in the Introduction, pages 1–11.

1942
'The Robinsons' begins on the BBC Light Programme, having first been broadcast under the title 'Front Line Family' on the BBC North American Service (ends 1947)

1947
'The Robinsons' ends

1948
5 January: 'Mrs Dale's Diary' (becomes 'The Dales' in 1962; ends in 1969)

1950
1 January: 'The Archers'

1952
October: 'The Appleyards' (until 1957)

1954
2 April: 'The Grove Family' (until 1957)

1955
22 September: Death of Grace Archer eclipses birth of Independent Television

1957
27 February: 'Emergency – Ward Ten' (until 1967)
April: 'The Appleyards' ends
June: 'The Grove Family' ends

1958
March: 'Starr and Company'

1960
9 December: 'Coronation Street'

1961
'Ben Casey' (until 1966)
'Dr Kildare' (until 1966)

1962
January: 'Compact' (until 1965)

1963
Jessie Matthews becomes Mrs Dale

1964
13 May: Martha Longhurst expires in her milk stout
2 November: 'Crossroads' begins (becomes Crossroads King's Oak' in 1987; ends in 1988)

1965
First appearance of Amy Turtle in 'Crossroads'
'Peyton Place' (until 1970)
12 June: Violet Carson, OBE, becomes first soap star to receive an honour
July: 'Compact' ends
October: 'The Newcomers' (until 1967)
October: 'United!' (until 1967)

1966
'Ben Casey' ends
'Dr Kildare' ends

1967
7 January: 'The Forsyte Saga' (until July)
March: 'United!' ends
June: 'Emergency – Ward Ten' ends
November: 'The Newcomers' ends

1969
April: 'The Dales' ends
28 April: 'Waggoners Walk' (until 1980)
November: 'The Doctors' (until 1971)

1970
'Peyton Place' ends (in most ITV regions)

1971
27 January: Death of Valerie Barlow
June: 'The Doctors' ends

1972
March: 'The Brothers' (until 1976)
September: 'General Hospital' (until 1979)
October: 'Emmerdale Farm'

1974
'Rooms' (until 1977)

1975
Meg marries Hugh Mortimer
July: Deirdre marries Ray Langton
October: Coronation Street evacuated as warehouse blazes

1976
April: Minnie Caldwell leaves 'Coronation Street'
7 September: 'Angels' (until 1983)
November: Mavis writes a romantic novel, *Song of a Scarlet Summer*
Christmas: 'The Brothers' ends

1977
'Rooms' ends
April: Rita marries Len Fairclough

1978
11 January: Ernest Bishop dies in wages snatch
Ena Sharples leaves 'Coronation Street'
5 September: 'Dallas' begins in Britain
15 September: 'Soap' starts on ITV

1979
'Crossroads'' Benny suspected of murder
May: 'Emmerdale Farm' part of Ilkley Literature Festival
26 January: 'General Hospital' ends
November: Gail marries Brian Tilsley. Meg's husband killed by international terrorists

1980
'Take the High Road'
March: J. R. Ewing shot
April: 'Knots Landing'
June: 'Waggoners Walk' ends

1981
Death of Roger Tonge
January: 'Triangle' (until 1983)
September: 'Taff Acre' (until December)
5 November: Crossroads Motel burns down; Meg Richardson sails off in QE2

1982
May: 'Dynasty'
2 November: 'Brookside'
'Flamingo Road' (until 1983)
The long agony of Arthur Brownlow ends when he is hit by a car as he staggers home from his retirement party

1983
Soap's first test-tube baby born to 'Crossroads'' Glenda
January–February: Deirdre Barlow's torrid affair with Mike Baldwin
April: 'Triangle' ends
December: 'Angels' ends
7 December: Len Fairclough killed off

1984
January: Elsie Tanner's final appearance in 'Coronation Street'
January: 'Miracles Take Longer' (until May)
13 May: Death of Albert Tatlock
October: Mavis chickens out of her wedding to Derek
21 November: Death of Stan Ogden

1985
Brian Cowgill of Thames Television tries to buy latest series of 'Dallas' from under the nose of the BBC
First thrilling episode of 'Acorn Antiques' as part of 'Victoria Wood – as Seen on TV'
May: Carrington clan escape unscathed from the Great Moldavian Massacre
January: 'The Practice' (second series 1986)
January: 'Gems'
19 February: 'EastEnders'
13 April: Death of Noele Gordon
20 June: Cot death of Hassan Osman
August: 'Albion Market' (until 1986)

September: 'Howards Way'
3 October: Michelle Fowler tells Dennis Watts that he is about to become a father

1986
Rover's Return burns down
January: 'The Colbys' (until 1987)
August: 'Albion Market' ends
14 August: Andy O'Brien killed off
September: 'Casualty' starts
Pat Sugden killed by hit-and-run driver
October: 'Neighbours'
Christmas Day: Arthur Fowler's nervous breakdown
Angie Watts walks out on Den

1987
'Santa Barbara'
Peyton Place: The Next Generation (film, 1985)
'Prisoner: Cell Block H'
'The Colbys' ends; Fallon is taken for a ride in a flying saucer
September: 'Crossroads' becomes 'Crossroads King's Oak'
27 October: 'Citizens'
January: 'Châteauvallon' (until June)
'Emmerdale Farm' villagers fight nuclear-waste dump
November: 'Damon and Debbie' spin-off from 'Brookside', which ends with Damon's death
December: Pam Ewing burned to a crisp
Christmas Day: Hilda Ogden leaves Coronation Street

1988
January: 'Black Forest Clinic' (until April)
'Neighbours' moves to evening slot and becomes Britain's second most popular soap
24 March: Sue Osman gives birth to Ali, jnr. Lofty is midwife
4 April: 'Crossroads King's Oak' ends
5 April: Myra de Groot dies of cancer
26 April: David Scarboro, 'EastEnders'' Mark, commits suicide
May: Lofty leaves Albert Square. Angie leaves for Majorca with new man, Sonny
Bobby Grant leaves 'Brookside'
Annie Sugden trapped in fire at Crossgill Cottage
Mary leaves Albert Square
13 June: Ivy Tilsley marries Don Brennan
29 June: Someone – Pam? – looms in Bobby Ewing's shower
19 July: 'The Bill' begins on Tuesdays and Thursdays on ITV

BIBLIOGRAPHY

Adams, Leon, *Larry Hagman: A Biography* (London: W. H. Allen, 1987).

Buckman, Peter, *All for Love* (London: Secker & Warburg, 1984).

Cantor, Muriel, and Pingree, Suzanne, *Soap Opera* (New York: Sage, 1983).

Katter, Suzy, *The Complete Book of 'Dallas'* (New York: Abrams, 1986).

Nown, Graham (ed.), *Coronation Street: 25 Years* (London: Ward Lock, 1985).

Redmond, Phil, *'Brookside': The Official Guide* (London: Weidenfeld, 1987).

Riley, Lee, *Patrick Duffy: The Man Behind Bobby Ewing* (London: W. H. Allen, 1987).

Smethurst, William, *The New Official 'Archers' Companion* (London: Weidenfeld, 1987).

Smith, Julia, and Holland, Tony, *'EastEnders': The Inside Story* (London: BBC Publications, 1987).

INDEX OF CHARACTERS

PICTURE ACKNOWLEDGEMENTS

The majority of photographs reproduced in this book are the copyright of Mirror Group Newspapers. The author and publishers also wish to make particular acknowledgement to the following: BBC Television: *EastEnders*, *Compact*. Central Independent Television: *Crossroads*. Jim Globus. Granada Television: *Coronation Street*. Grundy Television: *Neighbours*. ITC Entertainment Ltd: *General Hospital, Emergency – Ward 10*. Lorimar Television: *Dallas, Falcon Crest, Knots Landing*. MGM/Arena: *Dr Kildare*. The Mersey Television Company: *Brookside*. MTM Productions/Gilson International: *St Elsewhere*. Ken Sax. Twentieth Century Fox TV: *Peyton Place*. ZDF Mainz, W. Germany: *Black Forest Clinic*.